Chronicles and the Priestly Literature of the Hebrew Bible

Edited by Jaeyoung Jeon and Louis C. Jonker
This edition edited by Anthony Uyl MTS

Devoted Publshing
Ingersoll, Ontario, Canada 2023

Chronicles and the Priestly Literature of the Hebrew Bible

Edited by Jaeyoung Jeon and Louis C. Jonker
This edition edited by Anthony Uyl MTS

This book was originally published by Walter de Gruyter GmbH, Berlin/Boston.

The reformatted text of Chronicles and the Priestly Literature of the Hebrew Bible is all protected under Copyright ©2023 Devoted Publishing. The covers, background, layout and Devoted Publishing logo are Copyright ©2023 Devoted Publishing. This edition is published by Devoted Publishing a division of 2165467 Ontario Inc.

Note on Creative Commons 4.0 Attribution status: Although all the text in this document is from the CC-BY, the layout, formatting and note changes makes this book a copyrighted work. The original document remains in the CC-BY and can be found here:

https://doi.org/10.1515/9783110707014

For details on CC-BY go to http://creativecommons.org/licenses/by/4.0/.

Unless written permission is given for any material, all use of this material to be reproduced, stored in a retrieval system, or transmitted in any form by any means, electronic, mechanical, photocopying, recording or otherwise is forbidden. All rights reserved.

Drop Cap and Table of Contents fonts are AnglicanText by Typographer Mediengestaltung and used under a Free For Commercial Use License (FFC).

ISBN: 978-1-77356-488-3

Contact Us Online:
Email: office@devotedpub.com
For more information on Biblical Demonology and issues with the occult in modern evangelicalism, check out the editors' Substack Blog
Reformed Demonology: reformeddemonology.substack.com

Table of Contents

Abbreviations – 11

Preface – 13

Introduction – 15
   I – 15
   II – 19

Part 1: Consonance and Dissonance – 27

The Book of Chronicles through the Ages: A Cinderella or a Sleeping Beauty? – 29
   1. Introduction – 29
   2. Early rabbinic exegesis – 31
   3. Negative opinions – 33
   4. Wilhelm Martin Leberecht de Wette (1780–1849) – 34
   5. The Aftermath of de Wette's Proposition: Enthusiasm and Antagonism – 39
   6. Change in Perspective: Archaeology and Assyriology – 43
   7. Change in perspective: History "wie es gewesen war" or "wie es geschrieben ist"? – Gerhard von Rad – 46
   8. Change in perspective: The Chronicler, a historian "in his own right" according to Martin Noth – 51
   9. Change in Perspective: Literarkritik and Literary Criticism – Source and Discourse – 54
   10. Change in Perspective: Qumran and Scribal Work – 57
      10.1. Text criticism – 57
      10.2. Rewritten Bible – 58
      10.3 Additions and Omissions in Chronicles – Juha Pakkala – 61
      10.4 Importance of the cult, of the monarchy and of Moses' Law – 63
   11. Conclusion – 63

I. Consonance, Continuity, and mutual Influence – 65

Theocratic Reworking in the Pentateuch – 67
   1. Introduction – 67
   2. Divine Kingship in the Postexilic Composition of the Hexateuch – 69
   3. Divine Kingship, a Holy Nation, and a Kingdom of Priests in Late-Postexilic Layers of the Pentateuch – 73

4. The Proto-Chronistic and Chronistic Genealogy of the Zadokites in the Theocratic Reworkings of the Pentateuch – 76
  5. The Hierocratic Institution of the High Priest in the Theocratic Reworking of the Pentateuch – 86

Numbers and Chronicles: Close Relatives 2 – 95
  1. The (Two) Silver Trumpets – 96
  2. Korah (and Company) – 100
  3. The Covenant of Salt – 101
  4. Artificial Proper Names – 102
  5. War, Looting, and Spoils of War – 103
  6. Families, Women, Daughters, and Questions Related to Heritage – 105
  7. (High) Numbers – 118

נפש אדם and the Associations of 1 Chronicles 5 in the Hebrew Bible – 125
  1. Introduction – 125
  2. Translation issues – 126
  3. Triangular relationship? – 127
     3.1 1 Chronicles 5 and Joshua 22 – 130
     3.2 Numbers 31: a major locus for נפש אדם – 130
  4. Camels, capture, and divine aid in Chronicles – 131
     4.1 Key terms – 131
     4.2 Arabic, camels, and corpses – 132
     4.3 חיים in 2 Chronicles 25, מחיה in 2 Chronicles 14, and נפש in 1 Chronicles 5 – 132
  5. Development in 1 Chronicles 5:1–26 – 134
     5.1 From Reuben alone to Reuben/Gad/half-Manasseh – 134
     5.2 אדם, נפש, and שבה in Solomon's prayer – 136
  6. Some conclusions – 137
     6.1 1 Chronicles 5 in light of Numbers and Joshua – 137
     6.2 Victory and booty and life in Chronicles – 139
     6.3 A 'midrash' indebted to Solomon – 139

II. Dissonance, Discontinuity, and Alteration – 143

The High Priest in Chronicles and in the Priestly Traditions of the Pentateuch – 145
  1. Introduction – 145
  2. The high priest and the sanctuary in Chronicles – 147
     2.1 The high priest and the rituals performed inside the sanctuary – 147
     2.2 Other high priestly roles in the administration of the

    sanctuary – 155
  3. The high priest and communal leadership: the case of Jehoiada – 160
  4. The missing high priest: the case of royal reforms in Chronicles – 167
  5. Conclusion: the high priest in Chronicles and in the priestly texts of the Pentateuch – 173

The Tribes of Israel in Ezekiel and Chronicles – 177
  1. Introduction – 177
  2. Tribes and Territories – Ezekiel 47–48 – 179
    2.1 Putting the Land on the Map – 179
    2.2 Equality as the Principle? – 180
  3. Tribes and Genealogies – 1 Chronicles 1–9 – 182
    3.1 The Arrangement of the Tribes – 183
    3.2 Justifying the New Order – 184
  4. What and Who is Israel? – 186
    4.1 The Lasting Significance of the Tribal System – 187
    4.2 Tradition not Innovation – 188
    4.3 Tribal Hierarchy – 189
    4.4 Conflicting Concepts of Israel – 189
  5. Conclusion – 191

Sacrifices in Chronicles: How Priestly Are They? – 193
  1. Introduction – 193
  2. A brief overview of Levitical sacrifices in Chronicles – 195
  3. Hezekiah's reform – 199
  4. More stories about impurity – 207
  5. Ritual and moral impurity – 210
  6. Conclusion – 214

Part 2: Interpreting the Consonance and Dissonance – 217

III. Inclusive Reception and Creative Interpretation – 219

Scribes in the Post-Exilic Temple: A Social Perspective – 221
  1. Introduction – 221
  2. The Scribal Model – 222
    2.1 Scribes in the Hebrew Bible – 222
    2.2 Other Scribes in a Jewish Context – 224
    2.3 Scribes in Mesopotamia – 224
    2.4 Scribes in Egypt – 226
    2.5 Example of Homeric Poems – 229
    2.6 Summary about Scribes – 230
  3. Scribes and the Production of Literature – 231

4. Examples of Scribal Literary Development – 232
  5. My Proposal for Connecting Chronicles and P – 236
  6. Conclusions – 238

Atonement, Sacred Space and Ritual Time: The Chronicler as Reader of Priestly Pentateuchal Narrative – 241
  1. Introduction – 241
    1.1 Methodology and Premises – 242
    1.2 Disconnect between P and Chronicles? Preliminary Survey – 246
  2. Narrative Context of Priestly Day of Atonement and Passover – 247
    2.1 The Day of Atonement in Narrative Context of the Pentateuch – 248
    2.2 Exceptional Passover in Numbers 9:1–14 – 252
  3. Leviticus 8–10 and 16 as Background for Altar Violations and Atonement in Chronicles – 254
    3.1 Hezekiah's Temple Repurification and Passover (2 Chronicles 29–31) – 254
    3.3 Uzziah Is Not Quite Nadab or Qoraḥ (2 Chronicles 26:16–23) – 258
    3.4 Solomon's Temple Established (2 Chronicles 5–8) – 259
  4. Implications for the Chronicler's Relation to Priestly Literature – 262

Grundgeschichte und Chronik – Kontinuität und Diskontinuität in Altisraels Geschichtsschreibung – 265
  1. Das Neue im Alten – die Fragestellung der biblischen Chronikbücher – 265
  2. Mosezeit und Davidszeit – 266
  3. Mose in Davids Israel – 268
  4. Levi in Davids neuem Israel – 270
  5. "Grundgeschichte" und Chronik nach chronistischem Selbstverständnis – 276

Conversational Implicatures in the Book of Chronicles: The Pentateuch as horizon of the Chronicler – 279
  1. Introduction – 279
  2. Saying and Meaning: The Gricean Theory of Conversational Implicatures – 282
  3. Conversational Implicatures in 2 Chronicles 26:16–21 – 286
  4. Conclusion – 302

Levites of Memory in Chronicles and Some Considerations about

Historical Levites in Late-Persian Yehud – 303
1. Introduction – 303
2. Levites of Memory: Matters of Background, Texts, Memories and Mental Libraries – 304
3. Constructing Historical Reconstructions of Late-Persian Yehud Levites and Barriers to the Acceptance of the Mentioned Common Positions – 310
4. Exploring a Different Approach – 316

IV. Ideological Conflicts and Scribal Debates – 329

Genealogies as Tools: The Case of P and Chronicles – 331
1. Introduction – 331
2. Genealogies and their functions from a social-anthropological perspective – 332
3. Genealogies in P and Chronicles – 335
4. The struggle for interpretative supremacy in the Achaemenid period – 340
5. Conclusion – 345

David in the role of a second Moses – The revelation of the temple-model (*tabnît*) in 1 Chronicles 28 – 347
1. Introduction – 347
2. David as Cult founder in the books of Chronicles – 349
   2.1 David receives from YHWH a plan or blueprint (tabnît) of the future sanctuary (1 Chron 28) – 349
   2.1.1 1 Chronicles 28:11 – 350
   2.1.2 1 Chronicles 28:12 – 350
   2.1.3 1 Chronicles 28:18 – 351
   2.1.4 1 Chronicles 28:19 – 352
   2.1.5 Originality of the Literary Composition in 1 Chronicles 28 – 353
   2.2 David takes the initiative for the generous donation in favor of the projected Temple (1 Chron 29) – 354
   2.3 Appointment and diversification of the Levites by David (1 Chron 23–27) – 355
3. David as a second Moses: The Chronicler's handling of the Pentateuchal cultic tradition – 356
4. The Chronicler's ideological agenda – 358

The righteousness of the Levites in Chronicles and Ezekiel – 363
1. Introduction – 363
2. Second Chronicles 29 – 365
3. Ezekiel 44 – 366

    4. Returning to 2 Chronicles 29 – 367
    5. Priests and Levites – 368
    6. Historical development of the priesthood? – 372
    7. Conclusion – 373

The Levites and Idolatry: A Scribal Debate in Ezekiel 44 and Chronicles – 375
    1. Introduction – 375
    2. The Accusation of Idol Worship Against the Levites – 376
        2.1 The Lateness of the Zadokite Redaction – 376
        2.2 The Guilt of the Levites – 380
        2.2.1 A Historical or Literary Reference? – 380
        2.2.2 Understandings of the Levites's Guilt by the Audiences/Readers of Yehud – 382
    3. Ezekiel and Chronicles – 384
    4. The Levites and Idolatry in Chronicles – 387
        4.1 No Idols (גלולים) in Chronicles – 387
        4.2 Jeroboam's Golden Calves – 389
        4.3 Josianic Reform – 393
    5. Some Sociological Observations – 397
        5.1 Zadokites' Symbolic Capital – 397
        5.2 Active Remembering, Reshaping, and Forgetting – 400
    6. Conclusion – 401

V. Ezra-Nehemiah: Between P and Chronicles – 403

The Role of Priests and Levites in the Composition of Ezra-Nehemiah: Some Points for Consideration – 405
    1. Introduction – 405
    2. Priests and Levites in Ezra-Nehemiah – 407
        2.1 Ezra 1 and Nehemiah 13: The Introduction and Conclusion of the Priests and Levites – 408
        2.2 Ezra 3 – 411
        2.3 Ezra 7 and 8 – 412
        2.4 Nehemiah 8 and 9 – 414
        2.5 Nehemiah 12 – 416
        2.6 Nehemiah 13 (again) – 416
    3. The Priests and Levites in Ezra-Nehemiah Compared – 417
    4. Conclusion – 418

Levites, Holiness and Late Achaemenid/Early Hellenistic Literature Formation: Where does Ezra-Nehemiah fit into the Discourse? – 421
    1. Introduction – 421

2. Holiness and the Levites in Ezra-Nehemiah – 424
    2.1 The Temple-building Account (Ezra 1–6) – 425
    2.2 The Ezra Material (Ezra 7–10, Neh 8) – 426
    2.3 The Nehemiah Memoir (Neh 1–7; 9–13) – 427
3. Diachronic ordering of textual material – 432
    3.1 The formation of Ezra-Nehemiah – 432
    3.2 The ordering of the texts of Ezra-Nehemiah – 436
    3.3 Synthesis – 444
    3.3.1 Later references (during the 4th century BCE) – contemporaneous with Chronicles – 445
    3.3.3 Summary – 448
4. Conclusion – 450

ABBREVIATIONS

This work employs the standard abbreviations listed in the SBL Handbook of Style (2nd ed.), in addition to the following:

AThANT – Abhandlungen zur Theologie des Alten und Neuen Testaments
ATM – Altes Testament und Moderne
ATSAT – Arbeiten zu Text und Sprache im alten Testament
BEAT – Beiträge zur Erforschung des Alten Testaments und des antiken Judentums
BHTh – Beiträge zur historischen Theologie
BWANT – Beiträge zur Wissenschaft vom Alten und Neuen Testament
CO OT – Coniectanea biblica. Old Testament series
ExT – *The Expository Times*
HBOT – *Hebrew Bible/Old Testament: The History of Its Interpretation.*
HThK – Herders Theologischer Kommentar
JAJ – *Journal of Ancient Judaism*
PNAS – *Proceedings of the National Academy of Sciences*
RB – Rivista biblical
STAR – Studies in Theology and Religion
STDS – Studies on the Texts of the Desert of Judah
ThW – Theologische Wissenschaft
TSHB – Textpragmatische Studien zur Literatur- und Kulturgeschichte der Hebräischen Bibel
UBCS – Understanding the Bible Commentary Series
WANEM – Worlds of the Ancient Near East and Mediterranean

Preface

This book is the result of the collaboration of two scholars on a research topic of common interest. Jaeyoung Jeon of the Université de Lausanne, Switzerland, through a grant from the Swiss National Science Foundation (SNSF) for a project titled "A Bible born out of conflict" initiated the idea of bringing scholarship on the Priestly literature and Chronicles together in a critical and creative interaction. He approached Louis Jonker of Stellenbosch University, South Africa, who has called for interaction between Chronicles and Pentateuchal scholarship in the past, and who specializes in Chronicles to jointly organize a project on this research idea.

After identifying scholars working in these two related fields, they jointly organized an in-person meeting of participants where specialists on Priestly literature and on Chronicles respectively, could test their ideas in dialogue with one another. Thereafter, participants in the dialogue were requested to formulate their ideas on paper, in the wake of the oral in-person interaction. The papers were submitted to Jeon and Jonker who acted as editors of this volume that documents the outcome of the project group's joint deliberations.

After receiving the submissions, the editors submitted each contribution to two independent reviewers who did not participate in the in-person dialogue. They also invited two more contributions on aspects that were not sufficiently covered in the initial round of dialogue. The last-mentioned contributions were also, like the former, submitted to the double-blind peer reviewing process. The feedback of this process was communicated to each author who had the task of revising her/his contribution in light of the critical engagements of the peer reviewers.

This volume is thus the result not only of collaboration between two fields of Hebrew Bible specialization, but also of the scholarly engagement within the wider project team, as well as with a group of independent peer reviewers. As editors and contributors, we want to thank the following persons who acted in this capacity: Erhard Blum, Mark Brett, Christian Frevel, Sara Japhet, Jurie le Roux, Yigal Levin,

Reinhard Müller, Manfred Oeming, Eckart Otto, Thomas Römer, Konrad Schmid, Dalit Rom-Shiloni, Jeffrey Stackert, Hermann-Josef Stipp, Ian Wilson, and Jacob Wright. There critical engagements certainly contribute to the scientific quality of this book.

As editors, we also want to thank the series editors of BZAW, John Barton, Reinhard G. Kratz, Nathan MacDonald, Sara Milstein and Markus Witte, for accepting our volume in this prestigious series. As always, it was a great pleasure to work with the publishing team of De Gruyter, in particular Sophie Wagenhofer.

Jaeyoung Jeon and Louis C. Jonker
July 2021

INTRODUCTION

I

The biblical traditions of the Yahwistic cult, especially concerning temples, sanctuaries, ritual, and cultic personnel, are among the major cornerstones for reconstructing the literary history of the Hebrew Bible and the history of Israelite religion. While most of the biblical texts are somehow related to those issues, three texts (or text groups) deal with them extensively: the "Priestly" text within the Pentateuch ("P"), Ezekiel 40–48, and Chronicles. These three texts address these issues from three different cultic centers of different periods. P establishes the cultic institutions and regulations for the wilderness sanctuary – the Tent of Meeting (Tabernacle) – in the formative period of biblical Israel. The fundamental regulations of sacrificial rituals, priesthood, and other clerical duties center around this mobile tent-sanctuary. The high priest Aaron and his sons are the central figures in this cultic system and their exclusive prerogatives are secured across the various literary layers of P. The major cultic site of Chronicles is the "Solomonic" temple of Jerusalem during the monarchic period. Chronicles extensively describes the establishment of the temple cult by King David, depicting his reign as another, or even *the*, formative period for Israel's cult. David's temple cult both recognizes and implements the P regulations while also modifying the "old" system and inventing a new system of cult. Though the priestly prerogatives are not denied, they are much less present, and a considerable emphasis is laid on the roles of the Levites. The third text, Ezekiel 40–48, projects a new cultic program to an envisioned future temple. The new temple and its structure and system are the center of an imaginary reorganization of the entire land of Israel under hierarchical clerical and tribal systems. The vision of the new temple exhibits a close affinity to P in its language and hierarchical concepts of holiness and clergy. In this vision, however, neither a high priest nor the "Aaronite" priests are mentioned, but the Zadokite priests are introduced as the privileged party in contrast to the rest of the Levites.

The three texts not only share similar subject matter; recent studies indicate that they were composed or reworked in an overlapping time period of the mid-/ late Persian period, most likely in Yehud, and Jerusalem in particular. The earliest "Priestly Source" (P^G) in the Pentateuch has recently been thought to extend only to the Sinai pericope, so that the texts previously regarded as "Priestly" in (Leviticus-) Numbers are assigned to later generations of priestly scribes during the mid-/late Persian period.[1] The final section of Ezekiel (chs. 40–48) is also regarded as a late addition to Ezekiel, expanded through multiple stages during, as many scholars agree, the mid-/late Persian period.[2] For Chronicles, the majority of scholars assume the mid-/ late Persian period or late Persian and early Greek period. If we were to attempt a dating of the three biblical texts, it could be reasonably conjectured that the texts were composed temporally close to each other, or even simultaneously: for some sections, during the mid-/late Persian period. Since we may posit the existence of several scribal circles rather than a great number of literate elites in Yehud in this period, these scribes were probably well acquainted with important religious texts and traditions from other circles or families. The priestly authors and redactors especially of the late strata of P, the tradents of the "Ezekiel school," and the Chronicler were likely among this relatively small number of literate elites. Living and working in temporal and spatial proximity to one another, they would have been familiar with each other's literary works, which were becoming and/ or had already become common religious and intellectual assets of the community. Consequently, when these scribal groups wrote on similar subject matters from different perspectives, they were likely engaged in a dialogical relationship – either unidirectional or multidirectional, consciously or unconsciously reflecting and responding to the others' voices. Research on the possible interactions between them would therefore provide us not only with insights on their literary history but also with clues for reconstructing the socio-historical circumstances around them.

Nonetheless, while the literary relationship between P and Ezekiel has been much discussed, the possible interactions between Chronicles and these "priestly" literary works in a broader sense have thus far

---

1. For further, see, e. g., Reinhard Achenbach, *Die Vollendung der Tora: Studien zur Redaktionsgeschichte des Numeribuches im Kontext von Hexateuch und Pentateuch*. Beihefte Zur Zeitschrift für Altorientalische und Biblische Rechtsgeschichte, Bd. 3. Wiesbaden: Harrassowitz, 2003; Jaeyoung Jeon, "The Promise of the Land and the Extent of P." ZAW 130 (2018): 513–28.

2. For further details with references, see Jaeyoung Jeon, "The Levites and Idolatry: A Scribal Debate in Ezekiel 44 and Chronicles" in this volume.

not received appropriate scholarly attention. The studies of the Pentateuch, Ezekiel, and Chronicles have been conducted rather separately to one degree or another; particularly, the priestly literature (P and Ezekiel) and Chronicles have been regarded as though they are from different fields of study. Comparative approaches for Chronicles have mainly focused on Samuel and Kings or the Deuteronomistic History.[3]

This volume has been organized against this backdrop. In order to initiate in-depth discussions on this important but thus-far neglected subject, this volume raises two major questions: (1) Are Chronicles and the priestly literature consonant with each other? (2) How may one interpret the agreement and/or dissonance between them? The former question is discussed in Part I of the volume; the latter is addressed in Part II. The first question should primarily be addressed in terms of the literary relationship between them, which is a tricky task. To be sure, there are explicit references to the Torah in Chronicles, especially in connection with cultic regulations and the Mosaic wilderness sanctuary, though the latter is mentioned only sporadically. The priesthood in Chronicles is anchored in and legitimized by the P tradition of the Aaronite priests. On the contrary, Chronicles deliberately skips the period of the exodus and wilderness wandering, which is the formative period of the nation according to the Pentateuch, in its genealogical presentation of the early history.[4] The cultic regulations often diverge from the P laws in the Pentateuch. It is rather King David who stipulates new rules for the temple; these rules and regulations are held in even higher regard. Furthermore, the exclusive priestly prerogatives guaranteed in P are not always obvious in Chronicles and are often diminished in favor of the kings, people, and, especially, the Levites. Such ambivalence toward the Mosaic law and institutions provides us with diverse interpretive possibilities concerning their literary relationship. For instance, one may argue that Chronicles stands in accord with the P cultic regulations, harmoniously complementing the latter for the new post-Mosaic sanctuary. This position is taken by Reinhard Achenbach and Hans-Peter Mathys in this volume. One may, however, also weight the dissonance more heavily, as do Kristin Weingart, Christophe Nihan, and Esias Meyers and as Deirdre Fulton does for Ezra-Nehemiah. There is also the important question

---

3. See Jonker's plea that Chronicles and Pentateuch scholarship should be brought within hearing distance of one another: Louis C. Jonker, "From Paraleipomenon to Early Reader. The Implications of Recent Chronicles Studies for Pentateuchal Criticism," in *Congress Volume Munich 2013*, ed. Christl Maier, VTS 177 (Leiden: Brill, 2014), 217–54.

4. See further Thomas Willi, "Grundgeschichte und Chronik – Kontinuität und Diskontinuität in Altisraels Geschichtsschreibung" in this volume.

of the direction of literary influences: Was there only unidirectional influence from the priestly literature to Chronicles? Or did the influence move in both directions? The contributions by Graeme Auld and Louis Jonker take the latter position, while some others explicitly advocate for the former option.

Part II of this volume deals with other sets of questions. Since Gerhard von Rad shifted the scholarly approaches to Chronicles from any historical reliability to the Chronicler's own interpretation of history and *Tendenz*, the book has been perceived as a heavily ideological and theological scribal work.[5] This specific character of Chronicles enables interpreting the issue of literary consonance and dissonance at levels of ideology and theology as well as the socio-historical context in which they originated. For example, the priestly scribal works promote a worldview centered on the sanctuary-temple, and especially the late layers of P advance a theocratic ideology for priestly rule over the community. Chronicles is also marked by its temple-centered view of history, yet the book does not appear to be in complete agreement with priestly ideology. How, then, should one evaluate the similarities and differences? Should the two (or three, including Ezekiel) ideologies be understood as harmonious and complementary with each other? Or, could one consider the two (or three) as conflicting positions? The contributions of Lester L. Grabbe, Benjamin Giffone, Thomas Willi, and Lars Maskow take the former position, while Joachim Schaper, Jürg Hutzli, and Christine Mitchell are more sympathetic to the latter.

Another critical issue to be discussed is the differing treatments of the Levites. The priestly literature endeavors to perpetuate the division between the Aaronite (P) or Zadokite (Ezek) priests and the second-tier Levites. The so-called Levitical treaties in Numbers 3–4, 8 grant the Levites second-best, but still sacred, status; the priestly scribes also levy harsh polemics against the Levites (e. g., Num 16; Ezek 44). The Chronicler, however, projects the voice of the Levites. While accepting the distinction between the Levites and priests, Chronicles describes the status of the Levites almost as equal to, or at times even better than, the priests. The priestly right to serve in the inner sanctum and for the sacrificial ritual is secured; the remaining temple service and management are governed by the Levites. The different attitudes towards the Levites raises another important question of whether they reflect a socio-religious struggle between the priestly and Levitical

---

5. Gerhard von Rad, *Das Geschichtsbild des chronistischen Werkes*, BWANT 54 (Stuttgart: Kohlhammer, 1930). For further, see the contribution by Jean-Louis Ska, "The Book of Chronicles through the Ages: A Cinderella or a Sleeping Beauty?" in this volume.

scribal circles. Jaeyoung Jeon advocates for this view, whereas Ehud Ben Zvi opposes this possibility.

II

The structure of this volume and the contents of the contributions can briefly be summarized as follows. The volume consists of two parts and five subsections. The introduction is followed by a useful overview of research history of Chronicles by Jean-Louis Ska, "The Book of Chronicles through the Ages: A Cinderella or a Sleeping Beauty?" Ska traces the developments and changes of the views on Chronicles from early rabbinic traditions to recent critical studies. He selects major works that marked significant shifts in trends, such as Baruch Spinoza, Wilhelm M.L. de Wette, Gerhard von Rad, and Martin Noth, in addition to more recent critics. For these major junctures, Ska provides the intellectual and social backgrounds as well as the influences for important progressions in the study of the Hebrew Bible.

As discussed above, Part I is divided into two subsections that focus on literary relationships between Chronicles and the priestly literature. The first subsection contains three articles examining literary harmony, continuity, and (mutual) influence between the texts. In his article, "Theocratic Reworking in the Pentateuch: Proto-Chronistic Features in the Late Priestly Layers of Numbers and Their Reception in Chronicles," Reinhard Achenbach presents his chronological scheme of the formation of the Hexateuch and Pentateuch with three main stages of reworkings: the Hexateuchal Redaction, the Pentateuchal Redaction, and the Theocratic Revision (ThR). He then suggests that the ThR text especially in Numbers, formulated during the fourth century BCE, exhibits close literary affinities with Chronicles, which he defines as "proto-Chronistic" features. This is a unidirectional model of literary influence from the Late P texts to Chronicles.

Hans-Peter Mathys takes a similar approach to the relationship between Chronicles and, especially, the Late Priestly texts in Numbers. In his article, "Numbers and Chronicles: Close Relatives 2," which is a follow-up of his earlier work (2008),[6] Mathys compares several common motifs found in both texts, such as the two silver trumpets (Num 10; 2 Chr 13; 20; 29), Korah and his descendants (Num 16; 26; 1 Chr 9), the covenant of salt (Num 18; 2 Chr 13), artificial proper names (Num 11; 1 Chr 24; 25), exaggerated numbers (Num 1; 26; 1

---

6. Hans-Peter Mathys, "Numeri und Chronik: nahe Verwandte," in *The Books of Leviticus and Numbers*, ed. Thomas Römer, BETL 215 (Leuven: Peters, 2008), 555–78.

Chr 5; 9, etc.), and the concerns for families and women (Num 5; 12; 30; 2 Chr 11; 13; 21; etc.). Through these comparisons, Mathys highlights the common features between the two texts, which are unique to them in the Hebrew Bible.

Graeme Auld, however, advises caution in defining the direction of literary influence between the texts. In his contribution, "נפש אדם and the Associations of 1 Chronicles 5 in the Hebrew Bible," Auld performs a detailed examination of the usage of the term נפש אדם in Num 31, Josh 22, and 1 Chr 5. He concludes that (1) the material in 1 Chr 5:1–26 is relatively early for Chronicles and that (2) the material influenced both Num 31 and Josh 22. Auld then calls for not automatically giving priority to Numbers and Joshua when studying similar materials in Chronicles based on the familiar categories of the "Primary History" (Gen–Kgs) and the "Secondary History" (Chr–Ezra–Neh).

The second subsection consists of three articles that underscore the discontinuity and dissonance between Chronicles and the priestly literature. In his article, "The High Priest in Chronicles and in the Priestly Traditions of the Pentateuch," Christophe Nihan examines the Chronicles passages that mention the high priests (2 Chr 13; 19; 16; 23; 26; 31) and compares them with the descriptions of the prerogatives and roles of high priest in the Priestly text of the Pentateuch. Although Chronicles' description of high priestly roles is largely based on priestly materials, according to Nihan, there are significant differences between them as well. He demonstrates that (1) extra-sanctuary roles for the high priest are significantly limited in Chronicles compared to those in P and that (2) whereas the high priest in P is solely responsible for maintenance of the sanctuary's purity and sanctity, cultic reforms and maintenance of the sanctuary in Chronicles are royal initiatives made in cooperation with the Levites.

Kristin Weingart compares the tribal system in Ezek 47–48 and 1 Chr 1–9 in her contribution, "The Tribes of Israel in Ezekiel and Chronicles." She argues that both texts utilize the traditional twelve-tribe system in order to communicate their specific perspectives on Israel's definition and identity. The Ezekiel and Chronicles texts equally emphasize the prominent status of three tribes, Judah, Levi, and Benjamin, which are expressed through envisioned geography and genealogy, respectively. Nonetheless, Weingart finds a significant difference between them in their treatment of the former Northern tribes and the Northern province of Samaria in particular. Whereas Israel continues to exist in Samaria to the Chronicler, Samaria has nothing to do with the future of Israel in Ezek 47–48. In this regard, she argues, the two texts represent opposing positions in a pressing issue of their time: the status, or the "Israelite-ness," of the Samarians.

Esias E. Meyer's contribution, "Sacrifices in Chronicles: How Priestly Are They?" examines the language of purity and cleansing, טהר and טמא (both in *piel*), accompanying the sin offering and reparation offering in the Chronicles account of the temple cleansings by Hezekiah (2 Chr 29) and Josiah (2 Chr 34). Compared with the usage of the terms in Leviticus, Meyers observes that their uses in the Chronicler's accounts of Hezekiah and Josiah are not so clear about the kind of impurity at stake and, therefore, are used imprecisely and inadequately from the perspective of Leviticus. He concludes that although there might be some overlap of the notions of purity and cleansing in Leviticus and Chronicles, there are also some significant differences.

Part II contains three subsections dealing with interpretation of the agreement and dissonance in different ways. The first section includes four articles that understand the agreement-dissonance issue in terms of Chronicles' inclusive reception and creative interpretation of priestly traditions. Firstly, Lester L. Grabbe's contribution, "Scribes in the Post-Exilic Temple: A Social Perspective," approaches the present issue from the perspective of priestly scribal culture. Reviewing the scribal models from Egypt and Mesopotamia, he narrows the focus to priestly scribes in Yehud; from Homeric studies, Grabbe finds a model of transcribing oral traditions applicable to the formation of the biblical texts. He concludes that P was produced during the Persian period by priestly scribes, whereas Chronicles was written in the early Greek period, a century or two later than P, by an individual or individuals close to the priesthood. For the relationship between them, Grabbe argues that the Chronicler(s) inclusively used different sources – not only the P document, but also a version of Samuel-Kings, oral forms of priestly and temple traditions, and a utopian vision of theocratic paradise.

The contribution by Benjamin D. Giffone, "Atonement, Sacred Space and Ritual Time: The Chronicler as Reader of Priestly Pentateuchal Narrative," reads and interprets accounts in Chronicles in light of the Priestly and Ezekiel texts. He explains the motif of atonement and the extended period of the festival in the Chronicles account of Hezekiah's Passover (2 Chr 29) with a reading of Lev 8–10 immediately followed by Lev 16 as well as Ezek 43–45. Similarly, Giffone understands the account of Uzziah's incense (2 Chr 26:16–23) in connection with Lev 10 and Num 16, while he suggests a solution for the potential overlap between the Day of Atonement and Solomon's dedication of the temple (2 Chr 5–8) with the appearance of the glory of Yhwh (Exod 40; 43). Giffone concludes that, as an early interpreter of Torah, the Chronicler seems to have charted a path inclusive of both Deuteronomistic and Priestly traditions (understood broadly), and of both Levites and Zadokite priests in their own specific, necessary roles.

Thomas Willi's contribution "Grundgeschichte und Chronik: Kontinuität und Diskontinuität in Altisraels Geschichtsschreibung" argues for an innovation in Chronicles according to the Torah of Moses. Willi claims that, on the one hand, Chronicles – composed in the late fifth century BCE – views David's Israel as a critical period of cultic transition from the movable tent to the fixed house (e. g., 1 Chr 17), with the tribe of Levi as a whole, rather than a specific priestly family, holding the central position in this transition. On the other hand, Willi maintains that David's preparation of the new sanctuary somehow follows the Mosaic tradition: For instance, the Levites' physical activities are now spiritualized in their handling of the Torah. For Willi, therefore, the Pentateuchal (P) cultic system is a measure for the new system of the temple of Jerusalem, which is the final destination of the wilderness sanctuary.

The contribution by Lars Maskow, "Conversational Implicatures in the Book of Chronicles: The Pentateuch as Horizon of the Chronicler" suggests an interpretive model for implicit references to the Torah in Chronicles based on the Grice-Rolf theory of conversational implicature. Maskow examines the account of Uzziah's leprosy (2 Chr 26:16–21) as a test case and suggests that it is an implicit discourse on leadership between the high priest and king. For him, this interpretation is enabled by the relevant P accounts of incense offering and leprosy in Lev 10; 16; Num 12; 16 as well as the symbolic importance of Aaron's forehead (Exod 28:36–38), which together diminish Uzziah's authority. However, the Chronicler participates in this discourse only implicitly, out of caution not to elevate the dispute between king and priest. Maskow presents a case in which the Chronicler creatively uses the P traditions for promoting his own agenda.

In his article, "Levites of Memory in Chronicles: And Some Considerations about Historical Levites in Late-Persian Yehud," Ehud Ben Zvi presents his view on the Levites in Chronicles as the "complementary other" of the priests imagined by the Chronicler, rather than as the conflicting counterpart in reality. He reviews the biblical and post-biblical sources about the Levites, claiming that the Levites (singers and gatekeepers) were never as influential of a group as the priests were. Ben Zvi then interprets the Chronicler's depiction of the Levites as a "normalization" of social memory for social cohesion by the small group of literati in late Persian-period Jerusalem. Namely, the Chronicler's depictions reflect the literati's expectation of how the Levites should have been seen in the monarchic period according to their authoritative repertoire (including the Pentateuch and Ezekiel).

The second subsection of Part II consists of four articles that find scribal conflicts and ideological struggles in the relationship between Chronicles and the priestly literature. Joachim Schaper's contribution, "Genealogies as Tools: The Case of P and Chronicles," examines the function and purpose of the Levitical genealogy in 1 Chr 5:27–41. He observes that the genealogy integrates the Zadokite priesthood into the "Levi"-construct and artificially unifies historically separate Judahite priesthoods, while completely ignoring the distinction between priests and second-rank functionaries, i. e., Levites. Schaper argues that the genealogy represents a struggle for interpretative supremacy between the priests and the Levites conducted to a significant degree by means of scribal works – an attempt by one group of temple personnel to subtly subvert the power of another. The Levitical (later Pharisaic) scribes, according to Schaper, were not entirely hostile towards the priesthood but wary of the priests becoming too powerful.

Jürg Hutzli's contribution, "David in the Role of a Second Moses: The Revelation of the Temple-model (*tabnît*) in 1 Chronicles 28" highlights similarities and contrasts between the roles of David in the construction of the temple and Moses in the construction of the Tabernacle. Chronicles describes David as a "new Moses" for this task, in that he receives *tabnît* (תבנית) of the temple from Yhwh, which parallels Moses (e. g., Exod 25:9, 40); however, David is also contrasted to Moses through his own (very generous) tribute to the construction project and his appointments of the Levites into highly esteemed positions. Hutzli interprets these features in terms of ideological, theological, and political purposes aimed at providing better legitimation for the temple and its novelties and claiming exclusive legitimacy of the temple of Jerusalem vis-à-vis that of Gerizim.

Christine Mitchell compares the notion of righteousness in Ezek 44 and 2 Chr 29 in her article, "The Righteousness of the Levites in Chronicles and Ezekiel," and suggests that the two texts have a polemical relationship with each other. The Chronicles text – the account of

Hezekiah's Passover – justifies Levitical participation in the sacrificial ritual by praising them as opposed to the priests: לבב להתקדש מהכהנים כי הלוים ישרי ישדת (2 Chr 29:34 bβ). The term ישר (upright) is a pun on the root שרת, with the "service" or "ministry" linked to Ezek 44:11–14, where the root שרת occurs in the blunt polemic against the Levites. The term ישר is also paired with *tsedeqah/tsadiq* (or similar from the root צדק) in the scribal curriculum of the Chronicler. By making use of a phrase ישרי לבב (upright of heart) that evokes the Zadokites' name, the Chronicler polemicizes the Ezekielian distinction between the Zadokites and Levites in favor of the former.

Jaeyoung Jeon's contribution, "The Levites and Idolatry: A Scribal Debate in Ezekiel 44 and Chronicles" also starts with the "Zadokite" accusation against Levites' idolatry in Ezek 44 and investigates the Chronicler's response in favor of the Levites. Jeon argues that the Levites are totally separated from the idolatrous Northern cult (2 Chr 11:13–17); the Chronicler deliberately avoided the use of the term גילולים that invokes the Zadokite accusation (Ezek 44:11–14); in addition, the account of Josiah's reform (2 Chr 34:3–7) omits the motif of the local priests in Jerusalem. Employing the social theory of Pierre Bourdieu, Jeon interprets the Zadokite redaction in Ezekiel as an attempt to perpetuate their exclusive priestly rights through a class distinction from the rest of the Levites; Chronicles represents a resistance by the Levitical scribal circle against the symbolic violence of the priestly scribes as well as Levitical attempts to accumulate their own symbolic capital.

The final subsection of Part II examines interpretive possibilities that Ezra-Nehemiah may provide in understanding the relationship between Chronicles and the priestly literature. In "The Role of Priests and Levites in the Composition of Ezra-Nehemiah: Some Points for Consideration," Deirdre Fulton observes the diminished roles of the priests and an improved treatment of the Levites. In Ezra 1 and Neh 13, for instance, the purification of the community is performed by non-cultic officiants: Sheshbazzar and Nehemiah. Equally, Fulton observes, priests are assigned certain communal roles, which is rather balanced with that of the Levites (Ezra 7–8); whereas the account of the Festival of Booths in Ezra 3:1–6 depicts proper priestly cultic performance, the account in Neh 8 never mentions sacrificial activity and downplays the role of the priests – the festival is "democratized" by the roles of the Levites and the people. She further argues that the accounts in Neh 13 diminish priestly power in favor of community power or the authority of Nehemiah. As a conclusion, Fulton assigns the authorship of Ezra-Nehemiah to the Judean literati in conversation with the Jerusalem temple community consisting of Levites as well as priests.

The contribution by Louis Jonker, "Levites, Holiness and Late Achaemenid / Early Hellenistic Literature Formation: Where Does Ezra-Nehemiah Fit into the Discourse?" diachronically aligns different literary strata in Ezra-Nehemiah in relation to Chronicles and (Late) Priestly texts. Jonker builds his argument upon his earlier work, according to which Chronicles was contemporaneous with and in interaction with the Late Priestly layers but earlier than Num 16–18 and Ezek 40–48.[7] He argues that parts of Ezra-Nehemiah draw directly from the Holiness legislation ("H"), while others seem to engage with the "democratizing" tendency in H via Chronicles. Jonker distinguishes between three stages according to this criterion: pre-Chronistic references (e. g., Neh 11–12*; second half of the fifth century BCE), later references contemporaneous with Chronicles (e. g., Ezra 2; 6; 8*; 9*; Neh 7; fourth century BCE), and post-Chronistic references (Ezra 6:20; Neh 10:29; 13; end of the fourth to middle of the third centuries BCE).

As briefly presented above, the contributions in this volume represent different positions on the major issue at hand. For instance, some authors emphasize the similarity and literary continuity between the two texts, while others stress the discontinuity and differences. While many authors posit a direction of influence running from the priestly literature to Chronicles, some contributions presuppose or argue for mutual interaction between Chronicles and certain priestly texts. Some authors see a harmonious coexistence between the two texts/traditions as well as between the priests and Levites, while others take more seriously conflicting and polemical relations between them. Presumably, the present organization of the volume – putting the contrasting voices together – is precisely the way our source text manifests itself: a Bible born out of conflict.

---

7. Louis C. Jonker, "Holiness and the Levites. Some Reflections on the Relationship between Chronicles and Pentateuchal Traditions," in *Eigensinn und Entstehung der Hebräischen Bibel. Erhard Blum zum Siebzigsten Geburtstag*, ed. Joachim J. Krause, Wolfgang Oswald, and Kristin Weingart (Tübingen: Mohr Siebeck, 2020), 457–74.

Part 1: Consonance and Dissonance

THE BOOK OF CHRONICLES THROUGH THE AGES: A CINDERELLA OR A SLEEPING BEAUTY?

Jean-Louis Ska

1. INTRODUCTION

That Cinderella of the Hebrew Bible, Chronicles, has at last emerged from years of obscurity and scorn. Early last century she was all the rage among scholars who used her quite shamelessly in their battles over the reconstruction of Israelite history. But then, when the conflict was over, Wellhausen turned on her in favour of her Deuteronomistic stepsister and sent her packing for her unfashionable love of ritual and family ties, and for allegedly playing fast and loose with the facts. How things have changed over the last decade! She may not yet be the belle of the academic ball, but she has, at least, been noticed in her own right once again and has received long overdue attention from the scholarly community.[1]

---

1. John W. Kleinig, "Recent Research in Chronicles," *Currents in Research. Biblical Studies 2* (1994): 43–76, here 43. Among recent works used for this short survey, we must mention, besides Kleinig's article and, among others, some important studies and monographs by Dietmar Mathias, *Die Geschichte der Chronikforschung im 19. Jahrhundert unter besonderer Berücksichtigung der exegetischen Behandlung der Prophetennachrichten des chronistischen Geschichtswerkes. Ein problemgeschichtlicher und methodenkritischer Versuch auf der Basis ausgewählter Texte* (Dissertation zur Promotion A; Leipzig: Karl-Marx-Universität, 1977); Sara Japhet, "The Historical Reliability of Chronicles: The History of the Problem and its Place in Biblical Research," *JSOT* 33 (1985): 83–107; Hugh G.M. Williamson, "Introduction," in Martin Noth, *The Chronicler's History*. Translated by Hugh G.M. Williamson with an introduction, JSOT.S 50 (Sheffield: JSOTPress, 1987), 11–26; Kai Peltonen, *History Debated: The Historical Reliability of Chronicles in Pre-Critical and Critical Research* 2. Vols. Publications of the Finnish Exegetical Society 64 (Helsinki: The Finnish Exegetical Society, 1996); Thomas Willi, "Zwei Jahrzehnte Forschung an Chronik und Esra-Nehemia," *Theologische Rundschau* NF 67 (2002): 61–110; Rodney K. Duke, "Recent Research in Chronicles," Currents in Biblical Research 8 (2009): 10–

This quotation from John W. Kleinig (North Adelaide, Australia) captures in expressive images the changes of attitude towards Chronicles that occurred in the past fifty years. For a long time, the Book of Chronicles was never at the center of attention in biblical research. From the beginnings of exegesis, as early as the Greek translation of the Septuagint (2nd century BCE), Chronicles is something like a stepchild since it receives the title *Paralipoménōn* (Greek: Παραλειπομένων, lit. 'things left on one side,' or something like 'left overs'). This title suggests that the Greek translators found in these books mainly materials not present elsewhere, namely in the Pentateuch and especially in Samuel-Kings.

The usual title "Chronicles" goes back to Jerome's translation into Latin in the 5th century. The title evokes the presence of archives, records, accounts classified or organized in a chronological order – from the Greek word χρόνος, "time."[2] The temporal dimension of the Books was essential for Jerome. Chronicles begins with Adam's genealogy, and concludes with Cyrus the Great's edict (ca. 539 BCE). In a certain sense, we are invited to see in Chronicles a compilation of records about a history beginning with Adam's creation and ending with Cyrus the Great's edict. This is obviously just one way of characterizing the book that closes the third part of the Hebrew canon in several manuscripts, but not in all of them.[3]

The Book of Chronicles is rarely treated in a positive way, and this is the case already in rabbinical and patristic exegesis. There are several reasons for this state of affairs. One aspect of the question may explain, to a certain extent, why this book was often considered as a kind of second-class member of the canon. Chronicles, in fact, repeats several parts, or seems to re-use many elements present in other biblical books, partly in the Pentateuch and more fully in Samuel-Kings. These books were already considered as inspired and author-

---

50; Isaac Kalimi, *The Retelling of Chronicles in Jewish Tradition and Literature: A Historical Journey* (Winona Lake, IN: Eisenbrauns, 2009); Louis C. Jonker, "Within Hearing Distance? Recent Developments in Pentateuch and Chronicles Research," *Old Testament Essays* 27 (2014): 123–46; Louis C. Jonker, "From Paraleipomenon to Early Reader: The Implications of Recent Chronicles Studies for Pentateuchal Criticism," in *Congress Volume Munich 2013*, VTSup 163, ed. Christl M. Maier (Leiden: Brill, 2014), 217–54.

2. For more details on this point, see, among others, Gary N. Knoppers, *1 Chronicles 1–9*, AB 12.1 (New York: Doubleday, 2003), 47.

3. See, for instance, Edmon L. Gallagher, "The End of the Bible? The Position of Chronicles in the Canon," *Tyndale Bulletin* 65 (2014): 181–99; see also Gary N. Knoppers, "Chronicles and Canon," in Knoppers, I Chronicles 1–9, 135–7; Greg Goswell, "The Order of the Books in the Hebrew Bible," *JETS* 51/4 (2008): 673–88. In the Aleppo Codex and in the Saint-Petersburg Codex, the last book is Ezra-Nehemiah.

itative, especially the Pentateuch. Now, there are noticeable differences between Chronicles and these other writings. The tendency was, spontaneously, to give preference to the most respected books of the *Tanakh* at the expense of Chronicles that was relegated among the *Ketûbîm*. The history of exegesis will confirm this view and, in certain cases, add some nuances.

My purpose, in this short essay, is not to supply the reader with a complete and exhaustive history of research about Chronicles. This is impossible. On the other hand, several studies or monographs mentioned in the footnotes will provide the interested reader with all the pieces of information needed. Moreover, the numerous recent commentaries on Chronicles contain excellent introductions and *status quaestionis* (*inter alia* Japhet, Johnstone, Knoppers, Klein, Levin, Willi, Dirksen, Tuell, Williamson). It is not necessary to repeat here what others have exposed with much competence. My purpose is rather to explain what the major steps in the exegesis of Chronicles are and to inquire about the main cultural and intellectual factors that influenced it. Biblical studies do not develop within a vacuum, they breathe the air of their time and hum the popular melodies of their age.

2. EARLY RABBINIC EXEGESIS

According to the Talmud, Chronicles forms only one book and its redaction is attributed to Ezra, an attribution that would last for long (*Baba Bathra* 15a).[4] As for its intrinsic value, Rabbinical and Talmudic authorities already distrusted Chronicles' historical accuracy. The reasons are twofold. First, they were of the opinion that this book was meant for homiletic interpretation rather than for other, more precise, purposes (Lev. R. i.3; Ruth R. ii., beginning; cf. Meg. 13a). Second, the personal names were treated with great freedom, for instance in the genealogies. In some cases, names which had clearly been ascribed to different persons were declared, in other places, to designate one and the same man or woman (Soṭah 12a; Ex. R. i. 17, *et passim*).[5]

We perceive here the first signs of a critical attitude towards Chronicles. Rabbis compared Chronicles with the other books of the *Tanakh* or elements present in different parts of Chronicles, detected tensions and contradictions, and concluded that Chronicles was inaccurate.[6]

---

4. For more details on the place of Chronicles in Jewish tradition, see, for instance, Isaac Kalimi, *The Retelling of Chronicles in Jewish Tradition and Literature: A Historical Journey* (Winona Lake, IN: Eisenbrauns, 2009), 141–54.

5. Jewish Encyclopedia http://www.jewishencyclopedia.com/articles/4371-chronicles-books-of–consulted 07/09/2019.

6. Kalimi, *The Retelling of Chronicles*, 145–8.

This may also explain the reason why Chronicles was rarely commented in Antiquity. We have to wait until the time of Saadia Gaon (882–942), Rashi (1040–1105) and David Kimhi (1160–1235) to have the first rabbinic commentaries on Chronicles.[7] To be sure, the commentary ascribed to Rashi was written by someone else, most probably in Germany, and therefore called Pseudo-Rashi's commentary.[8] Another commentary, but preserved only in fragments, was written by Joseph Kara (c. 1065–c. 1135), Rashi's companion and colleague. Pseudo-Rashi alludes to this work.[9] David Kimhi (Radak), following the Talmud's opinion, considered that Chronicles was written by Ezra who used earlier sources in composing his work.[10] Radak's opinion is of a certain value because he takes the lead of those exegetes who saw in Chronicles mainly a historian. This view was contradicted some time later by Isaac Abravanel (1437–1508) who insisted more on the theological flavour of the book.[11] As we will see, views on Chronicles would oscillate frequently between these two positions, history or theology.[12]

---

7. See Eran Viezel, "The Anonymous Commentary on the Books of Chronicles Attributed to a Student of Sa'adia Gaon: Its Status in the History of the Jewish Peshat Exegesis," *Tarbiz* 76 (2007): 415–34; Kalimi, *The Retelling of Chronicles*, 193–7.

8. See Eran Viezel, *The Commentary on Chronicles Attributed to Rashi* (Jerusalem: Magnes Press, 2010) [Hebrew]. For the original text, see the site https://www.sefaria.org/Rashi_on_I_Chronicles?lang=bi – consulted 29/08/2019; Avraham Grossman, "Solomon Yishaqi/Rashi (1040–1105)," in *Hebrew Bible/Old Testament: The History of Its Interpretation*. I/2: *The Middle Ages* [hereafter *HBOT* I.2], ed. Magne Sæbø (Göttingen: Vandenhoek & Ruprecht, 2000), 332–46, here 333. Cf. Kalimi, *The Retelling of Chronicles*, 199–209.

9. On this author, see https://www.jewishvirtuallibrary.org/kara-joseph–consulted 29/08/2019. See also Avraham Grossman, "Joseph Kara," in *HBOT* I.2, 346–56. Cf. Kalimi, *The Retelling of Chronicles*, 238.

10. On David Kimhi/Radak, see Mordecai Cohen, "The Qimhi Family," in *HBOT* I.2, 388–415 – espec. "David Qimhi (Radak)," 396–415. For his commentary on Chronicles, see Yitzhak Berger, *The Commentary of Rabbi David Kimhi to Chronicles: A Translation with Introduction and Supercommentary* (Providence, RI: Brown University, 2007). Cf. Kalimi, The Retelling of Chronicles, 220–9.

11. The texts can be found in the *Biblia rabbinica or Mikraot Gdolot* (Venice: Daniele Bomberg, 1516–1517; reprinted in 1568); *Biblia Rabbinica con Targums*, Revised by Leon of Modena with a foreword (Venice: Pietro e Lorenzo Bragadin, 1617–1619).

12. See Thomas Willi, *Chronik: 1. Teilband 1. Chronik 1,1–10,14*, BK XXIV/1 (Neukirchen-Vluyn: Neukirchner, 2009), vii. On Isaac Abravanel, see Eric Lawee, "Isaac Abarbanel: From Medieval to Renaissance Jewish Biblical Scholarship," in *Hebrew Bible/Old Testament: The History of Its Interpretation*. II: *From Renaissance to Enlightenment* [hereafter *HBOT* II], ed. Magne Sæbø (Göttingen: Vandenhoeck & Ruprecht, 2008), 190–214.

3. NEGATIVE OPINIONS

Joseph Solomon del Medigo o Delmedigo (Candia, Crete, 16 June 1591 – Praga, 16 October 1655), a Jewish scholar, physician, astronomist and mathematician, expresses an opinion about Chronicles which is representative of what most intellectuals thought in that time.[13] For him, the writer of Chronicles is fundamentally unreliable for one main motive, namely that he lived a long time after the destruction of the First Temple. This is the reason why he was included into the *Ketûbîm* or Hagiographa. Moreover, there is much disagreement between the different versions of the same event in these late compositions. We may notice a critical spirit in these remarks, a rational or rationalist spirit stemming from Greek historians and philosophers.[14] Here is his opinion in a few sentences:[15]

> [The writer of Chronicles] lived a long time after the first destruction […] and therefore it was included among the Hagiographa […] and you should know these post – destruction stories, how they vary, like most of the modern historiographies, where you will find no two in agreement on one single event.

We find a similar reaction in Baruch Spinoza (1632–1677):[16]

> But about the two books of Chronicles I have nothing certain and worthwhile to say except that – contrary to a tradition that makes Ezra their author – they were written long after Ezra, and perhaps after Judas Maccabee restored the temple. […] Nothing is apparent to me about the true writer of these books, or about their authority, their utility or their

---

13. On del Medigo, see Isaac Barzilay, *Yoseph Shlomo Delmedigo (Yashar of Candia): His Life, Works and Times*, Studia Post-biblica 25 (Leiden: Brill, 1974); Jacob Adler, "Joseph Solomon Delmedigo: Student of Galileo, Teacher of Spinoza," *Intellectual History Review* 23.1 (2013): 141–57. Delmedigo was a great traveler. We count Venice, Alexandria and Cairo (Egypt), Istanbul, Wilna, Hamburg, Amsterdam, Frankfort-on-the-Main, and Praga among the cities he visited.

14. See Japhet, "Historical Reliability," 83–4. Source: Yoseph Shelomo del Medigo, *Matzref Lahochma*, ed. Sh. Ashkenazi (Basel: Ashkenazi, 1629), 29b. On the man and his works, see Issac Barzilai, *Yoseph Shlomo Delmedigo (Yashar of Candia)*, Studia Post-Biblica 25 (Leiden: Brill, 1974), esp. 299–304; David Geffen, "Insights into the Life and Thought of Elijah Medigo Based on His Published and Unpublished Works," *Proceedings of the American Academy for Jewish Research* 41/42 (1973–1974): 69–86. Cf. Kalimi, *The Retelling of Chronicles*, 294–6.

15. Japhet, "Historical Reliability," 83.

16. On Spinoza, see Rudolf Smend, "Baruch de Spinoza (1632–1677)," in Rudolf Smend, *Kritiker und Exegeten. Porträtskizzen zur vier Jahrhunderten alttestamentlicher Wissenschaft* (Göttingen: Vandenhoeck & Ruprecht, 2017), 50–66. See also Steven Nadler (ed.), *Spinoza and Medieval Jewish Philosophy* (Cambridge: Cambridge University Press, 2014); Jeffrey L. Morrow, *Three Skeptics and the Bible: La Peyrère, Hobbes, Spinoza, and the Reception of Modern Biblical Criticism* (Eugene, OR: Pickwick, 2016). Cf. Kalimi, The Retelling of Chronicles, 296–302.

doctrine. In fact, I am amazed at their being accepted as sacred by the people who removed the Book of Wisdom, Tobias, and the rest of the so-called apocrypha from the canon of sacred books. But I am not trying to lessen their authority; everyone accepts them, so I leave it at that.[17]

Two points are of importance. First, Ezra is no longer considered the author of Chronicles; second, the date of composition is pushed as late as the time of the Maccabees, in the 2nd century BCE. Of course, this statement undermines even more the historical value of the book since there is a longer temporal distance between Chronicles and the events recounted therein. Spinoza, as we know, was condemned by the authorities of the Synagogue, by the Church and even by the civil authorities of his city, Amsterdam. His ambivalent statement explains partly why he had little effect on the exegesis of Chronicles in his time. Anyway, Chronicles was surely not at the center of attention either.

Spinoza's doubts about the inspiration of Chronicles, however, were taken seriously by some other scholars, among them Georg Ludwig Oeder (1694–1760) who tried to prove that Chronicles was not divinely inspired and, therefore, had no place in the canon of Scriptures.[18] After being located to the bottom floor of Scriptures, Chronicles was about to be expelled to the street.

4. WILHELM MARTIN LEBERECHT DE WETTE (1780–1849)

A major turn in the exegesis of Chronicles occurred with Wilhelm Martin Leberecht de Wette who undoubtedly determined the study of the book for a long time.[19]

De Wette published his *Beiträge zur Einleitung in das Alte Testament – Contributions to the Introduction into the Old Testament* in 1807.[20] There were two volumes, and the subtitles reveal the exact

---

17. Baruch Spinoza, *Tractatus theologico-politicus* (Hamburg: Kühnrat, 1670), ch. 10. Quotation from Baruch Spinoza from J. Israel and M. Silverthorne, *Theological-Political Treatise*, Cambridge Texts in the History of Philosophy (Cambridge: Cambridge University Press, 2007), with some slight modifications to clarify Spinoza's thought. For a translation on the web, see https://www. earlymoderntexts.com/assets/pdfs/spinoza1669.pdf–consulted on 29/08/2019.

18. Georg Ludwig Oeder, *Freye Untersuchungen über einige Bücher des Alten Testament* (Hrsg. Georg Johann Ludwig Vogel) (Halle: Hendel, 1771), 137–246; Rudolf Smend, *Wilhelm Martin Leberecht de Wettes Arbeit am Alten und am Neuen Testament* (Basel: Helbing & Lichtenhahn, 1958), 41. Georg Ludwig Oeder was active in Heilbronn, Ansbach and Feuchtwangen.

19. On De Wette, see Rudolf Smend's work cited in the previous note; John W. Rogerson, *W.M.L. de Wette, Founder of Modern Biblical Criticism: An Intellectual Biography* (Sheffield: Academic Press, 1992).

20. Wilhelm Martin Leberecht de Wette, *Beiträge zur Einleitung in das Alte Tes-

purpose of the work. The first volume is entitled *Kritischer Versuch über die Glaubwürdigkeit der Bücher der Chronik mit Hinsicht auf die Geschichte der Mosaischen Bücher und Gesetzgebung. Ein Nachtrag zu den Vaterschen Untersuchungen über den Pentateuch – Critical Essay on the Reliability of the Books of Chronicles with Respect to the History of the Mosaic Books and Legislation: A Supplement to Vater's Investigation on the Pentateuch* and the second, *Kritik der Mosaischen Geschichte – Critique of the Mosaic History*.

The important word in the first subtitle is *Glaubwürdigkeit – Reliability*. We are dealing with a historical inquiry and de Wette's endeavours to find out whether we can rely on the Books of Chronicles, especially in what it says about the law of Moses. There were many discussions at that time about the Mosaic authorship of the Pentateuch, a problem connected with the authority and inspiration of the *Torah*. This problem was hotly debated, as everyone knows. But why does de Wette starts his inquiry with the Books of Chronicles? The reason is that the Old Testament offers two parallel histories of ancient Israel, Samuel-Kings on the one side and Chronicles on the other side. One of the main differences between the two presentations is that Chronicles, contrary to Samuel-Kings, contains many references to Moses' law. This law is constantly presented as the blueprint for the building of the temple and the organization of the cult. It is as if David and Solomon were constantly consulting the law of Moses before taking any decision in cultic matters. Every item in the building of the temple and every element in the cult conform to the prescriptions found in Moses' law.[21] The allusions are moreover to 'what is *written* in Moses' Law.'[22]

This fact was used by many scholars to show the antiquity of Moses' law since, according to Chronicles, it must have been known at the time of David and Solomon. On the other hand, it seems that Samuel-Kings ignore almost completely Moses' Law, apart from a very few exceptions (cf. 2Kgs 14:6). De Wette, for his part, opts for

tament (Halle: Schimmelpfennig, 1807; Hildesheim: Georg Holms, 1971).

21. Moses is mentioned in 1 Chr 6:34, 15:15, 21:29, 22:13, 23:15, 26:24, 2 Chr 1:3, 5:10, 8:13, 23:18, 24:6, 9, 25:4, 30:16, 33:8, 34:14, 35:6, 12 (18x). The legislation of Moses is mentioned explicitly in 2 Chr 8:13, 23:18, 25:4, 30:16, 33:8, 34:14, 35:6, 12.

22. 2 Chr 23:18; 25:4; 30:5, 18; 31:3; 35:12, 26. For more details on this point, see Arthur Charles Hervey, *The Book of Chronicles in Relation to the Pentateuch and "Higher Criticism"* (London: Society for Promoting Christian Knowledge – New York: Brighton, 1892); Thomas Willi, "'Wie geschrieben steht' – Schriftbezug und Schrift. Überlegungen zur frühjüdischen Literaturwerdung im perserzeitlichen Kontext," in Thomas Willi, *Israel und die Völker. Studien zur Literatur und Geschichte Israels in der Perserzeit*, SBAB 55 (Stuttgart: Verlag Katholisches Bibelwerk, 2012), 101–22; Knoppers, I Chronicles 1–9, 123–6 ("As It Is Written: The Chronicler's Source Citations").

Samuel-Kings and undermines Chronicles radically, insisting on its ideological and theological biases. Chronicles was also written much later than the events described and is, for this reason, untrustworthy. Altogether, Chronicles is a negligent, inaccurate, work that reveals patent tendentiousness, expressed for instance in the author's preference for the Levites, his predilection for the temple and the cult, his fondness for Judah and his hostility towards Israel.

We may ask, however, why de Wette wanted to demonstrate that the Pentateuch was written much later than Moses and was not a source of historical information. Three elements in de Wette's formation are essential for the understanding of his exegesis.

(1) First, de Wette was influenced much by Immanuel Kant's philosophy that he read during his studies in Jena.[23] This was a major element in his education although he also met with other great writers and philosophers in Weimar, for instance Wolfgang Goethe, Friedrich Schiller and especially Johann Gottfried von Herder,[24] or in Jena where he was in touch with Johann Gottlieb Fichte, Georg Wilhelm Friedrich Hegel, Friedrich Schelling and Jakob Friedrich Fries, the latter being a disciple of Kant. After reading de Wette, one cannot avoid noticing the parenthood between his ideas and Kant's theory of a *Die Religion innerhalb der Grenzen der bloßen Vernunft – Religion within the Boundaries of Mere Reason* (1793). This title expresses very well what was the intellectual atmosphere in that time and also explains why there was a strong suspicion towards every supranatural phenomenon, either miracle or oracle, in academic circles. The tendency was to look, first of all, for rational or natural explanations for such phenomena. Other scholars may have had some influence on de Wette's formation, as for instance, still in Jena, Johann Jakob Griesbach (1745–1812), a disciple of Semmler, Heinrich Eberhard Gottlob Paulus (1761–1851), Johann Philipp Gabler (1753–1826) and Karl David Ilgen (1763–1834), a very critical spirit, who probably encouraged de Wette to meet with Johann Severin Vater (1771–1826).

23. For these pieces of information, see Rudolf Smend, "Wilhelm Martin Leberecht de Wette (1780–1849)," in Kritiker und Exegeten, 192–206. See also Rogerson, *W.M.L. de Wette*, 19–63. On Kant's influence on biblical interpretation, see, among others, Jan Rohls, "Historical, Cultural and Philosophical Aspects of the Nineteenth Century with Special Regard to Biblical Interpretation," *Hebrew Bible/Old Testament: The History of Its Interpretation*. III/1: *The Nineteenth Century – A Century of Modernism and Historicism* [hereafter HBOT III.1], ed. Magne Sæbø (Göttingen: Vandenhoeck & Ruprecht, 2013), 31–63, esp. 34–5.

24. On Herder, see, for instance, Thomas Willi, *Herders Beitrag zum Verstehen des Alten Testaments*, Beiträge zur Geschichte der biblischen Hermeneutik 8 (Tübingen: Mohr Siebeck, 1971); Henning Graf Reventlow, "Johann Gottfried Herder – Theologian, Promotor of Humanity, Historian," in HBOT II, 1041–50; Smend, *Kritiker und Exegeten*, 154–75.

Vater's work duplicated that of de Wette to a certain extent since de Wette was, for a while, a "fragmentist" just as Vater.[25]

Paulus, to come back to this New Testament scholar, was another disciple of Kant, and he applied theological rationalism to the Scriptures, eliminating for instance any supranatural reference from the gospels. Gabler, for his part, is often considered as the founder of biblical theology as a discipline independent from dogmatic theology, in his writing *De justo discrimine theologiae biblicae et dogmaticae regundisque recte utriusque finibus – On the Correct Distinction between Dogmatic and Biblical Theology and the Right Definition of Their Goals* (1787). All these scholars helped de Wette sharpen his critical sensitivity in reading biblical texts especially in historical matters.

(2) The second important element in de Wette's formation is the idea of "myth" which becomes central especially in his understanding of the Pentateuch.[26] The word "myth" in de Wette's work has a precise meaning. "Myth" is a scenic, picturesque expression of a worldview and of a self-understanding in a given culture. This type of thinking is characteristic of ancient cultures, for instance in Greece and in the Ancient Near East. The idea itself does not come from de Wette, but from Christian Gottlob Heyne (1729–1812), a specialist of Homer. Once again, we must admit that many leading ideas in biblical exegesis stem from classical studies, especially Homeric studies.[27] This was already the case in antiquity. We may remember that Karl David Ilgen was also a specialist of Homer and taught classical literature in Jena.

The concept of myth, developed by Christian Gottlob Heyne (1729–1812), was first adopted by Johann Gottfried Eichhorn (1752–1827) who taught in Jena and Göttingen.[28] De Wette knew Eichhorn and was often in dialogue with him. More concretely, de Wette

---

25. De Wette mentions explicitly Ilgen and Vater among his predecessors and inspirers (*Beiträge*, iv).

26. "Was man vielleicht für zu kühn erkennen wird, daß ich den ganzen Pentateuch von Anfang bis zu Ende in mythischer Bedeutung nehme, ist doch weiter nichts als Konsequenz: denn wie das Einzelne, so auch das Ganze" (Beiträge, iv) – italics mine.

27. See, for instance, Margalit Finkelberg and Guy G. Stroumsa (eds.), *Homer, the Bible, and beyond: Literary and Religious Canons in the Ancient World*, Jerusalem Studies in Religion and Culture 2 (Leiden – Boston: Brill, 2003); Maren R. Niehoff (ed.), *Homer and the Bible in the Eyes of Ancient Interpreters*, Jerusalem Studies in Religion and Culture 16 (Leiden: Brill, 2012). For earlier essays in the field, see Cyrus Gordon, "Homer and the Bible," HUCA 26 (1955): 43–108; Umberto Cassuto, *The Documentary Hypothesis and the Composition of the Pentateuch* (Jerusalem: Magnes Press – Hebrew University, 1961) (Hebrew: 1941), 10–1.

28. Cf. Smend, Kritiker und Exegeten, 186–7. On Eichhorn, see Smend, *Kritiker und Exegeten*, 176–91.

disagreed with Eichhorn on the way of interpreting the presence of "myths" in biblical literature. Eichhorn tried to trace a middle path between supernaturalism and orthodoxy, on the one hand, and rationalism and enlightenment on the other. More concretely, he tried to find some historical kernels in biblical narratives, especially in the Pentateuch. For de Wette, on the contrary – and in a way like Ilgen and Paulus – it was impossible to find history behind ancient myths. Under the mythical language, or under the mythical varnish, we discover religion, not history. There are therefore two sides in de Wette's exegesis. The first is negative, and its purpose is to demonstrate the absence of history – in the modern sense of the word – in the Pentateuch. The more positive side is the exposition of the religious ideas and ideals in the texts. This second part is perhaps not sufficiently developed in de Wette's work, but this aspect was essential to him.

To come back to classical studies and its influence on biblical exegesis, de Wette considers the author of Genesis 24 as a "Canaanite Homer," he compares Jacob's journey to that of Ulysses, and finds similarities between classical epics, for instance Virgil's Aeneid, and the Elohist (the future Priestly Writer).[29] All this means that we can hardly treat the Pentateuch as a historical document or as a source of historical, accurate, information.

(3) This leads us to the third aspect of de Wette's research. Along the same line as Herder, after discussions with Friedrich Lücke (1791–1855) and especially Friedrich Daniel Ernst Schleiermacher (1768–1834) in Berlin, de Wette looked for some new ways to solve the conflict between orthodoxy and rationalism.[30] In his choice, he was guided by Immanuel Kant's third important work, *Die Kritik der Urtheilskraft – The Critique of the Judgement* (1790) and found there the lineaments of a conception of religion based on sensitivity (*Gefühl*) and aesthetics. This idea was also fostered by Jakob Friedrich Fries, Kant's disciple and de Wette's colleague. To give only one example of this way of thinking, de Wette affirms that there is no history in Genesis 22, but we should not forget the "beautiful meaning" of this poetic narrative: "Diese Mythe ist eine der schönsten in der Genesis" – "This myth is one of the most beautiful in Genesis." And Abraham is "das Vorbild hebräischer Frömmigkeit" – "the model of Hebrew piety."[31] All in all, for de Wette, the roots of authentic religion are not to be looked for in historical facts or in rational arguments. Its roots are elsewhere, especially in the aesthetic and artistic aspect of biblical narratives.

---

29. De Wette, *Beiträge*, 116, 123, 32.

30. On Schleiermacher, see Jan Rohls, "F.E.D. Schleiermacher – His Criticism of the Old Testament," in *HBOT* III.1, 38–44.

31. De Wette, *Beiträge*, 103.

All this may help us understand the reason better why de Wette insisted forcefully on the fact that Chronicles is no reliable source for Israel's ancient history. We have "myth" in the Pentateuch, we do not have history. The Pentateuch is the expression of Israel's religion, of Israel's convictions, worldview and self-consciousness. For this reason, it was essential for de Wette to demonstrate the unreliability of Chronicles, since these books affirmed, time and again, that the law of Moses, the written law, was known as early as the reign of David and Solomon. De Wette endeavored to free Israel's religion from too close an association with history and also, from some other forms of religion, such as legalism and ritualism, as in Kant and in liberal Protestantism.

5. The Aftermath of de Wette's Proposition: Enthusiasm and Antagonism

Handbooks usually mention de Wette's work as a turning-point in the exegesis of Chronicles but ignore or pass over in silence all the negative reactions this position provoked. *Falsa est de Wettii de Pentateucho sententia* is, to take just one example, the first sentence of a thesis defended in Bonn in 1823 by Ernst Wilhelm Hengstenberg (20 October 1802–28 May 1869).[32] Other authors attacked de Wette directly and tried by all means to save the validity of Chronicles as source for a history of Israel.[33] Among these authors, we may notice the names of Johann Gottfried Eichhorn and of Carl Friedrich Keil, Franz Delitzsch's disciple and colleague. The main problem, at that time, was the historicity of Chronicles, fiercely defended by all these authors who affirm that the book used reliable sources.[34]

32. On Hengstenberg, see Matthias A. Deuschle, *Ernst Wilhelm Hengstenberg. Ein Beitrag zur Erforschung des kirchlichen Konservatismus im Preußen des 19. Jahrhunderts*, BHTh (Tübingen: Mohr Siebeck, 2013); Smend, *Kritiker und Exegeten*, 240–57.

33. Johann Gottfried Eichhorn, *Einleitung in das Alte Testament* (Leipzig: Weidmann, 1780–1783, 41823), iii, 495–8; Johannes Georg Dahler, *De Librorum Paralipomenon Auctoritate atque Fide Histórica Disputatio* (Strassburg und Leipzig: Gleditsch, 1819); J.M. Hertz, *Sind in den Büchern der Könige Spuren des Pentateuch und der Mosaischen Gesetze zu finden? Ein Versuch zur Vertheidigung der Bücher der Chronik wie auch des Alterthums der Mosaischen Gesetze* (Altona: Hammerich, 1822); Carl Peter Wilhelm Gramberg, *Die Chronik nach ihren geschichtlichen Charakter und ihrer Glaubwürdigkeit neu geprüft* (Halle: Eduard Anton, 1823; Florence: Nabu Press, 2012); Carl Friedrich Keil, *Apologetischer Versuch über die Bücher der Chronik und über die Integrität des Buches Ezra* (Berlin: Oehmigke, 1833; Warsaw: Andesite Press, 2017).

34. See, on this point, besides the article by Sarah Japhet (note 1), M. Patrick Graham, *The Utilization of 1 and 2 Chronicles in the Reconstruction of Israelite History in the Nineteenth Century*, SBLDS 116 (Atlanta, GA: Scholars Press, 1990); M.

Things change, eventually, with Karl Heinrich Graf[35] and Julius Wellhausen.[36]

Both picked up de Wette's thesis and built their theories on it. For Wellhausen, it was crystal-clear that Chronicles cannot be used as reliable source for a reconstruction of Israel's past. His main reasons are the following: (1) In Chronicles, Israel's past is seen through a Judaic lense, i. e. Chronicles projects into the past a picture of the Judaean post-exilic community; (2) The differences between Chronicles and 1–2 Samuel/1–2 Kings are best explained by the influence of the Priestly Code and its interest in cultic and legal matters; (3) It is not possible to prove that Chronicles had made use of valid, ancient, and trustworthy sources. All in all, Chronicles remained the Cinderella or the stepchild of biblical exegesis, especially because of its historical biases in favor of Judah and Jerusalem, and its predilection for the cult of the temple and all its paraphernalia. For Wellhausen, Chronicles was a midrash that grows like a green ivy around a dead trunk, the ivy being Chronicles and the dead trunk the old traditions.[37] The word "midrash" would have some success subsequently.

Patrick Graham, Kenneth G. Hoglund, and Steven L. McKenzie (eds.), *The Chronicler as Historian*, JSOT.S 238 (Sheffield: Academic Press, 1997); Thomas Willi, *Israel und die Völker. Studien zur Literatur und Geschichte Israels in der Perserzeit*. Herausgegeben von Michael Pietsch, Stuttgarter biblische Aufsatzbände 55 (Stuttgart: Katholisches Bibelwerk, 2012).

35. Karl Heinrich Graf, "Das Buch der Chronik als Geschichtsquelle," in Karl Heinrich Graf, *Die Geschichtlichen Bücher des Alten Testaments. Zwei historisch-kritische Untersuchungen* (Leipzig: T.O. Weigel, 1866), 114–247. ["Die Bestandteile der historischen Bücher von Genes. 1 bis 2 Reg. 25" ("Pentateuch und Prophetae priores")].

36. Julius Wellhausen, *Prolegomena zur Geschichte Israels* (Berlin: Georg Reimer, 1878, ²1883; ⁵1899; de Gruyter Studienbuch; Berlin – New York: de Gruyter, 2001); English translation: *Prolegomena to the History of Israel*. Translated by S. Black and A. Menzies (Edinburgh: A. & C. Black, 1885), 171–227. Here again, there was strong opposition to Wellhausen's views. See, for instance, Wilhelm Möller, *Historisch-kritische Bedenken gegen die Graf-Wellhausensche Hypothese. Von einem früheren Anhänger den Studierenden der Theologie gewidmet. Mit einem Begleitwort versehen von C. von Dressi* (Gütersloh: Bertelsmann, 1899); English translation: *Are the Critics Right? Historical & Critical Considerations against the Graf-Wellhausen Hypothesis*. With an introduction by C. von Orelli; translated from the German by C.H. Irwin (London: The Religious Tract Society, 1903).

On Graf, see Joachim Conrad, *Karl Heinrich Grafs Arbeit am Alten Testament: Studien zu einer wissenschaftlichen Biographie* (BZAW 425; Berlin: de Gruyter, 2011).

On Wellhausen, see, among many others, Rudolf Smend, *Julius Wellhausen: Ein Bahnbrecher in drei Disziplinen* (München: Carl von Friedrich Siemens Stiftung, 2006).

37. Wellhausen, Prolegomena, 223: "Wie Efeu umgrünt derselbe [der Midrasch der Chronik] den abgestorbenen Stamm mit fremdartigen Leben, Altes und Neues in sonderbarer Vereinigung mischend."

Wellhausen had several followers and his influence lasted for a long a time. One question, however, received a different treatment and deserve some attention, namely the question of authorship. From the time of the Talmud (*Baba Bathra* 15a), Ezra was supposed to have written Chronicles or, in other words, the author of Ezra-Nehemiah composed Chronicles as well. This changed with the Jewish scholar Leopold Zunz (1794–1886). Together with other young men, among them the poet Heinrich Heine, alongside Joel Abraham List, Isaac Marcus Jost, and Eduard Gans, Zunz founded the *Verein für Kultur und Wissenschaft der Juden* ("The Society for the Culture and Science of the Jews") in Berlin in 1819. He was also the editor of the *Zeitschrift für die Wissenschaft des Judenthums*. For Zunz, Ezra was not the author of Chronicles. On the contrary, the Chronicler was the author of Ezra-Nehemiah.[38] His main reason is that these books – and Zunz still considered them as one literary composition – describe a historical situation from a distant viewpoint and are therefore written a long time after the events. Therefore, they cannot have been written by Ezra who is contemporary with the events. Hereby, we return, in a certain way, to Spinoza's conclusion.[39]

Along the same line, and independently from Zunz, Franz Karl Movers (1806–1856), a German Roman Catholic and Orientalist, reached similar conclusions. However, he attributed only Ezra 1–10 to the Chronicler. Movers had studied theology in Münster and was then professor of Old Testament theology in the Catholic faculty at Breslau (now Wrocław) from 1839 to his death. He had interest in the Phoenicians and in the two recensions of the Book of Jeremiah, the Masoretic text and the Greek text of the Septuagint.[40] Movers was at the same time concerned with Ancient Near Eastern history, text criticism and comparative philology. All these elements would play a role in his ensuing study of Chronicles.

Among Wellhausen's followers who doubted the historical trustworthiness of Chronicles, we must mention Charles C. Torrey, historian, orientalist, archaeologist and founder of the American School of Archaeology in Jerusalem in 1900–1901, a very critical spirit. He taught Semitic languages at the Andover Theological Seminary (1892–1900) and at Yale University (1900–1932). He was also a specialist of

---

38. Leopold Zunz, *Die gottesdienstlichen Vorträge der Juden, historisch entwickelt. Ein Beitrag zur Alterthumskunde und biblischen Kritik, zur Literatur- und Religionsgeschichte* (Berlin: A. Asher, 1832; Hildesheim: Georg Olms, 1966). See Japhet, "Historical Reliability," 88–9.

39. Cf. Japhet, "Historical Reliability," 103, note 31.

40. Franz Karl Movers, *Kritische Untersuchungen über die biblische Chronik. Ein Beitrag zur Einleitung in das Alte Testament* (Bonn: T. Habicht, 1834). See Japhet, "Historical Reliability," 103, note 32.

the Koran.⁴¹ Here is a summary of his opinion on Chronicles:⁴²

> No fact of Old Testament criticism is more firmly established than this, that the Chronicler as a historian is thoroughly untrustworthy. He distorts facts deliberately and habitually, invents chapter after chapter with the greatest freedom, and what is most dangerous of all, his history is not written for its own sake, but in the interest of an extremely one-sided theory.

According to Torrey, and this was a common opinion at that time since Zunz, the Chronicler was also the author of Ezra-Nehemiah, and these works were unreliable from the point of view of history. This led to the complete denial of the return from the exile and the restoration of "Israel":

> The exile was a limited phenomenon; there was no restoration at all; Ezra the Scribe is a fictitious figure; the edict of Cyrus and the letter of Artaxerxes are later forgeries; the story about the bringing of the Torah from Babylon is pure imagination; the expulsion of the foreign wives is an unfounded invention; and so on.⁴³

This is probably one of the most scathing and disparaging opinions on Chronicles that we meet in our history of research.

Other scholars were less radical in their conclusions, for instance, Albin van Hoonacker (Bruges, 19 November 1857 – Bruges, 1 November 1933), a Roman Catholic theologian, professor at the Faculty of Theology of the Catholic University of Leuven (Belgium).⁴⁴ He came to discuss the value of Chronicles in his dialogue with Abraham Kuenen, Graf and Wellhausen about the composition of the Pentateuch, a debate that caused him some difficulties with the Church authorities in Rome. Albin van Hoonacker raised doubts about the historical framework of Ezra-Nehemiah and he placed Ezra after Nehemiah.⁴⁵ Albin van Hoonacker is also one of the scholars who used

---

41. Charles Cutler Torrey, *The Composition and Historical Value of Ezra-Nehemiah*, BZAW 2 (Giessen: Ricker, 1896); Charles Cutler Torrey, *The Chronicler's History of Israel: Chronicles-Ezra-Nehemiah Restored to Its Original Order* (New Haven, CT: Yale University Press, 1954; Port Washington, NY: Kennicat Press, 1973); Charles Cutler Torrey, *Ezra-Studies* (Chicago, IL: University of Chicago Press, 1910).

42. Torrey, *Composition*, 52; cf. Japhet, "Historical Reliability," 88.

43. Torrey, *Composition*, 49–50; cf. Japhet, "Historical Reliability," 90.

44. Albin van Hoonacker was appointed to a newly created chair, that of the *Histoire critique de l'Ancien Testament*, due to his involvement in the debate on the origin and authorship of the Pentateuch.

45. See Albin van Hoonacker, *Néhémie et Esdras. Nouvelle hypothèse sur la chronologie de l'époque de la restauration* (Gand: H. Engelcke, 1890); *Néhémie en l'an 20 d'Artaxerxes I. Esdras en l'an 7 d'Artaxerxès II. Réponse à un mémoire de A. Kuenen* (Gand: H. Engelcke, 1892); *Zorobabel et le second temple. Étude sur la chronologie des six premiers chapitres du Livre d'Esdras* (Gand: H. Engelcke, 1892);

the Elephantine papyri in his research, an element of clear importance in the study of postexilic Israel.[46]

Along the same line and in a neighboring country, in the Netherlands, Willem Hendrik Kosters (Enschede 1843–Enscede 1897), a colleague of Kuenen in Leiden, came to somewhat more radical conclusions. For instance, he questioned the historicity of the restoration (cf. Torrey) and the reliability of Ezra 1–4.[47]

6. Change in Perspective: Archaeology and Assyriology

With Charles Torrey, we may have reached a nadir in the exegesis of Chronicles. The books are unreliable for the historian, disappointing for the theologian and dreary for the literary critic. As several other cases, a change in perspective comes both from internal developments and external factors. In the nineteenth century, the main interest was more history than literature and theology. The study of both the Pentateuch and Chronicles was guided by the search for reliable sources in the reconstruction of a history of Israel. Wellhausen's major work was entitled *Prolegomena zur Geschichte Israels*, and this title is revelatory of his intention.

In the course of the nineteenth century, however, an important shift in perspective occurred because of the numerous archaeolog-

Nouvelles études sur la restauration juive après l'exil de Babylone (Paris: Leroux, 1896). See Japhet, "Historical Reliability," 103, note 37. On Albin van Hoonacker, see Joseph Coppens, *Le Chanoine Albin Van Hoonacker. Son enseignement, son œuvre et sa méthode* (Paris: Desclée de Brouwer, 1935); Johan Lust, "A. van Hoonacker and Deuteronomy," in Norbert Lohfink (ed.), *Das Deuteronomium. Entstehung, Gestalt und Botschaft*, BETL 68 (Leuven: Peeters, 1985), 13–23. On the discussions in this period, see, among many others, Richard Jude Thompson, *Moses and the Law in a Century of Criticism since Graf*, SVT 19 (Leiden: Brill, 1970), 89–90.

46. See Albin van Hoonacker, *Une Communauté Judéo-Araméenne à Éléphantine, en Égypte aux VIe et Ve siècles av. J.-C.*, The Schweich Lectures (London: British Academy, 1915). The discoveries at Elephantine surely created a surprise among scholars. See, for instance, Arthur Cowley, *Aramaic Papyri of the Fifth Century B.C.* (Oxford: The Clarendon Press,1923; Eugene, OR: Wipf & Stock Publishers, 2005), xxiii: "So far as we learn from these texts Moses might never have existed, there might have been no bondage in Egypt, no exodus, no monarchy, no prophets. There is no mention of other tribes and no claim to any heritage in the land of Judah. Among the numerous names of colonists, Abraham, Jacob, Joseph, Moses, Samuel, David, so common in later times, never occur (nor in Nehemiah), nor any other name derived from their past history as recorded in the Pentateuch and early literature. It is almost incredible, but it is true."

47. Willem Hendrik Kosters, *Het herstel van Israël in het Perzische tijdvak. Eene studie* (Leiden: E.J. Brill, 1893) = *Die Wiederherstellung Israels in der persischen Periode*. Übersetzt von A. Basedow (Heidelberg: Hörning, 1895). See Japhet, "Historical Reliability," 103, note 37.

ical discoveries, especially in Israel, in Egypt and in Mesopotamia. Newly deciphered documents and new architectural elements obliged scholars to revise and complement the pieces of information coming from the Bible alone. As for the postexilic period, the discovery of the Elephantine papyri around 1870 is of paramount importance.[48] These discoveries obliged scholars to revise their opinions on the postexilic period and, consequently, on the value of Chronicles as witness of the spirit of that time. The Elephantine papyri provided exegetes and orientalists with fresh information about the Persian period and about a Jewish community of the diaspora. Until then, the Bible was almost the only source of information about the postexilic period. Now, documents were revealing important aspects of society, law, justice and religion, and details about Jerusalem, the temple, the Persian authorities, and the celebration of some liturgical feasts, for instance Passover. These papyri shed new light on the content of Ezra-Nehemiah, and conversely also on Chronicles.

One of the first authors who is witness to this shift in perspective is probably the Assyriologist Hugo Winckler, professor at the University of Berlin.[49] He is famous for having excavated the Hittite capital Ḫattuša, close to Boğazköy, in Turkey, from 1906 onward. He is also renowned for his translation of the Code of Hammurabi and the letters from Tel-Amarna. As a specialist of cuneiform documents, he was persuaded that these materials would force historians to revise their image of the history of the Ancient Near East.[50] As for Chronicles,

---

48. See, for instance, among the first publications on this topic, Martin Sprengling, *Chronological Notes from the Aramaic Papyri*; *the Jewish Calendar*; *Dates of the Achaemenians* (*Cyrus-Darius III*), Miscellanea papyrorum Elephantine 11 (Chicago, IL: University of Chicago Press, 1911); Eduard Sachau, *Aramäische Papyrus und Ostraka aus einer jüdischen Militär-Kolonie zu Elephantine. Altorientalische Sprachdenkmäler des 5. Jahrhunderts vor Chr.* (Leipzig: Hinrichs, 1911); Stanley A. Cook, "The Significance of the Elephantine Papyri for the History of Hebrew Religion," *The American Journal of Theology* 19/3 (1915): 346–82; Albin van Hoonacker, *Une Communauté Judéo-Araméenne à Éléphantine, en Égypte aux VIe et Ve siècles av. J.-C.* (London: Oxford University Press, 1915). For a more recent treatment of the documents, see Bezalel Porten, with J.J. Farber, C.J. Martin, G. Vittman (eds.), *The Elephantine Papyri in English*: *Three Millennia of Cross-Cultural Continuity and Change*, (Leiden: Brill, 1996; Atlanta, GA: Society of Biblical Literature, 2011).

49. Among Hugo Winckler's chief publications, mention must be made of *Keilinschriftliches Textbuch zum Alten Testament*, Hilfsbücher zur Kunde des Alten Orients 1 (Leipzig: J.C. Hinrichs'sche Buchhandlung, 1892, 31909); *Die Gesetze Hammurabis in Umschrift und Übersetzung*, Der Alte Orient 4 (Leipzig: J.C. Hinrichs'sche Buchhandlung, 1904).

50. See his significant work in the field, *Der alte Orient und die Geschichtsforschung*, Mitteilungen der Vorderasiatischen Gesellschaft 11,1 (Berlin: Wolf Peiser, 1906). See also "Zur Geschichte und Geographie Israels" in *Altorientalische Forschungen* (Helsingfors: Verlag von Eduard Pfeiffer, 1902), 249–73.

Winckler remained cautious, but admitted that the negative views of his predecessors were exaggerated in several aspects.

He acknowledged, however, the general view that Chronicles is prejudiced and tendentious in most cases. He limited his inquiry, therefore, to a very restricted number of texts, the sections unique to Chronicles, i. e. the material added to Samuel-Kings. Even in this case, he put the texts under close scrutiny and used them only when they proved to be free from historical biases. More importantly, Winckler was convinced that the new discoveries in the Ancient Near East had a special bearing on "historical reliability" or "historical probability" and that these new elements had some consequences for the way of reading Chronicles as well.[51] This attitude brought about a change in mentality in the field and, in particular, scholars ceased to disqualify Chronicles *a priori* as a source of information about the postexilic period. Comparison with other sources and further inquiries became indispensable.

After Winckler, several scholars treated Chronicles with more sympathy, for instance Immanuel Benzinger and Rudolf Kittel in Germany, or Edward Lewis Curtis and Albert Alonzo Madsen in the United States.[52] Archaeology had a definite place in these publications since Immanuel Benzinger (Stuttgart, 1865 – Riga, 1935), for instance, travelled to Palestine and taught in Jerusalem. He participated in the revision of the *Baedeker* for Palestine and Syria. Rudolf Kittel (1853–1929), active in Tübingen, Breslau (Wrocław), and Leipzig, also studied the archives of El-Amarna and the Code of Hammurabi. He is more famous for his *Biblia Hebraica*, but he also published on the history and the religion of Israel. He was rather conservative and opposed to Wellhausen's opinions.[53]

---

51. See Hugo Winckler, "Bemerkungen zur Chronik als Geschichtsquelle," *Alttestamentliche Untersuchungen* (Helsingfors: Verlag von Eduard Pfeiffer, 1891), 157–67; cf. Japhet, "Historical Reliability," 91.

52. See Immanuel Benzinger, *Die Bücher der Chronik*, KHAT (Tübingen und Leipzig: J.C.B. Mohr [Paul Siebeck], 1901), xxiii; Rudolf Kittel, *Die Bücher der Chronik*, HAT (Göttingen: Vandenhoeck & Ruprecht, 1902), x–xvi; English Translation: *The Books of the Chronicles* (Baltimore, MD: The Johns Hopkins Press; London: David Nutt, 1895); Edward Lewis Curtis and Albert Alonzo Madsen, *A Critical and Exegetical Commentary on the Books of Chronicles*, ICC (Edinburgh: T&T Clark, 1910, 1976), 14–6. Cf. Japhet, "Historical Reliability," 91 and 104, note 44.

53. See Rudolf Kittel, *Geschichte der Hebräer*. 2 vol. 1. *Quellenkunde und Geschichte der Zeit bis zum Tode Josuas*. 2. *Quellenkunde und Geschichte der Zeit bis zum babylonischen Exil* (Gotha: Perthes, 1888–1892; 21909–1912; 31922–1923); *Geschichte des Volks Israel*. Band 1. *Palästina in der Urzeit, Das Werden des Volkes, Geschichte der Zeit bis zum Tode Josuas* (Stuttgart: Kohlhammer, 1932); Band 2. *Das Volk in Kanaan, Geschichte der Zeit bis zum babylonischen Exil* (Stuttgart: Kohlhammer, 1925); Band 3. *Die Zeit der Wegführung nach Babel und die Aufrichtung*

But things change slowly, and this is evident in the case of William Foxwell Albright (1891–1971), to take just one example.⁵⁴ He held the traditional view about the unreliability of Chronicles, as it is confirmed by the following statement:

> Up to the present no archaeological discoveries have confirmed the facts added by the Chronicler to his liberal excerpts from the canonical books of the Old Testament. Some of his statements, especially his lists of towns and clans, have doubtless historical value, though their exact source remains unknown [...] It is still however too early for a categorical denial of historical nuclei in these fantastic stories [...]⁵⁵

Albright had access to the newly discovered and edited Elephantine documents.⁵⁶ For this reason, he was ready to revise his negative judgment in the hope of finding new elements to confirm the validity of a research that would take Chronicles into account as one of the key elements in a description of the postexilic Israel's worldview. We are now in a troubled and frantic period between the two World Wars, mainly in Europe. This is also a time of heated discussions in political and academic circles about radical and totalitarian ideologies. This atmosphere had an impact on biblical exegesis as well.⁵⁷ As for Chronicles, the main developments took place in Germany with Gerhard von Rad and Martin Noth.

7. Change in perspective: History "wie es gewesen war" or "wie es geschrieben ist"? – Gerhard von Rad

> [Die Chronik] schildert nicht "wie es gewesen," sondern pragmatisch; die Logik der Ereignisse, der Zusammenhang von Ursache und

---

der neuen Gemeinde (Stuttgart: Kohlhammer, 1929); *Die Religion des Volkes Israel* (Leipzig: Quelle und Meyer, 1921).

54. On Albright, see, for instance, David Noel Freedman, Robert B. MacDonald, and Daniel L. Mattson, *The Published Works of William Foxwell Albright: A Comprehensive Bibliography* (Cambridge, MA: American Schools of Oriental Research, 1975); Gus W. van Beek, *The Scholarship of William Foxwell Albright: An Appraisal* (Atlanta, GA: Scholars Press, 1989); Peter Douglas Feinman, *William Foxwell Albright and the Origins of Biblical Archaeology* (Berrien Springs, MI: Andrews University Press, 2004); Thomas Levy and David Noel Freedman, *William Foxwell Albright 1891–1971: A Biographical Memoir* (Washington, DC: National Academy of Sciences, 2008).

55. William Foxwell Albright, "The Date and Personality of the Chronicler," *JBL* 40 (1921): 104–24, here 104, note 1.

56. Albright, "Date," 107, 117–8.

57. See, among others, Horst Junginger, *The Study of Religion under the Impact of Fascism*, Numen Book Series 117 (Leiden – Boston: Brill, 2008).

> Wirkung wird unbedenklich zerschnitten, sei es, daß die eigentlichen Wirkungen von Ereignissen fehlen, sei es, daß weitgehend für Wirkungen theoretisch Ursachen erdichtet werden.[58]

> Chronicles does not depict the events "as they happened," but in a pragmatic way. The logic of the events, the connection between cause and effect, is cut without much scruple, either since the effects of the events are missing, or since causes are concocted, theoretically and to a large extent, for the effects.

This reflection by Gerhard von Rad marks a turning-point in the history of research on Chronicles.[59] Everyone has noticed the quotation of Leopold von Ranke's famous saying that the historian should report the events "wie es eigentlich gewesen war," without introducing personal, moral or philosophical, considerations into the presentation of the facts. Consciously or not, previous generations of exegetes condemned Chronicles for being biased, tendentious, ideological and therefore for not corresponding to Ranke's ideal of history writing. Gerhard von Rad is aware of the problem, obviously, but he focuses his study precisely on the Chronicler's ethical and religious background that characterizes his work. He speaks of the Chronicler's "image of history" (Geschichtsbild) and of "tendency" (Tendenz). Another quotation is of great significance:

> Man weiß, daß der Chronist den Ablauf der geschichtlichen Ereignisse nach eigenem Willen weithin neu geformt hat, teils nach Maßgabe vorhandener zeitgenössischer Verhältnisse, teils seinen eigenen noch nicht realisierten Tendenzen entsprechend.

> One knows that the Chronicler reshaped the course of the historical events by and large according to his own will, partly in relation to contemporaneous existing situations, partly in correspondence with his tendencies that had not yet become reality.

Gerhard von Rad adds a final, concluding, reflection about the Chronicler's way of writing history:

> [...] dann verschwimmt die von uns heutigen schärfer empfundene Grenze zwischen objektiver historischer Tatsache und später eingetragener Deutung oder gar Korrektur.

> [...] therefore, the borderline between objective historical fact and in-

---

58. Gerhard von Rad, *Das Geschichtsbild des chronistischen Werkes*, BWANT 54 (Stuttgart: Kohlhammer, 1930), 2.

59. For more details, see, for instance, Gerhard von Rad, *From Genesis to Chronicles*: *Explorations in Old Testament Theology* (ed. Kenneth C. Hanson), Fortress Classics in Biblical Studies (Minneapolis, MN: Fortress, 2005). On Gerhard von Rad, see especially Smend, *Kritiker und Exegeten*, 794–824.

terpretation, later introduced, or even correction, tends to disappear, a borderline which is perceived more acutely by us today.

These quotations reveal von Rad's sensitivity for a type of history that departs from the tenets of an ideal, objective history that was dominant in the 19th century and linked especially with the names of Leopold von Ranke (1795–1886) and Theodor Mommsen (1817–1903), a history based not on ideas but on a rigorous examination of documents.[60] The Chronicler, on the contrary, rarely distinguishes facts from interpretation, and this is the reason why the exegesis of the 19th century had little appreciation for this kind of "history." As we saw, von Rad is interested, instead, precisely in what characterizes the Chronicler's interpretation of history. For instance, he inquires about the way the Chronicler speaks of God, the people of Israel, the law, and how he retells Israel's history from the beginning until David.

In this, von Rad is close to a new way of understanding historical research that is aware of the fact that objective history does not exist as such since, on the one side, facts are always documented facts, necessarily seen and interpreted through the lens of the witnesses, and, on the other, that there is no history without the positive contribution of the historian who unravels the connections between facts and introduces a logic in the mere chronological succession of events. History is a reconstruction, according to Wellhausen's famous saying: "Konstruiren muß man bekanntlich die Geschichte immer [...]. Der Unterschied ist nur, ob man gut oder schlecht konstruirt" – "But history, it is well known, should always be constructed [...]. The question is whether one constructs well or not."[61]

This view of history is not completely new. Let me mention at least two names. The first personality to be remembered is that of the Swiss historian Jacob Burckhardt (Basel, 1818–1897).[62] He had studied in

60. On this, see, among others, Andreas D. Boldt, *The Life and Work of the German Historian Leopold von Ranke (1795–1886): An Assessment of His Achievements* (Lewiston, NY: Edwin Mellen Press, 2015). On the evolution in the field of the history of Israel, see Richard S. Hess, "Introduction: Foundations for a History of Israel," in *Ancient Israel's History: An Introduction to Issues and Sources*, eds. Bill T. Arnold and Richard S. Hess (Grand Rapids, MI: Baker Academic, 2014), 1–22; Jean Louis Ska, "Questions of the 'History of Israel' in Recent Research," in *Hebrew Bible/Old Testament. The History of Its Interpretation. Volume III. From Modernism to Post-Modernism (The Nineteenth and Twentieth Centuries).* Part 2. *The Twentieth Century – From Modernism to Post-Modernism* [hereafter *HBOT* III.2], ed. Magne Sæbø (Göttingen: Vandenhoeck & Ruprecht, 2014), 391–432.

61. Julius Wellhausen, *Prolegomena zur Geschichte Israels* (Berlin: Reimer ²1883; repr. Berlin: de Gruyter 2001), 365. English translation: *Prolegomena to the History of Israel*, Reprints and Translations (Atlanta, GA: Scholars Press 1994), 367.

62. On Burckhardt, see, for instance, René Teuteberg, *Wer war Jacob Burckhardt?* (Basel: Druckerei Ganzmann, 1997); Stefan Bauer, *Polisbild und Demokrati-*

Berlin under Leopold von Ranke, but soon became interested in culture and civilization, especially in the history of art, without neglecting economical and political developments, however. He is famous for his history of the Italian Renaissance.[63] Jacob Burckhart was in contact with Wilhelm de Wette who started teaching theology in Basel in 1822, and was appointed more than once as rector of the university. Actually, Jacob Burckhardt who was studying theology decided to shift to history because de Wette's esprit critique shuddered the foundations of his religious convictions.[64] What matters for our topic is that Jacob Burckhardt is exemplary of a shift in historical research that reconciles history with art and culture. This new spirit would suffuse the academic world especially after the First World War and would influence the studies on Israel's history in general and the Book of Chronicles in particular, and this in a direct or indirect manner.

The second name is that of Karl Gotthard Lamprecht (25 February 1856 Jessen – 10 May 1915 Leipzig) who taught for a long time in Leizpig and published a *History of Germany* in twelve tomes and nineteen books.[65] He reacted strongly against the Neo-Rankian historians who were too much interested in important events of national and international politics. He developed his own vision of history in several writings, enhancing the importance of society, culture and economy which were for him more important than political and personal history.[66] Albrecht Alt and Noth studied in Leipzig, and von Rad taught in this university as Privatdozent, from 1930 till 1934. Whether they came in touch with Lamprecht's vision of history is difficult to determine with certainty. There is however a certain parenthood between, for instance, von Rad's interest in the main cultural and religious conceptions underlying the Chronicler's work and Lamprecht's insistence on cultural history.

Burckhardt and Lamprecht were forerunners of a movement that took shape in France after the end of the First World War, the well-

everständnis in Jacob Burckhardts «Griechischer Kulturgeschichte», Beiträge zu Jacob Burckhardt 3 (Basel: Schwabe – München: C. H. Beck, 2001).

63. Jacob Burckhardt, *Die Cultur der Renaissance in Italien: Ein Versuch* (Basel: Schweighauser, 1860); *Geschichte der Renaissance in Italien* (Stuttgart: Vlg. Ebner & Seubert, 1878).

64. On this point, see Thomas Albert Howard, *Religion and the Rise of Historicism: W. M. L. de Wette, Jacob Burckhardt, and the Theological Origins of Nineteenth-Century Historical Consciousness* (Cambridge: Cambridge University Press, 1999, 2009).

65. Karl Gotthard Lamprecht, *Deutsche Geschichte. Zwölf Bände in neunzehn Büchern* (Berlin: Hermann Heyfelder & Weidmannsche Buchhandlung, 1906–1911).

66. Karl Gotthard Lamprecht, *Alte und neue Richtungen in der Geschichtswissenschaft* (Leipzig: Gaertner, 1896); *Die kulturhistorische Methode* (Berlin: Gaertner, 1900).

known *École des Annales* ("The Annals School"). In a few words, the tragic experience of the First World War showed that history is not only written by kings, emperors, or heads of states, in royal courts or on battlefields. The real subject of history is the life of the peoples, especially in its social and economic aspects. Developments, in this field, are much slower than in a history focused on specific political or military events. The historians belonging to this school distinguish therefore the *histoire événementielle* ("history of events") from the *histoire de moyenne or longue durée* ("medium or long term history"). This second kind of history pays attention to slow evolutions linked with changes in climate, techniques, economy, and society. The attention shifted from the royal courts and battlegrounds to the mentalities and conditions of daily life. These historians also introduced new quantitative methods to measure with more precision the evolution of societies or human groups. The important names are those of Marc Bloch (1886–1944), Lucien Fèbvre (1878–1956), Fernand Braudel (1902–1985), George Duby (1919–1996) and Jacques Le Goff (1924–2014). We may add to this group the Belgian scholar Henri Pirenne (1862–1935).[67]

Naturally, it is difficult if not impossible to trace a direct influence of the Annales School on the exegesis of Chronicles. Nonetheless we may safely affirm that the academic atmosphere was different when Gerhard von Rad published his pamphlet on these biblical books. As we could see, his viewpoint is less positivistic than that of the former generation and he is also less negative in his judgment because, at that time, scholars were more sensitive to other aspects of history-writing. According to this new vision, ancient historians, and this holds true for ancient Israelite "historians," through their recording of the past present a way of understanding the roots of the present and of shaping (or of trying to shape) it accordingly. The cultural, moral, ideological, and theological background of both the writers and the audience are essential elements of these "histories."

All this was made partly possible because the discussions about the composition of the Pentateuch and the relative chronology of the

---

67. On this school, see Peter Burke, *The French Historical Revolution: The Annales School 1929–89* (Stanford, CA: Stanford University Press, 1990); André Burguière, *L'École des Annales. Une histoire intellectuelle* (Paris: Odile Jacob, 2006); English translation: *Annales School: An Intellectual History* (Ithaca, NY: Cornell University Press, 2009); François Dosse, "À l'école des Annales, une règle: l'ouverture disciplinaire," *Hermès* 67 (2013): 106–12. Among the precursors of this school, we may count, in France, Voltaire, in his *Nouvelles considérations sur l'histoire* (1744); François Guizot, *Histoire générale de la civilisation en Europe* (1828) and François-René de Chateaubriand, *Études historiques* (1832). All of them insist on the social and economic aspects of history.

different sources had come to a – relative – rest. Hermann Gunkel, the *formgeschichtliche Schule* and the *Religionsgeschichtliche Schule* had introduced new questions and opened new areas of research, especially about the oral origins of ancient Israel's traditions.[68] History or historical "truth" was no longer the major or the unique focus of interest in biblical studies.

More importantly, perhaps, and easier to determine, is the impact of the political situation on von Rad's research. His monograph on Chronicles was published in 1930 when he was *Privatdozent* at Leipzig, a university where he had studied under the guidance of Albrecht Alt (1883–1956). Already at that time, von Rad was concerned by the anti-Semitic and anti-Old Testament bias that began to creep in among German scholars and he reacted in defending the vital significance of the Old Testament for Christian faith.[69] As a disciple of Karl Barth and as an expert in dialectic theology, he insisted on the religious value of every part of the Old Testament, and this is probably the reason why he wrote an essay on Chronicles, a book that was often presented as a compendium of Jewish legalism and ritualism.[70] He did not look for "hard facts" in Chronicles, but for an expression of Israel's deep convictions.

All in all, the Chronicler has a theological, dogmatic and didactic purpose, namely to legitimate the cult of the Second Temple trough a "David-Arch (of covenant)-Levites-tradition."[71] This cult is centered not on sacrifice and expiation, but on praise and gratitude for God's promised grace.[72] Von Rad's ideas were influential especially because they highlighted the positive side of the Chronicler's message.

8. Change in perspective: The Chronicler, a historian "in his own right" according to Martin Noth

We follow the same line when coming to Noth, the direct successor of

---

68. See, for instance, Japhet, "Historical Reliability," 96–7.
69. On this point, but more on Gerhard von Rad's career in Jena (1934–1945), see Bernard M. Levinson, "Reading the Bible in Nazi Germany: Gerhard von Rad's Attempt to Reclaim the Old Testament for the Church," *Interpretation: A Journal of Bible and Theology* 62 (2008): 238–54. As it is well-known, National-Socialism took power in 1933 in Germany.
70. On the influence on Karl Barth, see John Barton, "Karl Barth and the Canonical Approach," in *HBOT* III.2, 101–8; Manfred Oeming, "Karl Barth," HBOT III.2, 174–81.
71. Von Rad, *Geschichtsbild*, 134.
72. Von Rad, *Geschichtsbild*, 136.

von Rad.[73] He went along with his predecessor in many respects. For instance, he insisted on the necessity to judge the Chronicler "in his own right" and according to the literary standards of his time. The following paragraph is telling in this regard:[74]

> In all the features of Chr.'s composition discussed so far, no so-called bias (*Tendenz*) is to be perceived. They lead us, rather, to the conclusion that Chr. was always making an effort to go beyond the Vorlagen at his disposal by enlivening and giving graphic portrayal to the historical narrative. As is only to be expected, he sought to achieve this aim by making use of the conceptual horizon and interests of his own day, for there was no possibility of his giving a faithful historical picture of those older times which he had in view at any given moment. However, in the interests of an accurate appraisal of Chr.'s work it is also important to appreciate that he deserves recognition as an independent narrator in his own right. His work manifestly displays a purely literary concern, and this concern has influenced the content of his historical presentation in matters of detail. [...] His aim was not to entertain but to give teaching about various specific consequences which could be drawn from past history and which were of relevance to the present.

Noth's appraisal of the Chronicler's work is the exact opposite of that of Torrey on two main points. First, Noth highlights the narrative and literary qualities of his work, trying to understand its real purpose instead of looking only for "objective history." Second, Noth emphasises the Chronicler's didactic intention. The Chronicler purports neither to entertain nor to inform about the past as such. His intention is definitely to draw useful lessons from the past for his contemporaries.

Another point in Noth's research may have importance, namely his attention to the function of discourses in the Chronicler's writings. Discourses by important personalities were also determinative in the Deuteronomistic History. In this respect, we find close parallels between biblical literature and ancient historical works, especially in classical Greek and Roman histories.[75] Discourses were often used by

---

73. On Martin Noth, see Smend, *Kritiker und Exegeten*, 825–846.

74. Martin Noth, *The Chronicler's History*. Translated by H.G.M. Williamson with an Introduction, JSOT.S 50 (Sheffield: JSOTPress, 1987), 80. The German original is the second part of *Die Überlieferungsgeschichtliche Studien. Die sammelnden und bearbeitenden Geschichtswerke im Alten Testament*, SKGG 18,2 (Halle [Saale]: Niemeyer, 1943; Tübingen: Niemeyer, 1957; Darmstadt: Wissenschaftliche Buchgesellschaft: 31967) entitled *Das chronistische Geschichtswerk*.

75. On this point, see Kenneth G. Hoglund, "The Chronicler as Historian. A Comparative Perspective," in *The Chronicler as Historian*, eds. M. Patrick Graham, Kenneth G. Hoglund and Steven L. McKenzie, JSOT.S 238 (Sheffield: Sheffield Academic Press, 1997), 19–29, who explores the elements common to Chronicles and Hellenistic historiography. On discourses in Chronicles as such, see Mark A. Throntveit, "The Chronicler's Speeches and Historical Reconstruction," in *The Chronicler*

ancient historians to convey their own vision in specific fields.[76]

Noth is more interested in historical and literary questions than von Rad. He inquires about the original form of the text, its sources, and its dating before coming to its literary characteristics, its historical presuppositions, its reworking of its sources and, eventually, its theology. In his conclusion, he explicitly parts ways with von Rad about the theology of the book. For Noth, the Chronicler's work was composed to defend Jerusalem as the unique legitimate cultic centre for all Israel over against the claims of the Samaritans.[77] Therefore, Chronicles is more historical than merely theological. Noth insists on the Chronicler's "clear intention of giving information about what really happened" – "seine[...] offenkundige [...] Intention, wirklich Geschehenes mitzuteilen."[78] We hereby return to a vision of Chronicles as a historical work and to a conception of history closer to that of von Ranke, although surely not in the modern sense of the word, because Chronicles "believed [...] that only in this way would he be able to serve the concerns of his own time."[79] History is the only valid way of authenticating the institutions of the Second Temple period.

This discussion between von Rad and Noth is more than a typical example of different attitudes or different temperaments. From the very beginning of the exegesis of Chronicles, we find two main directions in the history of research. On the one side, some scholars read more theology (or ideology) than history in Chronicles, whereas others look at Chronicles as mainly a work of history. This was already the case with David Qimhi (ca. 1160–1235) and Isaac ben Jehuda Abravanel (1437–1508), as we saw earlier. This same contrast is observable in two more recent collective publications, *The Chronicler as Historian*[80]

as Historian, 225–45. For a short bibliography on the topic, see 227, note 9. On the role of discourses in classical literature, see, among others, N.P. Miller, "Discourses. Dramatic Speech in the Roman Historians," *Greece & Rome* 22 (1975): 45–57; Cynthia Damon, "Rhetoric and Historiography," in *A Companion to Roman Rhetoric*, ed. W. Dominik and J. Hall (Oxford: Blackwell Publishers, 2006), 439–50; Cristina Pepe, *The Genres of Rhetorical Speeches in Greek and Roman Antiquity*, International Studies in the History of Rhetoric 5 (Leiden: Brill, 2013). In the New Testament, see Martin Dibelius, "The Speeches in Acts and Ancient Historiography," in *Studies in the Acts of the Apostles*, ed. E. Greenwen (New York: Charles Scribner's Sons, 1956), 138–45.

76. The most famous example is, probably, Pericles' funeral oration in Thucydides' *History of the Peloponnesian Wars*, 2.35–46.

77. Noth, *Chronicler's History*, 97–8.

78. Noth, *Chronicler's History*, 98; German original: *Überlieferungsgeschichtliche Studien*, 172.

79. Noth, *Chronicler's History*, 98.

80. Patrick M. Graham, Kenneth G. Hoglund and Steven L. McKenzie (eds.), *The Chronicler as Historian*, JSOT.S 238 (Sheffield: Academic Press, 1997). See also Isaac Kalimi, *An Ancient Israelite Historian: Studies in the Chronicler, His Time,*

and *The Chronicler as Theologian*.[81]

It is perhaps of some interest to know that North published this short monograph in 1943. He served in the *Wehrmacht* (military) during the Second World War from 1939 till 1941, and again from 1943 until 1945. He therefore wrote this book in Königsberg (today Kaliningrad) between two periods of military service.

9. Change in Perspective: Literarkritik and Literary Criticism – Source and Discourse

A second element contributed to a change in mentality, namely the growing importance of literary studies on biblical texts. Already in 1938, in his well-known essay, *Das formgeschichtliche Problem des Hexateuchs*,[82] von Rad stated that "So far as the analysis of source documents is concerned, there are signs that the road has come to a dead end."[83] This is the reason why he decided to ask central questions about the "final form [of the Hexateuch] as we have it".[84] We find a similar reflection in his work on Chronicles, when he criticizes Wilhelm J. Rothstein's commentary because of an overstated interest in sources, layers, additions, etc. that reduces the book to a "Unsumme von disjecta membra" – "a vast sum of disjecta membra."[85] According to von Rad, the imperative of a theological interpretation as well as of historical research is to supplement this analytical process with an ef-

---

Place and Writing, Studia Semitica Neerlandica 46 (Assen: Van Gorcum, 2005); Sara Japhet, "Chronicles: A History," in *Das Alte Testament. Ein Geschichtsbuch? Beiträge des Symposiums "Das Alte Testament und die Kultur der Moderne," anläßlich des 100. Geburtstag Gerhard von Rads*, eds. Erhard Blum, William Johnstone and Christoph Markschies, Altes Testament und die Kultur der Moderne 10 (Münster: Lit Verlag, 2005), 129–46.

81. Patrick M. Graham, Steven L. McKenzie and Gary N. Knoppers (eds.), *The Chronicler as Theologian: Essays in Honor of Ralph W. Klein*, JSOT.S 371 (London: T&T Clark, 2003). See also John Goldingay, "The Chronicler as a Theologian," *Biblical Theology Bulletin* 5 (1975): 99–126.

82. Gerhard von Rad, *Das formgeschichtliche Problem des Hexateuchs*, BWANT 78 (Stuttgart: Kohlhammer, 1938); reprinted in *Gesammelte Studien zum Alten Testament*, TB 8 (München: Kaiser Verlag, 1958), 9–86; English translation: "The Form-Critical Problem of the Hexateuch," in *The Problem of the Hexateuch and Other Essays* (New York: McGraw-Hill, 1966; London: SCM, 1984), 1–78.

83. Von Rad, "Form-Critical Problem," 1.

84. Von Rad, "Form-Critical Problem," 1. The German expression for "final form" is *Letztgestalt* or *Endgestalt*.

85. Von Rad, Geschichtsbild, 133. The commentary discussed is by Wilhelm J. Rothstein, *Kommentar zum ersten Buch der Chronik*, KAT 18.2 (Leipzig: Deichert, 1927).

fort of understanding synthetically the biblical work ("das Bemühen um ein synthetisches Verstehen des Schriftwerkes.")[86]

The studies on the "final form" of the text had some forerunners, for instance Richard G. Moulton, who specialized in the study of Shakespeare[87] before publishing several monographs on a literary reading of the Bible.[88] Gunkel also had a strong influence since he shifted the attention from the genesis of the text to its original, oral, form and its typical style. For Gunkel, we may note, "exegesis is more an art than a science" and literary questions are much more important than historical questions.[89] Later on, in 1968, James Muilenburg delivered an impressive presidential address at the annual meeting of the Society of Biblical Literature, at Berkeley, California, on December 18, 1968. The text was published afterwards with the telling title: "Form Criticism and Beyond".[90] In a few words, Muilenburg promoted a study of stylistic features and structural compositions of biblical texts, especially poetic texts. He proposed to call this method – but this is perhaps not the most felicitous appellation – "rhetorical criticism". Here is a short summary of his program:

> Persistent and painstaking attention to the modes of Hebrew literary composition will reveal that the pericopes exhibit linguistic patterns, word formations ordered or arranged in particular ways, verbal sequences which move in fixed structures from beginning to end. Clearly, they have been skillfully wrought in many ways, often with consummate skill and artistry. It is also apparent that they have been influenced by conventional rhetorical practices.[91]

---

86. Von Rad, *Geschichtswerk*, 133.

87. Richard G. Moulton, *Shakespeare as a Dramatic Artist*: *A Popular Illustration of the Principles of Scientific Criticism* (Oxford: Clarendon Press, 1885). See also *The Ancient Classical Drama*: *A Study in Literary Evolution Intended for Readers in English and in the Original* (Oxford: The Clarendon Press. 1890).

88. Richard G. Moulton, *The Literary Study of the Bible*: *An Account of the Leading Forms of Literature Represented in the Sacred Writings* (London: Ibister and Company, 1896). See also *Select Masterpieces of Biblical Literature* (New York: The Macmillan Company; London: Macmillan & Co., 1901); *A Short Introduction to the Literature of the Bible* (Boston, MA: D. C. Heath & Co., 1901); *The Modern Reader's Bible Translation* (New York: The Macmillan Company, 1907); *The Bible at a Single View. With an Appendix, How to Read the Bible* (New York: The Macmillan Company, 1918). On this author, see Sarah Lawall, "Richard Moulton and the 'Perspective Attitude' in World Literature," in *The Routledge Companion to World Literature*, eds. Theo D'haen, David Damrosch and Djelal Kadir (London: Routledge, 2011), 32–40.

89. "Denn Exegese im höchsten Sinne ist mehr eine Kunst als eine Wissenschaft" (Hermann Gunkel, "Ziele und Methoden der Erklärung des Alten Testaments," in *Reden und Aufsätze* [Göttingen: Vandenhoeck & Ruprecht, 1913], 11–29, here 14).

90. James Muilenburg, "Form-Criticism and Beyond," *JBL* 88 (1969): 1–18.

91. Muilenburg, "Form-Criticism," 18.

In the exegesis of Chronicles, the attention to its specific style is witnessed by this outstanding remark found in Roddy Braun's commentary on Chronicles published in 1986: "[The Chronicler is] a person of much greater literary skill than usually attributed to him".[92] Two important works developed this insight. The first follows the path traced by James Muilenburg. The article stems from Leslie C. Allen (Pasadena, CA) and is devoted to stylistic devices such as chiasm, inclusion, and key words in structuring narrative units in Chronicles.[93] The second, by Rodney K. Duke (Appalachian State University, Boone, North Carolina), chooses a different direction, namely Aristotle's treatise on rhetoric and endeavors to apply these Greek categories to Chronicles.[94] Classifying Chronicles as belonging to the genre of deliberative rhetoric, he analyses the text according to Aristotle's three basic modes of persuasion, the rational, the ethical and the emotional. Despite laudable efforts, it seems that this work was not entirely successful.[95] We have here two of the chief directions in the field of stylistic analysis. On the one side, scholars proceed intuitively and inductively, looking for devices and features observed mainly in Hebrew and Semitic pieces of literature or, on the other side, they adopt a more systematic and deductive method, consulting first handbooks of ancient or more recent rhetoric, and applying these categories to biblical texts, and to Chronicles in particular.[96]

One of the main consequences of this new way of reading Chronicles is the major attention to its techniques of composition. A significant title to be mentioned in this context is *The Chronicler as Author: Studies in Text and Texture*.[97] The Chronicler is now an author, after being a historian and a theologian. To this internal development, that is, a new or renewed literary sensibility, we must add now another, external, factor, the discovery of the Dead Sea Scrolls.

---

92. Roddy Braun, *1 Chronicles*, WBC 14 (Waco, TX: Word Books, 1986), xxv, quoted by Kleinig, "Current Research," 49.

93. Leslie C. Allen, "Kerygmatic Units 1 & 2 Chronicles," *JSOT* 41 (1988): 21–36.

94. Rodney K. Duke, *The Persuasive Appeal of the Chronicler: A Rhetorical Analysis*, JSOT.S 88 (Sheffield: The Almond Press, 1990).

95. See Kleinig, "Current Research," 49; Duke, "Recent Research," 33–6.

96. For more details on the literary approach to Chronicles, see Kleinig, "Current Research," 49–51.

97. Patrick M. Graham and Steven L. McKenzie (eds.), *The Chronicler as Author: Studies in Text and Texture*, JSOT.S 263 (Sheffield: Academic Press, 1999).

10. Change in Perspective: Qumran and Scribal Work

The impact of the Dead Sea Scrolls was progressive, but also impressive.[98] Scholars noticed, for instance, similarities between the biblical commentaries or biblical interpretations found in the Dead Sea Scrolls and some biblical texts. This was the case especially with Chronicles, and suddenly, the interest for these late writings grew very fast. Chronicles became soon a field of research for all those interested in scribal work, in *Fortschreibung*, and in "Rewritten Bible". Let us give some examples of these recent tendencies in research.

10.1. Text criticism

Here is a statement by George Brooke that aptly summarizes the present situation:

> [...] it seems as if the Chronicler worked from a text of Samuel other than that found in the MT. Cross long ago suggested that 'examination of the passages of the large Samuel manuscript (4QSam^a) which are paralleled in Chronicles gives direct evidence that the Chronicler often utilized an edition of Samuel closer to the tradition of the Cave IV scroll than to that which survived in the Masoretic recension.'[99]

The Hebrew text of Chronicles is closer to the Qumran fragments and the Old Greek in minor and major points.[100] The consequence is that we have here one more example of the importance of some versions, concretely of the Old Greek. Moreover, we have to admit that the differences between Samuel-Kings and Chronicles can be explained otherwise than by attributing them all to a biased and partisan work by the Chronicler. In the Pentateuch as well, we have some examples where the Old Greek may have preserved a different form of the text, as in

---

98. See, for instance, George J. Brooke, "The Books of Chronicles and the Scrolls from Qumran," in *Reflection and Refraction: Studies in Biblical Historiography in Honour of A. Graeme Auld*, eds. Robert Rezetko, Timothy H. Lim and W. Brian Aucker, SVT 113 (Leiden – Boston, MA: Brill, 2007), 35–48. See also Knoppers, *I Chronicles 1–9*, 52–5.

99. Brooke, "Chronicles and Qumran," 36. The reference to Cross' work is Frank Moore Cross, *The Ancient Library of Qumran and Modern Biblical Studies* (Garden City, NY: Doubleday, 1958; The Biblical Seminar 30; Sheffield: Sheffield Academic Press, ³1995), 141 (139 in Sheffield's third edition). Cf. also this reflection by F.M. Cross: "Among other things it means that we can control better the Chronicler's treatment of his sources. The usual picture painted of the Chronicler violently or willfully distorting Samuel and Kings to suit his fancy must be radically revised." See Frank Moore Cross, "The History of the Biblical Text in the Light of Discoveries in the Judaean Desert," *HTR* 57 (1964): 281–99, here 294, note 41.

100. See, among others, Knoppers, *I Chronicles 1–9*, 52–65 ("The Relevance of Text Criticism").

Exodus 37–40.[101] Is it just a case that these chapters describe the construction of the tent, Israel's sanctuary?

These observations bring momentum to Graeme A. Auld's mill who defends the idea that Chronicles does not depend on or rework the actual text of Samuel-Kings, but a different source, common to Samuel-Kings and Chronicles.[102]

10.2. REWRITTEN BIBLE

The term "Rewritten Bible" – "umgeschriebene Bibel" – was introduced and popularized by Geza Vermes in 1961, in *Scripture and Tradition in Judaism: Haggadic Studies*.[103] His point of departure was the Sefer ha-Jaschar, "The Book of the Righteous," an anonymous medieval, Jewish, book of circa the 11th century, which retells the Pentateuch and the Book of Joshua, adding numerous midrashic and folkloristic elements. There are several definitions of "Rewritten Bible".[104] Here is what Gary Knoppers offers in his commentary on Chronicles:

> [This category refers to works] that take as point of departure an earlier biblical book or collection of books. They select from, interpret, comment on, and expand portions of a particular biblical book (or group of books), addressing obscurities, contradictions, and other perceived problems with the source text. Rewritten Bible texts normally emulate the form of the source and follow it sequentially. The major intention of such works seems to be to provide a coherent interpretative reading of the biblical text.[105]

The examples most frequently proposed by specialists in the field are,

---

101. See the fundamental article by Pierre-Maurice Bogaert, "L'importance de la Septante et du 'Monacensis' de la Vetus latina pour l'exégèse du livre de l'Exode (Chap. 35–40)," in Marc Vervenne (ed.), *Studies in the Book of Exodus. Redaction – Reception – Interpretation*, BETL 126 (Leuven: Peeters, 1996): 399–428.

102. See, for instance, Graeme A. Auld, *Life in Kings: Reshaping the Royal Story in the Hebrew Bible*, Ancient Israel and Its Literature (Atlanta, GA: Society of Biblical Literature, 2017).

103. Geza Vermès, *Scripture and Tradition in Judaism: Haggadic Studies*, Studia Post-biblica 4 (Leiden: Brill, 1961, ²1973).

104. For an overview on this term, see, for instance, George J. Brooke, "Rewritten Bible," in Lawrence Schiffman and James C. VanderKam (eds.), *The Encyclopedia of the Dead Sea Scrolls* (New York: Oxford University Press, 2000): 777–81; Moshe J. Bernstein, "'Rewritten Bible': A Generic Category Which Has Outlived Its Usefulness," Textus 22 (2005): 169–96; József Zsengellér (ed.), *Rewritten Bible after Fifty Years: Texts, Terms, or Techniques?* JSJ.S 167 (Leiden: Brill, 2014); Daniel Stökl Ben Ezra, *Qumran: Die Texte vom Toten Meer und das antike Judentum*, UTB 4681 (Tübingen: Mohr Siebeck, 2016), 216–23. About Chronicles as 'Rewritten Bible,' see Knoppers, *I Chronicles 1–9*, 129–34 ("Chronicles: A Rewritten Bible?"). The answer is negative.

105. Knoppers, *I Chronicles 1–9*, 130; quoted by Jonker, "From Paraleipomenon to Early Reader," 224.

(1) outside of the Bible, Josephus' *Jewish Antiquities*; Pseudo-Philo's *Liber Antiquitatum Biblicarum* ("Book of Biblical Antiquities"); *Joseph and Aseneth*; and the Book of Jubilees; (2) in Qumran, *Genesis Apocryphon*; the *Temple Scroll*; *Jeremiah Apocryphon*; and *Pseudo-Ezechiel*; (3) in the Bible itself, 1–2 Chronicles; and 2 Maccabees; (4) in the New Testament, the Gospels of Matthew and Luke "rewriting" – to a certain extent – the Gospel of Mark.

This concept is close, but not completely identical with that of *Inner-biblical exegesis*,[106] since it applies to longer texts or longer portions of texts. Inner-biblical exegesis applies mostly to single elements or short sections. But there are zones of overlapping, obviously. The idea, or a similar idea, is developed, by Thomas Willi, *Die Chronik als Auslegung. Untersuchungen zur literarischen Gestaltung der historischen Überlieferung Israels*.[107]

Knoppers, among others, uses this concept in his commentary, but shows some dissatisfaction with the term because there is no clear definition of it. Moreover, Chronicles cannot be a "Rewritten Bible" because there was no "Bible" by the time Chronicles is put in writing. Besides this, Chronicles treats the Pentateuch and Samuel-Kings in a different way. The Pentateuch is already authoritative Scripture, whereas Samuel-Kings has less weight. Moreover, the first part of 1 Chronicles does not rewrite the corresponding parts in the Pentateuch and there are also important differences between Chronicles and its alleged "sources". Ehud ben Zvi discusses the problem of applying the concept of "Rewritten Bible" to Chronicles at length and concludes in a negative way.[108]

A first quotation will clarify ben Zvi's position:

> In fact, I worry on the basis of my reading that before too long the field will be flooded with references to Chronicles as "rewritten Bible" and this will become a cherished piece of our "widely shared knowledge." I suggest that we stop for a moment and reflect on the matter before it is too late.[109]

---

106. Concept popularized by Michael Fishbane, *Biblical Exegesis in Ancient Israel* (Oxford: Clarendon Press, 1985). For some clarification about the vocabulary, see Russell L. Meek, "Intertextuality, Inner-Biblical Exegesis, and Inner-Biblical Allusion: The Ethics of a Methodology," *Bib* 95 (2014): 280–91.

107. Thomas Willi, *Die Chronik als Auslegung. Untersuchungen zur literarischen Gestaltung der historischen Überlieferung Israels*, FRLANT 106 (Göttingen: Vandenhoeck & Ruprecht, 1972).

108. Ehud ben Zvi, "In Conversation and Appreciation of the Recent Commentaries by Steven L. Mckenzie and Gary N. Knoppers," in "New Studies in Chronicles: A Discussion of Two Recently Published Commentaries," ed. Melody D. Knowles, *JHS* 5 (2005): 21–45, esp. 31–36 ("The Matter of the Rewritten Bible"). Sites: http://www.jhsonline.org and http://purl.org/jhs.

109. Ben Zvi, "Conversation and Appreciation," 31.

And here is his conclusion on the matter:[110]

> Incidentally, some aspects of the relation of the book of Chronicles to Samuel-Kings or the Primary History in Persian Yehud may be heuristically approached by using an analogy of the relation between Deuteronomy and other legal pentateuchal material (especially what we call the Covenant Code) in the same Persian Yehud. In both cases, we are talking of co-existing texts, each with its own linguistic voice, and above all of a textually centered community of literati in which different ideological voices are seen as, and are meant to be seen as, complementary rather than exclusive of each other. Instead of Rewritten Bible, perhaps it is better to refer to texts as products of an ever evolving scripturing community.

In his answer, Knoppers agrees to a large extent with Ehud ben Zvi, saying,

> Chronicles is much more than an exegesis, paraphrase, and elaboration of earlier writings. I think that Ben Zvi and I are in essential agreement on this larger issue so I do not want to belabour this point any further.[111]

One aspect of the problem is perhaps the question of the existence and use of written texts in post-exilic period. Scholars already noticed differences between the Masoretic Text of Chronicles and that of Samuel-Kings. We may ask, therefore, which text was used by the authors of Chronicles. More importantly, as some studies in recent years have firmly established, scribes and copyists did often work from memory rather than exclusively from written sources. People did not work with word-processing programs or photocopy-machines, and we must avoid several anachronistic views.[112] Copying is not photo-

---

110. Ben Zvi, "Conversation and Appreciation," 35–6.

111. Gary N. Knoppers, "Of Rewritten Bibles, Archaeology, Peace, Kings, and Chronicles," in Melody D. Knowles (ed.), "New Studies," 69–93, here 75.

112. For a recent publication on the topic orality-literacy, see Brian B. Schmidt (ed.), *Contextualizing Israel's Sacred Writings: Ancient Literacy, Orality, and Literary Production*, Ancient Israel and Its Literature 22 (Atlanta, GA: Society of Biblical Literature, 2015). Some earlier and important works are William A. Graham, *Beyond the Written Word: Oral Aspects of Scripture in the History of Religion* (Cambridge: University Press, 1987); Susan Niditch, *Oral World and Written Word: Ancient Israelite Literature*, Library of Ancient Israel (Louisville: Westminster John Knox, 1996); William M. Schniedewind, *How the Bible Became a Book: The Textualization of Ancient Israel* (Cambridge: University Press, 2004); David M. Carr, *Writing on the Tablet of the Heart: Origins of Scripture and Literature* (Oxford: Oxford University Press, 2005); Martin S. Jaffee, *Torah in the Mouth: Writing and Oral Tradition in Palestinian Judaism, 200 BCE–400 CE* (Oxford: Oxford University Press, 2001); Annette Weissenrieder and Robert B. Coote (eds.), *The Interface of Orality and Writing: Speaking, Seeing, Writing in the Shaping of New Genres*, WUNT 260 (Tübingen: Mohr Siebeck, 2010). For the history of research, the major works are Eduard Nielsen, *Oral Tradition*, Studies in Biblical Theology 11 (London: SCM Press, 1954);

copying. In a few words, to say it with Werner H. Kelber, concluding a review of seven books on orality in the biblical world:[113]

> There is a palpable discrepancy between the dominantly print medium of modern scholarship and the oral-scribal communication world of its subject matter, with the former encroaching upon the latter. The seven books under review challenge us to (re)consider the Bible in its Jewish and Christian provenance, the biblical and the rabbinic tradition in the media context of the ancient Near Eastern and Mediterranean communications history.

This conclusion may have some consequences in several fields, for instance when speaking of "Rewritten Bible" or "innerbiblical exegesis". To put it with Louis C. Jonker,[114]

When one takes the simultaneity of oral and literate cultures in postexilic Israel seriously, it follows that the Chronicler's engagement with the Pentateuch most probably was not primarily with written documents, but rather with fluid memories of those written documents, which nevertheless had authority as transmitted traditions of the past.

10.3 ADDITIONS AND OMISSIONS IN CHRONICLES – JUHA PAKKALA

The forty pages dedicated to Chronicles in a recent monograph by Juha Pakkala are worth mentioning for their methodological and systematic approach.[115] The subtitle of the book exposes its program, *Omissions in the Tansmission of the Hebrew Bible*. Actually, the book's purpose is wider since it discusses several ways of copying, rewriting and transmitting biblical texts. At the outset of the section dedicated to Chronicles, Juha Pakkala discusses previous attempts to define the literary nature of Chronicles. He shows some dissatisfaction with proposals such as "interpretation" ("Auslegung"),[116] Midrash[117] or rewrit-

---

Werner H. Kelber, "Orality and Biblical Studies: A Review Essay," *RBL* 12 (2007): http://www.bookreviews.org/pdf/2107_6748.pdf; Robert D. Miller II, *Oral Tradition in Ancient Israel*, Biblical Performance Criticism Series 4 (Eugene, OR: Cascade, 2011).

113. Werner H. Kelber, "Orality and Biblical Studies: A Review Essay," *RBL* 12 (2007): http://www. bookreviews.org

114. Jonker, "From Paraleipomenon to Early Reader," 225.

115. Juha Pakkala, *God's Word Omitted: Omissions in the Transmission of the Hebrew Bible*, FRLANT 251 (Göttingen: Vandenhoeck & Ruprecht, 2013), especially chapter VIII: "Chronicles as a Witness to the Editorial Process," 253–94.

116. Thomas Willi, *Die Chronik als Auslegung* (see note 63). See Pakkala, *God's Words Omitted*, 255–5.

117. Isaac Kalimi, *An Ancient Israelite Historian: Studies in the Chronicler, His Time, Place and Writing*, SSN 46 (Leiden – Boston, MA: Brill, 2005), 22, observes the presence of midrashic elements in Chronicles, but refuses to call this book a Mid-

ten Bible[118] because the terminology is too vague. He prefers the theory of replacement, in the sense that Chronicles intends to replace an earlier presentation of Israel's past with a new and more satisfactory one: "[…] the Chronicler wanted to provide a theologically more correct account of Israel's past and thereby replace at least 1–2 Kings as the current and most authoritative account." The Chronicler does more than interpret or supplement his sources.[119]

The Chronicler's method in rewriting 1–2 Kings is variegated. He can reproduce very faithfully his sources, he can omit certain, often short, parts of the text, or introduce new elements and rework entire sections to adapt them to his theology and world-view: "The Chronicler's position towards the source is somewhere between what is assumed of a classical redactor who made mainly expansions and an author of a new literary work."[120] For this reason, "A clear-cut division between the redactors and the authors of a new composition is artificial and hazardous."[121] The cases studied by Juha Pakkala[122] show that the Chronicler did not proceed exactly as the redactors of more ancient parts of the Hebrew Bible: "[…] the principle of preservation seems to have been repeatedly challenged in Chronicles, while the text-critical evidence of the Pentateuch, 1–2 Samuel, and 1–2 Kings shows only isolated instances of such cases and they are more limited in the number of words that are omitted."[123]

Pakkala's conclusion draws our attention on some dangers in applying too quickly the Chronicles' model to other parts of the Hebrew Bible:[124]

> It should be stressed that Chronicles cannot be used slavishly as a model in the sense that each fundamental change in the society would necessarily cause radical changes in all the texts. It provides an example that fundamental changes must be considered a possibility in the transmission of the Hebrew scriptures, especially in those situations where the fundaments of the society were shaken. Chronicles should thus be included in the construction of a model for the transmission of the Hebrew scriptures and should certainly not be neglected as irrelevant.

---

rash. See Pakkala, *God's Words Omitted*, 256, note 10. See also the authors quoted in note 11, Pancratius C. Beentjes, Simon De Vries, and Stephen McKenzie.

118. Pakkala, *God's Words Omitted*, 256, note 11. But, unfortunately, Pakkala does not seem to know Gary N. Knoppers' commentary on Chronicles.

119. Pakkala, *God's Words Omitted*, 257.

120. Pakkala, *God's Word Omitted*, 260.

121. Pakkala, *God's Word Omitted*, 289.

122. 1 Kgs 22:51 and 2 Kgs 8:16–24 // 2 Chr 21:1–20; 2 Kgs 11:1–18 // 2 Chr 22:11–23:18; 2 Kgs 12 // 2 Chr 24.

123. Pakkala, *God's Words Omitted*, 289.

124. Pakkala, *God's Words Omitted*, 294.

10.4 IMPORTANCE OF THE CULT, OF THE MONARCHY AND OF MOSES' LAW

For several scholars, we find in Chronicles a double attempt of justifying a postexilic form of cult and religion.[125] First, the organization of the cult goes back to the origin of Israel's united monarchy, to David even more than to Solomon, the latter carrying out David's project. Second, David himself did not invent the organization of the cult. He found its blueprint in Moses' *Torah*, and followed exactly the prescriptions *as they are written* in this *Torah*. This supposes that, for Chronicles, the monarchy is subordinated to Moses' law and that there is already some form of written Pentateuch at the writer's disposal. This opens the questions of the relationship between Chronicles and the cultic, religious, texts in the Pentateuch. Does the Chronicler refer to existing texts when describing the temple's construction and the temple's service? Or, were some sections of the Pentateuch composed to legitimate the postexilic religion in the Second Temple period? Or, do we have to deal with a simultaneous process of using, reinterpreting and completing cultic traditions and/or texts in the Pentateuch when Chronicles was composed? The palpable differences between Exodus 37–40 in the Masoretic Text and in the Old Greek (and Old Latin) could be explained in this context.

11. CONCLUSION

Let me summarize this short history of research in three main points, knowing that much more could be said.

(1) "The older, the better". Chronicles is a witness of an exegetical activity of reinterpreting the past in the Second Temple period, when the Pentateuch slowly became authoritative.[126] Chronicles refers to several legal traditions as foundation and the legitimation of the cult and religious institutions it describes, subordinating both the monarchy and the cult itself to Moses' *Torah*. This means that, in this time, Israel looks towards the past to justify and shape its present. "The older is better," to put it with Luke's Gospel (5:39). But one cannot but notice the major importance of David in this re-reading or rewriting of the origins of the Jerusalem cult: "Even though Moses and the Mosaic tradition would continue in honor, it is David who ordained

---

125. Cf. the seminal article by Simon J. De Vries, "Moses and David as Cult Founders in Chronicles," *JBL* 107 (1988): 619–39. See also Benjamin D. Giffone, "According to Which 'Law of Moses'? Cult Centralization in Samuel, Kings, and Chronicles," *VT* 67 (2017): 432–47.

126. On this very point, see now Lars Maskow, *Tora in der Chronik. Studien zur Rezeption des Pentateuchs in den Chronikbüchern*, FRLANT 274 (Göttingen: Vandenhoeck & Ruprecht, 2019).

the Levites to their office who brought the worship of Yahweh to its highest perfection and its true fulfillment," according to Simon J. De Vries.[127]

(2) Text criticism and literary criticism are twins. We noticed that the borderline between text criticism and literary criticism is difficult to trace with precision. This was already noticed by Wellhausen in his work on the Books of Samuel.[128] It was repeated by Dominique Barthélemy more recently. This means that we probably have to revise some of our presuppositions when trying to identify sources, redactions, additions and omissions in biblical texts. The importance of old versions, such as the LXX and the Old Latin is growing in many exegetical circles.

(3) Copying is not photocopying. Again, recent discoveries, as for instance the Elephantine papyri and the Dead Sea Scrolls, oblige us to revise traditional opinions about the dividing line between orality and literacy. Some problems in the Pentateuch as in Chronicles could find more satisfactory explanations if we take into account the importance of collective memory and oral transmission in ancient times. What is called intertextuality is perhaps to be revised too. A text does not refer necessarily to another text, but perhaps more simply to a collective memory and shared oral traditions.

All in all, we may say that we have more questions than answers and that there is still a lot to be done. Nonetheless, our Cinderella may have met her Fairy Godmother and Sleeping Beauty may also hear from afar the sound of a galloping horse and the voice of her Prince Charming.

---

127. De Vries, "Moses and David," 639.
128. Julius Wellhausen, *Der Text der Bücher Samuelis* (Göttingen: Vandenhoeck & Ruprecht, 1871), xi: "[…] es ist schwierig, die Grenze zu finden, wo die Literarkritik aufhört und die Textkritik beginnt." Dominique Barthélemy, "Critique textuelle et critique littéraire," in Dominique Barthélemy, *Découvrir l'Écriture*, LD hors série (Paris: Le Cerf, 2000), 141–5; Dominique Barthélemy, "L'enchevêtrement de l'histoire textuelle et l'histoire littéraire dans les relations entre la Septante et le Texte Massorétique," in Barthélemy, *Découvrir l'Écriture*, 161–83; Emanuel Tov, *Textual Criticism of the Hebrew Bible* (Minneapolis, MN: Fortress Press, 32012), 313–49.

I. Consonance, Continuity, and mutual Influence

THEOCRATIC REWORKING IN THE PENTATEUCH
Proto-Chronistic Features in the Late Priestly Layers of Numbers and Their Reception in Chronicles
Reinhard Achenbach

1. INTRODUCTION

יהוה ימלך לעלם ועד Exodus 18:15

The idea of Yhwh's kingship roots in preexilic mythical concepts of the weather–god, Yhwh, as a divine warrior (Ps 24:7–10) who is proclaimed as king (Ps 93:1–5; 97:1–7), paid homage by the gods (Ps 29:1–10; 97:7), and acclaimed by the whole cosmos (Ps 98:4–9). He erected his throne above the flood (Ps 29:10). He receives the king and the congregation in an audience at his temple. He protects and nourishes gods, humankind, and the creation (Ps 36:7–10; 104:1–4, 10–11, 27–28, 30–33).[1] In the royal cult, the king's position and role were legitimated and confirmed by Yhwh, the divine king. The royal accession to the throne mirrors a divine accession, probably in a regular festival at new year (cf. Ps 97:1–7; 98:4–9).[2] In the postexilic period, when the Judean monarchy was not reinstated, the congregation of Zion worshipped Yhwh in the Second Temple as the divine and universal king, the only God and ruler of the nations (Ps 47:9–11; 48:10–12; 98:1–3). Regarding these verses, therefore, Reinhard Müller has applied the term "theocratic reworkings."[3]

---

1. Reinhard Müller, *Jahwe als Wettergott. Studien zur althebräischen Kultlyrik anhand ausgewählter* Psalmen, BZAW 387 (Berlin: De Gruyter, 2008), 244.

2. Müller, *Jahwe als Wettergott*, 178–180, continuing from Sigmund Mowinckel, *The Psalms in Israel's Worship I–II* (Oxford: Basil Blackwell, 1962), I,122; John Day, Psalms, OTG (Sheffield: Sheffield Academic Press, 1990), 67–85. See also Corinna Körting, *Der Schall des Schofar. Israels Feste im Herbst*, BZAW 285 (Berlin: De Gruyter, 1999).

3. Müller, *Jahwe als Wettergott*, 169–172, 191–192. The weather-god has become the ruler of the whole world, the "Weltenherrscher" (227–234).

Flavius Josephus, in his writing *Contra Apionem II*, 164–165, introduced the term *theocracy*:

> Some peoples have entrusted the supreme political power (*exousia*) to monarchies (*monarchia*), others to oligarchies (*oligôn dynasteia*), yet others to the masses. Our lawgiver (*nomothetes*), however, was attracted by non of these forms of polity, but gave to his constitution (*politeuma*) the form of what – if a forced expression be permitted – may be termed a "theocracy" (*theokratia*), placing all sovereignty (*arche*) and authority (*kratos*) in the hands of God.[4]

Josephus stressed the advantage of a hierocratic system that was independent of any other political superiority; cf. *Contra Apionem II*, 184–187:

> For us, with our conviction that the original institution of the Law was in accordance with the will of God, it would be rank impiety not to observe it. What could one alter in it? […] Could there be a finer or more equitable polity than one which sets God at the head of the universe (*hegemôn tôn holôn*), which asigns the administration of its highest affairs to the whole body of priests, and entrusts to the supreme high-priest (*archhieros*) the direction of the other priests? These men, moreover, woed their original promotion by the legislator to their high office, not to any superiority in wealth of other accidental advantages. No; of all his companions, the men to whom he entrusted the ordering of divine worship as their first charge were those who were pre-eminently gifted with persuasive eloquence and discretion. But this charge further embraced a strict superintendence of the Law and oft he pursuits of everyday life; for the appointed duties of the priests included general supervision, the trial of cases of litigation, and the punishment of condemned persons.[5]

---

4. Henry S. J. Thackeray, trans., *Josephus. I The Life – Against Apion*, LCL (Cambridge Mass.: Harvard University Press – London: William Heinemann Ltd., 1926 [repr. 1961]), 359.

5. Cf. Thackeray, trans., *Josephus*, 369. The hierocratic features are also described by Hecataeus (Diod. Sic. XL). For problems related to the term *theocracy* cf. Reinhard Achenbach, *Die Vollendung der Tora: Studien zur Redaktionsgeschichte des Numeribuches im Kontext von Hexateuch und Pentateuch*, BZAR 3 (Wiesbaden: Harrassowitz, 2003), 130–140, "Überlegungen zu den Ursprüngen der jüdischen Theokratie"; Hubert Cancik, "Theokratie und Priesterherrschaft. Die mosaische Verfassung bei Flavius Josephus, contra Apionem 2,157–198," in Hubert Cancik and Hildegard Cancik-Lindemeyer, *Religionsgeschichten. Römer, Juden und Christen im römischen Reich. Gesammelte Aufsätze II*, 2 (Tübingen: Mohr Siebeck, 1987), 72; Bernhard Lang, "Theokratie: Geschichte und Bedeutung eines Begriffs in Soziologie und Ethnologie," *Taubes* (1987), 12; Jan Assmann, *Herrschaft und Heil: Politische Theorie in Altägypten, Israel und Europa* (Darmstadt: Wissenschaftliche Buchgesellschaft, 2000), 28; Jan Assmann, *Ägypten. Eine Sinngeschichte*, München: Carl Hanser, 1996, 332–334; Reinhard Kratz, *Translatio imperii: Untersuchungen zu den aramäischen Danielerzählungen und ihrem theologiegeschichtlichen Umfeld*, WMANT 63 (Neukirchen-Vluyn: Neukirchener Verlag, 1987), 284; Markus Saur, *Die*

Josephus suggests that the order described in the *torah* of the Pentateuch had been established in Jewish institutions as part of a social and political constitutional reality. However, these primary texts to which Josephus refers present the results of an iterative conceptual development, symbolically represented by Israel in the desert. Thus, they arose more in a virtual than in a political reality. Such development can be traced in a diachronic analysis of the Pentateuch when comparison with other biblical texts.

2. DIVINE KINGSHIP IN THE POSTEXILIC COMPOSITION OF THE HEXATEUCH

In the postexilic period after the transfer of the Babylonian Province of Yehud to Persian jurisdiction, the Achaemenids did not allow the restoration of the kingdoms of Israel or Judah. Under the first administrator (*pæḥah* פחה), named Sheshbazzar, some of the exiled Judeans probably returned from Babylon (Ezra 1:5–8; 5:14). Another group seems to have returned together with a Jewish *pæḥah* Zerubbabel at the time of Darius I (Ezra 2:2; Neh 7:7). According to Haggai 1:1 Zerubbabel ben Shealtiel, as governor of Yehud, and Joshua ben Jehozadak, as high priest, initiated the building of the Second Temple (Hag 1:7–15; 2:4). In later rewritings, Zerubbabel was described as Yhwh's *signet* (חותם), as *chosen*, and as *servant* of God (Hag 2:23), and thus connoted with royal Davidic symbols, in a messianic perspective (Hag 2:20–23; Zech 4:6–14; 6:9–14).[6]

Samaria and Yehud each remained governmental districts (*medinah*) under Persian jurisdiction. The rebuilding of the Yhwh temple in Jerusalem was permitted only at the end of the 6th century BCE. Recent archaeological work has documented the later edification of a sanctuary for Yhwh on Mount Garizim in the middle of the 5th century BCE. As everywhere else, the Persians did not interfere in local religious issues or even local jurisprudence. Leading families cooperating with the authorities made sure that taxes were collected, a modest, rather poor local economy could develop, and young men

---

Königspsalmen. Studien zur Entstehung und Theologie, BZAW 340 (Berlin: De Gruyter, 2004), 275–77.

6. Ralf Rothenbusch, "Serubbabel im Haggaiund im Protosacharja-Buch. Konzepte der Gemeindeleitung im frühnachexilischen Juda," in *Literatur- und sprachwissenschaftliche Beiträge zu alttestamentlichen Texten. Symposion in Hólar í Hjaltadal, 16.–19. Mai 2005*, FS W. Richter, ed. Sigurður Ö. Steingrímsson et al., ATSAT 83 (St. Ottilien: Eos Verlag, 2007), 219–64; Reinhard G. Kratz, "Serubbabel und Joschua," in Reinhard G. Kratz, *Das Judentum im Zeitalter des Zweiten Tempels. Kleine Schriften 1*, FAT 42 (Tübingen: Mohr Siebeck, ²2013), 79–92.

were regularly mustered to serve in the Persian army.[7]

The community that generated collection oracles collected in Isaiah 40–55 ("Deutero-Isaiah") believed that Yhwh had chosen the Achaemenid King in order to rebuild Jerusalem (Isa 44:24–45:8). Yet, the traditional function of the Davidic Kings as "servants of Yhwh" ('*Ebed Yhwh*) was transfered to a representative of the people of Jacob-Israel. They believed that this representative could assume responsibility to claim the fundamental right for Jews to settle in their original realms and to establish a religiously independent ethnic unit (Isa 42:1–8). When this representative failed, the title of '*Ebed Yhwh* (עבד יהוה) was transferred to the community itself (Isa 44:1–5; 52:13–53:12). Their members reestablished themselves as a community of Zion, considering themselves witnesses to the kingdom of Yhwh, the only God (Isa 44:6–8; 54).

If the Deuteronomists who wrote the history of Samuel and Kings had hoped, based on the oracle of Nathan (2 Sam 7:16), for the reinstitution of Davidic kings after Jehoiachin's release (2 Kgs 25:27–30), their hope remained unfulfilled. In a further concept of the Deuteronomists the scribes propagated the legend that God had already revealed the Decalogue and the Deuteronomic Law on Mount Horeb, and thus described the condition of a broken and renewed Covenant (Horeb-Covenant Legend: Deut 5; 9–10) as a precursor to the settlement and life of all Israelites in the former promised land (Moab-Covenant Legend: Deut 1–3; 28:69*; 31*, 34). As a text written for the late exilic and postexilic generations, the Deuteronomistic Covenant Theology formed one of the persisting foundations for the restitution of Jewish religious life and society in the early postexilic period. According to Deuteronomy 12*, the rebuilt sanctuary in Jerusalem was believed to be the place that Yhwh had chosen to let his name dwell (Deut 12:10–11; cf. Josh 1; 13; 21:44; 1 Kgs 5:5; 8:20).[8]

---

7. Material culture and archaeological evidence show that the positive picture of the economic and social situation of Jerusalem and its temple as reported in the books of Ezra and Nehemiah is not very realistic; cf. Oded Lipschits, "Materialkultur, Verwaltung und Wirtschaft in Juda während der Perserzeit und die Rolle des Jerusalemer Tempels," in *Persische Reichspolitik und lokale Heiligtümer. Beiträge einer Tagung des Exzellenzclusters "Religion und Politik in den Kulturen der Vormoderne und Moderne" vom 24.–26. Februar 2016 in Münster*, BZAR 25, ed. Reinhard Achenbach (Wiesbaden: Harrassowitz, 2019), 185–208.

8. A literary-critical differentiation must be observed between *Urdeuteronomium* (preexilic, not in the style of a sermon of Moses), late-exilic deuteronomistic frames that introduce the fiction of a Mosaic parenesis (Horeb-Covenant Deut 5:9–10, Moab-Covenant Deut 1–3*, 31*, 34*), late-dtr "historical commandments" (Deut 6–8; 11*) and a post-dtr introduction into the composition of Gen–Josh* (Hexateuch-Redaction: Deut 31:9–13), a late postexilic priestly Pentateuch-Redaction (Deut 31:14–15, 23; 32:48–52; 34:10–12) and later additions (Deut 32:33); cf. Eck-

The Priestly Code developed a foundation myth for the belief that Yhwh had chosen to dwell in the midst of Israel (Gen 1–Exod 29, 40* [Lev 9]),[9] and introduced the legend that the ancient *Ark of God* (ארון האלהים) had its origin already in the time of Moses (Exod 25:10–16*). They held that the Ancient Israelite priesthood had its origin in the family of Aaron, whose members were anointed and ordained (Exod 29:29). Attempts to promote the position of the high priest in the sense of an early hierocratic system by a coronation were not completed (cf. Zech 6:9–15).[10]

From the reconstructed literary-historical development observed in the literary layers of the Pentateuch, it seems that scribes, having reestablished themselves at the Second Temple in the fifth century BCE, combined the Priestly and the Deuteronomistic foundation myths, together with pre-exilic narrative cycles, into a Hexateuchal composition. They modified the priestly claim to leadership in the Aaronite Legend of P when they combined it with the deuteronomistic narrative of violation and restoration of the covenant in Exodus 32–34* and Deuteronomy 9–10 (cf. Exod 32:21–25; Deut 9:20). Moses's relatives, the Levites, proved themselves to be the most dedicated to Yhwh and, therefore, were ordained and assigned the task of priesthood (Exod 32:26–29) – to carry the Ark that Moses had built (Deut 10:1–5, 9–10) – and to keep the tablets of the Decalogue and to preserve the scrolls of the Mosaic Torah (Deut 31:9).[11]

---

ard Otto, *Das Deuteronomium im Pentateuch und Hexateuch. Studien zur Literaturgeschichte von Pentateuch und Hexateuch im Lichte des Deuteronomiumrahmens*, FAT 20 (Tübingen: Mohr Siebeck, 2000); Eckard Otto, Deuteronomium, HThKAT, 4 vols. (Freiburg – Basel – Wien: Herder, 2012–2017). One of the painstaking achievements of Otto's commentaries is the insight that the (postexilic) deuteronomistically framed Deuteronomy can even be observed in post-deuteronomistic contexts and with post-deuteronomistic layers that are younger than the Priestly Code "*Grundschrift*" (P^g).

9. For the debate about the reconstruction and the place of the Priestly Code in the context of Pentateuch redactions cf. Christian Frevel, *Mit Blick auf das Land die Schöpfung erinnern. Zum Ende der Priestergrundschrift*, HBS 23 (Freiburg – Basel – Wien: Herder, 2000); Christoph Nihan, *From Priestly Torah to Pentateuch: A Study in the Composition of the Book of Leviticus*, FAT II/25 (Tübingen: Mohr Siebeck, 2007); Thomas Römer, "Der Pentateuch," in *Die Entstehung des Alten Testaments*, ThW 1, ed. Walter Dietrich et al. (Stuttgart: Kohlhammer, 2014), 53–93, especially 90–93; Reinhard Achenbach, "Priestly Law," in *The Oxford Handbook of Biblical Law*, ed. Pamela Barmash (Oxford: Oxford University Press, 2019), 177–98.

10. Thomas Pola, *Das Priestertum bei Sacharja. Historische und traditionsgeschichtliche Untersuchungen zur frühnachexilischen Herrschererwartung*, FAT 35 (Tübingen: Mohr Siebeck, 2003), 224–64.

11. Reinhard Achenbach, "Das Exodusbuch als Teil des Hexateuch und des Pentateuch," in *Wege der Freiheit. Zur Entstehung und Theologie des Exodusbuches. Die Beiträge eines Symposions zum 70. Geburtstag von Rainer Albertz (Münster, 10.–11. Mai 2013)*, AThANT 104, ed. Reinhard Achenbach, Ruth Ebach and Jakob Wöhrle

According to the original form of Deuteronomy (the preexilic *Urdeuteronomium*) the priest at the central century – together with a judge – had the task of maintaining justice, even by divine ordeal in cases of unsolvable lawsuits and conflicts in the local courts (Deut 17:8, 9b, 10–13*). In the postexilic reworking of this text in the contexts of the Hexateuchal Redaction and Deuteronomistic history, these priests were called "*levitical* priests" (הלוים הכהנים, Deut 17:9a*). Within their domain, they claimed to have an exemplary text for the reproduction of further copies of the Torah (Deut 17:18), they kept the right of priesthood (Deut 18:1–8), and it was believed that they had taken care of the ark, the symbol of the central sanctuary (Num 10:35–36; 14:44; Josh 8:33). Aaron – as the brother of Moses (Exod 7:1–2 P*) – is believed thus to be of Levitical origin too. Moses took on the role of the '*Ebed Yhwh* (Deut 34:5; Josh 1:1), who saved Israel from divine wrath by his intercessory prayers (Exod 32:7–14; Num 14:13–20). He became the first prophetic mediator of God's will, to be followed by Yhwh's chosen prophets (Deut 18:15–22). The concept of Second Isaiah, to accept the Achaemenid king as *Messiah* (Isa 45:1), was rejected: no foreigner could be king in Israel, only one of their *brothers* (Deut 17:14–15). Yet, the critical experiences with the historic kings deemed having a king unnecessary, unless he would strictly keep to the Torah of the Levitical priests (Deut 17:16–20).

The so-called "Law of the King" was formulated with respect to the late-dtr story of 1 Samuel 8, a text already critical towards kingship. The law was formulated as if it were destined to warn against the sins of Solomon (Deut 17:17//1 Kgs 11:1–13). It also reflects the warnings of Isaiah not to go down to Egypt for help and rely upon horses (Deut 16:16//Isa 31:1). According to the oracle in 1 Samuel 8:7, the wish to install a king responsible for the law according to the constitution of other nations (שימה-לנו מלך לשפטנו ככל-הגנים, 1 Sam 8:5) is itself even an iniquity, as the demand implies the rejection of Yhwh's kingship: אתי מאסו ממלך עליהם ("it is me they have despised as their king!"). Installing a king in the future could only mean that this king obeys the Torah administered by the levitical priests and, thereby, acknowledges the exclusive kingship of Yhwh.[12]

(Zürich: Theologischer Verlag Zürich, 2014), 51–72; Reinhard Achenbach, "Grundlinien redaktioneller Arbeit in der Sinai-Perikope," in *Das Deuteronomium zwischen Pentateuch und Deuteronomistischem Geschichtswerk*, FRLANT 206, ed. Eckard Otto and Reinhard Achenbach (Göttingen: Vandenhoeck & Ruprecht, 2004), 56–80; Reinhard Achenbach, "The Story of the Revelation at the Mountain of God and the Redactional Editions of the Hexateuch and the Pentateuch," in *A Critical Study of the Pentateuch. An Encounter Between Europe and Africa*, ATM 20, ed. Eckard Otto and Jurie le Roux (Münster: Litt-Verlag, 2005), 126–151.

12. Reinhard Müller, *Königtum und Gottesherrschaft. Untersuchungen zur*

3. DIVINE KINGSHIP, A HOLY NATION, AND A KINGDOM OF PRIESTS IN LATE-POSTEXILIC LAYERS OF THE PENTATEUCH

As the process of *Fortschreibung* of the Hexateuch Composition continued, a new concept of divine presence was introduced, possibly around 400 BCE. This new concept was, namely, the idea of *kabôd yhwh* independent from any sanctuary – or even the ark. This *kabôd yhwh* appeared as a pillar of fire veiled by a pillar of cloud (Exod 13:21–22). The legend says that, after the covenant had been broken at Mount Sinai, Moses left the contaminated camp and pitched a tent outside the camp as a "Tent of Meeting" (אהל מועד, Exod 33:7–11). Yhwh descended in the pillar of cloud and spoke to Moses face to face (פנים אל־פנים, v. 11). In a later account, Yhwh confirms Moses's exceptional position as a mediator of Yhwh's word and will (Num 12:6–8). When leading authorities of the people (נשיאים) and a group of Levites around Korah question the priestly authority of the Aaronides, the *kabôd* appears before the Tent of Meeting, and the rebels are punished (Num 16:19–24). At the end of Moses's life, Yhwh appears again in a pillar of cloud before the Tent of Meeting and installs Joshua as Moses's successor (Deut 31:14–15, 23). The scribes who introduced these motifs into the Pentateuch concluded the composition of Genesis to Deuteronomy in Deuteronomy 34:10–12 and affirmed, that *"never again did there arise in Israel a prophet like Moses – whom Yhwh singled out face to face"* (v. 10).

Whereas the earlier Hexateuch Composition had been open to the idea of a continous prophetic Torah in addition to the canonised Mosaic Law of the Covenant Code and Deuteronomy (cf. Deut 18:15–22), the priestly scribes who filled up the Pentateuch with priestly Torah drew a line between prophetic scribal revelation and Moses's Torah revelation. They stressed Aaron's central position as the keeper of the *kehunnah* and relegated the other Levitical clans to the role of *clerus minor* (Num 16:8–10). The narrative of Num 16* seems to be part of the new structure focusing on the Holiness Code given to the narrative strand of Genesis to Deuteronomy, so it seems apropriate to identify this group of scribes with the Pentateuch Composi-

---

alttestamentlichen Monarchiekritik, FAT II/3 (Tübingen: Mohr Siebeck, 2004), 119–47 and 177–96; for the secondary, postdtr character of the Law of the King in Deut 17:14–20, cf. Reinhard Achenbach, "Das sogenannte Königsgesetz in Deuteronomium 17,14–20," *ZAR* 15 (2009): 216–33. The Law of the King reflects the collapse of the historical institution of kingship, accepts that it is not a necessary institution for Israel, and marks out conditions for a renewal in the context of the Hexateuch Composition.

tion. These scribes sought to establish Israel not only as a holy people (עם קדוש, Deut 7:6), but as a holy nation (גוי קדוש). As such, priests would take the foremost responsibility for the administration of the covenantal law – including its sacral laws (ממלכת כהנים, Exod 19:6). This conception of a holy nation reconstructed the holy people into a congregational society of all Israelites (כל עדת בני ישראל, Lev 19:2a), with its whole oriented around the sacred. The formula "You shall be holy, for I, Yhwh, your God, am holy!" (יהוה אלהיכם קדשים תהיו כי קדוש אני, Lev 19:2) implies a process of the sacralisation of everyday life in the midst of a community that gathers regularly around a permanent sanctuary. Whereas the administration of the Mosaic Torah was in the purview of these Levitical priests (Deut 17–18), the concept of Deuteronomy's scribal reworkings and additions in the Holiness Code[13] can be called hierocratic.

When the Holiness Code was introduced into the Pentateuch – probably in the late fifth century BCE – the whole composition was integrated into a new hermeneutic framework. The narrative connects to the older layers of the Priestly Code (= Pg*, Lev 9:22–24*) in Lev 10 and 16. The narrative in Lev 10 about the sin and death of Aaron's firstborn sons – Nadab and Abihu – altered and expanded the foundation myth of Pg*[14] and provided the reason for constituting a series of *sacral laws of atonement* (Lev 16), *sanctification and sacralisation* (Lev 17–26 + 27), supplemented by *ritual obligations on offerings* (Lev 1–7) and *rules of purity* (Lev 11–15). The book of Leviticus barely mentions Levites; the focus is rather on the central role of an Aaronide priesthood. According to this teaching, Aaron's main responsibility is maintaining his purity (Lev 10:9; cf. Ezek 44:21) so that he will be able "to distinguish between the sacred and the profane, and between the unclean and the clean" (ובין החל ובין הטמא ובין הטהור ולהבדיל בין הקדש Lev 10:10). And so that he will be able "to teach the Israelites all the laws which Yhwh has imparted to them through Moses" (אלהים ביד־משה ולהורת את־בני ישראל את כל־החקים אשר דבר יהוה,

---

13. Cf. Christophe Nihan, "The Holiness Code between D and P. Some Comments on the Function and Significance of Leviticus 17–26 in the Composition of the Torah," in *Das Deuteronomium zwischen Pentateuch und Deuteronomistischem Geschichtswerk*, FRLANT 206, ed. Eckard Otto and Reinhard Achenbach (Göttingen: Vandenhoeck & Ruprecht, 2004), 81–122.

14. Nihan, *From Priestly Torah to Pentateuch*, 576–607; Achenbach, *Vollendung*, 93–97; Reinhard Achenbach, "Ursprungsmythen des Priestertums in der Hebräischen Bibel als Camouflage klerikaler Machtkämpfe," in *Sukzession in Religionen. Autorisierung, Legitimierung, Wissenstransfer*, ed. Almut-Barbara von Renger and Markus Witte, (Berlin: DeGruyter, 2017), 113–32; Lars Maskow, *Tora in der Chronik: Studien zur Rezeption des Pentateuchs in den Chronikbüchern*, FRLANT 274 (Göttingen: Vandenhoeck & Ruprecht, 2019), 296–299.

Lev 10:11).

The rule of Leviticus 10:8–11 has a parallel in the Zadokite tradition of Ezekiel 44, where it is preserved in an older and more extended version (Ezek 44:15–31). The scribes of the school of Ezekiel clearly rejected the idea that all Levitical priests should have priestly rights. For them only the descendants of Zadok are allowed to serve the sanctuary, "to teach the people of God to distinguish between holy and profane, and impart the knowledge about what is clean and what is unclean" (Ezek 44:23).[15]

The Zadokite rule in Ezekiel 44:24 demands the following in the form of a divine prescription:

> "Presiding in lawsuits (על ריב) it is they who stand (המה יעמדו) to act as judges (לשפט) in accordance with my law (במשפטי), and they shall decide them (ושפטהו); they shall preserve all my torot and my rules and all my holy days (ואת תורתי ואת חקתי בכל מועדי ישמרו), and they shall maintain the sanctity of my Sabbaths (ואת־שבתותי יקדשו)."

The high priest should not only have the central position in the cult, but also at the central court. Ezekiel 44 thus tends to emend the rules of Deuteronomy 17:8–9: the judge of the central court, who had to obey the oracle of a priestly ordeal should be replaced by the high priest himself. And this person may only be of Zadokite origin. Not Levitical priests in general, but the leading high priest should maintain the text and the scroll of the Torah, and – beyond the conception of Deuteronomy – administrate the cultic calendar and the sanctity of the Sabbath.

It seems that the legitimation legend of Leviticus 10 met – at least in part – these claims and demands. It demanded that Aaron enter the sanctuary in a state of purity (Lev 10:9//Ezek 44:21). His task is to teach holiness and purity (Lev 10:10// Ezek 44:23), and he had to teach Israel all the orders and rules of Yhwh in general (Lev 10:11// Ezek 44:24). However, Lev 10:11 only implies any clear demand that the high priest should preside over the central court. Within this new hermeneutical frame, the Mosaic speeches of Deuteronomy are understood as an explication of the Torah (Deut 1:5). Therefore – within this context – the older tradition of Deuteronomy 17:8–9 is preserved and *not* changed according the more radical intentions of Ezekiel 44.

15. Nihan, *From Priestly Torah to Pentateuch*, 590–93 has shown that Lev 10:10 represents a younger version compared to Ezek 44:23; cf. also Maskow, *Tora in der Chronik*, 169–70; see for further alternative positions with respect to the relation between Lev 10, Numb 18 and Ezek 44 Michael D. Konkel, *Architektonik des Heiligen: Studien zur Zweiten Tempelvision Ezechiels* (Ez 40–48) (BBB 129–Berlin: Philo, 2001); Nathan MacDonald, *Priestly Rule: Polemic and Biblical Interpretation in Ezekiel 44* (BZAW 476–Berlin: de Gruyter, 2015).

4. THE PROTO-CHRONISTIC AND CHRONISTIC GENEALOGY OF THE ZADOKITES IN THE THEOCRATIC REWORKINGS OF THE PENTATEUCH

Why, though, does Leviticus 10 report that these rules were proclaimed after the death of Aaron's two older sons? The reason must be that the priestly scribes wanted to prepare a genealogical rationale for the demand that a Zadokite should occupy the position of high priest. Zadok's genealogical origin was unclear in 1 Kings 2:35, where it is reported that Solomon installed Zadok and rejected the ancient Israelite priest Abjatar (1 Kgs 2:26–27). It is only in 1 Chronicles 5:27–41 that the scribes maintain firmly that Zadok was a descendant of Aaron's third son Eleazar and grandson Pinehas – and an ancestor of Jehozadak, the father of the first high priest after the exile, Joshua.[16]

This genealogical line is introduced into the Pentateuch in Exodus 6:16, 20[17] and explained in Leviticus 10:1–5 and Numbers 20:26–28, the narrative on Eleazar's succession.[18]

1 Chr 5:27–34	References
27 בני לוי גרשון קהת וּמררי	Sons of Levi: Gen 46:11; Exod 6:16; Num 3:17; 10:17; 26:57–62; Josh 21:1–41

---

16. It is not possible to discuss every detail of the composite text of Chronicles. For an orientation to this, cf. Gary N. Knoppers, *I Chronicles 1–9: A New Translation with Introduction and Commentary*, AB (New York – London – Toronto – Sydney – Auckland: Doubleday, 2003), 400–15; Thomas Willi, Chronik. 1 Chr 1–10, BK XXIV/1 (Göttingen: Vandenhoeck & Ruprecht, 2009), 188–240, on 1 Chr 5:27–7:5. The impression that these texts contain a series of additions is due to the scribal technique of rewriting given texts (sources) and filling them up with explanations (lat. *adiectio*), but also leaving out things (lat. *detractio*), changing sequences (lat. *transmutatio*) or even replacing parts of them (lat. *immutatio*); cf. Maskow, *Tora in der Chronik*, 43–50.

17. On the late dating and the assignment to Theocratic Reworking (ThR), cf. Achenbach, *Vollendung*, 110–24; the late dating was confirmed by Christoph Berner, *Die Exoduserzählung. Das literarische Werden einer Ursprungslegende Israels*, FAT 73 (Tübingen: Mohr Siebeck, 2010), 153–67, and Rainer Albertz, *Exodus, Band I: Exodus 1–18*, ZBK (Zürich: Theologischer Verlag Zürich, 2012), 116–32; for the correlation with Chronicles cf. Maskow, *Tora in der Chronik*, 289–96.

18. Num 20:22–29 traditionally is ascribed to P^g*, cf. Frevel, *Mit dem Blick auf das Land*, 237–48; for the late priestly and redactional origin, cf. Christoph Levin, *Der Jahwist*, FRLANT 157 (Göttingen: Vandenhoeck & Ruprecht, 1993), 379; Achenbach, *Vollendung*, 318–34.

1 Chr 5:27–34 — References

1 Chr 5:27–34		References
ובני קהת עמרם יצהר וחברון ועזיאל	28	Qohat: Gen 46:11; Exod 6:16, 18; Num 3:17, 19, 27, 29; 4:2, 4, 15; 7:9; 16:1; 27:57–58; Josh 21:5, 20, 26; 1 Chr 6:1, 3, 7, 23, 46, 51, 55; 23:6, 12
ובני עמרם אהרן ומשה ומרים	29	Amram: Exod 6:18, 20; Num 3:19, 27; 26:58–59; 1 Chr 5:28, 29; 6:3; 23:12–13; 24:20; 26:23
ובני אהרן נדב ואביהוא		Nadab and Abihu: Exod 24:1, 9; 28:1; Lev 10:1; Num 3:2, 4; 26:61; 1 Chr 5:29; 24:1
אלעזר		Eleazar: Exod 6:23, 25; 28:1; Lev 10:6, 12, 16; Num 3:2, 4, 32; 4:16; 17:2, 4; 19:3–4; 20:25–26, 28; 25:7, 11; 26:1, 3, 60, 63; 27:2, 19, 21–22; 31:6–54; 32:2, 28; 34:17; Deut 10:6; Josh 14:1; 17:4; 19:51; 21:1; 22:13, 31–32; 24:33; Ezra 7:5; 1 Chr 5:29–30; 6:35; 9,20; 24:1–6
ואיתמר		Itamar: Exod 6:23; 28:1; 38:21; Lev 10:6, 12; Num 3:2, 4; 4:28, 33; 7:8; 26:60; Ezra 8:2; 1 Chr 5:29; 24:1–6
אלעזר הוליד את פינחס	30	Pinehas: Exod 6:25; Num 25:7, 11; 31:6; Josh 22:13, 30–32; 24:33; Judg 20:28; Ps 106:30; Ezra 7:5; 8:2;1 Chr 5:30; 6:35; 9:20
פינחס הוליד את אבישוע		*Abishua*: Ezra 7:5; 1 Chr 5:30–31; 6:35
ואבישוע הוליד את בקי	31	*Bukki*: Ezra 7:4; 1 Chr 5:31; 6:36
ובקי הוליד את עזי		*Uzzi*: Ezra 7:4; 1 Chr 5:31–32; 6:36

1 Chr 5:27–34	References
32 ועזי הוליד את זרחיה	Zeahiah: Ezra 7:4; 1 Chr 5:31–32; 6:36
וזרחיה הוליד את מריות	Meraioth: Ezra 7:3; 1 Chr 5:32–33; 6:37
33 מריות הוליד את אמריה	Amariah: Ezra 7:3; 1 Chr 5:33,37; 6:37
ואמריה הוליד את אחיטוב	Ahitub: 2 Sam 8:17; Ezra 7:2; 1 Chr 5:33–34, 37–38; 6:37; 18:16
34 ואחיטוב הוליד את צדוק	Zadok: 2 Sam 8:17
וצדוק הוליד את אחימעץ	Ahimaaz: 2 Sam 15:27, 36; 17:20; 18:19–28; 1 Chr 5:34–35; 6:36.

The passage renders the genealogy of Aaron's successors. First Chronicles 6:35–38 repeats the special geneaology of Aaron's descendants because here the different roles of the high-priestly family and the other priestly Levitical families is reported according to the structure that is worked out in Numbers, cf. 1 Chronicles 6:33–38:

> ³³And their brothers, the Levites (אחיהם הלוים), were assigned (נתונים) to all the service of the Tabernacle of the house of God (משכן בית האלהים לכל עבדת). ³⁴As for Aaron and his sons, they were sacrificing upon the altar of burnt offering and upon the incense altar, for every work of the Holy of Holies, to atone for Israel according to all that Moses the servant of God had commanded. ³⁵And these are the sons of Aaron: Eleazar his son, Phineas his son, Abishua his son, ³⁶Buqqi his son, Uzzi his son, Zerahiah his son, ³⁷Meraioth his son, Amariah his son, Ahitub his son, ³⁸Zadoq his son, Ahimaaz his son.

In Genesis–Numbers the genealogy serves to introduce the genealogies of Levites and of Aaronides. Its roots are traced back to Genesis 46:11. In the context of the Exodus account, it is introduced in Exodus 6:16 after the priestly account on Moses's mission, the reception of the Holy Name (Exod 6:2–8), and the first appearance of Moses and Aaron before the Pharaoh (6:13), when both represent political and religious leadership of the Israelites. The narrative of the priestly reworked Pentateuch continued, after the introduction of the Holiness Code, in Numbers 1–10. Only at this point were priestly and Levitical tasks delineated in a detailed structure. The priestly reworking here creates a new legend about the Tabernacle. It does not remain in the desert, but – in addition to the symbol of the Ark of the Covenant, the Tent of Meeting, and the Cloud of Divine Presence in the fiery *kabôd* – now the Tent of Meeting is identified with the *mishkan*, the sanctuary built at Mount Sinai. And this *mishkan* is transported together with the Ark and other sacred precincts by Priests and Levites during their wandering in the wilderness and brought into the promised land (Num 3–4; 9:15–23; Josh 18:1; 19:51; 1 Kgs 8:4).[19] Numbers 10:17 mentions Levi's genealogy again with respect to the tasks of the Levites as *clerus minor*. Numbers 26:57 mentions it with respect to the mustering before the conquest. Again, Joshua 21:6, 27 presents it with respect to the Levitical towns, though it never appears in any deuteronomistic or priestly layer of other biblical books. But then it appears again in 1 Chronicles 5:27 and in the Davidic census of the Levites in 1 Chronicles 23:6. Thus Exodus 6:16 stands in the line of late priestly reworkings of the Pentateuch, which included some necessary *Fortschreibung* in the scrolls of the Enneateuch and a systematic reception in Chronicles. In this way, the late priestly reworkings in Numbers 3–4, 9–10, and 26 can be described as *proto-Chronistic* reworkings.[20]

The same literary level as the list of the three sons of Levi can be observed in continuity with the list on Kohath and his descendants. As Aaron is derived from this ancestor and his son Amram, the Kohathites are allowed to serve at the Most Holy (קדש הקדשים, Num 4:4),[21] which is now identified with the Tent of Meeting (אהל מועד). It remains the privilege of Aaron to touch the holy devices and the Tabernacle itself (Num 4:5, 15).

Amram is listed as the husband of Jochebed, a daughter of Levi, and as the father of Moses, Aaron, and Miriam (Exod 6:20; Num 26:59; 1 Chr 5:29). Even when compared with his brother Moses, the

---

19. The book of Joshua underwent a reworking from ThR, cf. Reinhard Achenbach, "Der Pentateuch, seine theokratischen Bearbeitungen und Josua – 2 Könige," in *Les dernières rédactions du Pentateuque, de l'Hexateuque et de l'ennéateuque*, BEThL CCIII, ed. Thomas Römer and Konrad Schmid (Leuven – Paris: Peeters, 2007), 225–54; for the late priestly reworking see also Rainer Albertz, "Die kanonische Anpassung des Josuabuches: Eine Neubewertung seiner sogenannten 'priesterschriftlichen Texte'", in *Les dernières rédactions du Pentateuque, de l'Hexateuque et de l'ennéateuque*, BEThL CCIII, ed. Thomas Römer and Konrad Schmid (Leuven – Paris: Peeters, 2007), 199–216. References to these late priestly additions are found only a few times in Sam–Kgs, but their concepts are reflected in Chr.

20. That the late layers in Numbers are proto-Chronistic also was seen by Hans-Peter Mathys, "Numeri und Chronik: Nahe Verwandte," in *The Books of Leviticus and Numbers*, BEThL 215, ed. Thomas Römer (Leuven – Paris – Deudley MA: Peeters, 2008), 555–78.

21. The *qodesh ha-qodashîm* is mentioned only in Exod 26:33–34; Num 4:4, 19; and 18:9 in connection with the desert shrine, and in 1 Chr 6:34 in connection with the Aaronide privilege of priestly accession to it. In 1 Kgs 6:16; 7:50; 8:6 (1 Chr 3:8, 10; 4:22; 5:7), in connection with the Solomonic temple; in Ezek 41:4 and Ezra 2:63; Neh 7:65 with the Second Temple.

high-priestly privilege is reserved for Aaron alone (1 Chr 23:13):

> The sons of Amram: Aaron and Moses. Aaron was set apart (ויבדל), he and his sons, forever, to be consecrated as most holy (קדש קדשים להקדישו), to burn incense (להקטיר)[22] to Yhwh and serve Him and pronounce blessings in His name (לשרתו ולברך בשמו) forever (עד עולם).

The assignment of the priestly service to the tribe of Levi (Exod 32:29), as well as their performing cultic worship and blessings (Deut 10:8–את־שבט הלוי ... לעמד לפני יהוה לשרתו לברך בשמו הבדיל יהוה), is – according to this priestly reworking – exclusively assigned to Aaron and his progeny as a permanent privilege, not merely for a limited period (cf. Deut 10:8b עד היום הזה). The daily burning of incense is a privilege reserved for the high priest that brings him closest to the holiest precinct in the sanctuary and, thus, to God's presence. This ancestral lineage serves to secure the exclusivity of the high-priestly family's position.

Interestingly enough, the construct of a pure Levitical geneaology for Aaron's sons is supplemented in Exodus 6:23. Here, Aaron's wife is identified as Elisheba the daughter of Aminadab and the sister of Nachshon, a Judean leader (Num 1:7; 2:3; 10:14). Thus, the concept of priestly leadership and political leadership is intertwined and harmonised by means of a construct of putative kinship.[23] Chronicles seems to correspond to this concept when it states that Zadok was anointed as high priest at the same time that Solomon was anointed as king (1 Chr 29:22).[24] The mother of Eleazar, Elisheba (Gr. Elisabeth), is not mentioned again anywhere in Chronicles, whether in the LXX or the MT.

Nadab and Abihu are regarded as the two elder sons of Aaron. According to Exodus 24:1, 9–11 – together with Moses, their father Aaron, and seventy elders of Israel – they have the privilege of partaking in the covenant ceremony at Mount Sinai. These verses are generally considered secondary priestly additions, although they

---

22. Exod 29:13, 15; 30:7–8, 20; Num 17:5; 18:17.
23. Cf. Maskow, *Tora in der Chronik*, 257–59 and 293–95.
24. Maskow, *Tora in der Chronik*, 545–46. The Judean concept of leadership as documented in Num 2, 7, and 10 is transferred to the priestly lineage. Maskow has clearly seen the connection between the two leadership concepts: "Es gibt im nachexilischen Juda zwei miteinander interagierende Herrschaftsdiskurse, den des aktuellen Hohenpriester und den des (reminiszenten) judäischen Königtums. Der judäische Herrschaftsdiskurs liefert dem hierokratischen Diskurs gewissermaßen die institutionelle Grundlage, wobei sich dieser nicht mehr personaliter realisiert, sondern durch die Übernahme in die priesterliche Konstruktion Geltung verschafft und die Hohenpriester durch genealogische Ableitung zu einem Gesalbten und höchsten Vertreter der Rechtsinstanz als *de facto* zum nachexilischen König macht." When Nachshon became David's ancestor (Ruth 4:20; 1 Chr 2:10–11), the anointed high priest and the Messiah became relatives (Exod 6:23); Maskow, *Tora in der Chronik*, 295 n. 10.

have no further connection with P^g because – according to this layer – Moses was alone when he ascended the mountain to approach the divine (Exod 24:15–18). The narrative points out that when Moses approached the Most Holy during the first revelation, the designated high priest Aaron and his sons shared this privilege together with seventy representatives of the seventy descendants of Jacob (Gen 46:27; Exod 1:5; Deut 10:22).[25] They even were honoured by sharing in the vision of God on his throne from beneath his footrest. This footrest consisted of a pavement of lapislazuli coloured sapphire, like the very sky in terms of purity (Exod 24:10), a metaphorical description of the heavenly dwelling that is attested only in the (Zadokite) Ezekiel tradition (Ezek 1:26–28; 10:1–2). They partook in the first cultic meal together with God (Exod 24:11).

Aaron's other sons Eleazar and Itamar did not take part in the ceremony, maybe because they were considered younger. However, when Aaron is assigned his office, the four sons are mentioned at his installation (Exod 28:1). The legend about Nadab and Abihu continues in Leviticus 10:1–3, which reports that they died after using foreign (impure) fire when offering incense to Yhwh. This legend has the function of justifying why Aaron's third son, Eleazar, becomes his successor. So all other references to the firstborn mention this event (Num 3:2, 4; 26:61). Neither Nadab nor Abihu is mentioned elsewhere in Chronicles (1 Chr 5:29; 24:1–2). Thus, it seems at least plausible to assume that Exodus 24:1, 9–11; Leviticus 10*; and Numbers 3; [26] are part of a reworking of the Pentateuch that is younger than P, D, HC, and is proto-Chronistic. Because the function of this legitimating construct is to confirm hierocratic leadership in the context of the Mosaic Torah, this layer can be called a *theocratic reworking* (ThR).[26]

Exodus 6:25 already expounds Eleazar's lineage, mentioning his marriage with a daughter of Putiel and the birth of Phineas. Putiel is

---

25. The concept that Israel could be represented by seventy elders was not reflected anywhere else in dtr or prophetic literature, except in Ezek 8:11, where a group of seventy elders is blamed for idolatry in the temple during the time after 597 BCE. The Pentateuch Composition invented an institutional group of seventy elders in Num 11:16, 24–25, but the institution of the *gerousia* is attested only in the Hellenistic era. This underlines and confirms the assumption that Exod 24:1, 9–11 is a Fortschreibung from late priestly reworking.

26. The character of this reworking that adds a legend to the tabernacle in the wilderness, the order of priests, Levites, the congregation of Israel, and the division of land (ThR I, Num 1–4*; 10:11, 13–28, 34; [additions in Num 13–14; 16–18], 26–27; 32*; 33:50–56; 34–35; 36:13); later adds further rules on purity and rituals (ThR II, Num 5–6; 15; 19; 28–30*); and adds diverse legends on the origins of vessels and rules for the Second Temple congregation (ThR III, Num 3:11–13, 40–51; 7–9; 10:1–10; 30:2–27; 31; 33; 36), has been described in Achenbach, *Vollendung*, 37–172 and 443–638.

not mentioned anywhere else. Itamar's marriage and children are not mentioned in Exodus 6 because their lineage is not important for the genealogy of the high priest. The divine *torah* on the priestly duties after the death of Nadab and Abihu is addressed to Aaron, Eleasar, and Itamar (Lev 10:6, 16), and they have to share the cultic meal of the high priest (Lev 10:12). Consequently, in Num 3:2, 4 the scribe asserts that "Eleazar and Itamar served as priests in the lifetime of their father Aaron" and that Eleazar was the leading chieftain of Levi (נשיאי הלוי, Num 3:32). His task is described as the oversight of those attending to the duties of the sanctuary (משמרת הקדש פקדת שמרי). Before his father, he is responsible for assuring that the high priest is able to perform all his central duties (Num 4:16): He must take care that there is enough oil for the Menorah (שמן המאור, cf. Exod 27:20–21), aromatic incense for the daily incense offering (קטרת סמים, Exod 30:7), bread for the Tamid of the meal offering (מנחה התמיר, Exod 29:38–41), anointing oil (שמן המשחי, Exod 30:22–33), and for all other devices and vessels of the sanctuary (וכל אשר בו בודש וכליו).

The text of Numbers thus has the function of canonising the special responsibilities and tasks of the high priest's eldest son. The narrative of Numbers 17:1–5 then wants to show that this son is empowered to handle sacred vessels and holy fire. Thus, it reports that Eleazar removed the copper fire pans of the community following Korah after they had sanctified by the holy fire. They are hammered into plating for the altar as a reminder that no outsider, only Aaron and his offspring, is qualified and permitted to offer incense. Only Aaron or his offspring is also allowed to slaughter the red cow and thus prepare the material to produce the cleansing water that purifies those who have come into contact with the dead (Num 19:3). After the death of his father, Eleazar is invested with Aaron's vestments and becomes his successor (Num 20:25–29). The narrative about the zeal of Pinehas functions to confirm that Eleazar's son was also fit to take over the role of the high priest's eldest son and to succeed him in the holy office (Num 25:7, 11). Eleazar then stands at the side of Moses when Moses mandates the new census before the conquest of the land (Num 26:1, 3). Together with Moses he presides over the assembly of the Israelite community and their chieftains (העדה לפני הנשיאם וכל) in front of the Tent of Meeting (פתח אהל מועד) in the case of Zelophehad's daughters regarding the law of inheritance (Num 27:2). When Joshua is designated and commissioned as Moses's successor, Moses lays his hands upon him in the sight of Eleazar and the whole community (Num 27:18–23). He – as a political leader – is instructed that the high priest had the task to examine all fundamental decisions through the oracles of Urim and Tummim from God (v. 23). In questions of the highest legal authority and of war and peace (Num 31:6), the high priest now holds the ultimate authority. He, together with Joshua, apportions the land (Num 34:17). Other short additions also mark this leading role: Josh 14:1; 17:4; 19:51; 21:1; 22:31–32; 24:33. Judges 20:28 mentions Phineas as Eleazar's successor; cf. Josh 24:33[a] LXX.

After that, only the genealogies in Ezra 7:5; 1 Chronicles 5:29–30; and 9:20, as well as the narrative about the priestly obligations of the descendants of Eleazar and his brother Itamar (1 Chr 24:1–6) mention Eleazar again. Again, the Numbers narrative arc on the duties of the high priest's sons continues only in Chronicles.

Itamar, as Eleazar's younger brother, is named in the genealogies (Exod 6:23; 28:1; etc.) and has priestly duties (Lev 10:6, 12). In addition, his task is the oversight of the sanctuary's financial affairs (Exod 38:21; Num 7:8). The legend of 1 Chronicles 24 maintains that David divided the priestly offices among his sons, together with the Zadokite sons of Eleazar. Again, Chronicles takes up the line drawn from the priestly reworking of Numbers.

Phineas first appears in Exodus 6:25. Eleasar took a daughter of a certain Puti-El (פוטי־אל) as a wife, and she bore him Phineas. The hybrid name is only mentioned in this context. In analogy to the Egyptian name Poti-phera, Poti-phar (*P3-djp3-r*[ʿ] – "He whome Ra has given") the name means "*He-whom-El has given*", containing both an Egyptian and a West-Semitic name element. At least the name of Phineas's grandfather suggests an Egyptian cultural background. However, there is no further information about the scribes' intention in mentioning this name.[27]

The Hexateuch Composition narrative in Exodus 32:26–28 proves that the sons of Levi stand behind Yhwh without any doubt as to their loyalty. They are prepared to punish idolatry without compromise, and slay brother, neighbour, and kin (Exod 32:27).[28] Therefore, they are qualified for priesthood (cf. Exod 32:28; Deut 10:8–9). This tradition is confirmed in the Pentateuch Composition in the Blessing of Moses, Deuteronomy 33:9.[29] The hierocratic legend of Aaron's sons and grandsons in the priestly reworking of Numbers adds a tradition about the zeal of Phineas (Num 25:6–15): The Moabites and Midian-

---

27. Potiphera is known as priest from On (Heliopolis) and father-in-law of Joseph (Gen 41:45, 50; 46:20), Potiphar was the official who bought Joseph (Gen 37:36; 39:1). Rabbinic interpretation associates the name with Hebr פטר – someone who seperated and emancipated himself from idolatry and wrong passion (cf. Sot 43a; Mekh., Amalek 1).

28. Cf. Deut 13:7; 33:9.

29. Cf. Eckard Otto, *Deuteronomium 12–34. Zweiter Teilband: 23,16–34,12*, HThK (Freiburg – Basel – Wien: Herder, 2017), 2204–260, especially 2245–248.

ites try to seduce the Israelites to sexual intercourse and idolatry. Yhwh punishes the people with an epidemic. When the people gather before the sanctuary in rites of repentance and mourning, a Midianite woman and an Israelite man meet in a certain tent that may be associated with both sexual intercourse and pagan worship (*qubbah*). Phinehas stabs both through the belly (*qebah*) and thus stops the plague, profanation, and fornication (Num 25:1, 8). The priestly reworking of Numbers has its climax in the narrative on the *Covenant of Peace* (ברית שלום) and a *Covenant of Eternal Priesthood* (ברית כהנת עולם) with Phineas ben Eleazar ben Aaron and all his descendants (Num 25:10–13*). This covenantal relationship is affirmed because Pinehas had proven himself passionate enough to turn back God's wrath and was able to expiate (כפר) the Israelites' transgressions. The legend thus establishes a permanent genealogical measure for the legacy and legitimacy of Zadokite priesthood in the Pentateuch. A covenant of peace (ברית שלום) is mentioned in Isa 54:10 in parallel with the covenant of Noah (Gen 9:11–17): Yhwh promises not to bring a disatrous catastrophy over Israel again after the exile. Ezekiel 34:23–31 connects the promise of a covenant of peace (v. 25) with the promise to renew the Davidic kingdom, permanent blessing, welfare, and peace under the divine kingship of the shepherd Yhwh (v. 31). Ezekiel 37:25–27 connects the promise of the covenant of peace with the promise that this covenant will be permanent, an everlasting covenant (ברית עולם, v. 26), refering to the renewal of the Second Temple and an eternal presence of Yhwh, who sanctifies Israel (v. 27–28). Numbers 25:12–13 states that the promise of a covenant of peace has roots reaching back to the time of Phineas: By his zeal for holiness and purity he effects a divine covenant of peace for Israel in connection with an eternal covenant of priesthood (ברית כהנת עולם) with the descendants of Aaron, Eleazar, and Phineas. As priest, Phineas leads the war of retaliation against the Midianites, giving the divine signals with the holy trumpets (Num 31:6).[30] He leads the negotiations of the *'edah* with the Reubenites, never to build an altar for offerings (Josh 22:13–14, 30–34 – presumably a legend directed against the sanctuary of the Samaritans). He is Eleazar's successor (Josh 24:33) at the the Sanctuary of the Ark (Judg 20:27b–28). Again, Phineas is not mentioned in any other scripture

---

30. Num 10:1–10. The priestly trumpets are furthermore only mentioned in Ezra 3:10; Neh 12:35, 41; and in Chronicles (1 Chr 13:8; 15:24, 28; 16:6, 42; 2 Chr 5:12–13; 13:12, 14; 15:14; 20:28; 23:13; 29:26–28), where the motif has found its most marked reception; cf. Maskow, *Tora in der Chronik*, 373–76. Most significant is the connection between Num 10:10 and 1 Chr 15:24: "Was Mose aufgetragen wurde, nämlich am Tag der Freude (וביום שמחתכם) die Trompete zu blasen, wird in 1 Chr 15:24 umgesetzt, wo nach V. 16.25.28 ausdrücklich ein Tag der Freude annonciert wird."

beyond the genealogies in Ezra 7:5; 8:2, 33; and in 1 Chronicles 6:4, 50; 9:20, and in Psalm 106:30 reflecting Numbers 25:8.

The lineage between Phineas and Zadok continues only in the same chronistic contexts, about Abishua: Ezra 7:5; 1 Chronicles 5:30–31; 6:35; about Bukki: Ezra 7:4; 1 Chronicles 5:31; 6:36; about Uzzi: Ezra 7:4; 1 Chronicles 5:31–32; 6:36; about Zeahiah: Ezra 7:4; 1 Chronicles 5:31–32; 6:36; about Meraioth: Ezra 7:3; 1 Chronicles 5:32–33; 6:37; and about Amariah: Ezra 7:3; 1 Chronicles 5:33, 37; 6:37. Simply no other evidence exists for this lineage beyond these late contexts.

Ahitub is known as the father of Zadok in 2 Sam 8:17, a text which still mentions the lineage of the ancient Israelite priesthood of Ahimelekh ben Abiatar, too. Therefore, this name continues the traditional lineage in Chronicles (1 Chr 5:33–34, 37–38; 6:37; 9:11; Ezra 7:2).

It has long been observed that Zadok's background seems to place his roots in the ancient Jerusalemite priesthood. But he and his descendants remained the leading priests from Solomon's reign onwards after Abiatar's removal from his office and banishing (1 Kgs 2:26–27; 4:2). Zadok was therefore integrated into the legend of the Ark and described as being close to it from the beginning of David's reign (2 Sam 15:24–36). He was believed to have been the priest who was admitted to get the oil from the tent of the Ark and anointed Solomon together with Nathan the prophet (1 Kgs 1:32, 34, 39). His son Ahimaaz is associated with Jonathan, the son of Saul, the first king of Israel, and David's closest friend and favourite (2 Sam 15:27, 36; 17:20; 18:19–28; 1 Chr 5:34–35; 6:36).

The circle of scribes who developed the book of Ezekiel and its programmatic order for the Second Temple clearly favoured an exclusively Zadokite right to the priesthood against all other Levitical priestly lineages (Ezek 44:15; 48:11). The scribes of the Pentateuch canonised their choice in Exodus 6 and the late priestly layers of Numbers, whereupon a few additions in Joshua, Judges, and Kings, together with a clear choice in Chronicles for the Zadokites followed. As this program was introduced in the final stage of the Pentateuch's formation, we should assume that this was a post-dtr, post-P, and post-H proto-Chronistic stage in the fourth century BCE, possibly after Ezra's reforms.

The Levitical lineage described in Numbers 3:14–39 is not only important for identifying Levitical undertakings at the tabernacle (Num 4), but also for taking up (Num 35:16–34) the dtr rule of determining the cities of refuge for asylum seekers (Deut 19:1–13; 4:41–

43). It is then connected with the instruction to allocate land from the tribal holdings for the Levites for dwelling and pasture (Num 35:1–15). The ThR thus introduces rules for the subsistence of the increasing number of Levitical and priestly personnel at the Second Temple. ThR accordingly supplemented the dtr account in Joshua 21 with the account that settlements had been distributed to the Kohathite Aaronides (Josh 21:1–19), the other Kohathites (Josh 21:20–26), the Gershonites (Josh 21:27–33), and the Merarites (Josh 21:34–45). This connection is reflected, in addition, in the Aaronite genealogy in 1 Chronicles 6:39–66 (vv. 35–38), generally affirming the Aaronides' right to priestly possessions (Josh 21:1–4, 10–19//1 Chr 6:39–45), as well as that of all other Levitical clans (Josh 21:5–9//1 Chr 6:46–50), the Kohatites (1 Chr 6:51–55), the Gershonites (1 Chr 6:56–61), and the Merarites (1 Chr 6:62–66).[31] Again, the concepts of the ThR are incorporated into Chronicles and not recorded before.

5. THE HIEROCRATIC INSTITUTION OF THE HIGH PRIEST IN THE THEOCRATIC REWORKING OF THE PENTATEUCH

In the latest texts of the Pentateuch, Moses's position as the preeminent mediator of Divine Torah and Prophecy is illustrated in the Song at the Sea (Exod 15:1–18) and in the Song of Moses (Deut 32:1–43).[32] Moses proclaims Yhwh's kingship and uniqueness as God:

> Exodus 15:11 "Who is like You, Yhwh, among the gods, who is like You, majestic in holiness, awesome in splendour, working wonders! … 17 You bring them [your people] and plant them in the mountain of your heritage, the place You made to dwell in, Yhwh! The sanctuary, o Lord, which your hands established. 18 Yhwh will reign as king for ever and ever!"

When this prophetic hymn was placed before the song of the prophetess Miriam, the shorter prophetic version remains only as a repetition of what Moses has already envisioned and pronounced. At the end of his life as presented in the Pentateuch, Moses announces in his prophetic hymn the eschatological legal proceedings of Yhwh, the sole God, the creator, and the highest ruler over the world and over the nations, who proclaims himself as lord of the universe, ruling on life and death, Deuteronomy 32:39:

---

31. Knoppers, *I Chronicles 1–9*, 430–50.
32. John W. Watts, *Psalm and Story. Inset Hymns in Hebrew Narrative*, JSOTS 139 (Sheffield: Sheffield Academic Press, 1992).

"See now, that I, I am He, and there is no god beside me, I deal death and give life, I have wounded and I will heal, and none can deliver from My hand!"[33]

When, in the latest phase of reworking, priestly scribes introduced a new priestly hierarchical order into the narrative of the Pentateuch in connection with the introduction of priestly *torot*, they also introduced a legend about Aaron as Moses's successor in the task of Torah mediator. This meant his authority exceeded all other priestly, Levitical, prophetic, and scribal authority. The authorisation of Aaron superceded the authorisation of the prophets following Moses.

According to the Hexateuch Composition in Deuteronomy 18:15–22, prophetic authority was rooted in the legend about the covenant on Mount Horeb, which included the divine promise to raise a prophet like Moses for Israel and to put his words into the prophet's mouth (Deut 18:18; Jer 1:9; cf. also Isa 6:6–9; Ezek 3:1–4). When, according to the Pentateuchal reworking, the legend of the tent of meeting introduced a new perspective, it was believed that Moses's word directly delivered God's revelation, so that the Torah of Moses surpassed the prophetic word (Deut 34:10–12). The word of Moses became itself divine. In the theocratic priestly reworking of the Pentateuch, the narrative of Moses's call (Exod 3) therefore was supplemented in Exodus 4:10–17 with the assignment of Aaron the Levite, brother of Moses. Moses received the commandment from the beginning of his work, "speak to him and put the words in his mouth" (ודברת אליו ושמת את־הדברים בפיו, v. 15). God promised to be with the mouth of Moses as well as with the mouth of Aaron and instruct them both (v. 15). So when Aaron speaks to the people, he will be the mouth of Moses, and Moses will be for him a mediator in a divine position (הוא יהיה לך לפה ואתה תהיה לו לאלהים, v. 16). Before God promised to send the prophets, Aaron already had been assigned to be the first and *most high authority* to proclaim God's word through Moses. Thus, all *torot* of the Pentateuch, including the priestly torot on offerings and purity were also determined to supercede any further Torah proclaimed in the prophetic scrolls.

The priestly reworking of the Pentateuch effected scribal discourse between the prophetic and Pentateuchal scriptures. As an example, one may have a look at Jer 7:22–23, where it is denied that God commanded anything about burnt offerings or sacrifices on the way

---

33. Deuteronomy 32 is probably the latest text in Deuteronomy. The Song of Moses is a canonical and hermeneutical bridge between Torah, Prophets, Psalms, and Wisdom, announcing Yhwh's judgment over the nations and Israel's eschatological salvation. Cf. Otto, *Deuteronomium 23,16–34,12*, 2130–203; for a close reading cf. Petra Schmidtkunz, *Das Moselied des Deuteronomium. Untersuchungen zu Text und Theologie von 32,1–43*, FAT II/124 (Tübingen: Mohr Siebeck, 2020).

from Egypt to the promised land (cf. also Mic 6:6–8; Amos 5:25). The admission of foreigners to the cult was heavily disputed (Isa 56:3–8; Deut 23:2–9; Exod 12:48–49) and served as a reason to reject a general admission of Levites for worship at the center of the sanctuary and to degrade their majority to *clerus minor* (Ezek 44:9–11).

In the expansions of the priestly legends in Numbers, foundational legends serve to subsequently endow the hierocratic position of the high priest. They confirm that Aaron and his descendants have the *highest priestly authority* among the descendants of Levi and among all other tribes and chieftains of Israel. Numbers 16 reports about a rebellion of Korah the Levite, who claims the right of the priesthood to the assembly ('*edah*) and is rejected immediately (Num 16:1a, 3–5, 8–11, 16, 19–24, 28–34).[34] Thereby Aaron's preeminent position in the '*edah* is confirmed. When the '*edah* rails against Moses and Aaron in an assembly (Num 17:6–7), only Aaron is able to expiate their wrongdoing on their behalf and calm the wrath of Yhwh by the incense ritual (Num 17:8–15).

Numbers 16:2–3 reports about a rebellion of 250 chieftains (נשיאים) of the congregation (עדה), chosen by the assembly (קריאי מועד), against Moses and Aaron. With reference to the account of the Sinai covenant in Exodus 19:6 (תהיו לי ... גוי קדוש אתם) and the program of the Holiness Code (Lev 19:2 תהיו כי קדוש אני יהוה אלהיכם דבר אל־כל־עדת בני־ישראל ואמרת אלהם קדשים) the laity doubt the privileged position of Moses and Aaron over the *qahal*, the Assembly of the people (יהוה מדוע תתנשאו על־קהל, Num 16:3). In an ordeal, these laity try to offer incense, but – as in Leviticus 10:2 – "a fire went forth from Yhwh and consumed the 250 men" (Num 16:35). The legend proves that only Aaron and his descendants have the right to offer incense (Num 17:1–5). It is only he who is able to sanctify Israel before God by offering purifying incense. It is the Aaronide high priest alone who is allowed to come close to the adytum of the sanctuary every morning when he tends to the Menorah and offers incense (Exod 37:1–10).

The two legends are intertwined, and thus they make clear that Aaron is the head of the religious assembly ('*edah*) as well as over the subordinate political assembley (*qahal*). So he also represents the *highest political authority* of all Israelites. When the chieftains

---

34. For literary-critical analysis, cf. Achenbach, *Vollendung*, 37–123; recent research tends to assume that the motif of Korah's rebellion was intertwined with the narrative on a rebellion of 250 *nesi'îm*; cf. Christoph Berner, "Vom Aufstand Datans und Abirams zum Aufbegehren der 250 Männer. Eine redaktionsgeschichtliche Studie zu den Anfängen der literarischen Genese von Num 16–17," BN 150 (2012): 9–33; Katharina Pyschny, *Verhandelte Führung. Eine Analyse von Num 16–17 im Kontext der neueren Pentateuchforschung*, HBS 88 (Freiburg – Basel – Wien: Herder, 2017).

of Israel representing the twelve tribes lay down their staffs and the document of covenantal law (העדות, Num 17:19) before the ark as a symbol of their authority, Aaron's staff brings forth sprouts and blossoms of Almonds (שקדים, v. 18). From Jeremiah 1:11–12 the symbol of the blossoming almond branch is a traditional symbol for Yhwh watching his people (שקד); it seems that the prophetic connotation and the political context have been transferred to the Aaronide high priest in the legend of Numbers 17: He represents the highest authority in the assembly of Israel in religious and in political perspective; he represents Yhwh's watchfulness even over the prophetic tradition.

The Aaron legend of the older layers of the Priestly Code was worked out to confirm the high priest in his succession as the *highest legal authority* in the congregation of Israel (*'edah*, עדה). The general assembly of the people (*qahal*, קהל)[35] was subordinate to the assembly of the people as a religious community (*'edah*).[36] Since there is no annointed king (משיח), the high priest is the highest and only anointed authority in the society of the Second Temple.[37] His vestments express a divine kingly authority. The high priest's turban (Exod 28:40) is designated with a *diadem of the sanctuary* (נזר הקדש; as a representation of Zion, cf. Isa 61:10); he and his sons should, according to the Pentateuch *torah*, be the only annointed authorities (Exod 28:41; 29:7–9; 30:31–33; Lev 9:8–12; Isa 61:1). The clothes for the priestly investiture resemble, on the other hand, a series of symbols that represent Israel before God (Exod 28:12, 29).[38] He wears a breastplate as

---

35. *qahal*: Deut 5:22; 9:10; 10:4; 18:16; 23:2–9; 31:30; Josh 8:35; 1 Kgs 8:14 as a general term for the assembly of Yhwh's people; in Exod 12:6; Num 14:5 the term is subordinate to the term 'edah (לפני כל קהל עדת בני ישראל); cf. also Lev 4:13, 21; 16:17, 33; 16:3, 33; 17:12; 19:20; 20:6.

36. *'edah*: Exod 12:3, 6, 19, 47; 16:1, 2, 9–10, 22; 17:1; 35:20; 34:31; 35:1, 4; 38:25; Lev 4:15; 8:3, 5; 10:6, 17; 16:5; 19:2; Num 1–10; 15; 16–17; 29; 20; 25–35; not in Deuteronomy.

37. Cf. also Isa 61:1–11. The text is a self-proclamation of a person who is "anointed by Yhwh" and bestowed with the "spirit of Lord Yhwh," i. e., charisma to perform his office and to prove his authority by proclaiming a derôr, i. e., a release. The concept of this text is thus clearly connected with an early hierocratic program (cf. Henri Cazelles, "Royaume des prêtres et nation consacrée (Exode 19,6) in: "*Humanisme et foi chrétienne*": *Melanges scientifique de l'Institut Catholique Paris*, ed. Charles Kannengiesser/Yves Marchasson, Paris: Beauchesne 1976, 541–545; Pierre Grélot, "Sur Isaie LXI: la première consecration d'un grande prêtre, (RB 97, Leuven 1990, 414–431; R. Achenbach, "König, Priester und Prophet. Zur Transformation der Konzepte der Herrschaftslegitimation in Jesaja 61," in: R. Achenbach – Martin Arneth – Eckart Otto, *Tora in der Hebräischen Bibel. Studien zur Redaktionsgeschichte und synchronen Logik diachroner Transformationen* (BZAR 7 – Wiesbaden: Harrassowitz 2007, 196–244).

38. In Isa 61:10 the annointed thus appears "like a bridegroom adorned with a turban," i. e., a representative of the (divine) royal authority with respect to the con-

a symbol for the *highest authority over ordeals and the law* (המשפט חשן, Exod 28:30) together with the lots to explore and "obtain God's decision on important questions on which human judgment was found inadequate, such as military actions, allocation of land, legal verdicts in the absence of evidence, and choice of leaders"[39] They are called *urîm* and *tummim* (Exod 28:30; Lev 8:8), possibly representing a symbol for lights (אור > אורים) and for perfection and integrity (תמים > תמם / תם). They express the will of Yhwh as the creator of light (Gen 1:3–5, 18) and the origins of blessings (Num 6:23–27) and life (Ps 36:10), and as the God of complete revelation (תמם, Deut 31:24, 30), who has power to watch over integrity and righteousness (Gen 6:9: נח איש צדיק תמים) and to determine the end of life (Num 14:35; 17:28; 32:13). The application of the lots in preexilic contexts is mentioned in 1 Sam 14:41 (LXX*) and 2 Sam 28:6 in the context of *divination* during war. In the context of the late priestly reworking of Numbers they mark out a decisive function because it is Eleazar the high priest who seeks the decision of the *urîm* and *tummim* before Yhwh in situations of war and – more importantly – the division of the land, that is, the irrevocable inheritance of land for Israelite families. In remembrance of the postexilic history the administration of *urîm* and *tumim* was decisive for all Jewish rights of personal possession and heritage (cf. Ezra 2:63; Neh 7:65). According to Numbers 20:28–29, immediately after the death of Aaron, the vestments were handed over to his next eldest son Eleazar. In the priestly legend about a legal case that intends revising the laws of inheritance (Num 27:1–11), the place of negotiations of the highest court is before the sanctuary in its function as the Tent of Meeting. The court is the full assembly of the congregation – of the 'edah (כל העדה) – all its representatives (לפני הנשיאים), presided over by Moses and Eleazar the high priest. The divine decision is requested and proclaimed by Moses.

The subsequent part of the narrative reflects on Joshua's succession again.[40] The designation of Joshua is described in several steps. gregation who is addressed as "priests of Yhwh" and "servants of our God" (v. 6), and – at the same time – "like a bride bedecked with her finery," the annointed is a representative of Zion with respect to Yhwh.

39. Jeffrey H. Tigay, "Exodus," in *The Jewish Study Bible*, ed. Adele Berlin, Marc Zvi Brettler and Michael Fishbane (Oxford – New York: Oxford University Press, 2004), 102–202, here 172–73, with references to Num 27:21; 1 Sam 14:37–42; Ezra 2:63; Exod 22:8; Josh 7:14–18; Judg 1:1–2; 20:18; 1 Sam 10; 20–22; 2 Sam 2:1; 5:23–24.

40. There are four versions of a succession story for Joshua: in Josh 1:1–6* (dtr. reworking of a predtr version); in Deut 31:7–8 (dtr.) with a *Fortschreibung* of the Hexateuch redactor (Deut 31:9–13*); a Fortschreibung of the Pentateuch redaction (Deut 31:14–15, 23); and a late priestly version by the ThR (Num 27:12–23; Deut 34:9).

Yhwh commands Moses to single out Joshua as a person qualified with special charisma and an inspired man (רוח בו, Num 27:18). In the ritual, he has to stand before Eleazar and the congregation, who have to witness the act (v. 19). Moses must lay his hands upon him (v. 23) and transfer a part of his authority to him (ונתתה מהודך אליו, v. 20a), so that the community will obey him. By this act he is filled with a "spirit of wisdom" (רוח חכמה, Deut 34:9) and qualified as a political leader. But when he has to make decisions, he is obliged to request the divine decision first from Eleazar the priest via the "legal decision by *urîm* before Yhwh" (ושאל לו במשפט האורים לפני יהוה, v. 21a). This will impact all his undertakings in times of peace and war (v. 21b), and this will concern especially the decisions about the allotment of land and inheritance in Israel (Num 34:16–17). The role to augur divine decisions and thus to assign ultimate authority in lawsuits and to answer questions of law and justice has not been transferred to Joshua, but to Eleazar – and thus to the high priest.

The institutional power is specifically represented by the legend of a portable shrine, where cultic, ritual, and legal activities can be performed. Therefore, the theocratic reworking of the Pentateuch identified the Tent of Meeting (מועד אהל) with the desert shrine (משכן).[41] These editors also assumed that priests and Levites had transported the shrine through the desert during the forty years and had brought it into the promised land (Num 1–10*, 15–19*, 26–31, 33–35). The idea of already recognising the priestly institutions as a fundamental part of Israel's constitution from the beginning led to the narrative not only of the wandering kabôd of Yhwh, but also of a wandering *sanctuary*.

In Chronicles, the identification of the divine dwelling (משכן) with the Tent of Meeting (אהל מועד) is connected with the temple building in the rules of the temple offices in 1 Chronicles 6:16–17:

> 16 "These are the persons whom David put in charge of the service of song in the temple of Yhwh (בית יהוה), after the ark came to rest (הארון ממנוח),[42] 17 that they ministered with song before the tabernacle of the tent of meeting (משכן אהל מועד) …"[43]

They believe that the final resting place of the ark before it was transferred to Jerusalem was Gibeon (1 Chr 16:39; 21:29), because according to 1 Kings 3:4 Solomon had brought sacrifices there and Yhwh appeared to him (cf. also 1 Kgs 9:2). Chronicles does not mention the

---

41. Cf. Reinhard Achenbach, "*Mishkan – 'Arôn – 'Ohael Mo'ed*. Concepts of Divine Presence in the Pentateuch," ZAR 23 (2017): 151–61.

42. Cf. Num 10:33.

43. LXX confuses the functions once again, translating with ἐναντίον τῆς σκηνῆς οἴκου μαρτυρίου "before the tent of the house of witness".

former sanctuary in Shiloh, which had become unclean because of the wicked priests (1 Sam 1:3, 9, 24; 2:14–4:12; 14:3; 1 Kgs 2:27). According to 2 Chronicles 1:3, 13, after Solomon became king, he visited the sanctuary of the "Tent of Meeting, which Moses the servant of Yhwh had made in the wilderness" there. Before Solomon had built the temple as a permanent house, Yhwh had been worshiped in several tent sanctuaries (1 Chr 17:5 ואהיה מאהל אל־אהל וממשכן). When the ark was transferred to Jerusalem, the *mishkan* remained in Gibeon, so that the obligatory offerings could be offered (1 Chr 16:37–40). The Levites continued their service as guardians at the entrance of the tent, where the ark is placed (1 Chr 9:19–35), as they did before under the surveillance of Phineas ben Eleazar (1 Chr 9:20: עליהם לפנים יהוה עמו ופינחס בן אלעזר נגיד היה). Even descendants of Korah are found among them (v. 19), corresponding to the remark in Numbers 26:9 that "the sons of Korah did not die." In order to harmonise 2 Sam 6:17–19 and the narrative of Numbers, the Chronicler assumes that David had prepared a separate tent for the ark (1 Chr 15:1), where burnt offerings and *shelamîm* were brought before God after the transfer had been completed (1 Chr 16:1–3//2 Sam 6:17–19). Chronicles thus takes up the motifs of the theocratic reworking (ThR) in Numbers and tries to harmonise them with the dtr texts, that had already been reworked by ThR, rewriting and continuing Dtr in *Fortschreibung* from the perspective of ThR. With respect to the orders of offices in the Second Temple during the late Persian period, the roles of the Levite take on renewed weight.[44]

In the ancient dtr report on the consecration of Solomon's temple, the priests bore the ark from David's tent into the building and deposited it beneath the throne of cherubim that served as symbol for divine presence (1 Kgs 8:3b, 6). Late priestly scribes inserted 1 Kings 8:4, 6 (קדש הקדשים / ברית יהוה) and vv. 10b–11 with respect to Exod 40:34–35, bringing in late elements from the late priestly narrative of the ThR.[45] Since, according to Numbers 4:15, 19b, the Aaronide priests are responsible for organising the duties for each Levitical unit, priests and Levites are responsible for the transport of the tabernacle (1 Kgs

---

44. Gary N. Knoppers, "Hierodules, Priests, or Janitors? The Levites in Chronicles and the History of Isrealite Priesthood," *JBL* 118 (1999), 49–72. For a closer discussion, cf. Jaeyoung Jeon, "The Priestly Tent of Meeting in Chronicles: Pro-Priestly of Anti-Priestly?" *JHS* 18, Article #7 (DOI:10.5508/jhs.2018.v18.a7). Jeon assumes continuous conflicts between Zadokites and Levites. Cf. Jaeyoung Jeon, "The Zadokite and Levite Scribal Conflicts and Hegemonic Struggles," in *Scripture as Social Discourse*: *Social-Scientific Perspectives on Early Jewish and Christian Writings*, ed. Todd Klutz et al. (New York: T&T Clark, 2018), 97–110.

45. Achenbach, "Der Pentateuch," 225–54. See also Albertz, Die kanonische Anpassung des Josuabuches," 199–216.

8:4b). The priests take care that the other Levites do not touch the holy artifact, and they take care of the holy oil and the Menorah (Num 4:16), but the Levites have to bear the ark and the *mishkan* (Num 4:15b, 17–33). And since they had guarded the ark while the *mishkan* had remained in Gibeon, Chronicles assigns the responsibility for bearing it to them (2 Chr 4:4b). However, since the holy vessels are in the hands of the priests, it is the common responsibility of all "the levitical priests", הכהנים הלוים, Zadokites and Levites (Ezek 44:15), to bring everything up into the temple building (2 Chr 4:4b, leaves out the waw, but is corrected again in several manuscripts).

1 Kgs 8:3b–4, 6, 10b–11[46]	2 Chr 5:4b–5, 7, 13b, 14
3 ... וישאו הכהנים את־הארון הקד	4 ... וישאו הלוים את הארון
4 ויעלו את ארון יהוה ואת אהל מועד	5 ויעלו את ארון ואת אהל מועד
ואת כל כלישׁ אשׁר באהל	את כל כלי הקדשׁ אשׁר באהל
ויעלו אתם הכהנים והלוים ...	ו העלו אתם הכהנים הלוים
6 ויבאו הכהנים את ארון ברית יהוה	7 ויביאו הכהנים את ארון ברית יהוה
אל דביר הבית אל קדשׁ הקדשׁים אל מקומו	אל מקומו אל דביר הבית אל קדשׁ הקד שׁים
אל תחת כנפי הכרובים	אל תחת כנפי הכרובים
10 ... והענן מלא את בית יהוה	13 ... והבית מלא ענן בית יהוה
11 ולא יכלו הכהנים לעמד לשׁרת מפני הענן	14 ולא יכלו הכהנים לעמוד לשׁרת מפני הענן
כי מלא כבוד יהוה את בית יהוה	כי מלא כבוד יהוה את בית האלהים

When the temple was finished, the office of the Levites to transport the ark according to Numbers 4 ceases (1 Chr 23:16). Now the temple is the dwelling of Yhwh (2 Chr 1:5), even when the Israelites turn their faces away from it (2 Chr 29:6).

Chronicles takes up issues from ThR in Numbers and thus documents further scribal reception and debate, as Hans-Peter Mathys has already shown.[47] The position of the Levites is under on-going debate in Chronicles (cf. Num 18:3–4; 2 Chr 29:16, 34; 30:16; 35:11), and the Chronicler even added to the descriptions of Levitical tasks at Pesach (2 Chr 30:16; 35:11). Second Chronicles 30:2, 15 are the only other texts where the rules on a second *Pesach* (Numbers 9:10–13) are

---

46. 1 Kgs 8:4 is missing in LXX. In v. 6 אל קדשׁ הקדשׁים is missing in LXX. And instead of יהוה ארון ברית in v.6, LXX only had הארון in its *Vorlage*, and instead of יהוה בית just הבית, v. 10b, 11b.

47. Mathys, "Numeri und Chronik," n. 10, 20.

referred to in the Hebrew Bible. Levites not only receive the tithes (cf. Num 18:21–24), but also guard and administer them (2 Chr 31:11–13).

In his work on Torah in Chronicles, Lars Maskow has described how this narrative was received and expounded in Chronicles.[48] Here the Levitical genealogies, the sanctuary, the ark, the holy vessels, and the cultic calendar were transferred into the narratives received from the already reworked dtr tradition and described in further detail. The proto-Chronistic theocratic reworking of the Pentateuch led to the first extensive and complete work of "Rewritten Bible" in the book of Chronicles.

---

48. Maskow, *Tora in der Chronik*, 239–550; on "Kult-Personal", 240–334, "Kult-Gegenstand", 335–384; "Kult-Kalender", 477–542.

NUMBERS AND CHRONICLES: CLOSE RELATIVES 2

Hans-Peter Mathys

In 2008 I published an article entitled "Numbers and Chronicles: Close Relatives",[1] where I showed that the two books share much in common in their content, but often take quite different approaches. I briefly presented nine topics:

1. The relationship between priests and Levites; 2. Pesach; 3. The tithe; 4. Temple financing; 5. The registration of the people; 6. No collective liability; 7. Holy war; 8. Agriculture; and 9. Narrative. My aim in the present contribution is to clarify three of these points: numbers 1 (priests and Levites), 5 (registration) and 7 (holy war); four additional issues will also be examined.

---

1. Hans-Peter Mathys, "Numeri und Chronik: nahe Verwandte," in *The Books of Leviticus and Numbers*, ed. Thomas Römer, BETL 215 (Leuven: Peters, 2008), 555–78. In his article "Numbers and Chronicles: False Friends or Close Relatives?" *Hebrew Bible and Ancient Israel* [*HeBAI*] 8 (2019): 332–77, Louis Jonker alludes to the title of my contribution. The publication of Jonker's essay overlapped with the preparation of the present contribution. I maintain the substance of my remarks as they were presented at the Lausanne conference. Regarding the dating of Chronicles, Jonker formulates almost apodictically (p. 339): "There is general agreement that the book of Chronicles also originated in the late Persian era, towards the end of the Achaemenid rule, in the first half or around the middle of the fourth century B.C.E." Later on, he somewhat softens this judgement. Note however that such a dating is by no means uncontested; see Hans-Peter Mathys, "Chronikbücher und hellenistischer Zeitgeist," in Hans-Peter Mathys, *Vom Anfang und vom Ende. Fünf alttestamentliche Studien*, BEAT 47 (Frankfurt a.M.: Lang, 2000), 41–155 for dating Chronicles to the early Hellenistic period. Georg Steins, *Die Chronik als kanonisches Abschlussphänomen. Studien zur Entstehung und Theologie von 1/2 Chronik*, BBB 93 (Weinheim: Beltz Athenäum 1995) proposes an even later date (in the Maccabean period); see also Israel Finkelstein, *Hasmonean Realities Behind Ezra, Nehemiah, and Chronicles*, Ancient Israel and Its Literature 34 (Atlanta: SBL Press, 2018). For the general assumptions underlying the present contribution, see my first paper on the topic.

1. THE (TWO) SILVER TRUMPETS

According to Numbers 10:1–2,[2] Yahweh gives Moses the order to make two silver trumpets of "hammered work" (שתי חצוצרת כסף מקשה). They serve to summon the congregation and signal for its departure. When the Israelites begin a war in the land, they are to give its signal by sounding the trumpets. However, the instrument is also used for ritual occasions (Num 10:10):[3]

> Also on your days of rejoicing, at your appointed festivals, and at the beginnings of your months, you shall blow the trumpets over your burnt offering and over your sacrifices of well being...

The following sentence makes clear the importance of these trumpets, which are reserved for the priests (Num 10:8):

> The sons of Aaron, the priests, shall blow the trumpets; this shall be a perpetual institution for you throughout your generations.

The second-most frequent occurrence of the noun, after Numbers 10, is found in Chronicles. The trumpets are sounded after Jehoshaphat's successful war against the Moabites and Ammonites (2 Chr 20:28):

> They came to Jerusalem, with harps and lyres and trumpets, to the house of Yhwh.

However, the trumpets are much more frequently used for cultic and cult-adjacent occasions. Their importance is shown by the fact that the priests are responsible for playing the instrument, not the Levites. Two examples: When the Ark is brought up to Jerusalem for the second time, priests mentioned by name play the trumpet before the Ark (1 Chr 16:6).

A fine example of the trumpet's use in the cult can be found in the description of the Passover held under King Hezekiah (2 Chr 29:27–28):

> Then Hezekiah commanded that the burnt offering be offered on the altar. When the burnt offering began, the song to Yhwh began also, and the trumpets, accompanied by the instruments of King David of Israel. The whole assembly worshiped, the singers sang, and the trumpeters sounded; all this continued until the burnt offering was finished.

The trumpet has replaced the שׁוֹפָר as the signal instrument and has also partly replaced it in cultic practice. Although there are also two pas-

---

2. Sir 50:16 refers to this chapter: "Then the sons of Aaron shouted; they blew their trumpets of hammered metal; they sounded a mighty fanfare as a reminder before the Most High."

3. Translation of biblical passages according to NRSV.

sages in Kings (1 Kgs 11:14 [2x]; 12:14), one in Hosea (Hos 5:8) and one in the Psalter (Ps 98:6) that mention the trumpets, the use of חֲצֹצְרֹת is nevertheless clearly concentrated in post-exilic texts, in Numbers[4] as well as Chronicles.[5] In addition, the noun is attested in both Ezra (3:10) and Nehemiah (12:35, 41). I do not rule out the possibility that trumpets were used early in Israel and that the horn was used in post-exilic times. I would simply like to indicate that on the literary level, the trumpet appears almost exclusively in late texts, and that to a certain extent, this should be interpreted as an indication of the trumpet gaining importance in the cult of the Second Temple – as did temple music and singing in general.[6] 1–2 Kings offer little in this respect, and the laws of Exodus, Leviticus and Numbers contain only one single provision concerning temple music. According to Chronicles, in the absence of Mosaic laws, temple music and singing are regulated by King David (1 Chr 16).

The importance of the two trumpets in the Second and Herodian temples is also made clear by coinage as well as the Arch of Titus in Rome, which depicts the Romans carrying off loot from the temple of Jerusalem. Among the spoils shown on the Arch are two trumpets alongside the seven-branched menorah and the tables of the bread of the presence.[7]

Here, questions arise concerning the trumpets of whether the Chronicler consciously took up Numbers 10 and whether he would have also incorporated the trumpets into his work had Numbers 10 and Numbers 31:6 not yet existed. The first possibility is supported by the fact that in Chronicles, the trumpets actually find use on occasion, while Numbers 10 merely envisages them being played. There are four occasions for which Numbers stipulates sounding the trumpets: 1) gathering the congregation; 2) setting up the camp; 3) signaling war; and 4) various ritual occasions, including days of rejoicing. Inter-

---

4. Num 10:2, 8, 9, 10; 31:6. The bulk of the attestations are concentrated in one chapter.

5. 1 Chr 13:8; 15:24, 28; 16:6, 42; 2 Chr 5:12, 13; 13:12, 14; 15:14; 20:28; 23:13; 29:26–28.

6. For a general overview see Hans Seidel, *Musik in Altisrael*, BEATAJ 12 (Frankfurt a.M.: Lang, 1989); Joachim Braun, *Die Musikkultur Altisraels/Palästinas. Studien zu archäologischen, schriftlichen und vergleichenden Quellen*, OBO 164 (Freiburg i.Ü.: Universitätsverlag, 1999).

7. Whether the two instruments depicted upon the Arch of Titus in Rome are actually the two trumpets of Num 10 has proven controversial. They could instead be the *tuba sacrum* known in Rome. This thesis is seemingly supported by the fact that the menorah on the Arch does not correspond to the lampstand as represented in the Old Testament; see Lars Maskow, *Tora in der Chronik. Studien zur Rezeption des Pentateuchs in den Chronikbüchern*, FRLANT 274 (Göttingen: Vandenhoeck & Ruprecht, 2019), 376 and literature cited.

estingly, the trumpets in the book of Numbers do not resound when the people (are summoned and) depart throughout their desert march (though perhaps the text takes this for granted). Since the Chronicler omits the entire march through the desert in his work, the trumpets cannot resound at all on this occasion. They do so for the first time at the Ark's transfer to Jerusalem. Yet the configuration of the orchestra accompanying them in this procession differs between 2 Samuel 6:5 and 1 Chronicles 13:8: In 2 Samuel 6:5, various juniper woods are used, i. e. wind instruments, while the orchestra of the Chronicler also includes his beloved singers as well as the trumpets, which do not replace the ram horns like elsewhere. According to Maskow, the Chronicler introduced the trumpets in this passage because he saw a parallel between the march through the desert and the procession of the Ark.[8] This is a daring interpretation. In the second, successful attempt to transfer the Ark, seven (!) priests are named who blow the trumpet (1 Chr 15:24; without parallel in 2 Samuel 6), in the final act of which the Chronicler again uses an impressive orchestra (v. 28: shouting, horns, trumpets, cymbals, harps, and lyres), while the original in Samuel is content with shouting and horns (2 Sam 6:15). One gets the impression that the Chronicler mentions almost all of the instruments of an orchestra from his time period.

Trumpets resound in two wars: that of Abijah against Jeroboam (2 Chr 13:12, 14), and that of Jehoshaphat against a Transjordanian coalition (2 Chr 20:28). In the former case, only the trumpet is used, played by priests according to v. 14. In 2 Chronicles 20:28, the trumpets are merely one of several instruments. After their victory, the Judeans return to Jerusalem accompanied by an orchestra; before the hostilities, only the singers were in action.

The remaining passages concern the cult. The dedication of the Jerusalem temple is a crucial event in the Chronicler's history of the cult. At the end of the ceremony, the priests proceeded out of the sanctuary, while the Levites, who were singers and their brothers, stood east of the altar with cymbals and harps and lyres, and with them a hundred and twenty priests blowing trumpets; trumpeters and singers "sang with one voice" (2 Chr 5:12–13). When renewing the covenant with God under King Asa (2 Chr 15), the congregation swore to Yhwh with a loud voice and with rejoicing and with trumpets and horns (v. 14). It is irrelevant here who plays which instrument; the Chronicler may implicitly assume that the trumpets were reserved for priests.

The end of Athaliah's illegitimate rule is framed musically. She watches as the king stands on a pedestal, "and the trumpeters beside

---

8. Maskow, *Tora in der Chronik*, 373.

the king, and all the people of the land rejoicing and blowing trumpets, and the singers with their musical instruments leading in the celebration" (2 Chr 23:13–14). The people playing instruments reserved for priests in this passage is astonishing and should not be dismissed by the flippant idea that they acted in exuberance of emotions.

Of course, the Passover celebration under King Hezekiah is framed musically as well (2 Chr 29). However, very different statements follow each other in the report of this event: Hezekiah stations the Levites in the house of Yhwh with cymbals, harps and lyres (v. 25); the Levites stand in line bearing the instruments of David, while the priests wield the trumpets (v. 26); at the burnt offering, the singing and trumpeting begins, alongside the instruments of David (v. 27); the only performers are the singers and the trumpeters (v. 28).

What a confusing picture! No two passages correspond with one another. The result is best explained as follows: In his work, the Chronicler depicted the cultic realities of his time, while at the same time sketching an ideal image of it. The ideal element clearly dominates in the war reports, which are strongly cultic in tone.

The preceding observations have important consequences for the assessment of the relationship between Numbers 10 and the book of Chronicles. An evaluation of this relationship cannot be made without taking into account the cultic realities from the time of the Chronicler, which are difficult to assess, and there are few sources available other than Numbers 10 and Chronicles themselves. The most important of these are the three attestations of the "trumpet" in Ezra and Nehemiah and the almost complete absence of the instrument in the Deuteronomistic literature, the only attestations being 2 Kings 11:14 (2x); 12:14. The only conclusion that can be drawn from this is certainly what has already been established, namely that the trumpet played a much more important role in (late) postexilic times than in the time of the Temple of Solomon. Numbers 10 and Chronicles adopt this reality in different ways: The author of Numbers 10 considers what role the trumpet might have played with the Israelites before they conquered the land they were promised and before they built the temple in Jerusalem. The feasts to be celebrated in the future and the use of the trumpet in war could only be addressed in general terms. The most concrete and precise expression of the Chronicler's views on the past is found with the people's departure in the desert: a long time ago, far enough that no one can check whether it constitutes an accurate reflection of the past itself. We do not know why Moses makes only two trumpets at the command of Yhwh. The Chronicler reckons with bigger, but offers different numbers. Even the priestly privilege of blowing the trumpet, established in Numbers 10:8, is not something to which the Chronicler adamantly adheres. This may perhaps reflect a rich cultic reality. However, under no circumstances should the attestations of the trumpets be considered a mere continuation of Numbers 10. This would mean applying the principle of *scriptura sui ipsius interpres* where it has no place.

2. Korah (and Company)

In 2008, I discussed briefly and very generally the relationship between Levites and priests in the books of Numbers and Chronicles. In the present contribution, I would like to clarify one point, namely the history of the Korahites. The story of Korah and "all his company" in Numbers 16 is well-known. More relevant to the present context, however, is a brief recapitulation of the incident in Numbers 26. It concludes in v. 11 as follows:

> Notwithstanding, the sons of Korah did not die.

For the Chronicler, this sentence is of central importance. According to 1 Chronicles 9, which lists the inhabitants of Jerusalem, Levites also lived in the city. Verses 17–20 are particularly revealing:

> The gatekeepers were: Shallum, Akkub, Talmon, Ahiman; and their kindred Shallum was the chief, stationed previously in the king's gate on the east side. These were the gatekeepers of the camp of the Levites. Shallum son of Kore, son of Ebiasaph, son of Korah, and his kindred of his ancestral house, the Korahites, were in charge of the work of the service, guardians of the thresholds of the tent, as their ancestors had been in charge of the camp of Yhwh, guardians of the entrance. And Phinehas son of Eleazar was chief over them in former times; Yhwh was with him.

Shallum occupies a crucial position in this section. Numbers does not reveal whether the Korahites could still perform the functions originally assigned to them. The Chronicler's answer to this question is unequivocal: Of course they could! In 1 Chronicles 9:22, the Chronicler also states that a descendant of Shallum by the name of Zechariah was appointed by David and Samuel. He also draws attention to the fact that the family was stationed at the King's Gate in the east of the city and had fulfilled its duties to the Chronicler's own day.

Note that the Korahites in 1 Chronicles 9:19 are called "guards at the thresholds of the tent" (שֹׁמְרֵי הַסִּפִּים לָאֹהֶל). This formulation is unusual and anachronistic. It creates a link from the time of composition to the time of the wanderings in the desert. There is a continuum between these periods: during all this time, the Korahites served as guards at the thresholds of the tent. The prominent position taken by Phinehas in 1 Chronicles 9:20 may be explained by the fact that, according to Numbers 25:7–8, he performed a heroic deed by killing the Israelite man and the Midianite woman who had committed adultery together.

3. THE COVENANT OF SALT

Salt and religion are closely connected. The Old Testament prescribes salt for sacrifices (Lev 2:13; Ezek 43:24). Salt makes food more durable and therefore represents a permanence and inviolability; the term "salt" is therefore very well suited for the characterization of covenants, which are eternally valid by nature and inviolable by claim.[9] Not only is this close relationship between covenant and salt characteristic of the Old Testament, but, as Wellhausen points out, it is also attested among Arab tribes.[10] In this regard, the Arabic term *milcha* "covenant" speaks for itself.[11]

In the Old Testament, the term "covenant of salt" is first used in Numbers 18, a chapter which regulates the maintenance of priests. Verse 19 reads as follows:

> All the holy offerings that the Israelites present to Yhwh I have given to you, together with your sons and daughters, as a perpetual due; it is a covenant of salt forever (מלח עולם לחק עולם ברית) before Yhwh for you and your descendants as well).

The claims of the priests and their families are thus safeguarded. In this passage, note, besides the "covenant of salt," the two attestations of עוֹלָם, reinforcing the aspect of duration.

The Chronicler introduces the notion of a "covenant of salt" where one would not necessarily expect it: 2 Chronicles 13:5, concerning Abijah, the successor to King Rehoboam:

> Do you not know that Yhwh God of Israel gave the kingship over Israel forever to David and his sons by a covenant of salt (בְּרִית מֶלַח)?

There is no doubt that the Chronicler, strongly departing from his Deuteronomistic source, was inspired by Numbers 18:19. Japhet's interpretation is nearly correct: "The parallelism is clear: a divine grant (holy offerings//kingship) to a favoured beneficiary (Aaron//David)

---

9. Jonker, "Numbers and Chronicles," 349–50.
10. Julius Wellhausen, *Reste arabischen Heidentums* (Berlin: De Gruyter, ³1961), 186.
11. Hans Wehr, *Arabisches Wörterbuch für die Schriftsprache der Gegenwart. Arabisch-Deutsch* (Wiesbaden: Otto Harrassowitz, ⁵1985), 1219.

sealed by an eternal commitment."[12] Interestingly, the Chronicler, while adopting the term "salt covenant", omits the term "eternal." This is all the more surprising since "eternal covenant" is attested quite often in the Old Testament.[13] This "quote" weighs all the more heavily since the indirect parallelization of Aaron and David constitutes striking and unexpected evidence of the importance that the Chronicler bestows upon the priests. It is not by chance that the Chronicler uses the term "covenant of salt" and not "eternal covenant" in this passage. He thereby underpins Abijah's claim to reign over the northern and southern kingdoms, which form but one realm.

4. ARTIFICIAL PROPER NAMES

Artificial proper names can be found in many parts of the Old Testament, and this is true of Numbers and Chronicles to a remarkable extent.[14] This can be counted as another point that they share in common with one another, as they each contain whole groups of artificial names. In Numbers, see the list of tribal princes (Num 1), names containing El and Shaddai as theophoric elements: Eliab, Eljasaph, Elizur, Elishama, Gamliel, Deuel, Nethanel, Pagiel, Shelumiel, Ammi-shaddai, Zurishaddai, Shedeur. How can this be explained? In my opinion, Ziemer has provided the right answer to this question by pointing to a principle of the final composition, that there were no names of persons containing the theophoric element Yhwh in pre-Mosaic times.[15]

The example from Chronicles is even more spectacular. In 1 Chronicles 25:4, there is a series of ten (!) proper names of temple singers which, read one after the other, constitute a short psalmic prayer:

> Be gracious to me, O Yhwh (חנניה), be gracious to me (חנני), thou art my God (אליאתה), I have made great (גדלתי), I have raised up (ורממתי) (your) help (עזר); when I sat in distress (ישבקשה), I said (מלותי): Give abundance (הותיר) of manifestations (מחזיאות).

Some of these proper names belong to the common Hebrew onomas-

---

12. Sara Japhet, *I & II Chronicles. A Commentary*, The Old Testament Library (London: SCM Press, 1993), 691.

13. Gen 9:16; 17:7, 13, 19; Ex 31:16; Lev 24:8; Num 18:19; (25:13); 2 Sam 23:5; Isa 24:5; 55:3; 61:8; Jer 32:40; 50:5; Ezek 16:60; 37:26; Ps 105:10; 1 Chr 16:17.

14. Hans-Peter Mathys, "Künstliche Personennamen im Alten Testament," in "...*der seine Lust hat am Wort des Herr*n!". *Festschrift für Ernst Jenni*, ed. Jürg Luchsinger, Hans-Peter Mathys and Markus Saur, AOAT 336 (Münster: Ugarit-Verlag, 2007), 218–49. The proper names mentioned and treated below are listed in alphabetical order in this paper.

15. Benjamin Ziemer, *Abram – Abraham. Kompositionsgeschichtliche Untersuchungen zu Genesis 14, 15 und 17*, BZAW 350 (Berlin: De Gruyter, 2005), 322–23.

ticon, such as חנניה, while others do not belong to it at all, such as מלותי "I have spoken." Incidentally, this passage is a variation of the proverb "*nomen est omen*": "Tell me your name, and I'll tell you what you do."

As another example, Numbers 11 reports how Moses takes the spirit that rests on him and lays it on the seventy men, the elders. The story then continues as follows (vv. 26–30):

> Two men remained in the camp, one named Eldad, and the other named Medad, and the spirit rested on them; they were among those registered, but they had not gone out to the tent, and so they prophesied in the camp. And a young man ran and told Moses, "Eldad and Medad are prophesying in the camp." And Joshua son of Nun, the assistant of Moses, one of his chosen men, said, "My lord Moses, stop them!" But Moses said to him, "Are you jealous for my sake? Would that all Yhwh's people were prophets, and that Yhwh would put his spirit on them!" And Moses and the elders of Israel returned to the camp.

The point here is not the content of this story, although it is highly interesting. We are only interested in the two men, Eldad and Medad. Their names, which rhyme, are probably formed from the root ידד "love".[16] Yet this does not matter to us either. Rather, the two men serve the same function; they keep apart from the seventy, and in their similarity, they therefore also bear similar, almost identical names.

Let us turn to the parallel example in Chronicles.[17] According to 2 Kings 12:21–22, King Joash died at the hands of two conspirators. According to the Masoretic Text, their names are "Jozabad" and "Jehozabad," but on the authority of many Hebrew manuscripts, the Septuagint, Vulgate and Targum Jonathan, "Jozabad" should probably read "Jozacar." The Chronicler has appropriated this story, but calls the first conspirator "Zabad" rather than "Jozacar" (2 Chr 24:26), so that the two murderers each have a name formed from the same root, זבד: "Zabad" and "Jehozabad." Since they are involved in the same action, they must also be called similarly. However, the change of name is also facilitated by the fact that ב and כ are very similar in appearance. BHS suggests reading the first name as Jozacar with reference to the parallel in 2 Kings 12 and the translations (reckoning with a haplography). The Chronicler's theology speaks against this emendation.

5. WAR, LOOTING, AND SPOILS OF WAR

The Old Testament relates countless wars, from local skirmishes to the

---

16. Cf. Johann Jakob Stamm, *Beiträge zur hebräischen und altorientalischen Namenkunde*, ed. Ernst Jenni and Martin A. Klopfenstein, OBO 30 (Freiburg i.Ü.: Universitätsverlag, 1980), 26–7, 38.

17. On this example, see Hans-Peter Mathys, "Philologia sacra: das Beispiel der Chronikbücher," ThZ 53 (1997): 67.

"World War" of Gen 14 as well as fantastic depictions such as that of Josh 6, the conquest of Jericho. In many wars, the victors take spoils, either for the temple or for the warriors, and occasionally for both. The spoils may be large or small, containing merely a single item or a much wider range of loot. The actual war is waged only by men, but women and children may also appear in connection with these conflicts. Last but not least, it is important to distinguish between ordinary wars and those resembling a worship service; the latter can also be associated with elements of the "war of Yhwh." In reviewing every important war in the Old Testament, two emerge, each with a specific profile, that are very closely related but stand very much on their own: the Israelites' war against the Midianites in Numbers 31 and the war that Jehoshaphat waged against a Transjordanian coalition (2 Chr 20).[18] Closest to these two texts comes the conquest of Jericho, as described in Josh 6. Note that this observation should help to further liberate this text from its "Deuteronomistic captivity" than has been done so far. I would like to draw the attention to two similarities and one important difference.

Both campaigns are religious undertakings. The expression "holy war," as I described these wars in my first publication on the subject, is perhaps infelicitous, since it falls a little short of the mark. In the campaign against the Midianites, the priests Phinehas and Eleazar perform important functions; the army goes to war with holy instruments and trumpets. In Jehoshaphat's war against the Transjordanian coalition, the Levites – i. e. the Kohathites and the Korahites, much appreciated by the Chronicler – have an important task: to praise Yhwh with song, harp, lyre and trumpet.

In no other wars are the spoils so large. The Chronicler's description of the loot is rather general (2 Chr 20:25):

> When Jehoshaphat and his people came to take the booty from them, they found livestock in great numbers, goods, clothing, and precious things, which they took for themselves until they could carry no more. They spent three days taking the booty, because of its abundance.

Numbers 31:32, on the other hand, gives a list: 675,000 flock animals, 72,000 cattle (approximately 5 % of today's Swiss cattle livestock!) and 61,000 donkeys. The spoils are distributed among the warriors, the rest of the congregation, and the temple. 2 Chronicles 20 contains no information about distribution, but to assume that the temple did not receive part of it is as daring as to assume that the soldiers themselves did not receive any share. The motif of important spoils is, by the way, very widespread in Chronicles as a whole.

18. See Jonker, "Numbers and Chronicles," 367–8.

It is not only men who are present when Jehoshaphat preaches his sermon on war. The Chronicler explicitly states (2 Chr 20:13):

> Meanwhile all Judah stood before Yhwh, with their little ones, their wives, and their children.

In Numbers 31, the latter are not explicitly mentioned, but they are implicitly present in v. 3 (note the term "men"):

> So Moses said to the people, "Arm some of your men for the war, so that they may go against Midian, to execute Yhwh's vengeance on Midian."

However, there is also an important difference between the two texts concerning the role of God in these conflicts: In Numbers 31, though the initiative for war is taken by Yhwh, many of the usual elements of the "holy war" are missing. In 2 Chronicles 20, however, Jehoshaphat must wage a defensive war; it contains elements of the "war of Yhwh," such as an invitation to the warriors not to be afraid, and the promise of divine assistance (v. 20). In Numbers 31, the Israelites themselves wage war and kill their enemies; in 2 Chronicles 20, Yhwh does so indirectly by setting an ambush and allowing the enemies to kill each other.

6. Families, Women, Daughters, and Questions Related to Heritage

More than the other books of the Old Testament, Numbers and Chronicles take a great interest in families, especially women and daughters, not only in individual persons. The *Sondergut* of Numbers contains six texts dealing with women: First, there is Numbers 5:11–31, the jealousy offering by which a woman must prove that she has not committed adultery; then Numbers 30, a chapter that regulates the vows of men briefly and those of women very extensively; I will handle neither the strange story of the pierced Midianite woman (Num 25) nor Miriam and Aaron's jealousy of Moses (Num 12). The best-known texts dealing with women are Numbers 27:1–11 and Numbers 36, both of which regulate the hereditary rights of daughters in the event of no male offspring or the premature death of one.

I will also treat neither the jealousy sacrifice nor the story in Numbers 12 in the present article. However, let me make a few brief remarks about the vows:[19] Among other things, Numbers 30 provides

---

19. On this text see, e. g., Horst Seebass, *Numeri. 3. Teilband Numeri 22,2–36,13*, BK IV/3 (Neukirchen-Vluyn: Neukirchener Verlag, 2007), 265–82 (with extensive bibliography).

the circumstances under which a father/husband can invalidate the vow of his daughter/wife. Whether these provisions are misogynous or, to the contrary, women-friendly is a matter of controversy, and opinions are divided even on what Numbers 30 says about the position of women. After all, women can make vows without first having to ask the respective male authorities, whether a father or husband. Widows and women rejected by their husbands must stand for their own vows. The position of these women, however, is not as dire as it would seem at first sight. Levine even contends that Numbers 30 expresses misgivings about the overly strong entrepreneurial freedom of women.[20] Nevertheless, we are left only to speculate about the specific background of Numbers 30. For example, certain scholars believe that women were fascinated and attracted by religious foundations, and that the men responsible for them would therefore have been required to "foot the bill" as legal householders.[21] Whatever the case may be, vows made by women seem to have been of considerable importance: They are still addressed at considerable length in the Talmud.[22] Thus, vows may have played a far more important role in the (religious) life of the Israelites than the Old Testament texts would suggest.

In Chronicles, women and children (especially daughters) also play an important role outside the genealogical lists. These texts often include detailed genealogical information on Judean kings from the Chronicler's *Sondergut*, namely Rehoboam, Abijah, Jehoshaphat and perhaps also Joash. The information is most precise concerning Rehoboam (2 Chr 11:18–23). According to the Chronicler, Rehoboam had two wives, Mahalath and Maacah, with the latter being his preferred wife. With the two of them in addition to sixteen other wives and sixty concubines, he fathered a total of 28 sons and 60 daughters; we only know the names of Mahalath's and Maacah's children. Rehoboam arranged his succession in such a way that he appointed Abijah, the firstborn of Maacah, heir to the throne and politically quashed his other sons by appointing them as governors and by generously endowing them with food and women. The information on Mahalath and Maacah seems credible, but the large number of Rehoboam's wives (eighteen) and even more the round number of his concubines and daughters – sixty each – seems less so. Commentators evaluate this section in completely different ways. According to

---

20. Baruch A. Levine, *Numbers 21–36. A New Translation with Introduction and Commentary*, AB 4A (New York: Doubleday, 2000), 436.

21. See Levine, *Numbers 21–36*, 436: "Or, was there an increase in religiosity affecting women…?"

22. See Talmudic tractate Nedarim.

Japhet, women and children are "signs of God's blessing."[23] Rudolph, who considers the verses to be an addition by a later author,[24] sees Rehoboam's "Haremswirtschaft"[25] presented here as serving as an example for Rehoboam's apostasy against Yahweh. In the text, however, there is no such criticism. The question then arises of why this insertion happens in Chronicles but not in Kings, as well as the even more fundamental question of why it happens at all. It is particularly astonishing how soberly the passage assesses the king's "Realpolitik," which its author qualifies as "wise." The information is so precise that one supposes a specific contemporary historical situation to stand behind it, though such a situation is impossible to identify.

The Chronicler's information about King Abijah is less precise (2 Chr 13:21). After coming to power, he reportedly took fourteen wives and conceived twenty-two sons and sixteen daughters with them. Although this information, written in typical Chronistic style, does not mention any names, it is generally regarded as trustworthy.[26]

As with Rehoboam, the information about Jehoram also concerns the succession to the throne. The Chronicler first relates Jehoram's accession, and then lists the other five sons of Jehoshaphat, to whom he gives many gifts – together with fortified cities in Judah. Yet Jehoram does not seem to trust his brethren and kills them all (2 Chr 21:3–4). In vv. 1–4, only sons and brothers play a role:

---

23. Japhet, *I & II Chronicles*, 663.

24. Wilhelm Rudolph, *Chronikbücher*, HAT 1. R. 21 (Tübingen: Mohr Siebeck, 1955), 233; cf. Martin Noth, *Überlieferungsgeschichtliche Studien. Die sammelnden und bearbeitenden Geschichtswerke im Alten Testament* (Tübingen: Max Niemeyer, 31967), 143, n. 1: "die in diesen Abschnitten vorkommenden Namen gehören, soweit sie nicht aus der alten Überlieferung stammen, zum nachexilischen Typ".

25. Rudolph, *Chronikbücher*, 233.

26. See Rudolph, *Chronikbücher*, 239: "Der Schwächung Jerobeams entspricht die Erstarkung Abias (21); zu den Zeichen des göttlichen Segens rechnet der Chr. auch seine große Kinderzahl, deren Geschichtlichkeit nicht zu bezweifeln ist; daß ihm alle Kinder nicht erst während seiner dreijährigen Regierungszeit geboren wurden, liegt auf der Hand, die gegenteilige Meinung (Wellhausen, Prol. 216) gehört einer Zeit an, wo man dem Chr. jede Dummheit zutraute." Japhet, *I & II Chronicles*, 699, also assumes that the Chronicler may have had sources unavailable to the author of the Deuteronomistic History. Although she admits that "the passage reflects Chronistic idiom…and conforms to the Chronicler's view that children are a sign of blessing, these are hardly sufficient reason to doubt the information itself. The similar accounts for Rehoboam (II Chron. 11.18–21) and Jehoshaphat (II Chron. 21.2–4) indicate that systematic family records were kept for all the Davidic kings (except Asa) who reigned before the major crisis in the days of Athaliah. One wonders whether the Chronicler had access to a source with this genealogical information, which the Deuteronomistic author of Kings simply ignored, or whether these were fragmentary records which somehow survived to the Chronicler's time." These are all very daring assumptions – even if Chronicles is dated very early.

> Jehoshaphat slept with his ancestors and was buried with his ancestors in the city of David; his son Jehoram succeeded him. He had brothers, the sons of Jehoshaphat: Azariah, Jehiel, Zechariah, Azariahu, Michael, and Shephatiah; all these were the sons of King Jehoshaphat of Judah. Their father gave them many gifts, of silver, gold, and valuable possessions, together with fortified cities in Judah; but he gave the kingdom to Jehoram, because he was the firstborn. When Jehoram had ascended the throne of his father and was established, he put all his brothers to the sword, and also some of the officials of Israel.

The historicity and accuracy of this information is hardly disputed by the commentators, though there may well be cause for doubt.[27] Jehoram's brothers are likely called "sons of Jehoshaphat" because they are only half-brothers to the future king. King Jehoshaphat acts sensibly in giving rich gifts to the brothers of the future ruler; he probably seeks to prevent them from striving for the throne themselves. However, Jehoram distrusts his brothers and subsequently kills them. Finally, attention must be drawn to 2 Chronicles 24:3; the verse belongs to the *Sondergut*:

> Jehoiada got two wives for him / himself (לוֹ), and he became the father of sons and daughters.

It is not quite clear whether לוֹ refers to the priest Jehoiada or King Joash – grammatically, both translations are possible. However, in agreement with Japhet, the second possibility appears more likely. On the one hand, the verse emphasizes Jehoiada's strong commitment to the king while on the other hand making clear how much the Chronicler is concerned about the king's family. The information is so general that even Japhet does not exclude the possibility "that these biographical data are the Chronicler's own surmises."[28]

If this startling information about Rehoboam and Jehoram is correct, why has only the Chronicler included such in his work? Did the confusion surrounding the succession of Alexander the Great[29] raise the specter of similar events in Judah's past?

The passages handled immediately above, especially the references to large numbers of descendants, do not restrict themselves to royal lineages, as shown by 1 Chronicles 25:5:

---

27. For example, compare the simultaneous occurrence of the two personal names וִיהָרְנֶהָי and עָרְנֶעָ.

28. Japhet, I & II Chronicles, 841.

29. See e.g. *The Cambridge Ancient History. Volume VII. Part I The Hellenistic World*, ed. Frank W. Walbank, A.E. Astin, M.W. Frederiksen and R.M. Ogilvie (Cambridge: Cambridge University Press 21984), 23–61 (Chapter 2: The Succession to Alexander, Edouard Will).

> All these were the sons of Heman the king's seer, according to the promise of God to exalt him; for God had given Heman fourteen sons and three daughters.

Although the daughters are not mentioned by name, it is notable that they are mentioned at all. It is difficult to find a specific reason for this. The explanation most often advanced may be correct, that "the intention is simply to emphasise the blessing of Heman's family."[30] This interpretation is all the more probable as Job, after his restitution, is also blessed with seven sons and three daughters (Job 42:13). We will return to this passage below.

Numbers and Chronicles contain further texts in which women play a special role. These texts are of particular interest in cases where they interpret preexistent texts. As one case, Budd and Kellermann have shown that Numbers 5:5–10 is "some kind of halakhic comment on Lev 5."[31] Only here are men and women named separately (Num 5:5–6):

> Yhwh spoke to Moses, saying: Speak to the Israelites: When a man or a woman wrongs another, breaking faith with Yhwh, that person incurs guilt.

A similar case is found in Deut 23:22 and Numbers 6:1, as the juxtaposition of the two texts shows:

> Deut 23:22
> If you make a vow to Yhwh your God, do not postpone fulfilling it; for Yhwh your God will surely require it of you, and you would incur guilt.

> Numbers 6:1–2
> Yhwh spoke to Moses, saying: Speak to the Israelites and say to them: When either men or women make a special vow, the vow of a nazirite, to separate themselves to Yhwh,

Numbers addresses the remuneration of a priest's family members (including women!) more often than the book of Leviticus does, with the latter not being particularly helpful in this respect. Leviticus contains only scattered information on this subject (see, e. g. Lev 2:3; 7:6, 14; 22:7). In contrast, Deuteronomy contains more provisions, and – particularly important – a full, coherent section: Deut 18:1–8. However, even more extensive is Numbers 18. In the present context, it is par-

---

30. Hugh G. M. Williamson, *1 and 2 Chronicles*, NCB (Grand Rapids: Wm.B. Eerdmans, 1982), 168.

31. Philip J. Budd, *Numbers*, WBC 5 (Waco: Word Books Publisher, 1984), 57; cf. Diether Kellermann, *Die Priesterschrift von Numeri 1,1 bis 10,10 literarkritisch und traditionsgeschichtlich untersucht*, BZAW 120 (Berlin: De Gruyter, 1970), 66–69.

ticularly important that the sons and daughters of the clergy are also mentioned (Num 18:11, 19):

> ¹¹This also is yours: I have given to you, together with your sons and daughters, as a perpetual due, whatever is set aside from the gifts of all the elevation offerings of the Israelites; everyone who is clean in your house may eat them.

> ¹⁹All the holy offerings that the Israelites present to Yhwh I have given to you, together with your sons and daughters, as a perpetual due; it is a covenant of salt forever before Yhwh for you and your descendants as well.

The inclusion of sons and daughters is all the more remarkable, as it "[n]icht [um] die Versorgung der Priester, sondern [um] die Heiligkeit der ihnen zufallenden Opferanteile [geht]".[32] Milgrom defines the social and economic background of v. 11 as follows:

> *daughters that are with you*: The implication is that married daughters who have joined their lay husband's households are not eligible to partake of sacred food (see Lev 22:12–13). All other members of the priest's household, including his slaves (Lev 22:11) – but not his hired laborers since they maintain their own household (Lev 22:10) – may also share his sacred food.[33]

After victorious efforts in battle, the question always arises of how to divide the spoils. The basis provision can be found in Deut 20:13–14:

> (…) and when Yhwh your God gives it into your hand, you shall put all its males to the sword. You may, however, take as your booty the women, the children, livestock, and everything else in the town, all its spoil. You may enjoy the spoil of your enemies, which Yhwh your God has given you.

The Israelites adhere to these regulations in the war against the Ishmaelites, during which they act as follows (Num 31:9–12):

> The Israelites took the women of Midian and their little ones captive; and they took all their cattle, their flocks, and all their goods as booty. All their towns where they had settled, and all their encampments, they burned, but they took all the spoil and all the booty, both people and animals. Then they brought the captives and the booty and the spoil to Moses, to Eleazar the priest, and to the congregation of the Israelites, at the camp on the plains of Moab by the Jordan at Jericho.

---

32. Horst Seebass, *Numeri. 2. Teilband Numeri 10,11–22,1*, BK IV/2 (Neukirchen-Vluyn: Neukirchener Verlag, 2003), 221.
33. Jacob Milgrom, *The JPS Torah Commentary. Numbers* במדבר (Philadelphia: The Jewish Publication Society, 1990), 151.

Most striking in this passage is the level of detail with which the spoils are listed.

However, some verses later, a correction of the provision of Deut 20:13–14 is made when Moses criticizes the Israelites for having spared the women (Num 31:15–16). It is precisely they who, at the behest of Balaam, had made the Israelites fall away from Yhwh in Peor. He calls on the Israelites to kill all the boys, and then also every woman who has already consorted with a man. Only the virgins are to be spared.[34]

On the whole, it is astonishing how much attention women are given in the book of Numbers, both as individual figures as well as the collective of Israelite women. The same holds true for the book of Chronicles, though only a few examples must suffice to show this: 1) It is only 1 Chronicles 2:16–17 that enables determining the exact kinship of Zeruiah. The other passages where she is mentioned do not make perfectly clear that she is a sister of David. 2) Only 1 Chronicles 2:26 knows of Atarah, the second wife of Jerahmeel. 3) The following sentence is found in two passages – with almost identical wording (1 Chr 8:29; 9:35):

> Jeiel the father of Gibeon lived in Gibeon, and the name of his wife was Maacah.

Maacah is not mentioned anywhere else, and no commentators say anything about the presence of Maacah in this verse. 4) 1 Chronicles 25:5 is a particularly remarkable passage:

> All these were the sons of Heman the king's seer, according to the promise of God to exalt him; for God had given Heman fourteen sons and three daughters.

5) Finally, we should also mention the passages from the *Sondergut* of the Chronicler, where women (and children) are explicitly included in the congregation of the Israelites. As part of a covenant renewal during the reign of King Asa, the Israelites pledge (2 Chr 15:12–13):

> (…) to seek Yhwh, the God of their ancestors, with all their heart and with all their soul. Whoever would not seek Yhwh, the God of Israel, should be put to death, whether young or old, man or woman (ועד אשה למן קטן ועד גדול למאיש).

The speech of Azariah, in which this passage is found, occurs in a literary vacuum of sorts. The fact that women and children are also punished for violating the covenant is a significant "upgrade" in status for them.

---

34. This is exactly what happens; see v. 35.

War is basically a matter for men, and the exceptions confirm this rule. These include, to a certain extent, the war against the Transjordanian coalition (2 Chr 20). In the assembly of Judah and Jerusalem, Jehoshaphat offers a prayer of supplication to God (vv. 5–12). The report of the Chronicler continues as follows (v. 13):

> Meanwhile all Judah stood before Yhwh, with their little ones, their wives, and their children (גם טפם נשיהם ובניהם).

One might also translate it as "even their little ones…". Yet they play no role throughout the remaining course of events, much less a major role. They appear on stage for a short time because families are important to the Chronicler. For a moment, he forgets that the text is about a war and addresses the community gathered in the temple precinct.

A *crux interpretum* in 1 Chronicles 21:20 is the king hiding with his four sons. It could be a misspelling of "and when he saw him",[35] though this is anything but certain. Could it be that even in this passage, the Chronicler is thinking of the family, one of his favorite subjects?

The two laws regarding Zelophehad's daughters, Numbers 27:1–11 and Numbers 36 are two of the most well-known texts in Numbers. In the present context, I cannot deal with the controversial interpretation of these two chapters, even less so with the details of interpretation. However, I would like to show how infertility, and more precisely the absence of male heirs, connects the books of Numbers and Chronicles.

Although numerous Old Testament stories concern the absence of a male heir, they usually end positively, as is particularly clear in the stories of the patriarchs and in 1 Samuel 1–2. However, matters are different in Numbers and Chronicles.

Numbers 26:33 reports that Zelophehad had only daughters and no sons, and mentions the daughters by name. The *Sondergut* of Chronicles contains some passages reporting absences of male offspring; the author also briefly discusses the case of Zelophehad. The passages read as follows:

> 1 Chr 2:30
> The sons of Nadab: Seled and Appaim; and Seled died childless (בנים לא).

> 1 Chr 2:32
> The sons of Jada, Shammai's brother: Jether and Jonathan; and Jether died childless (לא בנים).

---

[35] See commentaries.

1 Chr 2:34–35
Now Sheshan had no sons, only daughters (ולא היה לששן בנים כי אם בנות); but Sheshan had an Egyptian slave, whose name was Jarha. So Sheshan gave his daughter in marriage to his slave Jarha; and she bore him Attai.

1 Chr 7:15
And Machir took a wife for Huppim and for Shuppim. The name of his sister was Maacah. And the name of the second was Zelophehad; and Zelophehad had daughters (ותהינה לצלפחד בנות).

1 Chr 23:22
Eleazar died having no sons, but only daughters (היו לו בנים כי אם בנות ולא); their kindred, the sons of Kish, married them.

1 Chr 24:2.
But Nadab and Abihu died before their father, and had no sons (היו להם ובנים לא); so Eleazar and Ithamar became the priests.

This passage recapitulates Numbers 3:4:

> Nadab and Abihu died before Yhwh when they offered unholy fire before Yhwh in the wilderness of Sinai, and they had no children (היו להם ובנים לא). Eleazar and Ithamar served as priests in the lifetime of their father Aaron.

Let us look briefly beyond these two books. Josh 17 reports how the claims of Zelophehad's daughters, who invoke Yhwh's command, are fulfilled. The text quite clearly and extensively engages Numbers 27:1–11; 36, a further indication of how crucial the subject of a missing male heir was at a certain period. In some aspects, Josh 17 can be regarded as the "*Vollendung*",[36] or rather the "second *Vollendung*" of the Torah. Only after reading this text do we discover how the claims of Zelophehad's daughters are finally realized.

This likewise applies to the establishment of asylum cities. Though there are three laws governing the asylum procedure, it is Josh 20 in its Masoretic version that makes perfectly clear how this procedure works.[37] In other words, Josh 20 answers the questions that remain unanswered following Exod 21:12–14; Deut 19 and Numbers 35.

A second digression: The issue of daughters and their right to inherit also plays a role in the book of Job, which probably dates to the Achaemenid period. At the very beginning of the book, its author states that Job has seven sons and three daughters (Job 1:2); he is a

---

36. See Reinhard Achenbach, *Die Vollendung der Tora. Studien zur Redaktionsgeschichte des Numeribuches im Kontext von Hexateuch und Pentateuch*, BZAR 3 (Wiesbaden: Harrassowitz, 2003).

37. See Hans-Peter Mathys, "Homizid und nicht Asyl / Asylstädte. Das Thema von Numeri 35, 9–34," *ThZ* 76 (2020): 122–3.

blessed man! The same number of sons and daughters are given to him after his recovery (Job 42:13). Note that these numbers of Job's descendants are reminiscent of the fourteen sons and three daughters of Heman (1 Chr 25:5). It is both interesting and irritating that the three daughters of Job receive much more attention than his seven sons. The author of the book of Job goes even further than Numbers 25:1–11 and 36 concerning the inheritance rights of daughters (Job 42:15):

> In all the land there were no women so beautiful as Job's daughters; and their father gave them an inheritance along with their brothers.

What is the social and economic background that explains the improved position of daughters and their right to a share of inheritance, whether linked to the absence of a male heir or not? Most interpreters shun this question. One reason for this caution is given by Raik Heckl: "Verblüffend sind die nachfolgenden zwei Verse, deren Intention wahrscheinlich nicht vollständig zu ergründen ist."[38] A remarkable proposal was made by Lipiński, according to whom Job 42:13–15 might reflect the custom whereby a rich father also gave his daughters a share of the inheritance.[39]

Some commentators have pointed out that in the ancient Near East, daughters could sometimes inherit, usually in the absence of a male heir. They refer to parallels from Nuzi, Ugarit, Alalah and Deir el-Medina,[40] though these parallels call for a certain amount of skepticism due to the large gap in time separating Numbers from these texts. Fohrer considers the frame of Job to be old and thus argues the opposite, that Job 42:15 bears witness to an older practice than that required in the texts of Numbers.[41] However, this older "Volksbuch" has completely disappeared from scholarly literature on the book of Job. The books of Numbers and Job are quite closely related in their dates; they both belong to the Achaemenid period. Therefore, potential parallels must first and foremost be sought in the fifth and fourth

---

38. Raik Heckl, Hiob – *vom Gottesfürchtigen zum Repräsentanten Israels*: *Studien zur Buchwerdung des Hiobbuches und zu seinen Quellen*, FAT 70 (Tübingen: Mohr Siebeck, 2010), 309.

39. Edward Lipiński, Art. לחז, TWAT V (Stuttgart: Kohlhammer, 1986): 348.

40. See, e. g., Kenneth Numfor Ngwa, *The Hermeneutics of the 'Happy' Ending in Job 42:7–17*, BZAW 354 (Berlin: De Gruyter, 2005), 114–15. For a theological interpretation of Job 42:13–15, see Jürgen Ebach, "Hiobs Töchter. Zur Lektüre von Hiob 42,13–15 (auch eine Art Brief an Luise Schottroff)," in Jürgen Ebach, *Hiobs Post. Gesammelte Aufsätze zum Hiobbuch zu Themen biblischer Theologie und zur Methodik der Exegese* (Neukirchen-Vluyn: Neukirchener Verlag, 1995), 67–72.

41. Georg Fohrer, *Das Buch Hiob*, KAT XVI (Gütersloh: Gütersloher Verlagshaus Gerd Mohn, 1963), 544–45.

centuries BCE. These can be found in Greece and Sparta. Close (and more distant) parallels are so numerous and varied that they can only be presented here in extracts and in simplified form.[42]

Before addressing these parallels, some general observations must be noted. Functioning families formed the backbone of a society's prosperity, and this is unlikely to have been very different in ancient Israel. Questions of inheritance are of relatively little importance in the Old Testament. In the everyday life of the Israelites, however, they certainly played a much more prominent role than, for example, capital crimes. In this respect, ancient Greek texts are a better mirror of reality than the Old Testament. This is especially true for one point: The laws were not always followed, as the sources occasionally attest. The fact that the inheritance rights of daughters both in Greece and in the Old Testament occupy an important place has a simple explanation that most commentators of Numbers do not consider worth mentioning: In quite many families, there have been "only" daughters, as the following statistical considerations make clear: If one assumes quite correctly that boys and girls each account for 50% of births, the following applies: Two-child families have a 25% chance of having all-male offspring and a 25% chance of all-female offspring; in three-child families, this number is 12.5%, etc. Zelophehad had five daughters, which corresponds to 3.125% – much more likely than one would generally assume.

I will now compile and briefly interpret the regulations concerning the hereditary daughters in Greece. It should be noted in advance that, as in Israel, the passing of paternal inheritance to a son was regarded as the normal or ideal case in Greece (understood in the broadest sense of the term). The importance of hereditary daughters is shown by the fact that in Athens, there was a *terminus technicus* for them, ἐπίκληρος.[43] If a father preferred not to adopt a son, his daughter was entitled to inherit. We know very little about the hereditary daughters in Sparta. According to Herodotus (VI:57), one of the many privileges of the Spartan king was to appoint a husband for a daughter if her

---

42. A selection of relevant books: Alick Robin Walsham Harrison, *The Law of Athens: The Family and Property* (Oxford: Oxford University Press, 1968), especially 122–62; Stephen C. Todd, *The Shape of Athenian Law* (Oxford: Clarendon Press, 1993), 228–231; Cynthia B. Patterson, *The Family in Greek History* (Harvard: Harvard University Press, 1998); Cheryl Anne Cox, *Household Interests. Property, Marriage Strategies, and Family Dynamics in Ancient Athens* (Princeton: Princeton University Press, 1998; see index: "heiress daughters"); Josine Blok, *Citizenship in Classical Athens* (Cambridge: Cambridge University Press, 2017).

43. Short information in Gerhard Thür, "Epikleros," *Der Neue Pauly* 3 (Stuttgart: J. B. Metzler, 1997): 1117–18.

father had not already done so, thus acting as a "surrogate father."⁴⁴ In his criticism of the "Spartan property system," Aristotle pointed out that about 40% of the land was owned by women. As one reason for this, he mentions the high number of ἐπίκληροι (Pol. 1270a).

The Gortyn Code dates to the fifth century BCE as the oldest collection of laws in Europe⁴⁵ and contains surprisingly detailed provisions concerning hereditary daughters (IV–VI). See the following in particular: "The *patroikos* is given in marriage to the oldest brother of her father. If there is no brother, she is given to the brother's son. If there are more than one *patroikos* or more than one son of the brother, then order of age rules. And the *epiballon* shall have one *patroikos* and not more."⁴⁶ The elaborate (and even quite complicated) rules that apply if these principles cannot be implemented need not be addressed here.

It is said that Solon, who tried to stabilize the polis of Athens through the establishment of laws, had already promulgated provisions concerning the *epikleroi* (Aristotle, Ath. Pol. 9.2). The veracity of this assertion is not necessary to examine here, though it is likely. The most exact "rule on the *epikleros*" is related by Isaeus, who lived from approximately the end of the fifth to the middle of the fourth centuries BCE and was numbered among the Ten Attic Orators.⁴⁷ His extant speeches unexceptionally deal with inheritance matters, including the validity of wills and the succession of heirs. This rule is as follows: "For we consider that the next-of-kin ought to marry this woman, and that the property ought for the present to belong to the heiress, but that, when there are sons who have completed their second year after puberty, they should have possession of it."⁴⁸ The pool of pretenders who were eligible as spouses for the hereditary daughter was much wider in Athens than in Gortyn; it included descendants of the uncle and aunt on the father's side as well as descendants of the uncle and aunt on the mother's side. The Athenians were not particularly interested in passing property only patrilineally. Patrilineality thus only played an important role in the political domain. In passing inheritance, the interests of the ἀγχιστεία were paramount, consisting

---

44. Patterson, *The Family in Greek History*, 101.
45. Ronald F. Willetts, *The Law of Gortyn*, Kadmos Supplement 1 (Berlin: De Gruyter, 1967); Anselm C. Hagedorn, *Between Moses and Plato. Individual and Society in Deuteronomy and Ancient Greek Law*, FRLANT 204 (Göttingen: Vandenhoeck & Ruprecht, 2004; text of the code and English translation according to Willetts: 285–99).
46. Patterson, *The Family in Greek History*, 93.
47. Short information in Michael Weißenberger, "Isaios," *Der Neue Pauly* 5 (Stuttgart: J.B. Metzler, 1998): 1115–16.
48. Edward Seymour Forster, *Isaeus, with an English Translation*, LCL 202 (Cambridge: Harvard University Press, 1983), 475.

more of a "branching web of relationships rather than a 'line'."[49]

Plato's innovative solution need not be presented here. For him, "the preservation of a stable property system is a key concern,"[50] which is most likely to be guaranteed if there is only one male heir (Leg. 924–925).

A comparison between the Greek provisions concerning the hereditary daughters and those of the Old Testament shows interesting similarities and differences:[51] Numbers 27:1–11 does not address the question of who should marry the daughters. This gap is closed by Numbers 36, which states that only a man from a clan of the father's tribe is eligible and not a man from another tribe; otherwise the clan would lose a part of its נַחֲלָה. Broadly speaking, Numbers 36 is concerned with specific provisions implementing the general provisions of Numbers 27.

Some questions concerning the daughters of Zelophehad are still unresolved. Four of them bear names that are also documented as names of villages. If Numbers 27 was only about the right of inheritance in families, and especially about the right of daughters to inherit, this amendment would probably not call for five daughters. How the inheritance is divided among them is of little importance. Moreover, Numbers 27:1 offers a detailed genealogy of Zelophehad, which is of no interest for the division of the inheritance. Although his daughters are vocal in their demand, as soon as they receive what they desire, they disappear and the remaining inheritance is arranged in case a man has left no heirs at all. Numbers 27 is best understood as an amendment to an inheritance law in which daughters were left with nothing. In this passage, they (or rather, the representatives of their interests) forcefully impose this new law. This lobbying must have been massive, as the singular structure of Numbers 27 makes clear: The five daughters present their case before Moses, the priest Eleazar, the princes, and the whole congregation – a comprehensive body. However, it is not the congregation who makes the decision as expected, but Yhwh, who authoritatively intervenes on the side of the five daughters (v. 7). This divine intervention seems to end any discussion. In order to rein-

---

49. Patterson, *The Family in Greek History*, 98.
50. Patterson, *The Family in Greek History*, 103.
51. So far, this relationship has only been mentioned in passing; see Hagedorn, *Between Moses and Plato*, 208, n. 59. Studies comparing Greek and biblical law focus on Deuteronomy; see Hagedorn and Leonhard Burckhardt, "Elemente der Vergleichbarkeit von Gesetzgebung. Deuteronom – Gortyn – XII-Tafelgesetze. Eine Skizze," in *Gesetzgebung in antiken Gesellschaften*, ed. Leonhard Burckhardt, Klaus Seybold and Jürgen von Ungern-Sternberg, Beiträge zur Altertumskunde 247 (Berlin: De Gruyter, 2007), 1–65. The gap in research is due to the fact that the book of Numbers has long been a Cinderella in research.

force this point further, v. 11 stipulates: "It shall be for the Israelites a statute and ordinance, as Yhwh commanded Moses." Yet, this decision by Yhwh does not please the Gileadites, and they make clear to Moses and the princes of the tribal chiefs that it must be corrected – by keeping daughters of heirs from marrying members of other tribes; otherwise, there would be a danger that one tribe might lose parts of its inheritance to another tribe. This makes sense to Yhwh; he agrees with the Gileadites. Here, he no longer speaks directly, but through Moses (Num 36:5: "Then Moses commanded the Israelites according to the word of Yhwh, saying, 'The descendants of the tribe of Joseph are right in what they are saying.'"). Verse 5 unmistakably references Numbers 27:7; this is made clear by the same unusual formulation:

Num 36:5 כן מטה בני יוסף דברים
Num 27:7 כן בנות צלפחד דברת

The two hereditary laws in Numbers 27:1–11 and Numbers 36 do indeed have the divine placet, but they do not ultimately proceed from it. Numbers 36 is further characterized by the fact that the correction of the law in Numbers 27 ultimately receives a rational justification. One could indeed argue that God has assigned the individual tribes their settlement areas – but the author of Numbers 36 does not do this, and accusing him of implicitly doing so would be a bold assertion. Apart from these two chapters, there are no other Old Testament legal texts that have such a strong rational foundation rather than being based primarily on theological/ethical motives.

Numbers 27, 36 and the Greek laws/texts I briefly presented above agree with each other on two additional points: They deal extensively with the succession of heirs in the event that a man dies without any male heirs, and they are characterized by a high degree of regulation. In both areas, it is not only a matter of the interests of the "nuclear" family, but also of smaller and larger political groups. In both chapters, Numbers 27 and 36, the problem of the daughters of Zelophehad is not definitely solved. This only happens in Jos 17:3–6.

7. (High) Numbers

Another characteristic of the books Numbers and Chronicles is their affinity for numbers, especially high ones.[52] This, of course, is direct-

---

52. On (high/fantastic/symbolic/incredible) numbers in Chronicles and their explanation, see Jonker, "Numbers and Chronicles," 344–7; Ralph Walter Klein, "How Many in a Thousand," in Graham M. Patrick, Kenneth G. Hoglund, Steven L. Mc Kenzie, ed., *The Chronicler as Historian*, JSOTSup 238 (Sheffield: Sheffield Academic Press, 1997), 270–82; Gary N. Knoppers, *I Chronicles 10–29*, AB 12 A (New York: Doubleday, 2004), 569–71 (lit.). According to the most credible thesis, pro-

ly related to their subject matter, such as censuses as well as religious services and the many sacrifices offered on these occasions. Here too, the two books differ considerably from other Old Testament writings. In order to meet the needs of the present essay, it is sufficient to list only the most important passages to offer brief comments, and if necessary, compare them with other passages.

The book of Numbers opens with a census of the tribes of Israel (with the exception of Levi). As is generally recognized, these numbers are fantastic and greatly exaggerated, clearly shown by the total alone: 603,550 (v. 46). The second chapter contains the same figures, though presented here according to the locations of the individual tribes within the camp. Chapter 3 lists the figures for the Levites, who were excluded from the general census. Chapter 4, describing the service of the Levites, also contains information on the number of those who were mustered. The gifts offered by the princes of the tribes (Num 7) are identical, but the author of the chapter lists them for each tribe, together with the numbers. There is a remarkable figure contained in Numbers 25:9: 24,000 men who died of a plague because of fornication with Moabite women. Interestingly, there has never been any mention of this plague before. After the plague, a second census of the people is carried out, again documented by precise numbers (Num 26). The report of the vendetta against the Midianites (Num 31) contains an exceptionally high number of figures. Each tribe must muster 1,000 men to go to war against them. In the war, Israel takes a great deal of spoils. Interestingly, God orders the spoils to be counted exactly and decides on its distribution in detail. This is the most precise and longest list of spoils of war in the Old Testament.

Unlike the book of Numbers, Chronicles does not begin with a census, but with genealogies, and thus does not give figures. This changes in 1 Chronicles 5:18–22, a passage which tells of Reuben warring against Transjordanian populations. 44,760 Reubenites go to war against them, taking 50,000 camels, 250,000 sheep, 2,000 donkeys, and 100,000 people. In a certain sense, this is a short edition of Numbers 31 – but without any religious coloring, much less any justification.

While the genealogies at the beginning of Chronicles do not contain any numbers, this changes in 1 Chronicles 7. Japhet explains this by stating that some of the numbers mentioned in this chapter (may have) come from a military census.[53] Wilhelm Rudolph, however,

---

posed by Braun, Levine, Fouts, Skolnic, Klein, and Heinzerling, "[t]he incredible numbers are a literary convention or a scribal embellishment" (570).

53. Japhet, *I & II Chronicles*, 169.

notes that the numbers do not fit this kind of genealogy.[54] 1 Chronicles 8:40 mentions not only the number of sons and grandchildren of Ulam (150),[55] but also explicitly states that he had many sons and grandchildren. 1 Chronicles 9 lists the inhabitants of Jerusalem. For some of the groups living there, the chapter also lists how many members they counted (vv. 6, 9, 13, 22).

The passages in which the Deuteronomistic History and Chronicles run parallel to each other rarely differ in their figures. Many (especially high) numbers are to be found in the Sondergut of the Chronicler. In the present section we will first deal with parallel passages, then with the Chronicler's *Sondergut*.

When the Chronicler draws on *Vorlagen*, he typically also maintains the numbers given in them.[56] After all, numbers cannot be manipulated at will. Deviations from the *Vorlage* in Chronicles are often easily explained, not infrequently by accidents through the course of the textual transmission.[57] Some differences, however, require further explanation.

How exactly should the different figures in the census conducted under King David be explained? This can no longer be answered with absolute certainty, and there are some text-critical problems as well. According to 2 Samuel 24:9, there were 800,000 Israelite soldiers able to take up arms, and those of Judah were 500,000. The Chronicler (1 Chr 21:5–6) offers the following total numbers: 1,100,000 in "all Israel" and 470,000 in Judah. However, according to him, Levi and Benjamin were not counted among the number. He seems to have thought that 800,000 and 500,000 "represented a total of 100,000 for each tribe (twelve tribes, plus the tribe of Levi) … he may have

---

54. Rudolph, *Chronikbücher*, 64.

55. Gary N. Knoppers, *1 Chronicles 1–9*, AB 12 (New York: Doubleday 2004), 486: "The number is quite low by the Chronicler's standards and pales in comparison with the size of the three Benjaminite phratries (7:7, 9, 11). The small number may be compared with some numbers in the list of Ezra 2||Neh 7."

56. See the following parallels: 2 Sam 23:18 || 1 Chr 11:20; 2 Sam 18:13 || 1 Chr 18:12; 2 Sam 10:18 || 1 Chr 19:18 (partially differing); 2 Sam 24:15 || 1 Chr 21:14; 2 Sam 12:30 || 1 Chr 20:2; 2 Sam 24:15 || 1 Chr 21:14; 1 Kgs 3:4 || 2 Chr 1:6; 1 Kgs 10:26 || 2 Chr 1:14; 1 Kgs 10:29 || 2 Chr 1:17; 1 Kgs 5:29 || 2 Chr 2:1 (different numbers of overseers; 1 Kgs 5:30); 1 Kgs 5:27–28 || 2 Chr 2:17 (The Chronicler omits the forced labor, which according to him should not exist in Israel); 1 Kgs 8:62–63 || 2 Chr 7:4–6; 1 Kgs 10:10 || 2 Chr 9:9; 1 Kgs 10:14 || 2 Chr 9:13; 1 Kgs 22:6 || 2 Chr 18:5; 1 Kgs 10:16–17 || 2 Chr 9:15–16 (partially differing); 1 Kgs 12:21 || 2 Chr 11:1.

57. 2 Sam 23:8 || 1 Chr 11:11; 2 Sam 8:4 || 1 Chr 18:4; 2 Sam 10,6 || 1 Chr 19,6 (It is also possible that the Chronicler makes 32,000 men and 1,000 talents of silver out of 33,000 men); 1 Kgs 7:26 || 2 Chr 4:5 (However, the different figures may also be based on different calculation methods); 1 Kgs 9:23 || 2 Chr 8:10; 1 Kgs 9:28 || 2 Chr 8:18; 1 Kgs 5:6 || 2 Chr 9:25.

concluded that the deletion of Levi and Benjamin should reduce the census total by 200,000 men".[58]

The Chronicler's report on the construction of the temple is very different from its *Vorlage*; above all, he shortens it considerably, which complicates the comparison between the two versions. The height of the temple according to Chronicles was 120 cubits (approx. 60 meters, 2 Chr 3:4), which seems completely implausible; it is often reduced to 20 cubits (approx. 10 meters) by a text-critical operation. However, the evidence for this correction is meagre. According to 2 Chronicles 3:15, the columns Boaz and Jachin are 35 cubits high, but according to the *Vorlage* (1 Kgs 7:15) only 18 cubits, which is more likely to be the case architecturally. The number 35 can be explained as the addition of the three numbers of 1 Kings 7:15–16: $18 + 12 + 5$ (Has the Chronicler not correctly understood the construction principle of the two pillars? …).[59]

The situation is quite different with the *Sondergut* of the Chronicler, which contains countless exaggerated numbers. These concern, among other things, wars and other conflicts, whether religiously motivated or not. The first example in Chronicles is the conflict between Reuben, Gad and the half-tribe of Manasseh versus a coalition of native Transjordanian peoples (1 Chr 5:18–22). The numbers are abnormally large. The Israelite tribes of the Transjordan lead 44,760 men into battle and capture 50,000 camels, 250,000 sheep, 2,000 donkeys and 100,000 people. Williamson tries to explain the gigantic number of Israelites by comparing them to even larger numbers in Numbers 1 and Numbers 26.[60] In 1 Chronicles 12:24–39, the numbers of the divisions of the armed troops who came to David in Hebron were 120,000 from the Transjordanian tribes and 340,822 in total muster. According to 1 Chronicles 27:2–15, David led 12 divisions of 24,000 men each, with each serving one month.

"Great enemy, great honor": The enemy may also sometimes dispose of an impressive army. This is the case of Pharaoh Shishak. In the fifth year of King Rehoboam's reign, Shishak went up to Jerusalem with 1,200 chariots, 60,000 horsemen, and countless people (2 Chr 12:3). Even more impressive was the army with which Jeroboam fought against Abijah, who could only muster half as many people for the battle: 800,000 Israelites against 400,000 Judahites. Nevertheless, Judah wins through Yahweh's partiality (2 Chr 13:5). However much the Chronicler appreciates high numbers, they are of no use when

---

58. Knoppers, *1 Chronicles 10–29*, 753. For further explications and details, see also Klein, "How Many in a Thousand?": 275.

59. Cf. Rudolph, *Chronikbücher*, 204.

60. Williamson, *1 and 2 Chronicles*, 66.

Yhwh enters the stage. Yet even if Yhwh's intervention is decisive, the Chronicler does not do without large numbers – not even without the 500,000 Israelites who remain lying dead on the battlefield (v. 17).

Abijah is the king of numbers *par excellence*. His army comprises 300,000 Judeans and 280,000 Benjaminites (2 Chr 14:7). In the following verse we are told that an army of the Cushite Serah is advancing against him consisting of no less than 1,100,000 (!) men and 300 chariots. Likewise, a census of the Judeans in the time of Amaziah yields a number of 300,000 warriors in addition to 100,000 Israelite mercenaries (2 Chr 25:5–6).

The cult, too, gives the Chronicler the opportunity to record high numbers.[61] David alone donates 100,000 *kikkar* of gold, 1,000,000 *kikkar* of silver, and much more to the temple (1 Chr 22:14). 1 Chronicles 29 records immense donations made by David and the people to build the temple (1 Chr 29:4–7). 1,000 young bulls, rams, and lambs are offered as burnt offerings at the sacrificial service that follows, along with sacrificial offerings in abundance (1 Chr 29:21). The figures of the sacrifice that Asa offered in the fifteenth year of his reign are significantly lower: 700 cattle, 7,000 sheep (2 Chr 15:11). The most significant sacrificial service ever held in the history of Israel is undoubtedly the one that took place during the dedication of the Temple of Solomon (2 Chr 7:5). Yet the number of animals sacrificed on the occasion of the Passover celebrations under Hezekiah and Josiah is also quite impressive:

> 2 Chr 30:24
> For King Hezekiah of Judah gave the assembly a thousand bulls and seven thousand sheep for offerings, and the officials gave the assembly a thousand bulls and ten thousand sheep.

> 2 Chr 35:7–9
> Then Josiah contributed to the people, as passover offerings for all that were present, lambs and kids from the flock to the number of thirty thousand, and three thousand bulls; these were from the king's possessions. His officials contributed willingly to the people, to the priests, and to the Levites. Hilkiah, Zechariah, and Jehiel, the chief officers of the house of God, gave to the priests for the passover offerings two thousand six hundred lambs and kids and three hundred bulls.

It is no surprise that the figures for Josiah are significantly higher than those for Hezekiah: the more sacrifices a king makes, the more im-

---

61. The remunerations which Solomon pays the Tyrians for their services in the building of the temple according to 1 Kgs 2 and 2 Chr 2 are incomparable with each other. In one case, it is a regular payment, while in the other case, it is a one-time payment.

portant he is. As the discussion above should make clear, (high) numbers are most definitely an important issue in the book of Numbers and Chronicles.

In conclusion, it is undisputed that Numbers and Chronicles are closely related in terms of the contents that they address, and there is likewise a consensus that the positions on certain topics taken by the Chronicler and the authors of Numbers often differ considerably. However, there is also disagreement as to how these similarities should be explained. This article, like my first one on the subject, concentrates on content and, for practical reasons, largely ignores the justifiable questions of whether the similarities can (also) be explained in a literary-critical way – and if so, how they could be explained. We have primarily been concerned with identifying the topics that were of particular, possibly even preoccupying, interest to the authors of Numbers and Chronicles, who do not seem to have been too far temporally removed from each other. The three most important findings of this paper are as follows: Among these issues were certainly those relating to family law, in particular the law of succession of daughters in the absence of male heirs. This question also preoccupied the legislator of Gortyn, who authored his codex at approximately the same time as the authors of Numbers; the absence of male heirs also features prominently in Chronicles. We dare not even express hypotheses accounting for this striking correlation. The fact that women (and families) generally are common subject matter in Numbers and Chronicles can be explained – again in very general terms – by the fact that this also corresponds to some extent to the place they occupied in society at the time when the present texts were written. In any case, the fact that "artificial" proper names are not only well-documented in Numbers and Chronicles, but are sometimes even key elements of their stories, must be explained as being due to the Zeitgeist of their period of composition. The case is different with the trumpets, which are prominently represented in Numbers and Chronicles. It can be debated whether the Chronicler adopted them from Numbers or whether he so variously used them not only out of interest of Numbers 10, but because he would have introduced them into his work even if they were missing in Numbers or mentioned only in passing.

נפש אדם AND THE ASSOCIATIONS OF 1 CHRONICLES 5 IN THE HEBREW BIBLE

Graeme Auld

1. INTRODUCTION

The combination of *nephesh* and *'adam* (נפש אדם) occurs only once in the books of Chronicles: in 1 Chr 5:21, almost at the centre of 1 Chr 1–9 (at v. 197 out of 407). Although both components are unremarkable nouns, they are combined only rarely in the Hebrew Bible. As in Chronicles, נפש אדם is found in only one context in each of books. (a) Lev 24:17–18 distinguishes between killing 'any human being' (כל־נפש אדם) and killing an animal: [נפש־] מות יומת ומכה בהמה ישלמנה איש כי יכה כל־נפש אדם (LXX does not attest the repetition of שפנ in v. 18). There is a difference in penalty: death for killing a human but payment for an animal. (b) Ezek 27:13 talks of humans being traded, humans as articles of exchange in Tyre's commerce: נתנו מערבך בנפש עדם וכלי נחשת. Lev 24 makes a distinction between humans and animals; however, by contrast, Ezekiel lumps humans along with lifeless bronze items as joint items of Tyre's trade. Then we find them on three occasions in Numbers: in Num 9:6 and 19:11, 13 in definitions of ritual uncleanness; and in Num 31:35, 40, 46 alongside animals, as in 1 Chr 5:21, among the prizes of war. Leviticus and Numbers are among the broadly 'priestly' books of the Pentateuch; and Ezekiel and Chronicles have many affinities with the priestly literature. Yet such priestly links may prove quite irrelevant to understanding how the few instances of נפש אדם are related.

Translations of 1 Chr 5:21 will be reviewed next (2). Then the wider paragraph (18–22) will be discussed under three main headings: Transjordanians and Levites in the books of Numbers, Joshua, and Chronicles (3); stories of victory, booty, and survival in Chronicles

(4); and the sources of 1 Chr 5:18–22, 25–26 (5). Some conclusion will then be drawn (6).

2. TRANSLATION ISSUES

נפש אדם may be near central in the Chronicler's prologue, but what does it mean? 1 Chr 5:21 is often paraphrased rather than translated literally. Roddy Braun's translation[1] is not untypical:

וישבו מקניהם	So they seized their cattle
גמליהם חמשים אלף	(fifty thousand camels,
וצאן מאתים וחמשים אלף	two hundred and fifty thousand from their flocks
וחמורים אלפים	and two thousand asses),
ונפש אדם מאה אלף	together with one hundred thousand men whom they took alive.
כי־חללים רבים נפלו	Many others fell …

1. מקנה overwhelmingly in HB refers to domestic animals, and the widespread choice to render מקנה by cattle/*Vieh*/livestock[2] gives priority to this usage over the primary sense of property or 'possessions', as rendered by Jacob Myers.[3]

2. Many agree in making a distinction between animals and humans – but that does not come straightforwardly from the simple Hebrew ־ו. Myers and Gary N. Knoppers[4] seem to me to be correct when they include humans straightforwardly in the list of מקניהם.

3. כי at the start of 22 is taken as causal by some and emphatic by others.

4. How do the fallen רבים relate to what has gone before? Are they contrasted with the immediately preceding נפש אדם, or does their great number help to explain how the Transjordanians were able to take such huge amounts of plunder, including human slaves?

5. Whatever the answer to 4., the 'many fallen slain' at the start of 22 have influenced Braun, Willi, and Knoppers[5] to give separate value to נפש from אדם in translation.[6] However, Myers ('men') and Ralph W.

---

1. Roddy Braun, *1 Chronicles*. WBC 14 (Waco: Word Books, 1986), 70.
2. Rendering מקניהם at the start by '*livestock*' (as also NRSV) may not be sensitive to the issues of life and death in the context – simply 'stock' would be better.
3. Jacob M. Myers, *1 Chronicles*. AB (New York: Doubleday, 1965), 33.
4. Myers, 33 and Gary N. Knoppers, *1 Chronicles* AB (New York: Doubleday, 2004), 376.
5. Braun, 70, Thomas Willi, *Chronik* BK xxiv.1 (Neukirchen: Neukirchener Verlag, 1991), and Knoppers, 376.
6. Braun's expansive 'whom they took alive' corresponds more closely to שבו

Klein ('people') take נפש אדם as a single semantic unit.[7]

מקניהם can be read strongly as defining the possessed status of all the living creatures that follow:

They captured their stock	their camels 50,000	גמליהם חמשים אלף	וישבו מקניהם
	and sheep 250,000	וצאן מאתים וחמשים אלף	
	and asses 2,000	וחמורים אלפים	
	and humans 100,000	ונפש אדם מאה אלף	

So read, נפש אדם may have been slaves of the Hagrites, a fourth element of Hagrite property. However, if the 100,000 were surviving Hagrites who escaped being among the many who fell (5:22), then אדם נפש is a second object of וישבו,[8] and co-ordinate instead with מקניהם:

The captured their stock:	their camels 50,000	גמליהם חמשים אלף	וישבו מקניהם
	and sheep 250,000	וצאן מאתים וחמשים אלף	
	and asses 2,000	וחמורים אלפים	
and humans	100,000	מדא שפנו	פלא האמ

The absolute numbers are extraordinary, and even the proportions surprising. 100,000 human captives alongside a total of 302,000 animals is just credible. But Klein's extraordinary suggestion[9] that these 100,000 humans may all have been virginal females surely constitutes one argument against joining him in reading 1 Chr 5 in light of Num 31:35, 40, 46.[10]

3. TRIANGULAR RELATIONSHIP?

נפש אדם would be even closer to the centre of 1 Chr 1–9 if ch. 5 were

---

חיים [עשרת אלפים] in 2 Chr 25:12 (see section 4.3 below).

7. I am puzzled that Sara Japhet (*I & II Chronicles*. OTL [Louisville: Westminster John Knox, 1993], 139) finds in this verse 'the only occurrence in Chr of נפש alone meaning "person", which is the more common usage in the priestly stratum'; and I suspect that her Hebrew has suffered in English translation.

8. *Die Bibel* (*in heutigem Deutsch*), 435 supplies a second verb for the second object: *Sie erbeuteten von ihnen ... und nahmen 100,000 Mann gefangen*.

9. Ralph W. Klein, *1 Chronicles*. Hermeneia (Minneapolis: Fortress, 2006), 168.

10. See section 3.2 below.

organised more logically: vv. 23–24 belong logically with vv. 1–17, while vv. 25–26 naturally link with vv. 18–22.

5:1–10	Reuben
5:11–17	Gad
5:18–22	all three together
5:23–24	half-Manasseh
5:25–26	all three together

However, to focus on the near-central location of נפש within the opening chapters of Chronicles would probably lead interpretation into a *cul de sac*. Yet there is more than one structural way to suggest significant links. Within the register of all Israel (1 Chr 4–8), we find Transjordan (5) and the Levites (5–6) at the centre: between the southern (4) and the northern (7–8) tribes west of the Jordan. A similar distinction between groups of tribes is achieved differently in Joshua by having Transjordan and Levites and refuge not separate south from north but set before (Josh 13–14) and after (20–22) south and north (15–19).

1 Chr 4–8	Josh 13–22
4 South	13–14 Transjordan and Levites
5A Transjordan	15 South
5B–6 Levites and refuge	16–19 North
7–8 North	20–22 Refuge, Levites, and Transjordan

It is the same two groups that receive special attention at the end of Numbers: Transjordan (Num 32) and Levites and refuge (Num 35). Some key terms have similar prominence in these same books.

– אחזה (holding/possession) is concentrated at the end of Numbers (and related end of Deuteronomy), in Josh 21–22, at the end of Ezekiel, and in Chronicles.[11]

– In seven contexts in the narrative books, מקנה (possession/ holding of livestock) denotes property belonging to David and subsequent kings in Jerusalem;[12] but ten times in the narratives listed below, all set between Exodus and monarchy, מקנה is exclusively associated with Israel in Transjordan or Reuben/Gad/half-Manasseh in particular.

Num	20:19	Israel and Edom

---

11. Num 27:4, 7; 32:5, 22, 29; 35:2, 8, 28; Deut 32:49; Josh 21:12, 41; 22:4, 9, 19, 19; 1 Chr 7:28; 9:2; 2 Chr 11:14; 31:1; and 14x in Ezek 44–48.

12. 1 Sam 23:5; 30:20; 2 Kgs 3:17; 1 Chr 28:1; 2 Chr 14:14; 26:10; 32:29. 1 Chr 7:21 provides the sole exception.

	31:9	Israel and Midian
	32:1, 4, 16, 26	Gad and Reuben
Deut	3:19	Reuben/Gad/half-Manassah
Josh	22:8	Reuben/Gad/half-Manassah
1 Chr	5:9, 21	Reuben, then Reuben/Gad/half-Manassaeh

An eleventh case (Josh 14:2–4) explains how the Levites relate to the 12 tribes understood as 9½ west of the Jordan +2½ east.[13]

There is further evidence of a triangular relationship between the end of Numbers, the framework of Josh 13–22, and 1 Chr. מעל often appears in these books in contexts that have already used מקנה.

	מקנה	מעל
Numbers	31:9; 32:1, 4, 16, 26	31:16
Joshua	14:4; 22:8	22:20, 31
1 Chr	5:9, 21; 7:21	2:7; 5:25; 9:1; 10:13

Itzhak Amar draws attention, within his discussion of how the Chronicler portrays exile differently for Judah, Israel, and the Transjordanians,[14] to the several similarities noted by Yair Zakovitch[15] between the portrayal of west and east in Num 32 and Josh 22. But he does not comment on the fact that Reuben and Gad are found in parts of these texts without half-Manasseh.

– They (mostly in the order Gad-Reuben) are the only players in Num 32:1–32, with half-Manasseh added only in 32:33–42.

– In Josh 22 MT, Reuben, Gad, and half-Manasseh feature throughout vv. 1–31 while only Reuben and Gad in the concluding vv. 32–34.[16]

– As already noted, 1 Chr 5 starts with Reuben alone, moves to Gad alone, then reports on all three together before a separate mention of half-Manasseh.

---

13. The Cisjordanians are described as 9½ tribes only in Num 34:13; Josh 13:7; 14:2.

14. Itzhak Amar, 'Expansion and exile in the Chronicler's narrative of the two and a half tribes (1 Chr. 5.1–26)', *JSOT* 44, 2020, 357–376 (see, 367).

15. Yair Zakovitch, *Joshua* (Tel Aviv: Revivim, 2000), 200.

16. LXX includes half-Manasseh throughout.

3.1 1 Chronicles 5 and Joshua 22

The kinship between these chapters is marked not just by shared terminology – an argument over substance is also implied. 1 Chr 5:25 straightforwardly attributes the exile of Reuben, Gad, and half-Manasseh to a gross though unspecified breach (מעל) with the god of their fathers. In Josh 22, however, a specific accusation of מעל is laid by the western majority against the eastern minority and is vigorously rebutted by them. The western tribes first charge these easterners with מעל over a structure near the Jordan, but then become persuaded they had been wrong in making such a complaint. Possibly 1 Chr 5:25 is a brief reference to the extended narrative in Josh 22. It is equally possible that the debate reported in Joshua between tribes east and west of the Jordan was created in response to the charge recalled in 1 Chr 5. That long account is told differently in MT and LXX, with some of the differences reflected in the variant retellings in Josephus and Pseudo-Philo – and, in MT at least, Joshua himself is absent from the story.[17]

3.2 Numbers 31: A major locus for נפש אדם

Num 31 deals with living booty, human and animal, taken by Israel from Midian, and in much greater detail than 1 Chr 5 from the Hagrites. And this long chapter of 54 verses immediately precedes the report in Num 32 of Moses settling the Transjordanians in a land entirely suitable for מקנה (32:1, 4, 16, 26 resonate with 1 Chr 5:9). The act of capture is stated in Num 31:9 using the same verb שבה as 1 Chr 5:21 (with the cognate noun שבי used in 31:12, 19, 26). The expressions for 'those going out to war', היצאים לצבא (31:27, 28) and היצאים בצבא (31:36), are similar to but not the same as the Chronicler's יצאי צבא (1 Chr 5:18; 7:11; 12:33, 36; 2 Chr 26:11). In fact, the Chronicler's usage is the same as we find when all Israel is counted earlier in Numbers (chs 1 and 26).

Later in the long chapter come instructions (unique to Num 31) about the division and taxation (מכס) of the booty (31:28, 37–41), both human (אדם) and animal (בהמה) – with the animals in three categories: herd (בקר), asses (חמרים), and flock (צאן). The taxation rate for all categories, animals and humans alike, is stated in v. 28 as one nefeš per five hundred (אחד נפש מחמש המאות).[18] The statement in v. 31 that 'Moses and Eleazar the priest did as Yahweh had commanded Moses' is at least an interim conclusion and may have marked the end of an earlier shorter draft. There are several shifts in terminology from the

---

17. Graeme Auld, "Re-telling the Disputed "Altar" in Joshua 22," in Ed Noort (ed.), *The Book of Joshua*. BETL CCX (Leuven: Peeters, 2012), 281–293.

18. The first half of this chapter uses נפש just once more: כל הרג נפש (v. 19).

first to the second part of the chapter:

– The totals of the taxable remainder are listed in 31:32–35 in reverse order from v. 28: sheep, asses, cattle, and humans.

– The humans are now termed not אדם but נפש אדם (vv. 35, 40, 46) and narrowly defined in 31:35 as women who had not experienced lying with males (לא־ידעו משכב זכר אשר).

– The tax due on the three categories of animal is stated as a simple numeral, for example there were 36,000 cattle 'and the tax on them for Yahweh was seventy-two' (ומכסם ליהוה שנים ושבעים). However, the tax on the 16,000 נפש אדם is given in v. 40 not as 'thirty-two' but as 'thirty-two *nefeš*' (שוים ושלשים נפש).[19]

4. CAMELS, CAPTURE, AND DIVINE AID IN CHRONICLES

In several respects, what the Transjordanians capture from the Hagrites anticipates several linked situations described in Chronicles.

4.1 KEY TERMS

A pattern of recurrent terms readily illustrates this:
מקנה 1 Chr 5:9, **21**; 7:21; 28:1; 2 Chr **14:14**; 26:10; 32:29
רכוש 1 Chr 27:31; 28:1; 2 Chr 20:25; 21:14, 17; 31:3; 32:29; 35:7
גמלים 1 Chr **5:21**; 12:41; 27:30; 2 Chr 9:1; **14:14**
שבה 1 Chr **5:21**; 2 Chr 6:36, 37, 38; **14:14**; 21:17; 25:12; 28:5, 8, 11, 17[20]
עזר 1 Chr **5:20**; 12[5x]; 18:5; 22:7; 2 Chr **14:10, 10**; 18:31; 19:2; 20:13; 25:8; 26:7, 13; 28:16, 23; 32:3, 8

As the numbers in **bold** make clear, the report of the confrontation between King Asa and the Cushites (2 Chr 14:9–15) provides the closest parallel. And the relevance of this link is further marked by similar resources available to Asa and the Transjordanians: נשאי מגן (shield-bearers) is unique in HB to 1 Chr 5:18 and 2 Chr 14:7, while דרכי קשת (bow-drawers) is found additionally only in Jer 50:14, 29 and 1 Chr 8:40. The combination מגן וחרב (5:18) is known elsewhere only in Ps 76:4, while the passive participle למוד (5:18) and the combination שעמהם (5:20) are unique. But there is one key difference: in the case of Asa, as often in the other subsequent passages, the humans or animals captured are said to be 'very many' (רב מאֹד) or 'in quantities' (לרב). In all of Chronicles, it is only in 1 Chr 5:21 that we are provided

---

19. מלקוח (31:11, 12, 26, 27, 32) is used elsewhere in HB only in Isa 49:24, 25.

20. Half the non-synoptic instances in Chronicles of שבה are in 2 Chr 28 – Judah under Ahaz suffers incursions from Aram (v. 5), Israel (vv. 8, 11), and Edom (v. 17).

with precise totals – as also in Num 31.

4.2 Arabic, Camels, and Corpses

The list of the defeated Hagrites starts with their camels, which can remind us of the joke that purports to explain how difficult it is to learn Arabic – because so many nouns in that language have at least four senses: a word means itself, and its opposite, and something obscene, and some part of a camel. And that observation, even if much exaggerated, leads back to the book of Numbers, even if not one camel can be found anywhere in its 36 chapters.

Num 9:4–5 opens: 'Moses spoke to all Israel of holding the Passover. And they held the Passover at first on the fourteenth day of the month …' The passage continues (9:6): לעשת־הפסח ביום ההוא – 'ויהי אנשים אשר היו טמאים לנפש אדם ולא יכלו – 'And there were men who had become unclean in respect of a נפש אדם and they were unable to perform the Passover on that day.' How can one become unclean by way of or in respect of a living human being? The more specific Num 19:11, 13 apparently clarifies the situation: נפש אדם וטמא שבעת ימים הנגע במת לכל – 'Whoever touches the dead of any human being will be unclean seven days.' It seems that נפש אדם, like any good Arabic word in the jest, can also mean its opposite; and certainly נפש in Qumran Hebrew (*DCH* V 733b), like its cognates in Aramaic and Arabic, can refer to a memorial for the dead.

4.3 חיים IN 2 CHRONICLES 25, מחיה IN 2 CHRONICLES 14, AND נפש IN 1 CHRONICLES 5

According to the synoptic narrative, Amaziah and his people struck down 10,000 men of Seir (2 Chr 25:11//2 Kgs 14:7). But the Chronicler adds in the next verse that they captured (ובש) a further 10,000 alive (חיים): אלפים חיים שבו בני יהודה ויך את־בני שעיר עשרת אלפים ועשרת. These they then threw to their destruction from the top of a rock. Klein interprets this action in light of the observation by the unnamed man of God that Yahweh could give Amaziah much more if he discharged his northern mercenaries.[21] Troy Cudworth cautions in response that Chr 'never praises mere brutality for its own sake'.[22] However that may be, 'alive' (חיים) in this supplement to the older story is the result of a skilful re-reading of the immediate synoptic context. The story shared

---

21. Ralph W. Klein, "The Chronicler's Theological Rewriting of the Deuteronomistic History: Amaziah, a Test Case," in K.L. Noll and Brooks Schramm (eds), *Raising Up a Faithful Exegete. Essays in Honor of Richard D. Nelson* (Winona Lake: Eisenbrauns, 2010), 237–245 (p. 242).

22. Troy D. Cudworth, *War in Chronicles. Temple Faithfulness and Israel's Place in the Land.* LHBOTS 627 (London: T&T Clark, 2016), 151.

with the book of Kings about Amaziah's success over the Edomites and subsequent challenge to Joash of Israel uniquely contained two of the very rare[23] synoptic instances of this 'life/living' word.

The first response by J[eh]oash to the presumptuous Amaziah was verbal: couched in the form of a fable (2 Chr 25:18//2 Kgs 14:9). As often in a parabolic warning (distinct from an allegory), the relationship between the characters in the story and those in the real-life situation it addresses is flexible. On first hearing/ reading the fable, we fairly suppose that the king of Israel is portraying himself as the cedar. But when he responds in action, he is experienced more like a 'wildlife' (חית השדה), an animal who would trample on a mere thistle. Defeat him he did; but the consequence was paradoxical: Amaziah out*lived* wild*life* Jehoash by fifteen years (25:25//14:17), till his reign ended in death in Lachish during an uprising against him. The Chronicler's addition to the Edom section of the story underlined a mismatch: between Amaziah's behaviour to 'the men of Seir' and his own lenient treatment at the hands of Jehoash. Ten thousand men of Seir were still alive after the battle; but, unlike Amaziah who would live fifteen more years after his defeat, they survived only to meet an immediate grisly fate.[24]

Asa's struggle with the Cushites is told in terms very reminiscent of 1 Chr 5. The defeat is no less decisive and is described in a single clause (2 Chr 14:12): 'and there fell of the Cushites till none of them had life' (ויפל מכושים לאין להם מחיה), though a great quantity of booty is also reported. Klein inserts 'wounded' in his paraphrase: 'some fell wounded beyond recovery'.[25] It should be stressed that מחיה in the Asa story and חיים in the Amaziah story are the only instances of words related to חיה in all of non-synoptic Chronicles.[26] The behaviour of kings Asa and Amaziah described in non-synoptic Chronicles matches that of their ancestor David in non-synoptic Samuel: in his southern raids (1 Sam 27:9, 11) 'he left alive neither man nor woman' (איש ואשה

---

23. There are seven at most: 2 Chr 6:31; 10:6; 18:13//1 Kgs 8:40; 12:6; 22:14; and 2 Chr 23:11; 25:18, 25//2 Kgs 11:12; 14:9, 17 (*Life in Kings*, 29–38). The seventh is 1 Chr 11:8, arguably part of a more original account of David taking Jerusalem than 2 Sam 5:6–9 (A. Graeme Auld, *1 & II Samuel*, OTL [Louisville: Westminster John Knox, 2011], 395–399).

24. The final synoptic instance of חיה was no less influential on the development of the book of Kings. I have argued that Amaziah's 15-year survival was the model for Hezekiah's survival from Sennacherib's invasion in his 14th year to his own death in the 29th year (*Life in Kings*, 184).

25. Ralph W. Klein, 2 Chronicles. Hermeneia (Minneapolis: Fortress, 2012), 208.

26. Given that the Chronicler did add forms of חיה twice to the source-material he shared with Sam-Kgs, it seems unlikely that he also stripped out of his source more than one hundred instances of this word. It is more likely that he knew a shorter and earlier form of the book of Kings that did not yet contain them.

ולא יחיה). The cases of Asa and Amaziah are cited here partly to caution against Braun's rendering of נפש אדם in 1 Chr 5:21b – 'together with one hundred thousand *men whom they took alive*'.[27] The Chronicler, supposing he was consistent in his usage, would have used some form of חיה to convey that meaning.

נפש and חיים are familiar in HB in poetic parallel, repeatedly so in Job 33.[28] Yet in Chronicles, these terms, each only sparsely used, are never found in proximity, whether in synoptic or non-synoptic contexts. While חיים largely corresponds to Latin *vita*, נפש in Chronicles might better be represented by *vitalitas*. In the case of the Transjordanians and Hagrites, booty is reported before casualties. The booty includes humans (נפש אדם) who, like the other livestock, will be found useful and not simply led off to a second stage of slaughter.

5. Development in 1 Chronicles 5:1–26

There are clear signs of development within this first section of 1 Chr 5. As in Num 32 and Josh 22, it appears that half-Manasseh has been added secondarily to Reuben (and Gad).[29]

5.1 From Reuben alone to Reuben/Gad/half-Manasseh

The account of joint action by Reuben/Gad/half-Manasseh in vv 18–22 – before half-Manasseh has even been mentioned as a separate unit – reuses each element of vv 9b-10 except for the specifics of place ('in the land of Gilead', 9b) and time ('in the days of Saul', 10a).

	1 Chr 5:9–10	>>5:18–22	
9b	כי מקניהם רבו בארץ גלעד		
10b	בימי שאול עשו מלחמה עם־ההגראים	ויעשו מלחמה עם־ההגריאים	19a
	ויפלו בידם	וינתנו בידם ההגריאים	20a
		וישבו מקניהם	21a

---

27. Section 2 above.

28. The densest cluster is in Job 33:20, 22, 28, 30; but there are several other instances in Job – 7:15; 9:21; 10:1; 12:10; 36:14.

29. See section 3 above.

1 Chr 5:9–10 >>5:18–22 >>

22a כי־חללים רבים
נפלו

'They made war with the Hagrites' (10a/19a) ends with the enemy 'in their hands' (10a/20a). But 'their possessions' at the start of 9b is resumed only in 21a, while the associated כי ... רבו (9b) is not resumed till 22a by כי ... רבים, where 'they fell' also resumes 10a. Time and place are not overlooked in this expansive retelling. However, they are apparently only rather loosely suggested in the concluding words (22b): 'and they settled instead of them[30] till the exile' – see further section 5.2 below.

Immanuel Benzinger already noted the link with Hagrites in 5:10.[31] Klein observes that '[t]he vague expansion of Reuben into the lands of the Hagrites in v. 10 is modified in vv. 21–22 by the acquisition of an enormous amount of booty and the notice that the two and one-half Transjordanian tribes settled in their territory'.[32] However, his further comment is rather odd: that '[t]he word "livestock" מקניהם echoes the abundant "cattle" מקניהם of the Reubenites in v. 9'.[33] Such a shift in rendering is certainly anticipated in LXX (and differently in B and L); but it seems perverse to translate מקניהם differently *precisely where* a relevant link is being asserted.

LXX^B		LXX^L	
5:9	κτήνη	5:9	κτήνη
5:21	ἀποσκευὴν	5:21	κτήσεις

We are not dealing with a simple expansion or supplementation of the earlier note. It is more like a 'midrashic' development of the conclusion of the section on Reuben. And this is not unique within 1 Chr 5:1–26. The still earlier note (5:6) about the Assyrian king exiling a Reubenite prince is reapplied to the exile of the Reubenites, Gadites, and half-tribe of Manasseh as the development of the whole section ends (5:26). In Amar's account of the narrative as chiastic, 'the exile of the two and a half tribes' (25–26) corresponds to 'Reuben ... deprived of

---

30. וישבו תחתיהם is anticipated in 1 Chr 4:41. Cf וישבו תחתם in Deut 2:12, 21, 22, 23 – also in a Transjordanian context.

31. Immanuel Benzinger, *Die Bücher der Chronik*. KHAT XX (Tübingen: Mohr Siebeck, 1901), 20.

32. Klein, 158.

33. Klein, 168.

his birthright' (1–2).³⁴ These opening verses of the section on Reuben are of course also secondary: the opening words of v. 1 are recapitulated in v. 3. Amar also notes unique links between the core account of Reuben and the preceding report on Simeon as also between Reuben and Levi. As to the first, both 4:38 and 5:6 use נשיא 'prince' and both 4:38–40 and 5:9–10 'describe an increase in population and livestock'.³⁵ And, as to the second, 5:6 and 5:41 are the only mentions of a *single* person taken into exile.³⁶ The links he notes might preserve evidence of a Simeon-Reuben-Levi textual substratum, that was developed later into the Transjordanian/Levite pairing explored in section 3 above. These were after all the three senior sons of Jacob listed before Judah in Gen 29:32–35; 35:23.

Amar himself does not venture into literary-historical remarks about 1 Chr 5:1–26. However, I find in his own remark that '[t]he exile of the two and a half tribes is mentioned in 2 Kgs 15:29' an echo of how the author of 5:18–22, 25–26 read 5:3–10.³⁷ The verse in Kings does not in fact mention Reuben, Gad, or half-Manasseh: it lists Gilead as one of several areas of Israel taken from Pekah by Tiglath-Pileser and exiled. It is because of Amar's prior knowledge that he reads all these tribes into a mention of Gilead. Somewhat similarly, the author of 1 Chr 5:1–26 expansively re-presented 5:3–10 in light of his knowledge of all the Transjordanian tribes. Whatever prompted the author of the longer report to produce an account of joint action by 'the sons of Reuben and Gad and half of the tribe of Manasseh', much of the content was developed from a very local source. The source of much of the rest was also close to hand.

5.2 אדם, נפש, AND שבה IN SOLOMON'S PRAYER

נפש אדם combines two common Hebrew words. It is of course possible that these were paired more frequently in classical Hebrew, even though this is rarely attested in HB. The author of 1 Chr 5:21 may even have been familiar with the passages already reviewed in Ezekiel or Leviticus or Numbers. But the more important question is not whether the Chronicler knew these texts, but whether in this detail he was influenced by them. We have already noted that 1 Chr 5:18–22 and 5:26 were spun in part from threads sourced very locally in 1 Chr 5:6, 9b–10a.

There are also several close links between this 'midrash' and the seventh and last request in Solomon's long prayer (2 Chr 6:36–39//1

---

34. Amar, 365.
35. Amar, 359.
36. Amar, 363.
37. Amar, 359 (n. 6).

Kgs 8:46–50a). Whether as part of the familiar book of Kings (the consensus view) or as one element of an older draft of Kings (my own view), Solomon's long prayer was part of the Chronicler's major source. נפש and אדם are both used in this final petition – separately. More significantly, the prayer includes alongside אדם (6:36) and נפש (6:38) the only synoptic instances of the verb שבה: twice in qal (36) and once in niphal (37). Not only so – a feature of this petition is the juxtaposition of the common and also assonant verb שוב ([re-]turn) with this repeated verb שבה (capture): והשיבו and ושבו are examples of שוב in v. 37, and נשבו and שבים of שבה; and in v. 38, ישבי is again related to שוב, but שבו and שבים to שבה.[38] Modelled on Solomon's intricate play, the 'midrash' concludes (5:22b) equally skilfully: עד־הגולה וישבו תחתיהם (and they dwelt in their place till the exile). גולה (exile) names the background implied in Solomon's plea; and וישבו (dwelt) is no less assonant with שבה than Solomon's שוב.

Num 31 also uses both שבה (v. 9) and נפש אדם (vv. 35, 40, 46), but not in the same immediate context. Then, though a long chapter, it uses neither of the assonant – and common – verbs שוב and ישב. Only Solomon's prayer in all of HB, like 1 Chr 5, uses both אדם and נפש (though not in actual combination), with שבה in close proximity.

6. Some conclusions

6.1 1 Chronicles 5 in light of Numbers and Joshua

Israel's Levites and the tribes east of the Jordan are odd associates from several points of view. Yet they share an important link that can be stated both negatively and positively. Neither has a share in the division of land west of the Jordan and both have requirements for grazing livestock. The holdings (מקנה) of the Transjordanians are described in terms of animals, while the Levites have a need for pasture (מגרש) near their appointed cities.

These two groups come to the fore in the final chapters of Numbers as joint exceptions within a 12-tribe Israel: counted once in Num 1 and again in Num 26 after forty years, this Israel is now facing the historical and topographical realities of settlement in a promised land west of the Jordan. In Josh 13–22, their exceptional situation is described before and after the division of that western land of promise; but in 1 Chr 5–6 they are listed at the heart of the people, between south (1 Chr 4) and north (7–8). For all that they are handled side by side in

---

38. Non-synoptic 2 Chr 28:11 repeats the wordplay: השביה אשר שביתם מאחיכם והשיבו.

Numbers and Joshua as well as at the start of Chronicles, there is one major difference in the Chronicler's treatment of the two exceptional groups. Levites and priests will play a large role throughout Chronicles while the Transjordanians are restricted to 1 Chronicles:[39] they do not reappear in the text after the death of David has been reported. This textual disappearance – the 'actual' disappearance will not occur till much later – may support Amar's reading the Transjordanian exile as one without return.

The inter-relatedness of Num 32, Josh 22, and 1 Chr 5 as they present the Transjordanians does not simply belong to the final stage in the development of these texts. There is some evidence in each that the half-tribe of Manasseh has been added to a prior Reuben-Gad pairing. The materials in 1 Chr 5:18–22, 25–26 about the eastern tribes as a group are additional to the traditions about the three separate units. A key source of their wording is the section on Reuben (5:3–10). Then 1 Chr 5:26 states that the easterners were exiled because of מעל, while Josh 22 debates such a charge against them and finally rejects it. The Chronicler may have misremembered the narrative in Joshua or disagreed with it. Alternatively, as suggested above, the extended narrative in Josh 22 may have taken the brief note reported in Chronicles as the opportunity for an extended discussion of centre and periphery, of the legitimacy or otherwise of (cultic) life outside the western heartland. I am no longer committed to the view that the list of Levitic cities in 1 Chr 6 was the source of Josh 21; but I still find it equally unlikely that Josh 21 (MT or LXX) was the source of the list in 1 Chr 6. The ideal number 48, stated in Num 35 (4 cities from each of 12 tribes), has been imposed on a prior list which it cannot fit: Judah and Simeon have 9 cities and the Aaronites 13.[40]

In most of Num 31 (in vv. 11, 26, 28, 30, 47), the term for human (as distinct from animal) is simply אדם. But in the supplementary section about taxation (vv. 32–46) this is replaced (in vv. 35, 40, 46) by נפש אדם (human [person?]). The end of the supplement is marked by recapitulating much of vv. 30–31 in v. 47, including a return to using the simple אדם. If the author of the so-called midrash in 1 Chr 5:18–22 did draw on the expanded text of Num 31–32 with its variation between אדם and נפש אדם, then his נפש אדם too may signify little different from אדם; and, even if נפש does have its own significance within the pairing, it will simply mean 'person' or 'individual'.[41]

---

39. 1 Chr 6:48, 63; 11:42; 12:9, 15, 38; 26:32; 27:16, 21.

40. A. Graeme Auld, "The Cities in Joshua 21: The Contribution of Textual Criticism," in *Textus XV* (1990), 141–152 (reprinted in *Joshua Retold. Synoptic Perspectives* [Edinburgh: T&T Clark, 1998], 49–62).

41. *As…ainsi que cent mille personnes* in La Bible: traduction oecuménique,

6.2 VICTORY AND BOOTY AND LIFE IN CHRONICLES

In the victory story of Amaziah, continued living (חיים) on the part of the vanquished is mentioned only to be immediately extinguished. In the victory story of Asa, life/survival (מחיה) is mentioned only to be denied. These, we need to remember, are the only two instances of חיה/'life' in non-synoptic Chronicles; and, in the Chronicler's version of the story of Jerusalem's monarchs, both Asa and Amaziah came to a bad end. However, for the two-and-a-half tribes east of the Jordan, 100,000 נפש אדם are a vital human resource.

The victory-plus-booty report in 1 Chr 5:18–22 is the first in a whole series of such narratives in Chronicles; yet it is also distinct from those that follow. It states precise thousands of animals and humans captured while other reports simply claim 'large numbers'. Then, even within the sub-group of three that deal with the issue of continued existence for the defeated humans, the report about the Transjordanians takes its own path. Defeated Edomites equal in number to those who died in battle do leave the field 'alive' (חיים), though only to be killed elsewhere. As for the defeated Kushites, no 'life' (מחיה) survived. The Chronicler took over from his source only a small number of forms related to חיה. It is only in these two notes that Chronicles adds to this already sparing usage; and in one of them חית השדה and ויחי were already part of the inherited synoptic context (2 Kgs 14:9, 17//2 Chr 25:18, 25). However, the continuation of human life after the Hagrite defeat in 1 Chr 5:21 is differently expressed. Here the Chronicler uses שבנ, a term similarly rare in both synoptic and non-synoptic Chronicles. 'Life' (חיים\מחיה) denotes the opposite of immediate death meted out by the troops of Amaziah or Asa. But human נפש has potential as a useful labour force. The Chronicler made at least a lexical distinction between the battlefield actions of the eastern tribes and of two kings in Jerusalem. Whether he intended thereby an ethical distinction is hard to determine. Unlike Achar/n before them (1 Chr 2:7) or Saul after them (10:13–14), their terrible fault (מעל) is left unspecified (5:25).

6.3 A 'MIDRASH' INDEBTED TO SOLOMON

Two features of 1 Chr 5 do invite comparison with Num 31: specification of booty-totals unique within Chronicles; and the use of נפש [אדם]. However, three further features of 1 Chr 5 – in addition to uniquely sharing the keywords אדם, נפש, and שבה – suggest an even closer relationship with the conclusion of Solomon's long prayer at the dedication of the temple: (1) The assonant play by Solomon on שבה and שוב is echoed in 1 Chr 5 by play on שבה with ישב. (2) The formula 'with all his/their heart and שפנ' from the source-prayer (2 Chr 6:38) is repeated almost verbatim three times in non-synoptic Chronicles – Solomon's words were clearly important to this author.[42] (3) Several other elements of vv. 18–22 and vv. 25–26 are also midrash-like developments, in their case of material in vv. 1–10. In the source text, נפש and אדם both have a distinct role. That makes it more likely that they retain a separate function in 1 Chr 5:21 and that combined נפש אדם was not simply, as in the extension to Num 31, an expanded alternative to אדם.

Typical of many key synoptic terms in the older book of Jerusalem's kings, the four instances of נפש come in two pairs, with each member of the pair relating to a different king.[43]

1a	1 Chr 11:19 (//2 Sam 23:17)	כי בנפשותם הביאום
1b	2 Chr 1:11 (//1 Kgs 3:11)	ולא־שאלת את נפש שנאיך
2a	2 Chr 6:38 (//1 Kgs 8:48)	ושבו אליך בכל־לבם ובכל־נפשם
2b	2 Chr 34:31 (//2 Kgs 23:3)	בכל־לבבו ובכל־נפשו

(1) David refuses to drink water brought by his heroes from Bethlehem at cost of their lives and Yahweh praises Solomon in his vision at Gibeon for not requesting the life of those who hate him.

(2) In each of the second pair, נפש reinforces לב:[44] Solomon asks Yahweh to listen if his future exiled people commit *their whole hearts and lives* in turning back to him and Josiah covenants *with his whole heart and life* to follow Yahweh.

The non-synoptic usage of each in Chronicles nicely illustrates the thesis of organic development from the synoptic core.[45] Four of the five non-synoptic instances maintain the synoptic inheritance or modify it only minimally:

---

42. Japhet rightly finds the usages in 1 Chr 22:19 and 28:9 'characteristic of the Chronicler' (p. 493, cf. 402), yet describes 2 Chr 15:12 as borrowing from a Deuteronomistic phrase (p. 726).

43. *Life in Kings*, 92–93 included 29 significant pairings. These נפש-pairs are two of more than 130 listed in "Tracing the Writing of Kings with Nadav Na'aman and Klaus-Peter Adam," to be published in SJOT 35, 2021.

44. One half of all the synoptic occurrences of 'heart' are found in Solomon's prayer: 2 Chr 6:7, 8, 8, 14, 30, 37, 38//1 Kgs 8:17, 18, 18, 23, [38,] 39, 47, 48. Of these, it is the culminating instance that is paired with נפש.

45. The thrust of my work on Sam-Kgs and Chr has been less interested in Chr as such and more in what comparison between Chr and Sam-Kgs helps us to understand about Sam-Kgs: both Sam-Kgs and Chr being organic developments from a much

– 1 Chr 11:19 simply repeats the synoptic usage within the same verse.

– 1 Chr 22:19; 28:9; 2 Chr 15:12 repeat or lightly modify the use of נפש to reinforce לב that is already synoptic in 2 Chr 6:38; 34:31 and is most familiar now in the Shema and related texts.

If this short narrative builds on material from the source of Chronicles, and specifically the water brought to David from Bethlehem or the seventh request in Solomon's prayer, נפש אדם will carry the stronger sense of 'live humans' or even 'lively humans'.

An ancient writer could re-present details of a more ancient report about Reuben in his own account of the two-and-a-half tribes. A modern scholar familiar with Numbers and Joshua could read Gilead in Kings as a reference to these two-and-a-half tribes. And it is natural for other contemporary readers, familiar with the categories Primary History (Genesis-Kings) and Secondary History (Chronicles-Ezra-Nehemiah), to give priority to Numbers and Joshua when studying similar materials in Chronicles.[46] However, this essay has advised double caution in relation to the development of 1 Chr 5:1–26. (1) Even the latest elements in this narrative are derived from earlier material within Chronicles. (2) While there are clear links with late elements in both Num 31 and Josh 22, the direction of influence in each case was arguably from 1 Chr 5 to these 'partner texts'. Each such relationship between materials in the so-called 'Primary' and so-called 'Secondary' Histories must be assessed on its own merits.[47]

---

earlier book of Kings. The book of Chronicles may be one of the latest books in HB. However, in several cases I suspect that it also contains evidence about earlier stages in the so-called 'Primary History' (Genesis-Kings). See further "Counting Sheep, Sins, and Sour Grapes: The Primacy of the Primary History?" (n. 46 below).

46. At the end of 'Counting Sheep, Sins, and Sour Grapes: The Primacy of the Primary History?', in Alastair G. Hunter and Philip R. Davies [eds], *Sense and Sensitivity: Essays on Reading the Bible in Memory of Robert Carroll*, JSOTS 348, 2002, 63–72, I probed these terms. 'Primary' in English is ambiguous: it can refer to greater authority (primacy) or simply greater age. Torah and Former Prophets (the Primary History) certainly have greater (canonical) authority; but does that necessarily derive from the greater age of all their materials?

47. Whichever way the influence runs between the 'generations' (תולדות) at the start of Genesis and the start of Chronicles, the fact that 1 Chr 1 and Gen 5 open with the same genealogy of Adam and that Gen 5 has a formal 'title' ('*This is the book* of the generations of Adam') may preserve evidence that 'the generations of heaven and earth' (Gen 1–4) are a later preface to the 'first' book of the Bible (A. Graeme Auld, '*imago dei* in Genesis', ExT 116, 2005, 259–262).

II. Dissonance, Discontinuity, and Alteration

The High Priest in Chronicles and in the Priestly Traditions of the Pentateuch

Christophe Nihan

1. Introduction

The high priest in Chronicles has not been the subject of much research. The main publications on the topic consist of a chapter in Deborah Rooke's 2000 monograph,[1] as well as an article by Steven J. Schweitzer from 2003.[2] Even studies devoted to the cult and the temple in Chronicles often pay minimal attention to the high priest, and sometimes even no attention at all. Furthermore, while the connections between descriptions of the cult in Chronicles and in the priestly traditions of the Pentateuch have often been addressed in the scholarly literature, the parallels and differences between the image of the high priest in these two corpora do not appear to have been subjected to a detailed analysis. The following essay will focus on two related themes: (a) the characterization of the high priest in Chronicles, and (b) its relationship to the description of the high priest in the priestly traditions of the Pentateuch.

Like many other topics in Chronicles, one key issue has to do with understanding the selection involved in the mentionings of high priests. The genealogy of Levi in 1 Chronicles 5:27–6:66 includes a comprehensive list of the high priests following Aaron, from Eleazar to Jehosadaq (1 Chr 5:27–41). Yet the Chronicler's account of the Judean monarchy in 1 Chronicles 10 to 2 Chronicles 36 only includes selected references to some high priests, as the following table shows:

---

1. Deborah W. Rooke, *Zadok's Heirs: The Role and Development of High Priesthood in Ancient Israel*, OTM (Oxford: Oxford University Press, 2000), 184–218.

2. Steven J. Schweitzer, "The High Priest in Chronicles: An Anomaly in a Detailed Description of the Temple Cult," *Biblica* 84 (2003): 388–402.

High priest	King	Text in Chronicles
Zadoq	David	1 Chr 12:29; 15:11; 16:39–40; 18:16; 24:3–6; 24:31; 27:17; 29:22
Amariah	Jehoshaphat	2 Chr 19:11
Jehoiada	Joash	2 Chr 22:10–24:16
Azariah (I)	Uzziah	2 Chr 26:16–21
Azariah (II)	Hezekiah	2 Chr 31:10
Hilkiah	Josiah	2 Chr 34:8–28; 35:8

It is probable that this difference is due to the fact that the high priestly genealogy in 1 Chronicles 5:27–41 was not part of the Chronicler's main composition but was added later, as it has often been suggested.[3] Yet even so, it remains significant that the addition of the genealogy did not lead to any sort of systematic referencing of the high priests in the Chronicler's account. Instead, within 1 Chronicles 10 to 2 Chronicles 36 references to the high priest of Jerusalem remain highly selective, as the Table above exemplifies. It is not easy, at first sight, to understand the logic underlying this selection, if there is any. Assuming a traditional view of the relationship between Chronicles and Kings,[4] it is likely that the Chronicler's references to the high priest are influenced by the reuse of materials from Kings, where a similar figure – the chief-priest of Jerusalem – is already mentioned. Yet this hardly accounts for all the references to the high priest in Chronicles, since comparison with Kings shows that Chronicles can either omit mentionings of the high priest or introduce new mentionings that have no parallels in Kings. Thus, for example, Chronicles ignores all mentionings of Zadok in connection with Solomon,[5] with the result that in

---

3. See, e. g., Thomas Willi, *Die Chronik als Auslegung*, FRLANT 106 (Göttingen: Vandenhoeck & Ruprecht, 1972), 214; and with more details Magnar Kartveit, *Motive und Schichten der Landtheologie in 1 Chronik 1–9*, ConBOT 28 (Stockholm: Almqvist & Wiksell, 1989), 77–87. In this view, the genealogy in 1 Chr 5:27–41 is a later addition within the Levitical genealogies, expanding upon the shorter list in 1 Chr 6:38–41. Alternatively, other scholars consider that the list in 1 Chr 5:27–41 is more likely to be chronologically prior; see, especially, Gary Knoppers, *1 Chronicles 1–9: A New Translation with Introduction and Commentary*, AB 12 (New York et al.: Doubleday, 2003), 407–10, with additional references.

4. Specifically, I am assuming that the authors of Chronicles knew a composition comparable to Samuel and Kings, but which was still transmitted in a Hebrew form distinct from the MT of these two books. For further details, see my discussion in Christophe Nihan, "Textual Fluidity and Rewriting in Parallel Traditions. The Case of Samuel and Chronicles," *JAJ* 4 (2013): 186–209.

5. Cf. 1 Kgs 1:8, 26, 32, 34, 38, 39, 44, 45; 2:35; 4:2, 4. In Chronicles, the only

Chronicles Zadok is almost exclusively associated with David's reign. Conversely, Chronicles introduces an account about the high priest Azariah under the reign of king Uzziah (2 Chr 26:16–21), of which the parallel account in Kings knows nothing. In short, the mentioning of high priests in Chronicles cannot be simply explained by comparison with the evidence in Kings. Rather, in order to understand this, we need to take into account the way in which high priests are characterized in Chronicles. The following discussion will seek to identify some major trends in this characterization.

2. THE HIGH PRIEST AND THE SANCTUARY IN CHRONICLES

2.1 THE HIGH PRIEST AND THE RITUALS PERFORMED INSIDE THE SANCTUARY

Except in the case of Jehoiada (2 Chr 22:10–24:16), who deserves a specific discussion (see below §3), most of the references to the high priest in Chronicles associate him closely to the sanctuary and the rituals performed there. In particular, various passages mention the high priest in contexts where sacrifices are performed. This view is already introduced in 1 Chronicles 6:34, a passage which is part of the genealogies and lists comprising 1 Chronicles 1–9.

1 Chronicles 6:34

ואהרן ובניו מקטירים על מזבח העולה ועל מזבח הקטרת לכל מלאכת קדש הקדשים ולכפר על ישראל ככל אשר צוה משה עבד האלהים:

> Aaron and his sons burnt (offerings) on the altar of burnt offering and on the altar of incense, (to perform) all the work of the most holy place, to effect *kippēr* (removal) for Israel, according to all what Moses the servant of the deity had commanded.

This verse is aptly located at the junction between the genealogies of the Levitical clans (v. 1–33) and the subsequent genealogy of the Aaronite line (v. 35–38).[6] The description of Aaronite duties focuses on

---

context where Solomon and Zadoq are mentioned together is in 1 Chr 29:22, which relates Solomon's appointment as David's successor. Incidentally, it is also the last notice mentioning Zadoq in the context of David's and Solomon's reigns. Of course, this has to do with the fact that Chronicles omits Kings' account of David's succession in 1 Kgs 1–2, where most of the references to Zadoq are found. Even so, however, it remains striking that Chronicles never mentions Zadoq in connection with Solomon's reign after the notice in 1 Chr 29:22.

6. For more details on the location of 1 Chr 6:34 and its significance, see, e. g., Sara Japhet, *I & II Chronicles. A Commentary*, OTL (Louisville: Westminster John Knox, 1993), 156; and more recently Lars Maskow, *Tora in der Chronik: Studien zur*

the offering of burnt offerings and incense on the corresponding altars, which is summarized with the expression לכל מלאכת קדש הקדשים, "(to perform) all the work of the most holy place".[7] The mention of the "altar of incense" refers to the practice prescribed in Exodus 30:7–8, where Aaron is instructed to offer incense every morning and evening on this altar located inside the outer-sanctum.[8] This is confirmed by the fact that the end of the verse explicitly refers to the Mosaic legislation, including the priestly ritual instructions (אשר צוה משה עבד האלהים ככל). While Exodus 30 exclusively mentions Aaron, the high priest, in this context other passages indicate that the high priest could be accompanied by other Aaronite priests when he performed rituals inside the outer-sanctum.[9] Presumably, this is what 1 Chronicles 6:34 has in view when it states that this ritual was performed by "Aaron and his sons." The reference to the altar of burnt offering, for its part, may include in principle all the sacrifices offered by the priests on behalf of Israel. However, the parallel with the altar of incense suggests that 1 Chronicles 6:34 may well have in view the daily ritual prescribed in Exodus 29:38–42 (see further Num 28:3–8), according to which Aaron and his sons must offer a whole burnt offering and accompanying grain offerings every morning and evening in the courtyard of the temple. Finally, the reference to the priests effecting the "removal" (of impurities, sins, etc.) from the community in the second half of the verse (ולכפר על ישראל) takes up a notion already present in the priestly traditions of the Pentateuch, where priests are described as performing *kippēr* (removal) by means of sacrifices.[10] In short, 1 Chronicles

---

Rezeption des Pentateuchs in den Chronikbüchern, FRLANT 274 (Göttingen: Vandenhoeck & Ruprecht, 2019), 281–2.

7. The lamed in לכל must probably be construed as expressing finality (thus, e. g., Thomas Willi, *Chronik* [*1 Chr 1,1–10,14*], BKAT XXIV/1 [Neukirchen-Vluyn: Neukirchener Verlag, 2009], 230). While some scholars (e. g., Knoppers, *1 Chronicles 1–9*, 425) opt to translate the phrase קדש הקדשים to mean "Holy of Holies," the formulation of this verse implies that its description refers to more than the rituals performed inside the inner-sanctum specifically. Therefore, it is arguably preferable to understand this phrase in a non-technical sense, as denoting the entirety of the temple compound. This usage of the phrase קדש הקדשים to denote the whole sanctuary is admittedly infrequent. It could be a case of metonymy, in which the sanctuary is designated through its most holy parts.

8. On this passage, and the offering of incense as a high priestly prerogative, see, e. g., the discussion by Menahem Haran, *Temples and Temple-Service in Ancient Israel* (Oxford: Clarendon, 1978), 208.

9. See, especially, Exod 27:21 concerning the daily disposal of the oil for the luminary. This is also suggested by Exod 31:20, which mentions both Aaron and his sons going inside the tent of meeting.

10. For this interpretation, see, e. g., Willi, *Chronik 1,1–10,14*, 230. For a recent restatement about the meaning of *kipper* in this context, see the helpful discussion by Marskow, *Tora*, 282–3.

6:34 provides a short but essential description of priestly duties, which claims a significant degree of continuity with the Mosaic legislation. The duties and prerogatives of the Aaronite priests are primarily defined in terms of the sacrifices they perform, and especially the rituals comprising the daily offering of burnt offerings and incense (Exod 29:38–42 and 30:7–8 respectively). Both rituals are placed under the authority of the high priest, but 1 Chronicles 6:34 emphasizes these rituals as a collaborative performance involving all Aaronite priests ("Aaron and his sons") rather than the sole high priest.

A very similar view is found a little later in the Chronicler's account, namely, in 1 Chronicles 16:39–40.[11] David, after bringing the Ark to Jerusalem, appoints Zadoq (who had been only briefly mentioned until now in the account, 1 Chr 12:29 and 15:11) and "his brothers the priests" to watch over the tabernacle which, at this point of the narrative, is staying in Gibeon according to Chronicles (see further 2 Chr 1:3–6; and for the reference to Gibeon, 1 Kgs 3:4).[12] Zadoq and the other priests are then appointed with the following task:

1 Chronicles 16:39–40

39 ואת צדוק הכהן ואחיו הכהנים לפני משכן יהוה בבמה אשר בגבעון:
40 להעלות עלות ליהוה על מזבח העלה תמיד לבקר ולערב ולכל הכתוב בתורת יהוה אשר צוה על ישראל:

> [39]Zadok the priest and his brothers the priests were before Yhwh's dwelling in the high place at Gibeon [40]to sacrifice burnt offerings to Yhwh upon the altar, the regular morning and evening burnt offering, according to all that is written in the Torah of Yhwh, which he prescribed to Israel.[13]

As in 1 Chronicles 6:34, the reference to the Mosaic legislation is explicit,[14] and the focus of priestly ritual activity is on the daily burnt offering (Exod 29:38–42; Num 28:3–8). The syntax of verse 40a is somewhat ambiguous as regards the relationship between the proposi-

---

11. The continuity between the conception stated in 1 Chr 16:39–40 with the earlier notice in 1 Chr 6:34 has already been noted by various scholars. Cf., e. g., Japhet, *Chronicles*, 158.

12. On this issue, see my discussion in Christophe Nihan, "Cult Centralization and the Torah Traditions in Chronicles," in *The Fall of Jerusalem and the Rise of the Torah*, ed. Peter Dubovský, Dominik Markl & Jean-Pierre Sonnet, FAT 107 (Tübingen: Mohr Siebeck, 2016), 253–88, here 267–75.

13. G preserves here a long plus, which is very likely secondary: ἐν χειρὶ Μωυσῆ τοῦ θεράποντος τοῦ θεοῦ, "by the hand of Moses, the servant of God."

14. Despite the recent detailed argument by Maskow, *Tora*, 73–4, I remain unconvinced that it is necessary to understand the reference to Moses' Torah as including all of v. 39–40, rather than the performance of the daily burnt offering specifically, as most scholars tend to assume. For the present discussion, however, this point is not decisive.

tion תמיד לבקר ולערב העלות עלות ליהוה על מזבח and the following clause העלה, referring to the daily burnt offering. Presumably, this construction should be understood in the sense that the primary duty of Zadoq and other priests is toward the continuous (תמיד) burnt offering presented twice every day to the deity, although this does not preclude the inclusion of other, more occasional burnt offerings presented in specific circumstances (see Lev 1).[15] Whether the omission of the offering of incense, which is mentioned together with the daily burnt offerings in 1 Chronicles 6:34, is significant, is difficult to say. It may have to do with the fact that the tabernacle has not yet arrived in Jerusalem, and that the cult is still missing some key components, such as the Ark.

At any rate, this brief episode highlights two related concerns of the Chronicler, namely, (a) that David already instituted a regular sacrificial cult for the wilderness sanctuary at Gibeon, long before that sanctuary was brought to Jerusalem by his son, Solomon; and (b) that he did so by establishing Zadoq and his kinsmen as the only legitimate agents of this sacrificial cult. A parallel is thus established with the conception stated in 1 Chronicles 6:34: just like "Aaron and his sons" were appointed by Moses to perform the required rituals in the tabernacle at Mount Sinai, "Zadoq and his brothers" were appointed by David when the tabernacle was in Gibeon. In this conception, the sacrificial monopoly enjoyed by Zadoq and the priests under his command goes back to the reign of David himself, and predates the building of the temple under Solomon (see 2 Chr 2–7). However, neither David nor subsequent kings have any part in the rituals performed daily at the sanctuary. This point is further emphasized by the split in the description of two kinds of ritual performance at this point in the Chronicles narrative: while Zadoq and the other priests are left in Gibeon to perform the daily sacrifices, David is leading the procession bringing the Ark back to Jerusalem (1 Chr 15:25–16:36).

A further key text as regards the sacrificial monopoly of priests in general, and the high priest in particular, is found in the account of 2 Chronicles 26:16–21 narrating the origins of king Uzziah's skin disease. According to this account, Uzziah, in the course of his reign, became arrogant and committed a sacrilege (מעל) by entering the temple in order to offer incense on the altar of incense, despite the warning addressed by the high priest Azariah and the priests accompanying him. As a result, he was struck by Yhwh with a form of serious skin disease (צרעת), and forced to live secluded the rest of his days.[16]

---

15. According to 2 Chr 1, Solomon himself offered whole burnt offerings upon the altar in Gibeon; cf. 2 Chr 1:6.

16. Like most scholars, I regard the text as a literary unity. For a different view, see Zwickel, *Räucherkult*, 321–322; for a defense of the text's unity, see Steins,

2 Chronicles 26:16–21

16וכחזקתו גבה לבו עד להשחית וימעל ביהוה אלהיו ויבא אל היכל יהוה להקטיר על מזבח הקטרת: 17ויבא אחריו עזריהו הכהן ועמו כהנים ליהוה שמונים בני חיל: 18ויעמדו על עזיהו המלך ויאמרו לו לא לך עזיהו להקטיר ליהוה כי לכהנים בני אהרן המקדשים להקטיר צא מן המקדש כי מעלת ולא לך לכבוד מיהוה אלהים: 19ויזעף עזיהו ובידו מקטרת להקטיר ובזעפו עם הכהנים והצרעת זרחה במצחו לפני הכהנים בבית יהוה מעל למזבח הקטרת: 20ויפן אליו עזריהו כהן הראש וכל הכהנים והנה הוא מצרע במצחו ויבהלוהו משם וגם הוא נדחף לצאת כי נגעו יהוה: 21ויהי עזיהו המלך מצרע עד יום מותו וישב בית החפשות מצרע כי נגזר מבית יהוה ויותם בנו על בית המלך שופט את עם הארץ:

> [16]But as he became strong, his heart grew proud, to the point of acting corruptly. [17]He acted disloyally toward Yhwh his god, and went into the temple of Yhwh to burn incense on the altar of incense. [17]Azariah the priest came after him, and with him eighty priests of Yhwh, men of valor. [18]They stood by Uzziah the king and said to him: "It is not for you, Uzziah, to burn incense to Yhwh, but for the priests, sons of Aaron, who sanctify themselves to offer incense. Go out from the sanctuary, for you have acted disloyally, and there will be for you no honor from Yhwh Elohim!" [19]Uzziah became furious: he had a censer in his hand, and when he became furious with the priests, a skin-disease (*ṣāraʿat*) broke out on his forehead before the priests in the house of Yhwh, beside the altar of incense. [20]Azariah the high priest and all the priests turned toward him, and behold: he had become a *mĕṣōrāʿ* (one affected by skin disease) on his forehead. They hastened him out from there, and he himself hastened to go out, for Yhwh had struck him. [21]Uzziah the king remained a *mĕṣōrāʿ* until the day of his death. He lived in separate quarters,[18] a *mĕṣōrāʿ*, for he was banned from the house of Yhwh. His son Jotham was in charge of the palace and ruled over the people of the land.

The motif of Uzziah's skin disease was taken from Kings' account; the parallel is all the more obvious since v. 21 (and the last two words of v. 20) are virtually identical with 2 Kings 15:5. Presumably, as several authors have surmised, the Chronicler was faced with the contradiction between Uzziah's length of reign (usually a sign of divine favor) and the tradition that he was severely struck by the deity. Consequently, he provided in a quasi-midrashic way an explanation for this tension.[19] At the same time, and as is often the case in Chronicles, the sto-

---

Chronik, 408–414.

17. For this translation, and the interpretation of *lĕhašḥît* as an intransitive form in Chronicles, see Japhet, *Chronicles*, 885; Ralph W. Klein, *2 Chronicles: A Commentary*, Hermeneia (Minneapolis: Fortress Press, 2012), 367.

18. With the majority of commentators, I follow the Qere *ḥḥpšyt* instead of the Ketib *ḥḥpšwt*, cf. also 2 Kgs 15:5.

19. E.g., Klein, *2 Chronicles*, 377. Alternatively, some scholars have surmised that the Chronicler would have made use here of an older legend about Uzziah's leprosy; cf., e. g., Japhet, *Chronicles*, 877. While this view is possible, it is not likely,

ry also serves to make an important point about the respective roles of priests and kings. While the main obligation of kings is toward the temple, which they are expected to finance and renovate,[20] this gives them no right to perform rituals inside that temple. On the contrary, those rituals are the exclusive prerogative of the Aaronite priests, who are led by the high priest.

The nature of the sacrilege committed by Uzziah and its consequences are also remarkable and deserve a brief comment in the context of this essay. According to v. 16, Uzziah's intent is to offer incense on the altar of incense. As already mentioned above, in the priestly traditions of the Pentateuch the offering of incense on the altar located inside the outer-sanctum is a privilege of the high priest (Exod 30:7–8), although he can be accompanied by other priests (see above). Presumably, it is this kind of cooperative priestly performance supervised by the high priest that the account of Chronicles has in view when Azariah and the other priests declare that the offering of incense is a prerogative of "the priests who sanctify themselves", and not just the high priest. This would also explain why Azariah is accompanied by no less than eighty priests described as בני חיל, a term that can be rendered as "men of valor" but also "men of standing" (*scil.* among the priests).[21] In this way, the claim placed in the mouth of Azariah and the eighty priests is consistent with the priestly legislation of the Pentateuch; but whereas the priestly texts tend to emphasize the daily offering of incense as a prerogative of the high priest specifically, the account of 2 Chronicles 16 highlights instead the collective dimension of this ritual, which is performed by the Aaronite priesthood as a whole.

---

especially since the language and themes used in this account are typical of Chronicles. See also on this point the detailed discussion by Hugh G. M. Williamson, *1 and 2 Chronicles*, NCBC (London: Marshall, Morgan & Scott; Grand Rapids: Eerdmans, 1982), 338–9.

20. See, e. g., David's donations to the temple in 1 Chr 29:2–5. On the role of kings as patrons of the Jerusalem temple in Chronicles more generally, see also Jozef Tiňo, *King and Temple in Chronicles. A Contextual Approach to Their Relations*, FRLANT 234 (Göttingen: Vandenhoeck & Ruprecht, 2010).

21. This interpretation highlighting the collective dimension of the performance of the daily burning of incense would remain correct even if the motif of the eighty priests following Azariah inside the sanctuary is secondary, as recently argued by Maskow, *Tora*, 527, following an earlier suggestion by Japhet, *Chronicles*, 877. However, Japhet's argument regarding the possibly secondary character of the eighty-priests-motif relates to the source used by the Chronicler, not the present account in 2 Chr 26:16–21. Once this account is viewed as being entirely a literary creation by the Chronicler, as Maskow would accept, there is little evidence for this claim. At any rate, the point remains that the key statement voiced in v. 18 refers to "the priests, sons of Aaron" as responsible for the daily burning if incense, not just the high priest.

The interaction with the traditions of the Pentateuch, and especially with priestly texts, is not restricted to the description of Uzziah's transgression, however, but also extends to the king's punishment. As various authors have observed, the motif that Uzziah was struck while approaching Yhwh with a censer (מקטרת) is reminiscent of the story of Nadab and Abihu in Leviticus 10, as well as of the 250 chieftains led by the Levite Korach in Numbers 16. In addition, the fact that Uzziah is sanctioned for his sacrilege by a severe skin disease (צרעת) is reminiscent of the story of Miriam in Numbers 12.[22] The parallel with Leviticus 10 and Numbers 16 is especially significant, since, as I have argued elsewhere,[23] these two accounts form a system of sorts with the legislation on Yôm Kippur in Leviticus 16, highlighting the point that the offering of incense on a censer before the deity is a privilege restricted to the high priest, when he enters the inner-sanctum once every year in order to purify it (see Lev 16:12–13). It seems likely, therefore, that the motif of Uzziah's being struck while he was holding a censer was introduced by the Chronicler in order to establish a link not only with the priestly legislation on the daily offering of incense in Exodus 30:1–10 but also with the grand ceremony of Leviticus 16. Finally, the fact that Uzziah's skin disease appears on his "forehead" (במצחו) may allude to the place of the golden plate worn by Aaron in Exodus 28:38.[24] In this case, the allusion would strengthen the contrast between the high priest and the king, as well as the impossibility for the king to take over the high priest's role: Whereas Aaron's golden plate exemplifies both his holiness (since the plate is engraved with the inscription "holy to Yhwh") and his ability to "bear" the sin of the Israelites with regard to cultic transgressions (Exod 28:38),[25] Uzziah's skin-disease on his forehead publicly manifests his own fault, resulting in extreme uncleanness (cf. the treatment reserved to the *měṣorāʿ* in Lev 13–14).

If this reading is correct, it suggests that the account in 2 Chron-

---

22. For these parallels, see, especially, the recent and comprehensive discussion by Maskow, *Tora*, 524–42, esp. 525–6 and 529–32. Regarding the parallel with Num 12, Maskow notes, in particular, the phraseological connection between 2 Chr 26:20a and Num 12:10b (Maskow, *Tora*, 531).

23. See Christophe Nihan, *From Priestly Torah to Pentateuch: A Study in the Composition of Leviticus*, FAT II 25 (Tübingen: Mohr Siebeck, 2007), 585–6.

24. As suggested, e. g., by Japhet, Chronicles, 887; see also the detailed discussion by Maskow, *Tora*, 532–4.

25. On the difficulties raised by the interpretation of this verse, and the reference to the "bearing of sin," see the discussion in Christophe Nihan & Julia Rhyder, "Aaron's Vestments in Exodus 28 and Priestly Leadership," in *Debating Authority, Concepts of Leadership in the Pentateuch and the Former Prophets*, ed. Katharina Pyschny and Sarah Schulz, BZAW 507 (Berlin/Boston: De Gruyter, 2018), 45–67, here 59–61.

icles 26:16–21 implies a fairly complex interaction with the priestly traditions of the Pentateuch – or at least more complex than it has sometimes been assumed. The Chronicler's choice to relate Uzziah's sacrilege with the offering of incense takes up and continues P's conception of incense as a key "marker" of the high priest's exclusive status and privilege (Exod 30:7–8). This textual strategy is further reinforced through the contrast built with the ceremony of Leviticus 16, and possibly the allusion to the golden plate worn by Aaron on his forehead in Exodus 28. At the same time, the key speech placed in the mouth of Azariah and the other priests in v. 18 emphasizes the offering of incense as a *collective* priestly task, in a way that is unparalleled in P.

One should note at this point that the same phenomenon can be observed in another key passage in Chronicles, 2 Chronicles 13:11, a verse which is part of king Abijah's speech to Jeroboam's army in 2 Chronicles 13:5–12.[26] Abijah's speech, whose programmatic function in Chronicles has long been recognized, consists of two main parts.[27] The first part (v. 5–7) states that Yhwh gave the "kingship over Israel" to David and his sons, "forever", as a "covenant of salt", i. e., an everlasting covenant (see v. 5). The second part (v. 8–12) illustrates this claim by asserting that the only legitimate cult is located in the kingdom of Judah. Significantly enough, in Abijah's speech Judah's cultic legitimacy is demonstrated by the presence of Aaronite priests ("the sons of Aaron") performing the following tasks:

2 Chronicles 13:11

ומקטרים ליהוה עלות בבקר בבקר ובערב בערב וקטרת סמים ומערכת לחם על השלחן הטהור ומנורת הזהב ונרתיה לבער בערב בערב כי שמרים אנחנו את משמרת יהוה אלהינו ואתם עזבתם אתו:

They offer to Yhwh burnt offerings every morning and every evening, as well as fragrant incense; (they set out) the stacks of bread[28] upon the

---

26. On this account, see, especially, the study by Gary N. Knoppers, "'Battling against Yahweh': Israel's War against Judah in 2 Chr. 13:2–20," *RB* 100 (1993): 511–532.

27. The distinction between two main parts in Abijah's speech is generally acknowledged, although the exact division between these sections remains somewhat disputed. For a justification of the present division, see my discussion in Nihan, "Cult Centralization," 276 n. 86.

28. Hebrew *mʿrkt* appears to be a variant form of the term *maʿărākāh*, which normally refers to a row. However, since the passage appears to refer to the ritual for the bread of presence, this rendering makes little sense here, as noted by various commentators. Compare, in particular, the detailed discussion by Jacob Milgrom, *Leviticus 23–27: A New Translation with Introduction and Commentary* (AB 3B; New York: Doubleday, 2001), 2096, on Lev 24:6, 7, where the term *mʿrkt* is already used for the arrangement of the bread of presence.

pure table, together with the golden lampstands and its lamps, so that they may burn every evening. For we are keeping the service of Yhwh, our god, whereas you have forsaken him (2 Chr 13:11).

As it has often been observed, all the elements in this description correspond to the four daily rituals prescribed in the priestly legislation: the daily burnt offering (Exod 29:38–42); the daily offering of incense (Exod 30:7–8); the disposal of the "bread of the presence" (לחם פנים) upon the golden table located inside the inner-sanctum (Exod 25:30; further Lev 24:5–9); and finally, the burning of the oil of the luminary (Exod 27:20–21). In other words, Judah's cultic legitimacy is expressed in 2 Chronicles 13:11 in terms of the performance of the daily rituals which, in the priestly texts, are all placed under the authority of the high priest. Yet in this passage the high priest is not specifically mentioned, and the Chronicler emphasizes instead the *collective* nature of the performance of these rituals by the "sons of Aaron" (2 Chr 13:10), i. e., the Aaronite priests.[29]

2.2 OTHER HIGH PRIESTLY ROLES IN THE ADMINISTRATION OF THE SANCTUARY

The passages discussed so far concern the role of the high priest in connection with the rituals performed inside the sanctuary. Other passages in Chronicles, however, indicate that his authority extends to other matters pertaining to the sanctuary, including administrative and legal ones. The account of 2 Chronicles 19:4–11 concerning king Jehoshaphat's appointment of judges in every town of Judah and the creation of a high court in Jerusalem (cf. Deut 17:8–13)[30] concludes with the appointment of the high priest Amariah (2 Chr 19:11).

2 Chronicles 19:11a
והנה אמריהו כהן הראש עליכם לכל דבר יהוה וזבדיהו בן ישמעאל הנגיד לבית יהודה לכל דבר המלך ושטרים הלוים לפניכם
Amariah the chief priest will be over you in every matter concerning

---

29. The only alternative would be to understand the expression בני אהרן in 2 Chr 13:10 to refer to those descendants of Aaron who became high priests in Jerusalem specifically. However, such reading would be entirely inconsistent with the usage of this construct elsewhere in Chronicles, where it is always used to denote *all* the priests claiming descent from Aaron, not the high priest specifically. It also stands in tension with the use of בני אהרן in the previous verse (2 Chr 13:9), where this construct is clearly used in a broad, collective sense to denote priests collectively (note, in particular, the parallel in this verse with the Levites).

30. For a detailed analysis of the reception of Deut 17 in 2 Chr 19:4–11 (especially v. 8–11), see Sarah J.K. Pearce, *The Words of Moses. Studies in the Reception of Deuteronomy in the Second Temple Period* (TSAJ 152; Tübingen: Mohr Siebeck, 2013), 252–263; as well as Maskow, *Tora*, 163–182.

Yhwh, whereas Zebadiah the son of Ishmael, the leader of the house of Judah, will be over you in every matter concerning the king, and the Levites present with you shall be your officials.

The distinction between דבר יהוה, "the matter of Yhwh," and דבר המלך, "the matter of the king" is not entirely clear and has been the subject of some debate. While we must be careful not to project a modern, anachronistic distinction between "religious" and "secular" matters, which would have been unknown in Antiquity,[31] there is something to be said for the view that the reference to דבר יהוה and דבר המלך has to do primarily with the legal and administrative matters concerning the temple and the palace respectively.[32] If this interpretation is correct, the high priest Amariah is acknowledged as having authority over the Levites, the priests and the heads of the families who comprise the high court in Jerusalem (see 2 Chr 19:8) for all the judicial matters that pertain to the temple and its cult. Like Zebadiah, however, he remains subordinated to the king, who is responsible for his appointment. In fact, as Yigal Levin aptly points out, both men are best described as representatives of the king in the high court.[33]

A similar situation is reflected in subsequent passages of Chronicles. 2 Chronicles 23:18–19 describes Jehoiada assigning priests and Levites their duties in the temple. While this description concludes the narration of Joash's accession to the throne in 2 Chronicles 23, which gives a prominent place to Jehoiada (more on this below), the notice in v. 18–19 is consistent with the view already expressed in 2 Chronicles 19:11 according to which the high priest is responsible for the overall administration of the temple, and as such has authority (at least in principle) over the various priestly and Levitical classes. Additionally, another notice earlier in the same account, 2 Chronicles 23:8, also suggests that for the Chronicler the high priest was responsible to oversee the shifts of the Levitical groups active inside the temple.[34] According to 2 Chronicles 31:10, under Hezekiah the high priest Azariah was in charge of managing the sacred donation, or contribution (תרומה) brought by the community to the temple. Further in the account, the same Azariah is described as נגיד בית האלהים, "leader of the house of the god" (2 Chr 31:13), a title which is reminiscent

---

31. As rightly pointed out, e. g., by Steven L. McKenzie, *1–2 Chronicles*, AOTC (Nashville: Abingdon Press, 2004), 294.

32. Thus McKenzie, *1–2 Chronicles*, 294, who speaks of a distinction between "cultic" and "non-cultic." In effect, this seems to be the majority view among scholars, compare also, e. g., Yigal Levin, *The Chronicles of the Kings of Judah. 2 Chronicles 10–36: A New Translation and Commentary* (London: Bloomsbury T&T Clark, 2017), 132.

33. Levin, *Chronicles*, 132.

34. As pointed out, in particular, by Schweitzer, "High Priest," 398–9.

of Zebadiah's title as נגיד לבית יהודה, "leader of the house of Judah," in 2 Chronicles 19:11.[35] Nonetheless, the account also implies that king Hezekiah has some degree of authority over the management of the temple, since it is he who orders that storerooms be prepared to gather the community's contribution (2 Chr 31:11). The supervision of the contributions stored in the temple is eventually placed under the joint authority of the king and the high priest (2 Chr 31:13). Finally, two passages in Chronicles, 2 Chronicles 24:11 and 34:9, describe the high priest being involved in the supervision of financial matters in the context of the reconstruction of the temple. In 2 Chronicles 24:11 the money collected by the Levites is brought to "the scribe of the king and the official of the high priest" (סופר המלך ופקיד כהן הראש), presumably to be counted by them (cf. 2 Kgs 12:10); whereas in 2 Chronicles 34:9, the money is presented to the high priest Hilkiah alone. Both notices, however, are based on a previous notice in Kings (2 Kgs 12:10 and 22:4 respectively), so that it is difficult to derive substantial conclusions for Chronicles on the basis of these passages. However, there is some evidence that Chronicles slightly emphasizes the status of the high priest Jehoiada in the first account. Jehoiada is now provided with an official seconding him, like the king (2 Chr 24:11);[36] and he is responsible, together with the king, for handing over the money to the workers appointed for the repairs of the temple (2 Chr 24:12).[37]

Overall, despite the selective nature of the references to the high priest in Chronicles and the absence of a comprehensive description of this figure and its main duties and prerogatives, a fairly coherent picture nonetheless emerges. Various passages describe the high priest as enjoying leadership over the sanctuary not only in ritual matters, but in legal, administrative and financial matters as well; and this conception is somewhat exemplified by the designation of the high priest Azariah in 2 Chronicles 31:13 as נגיד בית האלהים. At the same time, some passages suggest that the king preserves a substantial degree of control over the temple, as far as legal and administrative matters are concerned. In particular, the appointment of Amariah

---

35. For a detailed justification of the translation of נגיד as "head" or "leader" in this context, see Levin, *Chronicles*, 126–8.

36. As Klein, *2 Chronicles*, 342, aptly comments: "One suspects that the Chronicler invented this official [...] because he thought that the chief priest should not be involved in something as menial or mundane as counting money" (cf. 2 Kgs 12:10).

37. As pointed out by several scholars; compare, e. g., Klein, *2 Chronicles*, 342; Levin, *Chronicles*, 207. However, it may have been the Chronicler's understanding that Jehoiada was included in the third person masculine plural used in the corresponding passage, 2 Kgs 12:11, especially since this priest was mentioned immediately before (v. 10). At any rate, Chronicles makes the involvement of Jehoiada more explicit at this point of the account.

by Jehoshaphat in the notice of 2 Chronicles 19:11 indicates that the high priest receives from the king his authority in judicial matters pertaining to the temple and the cult. Likewise, the account in 2 Chronicles 31:11–13 implies that king Hezekiah could legitimately involve himself in the management of the temple, at least in specific circumstances like the ones described in 2 Chronicles 31. Finally, Chronicles does not revise Kings' tradition according to which the repairs of the temple in Jerusalem were initiated by the king, not the high priest (2 Chr 24:4–14 // 2 Kgs 12:4–16; 2 Chr 34:8–14a // 2 Kgs 22:3–7). Nonetheless, Chronicles does highlight the role of Jehoiadah to some extent by explicitly presenting him and the king in 2 Chronicles 24:11 as financing together the builders appointed for the repairs of the sanctuary. All in all, one gets the impression that Chronicles aims toward a balance of sorts between royal and high priestly supervision of the sanctuary. The king, as the patron and financial sponsor of the temple, retains a substantial degree of authority over its management; but he cannot do without the collaboration of the high priest, who is in effect the main administrator of the temple. This conclusion is consistent with the view, already expressed by some scholars, that those passages describing the king and the high priest working together for the benefit of the temple, such as 2 Chronicles 24:11–14 or 31:9–13, represent something of an ideal scenario in Chronicles.[38] In some ways, this can be seen as a compromise between the situation prevailing in monarchic times, where the temple of Jerusalem was presumably much more strictly controlled by the kings of Judah,[39] and the priestly ideal of a temple fully controlled by the high priest and his family. It may also reflect the situation at the time of the Chronicler, since some traditions suggest that the management of the temple was disputed between the high priest and the representative of the foreign ruler in the Late Persian and Early Hellenistic periods.[40] In

---

38. E.g., Klein, *2 Chronicles*, 451, in the case of 2 Chr 31:9–10: "This is the Chronicler's understanding of an ideal sharing of power."

39. The book of Kings, in particular, consistently shows the chief-priest of Jerusalem subordinated to the Judean kings. However, one may date these texts, there is little doubt that this motif reflects the situation effectively prevailing under the monarchy. See on this the detailed discussion by Deborah W. Rooke, *Zadok's Heirs. The Role and Development of the High Priesthood in Ancient Israel* (Oxford: Oxford University Press, 2000), 72–9, for the traditions about the period from the divided monarchy to the fall of Jerusalem; and cf. also James C. VanderKam, "Joshua the High Priest and the Interpretation of Zechariah 3," *CBQ* 53 (1991): 553–70, here 559.

40. This is suggested, in particular, by the tradition reported by Josephus in Ant. 11, 297–301 regarding the conflict between the Persian governor Bagoses (Bagohi) and the high priest Johannes (Yoḥanan). With various scholars, I consider it likely that Josephus has used a source for this account, which may go back to the Late Persian or Early Hellenistic period. See recently Rainer Albertz, "The Controversy between

this case, Chronicles' description may be intended to promote collaboration rather than conflict between the high priest and the local ruler with regard to temple management.

Matters are quite distinct with regard to the performance of rituals inside the temple. In this case, Chronicles acknowledges more fully the authority of the high priest. Nonetheless, the range of ritual activities with which the high priest is effectively associated is limited. Specifically, high priestly ritual performance appears to be consistently associated, in various passages of Chronicles, with the offering of sacrifices, and especially the daily burnt offering and the burning of incense. This view is already introduced in connection with Aaron in the notice of 1 Chronicles 6:34, which mentions the daily sacrifice of burnt offerings and incense by Aaron and his sons in the tabernacle. It is continued in 1 Chronicles 16:39–40, which refers to the daily burnt offering presented by Zadoq and the other priests in Gibeon; and it somehow culminates in the account of Uzziah's cultic transgression in 2 Chronicles 26:16–21, which establishes the exclusive privilege of the Aaronite priests led by Azariah to burn incense on the altar of incense (v. 18). While this point has not always been noted by scholars, the way in which Chronicles defines the ritual expertise and authority of the high priest in terms of the daily rituals performed inside the sanctuary, and especially the daily burnt offering and the burning of incense, is striking. It suggests that for the Chronicler much of the prestige and status of the high priest and his family were actually mediated by the continued performance of those daily rituals. Presumably, this may be the reason why the account of Jehoiada – certainly one of the most successful high priests in Chronicles – concludes with the mention that "burnt offerings were offered in the temple of Yhwh continuously during all the days of Jehoiada" (בבית יהוה תמיד כל ימי יהוידע ויהיו מעלים עלות, 2 Chr 24:14b). Apparently, for the Chronicler, the capacity of the high priest to maintain the daily burnt offering (and presumably other daily rituals as well) is a key marker of the success of his high priesthood. This conception may well reflect the situation effectively applying at the time of the Chronicler, in the sense that the high priestly family presumably exercised a monopoly of sorts over the regular sacrifices offered at the temple in Jerusalem

Judean Versus Israelite Identity and the Persian Government: A New Interpretation of the Bagoses Story (Jewish Antiquities XI.297–301)," in *Judah and the Judeans in the Achaemenid Period: Negotiating Identity in an International Context*, ed. Oded Lipschits et al. (Winona Lake: Eisenbrauns, 2011), 483–504, although I would disagree with some aspects of the interpretation that he offers. Another piece of evidence for the growing interest of the Persian governor for some degree of control over the temple of Jerusalem is provided by the account of Neh 13:4–9, which should likewise be dated to the Late Persian or Early Hellenistic period.

and derived a substantial portion of its economic and political status from this monopoly.

Additionally, this view is also consistent with the priestly ritual legislation, which likewise defines high priestly authority in terms of the performance of the daily rituals. This conformity is actually highlighted in Chronicles, which explicitly refers to the Mosaic legislation in connection with the daily rituals performed by the high priest (1 Chr 6:34; 16:39–40). However, the priestly texts have several other ways to express the ritual authority and even monopoly of the high priest within the sanctuary, such as the description of his holy vestments (Exod 28);[41] the ceremony of Yom Kippur (Lev 16); as well as specific laws pertaining to the high priest (Lev 21:10–15). None of this is mentioned in Chronicles, where high priestly ritual monopoly is more exclusively defined through the daily rituals performed inside the sanctuary. Another difference with the priestly traditions concerns the collective dimension of the rituals associated with the high priest. While the priestly texts are not entirely consistent on this point (cf. Exod 29:38–42), they tend nonetheless to highlight high priestly agency in the performance of the daily rituals. In effect, some texts, like Exodus 30:7–8 (daily offering of incense) or Leviticus 24:1–4 (the oil of the luminary) only mention Aaron (the high priest) as the ritual agent. By contrast, Chronicles never ascribes the performance of daily rituals to the high priest alone, but always mentions other priests alongside him (see 1 Chr 6:34; 16:39–40). Moreover, texts like 2 Chronicles 13:11 or 26:18 even ascribe the performance of those same rituals to "the priests, sons of Aaron," rather than the high priest himself. This is not to say, of course, that Chronicles seeks to challenge high priestly authority in regard to the performance of daily rituals. Rather, the Chronicler's point in this description seems to be to emphasize the *collective* nature of high priestly authority: namely, the ritual monopoly enjoyed by the high priest inside the temple cannot be dissociated from the support of other priests.

3. THE HIGH PRIEST AND COMMUNAL LEADERSHIP: THE CASE OF JEHOIADA

The discussion so far has concerned the description of the high priest in connection with the temple, its administration, and its rituals in Chronicles. We also need to ask, however, whether and to what extent Chronicles envisions a larger communal role for the high priest, alongside the king. The main piece of evidence for this is provided by

---

41. See on this Nihan and Rhyder, "Aaron's Vestments," 45–67.

the account of 2 Chronicles 22–24 about king Joash and the high priest Jehoiada, which is also the most extensive account about a high priestly figure in Chronicles.

A key issue here has to do with the way in which the Chronicler's account in 2 Chronicles 22–24 rewrites its source in 2 Kings 11–12.[42] It should be clear that, as is often the case, the Chronicler's rewriting does not pursue one, but *several* aims simultaneously. In particular, Chronicles highlights the joint involvement of the community and the clergy in the reinstatement of Joash on the throne;[43] it gives to the Levites a central role in protecting the king and acting like bodyguards for him;[44] and, most importantly, it makes explicit that the sanctity of the temple was preserved throughout the whole procedure.[45] Additionally, one may ask whether, and to what extent, this rewriting also confers an extended role to the high priest Jehoiada. This possibility is rejected by Deborah W. Rooke in her monograph,[46] but briefly mentioned by Schweitzer in his article on the high priest in Chronicles.[47] On closer examination, there is indeed some evidence

---

42. For a recent analysis of some key aspects of Chronicles' rewriting in 2 Chr 22–24, focusing on the account of Jehoiada's coup in 2 Chr 22:10–23:21, see Juha Pakkala, "Selective Transmission of the Past in Chronicles: Jehoiada's Rebellion in 2 Kings 11 and 2 Chronicles 22:10–23:21," in *Remembering and Forgetting in Early Second Temple Judah*, ed. Ehud Ben Zvi and Christoph Levin (FAT 85; Tübingen: Mohr Siebeck, 2012), 239–256.

43. Compare 2 Chr 23:1–11 with 2 Kgs 11:4–12. In 2 Chr 23:2, Chronicles adds a notice according to which the "officers of the hundreds" (2 Chr 23:1, cf. 2 Kgs 11:4) went through Judah to gather "the Levites from all the towns of Judah and the heads of the families of Israel." In v. 3, the covenant in support of Joash is made with "all the assembly," not just the military officers as in Kings. In v. 5, Chronicles adds a reference to "all the people" standing in the courts of the temple. In v. 8, the "officers of the hundreds" are replaced with "the Levites and all Judah." In v. 10, finally, Chronicles replaces the reference to "the guards" protecting Joash with "all the people." On this motif, see, e. g., the brief comments by Klein, *2 Chronicles*, 331.

44. Compare 2 Chr 23:4–7 with 2 Kgs 11:4–8. According to Kings, the "Carites and the runners" are arranged into three groups; in Chronicles' version, it is now the Levites who are divided into three groups. The implications of this change are made clear in 2 Chr 23:7 (cf. 2 Kgs 11:8), where it is now the Levites who are tasked with the protection of the king.

45. In particular, Chronicles' account in 2 Chr 23:1–11 makes clear that only the Levites enter the temple during the coup (cf. 2 Chr 23:6), whereas the rest of the community stands in the courts of the temple (cf. 2 Chr 23:5b). See on this, e. g., the comments by Levin, *Chronicles*, 195–196. Presumably, this is one of the reasons (albeit not the only one) for the replacement of the Carites with the Levites, as argued by Pakkala, "Selective Transmission," 247: "The change is understandable because the rebellion began in the temple, and it would certainly have disturbed the Chronicler to have foreign mercenaries enter an area where not even lay Judeans were allowed […]."

46. Rooke, *Zadok's Heirs*, 208–210.

47. Schweitzer, "High Priest," 397–399.

supporting the latter view.

(1) According to 2 Chronicles 22:11, Jehoshabeath, daughter of king Yoram, who is responsible for hiding Joash inside the temple and therefore protecting him from Athaliah (cf. 2 Kgs 11:2), was in fact the wife of Jehoiada. Despite some contrary views,[48] it is unlikely that this information has any historical basis.[49] It is more likely to have been introduced by the Chronicler. Presumably, as various scholars have surmised, the primary function of this motif is to explain the presence of Jehoshebat inside the temple.[50] In addition, it also accounts for the connection between Jehoshabeath and Jehoiada, which is implied but never explained in the text of Kings. In any case, the effect produced by this addition is to move Jehoiada much closer to the royal house, since in Chronicles' version he has now married into the Davidic line. This is all the more striking because, as already pointed out by some scholars,[51] Jehoiada's marriage with Jehoshabeath appears to stand in contradiction with the law of Leviticus 21, which requires that the high priest can only marry a virgin of his own "kin" (Lev 21:14).

(2) In 2 Chronicles 23:3, which substantially rewrites 2 Kings 11:4, the people gathered at the temple, presumably inside the court-yard (see 2 Chr 23:5), makes an alliance with the king. This alliance is accompanied by the following statement from Jehoiada: יהוה על בני דויד הנה בן המלך ימלך כאשר דבר, "Look, the son of the king will be king,[52] according to what Yhwh declared about the sons of David!"[53] While this addition serves to highlight that Joash's reinstatement was a legitimate procedure rather than a coup, it also serves simultaneously to position the high priest Jehoiada as the first supporter of the Davidic line.

(3) The description of Joash's installation in 2 Kings 11:10–12 has been subtly but nonetheless significantly rewritten in 2 Chronicles

---

48. E.g., Williamson, *Chronicles*, 314–315; Japhet, *Chronicles*, 828.

49. Compare, e. g., the recent discussions by Klein, *2 Chronicles*, 322; Pakkala, "Selective Transmission," 245–246.

50. Thus most recently Pakkala, "Selective Transmission," 246. Schweitzer, "High Priest," 397, aptly observes that this would not account for the problem raised by the presence of Joash inside the temple. This objection is based on a correct observation, but it does not necessarily rule out the usual explanation. As pointed out by Pakkala, it would have been difficult for the Chronicler to omit entirely the motif of Joash being hidden inside the temple, "because many details in the ensuing story were dependent on his [Joash's] hiding place."

51. E.g., Schweitzer, "High Priest," 397.

52. This translation of the first half of Jehoiada's statement follows the Masoretic accents; compare also the Greek text (G) of Chronicles.

53. This appears to refer to Chronicles' version of the promise to David, 2 Chr 17:12–14, which is repeated at several key passages in Chronicles' account of the Judean monarchy: 1 Chr 22:9–10; 28:6–7; 2 Chr 13:5. See Klein, *2 Chronicles*, 324.

23:9–11 to the benefit of Jehoiada.

2 Chr 23:9–10 MT	2 Kgs 11:10–11 MT
⁹ויתן יהוידע הכהן לשרי המאות את החניתים ואת המגנות ואת השלטים אשר למלך דויד אשר בית האלהים: ¹⁰ויעמד את כל העם ואיש שלחו בידו מכתף הבית הימנית עד כתף הבית השמאלית למזבח ולבית על המלך סביב:	¹⁰ויתן הכהן לשרי המאות את החנית ואת השלטים אשר למלך דוד אשר בבית יהוה: ¹¹ויעמדו הרצים איש וכליו בידו מכתף הבית הימנית עד כתף הבית השמאלית למזבח ולבית על המלך סביב:
⁹Jehoiada the priest gave to the officers of the hundreds the spears, the shields and the bow cases⁵⁴ (?) which belonged to king David, and which were in the house of the god. ¹⁰He stationed all the people round, each with a weapon in his hand, from the south side of the house to the north side of the house, around the altar and the house, around the king.	¹⁰The priest gave to the chiefs of hundreds the spears and the bow cases which were for king David, and which were in the house of Yhwh. ¹¹The runners stood, each with his weapon in his hand, from the left side of the house to the right side of the house, around the altar and the house, around the king.

In Chronicles' version, it is Jeohiada who is responsible for stationing the people in arms around the king, thereby highlighting his role in the whole procedure. Additionally, 2 Chronicles 23:9 adds the mention "Jehoiada" before הכהן, thus leaving no doubt that "the priest" responsible for providing weapons to the supporters of Joash is in effect Jehoiada.

The matter is more complex in the case the relationship between the next verse, 2 Chronicles 23:11 and 2 Kings 11:12. The MT version of 2 Kings 11:12 has the first two verbs in the singular (v. 12aα), then shifts to the plural. This suggests that Jehoiada is responsible for bringing Joash, for placing on him the diadem (נזר), and for giving to him the "testimony" (עדות), while the rest of the procedure is ascribed to the "officers of the hundreds" and the guards. In the main Greek versions of Kings, however, not just the first two verbs but all four verbs in v. 12a are in the singular, and therefore ascribed to Jehoiada.⁵⁵

54. For this rendering of שלטים, see Klein, *1 Chronicles*, 394 (at 1 Chr 18:7).

55. G^L has the reverse order for the third and fourth verbs in the singular: "he anointed him and made him a king". According to Steven L. McKenzie, *1 Kings 16 – 2 Kings 16* (IECOT; Stuttgart: Kohlhammer, 2019), 427, this reading is more logical and should be viewed as superior to G^B's reading, which agrees with MT and may represent a case of secondary alignment within the Greek tradition. While this is indeed possible, the fact that the sequence of verbs in G^L is more logical is not neces-

2 Kgs 11:12 MT	2 Kgs 11:12 LXX (G^B)
ויוצא את בן המלך ויתן עליו את הנזר ואת העדות וימלכו אתו וימשחהו ויכו כף ויאמרו יחי המלך	καὶ ἐξαπέστειλεν τὸν υἱὸν τοῦ βασιλέως καὶ ἔδωκεν ἐπ' αὐτὸν τὸ νεζερ καὶ τὸ μαρτύριον καὶ ἐβασίλευσεν αὐτὸν καὶ ἔχρισεν αὐτόν, καὶ ἐκρότησαν τῇ χειρὶ καὶ εἶπαν Ζήτω ὁ βασιλεύς.
He (Jehoiada) brought out the son of the king, put on him the diadem and the testimony;[56] they made him king and anointed him, they clapped their hands and said: "Long live the king!"	He (Jehoiada) brought out the son of the king, put on him the diadem and the testimony, made him a king and anointed him; they clapped their hands and said: "Long live the king!"

The MT version of the corresponding passage in 2 Chronicles 23:11, for its part, has all the verbs in the plural. In this case, the subject is most likely Jehoiada and his sons, who are mentioned at the beginning of v. 11b.[57] However, the Greek version of Chronicles preserves a different wording, according to which the first two verbs are in the singular, and therefore describe actions ascribed to Jehoiada alone, whereas the following verbs are ascribed to "Jehoiada and his sons."

2 Chr 23:11 MT	2 Chr 23:11 LXX (G^B)
ויוציאו את בן המלך ויתנו עליו את הנזר ואת העדות וימליכו אתו וימשחהו יהוידע ובניו ויאמרו יחי המלך	καὶ ἐξήγαγεν τὸν υἱὸν τοῦ βασιλέως καὶ ἔδωκεν ἐπ' αὐτὸν τὸ βασίλειον καὶ τὰ μαρτύρια, καὶ ἐβασίλευσαν καὶ ἔχρισαν αὐτὸν Ιωδαε καὶ οἱ υἱοὶ αὐτοῦ καὶ εἶπαν Ζήτω ὁ βασιλεύς.

---

sarily an argument for the priority of this reading. It could likewise represent a case of a facilitating reading. For the present discussion, this point is not significant and can remain open.

56. For the problem raised by the term עדות in this context, see the recent and detailed discussion by McKenzie, *1 Kings 16 – 2 Kings 16*, 439–440. McKenzie himself follows Wellhausen in emending עדות to צעדות, denoting "bracelets" or "armbands", which is attested together with the term נזר in 2 Sam 1:10.

57. The previous collective subjects in Chronicles' account are the "officers of the hundreds" mentioned in 2 Chr 23:9 and the people mentioned in v. 10. It is unlikely that Chronicles would have ascribed the actions described in v. 11, especially the crowning of the king and his anointing, to these groups. It is more likely, therefore, that all the verbs in the plural are implicitly ascribed to the other collective mentioned in v. 11, namely, Jehoiada and his sons.

2 Chr 23:11 MT	2 Chr 23:11 LXX (G^B)
Then Jehoiada and his sons brought out the son of the king, placed on him the diadem and the testimony; they made him king, they anointed him and said: "Long live the king!"	Then he (Jeoiada) brought out the son of the king, and gave him the kingdom and the testimony. Jehoiada and his sons made him king, they anointed him and said: "Long live the king!"

Several scholars consider that the Greek version of 2 Chronicles 23:11 should be preferred,[58] and this conclusion seems indeed likely. The Greek version effectively corresponds to 2 Kings 11:12 MT, except that the verbs in the plural are now effectively ascribed to "Jehoiada and his sons," rather than to the officers and the guards, as in Kings' version (see above). MT's version, for its part, could reflect a secondary attempt to harmonize the syntax of this verse by ascribing all the actions it narrates to the high priest Jehoiada and his sons. Even so, however, the difference merely concerns the extent of Jehoiada's personal involvement in the procedure described in 2 Chronicles 23:11. Both versions actually concur in placing this procedure under the high priest's authority, whether some actions are performed by Jehoiada alone (thus LXX, as in 2 Kgs 11:12 MT already), or Jehoiada is consistently assisted by other priests (thus MT). Either way, *Chronicles now places the entirety of the ceremony establishing Joash as king over Judah under the responsibility of Jehoiada.*

(4) In 2 Chronicles 23:16, the covenant concluded by Jehoiada after Athaliah's death contains a noticeable difference with the version of this covenant in Kings:

2 Kgs 11:17a MT	2 Chr 23:16 MT
ויכרת יהוידע את הברית בין יהוה ובין המלך ובין העם להיות לעם ליהוה	ויכרת יהוידע ברית בינו ובין כל העם ובין המלך להיות לעם ליהוה:
Jehoiada concluded the covenant between Yhwh, the king and the people, so that they should be Yhwh's people.	Jehoiada concluded a covenant between himself, all the people and the king, so that they should be Yhwh's people.

Again, the variation in Chronicles is subtle but nonetheless substantial. Chronicles' reading, replacing בין יהוה with בינו, presumably reflects an understanding that the high priest acts here as the representative of the deity.[59] Even so, however, the effect produced is significant:

---

58. See, e. g., Klein, *2 Chronicles*, 319 and n. 26–27; Levin, *Chronicles*, 185.
59. Thus, e. g., Raymond B. Dillard, *2 Chronicles* (WBC 15; Waco, Tx: Word

in Chronicles' formulation, Yhwh's implication in the covenant inaugurating Joah's reign is mediated by the high priest, and Jehoiada has now become a party to the covenant, alongside the king and the people.[60]

(5) After reinstating Joash on the throne, Jehoiadah is said in 2 Chronicles 24:3 to have procured two wives "for him": נשים שתים וישא לו יהוידע. Although the wording of this clause is ambiguous, the third masculine singular suffix (לו) clearly refers to king Joash, who is the general subject of the immediate context (2 Chr 24:1–3). This verse is entirely an addition by the Chronicler. While it has not received much attention, the idea of the high priest being responsible for providing wives for the king is quite unique. Within the Western Asian context, it is reminiscent of the kind of vertical relationship uniting a suzerain and his vassal.[61] This observation must however be balanced with the subsequent narrative in 2 Chronicles 24:4–14, which shows that Jehoiada remains de facto subordinated to the king (see, especially 2 Chr 24:6). Nonetheless, the notice added by the Chronicler in 2 Chronicles 24:3 does index a position of power and influence for Jehoiada visà-vis of Joash. Furthermore, this notice calls into question the view that, in the Chronicler's perspective, Jehoiadah's political power would have been limited to the period preceding Joash's enthronement.[62] On the contrary, 2 Chronicles 24:3 points to a more lasting influence for the high priest, extending into Joash's reign.

(6) Finally, according to the notice in 2 Chronicles 24:15–16, Jehoiada dies at the age of 130, which is more than Moses in Deut 34:7 (!), and also more than the maximal age set for humankind in Gen 6:3. What is more, Jehoiada is buried in the City of David, "together with the kings" of Judah (ויקברהו בעיר דויד עם המלכים), as a reward for the good he did during his life for "Israel, Yhwh and his temple". This notice is absolutely unique for a high priest in Chronicles (or in the Hebrew Bible for that matter), and appears to index again a royal or quasi-royal status for Jehoiada.[63] In effect, it is the only notice

Books, 1987), 178.

60. The other half of 2 Kgs 11:17 mentions a second covenant, this time between Joash and the people, which is not mentioned in 2 Chr 23:16. This omission is presumably due to the fact that the Chronicler had already mentioned a similar covenant in 2 Chr 23:3 (thus, e. g., Japhet, *Chronicles*, 835). Klein, *2 Chronicles*, 329, suggests that the Chronicler may have been dependent here on an alternate version of Kings, which did not contain this clause.

61. I am grateful to my colleague Ehud Ben Zvi (University of Alberta) for discussing this point with me.

62. Thus, e. g., Schweitzer, "High Priest," 398.

63. Schweitzer, "High Priest," 398, also suggests that this may reflect "a retrojection of Second Temple practice by the Chronicler." While this is an intriguing possibility, it cannot be demonstrated and remains speculative, as Schweitzer himself ac-

in Chronicles reporting the death and burial of a figure who is not a king.⁶⁴ Last but not least, the comparison with the notice for Joash in 2 Chronicles 24:25 provides an additional element of contextualization. Chronicles takes up Kings' notice in 2 Kings 12:22 according to which Joash was buried in the city of David, but corrects it by stating that he was not buried in the tombs of the kings (קברהו בקברות המלכים ולא). Chronicles' account of Joash and Jehoiada thus concludes with an exceptional situation, in which it is the high priest, instead of the king, who is buried in the royal tombs.

Taking this evidence together, it does not seem possible to avoid the conclusion that some sort of communal leadership, extending well beyond the boundaries of the sanctuary, is conferred to Jehoiada here. In effect, Jehoiada, who marries into the Davidic line, oversees and controls the whole procedure for Joash's establishment on the throne, provides wives for the king and is buried like a Judean king in the place of Joash himself, is somehow described in Chronicles as *the closest equivalent to a king*. However, this conclusion must be immediately qualified in two respects. Firstly, there is very little evidence for similar communal leadership in the case of other high priestly figures in Chronicles. Jehoiada may enjoy extended privileges and status, which bring him in close connection with royal figures, but he remains something of an exception in Chronicles. Secondly, Jehoiada is elevated in Chronicles only inasmuch as he remains loyal to the Davidic monarchy. In this respect, it is certainly significant that the plus in 2 Chronicles 23:3 reminding that kingship can only belong to the Davidic house is precisely placed in the mouth of Jehoiada, the high priest. In this way, the Chronicler's account also subtly recalls that high priests are normally not expected to take the place of kings.

4. THE MISSING HIGH PRIEST: THE CASE OF ROYAL REFORMS IN CHRONICLES

In order to understand Chronicles' discourse on the high priest, we need to look not only at the passages where the high priest is mentioned but also at those passages where he would be expected but is actually absent. Contrary to some kings, like Amaziah (2 Chr 25), Ahaz (2 Chr 28) or Manasseh (2 Chr 33:1–20), the high priest is never explicitly criticized in Chronicles; but his absence in some contexts seems nonetheless significant. This is the case, in particular, in the context of royal reforms. The importance of royal reforms in Chronicles has been highlighted by several studies, especially in the case of knowledges.

64. As finely noted by Klein, *2 Chronicles*, 344.

the reigns of Hezekiah and Josiah at the end of the Chronicler's account of the Judean monarchy.[65] While this point has not always been noted, it is striking to observe that the high priest plays a very limited role in both reforms.

The case of Chronicles' account of Hezekiah's reforms in 2 Chronicles 29–31 is especially instructive in this regard. While this account is complex, it presents nonetheless a logical structure. Following the notice introducing Hezekiah (2 Chr 29:1–2), the account begins by describing the purification of the temple (29:3–19), followed by sacrifices offered by Hezekiah and the officials of the city (29:20–30) as well as by the people (29:31–36). 2 Chronicles 30 continues with the celebration of Passover and Unleavened Bread in Jerusalem, which is also the occasion to eliminate from the city non-Yahwistic cult objects (30:14). In 2 Chronicles 31, finally, the whole land of Judah and Israel is purified (31:1),[66] and various provisions are made by Hezekiah for collecting contributions to the priests and the Levites (31:2–21). It is not possible to provide here a comprehensive discussion of this fascinating yet complex account. In the limits of this essay, two general observations will suffice.

Firstly, it is striking to observe that the high priest plays no part in the reforms themselves, even at points where one would expect to see him mentioned. According to 2 Chronicles 29, the purification of the temple (see 29:3–19) and the reinstatement of the sacrificial cult (29:20–36) were decreed by Hezekiah. However, according to other passages in Chronicles (see above), maintaining the purity and sanctity of the sanctuary and warranting the continued offering of sacrifices are duties that typically belong to the high priest,[67] who is none-

---

65. See, especially, Hee-Sook Bae, *Vereinte Suche nach JHWH. Die Hiskianische und Josianische Reform in der Chronik* (BZAW 355; Berlin/New York: de Gruyter, 2005); for Josiah's reform in Chronicles compare also Louis C. Jonker, *Reflections of King Josiah in Chronicles. Late Stages of the Josiah Reception in II Chr. 34 f.* (TSHB 1; Gütersloh: Gütersloher Verlagshaus, 2003). See further now Julia Rhyder, "The Reception of Ritual Laws in the Early Second Temple Period: The Evidence from Ezra-Nehemiah and Chronicles," in Text and Ritual in the Pentateuch: A Systematic and Comparative Approach, ed. Christophe Nihan and Julia Rhyder (Eisenbrauns: University Park, PA, 2021), 255–279, esp. 264–273, with additional references.

66. Thus, there is a clear concentric structure in the account of Hezekiah's reform, beginning with the purification of the temple (2 Chr 29:15–20) and extending gradually to the city (2 Chr 30:14) and finally the entire land (2 Chr 31:1). See further on this my discussion in Christophe Nihan, "Deuteronomic Alignment in Chronicles: Royal Reforms and the Elimination of Cultic Objects," in *Writing, Rewriting and Overwriting in the Books of Deuteronomy and the Former Prophets*, ed. Ido Koch, Thomas Römer and Omer Sergi (BEThL 304; Leuven et al.: Peeters, 2019), 309–336, here 319–324.

67. See, e. g., 2 Chr 26:16–21 for the first matter, and 1 Chr 16:39–40 for the second.

theless not mentioned in the context of 2 Chronicles 29. There are, however, good reasons for this absence of the high priest. In particular, Hezekiah's speech in 2 Chronicles 29:6–7 implies that the cult in Jerusalem has been completely discontinued, presumably as a consequence of Ahaz's impious actions as described immediately before, in 2 Chronicles 28.[68] As various scholars have observed, the discontinuation of the cult is a reversal of "the situation initiated by Solomon (cf. 2:4 and 4:7) and reaffirmed by Abijah (13:11)".[69] This reversal, in turn, justifies for the Chronicler the representation of Hezekiah as a new Solomon.[70] Just like Zadok takes virtually no part in the initial organization of the cult under David and Solomon,[71] there is apparently no need for the high priest alongside the king in Chronicles' account of Hezekiah's reestablishment of the cult. This conclusion is consistent with the fact that Azariah is effectively mentioned only *after* the cult has been reinstated and reorganized, in 2 Chronicles 31:10. As discussed above, this notice acknowledges the role of the high priest in the management of the temple's resources, and the account continues in 31:13 by showing Hezekiah and Azariah being jointly involved in the supervision of the storing of the contributions brought to the temple by the Israelites (cf. 31:4–7).

Secondly, while the high priest plays no role in the royal reform itself, it has often been observed that this reform provides an opportunity to highlight the role of the Levites. According to 2 Chronicles 29:4, Hezekiah gathered "the priests and the Levites", the subsequent speech placed in the king's mouth is exclusively addressed to "the Levites" (הלוים). It is very likely that הלוים is used here as a generic term, including all the members of the tribe of Levi, and not just the Levites, as various scholars have surmised.[72] Even so, however, this

---

68. This is suggested, in particular, by the fact that the description of the discontinuation of the cult in 2 Chr 29:7 begins with a reference to the doors of the temple having been shut, which corresponds to the action ascribed to Ahaz in 2 Chr 28:24–25. For the view that the discontinuation of the cult described in Hezekiah's speech in 29:6–7 goes back to Ahaz, see, e. g., Williamson, *Chronicles*, 353; further Klein, *2 Chronicles*, 416.

69. Williamson, *Chronicles*, 353.

70. On this topic, see, especially, Mark A. Throntveit, "The Relationship of Hezekiah to David and Solomon in the Books of Chronicles," in: *The Chronicler as Theologian: Essays in Honor of Ralph W. Klein*, ed. M. Patrick Graham, Steven L. McKenzie and Gary N. Knoppers, (JSOT.S 371; London/ New York: T & T Clark, 2003), 105–121.

71. The only partial exception is 1 Chr 24:3–6, where Zadok is associated, together with Ahimelek, to the division of Aaron's descendants by David. Note, however, that 1 Chr 24 is generally considered to be a later addition within Chronicles.

72. See, e. g., Japhet, *Chronicles*, 917; Klein, *2 Chronicles*, 415. *Contra* Antje Labahn, "Antitheocratic Tendencies in Chronicles," in: *Yahwism After the Exile. Per-*

usage of הלוים is significant. By recalling that priests and Levites share a common ancestor (Levi), it tends to provisionally bracket the differences between these two groups, suggesting that, at least in the context of Hezekiah's reform, Levites enjoy similar if not identical status as priests. This trend is continued in 29:12–14, which provides the genealogy of seven Levitical families (with the mention of two members for each family),[73] whereas nothing is said about the genealogy of the priests involved in the reform (who are merely mentioned as "the priests"). Later in the account, Levites are described as being involved in sacrificial roles which are normally reserved to the priests. According to 2 Chronicles 29:34, the Levites were allowed to assist the priests in skinning he animals brought by the community to be sacrificed as burnt offerings (see 29:31–36), because the priests were too few. In order to legitimize what is apparently a ritual innovation, Chronicles adds a further rationale, stating that "the Levites were more upright of heart in sanctifying themselves than the priests" (מהכהנים כי הלוים ישרי לבב להתקדש).[74] Later, in 30:16, Levites are also presented as handing the blood of the Passover sacrifices to the priests,[75] and in 30:17 they slaughter the Passover lambs on behalf of the participants to the festival who could not purify themselves.[76] The elevation of the Levites in this account culminates in 30:22, when the contribution of the Levites to the festival is acknowledged by Hezekiah himself, who "speaks to the heart of the Levites" (וידבר יחזקיהו על לב כל הלוים),[77] an expression apparently meaning that he speaks to them favorably,

---

spectives on Israelite Religion in the Persian Era. Papers Read at the First Meeting of the European Association for Biblical Studies, Utrecht, 6–9 August 2000, ed. Rainer Albertz and Bob Becking (STAR 5; Assen: Royal Van Gorcum, 2003), 115–135, here 118, who considers that הלוים refers here to the Levites alone.

73. For a detailed discussion of these families, see, e. g., Klein, *2 Chronicles*, 417–418.

74. On this verse and its implications, see, especially, the detailed discussion by Bae, *Vereinte Suche*, 125–128.

75. As observed by Japhet, *Chronicles*, 949–950, the Chronicler introduces two innovations here: (a) the idea that the blood of the Passover sacrifice must be sprinkled against the altar, like the blood of burnt and well-being offerings in P (Lev 1:5, 11; 3:2, 8, 13); (b) the notion that the Levites carry that blood from the place where the animal has been slaughtered to the priests. The statement in v. 16a that the priests and the Levites "stood in their posts according to their custom, according to the Torah of Moses, the man of God" has been much discussed. Presumably, this statement does not point to a specific commandment but, rather, to the general conformity of this procedure with the instructions of the Mosaic Law.

76. For a discussion of this passage, see Bae, *Vereinte Suche*, 130–133.

77. Contrary to 29:5, I see no reason here to interpret הלוים inclusively; the focus on the Levites is in keeping with the insistence on the readiness of the Levites throughout 2 Chr 29–30 (see, especially, 29:34). Compare, e. g., Bae, *Vereinte Suche*, 131–132; Klein, *2 Chronicles*, 439; *pace* Japhet, *Chronicles*, 954.

or encouragingly.⁷⁸ Overall, there is a clear tendency throughout the account of the purification of the temple, the reestablishment of the cult (2 Chr 29) and the celebration of Passover in Jerusalem (2 Chr 30) to highlight the role of the Levites in the success of these ceremonies, and especially their readiness to assist the king in his cultic and religious reform.

A very similar point can be made in the case of Josiah's cultic reform and celebration of the Passover (2 Chr 35). The high priest Hilkiah is mentioned in the account of the repairs of the temple (2 Chr 34:9, cf. 2 Kgs 22:4) and the finding of the "book of the law" (2 Chr 34:14–15, cf. 2 Kgs 22:7–8), as already in Kings.⁷⁹ But contrary to what is the case in Kings (2 Kgs 23:4) he is no longer mentioned in the context of the account of the purification of the temple, which is described more briefly in 2 Chronicles 34:3–7. The high priest likewise plays no significant role in the celebration of Passover under Josiah (2 Chr 35). He is merely mentioned among other temple authorities (נגידי בית האלהים, "leaders of the house of the god") who contribute to the sacrifices with a generous donation of animals (35:8), but no longer in the performance of the ceremony itself. Moreover, it is not even certain that the "Hilkiah" mentioned in this verse is the same person as the high priest with this name in 2 Chronicles 34.⁸⁰ By contrast, the Levites play a key role in the celebration of the festival described in 2 Chronicles 35, comparable to or even more important than in the case of Hezekiah's Passover in 2 Chronicles 30. The role of Levites is already prepared in 35:3–6, where they receive detailed instructions from Josiah himself for the celebration of Passover.⁸¹ In the account of the celebration (35:10–16), they are described in a variety of ritual roles. As in 2 Chronicles 30:17, they slaughter the Passover lamb and skin the animals (35:11; cf. already 29:34);⁸² they set apart the fat portions of the animals to be burnt by the priests (35:12); they cook the animals and bring them to the people gathered in Jerusalem (35:13); and last but not least they prepare portions for the priests, themselves (35:14), and even other Levites such as the singers and the gatekeepers

---

78. See Gen 50:21; Isa 40:2. Klein, *2 Chronicles*, 439, renders this expression with "tenderly".

79. See further 2 Chr 34:20–22 (// 2 Kgs 22:12–14), where Hilkiah, the high priest, is mentioned among the men sent by Josiah to seek an oracle from the prophetess Huldah.

80. See, e. g., Klein, 2 Chronicles, 521; Levin, *Chronicles*, 421 n. 133.

81. On this section and its function in the account of 2 Chr 35, see the detailed analysis by Bae, *Vereinte Suche*, 139–144. Compare also Rhyder, "Reception", 270–271.

82. As Bae, *Vereinte Suche*, 145–146, aptly observes, what was still an exceptional measure in 2 Chr 30 is now presented as a regular privilege for the Levites.

who are on duty and cannot leave their posts (35:15). In short, except for those ritual actions involving contact with the altar (namely, sprinkling the blood against the altar, and burning the fat portions of the sacrifices), which are reserved to the priests,[83] Levites are responsible for all the remainder of the ceremony. Their importance in the success of the ceremony is further emphasized by the notice in 35:9, which specifies that the "chiefs of the Levites" contributed animals to the Passover sacrifices with a donation of 5,000 sheep and 700 hundred bulls, which is roughly the double of the donation made by the leaders of the priests according to 35:8 (2,600 sheep and 300 hundred bulls).

All in all, while we must be cautious not to infer too much from omissions in Chronicles, some significant patterns can nevertheless be identified as regards the general omission of the high priest in the context of royal reforms. Both Hezekiah and Josiah are presented as being responsible for the reestablishment of the cult in Jerusalem, after it was discontinued by their predecessor on the throne (Ahaz in 2 Chr 28; Manasseh in 2 Chr 33). This situation provides the opportunity to compare them with David and Solomon, the founders of the royal dynasty and of the cult in Jerusalem, two domains which are deeply intertwined in Chronicles. By contrast, the high priest never plays any role in these reforms, and is exclusively mentioned in the context of issues related to the administration of the temple.[84] This suggests that in Chronicles *the foundation and renovation of the cult remains essentially a royal initiative, whereas the function of the high priest is much more associated with the management of the temple.* Furthermore, while royal reforms in Chronicles mobilize various ritual agents, the accounts in 2 Chronicles 29–30 and 2 Chronicles 35 show a clear preference for the Levites, who are presented as enjoying a special relationship to the king in the context of those reforms.[85] Levites are thus clearly positioned in Chronicles as privileged ritual agents in connection with the purification and refoundation of the cult, and this privileged position is explicitly affirmed in some passages which highlight the Levites' outstanding zeal during the royal reforms, such as 2 Chronicles 29:34.

Overall, while the accounts of Hezekiah's and Josiah's reform in Chronicles make repeated reference to the Mosaic Law and are partly consistent with the prescriptions laid in the priestly portions of the Pentateuch, the conception of the cult that emerges from these accounts is substantially distinct from that of the priestly texts. In the

---

83. See 2 Chr 35:11 and 12 respectively for these two ritual actions.
84. See 2 Chr 29:10, 13 (Azariah); 34:14–15, and perhaps 35:8 (Hilikiah).
85. This is apparent, in particular, from the royal speeches to the Levites in 2 Chr 30:22 and 35:3–6 (see above).

priestly texts, the high priest is basically at the head of the cult and is personally responsible for maintaining the sanctity and the purity of the sanctuary. This conception somehow culminates in the grand ritual of Leviticus 16, which can only be performed by the high priest, and which warrants in principle that the temple (16:14–19) and the community (16:20–22) are regularly purified and therefore can never become irremediably defiled.[86] In this system, Levitical families have a role to play in the preservation of the sanctuary's integrity, at least according to the Book of Numbers.[87] Yet they remain clearly subordinated to the high priest and his family, and can only undertake more menial tasks. The accounts of cultic reforms in Chronicles point therefore to a *different balance of power* between the priestly and Levitical families as is the case in Numbers. In Chronicles' conception the ritual monopoly of the Aaronite priests is recognized in principle, *but it is no longer enough to warrant the purity and sanctity of the temple and its cult.*

5. CONCLUSION: THE HIGH PRIEST IN CHRONICLES AND IN THE PRIESTLY TEXTS OF THE PENTATEUCH

The previous discussion provides a basis to address the issue of the relationship between the description of the high priest in Chronicles and in the priestly texts of the Pentateuch. Specifically, four aspects relevant to the comparison between Chronicles and the priestly texts can be briefly highlighted here.

(1) Like the priestly texts, Chronicles consistently emphasizes the high priest's role in the sanctuary. In fact, except for Jehoiada in 2 Chronicles 22–24 (on which see below), all the other references to high priests in Chronicles exclusively focus on their role in connection to the sanctuary and its management. Chronicles' description of high priestly roles with regard to the sanctuary presents a number of connections with the priestly texts, but also some substantial discontinuities. To begin with, Chronicles posits a distinction between non-ritual and ritual matters in the management of the sanctuary. While the high priest *de facto* operates as the main administrator of the sanctuary, several texts indicate that the king, as the patron and financial sponsor of the temple, retains a substantial degree of control over this institution and can even intervene in its actual management, at least in specific circumstances (see, e. g., 2 Chr 31:11–13, and the

---

86. See on this my discussion in Nihan, *Priestly Torah*, 370–379.
87. See, especially, Num 3–4 and 8.

discussion above

(2). This situation, however, does not confer any prerogatives to the king in ritual matters; the account of king Uzziah in 2 Chronicles 26 effectively establishes this point. Such distinction between non-ritual and ritual matters in the management of the temple is unknown to the priestly texts, which merely assume that the high priest and the main priestly families enjoy complete control over the sanctuary (compare, e. g., Num 18).

(2) With regard to ritual matters, specifically, Chronicles' description of high priestly roles is largely based on priestly materials, as one would expect, but these materials are reused both freely and selectively. In particular, high priestly ritual hegemony in Chronicles is expressed almost exclusively through reference to the performance of the daily sacrifices. Other key markers of the high priest's ritual hegemony in the priestly texts, such as the description of high priestly vestments (Exod 28), the ceremony of Yom Kippur (Lev 16) or specific laws pertaining to the high priest (Lev 21:10–15), are never mentioned in Chronicles. A further difference, which has not always been correctly noted, is that Chronicles tends to emphasize the collective nature of high priestly authority. Contrary to the priestly texts, Chronicles never ascribes the performance of daily rituals to the high priest alone, and always mentions other priests alongside him (see 1 Chr 6:34; 16:39–40). Moreover, texts like 2 Chronicles 13:11 or 26:18 even ascribe the performance of those same rituals to "the priests, sons of Aaron," rather than the high priest himself.

(3) Both the priestly texts and Chronicles consider larger communal, extra-sanctuary roles for the high priest, but they do it in entirely distinct ways. In the priestly texts, such roles are almost exclusively developed in the book of Numbers.[88] In particular, Numbers 17 recounts how Aaron performs a ritual inside the camp in order to ward off Yhwh's wrath, which is represented as a demonic force of sorts (cf. Num 17:6–15); Numbers 27 describes Eleazar casting lots for Joshua in order to determine when he must go to war (Num 27:21);[89] and other passages describe him involved in the division of the land.[90] None of these roles are mentioned in Chronicles for the high priest. Instead, Chronicles addresses this matter primarily

---

88. The only (partial) exception would concern Aaron's roles in Exodus, before Exod 19 and Israel's arrival at Mount Sinai.

89. On this verse and its significance within the context of Num 27:12–23, see further my discussion in Christophe Nihan, "Joshua and Eleazar in Numbers 27," in: *Bible and Politics. A Festschrift in Honor of Prof. Rev. Dr Olivier Artus on his 65th Birthday*, ed. Sophie Ramond and Joseph Titus (Bangalore: ATC Publishers, 2019), 77–97.

90. Num 32:28; 34:17–18; further Josh 14:1–2; 17:4; 19:51; 21:1.

through the figure of Jehoiada. As a matter of fact, Jehoiada is the only case where Chronicles effectively considers the possibility for a high priest to take extended communal roles. As argued above (§3), Chronicles' description of Jehoiada aligns him closely with a royal figure: he marries into the Davidic line, oversees and controls the whole procedure for Joash's establishment on the throne, provides wives for the king and is buried like a Judean king in the place of Joash himself. While not a king per se, Jehoiada is arguably construed in Chronicles as the closest equivalent to a king. However, there is no indication that the high priestly dynasty in Jerusalem could one day replace the Davidic dynasty. On the contrary, Jehoiada can take a quasi-royal role only because he is loyal to the Davidic dynasty, and pays lip service to the latter (2 Chr 23:3). Furthermore, there is likewise no evidence in Chronicles that other high priests could imitate Jehoiada or achieve equal status. Jehoiada in Chronicles is an exceptional high priest in exceptional circumstances, who steps up at a time when the Davidic monarchy is failing.

(4) Finally, a major difference between the descriptions of the high priest in the priestly texts and Chronicles concern his role in the maintenance of the sanctuary's purity and sanctity. In the priestly texts, the high priest is basically at the head of the cult and is personally responsible for maintaining the sanctity and the purity of the sanctuary. This conception somehow culminates in the grand ritual of Leviticus 16, which can only be performed by the high priest, and which warrants in principle that the temple (16:14–19) and the community (16:20–22) can never become irremediably defiled. In Chronicles, accounts about the defilement of the sanctuary and its subsequent purification play an important part, but the high priest plays no role in those stories (see above, § 4). In the accounts of Hezekiah (2 Chr 29–31) and Josiah (2 Chr 34–35), cultic reforms are expressly described as a royal initiative. While they involve various ritual agents, such as especially Levites and, to a lesser extent, priests and the rest of the community, the high priest is never mentioned among them: on the contrary, in the account of Hezekiah's reform he only comes into play after the cult has been reinstated (2 Chr 31:10). As a result, while Chronicles aligns with the priestly traditions in acknowledging the central role of the high priestly family in the management of the temple, a key difference is that in Chronicles this role is no longer construed as being sufficient to warrant the purity and sanctity of the temple and its cult. Instead, accounts of royal reforms provide the opportunity to present a *new balance of power*, which is substantially less vertical and more diverse than in the priestly texts. In this conception, high priestly manage-

ment of the temple is not possible without the continued support of the king, and without the assistance of dedicated ritual agents such as the Levites.

Taken together, these points indicate that the various continuities in language and conception that can be observed between the priestly texts and Chronicles with regard to the high priest should not blind us to the substantial discontinuities that exist between these two corpuses. Chronicles' description is clearly based on the priestly texts, and uses them as a key reference in its description of the high priest. But it also regularly branches off in order to pursue its own agenda. In the end, the overall picture of the high priest that emerges is quite distinct from the priestly texts. On the one hand, Chronicles acknowledges some form of ritual hegemony to the high priest in ritual matters inside the sanctuary, and occasionally even confers him some larger communal responsibilities (Jehoiada in 2 Chr 22–24). On the other hand, however, Chronicles also shows a clear concern to highlight the relational dimension of high priestly prerogatives within the sanctuary. Rituals inside the temple can only be performed with the assistance of other priests; temple management requires the cooperation between the high priest and the king; and the maintenance of the sanctuary's integrity likewise requires the intervention of other agents, like the Levites. The resulting picture is a description of high priestly leadership which is substantially less hegemonic, and more balanced, than in the priestly texts.

THE TRIBES OF ISRAEL IN EZEKIEL AND CHRONICLES
Kristin Weingart

1. INTRODUCTION

If one wants to understand Persian Period Israel – or, how Israel understood itself in the Persian Period – segmental structures, genealogies, or questions of descent come up frequently in one's investigations, and in quite a number of texts that are usually connected with this period. Among them are some obvious and expected examples:[1]

– The Book of Chronicles opens with extensive genealogical lists in 1 Chronicles 1–9, some aspects of which will be discussed in this paper.

– The so-called lists of returnees in Nehemiah 7 and Ezra 2 try to present all Israel as a returnees' Israel, and at the same time apply the criterion of lineage or descent when it comes to the question 'who is an Israelite' and who is not.[2] Nehemiah 7:61–63 lists families whose status was doubted, because "they were not able to tell their fathers' houses and their descent, whether they belonged to Israel" (מישראל הם לא יכלו להגיד בית אבותם וזרעם אם). Nehemiah 7:64 seems to imply that

---

1. How to relate constructions of collective, cultural identity or ethnicity to archaeological finds or material culture is a notoriously difficult issue and as such subject of ongoing debates (see e. g. the wide range of problems presented in Stephen Shennan, ed., *Archaeological Approaches to Cultural Identity* (London: Unwin Hyman LTD, 1989), or – directly relating to the Levant – Israel Finkelstein, "Pots and People Revisited: Ethnic Boundaries in the Iron Age I," in *Archaeology of Israel: Constructing the Past Interpreting the Present*, eds. Neil A. Silberman and David B. Small (Sheffield: Sheffield Academic Press, 2010): 216–37.

2. The lists which are presented as returnees' lists in the narrative (esp. so in Ezr 2) are in fact lists of inhabitants (see e. g. Hugh G. M. Williamson, *Ezra, Nehemiah*, WBC 16 [Dallas, Tex.: Word Books, 1985], 30–1). They reflect settlement structures in the late Persian or early Hellenistic periods; cf. Israel Finkelstein, "Archaeology and the List of Returnees in the Books of Ezra and Nehemiah," *PEQ* 140 (2008): 7–16.

there was a register of all Israel by means of which one could proof one's affiliation to Israel[3] or – for that matter – one's right to the priesthood. The parallel in Ezra 2 does not differ in this regard.[4]

– Undoubtedly, another strong indicator is the priestly literature in the Pentateuch with its characteristic interest in genealogies and lineages.[5]

Besides these obvious and well-known cases, there are also some more surprising finds, e. g. in the book of Ezra: While Ezra does not seem to attach any special importance to the notion of a twelve-tribe nation, the tribal system suddenly pops up in cultic matters: texts like Ezra 6:16–17; 8:24–35, or 8:35 presuppose the tribal system and Israel's kinship identity as a basic characteristic of Israel.

The undisputable prominence of genealogies and the tribal system in Persian Period texts has led a number of scholars to assume that the whole idea of Israel's kinship identity, of Israel's being a nation of twelve tribes, is a Persian Period invention[6] – a novel construction fabricated to provide the community within the Persian province of Yehud with some sense of belonging.

The pre-exilic history of the tribal system is not the issue here, neither is Israel's kinship identity as a whole.[7] Instead, the following remarks focus on the system of the twelve tribes and the way it is used in two different contexts, namely Ezekiel 47–48 and 1 Chronicles 1–9, in order to address the following questions: How is the tribal

3. For a discussion of the understanding of Israel reflected in the lists see Kristin Weingart, *Stämmevolk – Staatsvolk – Gottesvolk?*: *Studien zur Verwendung des Israel-Namens im Alten Testament*, FAT II 68 (Tübingen: Mohr Siebeck, 2014), 81–3.

4. The list was probably introduced in Neh 7 and later transferred to Ezr 2 (cf. Williamson, *Ezra*, 29–30), but it is a secondary insertion in its Nehemiah context as well (see Weingart, *Stämmevolk*, 81).

5. A discussion of P lies outside the scope of this paper but see the contribution by Joachim Schaper in this volume.

6. Two names must suffice to represent a broader phalanx of researchers: Christoph Levin argued on the basis of a redaction critical discussion of Genesis 29–30 that there is no literary trace of the system of the twelve tribes in any pre-exilic text. The system must therefore be a post-exilic construction (Christoph Levin, "Das System der zwölf Stämme Israels," in *Congress Volume, Paris 1992*, VT.S 61, ed. J.A. Emerton [Leiden: Brill, 1995], 163–78.). Philip Davies sees the whole idea of a greater Israel and with it the notion of a twelve-tribe Israel as an invention of post-exilic Judean scribes in their striving for indigenization and authority over the gola community (Philip R. Davies, *In Search of "Ancient Israel"*, JSOT.S 148 [Sheffield: Sheffield Academic Press 1992], or – more recently – *The Origins of Biblical Israel*, LHBOTS 485 [New York / London: T & T Clark, 2007]). For an overview of the current debates see Weingart, *Stämmevolk*, 8–37.

7. For a more comprehensive discussion of the pre-exilic origins of the tribal system as well as the recent debates regarding the alleged appropriation of the name of Israel and self-understanding as Israel in Judah, see Weingart, *Stämmevolk*.

system presented in these texts? What aim does it serve? And, do these texts which both feature the tribal system talk about the same Israel? In doing so, the paper will illustrate how Ezekiel 47–48 as well as 1 Chronicles 1–9 both utilize a basic understanding of Israel as a twelve-tribe nation in order to communicate their specific perspective on Israel's definition and identity.

2. Tribes and Territories – Ezekiel 47–48

Ezekiel 47–48 are the final chapters of the last section of the book of Ezekiel, which is introduced as a new prophetic vision of the temple in the beginning of chapter 40. It contains a detailed description of the new temple (40–42), various laws and regulations concerning the temple, its cult as well as the organization of the people (43–46) and ends with a great vision of the new land and its distribution to the tribes of Israel.[8] The whole section has been labelled "Verfassungsentwurf Ezechiels" by Hartmut Gese, in his seminal study from 1957.[9] It has long been recognized that Ezekiel 40–48 is a composition of its own, distinct and in all likelihood later than the main part of the book in 1–39.[10]

2.1 Putting the Land on the Map

Ezekiel 47–48 deal with the subject of the land. Ezekiel 47:1–12 envision its wonderful transformation into a well irrigated and fertile ground. Against this background, Ezekiel 47:13–48:29 develop a detailed program for the distribution of the now transformed land to the tribes of Israel. Ezekiel 48:30–34 finally turn to the city of Jerusalem and list its twelve gates named after the twelve tribes. Verse 48:35 concludes the section, providing the city with a new name: יהוה שמה.

The main section is marked by an inclusion: 48:29 reiterates and refers back to 47:13–14. Verses 13–14[11] function as a heading; the

---

8. For compositional structures within Ezek 40–48, see Michael Konkel, *Architektonik des Heiligen*, BBB 129 (Berlin / Wien: Philo, 2001), 23–7.

9. Hartmut Gese, *Der Verfassungsentwurf des Ezechiel* (Kap. 40–48): *Traditionsgeschichtlich untersucht*, BHTh 25 (Tübingen: Mohr, 1957).

10. So already Gese, *Verfassungsentwurf*, 1–2. See also Walther Zimmerli, *Ezechiel*: *2. Teilband Ezechiel 25–48*, BK XIII/2 (Neukirchen-Vluyn: Neukirchner Verlag 21969), 977–9; as well as the presentations of the history of research in Thilo A. Rudnig, *Heilig und Profan*: *Redaktionskritische Studien zu Ez 40–48*, BZAW 287 (Berlin / New York: de Gruyter, 2000), 5–28, or Konkel, *Architektonik*, 8–22. Against the broad consensus, Rudnig proposes a redaction critical model that sees at least one continuous redactional layer between Ezek 1–39 and 40–48 (for a critical appraisal of Rudnig's model, cf. Michael Konkel, "Die Gola von 597 und die Priester: Zu einem Buch von Thilo Alexander Rudnig," *ZAR* 8 [2008]: 357–83).

11. Read זה הגבול in 47:13; cf. App. BHS.

keywords גבול and נחלה point to the two segments of the paragraph: the borders of the land in 47:15–20, and the distribution of the land as hereditary property of the individual tribes in 47:21–48:29. Both segments form distinct units, but they are clearly coordinated and interlocked:[12] 48:1 and 28 utilize places named in 47:15–16 (לבוא חמת) (מתמר עד מי מריבות קדש נחלה אל הים הגדול) and 19 (מצר עינן and חתלן) in order to locate the regions given to the northern-most and southern-most tribes Dan and Gad.

2.2 EQUALITY AS THE PRINCIPLE?

Ezekiel 47:14 names the principle applied in the distribution of the land: אותה איש כאחיו ונחלתם. The aim seems to be a division of the land in which each tribe receives an equal share: The geographical region specified in 47:15–20 is to be divided into thirteen east-west "strips" of land. Twelve shares go to the twelve tribes, the central section south of Judah and north of Benjamin is set apart as תרומת הקדש (vv. 10, 20). It includes the city of Jerusalem and the land assigned to the priests, the Levites and the נשיא. Seven tribes receive territories north of the תרומה; these are – from north to south – Dan, Asher, Naphtali, Manasseh, Ephraim, Reuben, and Judah. Five tribes are situated south of the תרומה: Benjamin, Simeon, Issachar, Zebulon, and Gad (again from north to south).

A distribution like this is of course highly artificial, and the principle of equality is applied schematically regardless of the fact that the tribes might differ in size or the geographical conditions within the specific regions of the land might vary.[13] Although the text does not explain the rationale of the envisioned distribution, the identical size of the sections seems to be the sole criterium. All considerations of practicability or real-world conditions are set aside.

What are the reasons for the specific allocations to the tribes? Once again, there is no explanation, the criteria can only be deduced:

– The traditional settlement areas seem to play a role; Dan is located in the far north, Ephraim and Manasseh receive their territories in the area of the former Northern Kingdom, Simeon receives a share in the south. But there are also obvious deviations from the traditional territories. Why place Judah north of Jerusalem or Reuben south of Ephraim?

– In addition to traditional geography, also genealogical considerations seem to matter: The first-born Reuben is placed in greater prox-

---

12. Cf. Zimmerli, Ezechiel, 1220.

13. The problem is also pointed out by Thilo A. Rudnig in Karl-Friedrich Pohlmann, *Das Buch des Propheten Hesekiel* (*Ezechiel*), ATD 22,2 (Göttingen: Vandenhoeck & Ruprecht, 2001), 623.

imity to Jerusalem, the sons of Bilhah (Dan and Naphtali) and the sons of Zilpah (Asher and Gad) are moved to the margins.[14]

– Neither genealogical nor geographical considerations can account for the central positions of Judah and Benjamin. Walter Zimmerli proposed that the two tribes gain their centrality as "die eigentlichen Trägerstämme des vorexilischen Juda".[15] But one does not have to go back to pre-exilic Judah in order to account for the significance of these two tribes; the Persian period provides an equally or even more apt background: Judah and Benjamin (as well as Levi, who is of course situated within the תרומה) are the primary tribes within Persian period Yehud.[16] While real-world conditions are widely neglected in other facets of the vision, they seem to enter the picture when it comes to the hierarchy of the tribes.

– That hierarchy is an issue is confirmed by the probably most curious aspect of the allocation scheme, the positioning of Benjamin to the south and of Judah to the north of Jerusalem. The rationale of the setting has been intensely discussed. Zimmerli proposed that the name 'Benjamin' suggested a southern territory for the tribe, or that the territories of the Leah-sons Reuben, Levi and Judah should be kept in geographical proximity.[17] Moshe Greenberg introduced the aspect of hierarchy into the discussion; he read the placement of Judah on the site of Benjamin as the smallest tribe as an intentional humiliation of Judah.[18] Greenberg's idea highlights a decisive point, but the pragmatics have to be turned around: If hierarchy is of importance here, it is instructive that Judah is moved to an area bordering directly on the holy area of the תרומה district, therefore the tribe's territory has

---

14. So also Zimmerli, Ezechiel, 1231; Konkel, *Architektonik*, 219, 283–4.

15. Zimmerli, *Ezechiel*, 170.

16. While the precise territorial extent of Yehud remains a notorious question (cf. Charles E. Carter, *The Emergence of Yehud in the Persian Period. A Social and Demographic Study*, JSOT. SS 294 [Sheffield: Sheffield University Press, 1999], 75–113), there is no doubt that it comprised mainly the territory associated with the tribes Judah and Benjamin. See also Gary N. Knoppers, *I Chronicles 1–9. A New Translation with Introduction and Commentary*, AB 12, (New York et al.: Doubleday, 2003), 260–264.

17. So Zimmerli, *Ezechiel*, 1231–2. But why is Simeon set apart and placed in the south? He is also a son of Leah. Jon D. Levenson, *Theology of the Program of Restoration of Ezekiel 40–48*, HSM 10 (Missoula, Mont.: Scholars Press, 1976), 117–20, sees the whole design as an attempt to replace Judean hegemony: "[W]e suggest, that the hitherto unexplained reversal of Judah and Benjamin is owing to a concern that the royal tribe not oppress the North, that the North have a share in the House of David, and the House of David a share in the North. There was no better way to insure this than to move Judah above the 'Mason-Dixon line'."

18. Moshe Greenberg, "The Design and Themes of Ezekiel's program of Restoration," *Interpretation* 38 (1984): 181–208, here 200: "The most striking departure from preexilic order is the transposition of Judah and Benjamin, as though the royal tribe (Judah) were purposely removed to the place of the smallest (to humble it?)."

the closest proximity to the temple. Between the holy area and the area of Benjamin in the south lies the profane "cross bar" (48:15: הוא חל), which is designated as the living and working area for the city.[19] Placing Judah to the north of the תרומה is not a humiliation: Judah comes closest to the temple which illustrates its prominent status and special role among the tribes of Israel.

The whole idea of placing the tribes around the sanctuary has of course its closest parallel in Numbers 2. Here the tribes are all placed around the tabernacle: The Levites form an inner circle; all the other tribes are located around it, three on each side – Dan, Asher, and Naphtali in the north; Judah, Issachar, and Zebulon to the east; Reuben, Simeon, and Gad to the south; and Ephraim, Manasseh, and Benjamin to the west. A similar idea seems to have inspired the naming of the twelve gates of the city after the twelve tribes in Ezekiel 48:30–34, but once again, the allocation does not resemble the one of Numbers 2.

While the idea of placing the tribes around the sanctuary has its forerunners, Ezekiel 47–48 develop an own and innovative idea in implementing it. Geographical, genealogical and hierarchical considerations are combined in order to envision a new settlement pattern and to highlight the special importance of three tribes: Judah, Benjamin, and Levi.

3. Tribes and Genealogies – 1 Chronicles 1–9

While Ezekiel's account of the resettlement of the land by the tribes of Israel is highly visionary, the Chronicler's handling of the tribal system is rather down to earth, but not less ambitious. The Chronicler opens his book with the so-called "genealogische Vorhalle",[20] but other than this traditional designation might suggest, the registers form

---

19. For the inner structure of the תרומה-district see Gese, *Verfassungsentwurf*, 101–2, or Konkel, *Architektonik*, 219–21. The interdependency between the allocation of the tribes and the inner structure of the תרומה-district casts doubt on Rudnig's redaction-critical hypothesis that attributes 48:8–22 to a different layer than the distribution of the land to the tribes (*Heilig*, 181).

20. The designation seems to have been coined by J. Wilhelm Rothstein and Johannes Hänel, *Kommentar zum ersten Buch der Chronik*, KAT (Leipzig: Deichert, 1927), 2: "Den ersten Abschnitt…habe ich als 'Vorhalle' des chronist. Werkes bezeichnet. Daß das eigentliche Geschichtswerk mit c. 10 beginnt, kann ja nicht zweifelhaft sein; aber bedeutungslos sind darum c. 1–9 doch nicht, aber sie lagern sich vor das eigentliche Werk eben wie die Vorhalle vor das Heiligtum." A number of other designations have since been suggested, they are collected in Manfred Oeming, *Das wahre Israel: Die "genealogische Vorhalle" 1 Chronik 1–9*, BWANT 128 (Stuttgart/Berlin/Köln: Kohlhammer, 1990), 9–10.

an essential part of the book.[21] In literary terms, the opening chapters provide the framework and the stage on which only one act from the longer and wider history of Israel is played out: the history of the Davidic kingdom.[22]

1 Chronicles 1:1–2:2 place Israel within the greater world – or better: family – of nations. Very concise linear genealogies and more detailed segmental genealogies alternate. The secondary lines are placed before the main line: at first, the descendants of Japheth and Ham, then the descendants of Shem, up to the sons of Abraham and so on. In this way 1 Chronicles 1:1–2:2 narrows down on Israel. From the broader stock of all the descendants of Adam the focus finally reaches the sons of Israel. According to 1 Chronicles 1–9, the history of humankind thus genealogically leads up to Israel.[23]

1 Chronicles 2:1–2 name the twelve sons of Israel in a sequence that has no parallel in the Hebrew Bible. The closest proximity is to Genesis 35:22b–26 or Exodus 1:2–4, but Dan comes before Joseph and Benjamin. However, all twelve sons are there, and 2:1–2 serve as the conclusion of the genealogies of the nations and at the same time introduce the following lists, which are dedicated to the inner division of Israel.

3.1 THE ARRANGEMENT OF THE TRIBES

Accordingly, 1 Chronicles 2:3–9:2 provide segmental genealogies for the tribes of Israel. But the order does not correspond to 2:1–2. The Chronicler rather follows an independent ordering principle. The genealogies for Judah (2:3–4:23), Levi (5:27–6:66) and Benjamin (especially 8:1–40) are the most important blocks, set out by their sheer extent. They are also placed in prominent positions within the composition: beginning – Judah, center – Levi, and end – Benjamin.

The arrangement of the tribes within this basic framework is not as obvious. It is best explained – as Thomas Willi has done[24] – by applying a combination of kinship ties and settlement geography. At the beginning, the tribes of Judah (2:3–4:23) and Simeon (4:24–43) settling south are dealt with. This is followed by an eastern block of Reuben (5:1–10), Gad (5:11–22) and eastern Manasseh (5:23–26). Levi (5:27–6:66) and Lea's son Issachar (7:1–5) are at the center. The

---

21. So very persuasively Thomas Willi, *Chronik: 1. Teilband 1. Chronik 1,1–10,14*, BK XXIV/1 (Neukirchen-Vluyn: Neukirchner, 2009), 7–9. For an introduction into the Chronicler's genealogies cf. the excursus in Knoppers, *I Chronicles 1–9*, 245–264.

22. Cf. Ralph W. Klein, *1 Chronicles*, Hermeneia (Minneapolis: Fortress, 2006), 46.

23. Cf. Weingart, *Stämmevolk*, 117–21 with further references.

24. Willi, *Chronik*, 55 f.

geographical aspect fades somewhat into the background. The Levites settled in various tribal areas according to 6:39–66. The conclusion is formed by the Rachel-Bilhah sons Benjamin (7:6–11; 8:1–40), possibly Dan (7:12),[25] Naphtali (7:13), West-Manasseh (7:14–19) and Ephraim (7:20–29), as well as the Zilpah son Asher (7:30–40), who is probably moved to this place because of the geographical proximity to the great northern tribes Ephraim and Manasseh. Zebulon is missing.[26] Whether 7:12 really contains a genealogy of Dan or some remnant of it, remains doubtful. However, according to 1 Chronicles 9:1a, the listed tribes and clans constitute "all Israel."

3.2 Justifying the New Order

The arrangement and extent of the individual genealogies clearly show where the Chronicler sees the priorities: the most important tribes are Judah, Levi, and Benjamin. Judah gains the most prominent position. There is no other genealogical list of tribes in the Hebrew Bible which starts with Judah.[27] It is not surprising, that the arrangement of the tribes in 1 Chronicles 2–9 was by no means self-evident; it had to be justified, and the Chronicler does so in 1 Chronicles 5:1–2.[28]

The note is placed at the beginning of the genealogy of Reuben. The Wiederaufnahme of ובני ראובן בכור ישראל from v. 1 in v. 3 marks it as a digression interrupting the genealogical lists and offering some additional information.[29] Not in the beginning, where the genealogy

---

25. The conclusion בני בלהה in 7:13 seems to suggest that besides Naphtali also the other Bilhah son Dan is included in the list. Since 7:13 is clearly devoted to Naphtali, 7:12 remains the only likely place to look for a Danite genealogy (Oeming, *Israel*, 163–164, offers an overview over the discussion). The older proposal by August Klostermann to emend עיר into דן was recently taken up by Sara Japhet, *1 Chronik*, HThKAT, Freiburg / Basel / Wien: Herder, 2002), 188, and Willi, *Chronik*, 253.

26. There have been attempts to reconstruct a genealogy of Zebulon (see e. g. Georg Richter, "Zu den Geschlechtsregistern I Chronik 2–9," ZAW 50 [1932]: 130–40, here 133–134; Edward L. Curtis and Albert A. Madsen, *A Critical and Exegetical Commentary on the Books of Chronicles*, ICC [Edinburgh: Clark, ²1952], 145–9).

27. In Numb 2 (the camp order) as well as Numb 7 (a list of offerings connected to the dedication of the tabernacle) Judah is mentioned first. But in both cases the order does not follow genealogical considerations. Cf. already Martin Noth, *Das vierte Buch Mose: Numeri*, ATD 7 (Göttingen: Vandenhoeck & Ruprecht, 1966), 24–5, 59.

28. The short note has been intensely discussed, for the more recent debates see e. g. Piet B. Dirksen, "1 Chronicles 5:1–2," *JNSL* 25 (1999): 17–23; Michelangelo Tabet, "La preminenza a Giuda, la primogenitura a Giuseppe (1Chr 5,1b–2)," *RivBib* 55 (2007): 273–96, both with further references.

29. There is no need to assume a secondary expansion (against Martin Noth, *Überlieferungsgeschichtliche Studien: Die sammelnden und bearbeitenden Geschichtswerke im Alten Testament* [Tübingen: Niemeyer, ²1957], 120; Magnar Kartveit, *Motive und Schichten der Landtheologie in I Chronik 1–9*, CB OT 28 [Stockholm: Almquist och Wiksell, 1989], 65–6).

of Judah starts the lists, but only when he reaches Reuben, the Chronicler takes the readers to a meta level in order to explain and defend his arrangement of the genealogical register. He offers an argument in two steps which builds and expands upon Genesis 49. In using the phrase חלל יצוע for Reuben's offence, 1 Chronicles 5 adopts not only the concept but also the wording from Genesis 49. Genesis 49:3–4 in turn, refer to Genesis 35:22 and explain Reuben's loss of his birthright with reference to the latter's sexual intercourse with Bilhah.

According to Genesis 49, Reuben remains the first-born and is also the first to receive a "blessing",[30] but he loses the rights associated with his primogeniture. The two tribes or sons receiving the most important blessings in Genesis 49 are Joseph and Judah. They are thus distinguished from all the other brothers and find their role precisely in opposition to them. Judah (Gen 49:8–12) is promised dominion among the sons of Jacob (v. 8b: ישתחוו לך בני אביך). Accordingly, in the imagery of his blessing, he is presented as a lion and endowed with scepter and staff (v. 10a: לא יסור שבט מיהודה ומחקק מבין רגליו). Joseph is considered to be blessed in a special way by Jacob (Gen 49:25–26: … מאל אביך ויעזרך ואת שדי ויברכך), which sets him apart from his brothers.

But which of the two receives the right of the first-born taken away from Reuben? Genesis 49 does not answer the question, while both Judah and Joseph remain likely candidates. From a compositional point of view, Judah could be seen as the recipient. After Reuben's degradation and the curses on Simeon and Levi, Judah is the first son of Jacob to receive a positive evaluation. But other indicators point to Joseph: The blessing of Jacob lies stronger on him than on all the other brothers (cf. v. 26: ברכת אביך גברו). Primogeniture and paternal blessing usually belong together, at least according to Genesis 27:[31] Is the one who is blessed in a special way by the father not also the recipient of the birthright?[32] The Chronicler fills the gap left open by

---

30. The blessing is actually a reversal of Reuben's status. See the wordplay with the root יתר (cf. Jürgen Ebach, *Genesis 37–50*, HThKAT [Freiburg / Basel / Wien: Herder, 2007], 585). Reuben was שאת יתר (or שאה, cf. app. BHS) and יתר עז (49:3) among his brothers; now, Jacob decrees that he will lose his preeminence אל תותר (49:4).

31. It is almost a stock motif of the ancestral narratives that the firstborn does not receive the paternal blessing (so besides Reuben also Ishmael, Esau, and Manasseh). For discussions of the phenomenon cf. Roger Syrén, *The Forsaken First-Born: A Study of a Recurrent Motif in the Patriarchal Narratives*, JSOT.S 133 (Sheffield: Sheffield Academic Press, 1993); Benedikt Hensel, *Die Vertauschung des Erstgeburtssegens in der Genesis: Eine Analyse der narrativ-theologischen Grundstruktur des ersten Buches der Tora*, BZAW 423 (Berlin/New York: de Gruyter, 2011). However, all these stories create their narrative suspense by deviating from the rule they presuppose: the firstborn son is usually the receiver of the paternal blessing.

32. 1Chr 5:1–2 is the only text in the Hebrew Bible which addresses the question

Genesis 49 and explicitly assigns the בכרה to Joseph (5:2b).

The actual objective of the argument is not 5:2b, but 5:2a; the Chronicler is not so much concerned with Joseph but with Judah. It is not Reuben who lost his right as a first-born and also not Joseph who is now considered to be the first-born who gains the first place in the genealogical register: להתיחש לבכרה. The Chronicler differentiates between the birthright of the firstborn, the paternal blessing associated with it and the supremacy or preeminence among the brothers, which is expressed by a prominent place within the registers. In doing so, the Chronicler once again expands on Genesis 49: Joseph is the blessed one, but Judah takes the lead. And – comparable to Ezekiel 47–48 – the inner hierarchy of the tribes is once again an issue.

Which register does 5:1b refer to? It can only be an auto-reflective reference to the lists in 1 Chronicles 2–9, the only register featuring Judah at the head.[33] The Chronicler thus explains the most conspicuous point in his arrangement of the Israelite tribes, namely the top position of Judah. The latter is a result of the Chronicler's perspective on the historical development of the tribes (Reuben had long since become meaningless; Judah became a decisive factor of Israel's continued existence) and probably at the same time a reflection of the historical circumstances in the province of Yehud.[34] In addition, 5:1b provides a link to 9:1a, 2, the conclusion of the genealogical lists, which characterizes them as a register of all Israel (התיחשו וכל ישראל).[35]

4. WHAT AND WHO IS ISRAEL?

The two texts and their literary contexts are obviously only samples and they do not offer an exhaustive picture of everything that either Ezekiel or Chronicles had to say about the tribes of Israel. They belong to different genres and each has its specific pragmatics. But their similarities and differences illustrate interesting points and allow a glimpse into Israel's self-understanding and the discourses pertaining to it in the Persian period.

---

whether Reuben's הרוכב is reassigned or not. The answer frequently found in the rabbinical literature is that the primogeniture was reassigned and given to Joseph. See e. g. the discussion in bBaba Batra 123a,b.

33. Cf. Willi, *Chronik*, 164.

34. The same holds true for the lists themselves which not only collect data from older texts, but also incorporate settlement and segmental structures of the Chronicler's own time, especially in the genealogy of Judah. See Yigal Levin, "Who was the Chronicler's Audience?: A Hint from His Genealogies," *JBL* 122 (2003): 220–45.

35. 1Chr 9:1–2 display a number of difficulties, most of them created by the secondary insertion of 9:1b into an older context; cf. the discussion of the literary history and understanding of 9:1–2 in Weingart, *Stämmevolk*, 132–5.

4.1 THE LASTING SIGNIFICANCE OF THE TRIBAL SYSTEM

Both texts attest to the fact that the tribal system was and remained a decisive factor in Israelite collective identity. Both of them presuppose the same basic criterion for belonging to Israel, namely being a member – or more precisely – being born into one of the tribes of Israel. This means: the underlying construction of Israelite collective identity is an ethnic one, based on a putative common descent.[36]

Using the terms 'construction' and 'putative' in this regard hints to an understanding which does not see the genealogical system as a genetic description, but rather as a means of structuring social reality. Ethnological research has shown that genealogical systems are social constructions with a great deal of fluidity. They are able to incorporate changes of relation or alliances between communities or groups within a community into new genealogical systems. These are however perceived within the community as unchanged and persisting from the beginning of the genealogical line. They are considered as given and essential traits of the social world.[37]

The genealogies of the Chronicler are almost a textbook example of the mechanisms at play in such primordial genealogical codes. Once one leaves the top-level structure of the twelve tribes, there is a considerable amount of fluidity. The assignment of certain families and clans to one tribe or the other, can still vary. For example, Caleb belongs to Judah in 1 Chronicles 2 but is a Kenazite in Joshua 14. The inclusion of clans like the Calebites, Kenazites, and Kenites who are seen as non-Israelites in other texts, is accomplished by incorporating them into the genealogical structure.[38]

---

36. For a methodological overview of ethnic theory and its discussion pertaining to biblical texts, see Mark G. Brett, "Interpreting Ethnicity: Method, Hermeneutics, Ethics," in *Ethnicity and the Bible*, ed. M.g. Brett (Leiden: Brill, 1996), 3–22. The lasting significance of the tribal system as a basic trait of Israel's self-understanding in post-exilic times, is discussed in Weingart, *Stämmevolk*, 288–340.

37. For a discussion of a primordial code of collective identity, its underlying principles and differentiation from other possible codes, see Bernard Giesen, *Kollektive Identität. Die Intellektuellen und die Nation 2* (Frankfurt a.M.: Suhrkamp, 1999; Jonathan M. Hall, *Ethnic Identity in Greek Antiquity* (Cambridge: Cambridge University Press, 1998), or Weingart, *Stämmevolk*, 38–44.

38. Cf. Willi, *Chronik*, 88, 105, 130; Japhet, *Chronik*, 136; or Weingart, *Stämmevolk*, 127–31. For the functionality and pragmatics of genealogies (with regard to the study of the Hebrew Bible and ancient Israel), see e. g. Robert R. Wilson, *Genealogy and History in the Biblical World*, Yale Near Eastern Researches 7 (New Haven/London: Yale University Press, 1977). For a recent concrete investigation which brings together textual and epigraphical evidence pertaining to the tribe of Manasseh, see Erhard Blum, "The Israelite Tribal System – Social Reality or Literary Fiction?," in *Saul, Benjamin and the Emergence of Monarchy in Israel: Biblical and Archaeo-*

The same self-understanding of Israel stands behind Ezekiel's vision of the transformation and re-population of the land. Israel is a segmental society, structured into tribes, each of which receives its share. The Chronicler tries to assemble a register of all Israel, past and present, which is also structured as a family of tribes and embedded into an even greater family of nations. Each in its own way, the two texts attest to the fact, that in their view being an Israelite is a matter of birth and descent, and not of geographical provenance, shared values, or religious affiliation.

4.2 Tradition not Innovation

In addition, both texts clearly show that the tribal system is a tradition that could be used and was indeed used. It was also a tradition that had become fixed to a certain degree; the Chronicler as well as the author of Ezekiel 47–48 could rely on, and at the same time had to take into account their audiences' familiarity with the concept.

In Ezekiel this is apparent from the way the tribal system is presented. The author presupposes that there are twelve tribes. In 47:13, he allots two portions of the land to the tribe of Joseph: שבטי ישראל יוסף חבלים זה הגבול[39] אשר התנחלו את הארץ לשני עשר. Accordingly, the list features Ephraim and Manasseh in 48:4 and 5. But there is no explanation why Joseph is treated differently or why his name does not appear in the list. It must have been known by the addressees that Joseph is represented by Ephraim and Manasseh. On the other hand, in naming the gates of the city (48:31–34), the name Joseph appears alongside Levi. Both versions of the tribal system, which Martin Noth called System I – including Levi and Joseph – and System II – not including Levi but listing the Joseph-sons Ephraim and Manasseh in order to reach the total of twelve, stand side by side.[40] Both of them must have been commonly known on the side of the addressees so that they could identify and understand them as both representing the same Israel.

Equally, the Chronicler's treatment of the tribal system illustrates a familiarity with, but also an engagement with the received and traditional shape of the system. It could no longer be simply changed or adapted – at least not with regard to its basic structure and design as a genealogical system consisting of twelve specific tribes (see also 1Chr

---

logical Perspectives, AIL, eds. Joachim J. Krause, Omer Sergi and Kristin Weingart (Atlanta: SBL, In press).

39. MT reads גה גבול but is apparently corrupted; cf. app. BHS.

40. Martin Noth, *Das System der zwölf Stämme Israels*, BWANT 52 (Stuttgart: Kohlhammer, 1930), 7–23.

2:1–2).[41] When the Chronicler adapted the traditional system in his register, he could not simply ignore it, but had to justify the new position of Judah. As Gerhard von Rad already put it, the aim is an "interlocking of the old 12-tribe schema with the actual historical reality" at the time of the Chronicler.[42] The coordinates within the twelve-tribe system are shifted, but the system is retained as fundamental for Israel.

4.3 Tribal Hierarchy

The attempts to adapt the system, therefore, do not concern its general outline – despite the fact that some tribes were no longer, or have never been a factor in real life. The Chronicler's difficulty to provide genealogies for Dan or Zebulon are telling in this regard. Reuben is another notorious candidate.[43] The shifting of the coordinates concerns primarily the inner hierarchy of the tribes.

The Chronicler puts Judah in first place, and Levi and Benjamin gain prominent positions. The traditional ties between Benjamin and Joseph fade away. The social reality of Yehud leaves its mark on the way the genealogical system is presented.

If the analysis outlined above is correct, and the layout of the tribal territories envisioned in Ezekiel 47–48 reflects an inner hierarchy of the tribes, we find a similar picture in the two texts. Levi, Judah, and Benjamin gain the most prominent places around the sanctuary. Besides Levi, it is once again Judah who finds itself in the place of honor. The aim to symbolize Judah's supremacy – also over and against Benjamin – turns the traditional geographic allocation of Judah and Benjamin, quite literally, upside down.

4.4 Conflicting Concepts of Israel

Ezekiel 40–48 develop a vision. It deals with the new temple, the new Jerusalem and of course with Israel. Israel is a people structured into twelve tribes. Therefore, it includes more than the Judeans of the Golah who would have been Ezekiel's primary addressees. And it also

---

41. The fluidity noted above, is achieved by adjustments on the subsequent levels of clans and families.

42. Gerhard von Rad, *Das Geschichtsbild des chronistischen Werkes* (Stuttgart: Kohlhammer, 1930), 73: "In diesen wenig beachteten Sätzen [sc. 1Chr 5:1–2] hat also der Chronist in theoretischer Form sich über die Frage, wie die Hegemonie schließlich an Juda kam, Rechenschaft gegeben, und wir sehen die recht interessante dogmatische Verklammerung des alten 12-Stämmeschemas mit der tatsächlichen geschichtlichen Wirklichkeit, die der Chronist vorfand."

43. Cf. Ulrike Schorn, *Ruben und das System der zwölf Stämme Israels*, BZAW 248 (Berlin/New York: de Gruyter, 1997), who comes to the conclusion, that all texts dealing with Reuben originate from periods when the territories associated with the tribe no longer belonged to Israel (282).

includes more than just Judah, Benjamin and Levi as the tribes in Persian Period Yehud. The so-called northern tribes are an essential part of the Israel Ezekiel 47–48 have in mind. All twelve tribes are to come back, to resettle and to repopulate the land of Israel.

Ezekiel's vision has been called a utopia,[44] but the designation seems problematic. The land of Ezekiel 47–48 is not a "no place" like the Greek οὐ τόπος would imply. It is the land of Israel, which will be transformed and afterwards resettled by the tribes of Israel.[45] This in turn implies that in this vision, none of the tribes is in the land; all of them have to return and take possession of their new territories once the transformation of the land is completed. Right now, the land is empty,[46] there are no Israelites in it. All Israelites have to return first.

In Chronicles the situation is somewhat different. If one searches the genealogies for notions of deportation from the land, one learns in 1 Chronicles 5:25–26 about the deportation of Reuben, Gad, and one half of Manasseh, i. e. the tribes whose territories are situated east of the Jordan. One reads in 5:41 about the generation of the Levites in whose period Judah and Jerusalem had been exiled by Nebuchadnezzar, namely in the period of Yozadaq, the son of Seraya. 1 Chronicles 9:1, eventually, talks about the exile of Judah. While 9:1b might be a later gloss, it is consistent with the Chronicler's view of history. 1 Chronicles 5:42 allude to it and 2 Chronicles 36:20–21 express it clearly: Judah and Jerusalem went into exile.

So, while Ezekiel 47–48 and 1 Chronicles 1–9 both refer to the tribal system and both present Israel as a twelve-tribe nation and in doing so, transcend their historic realities, they show a slight albeit decisive difference regarding the shape of their communities or polities. Ezekiel's vision presupposes that there are no Israelites in the land. All of Israel have to come back from the outside. Then and only then, can the land be distributed anew. Because there are no Israelites yet, the territories of the tribes can be rearranged freely. According to the Chronicler, however, the northern tribes – with the exception of the east-Jordanian ones Reuben, Gad, and half of Manasseh – have

---

44. Cf. among others Ruth Poser, *Das Ezechielbuch als Traumaliteratur*, VT.S 154 (Leiden/New York/Köln, Brill, 2012), 1, or the title of Jürgen Ebach's dissertation: *Kritik und Utopie*: *Untersuchungen zum Verhältnis von Volk und Herrscher im Verfassungsentwurf des Ezechiel* (Kap. 40–48) (Univ. Diss, Hamburg 1972).

45. So already Iain M. Duguid, *Ezekiel and the Leaders of Israel*, VT.S 56 (Leiden/New York/Köln: Brill, 1994), 140: "In another sense, however, Ezekiel's plan is not strictly utopian. His promised land is not located 'nowhere' or even 'somewhere' but in the land of Israel, which Yahweh swore to the patriarchs."

46. For the concept of the "empty land", its historical difficulties and possible background, see Weingart, *Stämmevolk*, 307–14, with further references.

remained in the land.⁴⁷ In this respect, and with regard to any inhabitants in the area of the former northern kingdom, i. e. the Persian province of Samaria, the Israel of Ezekiel is not the Israel of Chronicles.

5. CONCLUSION

In conclusion, one might say: what we find in Ezekiel is only a vision and no portrayal of historical circumstances. But also a visionary text has its intended addressees who can share the vision and the hopes it conveys, and who may read it as an ideal worth striving for. For the Chronicler, Israel continues to exist in Samaria; in Ezekiel 47–48, Samaria has nothing to do with the future of Israel. In this regard – although this might not have been the primary pragmatics of the texts – they both represent opposing positions in a question which was a pressing issue in their time: the status, or better, the Israelite-ness of the Samarians.⁴⁸

---

47. Cf. also the short remarks in Klein, *1 Chronicles*, 46.

48. For discussions of the discourse and the texts pertaining to it, see Weingart, Stämmevolk, 296–340; Benedikt Hensel, *Juda und Samaria: Zum Verhältnis zweier nach-exilischer Jahwismen*, FAT 110 (Tübingen: Mohr Siebeck, 2016), as well as Kristin Weingart, "What Makes an Israelite an Israelite?: Judean Perspectives on the Samarians in the Persian Period," *JSOT* 42 (2017): 155–75.

Sacrifices in Chronicles: How Priestly Are They?

Esias E. Meyer

1. Introduction

As the title suggests the purpose of this chapter is to explore the depiction of the sacrificial cult in Chronicles in the light of the presentation of sacrifices in Leviticus. Scholars such as David Janzen and Sara Japhet agree on the centrality of the cult in Chronicles.[1] Thus Japhet would say concerning the temple that what strikes the reader "as almost every study has noted, is the book's emphasis on the subject."[2] To state that the cult is central in Leviticus is saying the very obvious. This essay aims to scrutinise the Chronicler's presentation of the sacrificial cult from the Priestly perspective of Leviticus. It will become clear that at times there is a fair amount of overlap or similarity between the cult presented by the Chronicler and the one described in Leviticus. At other times there are evident tensions between the two portrayals of the cult.

Why would one approach the presentation of the cult from the perspective of Leviticus? One answer could refer to historical context. Most scholars who engage with dating the final compilations of these books would date the Chronicler to a slightly later period than Leviticus.[3] Both are probably from the Persian Period, but the Chronicler

---

1. David Janzen, *The Social Meanings of Sacrifice in the Hebrew Bible: A Study of Four Writings*, BZAW 344 (Berlin: De Gruyter, 2004), 209; Sarah Japhet, *The Ideology of the Book of Chronicles and its Place in Biblical Thought*, trans. A. Barber, BEATAJ 9 (Berlin: Peter Lang; 1997; repr. Winona Lake, IN: Eisenbrauns, 2009). See also Ehud Ben Zvi, "Purity Matters in the Book of Chronicles: A Kind of Prolegomenon," in *Purity, Holiness, and Identity in Judaism and Christianity: Essays in Memory of Susan Haber*, eds. Carl S. Ehrlich, Anders Runesson and Eileen Schuller (Tübingen: Mohr Siebeck, 2013), 37–54, here 39.

2. Japhet, *The Ideology of the Book*, 175.

3. Scholars such as Klaus Grünwaldt, *Das Heiligkeitsgesetz Leviticus 17–26: Ursprüngliche Gestalt, Tradition und Theologie*, BZAW 271 (Berlin: De Gruyter, 1999), 379–81, whose work focused on the Holiness Code, dates this text to the middle of the

is later and takes us to the end of the Persian Period (if not the Hellenistic Period, as some would argue).[4] Both presentations of the cult thus derive from a similar historical context.

A further answer has to do with the fact that some Chronicles scholars have already argued that the Chronicler was drawing from both "the Deuteronomistic tradition (which formed the main source for his historical work) and the priestly tradition, probably in mimetic fashion."[5] The question is thus *how* did the Chronicler draw on the Priestly view of the cult in Leviticus.

One should keep in mind though that in terms of genre both texts are quite different. Apart from the fact that Leviticus is a mixture of apodictic and casuistic law with a narrative section here and there, Chronicles is another kind of text, mostly characterised by narratives and genealogies.[6] Both books also depict two different narrative settings. Leviticus tells the story of Sinai, which is primarily understood as fictional, but it retells this story in the Persian context. In this

---

fifth century BCE. At this time, most of Leviticus 1–16 was already in place. Christophe Nihan, *From Priestly Torah to Pentateuch*, FAT II 25 (Tübingen: Mohr Siebeck, 2007), 574, argues for the late fifth century for the completion of what he calls H. But then, the two dark horses of any attempt at diachronic reconstructions of the development of the text of Leviticus are chapters 10 and 27, which probably came later. Thomas Hieke, *Levitikus 1–15*, HTKAT (Freiburg: Herder, 2014), 70, like Grünwaldt, thinks it was the middle of the fifth century. I will not engage here with the dates put forward by members of the Kaufmann school. For the most recent challenge to that position see Konrad Schmid, "How to Identify a Persian Period Text in the Pentateuch," in *On Dating Biblical Texts to the Persian Period*, FAT II 101, eds. Richard J. Bautch and M. Lackowski (Tübingen, Mohr Siebeck, 2019), 101–18. Also see the diverse opinions in the contributions by Shimon Gesundheit, Erhard Blum, Jan Joosten, William M. Schniedewind, Thomas Römer, Noam Mizrahi, Jakob Wöhrle and Frank H. Polak in *The Formation of the Pentateuch*: *Bridging the Academic Cultures of Europe, Israel, and North America*, FAT 111, eds. Jan C. Gertz, Bernard M. Levinson, Dalit Rom-Shiloni and Konrad Schmid (Tübingen: Mohr Siebeck, 2016). My own understanding of dating Leviticus would be similar to the views of Blum, Römer, Wöhrle etc. which I suppose puts me very much in the European corner of this debate.

4. See the overviews provided by Louis C. Jonker, *1 & 2 Chronicles*, UBCS (Grand Rapids, MI: Baker Books, 2013), 8, or, Gary N. Knoppers, "Chronicles, First and Second Books of," NIDB 1:621–31, here 624. Both argue for the fourth century BCE. Also, Steven L. McKenzie, *1–2 Chronicles*, AOTC (Nashville: Abingdon, 2004), 29–31, regards "the second half of the fourth century (350–300 B.C.E.) being perhaps the most likely."

5. Louis C. Jonker, *Defining All-Israel in Chronicles*: *Multi-levelled Identity Negotiation in Late Persian-Period Yehud*, FAT 106 (Tübingen: Mohr Siebeck, 2016), 236. Jonker gets the idea of "mimetic fashion" from Gary N. Knoppers, "The Relationship of the Deuteronomistic History to Chronicles: Was the Chronicler a Deuteronomist?," in *Congress Volume Helsinki 2010*, ed. Martti Nissinen (Leiden: Brill, 2012), 307–41.

6. See Jonker, *1 & 2 Chronicles*, 5–6. Other genres mentioned are a letter and edict, prayers and speeches.

narrative world there are no kings, since they appear only later in the story, but incidentally, it is told in a historical context where there are no longer any kings (except for Persian ones). The Chronicler tells his story in a similar historical context, but in his part of the story there are kings, and they need to be portrayed as characters. They need to have some kind of relationship with the cult in that story. As we will see below, the depiction of the cult becomes most interesting when certain kings enter the story.

The chapter will first present a brief overview of how the five sacrifices of Leviticus 1–7 are portrayed in the books of Chronicles. These are not the only sacrifices in the Old Testament and they are not the only sacrifices mentioned in Chronicles. It would be possible to present the Chronicler's view of sacrifice by focusing on the sacrificial terms which feature in these books,[7] as Janzen did, for instance,[8] but this chapter will do this the other way around, taking Leviticus as point of reference.

This overview will eventually lead us to the narratives about Hezekiah and Josiah, and it will also lead us to considering issues of clean and unclean, concepts which for some reason virtually feature only in the stories about these two kings. If one were to look for the five offerings (עֹלָה, מִנְחָה, שְׁלָמִים, חַטָּאת and אָשָׁם) mentioned in Leviticus 1–7 then one finds the situation as discussed below.

2. A BRIEF OVERVIEW OF LEVITICAL SACRIFICES IN CHRONICLES

The first type of sacrifice found in the book of Leviticus is the עֹלָה usually translated as "burnt offering." It is regarded as one of the oldest and most prevalent sacrifices in the Old Testament.[9] The whole sacri-

---

7. One could, for instance, start by looking at how the verb זבח is used. The verb is found in 1 Chronicles *15:26*; *21:28*; 29:21; 2 Chronicles *5:6*; 7:4, 5; *11:16*; *15:11*; *18:2*; *28:4*, *23*(x2); 30:22; 33:16, *17*, *22*; *34:4*. Of these the ones in italics do not mention any specific kind of sacrifice, but in other cases we find reference to the עֹלָה (1 Chron 29:21) or the זֶבַח שְׁלָמִים (2 Chron 30:22; 33:16). Sometimes the verb is used to describe the wrong kind of sacrifices as in 2 Chronicles 28:4, 23; 33:17, 22; 34:4. In 2 Chronicles 18:2 the verb actually refers to "slaughter" and not "sacrifice". We also find the very general term זֶבַח (2 Chron 7:4, 5) as object of the verb. In Leviticus the term would usually be used in a construct relation with שְׁלָמִים. As a stand-alone term it is found only in Leviticus 17:16, 17; 23:37, which are all texts of the Holiness Code.

8. David Janzen, *The Social Meanings*, 209–42. In his discussion of sacrifice in Chronicles he focuses on two kinds of sacrifices namely "ad hoc" and "regular". Janzen also focuses more on 1 Chronicles 23–27 whereas the path taken in the present contribution rather leads to the narratives about Hezekiah and Josiah.

9. See overviews in Hieke, *Levitikus 1–15*, 82–4; James W. Watts, Leviticus 1–10, HCOT (Leuven: Peeters, 2013), 172–5; Jacob Milgrom, *Leviticus 1–16: A New*

ficial offering was burnt and nothing was left over. The עֹלָה is found in Leviticus 1, but also in many other famous stories in the OT; for instance, in the Akedah Isaac is saved from becoming an עֹלָה. But Jephthah's daughter is not so fortunate in Judges 11.[10] The first big disagreement between Samuel and Saul in 1 Samuel 13 was because Saul presented an עֹלָה and a שְׁלָמִים and Samuel thought that he was not supposed to do that. The עֹלָה is found in many other texts, including 43 occurrences in the book of Chronicles.[11] The first occurrence of the term tells us something of the Chronicler's view of priesthood:

1 Chronicles 6:34 (BHS SESB 2.0)	1 Chronicles 6:49 (NRSV)
¹⁴וְאַהֲרֹן וּבָנָיו מַקְטִירִים עַל־מִזְבַּח הָעוֹלָה וְעַל־מִזְבַּח הַקְּטֹרֶת לְכֹל מְלֶאכֶת קֹדֶשׁ הַקֳּדָשִׁים וּלְכַפֵּר עַל־יִשְׂרָאֵל כְּכֹל אֲשֶׁר צִוָּה מֹשֶׁה עֶבֶד הָאֱלֹהִים: פ	¹⁴But Aaron and his sons made offerings on the altar of burnt offering and on the altar of incense, doing all the work of the most holy place, to make atonement for Israel, according to all that Moses the servant of God had commanded.

This description follows after we had been told about which Levites were supposed to make music in the tabernacle. This text acknowledges that there are two altars in the sanctuary, and it is the job of Aaron's sons to burn sacrifices on them: the outside altar of the עֹלָה and the inside altar of incense. These are the same terms used in Exodus 30 and, for instance, in Leviticus 4 (but they do not occur in Lev 16).[12] It is also clear that the vocation of the sons of Aaron is to bring about reconciliation (כפר). This text sounds like a good summary of the sacrificial cult as portrayed by the authors of Leviticus.[13] In Leviticus the verb

---

Translation with Introduction and Commentary, AB 3 (New Haven: Yale University Press, 2009; repr., New York: Doubleday, 1991), 172–7.

10. Erhard S. Gerstenberger, *Das 3. Buch Mose. Leviticus*, ATD 6 (Göttingen: Vandenhoeck & Ruprecht, 1993), 22–3 speculates that the עֹלָה might have originated with human sacrifice.

11. 1 Chronicles 6:34; 16:1, 2, 40 (x2); 21:23, 24, 26 (x2), 29; 22:1; 23:31; 29:21; 2 Chronicles 1:6; 2:3; 4:6; 7:1, 7 (x2); 8:12; 13:11; 23:18; 24:14; 29:7, 18, 24, 27 (x2), 28, 31, 32 (x2), 34, 35 (x2); 30:15; 31:2, 3 (x3); 35:12, 14, 16.

12. For a detailed discussion of this issue, see Nihan, *From Priestly Torah*, 161–4. Nihan argues that Leviticus 4 and Exodus 30 belong to a younger P layer than, for instance, most of Leviticus 16 and Exodus 30. Or see the more recent overview in Julia Rhyder, *The Holiness Legislation and Cult Centralization in the Persian Period* (PhD Thesis, University of Lausanne, 2018), 32–5. She also engages with the text-critical debate.

13. See Knoppers "The Relationship," 329.

כפר is usually used to describe the result of a sacrificial process which leads to reconciliation or atonement.[14] Usually, the priest is the subject of the verb.[15] On one occasion (Lev 17:11) blood is the subject. Leviticus 1:4 says that the offerer must put his hand on the head of the עֹלָה so that it can bring about reconciliation (כפר) for the addressee.

In the rest of Chronicles the עֹלָה is found in combination with other sacrifices, such as the שְׁלָמִים and the חַטָּאת[16] The former combination is found quite frequently in the Old Testament, as mentioned before, but it is not common in Leviticus.[17] The combination of עֹלָה and חַטָּאת will be discussed in more detail below.

The second offering found in Leviticus, chapter 2, is the מִנְחָה, which in Leviticus usually means "grain offering". The noun occurs 11 times in Chronicles, but in most of these cases it means a gift or tribute, which is the more basic meaning of the noun, compared to the more technical sacrificial term found in Leviticus 2.[18] On three occasions we do read of the grain offering specifically. In 1 Chronicles 21:23 Ornan presents cattle as burnt offerings, and wood, and wheat for a grain offering to David. In 1 Chronicles 23:29 David gives the duty of taking care of the rows of bread and the choice flower for the grain offering to the Levites. Many of the terms which occur in 1 Chronicles 23:29 are found in Leviticus, where they are used to describe the duties of the Aaronides.[19] Levites "trespassing" into cultic territory reserved for priests in Leviticus seems to be an essential aspect of the portrayal of the cult in Chronicles. One should also add that despite the name of the book, Leviticus is not really interested in Levites. They, or their cities, to be exact, feature only in a few verses in chapter 25 (vv. 32–33). This issue of "promoted" Levites is

---

14. I will use both "reconciliation" and "atonement" as translations of כפר and thus as synonyms.

15. E.g. Leviticus 4:20, 26, 31, 35; 5:6, 10, 13, 16, 18, 26 etc.

16. Combined with the שְׁלָמִים, see: 1 Chronicles 16:1, 2; 21:26; 2 Chronicles 7:7; 29:35 and 31:2.

17. In Leviticus 4:26 and 35 the text says that the fat of the חַטָּאת should be treated like the fat of the שְׁלָמִים, but the two are not used in the same ritual. These two sacrifices are also listed together with the other three sacrifices in 7:37 in a concluding verse to that chapter. Both do feature in Leviticus 9 when Aaron and his sons are inaugurated, but so is the מִנְחָה and the עֹלָה.

18. David Clines, "מִנְחָה," DCH 5:350–1.

19. I am referring to the following words: 1) מַעֲרֶכֶת, which refers to the rows in which the bread is arranged, is found in Leviticus 24: 6 and 7. The same goes for the Hophal participle of the verb רבך or "mix" which also occurs in the verses from Leviticus just mentioned. Another term is מַחֲבַת or baking tray on which flat breads were baked, found in Leviticus 2:5; 6:14 and 7:9. Then there is רָקִיק or "flat bread" found in Leviticus 2:4; 7:12 and 8:26.

a general point of debate amongst scholars of Chronicles.[20] Knoppers, after discussing the role of Levites in 1 Chronicles 23:28–32, puts it as follows:[21]

> The Chronicler draws on Priestly terminology, but he does so to expand levitical responsibilities and to blur some of the clear distinctions advanced by the Priestly writers and defended by Ezekiel.

Although I cannot comment on Ezekiel, his argument about the expansion of Levitical responsibilities seems sound. We will return to this topic below. To return to the issue of the מִנְחָה, in 2 Chronicles 7:7, Solomon consecrated the middle court because the bronze altar could not hold all of the עֹלוֹת, מִנְחָה and שְׁלָמִים.

We read here of a מִנְחָה, a few עֹלוֹת and also the third offering found in Leviticus 3, the שְׁלָמִים. This latter term is found eight times in the books of Chronicles.[22] It is usually used in combination with the עֹלָה. Thus, David sacrifices both in 1 Chronicles 16:1–2 and also in 1 Chronicles 21:26 after he received them as gifts from (the just mentioned) Ornan. As mentioned before, this combination of עֹלָה and שְׁלָמִים is quite common in the narratives of the Old Testament, as in 1 Samuel 13, for instance, where Saul gets into trouble for sacrificing them, a story that the Chronicler does not narrate.

When Hezekiah celebrates the Passover, we read that in 2 Chronicles 30:22 the people ate of the שְׁלָמִים, but earlier in the chapter the priests did also bring some תוֹלַע. Both offerings are thus used on the same occasion. These are indeed strange sacrifices as Exodus 12 – the basic priestly instruction on the פֶּסַח – does not refer to them at Passover. The same is true of Leviticus 23. Numbers 28 presents a festival where some עֹלוֹת are involved and even a מִנְחָה, but no שְׁלָמִים, but the עֹלוֹת and מִנְחָה are actually associated with the festival of unleavened bread. This is despite 2 Chronicles 30:16 stating that the sacrifice was executed "according to the law of Moses the man of God." In light of this tension, Japhet argues that "the Chronicler did not refer to the written word as it stands, but rather to the way it was understood and interpreted, either by him or at his time..."[23]

But to return to the שְׁלָמִים, even Manasseh sacrifices a few שְׁלָמִים after his repentance in 2 Chronicles 33. It is possible, though, that the

---

20. See Gary N. Knoppers, "Hierodules, Priests, or Janitors? The Levites in Chronicles and the History of the Israelite Priesthood," *JBL* 118/1 (1999):49–72, especially pages 51–3, where he provides an overview of past debates.

21. Knoppers, "Hierodules, Priests, or Janitors?", 64.

22. See 1 Chronicles *16:1, 2*; *21:26*; 2 Chronicles *7:7*, *29:35*; *30:22*; *31:2* and 33:16. All the references in italics are when a שְׁלָמִים is used with the עֹלָה.

23. Sara Japhet, *I & II Chronicles: A Commentary*, OTL (London: SCM Press, 1993), 950.

שְׁלָמִים was in Chronicles, just as in Leviticus, the main sacrifice that provided food for the table of the person bringing the offering.[24]

In Leviticus the sacrifices just discussed would usually be called "voluntary", while the sacrifices found in chapters 4 and 5 are "required".[25] These latter sacrifices are often regarded as later exilic or post-exilic developments with their roots in the pre-exilic period.[26] They are the חַטָּאת, translated as sin offering or purification offering (but חַטָּאת is also the word for sin), and the אָשָׁם is translated as guilt offering or restitution offering. The אָשָׁם offering is absent from Chronicles, but one does find a female version of the noun אַשְׁמָה, which means guilt.[27] Although one finds the word חַטָּאת frequently in Chronicles, it usually refers to sin. But the sin or purification offering is mentioned on one occasion and that is during Hezekiah's restoration of temple worship.

In the rest of this essay, we will specifically focus on the narratives regarding Hezekiah and Josiah, which some scholars regard as a "literary climax" of sorts.[28]

3. HEZEKIAH'S REFORM

The Chronicler tells his story about the reform of Hezekiah over three chapters. For Ralf W. Klein, these chapters all go back to 2 Kings 18:4.[29] Thus, one verse in the Former Prophets becomes three chapters in which the Chronicler tells us about "the Purification of the Temple and the Restoration of the Cult" in chapter 29 and then in 30 about "The Passover of Hezekiah". The Chronicler concludes this long tale about Hezekiah's reforms with chapter 31 on "the comple-

---

24. Or, that is the impression one gets from a text such as 2 Chronicles 30:22. This is the only case where eating by the people is explicitly mentioned. In Leviticus the שְׁלָמִים is often regarded as the sacrifice which provides food for the table. See the discussion in Milgrom, *Leviticus 1–16*, 217–25, but especially 221. Also, Hieke, *Levitikus 1–15*, 95, who translates this sacrifice as *Heilsgemeinschaftsopfer*. As he puts it: "Die Gemeinschaft wird auch durch das gemeinsame Essen betont."

25. See, for instance, the overview of sacrifices found in Frank H. Gorman "Sacrifices and offerings," *NIDB* 5:23–6.

26. For a detailed discussion of this rather complex debate, see Nihan, *From Priestly Torah*, 166–198, on the חַטָּאת in Leviticus 4 and 5 and 237–56, on the אָשָׁם and Leviticus 5.

27. See Clines, "אַשְׁמָה," DCH 1:416–7.

28. Louis C. Jonker, "Holiness and the Levites: Some Relections on the Relationship between Chronicles and Pentateuchal Traditions," in *Eigensinn und Entstehung der Hebräischen Bibel. Erhard Blum zum siebzigsten Geburtstag*, eds. Joachim J. Krause, Wolfgang Oswald and Kristin Weingart (Tübingen: Mohr Siebeck 2000): 457–76, here 473.

29. Ralph W. Klein, *2 Chronicles: A Commentary*, Hermeneia (Minneapolis, MN: Fortress Press, 2012), 412.

tion of Hezekiah's Cultic Reforms; Provisions for Collection and Distributing Contributions to the Priests and Levites".[30] We have already referred to the Passover as described in chapter 30, and we will revisit that chapter in this part, but will focus especially on chapter 29. The חַטָּאת is mentioned for the first time in 29:21 and then again in verses 23 and 24. Before we get to these verses, we need to talk through the first 20 verses of chapter 29, which tell how the temple was "cleaned" or "cleansed" before the sacrifices were presented. I am using verbs like "clean" and "cleanse" (the ritualised version of "clean") rather loosely at this stage, but my discussion of them in this chapter will attempt to clarify their meaning.

In the first part of the chapter we read how the temple which was closed in the time of Ahaz (only mentioned in v. 19) has now been reopened by Hezekiah, but it first needs to be "cleansed". Hezekiah calls the priests and Levites together and the give a brief speech (vv. 5–11).[31] Hezekiah instructs them first to sanctify themselves (Hitp קדשׁ) and sanctify (Pi קדשׁ) "the house of YHWH the God of your fathers" and remove the נִדָּה (NRSV "filth", NKJV "rubbish") from the sanctuary. Verses 12–14 provide us with a list of the Levites who participated. In verse 15 they sanctify (Hitp קדשׁ) themselves and enter the sanctuary to cleanse (Pi טהר) it. Then in the next verse (v. 16) there seems to be a division of labour between priests and Levites, with the former going into the "inner part" (פְּנִימָה) of the "house of YHWH" once again to cleanse it (Pi טהר). The priests carry out הַטֻּמְאָה (NRSV "unclean things") to the court, and the Levites then carry it to Wadi Kidron. This whole process lasted sixteen days (v. 17), and when they finished, they reported to the king (v. 18) that they had indeed cleansed (Pi טהר) the house of YHWH and that all the utensils have been sanctified (Hi קדשׁ).[32] As Klein points out, there is no mention here of the

---

30. Headings from Klein, *2 Chronicles*, 409–56.

31. There is a discrepancy here in that the king assembles both groups in verse 4, but then in verse 5 he only speaks to the Levites. Japhet, *I & II Chronicles*, 917, argues that "Levites" has a broader meaning here, including "all the members of the tribe of Levi, constituting the clergy at large." Raymond B. Dillard. *2 Chronicles*, WBC 15 (Waco, TX: Word Books, 1987), 233, argues that either the text is highlighting the Levites, or the term includes both groups (as with Japhet), but also thinks that there is clearly some rivalry going on between the two groups. See also Klein, *2 Chronicles*, 413, who presents a similar argument to that of Japhet. Jonker, *Defining All-Israel*, 264, states that verse 12 shows that only the Levites (excluding the priests) respond. The question would then be why do the priests participate in verse 16? They actually went into the inner part of the temple.

32. Japhet, *I & II Chronicles*, 922, thinks that "'purify' denotes the cleansing, the deliverance of the Temple from a state of 'pollution', the removal of an essentially negative condition; 'sanctify' or 'hallow' goes beyond 'purity' and brings the Temple to the elevated state of sanctity." Although this interpretation makes sense from a

inner altar or ten golden lampstands, but these are probably included with the utensils (הַכֵּלִים).[33]

It is only after the Levites and priests had cleansed the temple that we read of a חַטָּאת in verse 21. We hear of seven bulls, seven rams, seven lambs and seven male goats presumably presented as חַטָּאת. Yet, if one also reads verses 22 to 24, it seems that only the seven male goats were חַטָּאת, whereas the other sacrifices were actually עֹלוֹת. Verse 22 describes how the bulls, rams and lambs were slaughtered and the blood dashed by the priests.[34] Then verse 23 singles out the male goats as חַטָּאת. The kings and the assembly laid hands on the goats before they were slaughtered by the priests. It seems that there are two kinds of sacrifices performed here and if one takes into account that verse 24 concludes by stating that the king commanded the עֹלָה *and* the חַטָּאת to be performed for "all Israel", then it seems that verse 22 actually referred to עֹלוֹת. This is how most commentators interpret these verses.[35] With regard to the חַטָּאת of verse 23, it is spelled out that the priests used the blood on the altar to bring about reconciliation (כפר) for all of Israel in verse 24. This is only the second time that כפר is used after 1 Chronicles 6:34 (BHS).[36]

The history of the חַטָּאת offering is complex and cannot be discussed here in detail. One could mention, though, that some scholars such as Jacob Milgrom and Christophe Nihan would argue that there are indeed two kinds of offering.[37] Here, with only one occurrence, there seems strictly semantic perspective, it is not clear that the Chronicler really distinguished between the two processes. It sounds as if the priests going into the "inner part" to purify and the description of starting to sanctify on the first of the month in verse 17 refer to the same event, which means that the Chronicler uses the two terms as synonyms.

33. Klein, *2 Chronicles*, 420.

34. An issue explored by most commentaries here is who slaughtered these burnt offerings. For Japhet, *I & II Chronicles*, 926, the "they" refers to laymen. Dillard, *2 Chronicles*, 236, and Klein, *2 Chronicles*, 421, both agree that in the light the Leviticus 1:4, 5 it could indeed be the laymen who did the slaughtering, but both allow for some ambiguity in the text.

35. Japhet, *I & II Chronicles*, 925; Klein, *2 Chronicles*, 421; Dillard, *2 Chronicles*, 235; Milgrom, *Leviticus 1–16*, 285. See also Rolf Rendtorff, "Chronicles and the Priestly Torah," in *Texts, Temples, and Traditions: A Tribute to Menahem Haran*, eds. Michael V. Fox, Victor A. Hurowitz, Avi Hurvitz, Michael L. Klein, Baruch J. Schwartz, and Nili Shupak (Winona Lake, IN: Eisenbrauns; 1996), 259–66, here 263.

36. A fascinating debate is why the change from "for Judah" in verse 21 to "for all Israel" in verse 24. For most scholars this is clear evidence of a more inclusive approach present in the two books of Chronicles. The mention of "all Israel" here also paves the way for the *manner* in which the Passover is celebrated in the next chapter with Northerners also invited. See discussions by Milgrom, *Leviticus 1–16*, 285–6; Klein, *2 Chronicles*, 422; Dillard, *2 Chronicles*, 236. For a more detailed discussion see Jonker, *Defining All-Israel*, 151–90.

37. Milgrom, *Leviticus 1–16*, 253–91; Nihan, *From Priestly Torah*, 179–186. Or, originally, see Jacob Milgrom, "Two Kinds of ḥaṭṭā't," *VT* 26/3 (1976):333–7.

to be one kind only and the חַטָּאת is brought only *after* the cleansing or sanctifying of the temple in the first 20 verses of the chapter. Another issue is how to translate the term; the options are the more traditional "sin offering" or as a "purification offering", a translation which seems to be more dominant in recent years.[38]

If one compares this elaborate ritual described in 2 Chronicles 29 with chapters 4, 5 and 16 of Leviticus, where the חַטָּאת is mostly found in Leviticus,[39] then it is important to note that there is no ritual in Leviticus prescribed for a scenario after the temple has been closed. There could not be, because Leviticus works within the fiction of Sinai and the tabernacle. As Japhet rightly points out:[40] "The ceremony as described is different from anything prescribed or described elsewhere in the Bible."

The Chronicler could, however, have drawn very loosely from Leviticus 16, which does describe the yearly ritual cleansing of the sanctuary.[41] As Benedikt Jürgens argues, the purpose of the use of the חַטָּאת in Leviticus 16 is to facilitate a yearly return to the "Zustand des Heiligtums" achieved originally with the consecration of the sanctuary in Leviticus 8–9.[42] Leviticus 16 uses the combination of עֹלָה and חַטָּאת, but does not include the number of animals listed in 2 Chronicles 29:21. There is no mention of a male sheep in Leviticus 16 and a bull is used as a חַטָּאת and not an עֹלָה. Yet, if the general aim of Leviticus 16 is to bring about the "permanent restitution of Yahweh's Pres-

38. See Milgrom, *Leviticus 1–16*, 253–8, for a detailed discussion, but already going back to Jacob Milgrom, "Sin-offering or purification offering?" VT 21/2 (1971):237–9. For further discussions on how to translate the term see, for instance, Hieke, *Levitikus 1–15*, 88–92, who opts for a more traditional translation of "Entsündigungopfer", or Watts, *Leviticus 1–10*, 302–16, who would also prefer to stick to the traditional translation of "sin offering". Other scholars such as Gorman, "Sacrifices and offerings," 25, Jay Sklar, *Leviticus: An Introduction and Commentary*, Tyndale (Downers Grove, IL: Inter-Varsity Press, 2013), 107–8; Gordon J. Wenham, *The Book of Leviticus*, NICOT (Grand Rapids, MI: Eerdmans, 1979), 88–9, follow Milgrom in this regard. It is also worth noting that not all commentators on Chronicles used here follow Milgrom. Japhet, *I & II Chronicles*, 925 and Dillard, *2 Chronicles*, 235 do not, whereas Klein, 2 Chronicles, 421 does.

39. חַטָּאת is found in the following instances in Leviticus: 4:3(x2), 8, 14(x2), 20, 21, 23, 24, 25, 26, 28(x2), 29(x2), 32, 33(x2), 34, 35; 5:6(x3), 7, 8, 9(x2), 10, 11, 12, 13; 6:10, 18, 19, 23; 7:7, 37; 8:2, 14, 15; 9:2, 3, 7, 8, 10, 15, 22; 10:16, 17, 19; 12:6, 8; 14:13, 19, 22, 31; 15:15, 30; 16:3, 5, 6, 9, 11, 15, 16, 21, 25, 27, 30, 34; 19:22(x2); 23:19; 26:18, 21, 24 and 28. Of these, the following refer to sin and thus not the sacrifice: 4:3, 14, 23, 26, 28(x2), 35; 5:6, 10, 13; 16:16, 21, 30, 34; 19:22(x2); 26:18, 21, 24 and 28. In some cases you have the two meanings in one verse such as 4:3, 14 and 5:6.

40. Japhet, *I & II Chronicles*, 924.

41. McKenzie, *1–2 Chronicles*, 341, also thinks the chapter is reminiscent of the "Day of Atonement".

42. Benedikt Jürgens, *Heiligkeit und Versöhnung. Levitikus 16 in seinem literarischen Kontext*. HBS 28 (Freiburg: Herder, 2001), 342.

ence in Israel",[43] then it seems like a suitable text to draw from. As Gorman puts it with regard to Leviticus 16:[44]

> The ritual clearly reflects the structure of a community rite of passage. More specifically, it reflects community passage to a renewed and re-ordered state of existence. Thus, it must be seen primarily as a ritual of restoration – it serves to restore the community to its prescribed and founded state.

In both Leviticus 16 and 2 Chronicles 29:24 we read that atonement is brought about for the people. In 2 Chronicles 29:24 atonement is for כָּל־יִשְׂרָאֵל, a term (as indicated above) which often leads to debates about inclusivity. The use of the verb כפר in Leviticus 16 is a much more complex issue, but it is used for both people and the sanctuary.[45] Even though the Chronicler did not mention the temple itself, at least he thought that the people (or more exactly כָּל־יִשְׂרָאֵל) needed כפר. Yet, initially in verse 21, we read that the purpose of the חַטָּאת was for (עַל) the kingdom, the sanctuary and Judah, but with the conclusion of the חַטָּאת in verse 24 כפר is only meant for כָּל־יִשְׂרָאֵל. It is not clear why the sanctuary is excluded in verse 24, but in the light of verse 21 I hesitate to argue that the Chronicler thought that only כָּל־יִשְׂרָאֵל needed atonement.

We are again reminded of the job of the priests and that is to play a crucial role in slaughtering the חַטָּאת and bringing about atonement for Israel. This links up with 1 Chronicles 6:49. Yet the role played here by the Levites is something not found in Leviticus and it is another case of "promoted" Levites.[46]

There is another ritual in 2 Chronicles 29 which is also (at least at first glance) reminiscent of Leviticus 16 and other texts in Leviticus, and that is the king and the assembly laying their hands on the

---

43. Nihan, *From Priestly Torah*, 370–1. The heading from Nihan does not refer to any historical context, though, but to the restoration of the new order created by Leviticus 8–9 "every time it is significantly transgressed." This new order is threatened by ritual impurities and moral faults.

44. Frank H. Gorman, *Ideology of Ritual: Space, Time and Status in the Priestly Theology*, JSOTS 91 (Sheffield: Sheffield Academic Press, 1990), 61.

45. Leviticus 16 usually uses the preposition בְּעַד when כפר is referring to people. Thus, in verses 6, 11 and 17 the חַטָּאת is used for Aaron and his house, but in verse 24 the עֹלָה is used for Aaron and the people. When applied to the sanctuary or other parts of it, one finds other prepositions. In verse 10, לְ is used in reference to the altar and the same goes for the sanctuary in verse 16, but in verses 17 and 27 בְּ is used in reference to the sanctuary. Then in the last few verses of the chapter עַל suddenly gets used with reference to people. Verses 29–34a are often regarded as a later layer in the text. See Thomas Hieke, *Levitikus 16–27*, HTKAT (Freiburg: Herder, 2014), 569–70. For a discussion of the use of the different prepositions see Milgrom, *Leviticus 1–16*, 255–6.

46. Jonker, "Holiness and the Levites," 457–76. Or for a more detailed discussion Jonker, *Defining All-Israel*, 263–7.

male goats for the חַטָּאת, before the priests slaughtered them. In Leviticus this act is performed in 1:4 by the person who brought the עֹלָה and also in Leviticus 3 with regard to the זֶבַח שְׁלָמִים. In Leviticus 4 the same is true of the חַטָּאת. On five occasions (vv. 4, 15, 24, 29 and 33) one reads of this act of laying a hand on the חַטָּאת that was about to be sacrificed. This action is also found in Leviticus 8 with the ordination of the priests, when Aaron and his sons lay hands on each of the three sacrifices found in that chapter. Here one also finds a combination of the עֹלָה and the חַטָּאת, but the unique מִלֻּאִים is added. Also, in Leviticus 16:21 Aaron lays his hands on the go-away goat, which is called a חַטָּאת, but it does not get slaughtered. But this ritual is different in the sense that it is usually regarded as an elimination ritual and is clearly not a sacrifice.[47] What exactly this act means has been debated extensively regarding Leviticus,[48] but with regard to Chronicles most of the commentators engaged with in this chapter are not really interested in this debate.[49] One cannot blame them, since the Chronicler did not tell us whether it was with one hand or two hands. The latter is stipulated in Leviticus 16:21.

Apart from Leviticus 16 and other texts where the חַטָּאת is mentioned in Leviticus, the Chronicler could also have drawn from other texts in the book of Numbers, or Ezekiel.[50] It is furthermore important to note that the number of animals referred to in this text is astounding and there is nothing in Leviticus that is similar, or in the Hebrew Bible for that matter. Rendtorff thinks that the number

---

47. For a more recent engagement with Leviticus 16, see Christian A. Eberhart, "To Atone or Not to Atone: Remarks on the Day of Atonement Rituals According to Leviticus 16 and the Meaning of Atonement," in *Sacrifice, Cult, and Atonement in Early Judaism and Christianity: Constituents and Critique*, eds. Henrietta L. Wiley and Christian A. Eberhart (Atlanta, GA: SBL Press, 2017), 197–232.

48. See the overview in Jürgens, *Heiligkeit und Versöhnung*, 229–31 or Milgrom, *Leviticus 1–16*, 150–3.

49. Or, that is how I interpret the virtual absence of discussion. Japhet, *I & II Chronicles*, 926, refers to this ritual in Leviticus 1:4 and 4:15, but does not engage with its meaning. Dillard, *2 Chronicles*, 235–6, offers no discussion. Klein, *2 Chronicles*, 421, opts for one of the possible interpretations, namely identifying with the victims, which is one that Milgrom, *Leviticus 1–16*, 151, rejects.

50. Japhet, *I & II Chronicles*, 925, refers to Numbers 7:88, where "[t]his particular combination of sacrifices – bulls, rams and lambs for burnt offering and he-goats for sin-offering – is prescribed …" In Numbers 7, this event only happens over one day, though. She also points out that the "additional sacrifices of the holidays" in Numbers 28 and 29 are similar and that these combinations of animals are also mentioned in Ezra 6:17 and 8:35 with the dedication of the second temple. Dillard, *2 Chronicles*, 236, argues that the "inclusion of the sin offerings finds its closest analog in the sin offerings mentioned in Ezekiel as part of the cleansing of the altar and sanctuary." He then refers to chapters 43 to 45. He does not provide any detailed support for his statement.

of animals is clearly "a product of the Chronicler's imagination."⁵¹ Rendtorff also argues that the Chronicler was not really interested in the חַטָּאת as such, as it is only mentioned at this point in the story.⁵² In response to this argument one could argue that the חַטָּאת is mentioned at a very crucial junction in the narrative of the Chronicler, if not even as some kind of "literary climax."

About the reference to חַטָּאת here, one could say that despite many differences, the Chronicler at least understood that a ritual solution would be necessary before the temple could be used again. This kind of thinking is not that far removed from priestly thinking and if one were to look for other examples (apart from Leviticus 16) of where the עֹלָה and the חַטָּאת are combined, they often occur in chapters where a ritual solution is provided for impurity, namely Leviticus 12 to 15. They are combined in Leviticus 12:6 when a woman is finally cleansed after giving birth. They are also combined (with an אָשָׁם and מִנְחָה) in Leviticus 14:10–14 in the final phase of the ritual for the cleansing of a person who had צָרַעַת. They are combined in 15:15 and 30 as part of a ritual in response to an irregular discharge in a man, or of a woman who suffers from an irregular זוֹב. Thus, one expects to find a combination of an עֹלָה and a חַטָּאת when you need to do some kind of ritual cleansing.⁵³

We need to take a closer look at how 'impurity' language is used in the first half of 2 Chronicles 29. This language in the earlier part of the chapter stands out for somebody who is more familiar with Leviticus, and this part of the chapter describes what takes place before the sacrifices are presented. It is indicated above that the verb טהר (Piel) is used in verses 15, 16 and 18. In verses 15 and 16 it refers to the Levites who will "cleanse" the temple, and in verse 16 to priests who go into the house of the lord to "cleanse" it. What does cleansing actually mean here? Basically, the priests are taking unclean things from the temple, which are also described with terms usually associated with impurity language. In verse 5 the king had already said that the נִדָּה needs to be taken from (Hif of יצא) the temple and in verse 16 the priests go in to remove (Hif of יצא) the טֻמְאָה from the temple. In Leviticus טֻמְאָה usually refers to impurities associated with biological processes such as menstruation or discharge from a woman (15:25;

---

51. Rendtorff, "Chronicles and the Priestly Torah," 263.
52. Rendtorff, "Chronicles and the Priestly Torah," 265.
53. See the discussion in Nihan, *From Priestly Torah*, 169–70. One of the questions in this debate is whether the clearly older עֹלָה always had an atoning function. Nihan would say yes. With regard to the combination, he puts it as follows: "The combined offering of a עֹלָה and a חַטָּאת for atonement is further found in Num 15:24–25; it also consistently occurs in the context of purification rites from a major source of pollution, see Lev 12:6–7a, 8; 15:15, 30, as well as Num 6:11; 8:12."

18:19) or a man (15:3) or צָרַעַת (14:19). נִדָּה[54] usually refers to menstruation in Leviticus and the usage of the term is very odd here.[55] Quite a few scholars have recently studied this term, often drawing from the perspective of gender studies. Thus Elizabeth W. Goldstein discusses three stages in the development of the meaning of the term with the usage here presenting the last phase.[56] Most of these scholars agree that in 2 Chronicles 29:5 the term no longer means menstruation, but refers to objects in the temple which made it unclean and therefore the temple needed cleansing from these objects and their polluting effect.[57] What were these objects?

Scholars usually refer to the next chapter on the Passover, or the even later story of Josiah's reform and the earlier one of Asa to answer the question.[58] These objects were illegitimate and associated with

54. See Clines, "טֻמְאָה," DCH 3:370–1.

55. In Leviticus the word is found in: 12:2, 5; 15:19, 20, 24, 25(x3), 26, 33; 18:19 and 20:21. The last example is an exception as the word is used to express a general feeling of disgust, similarly to other terms such as תּוֹעֵבָה, תֶּבֶל, or זִמָּה. Elizabeth W. Goldstein, *Impurity and Gender in the Hebrew Bible*. (New York: Lexington Books, 2015), 58 regards this latter occurrence as a gloss. As a member of the Kaufmann school, which dates the Holiness Code to the late pre-exilic period, she has no choice, because otherwise this meaning will not fit into the three phases she identifies in the development of the term, as explained in the next footnote.

56. Goldstein, *Impurity and Gender*, 54–58. The term initially only had the meaning of menstruation, which implies that it is a state which makes you unclean. The second stage was when the term gained a more figurative meaning, which presented revulsion as found in Lamentations 1:17 and Isaiah 30:22. The term now expresses something of the shunning of the menstruant which is applied to Jerusalem or images of idols which are to be shunned more or less like the proverbial "hot potato." For Goldstein these two phases are followed by a third, which she calls a "semantic broadening" in the Second Temple Period and now it refers to "sins threatening the fabric of the community" and in this regard she uses 2 Chronicles 29:5 as an example. In this period the word can either mean menstruation or this new broadened meaning expressing some kind of sin. See also the overview in Eve L. Feinstein, *Sexual Pollution in the Hebrew Bible* (Oxford: Oxford University Press, 2014), 181–3, who responds to Goldstein's argument (citing her PhD from 2010) and does not find all aspects convincing. For a further discussion of the term see Dorothea Erbele-Küster, *Body, Gender and Purity in Leviticus 12 and 15*, (New York: Bloomsbury, 2017), 117–37.

57. Thus Feinstein, *Sexual pollution*, 182 sketches this usage "to denote any type of pollution, with no particular connection to menstruation". Erbele-Küster, Body, Gender and Purity, 122, describes this usage of the term as "pejorative and polemical" and for her נִדָּה becomes "a literary indication of what is outside the system." See also the discussion in Christophe Nihan, "Deuteronomic alignment in Chronicles: Royal Reforms and the Elimination of Cultic Objects," in *Writing, Rewriting, and Overwriting in the Books of Deuteronomy and the Former Prophets*: Essay in honour of Cynthia Edenburg, eds. Römer, T., Sergi, O. and Koch, I. (Leuven: Peeters, 2019): 309–36, here 322.

58. Klein, *2 Chronicles*, 419 and Nihan, "Deuteronomic Alignment," 322 mention the altars destroyed in 30:14. Klein refers to both the reforms of Josiah which burned "illegitimate cult objects" or the burning of the image of Asherah during the

other gods. Incidentally, one also finds impurity language in the two following stories of Hezekiah's Passover and Josiah's reform, which we will now discuss briefly.

4. MORE STORIES ABOUT IMPURITY

Although references to sacrifices and offerings are not so prevalent in the rest of 2 Chronicles and the חַטָּאת is never mentioned again, one does find some references to purity language.[59] Whereas the cases just discussed seem closer to priestly thinking, things now change.

In 2 Chronicles 30:18 we read of a multitude of people who came to Hezekiah's Passover who did not cleanse (Hitpael of טהר) themselves. Most commentators seem unsure about what could have caused the people to be unclean.[60] In Leviticus, this stem of the verb is found a lot in chapter 14, where it is always a participle. It refers to the person who does not have צָרַעַת anymore and now has to go through the elaborate cleansing process described in that chapter. It is often translated with "the one who is to be cleansed." The text of the Chronicler is not clear on which rituals these people in 2 Chronicles 30 were supposed to perform, but verse 17 makes it clear that Levites had to offer the Passover lamb for those who were not clean. Verse 18 also says that Hezekiah prayed for them and the "good Lord pardoned all (NRSV)." Here the verb כפר is used again. In Leviticus that verb always follows a sacrifice, yet here one finds that a prayer by the king does the trick. This usage of כפר in Hezekiah's prayer is also in tension with 1 Chronicles 6:49, cited earlier, where the Aaronides are supposed to do the work of the holy place. Here a king can pray and all is forgiven. It is also different from 2 Chronicles 29:24, where it is the priests who slaughter and manipulate the blood to accomplish כפר. Rolf Rendtorff has the following to say on this:[61]

> I must confess that I do not understand what the Chronicler means, but in any case this use of *kippēr* is incompatible with any priestly theology. It is amazing that the Chronicler presents two totally different concepts of *kippēr* so close to each other.

For Japhet the fact that the text says that the Lord healed the people in verse 20 makes this "an explicit pronouncement that 'the setting of reign of Asa.

59. The עֹלָת features in 30:15; 31:2, 3; 35:12, 14 and 16. The זֶבַח שְׁלָמִים is mentioned in 30:22; 31:2 and 33:16.

60. Japhet, *I & II Chronicles*, 952, thinks it has to do with "the problem of the pilgrims". She argues that this was a major problem in the "second commonwealth." She also adds that what is presented here as irregular probably happened much more regularly.

61. Rendtorff, "Chronicles and the Priestly Torah," 265.

the heart' is of higher value than ritualistic purity."⁶² This seems to be an explicit critique of the Priestly view of atonement. As Ehud Ben Zvi puts it:⁶³

> Moreover, in the main case in which matters of ritual purity are saliently raised in Chronicles, namely in the account of Hezekiah's Passover – it is no coincidence that about half of the occurrences of words from the roots טהר and טמא occur in this account – the Chronicler seems to suggest that personal devotion, "setting one's heart," outweighs – although does not eliminate – matters of bodily purity.

But to complete my overview of the verb טהר, it is also found at another incident in 2 Chronicles where we read of the other great love of the Chronicler, namely king Josiah. 2 Chronicles 34 retells the tale of 2 Kings 22. Still, in Chronicles, even before Josiah discovered the book in the temple, he started with a process of cleansing the country of Judah and the city of Jerusalem. In 2 Chronicles 34:3–5 טהר (always in the Piel) is used on two occasions. In verse 3 we read that Josiah started to טהר Judah and Jerusalem from high places, sacred poles and cast images. Verse 5 recounts how Josiah burned the bones of priests on their altars, and thus he purged (טהר) Judah and Jerusalem.

Thus, before Josiah discovered the scroll, he started with this process of purging. In Leviticus only priests can be the subject of the Piel of טהר. Yet now the king is the subject and these actions are not followed by any rituals, but merely a removal of cultic sites belonging to other gods. The text never states that Judah was unclean, but it is presumed, since why would you clean something if it is not unclean? A few verses later, the same verb occurs again in verse 8, when we read that Josiah purged (טהר) the land. We now learn that after he had cleansed the land and the house, he started to repair the house of the Lord and only after that do they discover the scroll. This kind of thinking is reminiscent of the Holiness Code, especially the parenetic frame, where one reads of the threat that the land could become unclean.⁶⁴ In Leviticus 18:25 and 27 the land will become unclean (Qal of טמא) if (v. 24) the addressees make themselves unclean (Hitpael) by violating any of the taboos mentioned above, since the nations before them became unclean (Nifal) by doing these things. Thus, the Holiness Code refers to the land becoming unclean but does not mention the land becoming clean again like here in Chronicles. The land becoming

---

62. Japhet, *I & II Chronicles*, 953.
63. Ben Zvi, "Purity Matters," 41.
64. Eckart Otto, "Innerbiblische Exegese im Heiligkeitsgesetz Levitikus 17–26," in *Levitikus als Buch*, BBB 119, ed. Heinz–Josef Fabry and Hans–Winfried Jüngling (Bonn: Philo, 1999): 125–96, identifies 18:1–5, 24–30; 19:1–4; 20:7–8, 22–27; 22:8, 31–33; 25:18–19, 38, 42a, 55 and 26:1–2 (172–6) as such instances.

unclean leads to the land spitting out her inhabitants in Leviticus 18.

In Leviticus the verb טהר is often found in the Piel and in these cases a priest is always the subject of the verb and it usually means that the priest proclaims a person clean who had previously been unclean.[65] This declaration always follows the performance of certain cleansing rituals in especially Leviticus 12 to 15 where, as discussed before, we find combinations of the חַטָּאת and the עֹלָה. Thus, concerning the instruction of צָרַעַת in Leviticus 13:6, on the seventh day the priest shall examine a person who suffers from this ailment and if the disease has not spread, he shall declare the person clean. In this case the Piel of טהר is used and if the person did not get better, then the priest would declare him or her unclean, and in that case the Piel of טמא is used. There are many examples of this scattered throughout Leviticus 13, 14 and 16. Chapter 14 deals with cases where a person gets full-blown skin disease but then heals, and performs a very elaborate ritual of cleansing. This ritual includes a lot of washing and laundering, a ritual which involves two birds and more sacrifices involving four of the sacrifices described in Leviticus 1–7, namely עֹלָה, אָשָׁם, מִנְחָה and חַטָּאת. On one occasion, the priest declares the person clean (v. 7) and then three times we read that the person has now become clean (Qal, vv. 8, 9 and 20). Verse 20 follows after all the rituals had been concluded and all the sacrifices had been presented, and "thus the priest shall make atonement on his behalf, and he shall be clean."

The only other two cases of טהר in the Piel are found in Leviticus 16:19 and 30. In verse 19 we read that the blood of the goat of the חַטָּאת is sprinkled on the altar seven times to cleanse it (Piel of טהר) from the impurities of the sons of Israel and to sanctify it. Verse 30 is a much more complicated issue to which we will return later, but many scholars regard this verse as part of the same layer as the Holiness Code.[66]

The point is that this verb (Piel of טהר) is only used in a highly ritualised context with either priests or blood as the subject. In Chronicles, usage of the term seems to be a free for all. In the story of Hezekiah, it is indeed the priests and (promoted) Levites who do the cleansing, but without any sacrifices, as these follow only later. In the story of Josiah, he is the subject of the verb and cleansing is done without any sacrifices.

In all of these cases mentioned above in Leviticus the verb is used to get rid of impurity, but in the examples from the stories of Hezekiah and Josiah it is not so clear what kind of impurity is at stake. This takes

---

65. Cases of the verb in the Piel: Leviticus 13:6, 13, 17, 23, 28, 34, 37, 59; 14:7, 11, 48.

66. Thomas Hieke, *Levitikus 16–27*, 569–70.

us to the debate on the difference between ritual and moral impurity.

5. RITUAL AND MORAL IMPURITY

Ritual impurity usually refers to all the impurities indicated in Leviticus 11 to 15 (although chapter 11 and the rules on what to eat and what not is an in-between category).[67] These impurities are not sins, but are caused by things such as childbirth, skin disease and bodily fluids. They are all part of life and they can be managed with rituals, which is one of the reasons why they are referred to as "ritual impurities." Nihan calls them "physical impurities" because they are "various physical and biological phenomena that affect especially the human body."[68] It is in this context that the verbs טמא and טהר (especially in the Piel) occur. Yet there are also nouns and adjectives for these terms. These terms occur very rarely in both books of Chronicles. We have already mentioned 2 Chronicles 30:19, where people did not purify themselves, and this presumably refers to ritual impurity. Also, in the next verse, we read of the "cleanliness of the sanctuary" often translated with the "sanctuary's rules of cleanness" (טָהֳרָה). This is an example of the female noun, but the male form (טָהֹר) appears a few times and is usually used to refer to pure gold, although the male form is also found in 2 Chronicles 30:17 referring to the Levites who slaughtered the Passover lamb for those who were not clean.[69] Thus, it seems that this incident with Hezekiah's Passover is the only place where there is a clear reference to ritual impurity. However, the text is silent on any cleansing rituals.

But in Leviticus or more specifically in the Holiness Code (Leviticus 17–26) one also finds what some call "moral" impurities, which are usually regarded as caused by "the transgression of divine laws".[70] This takes us to something which could be viewed as a sin. In the heart of the argument one finds the idea that sins are defiling, or in other words, lead to what one could call moral contamination. Transgressing a particular law now makes you unclean, not some bodily function. Jonathan Klawans has elaborated on this distinction extensively and identifies five differences between "ritual" and "moral" defilement:[71]

67. See Christophe Nihan, "Forms and Functions of Purity in Leviticus," in *Purity and the Forming of Religious Traditions in the Ancient Mediterranean World and Ancient Judaism*, eds. Christian Frevel and Christophe Nihan (Leiden: Brill, 2013): 311–67, here 338.
68. Nihan, "Forms and Functions," 321.
69. See 1 Chronicles 28:17; 3:4; 9:7; 13:11.
70. Nihan, "Forms and Functions," 339.
71. Jonathan Klawans, *Impurity and Sin in Ancient Judaism*, (Oxford: Oxford University Press), 26. I am using terms such as "defilement", "impurity" and "pollu-

1. Ritual impurity is not a sin, but moral impurity is. Klawans talks of "grave sin". In the Holiness Code one finds examples of sexual immorality (Lev 18 – when you sleep with another man's wife) and idolatry (Lev 19:31 and 20:1–3), which in Leviticus means turning to wizards and mediums and sacrificing your children to Molech;

2. Ritual impurity is mostly the result of contact, but moral impurity does not entail any contact;

3. Ritual pollution leads to temporary impurity, but moral pollution causes longterm damage. The land spits out the people, as the parenetic frame of the Holiness Code has it, or they are exiled;

4. Ritual impurities are controlled by ritual solutions, but for moral impurity punishment follows. Moral impurity is best to be shunned;

5. In terms of terminology, the root טמא is always used to refer to ritual impurity, but for moral impurity other terms are also used such as תּוֹעֵבָה, which is found in Leviticus 18 but not in Chronicles at all.

The most crucial point here is that in all of the cases of moral impurity, one finds the verb טמא in the Qal. The verb is used to show that an immoral act made you unclean. But in light of the definition by Klawans, there is no way of undoing this kind of pollution. It leads to exile. The land spits you out. The Piel of the verb טהר is never used to refer to the reversal of moral impurity, with one exception. The one exception is the one already mentioned in Leviticus 16:30, which states atonement takes place to cleanse (Piel of טהר) of sin and that the addressees will be clean (Qal of טהר) before the Lord. This goes against what Klawans is arguing since it is a clear case of removing moral pollution utilising ritual.

To resolve this conundrum, Klawans falls back on diachronic arguments which make this verse part of a later layer that includes the Holiness Code.[72] The problem is that even if these verses are on the same diachronic level as the Holiness Code, they still contradict Klawans's understanding of the Holiness Code. He argues that references to moral impurity are found in the Holiness Code and that there is no cure for moral impurity in the Holiness Code, yet here it is in Leviticus 16:30. Still, it is only one verse, and apart from this verse, there is no further indication in Leviticus that one could be cleansed of moral sin, only of impurity. And indeed no solution or cleansing process is provided in the Holiness Code for dealing with the sexual sins and idolatry even if employing impurity language.

---

tion" as synonyms.

72. Klawans, *Impurity and Sin*, 172 n. 30 cites Milgrom, *Leviticus 1–16*, 1064–5 and we have already referred to Hieke, *Levitikus 16–27*, 569–70. One could also add Nihan, *From Priestly Torah*, 347–50.

One should also add that although many scholars have supported Klawans's arguments, many have been critical of his ideas. Just a brief overview of the scholars cited in this paper would provide different views about his work, some positive, some negative and some mixed.[73] A further point of critique would be that it seems that Klawans's categories do not work in the Chronicler's stories about Hezekiah and Josiah. The נִדָּה and טֻמְאָה in 2 Chronicles 29 referred to foreign cultic objects, which clearly references some kind of idolatry and thus a sin. The same goes for the cultic objects in the story of Josiah. This fits into Klawans's description of moral impurity in the Holiness Code, since there idolatry and sexual sin are described using impurity language. Still, points 2 and 3 of the summary above do not fit these narratives in Chronicles.

Let us start with point 3 first. Klawans says that there is no "cleansing" for moral impurity. Yet in 2 Chronicles 29 the Levites and priests go into the temple to remove all filth and to declare things clean (before any sacrifices). As shown above, the same words refer to ritualised cleansing in Leviticus. Josiah also simply removes the idolatrous objects from the temple and Jerusalem, and that counts as cleansing. Chronicles does not seem to be familiar with the difference between bodily and moral impurity and casually mixes categories. Interestingly, in his response to Klawans, Milgrom says the following about H's use of impurity language:[74]

> The truth is that H has no system! And why should it? H is not P. H is the product of a later school of priests bearing a new agenda (ignored by Klawans). The key to this enigma is that H has dissolved the terminological precision of P.

With a few adjustments, Milgrom's point seems like a good description of what the Chronicler also did with Priestly views of the cult. Chronicles used Priestly language of 'impurity' but applied it with no

---

73. Thus, Feinstein, *Sexual Pollution*, 33 thinks Klawans's distinction is too simple, but Goldstein, *Impurity and Gender*, 2–5, discusses his work and, despite identifying some shortcomings, builds further on it. Nihan, "Forms and Functions," 342–4, agrees to some extent, but identifies some clear weaknesses with regard to the interpretation of Leviticus 16. Hieke, *Levitikus 1–15*, 126–9, agrees. Jacob Milgrom, "Systematic Differences in the Priestly Corpus: A Response to Jonathan Klawans," *Revue Biblique* 112/3 (2005): 321–9, responded in an article and does not agree. Milgrom actually regards what Klawans calls "moral pollution" as having a metaphorical meaning and simply does not accept Klawans's argument against this metaphorical interpretation. See Klawans, *Impurity and Sin*, 32–6. For a fairly extensive critique see Andrian Schenker, "Unreinheit, Sünde und Sündopfer: Kritische Untersuchung zweier verbreiteter Thesen: befleckende Sünde (*moral impurity*) und Sündopfer *chaṭṭa't* als Reinigunsopfer für das Heiligtum," *Biblische Zeitschrift* 59/1 (2015): 1–16.

74. Milgrom, "Systematic Differences," 324.

terminological precision. The sons of Aaron can bring about כפר, but so can a praying king! Verbs used by Leviticus 1–16 for ritual impurity can describe idolatry. Why not? The Chronicler was certainly not P and did not pretend to be P either.

Point number 2 above, summarizing Klawans's view, does not seem applicable to the Chronicler's "imprecise" understanding of things either. If moral impurity such as idolatry cannot contaminate through contact, then how did the temple and Judah become polluted in the stories of Hezekiah and Josiah? By the presence of foreign cultic objects? But is that not contact? Similar to touching a dead body or a person with צָרַעַת etc.? I argue this is indeed a case of contact and that for the Chronicler the very fact that these foreign objects were carried into the temple and Jerusalem meant contamination which needed cleansing. Thus, impurity terms are used to describe a sin such as idolatry. What was the solution?

As I tried to argue concerning 2 Chronicles 29, the author has some idea of Priestly thinking and therefore needed at least the עֹלָה and חַטָּאת in some ritual reminiscent of the Yom Kippur. But this followed after some "cleansing" by simply removing what did not belong there. What cleanses here is not sacrifice, but merely stopping what you did wrong. Still, the Chronicler felt the need for sacrifice, even if afterwards. It could very well be that for the Chronicler טהר simply meant cleaning and not our ritualised cleansing. Still, I argue that the very fact that חַטָּאת as the purification offering and verbs such as טהר occur in such proximity means that the authors had some understanding of Priestly views of pollution. It is also noteworthy that after the mention of חַטָּאת towards the end of 2 Chronicles, impurity language is used for the first time.[75] In short, it seems that there was some kind of priestly thinking going on, but much more haphazardly than in Leviticus. Yet even if the Chronicler gives the impression that the problem of idolatry can be solved, it is clear that it was not a permanent solution as impurity language is used again toward the end:

---

75. As Ben Zvi, "Purity Matters," 41, points out, this kind of language is absent from stories about "cult foundational accounts" in 1 Chronicles 16 and 2 Chronicles 5–7. The focus in these stories was more on "joy, praise and thanksgiving than purity matters."

2 Chronicles 36:14 (BHS SESB 2.0)	2 Chronicles 36:14 (NRSV)
¹⁴וְגַם כָּל־שָׂרֵי הַכֹּהֲנִים וְהָעָם הִרְבּוּ לִמְעָול־ מַעַל כְּכֹל וַיְטַמְּאוּ אֶת־בֵּית יְהוָה אֲשֶׁר הִקְדִּישׁ הֹ וּגֹים בִּירוּשָׁלָ͏ִם:	¹⁴All the leading priests and the people also were exceedingly unfaithful, following all the abominations of the nations; and they polluted the house of the Lord that he had consecrated in Jerusalem.

The next verse starts to tell the story of the fall of Jerusalem. Thus, even if the texts where we find the verb טהר seem to indicate that moral pollution could be cleansed, the outcome is still the same as Klawans and the Holiness Code would have it, namely exile. The crucial question still is: how Priestly is the portrayal of sacrifice in Chronicles?

6. CONCLUSION

The short answer would be that the Chronicler's presentation of the sacrificial cult is fairly Priestly, but in a very imprecise way.

Concerning the priesthood, the Chronicler refers to Aaron and his sons, which agrees with Leviticus, and they are responsible for reconciliation. But in 2 Chronicles 30:18, a prayer by Hezekiah also leads to atonement, which is something not found in the book of Leviticus. The prayers of the kings thus compete with the role of the priests. The following point from Ben Zvi puts it clearly:[76]

> When matters of ritual purity and impurity finally come to the fore in a very limited number of accounts, the text seems to deemphasise them or subvert some aspect of the ideological logic that underpins them.

Whereas purity concerns are deemphasised, the role of the Levites is emphasised and they play a much bigger role, even encroaching on the terrain of the priests, an issue which has already been extensively discussed by Chronicles scholars.

Of the five sacrifices found in Leviticus, all the voluntary ones are present. Concerning the involuntary חַטָּאת and אָשָׁם, only the former occurs once during Hezekiah's cleansing of the temple. It is also in this chapter that we found the verb טהר in the Piel referring to the cleansing of the temple, something which happened before the sacrifices were performed. What this cleansing entailed is not clear, but if we take the story of Josiah into account, then it probably had to do with removing images of other gods, which thus implies that the cause

[76]. Ben Zvi, "Purity Matters," 43.

of the problem was idolatry. I have tried to show that these examples undermine attempts by scholars such as Klawans to distinguish between ritual and moral impurity.

I have also argued that behind 2 Chronicles 29, there must be some kind of thinking about clean and unclean akin to Priestly thinking on these matters. The combination of the עֹלָה and the חַטָּאת – as so often happens in Leviticus 12 to 15, but also in 16 – bears witness to this fact. This thinking does overlap somewhat with Priestly thinking. But the major difference is that that cleansing language occurs before any rituals have taken place and that cleansing language is not associated with sacrifices like in Leviticus. For the priests who wrote Leviticus, this "impreciseness" of Chronicles would simply not have been adequate.

For instance, in Leviticus 14, when the priest sees that the צָרַעַת is gone from the person, he cannot merely pronounce him clean as soon as the source of his uncleanness is gone. A ritual, including some sacrifice, is required. It is only after the ritual with the two birds, cedarwood, crimson yard and hyssop had been concluded that the priest would declare the person clean and then some more sacrifices and rituals would follow. Thus, although there might be some overlap, there are also significant differences.

In light of the debate on ritual or bodily impurity and moral impurity, Chronicles paints a complex picture. It is not clear that the Chronicler was familiar with this distinction, and if he were, he blurred the distinction. The most evident reference to ritual impurity seems to be chapter 30 and the celebration of the Pesach. The clearest reference to moral impurity is found in the two stories of Hezekiah and Josiah cleansing the temple, as well as the city and Judah (in the case of Josiah). Yet this very act of cleansing of moral impurity contradicts the usual definitions of moral impurity. In the end, though, the outcome is the same as for all moral impurity, namely the land and temple could not be cleansed, and this resulted in the people being removed from the land into exile.

Part 2: Interpreting the Consonance and Dissonance

III. Inclusive Reception and Creative Interpretation

Scribes in the Post-Exilic Temple: A Social Perspective

Lester L. Grabbe

1. Introduction

The basic question asked in this conference relates to how the priestly writings developed. This is a scribal question but one on which we have little information. The standard traditio-historical analysis is used by a number of papers in this volume, based on principles developed over a long time. The problem is that the results are hypothetical and depend on colleagues' accepting the result as plausible. What I want to do in this paper is go back to the basics and ask about what we can know about how scribes work. Can we support our traditio-historical results by actual evidence about how scribes carried out their duties?

Thus, in order to throw light on how literature such as Chronicles and the priestly writings may have arisen, an important consideration is the duties of scribes and how they carried them out. Yet a perennial problem is that our actual knowledge of the detailed workings of the Jerusalem temple[1] in practically any period is very small. On the other hand, scribes functioned in Egypt and Mesopotamian and also in Judah in the later Second Temple period. They also produced a great deal of literature that became conventional, if not canonical. This study will, first, assemble the few data that we have on scribes in the temple and, then, attempt to fill out the picture by cross-cultural comparisons with the work of scribes elsewhere in the ancient Near East. What happened in Judah can only be surmised, but surmise must

---

1. It is assumed here that the Jerusalem temple was probably the main place of worship and the location of the largest number of priests and scribes. Other temples also existed in pre-exilic times and are well catalogued for the Persian and Greek periods: Gerizim, Leontopolis, perhaps even Iraq al-Amir across the Jordan.

be based on as much evidence as can be assembled. One important question is whether this literature is a scribal product, if there was widespread literacy. A recent study suggested that the military hierarchy was literate down to the level of quartermaster.[2] This study invites a major discussion, but it is assumed here that a certain amount of leisure was required to compile, edit, or author texts, which was not the situation of even many literate individuals. Therefore, "scribe" is used here to mean any literate person who deals with the compiling or composition of texts, though it is assumed that this would normally be someone employed in this capacity, i. e., a professional scribe.

2. The Scribal Model

Many analogies for understanding the scribal process of producing literature are available to us in recent study in classical, folklorist, and ancient Near Eastern studies. Included here are a look at Mesopotamia, Egypt, and recent study on the Homeric poems, but we begin with the relevant data in the Hebrew Bible and attested for Jews elsewhere.

2.1 Scribes in the Hebrew Bible

Although we have no way of confirming the truth of all the statements in the Hebrew Bible, it shall be assumed that they are not far removed from describing the general scribal milieu among the Jews of Palestine from the 7th to perhaps the 4th centuries BCE.

First, a number of passages suggest that many scribes were temple personnel. These are primarily in the books of Chronicles and in Ezra. Levites as scribes are mentioned in a number of passages of Chronicles that have no parallel in Kings (many would argue that these passages should be dated to the Persian period and reflect the situation then): clans of scribes were said to live at Jabez (1 Chron 2:55); Shemaiah b. Nathanel the Levite was a scribe (1 Chron 24:6); the Levitical clans of the Izharites and Hebronites acted as scribal administrators (1 Chron 26:29–32); Jeiel the scribe mustered the army under Uzziah (2 Chron 26:11); some of the Levites were scribes, officials, and gatekeepers (2 Chron 34:13). Ezra is a scribe as well as a priest (Ezra 7:1–6). A scribe called Zadok is appointed to a panel by Nehemiah (Neh 13:13); his name might suggest he is a priest, but other members of the panel are identified as a priest and Levite while he is said only to be a scribe. The Hebrew Bible assumes scribes were used in the administrations of

---

2. Shira Faigenbaum-Golovin, Arie Shaus, Barak Sober, David Levin, Nadav Na'aman, Benjamin Sass, Eli Turkel, Eli Piasetzky, and Israel Finkelstein, "Algorithmic Handwriting Analysis of Judah's Military Correspondence Sheds Light on Composition of Biblical Texts," *PNAS* 113/17 (2016): 4664–69.

the kingdoms of Israel and Judah. We know of scribes who were part of the royal administration but are not designated as priests. Some of them may have been part of the temple personnel, but we do not have such information recorded. Seraiah was the main scribe in David's administration (2 Sam. 8:17), or was it Sheva (2 Sam. 20:25; 1 Chron. 18:16: Shavsha)? Solomon had Elthoreph and Ahijah, sons of Shisha, which may indicate the office was passed down in families (1 Kgs 4:2). The royal scribe was involved in the donation and use of money for the repair of the temple under the rule of Jehoash (2 Kgs 12:11; 2 Chron 24:11). Shebna, Hezekiah's scribe, was part of the group of officials who listened to the speech of the Rabshakeh (2 Kgs 18:18, 37; 19:2; Isa. 36:3, 22). Hezekiah then sent Shebna with a message to the prophet Isaiah (2 Kgs 19:2; Isa. 37:2). Josiah's scribe Shaphan was centrally involved in the activities surrounding the discovery of the book of the law in the temple and its authentication by the prophetess Huldah, as was Shaphan's son Ahikam (2 Kgs 22:2, 8–12, 14; 2 Chron 34:15, 18, 20). The scribe of the army commander was one of those executed by Nebuchadnezzar (2 Kgs 25:19; Jer. 52:25).

Jeremiah has a number of references to scribes: chamber of the scribe in the king's palace (36:12); Elishama the scribe (36:12, 20, 21); Baruch the scribe plays a prominent role (36:26, 32); Jeremiah was imprisoned in the house of Jonathan the scribe (37:15, 20). It is in the book of Jeremiah, however, that it becomes clear that in the last days of Judah a family of scribes were very important in the government and administration of the kingdom, the family of Shaphan. Shaphan was a royal scribe (2 Kgs 22:3, 8; Jer. 36:10–12). This family was an important support for the prophet Jeremiah, with the sons and grandson of Shaphan active in service to him (Jer. 26:24; 36:10–12; 2 Kgs 22:11, 14); for example, Baruch reads the divine words in the chamber of Gemariah son of Shaphan the scribe in the temple (Jer. 36:10). It is not certain that Shaphan was a priest or Levite, but the biblical data do not seem to exclude that possibility. On the other hand, because the king was the leading cultic figure and authority,[3] it is natural that the royal scribe would be involved in activities relating to the cult and temple, even if he was not of a priestly family. Things changed after the monarchy ceased, in that there were no longer royal scribes. The scribes described in the biblical text all seem to have been associated with the temple, but there were presumably scribes of the Persian administration, perhaps assisting the provincial governor. Yet there is nothing to prevent there being local people trained for this

---

3. Lester L. Grabbe, *Priests, Prophets, Diviners, Sages: A Socio-historical Study of Religious Specialists in Ancient Israel* (Valley Forge, PA: Trinity Press International, 1995), 20–40.

purpose, even priests.

2.2 OTHER SCRIBES IN A JEWISH CONTEXT

We also have contemporary information in the material culture, beginning at least with the Persian period. Ten seal impressions from a horde sold on the antiquities market have the name "to Jeremai the scribe".[4] These do not tell us a lot beyond the title, but we also have valuable data from the Jewish community at Elephantine in Egypt. "Scribes of the province" (ספרי מדינתא) are named alongside judges and other officials in a letter to Arsames the governor of Egypt;[5] we also have references to "scribes of the treasury"(ספרי אוצרא).[6] An individual, whose salary had not been paid and complained to the "officials", was told to complain to the scribes.[7] Especially interesting are a number of the documents dictated by Arsames: we know he dictated them because the name of the scribe who copied the specific document is also named.[8] On the other hand, many of the other letters in the collection do not name a scribe, suggesting that the person who sends the letter is also the scribe who wrote it (e. g., in the "Jedaniah Archive").[9]

2.3 SCRIBES IN MESOPOTAMIA

The scribal tradition in Mesopotamia is well documented, including the training of scribes.[10] As elsewhere scribal duties and positions ranged from the ordinary scribe with the duties of copying texts and perhaps involved in local (village) administration and the lowest level of the bureaucracy up to the ministers of state next to the king. The composing of literature was not in the remit of most scribes, but we

---

4. Nahman Avigad, *Bullae and Seals from a Post-Exilic Judean Archive*, Qedem 4 (Jerusalem: Hebrew University, 1976), 7.

5. Bezalel Porten and Ada Yardeni, *Textbook of Aramaic Documents from Ancient Egypt: 1–4*, Hebrew University, Department of the History of the Jewish People, Texts and Studies for Students (Jerusalem: Hebrew University, 1986–99), abbreviated *TAD*: A6.1:1, 6 (= A. Cowley, [1923] *Aramaic Papyri of the Fifth Century B.C.* [reprinted Osnabruck: Otto Zeller, 1967], abbreviated *AP*: 17:1, 6).

6. TAD B4.3:13//B4.4:12, 14 = *AP* 3:13//2:12, 14.

7. TAD A3.3:5 = *BM* 4:5.

8. E.g., *TAD* A6.2:28; A6.8:4; A6.10:10; A6.11:6; A6.12:3; A6.13:5 = *AP* 26:28; AD 4:4; 7:10; 8:6; 9:3; 10:5.

9. TAD A4.1–10.

10. E.g., Laurie E. Pearce, "The Scribes and Scholars of Ancient Mesopotamia", in *Civilizations of the Ancient Near East*, ed. Jack M. Sasson (New York: Scribners, 1995), 4: 2265–91; Christopher J. Lucas, "The Scribal Tablet-House in Ancient Mesopotamia," *History of Education Quarterly* 19 (1979): 305–32; Åke W. Sjöberg, "The Old Babylonian Eduba", in *Sumerological Studies in Honor of Thorkild Jacobsen on his 70th Birthday*, ed. Stephen J. Lieberman, AS 20 (Chicago: University of Chicago Press, 1976), 159–79; Samuel Noah Kramer, "Schooldays: A Sumerian Composition Relating to the Education of a Scribe," *JAOS* 69 (1949): 199–215.

have documentation that some scribes had duties of teaching and enhancing scribal skills and knowledge of philology: bilingual word lists needed to be compiled, in part to help apprentice scribes learn to read and copy Sumerian (which had apparently become only a learned language among scholars by about the end of the 2nd millennium BCE). But there were other texts that presented problems, such as divinatory texts and even literary wisdom texts that made use of rare and archaic vocabulary. Thus, one scribal enterprise was to compile commentaries on certain texts.[11] We also have evidence that some texts were edited to produce new versions for political and perhaps theological reasons. This is documented for the *Enuma Eliš*, the Babylonian creation epic, with its hero Marduk. Under the Assyrian ruler Sennacherib, the *Enuma Eliš* (as well as some other texts) were edited to make Aššur the hero of the epic and the chief city Baltil (= Aššur) rather than Babylon.[12]

One of the texts that – perhaps surprisingly – does not have commentaries is the *Epic of Gilgamesh*. One possible reason for this is that it was not just passed down unchanged but underwent a variety of developments and edits from its origins (perhaps in the mid-3rd millennium BCE). The development of the Gilgamesh story has been investigated at least twice in recent decades. The process can be fairly well documented because of the extent of preservation of copies of the epic over 1500 years.

First was by Jeffrey Tigay[13] who argues that the story begins with Sumerian texts (perhaps written in the Ur III period in the late 3rd millennium) that narrate individual episodes about Gilgamesh, such as *Gilgamesh and the Land of the Living, Gilgamesh and the Bull of Heaven, The Deluge, The Death of Gilgamesh, Gilgamesh and Agga,* and *Gilgamesh, Enkidu, and the Netherworld.* Some of these Sumerian episodes were translated into Akkadian. At some point, an author (apparently a single individual) took either the Sumerian tales or Akkadian translations of the Sumerian material and created the unified Gilgamesh epic in the Old Babylonian period. He did not just compile the epic but edited and rewrote existing material and perhaps even invented material to make a coherent single narrative subordinate to a single primary aim: "The plan of the integrated epic thus testifies to the working of a single artistic mind".[14] After the developments in

---

11. See especially Eckart Frahm, *Babylonian and Assyrian Text Commentaries: Origins of Interpretation*, Guides to the Mesopotamian Textual Record 5 (Münster: Ugarit-Verlag, 2011).

12. Frahm, *Babylonian and Assyrian Text Commentaries*, 347–54.

13. Jeffrey H. Tigay, *The Evolution of the Gilgamesh Epic* (Philadelphia: University of Pennsylvania Press, 1982).

14. Tigay, *The Evolution of the Gilgamesh Epic*, 42.

the Old Babylonian period, the epic continued to develop in a Middle Babylonian version, a late version that contains the flood story,[15] and the version in Berossus.[16]

More recently Daniel Fleming and Sara Milstein argue that the "Huwawa narrative" is at the core of the epic's growth.[17] They do not appear to rule out an oral stage, but an earlier Sumerian version of the tale was turned into an Akkadian version in the Old Babylonian period (early 2nd millennium BCE). This Akkadian version was not, however, a simple translation of the Sumerian but a new independent creation. This had material added before and after it, with some re-editing of the Huwawa narrative itself, to create the fuller Gilgamesh epic in the Old Babylonian period. Their study stops at this point and does not trace the further development of the epic after the Old Babylonian period.

In spite of the differences of the two analyses just outlined, there are substantial agreements. It seems clear that there was an oral stage of Gilgamesh traditions in the half millennium between a historical Gilgamesh, who seems to have been king of Uruk somewhere in the period 2700–2500 BCE, and the earliest Sumerian written texts with these traditions in the Ur III period. How the oral tradition was passed down and how it came to be written down are questions to which we have no answer. But it does seem that such an oral period of the various Gilgamesh traditions did exist. After the developments in the Old Babylonian period (as discussed above), the epic continued to develop, with a Middle Babylonian version, a late version that contains the flood story, and finally the version in Berossus.

2.4 SCRIBES IN EGYPT

The development of writing and scribalism in Egypt is well documented over three millennia and more.[18] In Egyptian inscriptions "scribe" and "administrator" are often used interchangeably. Briefly, scribes were initially in the service of the king and also took care of the affairs of the administration. They had a variety of different functions, just as the higher officials in the administration had functions different from the ordinary scribe at the bottom of the ladder, as their titles show:[19] at the lower level were those scribes who recorded the numbers of cat-

---

15. *ANET* 72–99, probably dated to the late 2nd millennium.
16. Stanley M. Burstein, *The Babyloniaca of Berossus*, SANE 1/5 (Malibu: Undena, 1978), late 4th century BCE.
17. Daniel E. Fleming and Sara J. Milstein, *The Buried Foundation of the Gilgamesh Epic: The Akkadian Huwawa Narrative*, Cuneiform Monographs 39 (Leiden: Brill; Atlanta: SBL Press, 2010).
18. E.g., Adelheid Schlott, *Schrift und Schreiber im Alten Ägypten*, Beck's Archäologische Bibliothek (Munich: Beck, 1989).
19. Schlott, *Schrift und Schreiber im Alten Ägypten*, 93–94.

tle or the yield of the harvest (primarily for tax purposes) and perhaps wrote letters for the illiterate at the village level. At the top were the high officials next to the king, but they employed a "middle level" of scribes who did the actual work of writing, recording, and translating. Although there are examples in which scribes rose in status in the hierarchy, generally the sons of those at the bottom of the hierarchy themselves remained also at the bottom, and so on.

In the New Kingdom a number of high scribes were responsible for recruiting for the army and even leading it as generals.[20] The Israelite "scribe of the army" had a similar function of "recruiting the people of the land (for the military)" (2 Kgs 25:19; Jer. 52:25). Because their tombs have been preserved, we have the "autobiographies" of some Egyptian high officials who designate themselves as scribes (e. g., Rechmire[21]). Military campaigns required a number of ordinary scribes to keep the "palace day book" in which the deeds of the king were recorded with regard to military operations (e. g., Thutmose III[22]).

When we look at the literature produced, we find a variety of genres. An important scribal product is the range of writings produced or selected as useful for teaching apprentice scribes.[23] In the First Intermediate Period we find writings, such as the *Admonitions of Ipuwer or the Prophecies of Neferti*, which have been interpreted as an expression of the consternation felt by many during those troubled times,[24] though not everyone agrees.[25]

We have another model for which we have good deal of information from the Ptolemaic period: the village scribe. We shall focus on one particular archive here, that of Menches, village scribe (κωμογραμματεύς) of Kerkeosiris in the Fayum.[26] Menches first

---

20. Schlott, *Schrift und Schreiber im Alten Ägypten*, 217–37.
21. See *Lexikon der Ägyptologie* 5:180–82.
22. Miriam Lichtheim, *Ancient Egyptian Literature: Volume II: The New Kingdom* (Berkeley/Los Angeles: University of California Press, 1976), 29–35.
23. Schlott, *Schrift und Schreiber im Alten Ägypten*, 196–208.
24. Schlott, *Schrift und Schreiber im Alten Ägypten*, 182–96.
25. Miriam Lichtheim, *Ancient Egyptian Literature: Volume I: The Old and Middle Kingdom* (Berkeley/Los Angeles: University of California Press, 1973).
26. A lengthier discussion of this figure is given in Lester L. Grabbe, "Scribes, Writing, and Epigraphy in the Second Temple Period", in *"See, I Will Bring a Scroll Recounting What Befell Me" (Ps 40:8): Epigraphy and Daily Life from the Bible to the Talmud, Dedicated to the Memory of Professor Hanan Eshel*, Journal of Ancient Judaism Supplement 12, ed. Esther Eshel and Yigal Levin (Göttingen: Vandenhoeck & Ruprecht, 2014), 105–21. A basic study is A. M. F. W. Verhoogt, Menches, *Komogrammateus of Kerkeosiris: The Doings and Dealings of a Village Scribe in the Late Ptolemaic Period* (120–110 B.C.), Papyrologica Lugduno-Batava 29 (Leiden: Brill, 1998). A recent study of village scribes that uses other examples, as well as Menches,

comes to our attention in a papyrus of about 120 BCE when his term of office is renewed, indicating that he had already held the office for an unknown period previously. A letter of appointment was written by the chief royal scribe (βασιλικὸς γραμματεύς) to the chief scribe of the toparchy.[27]

We do not know how Menches got the office. There is some evidence that he knew or was related to someone substantial in the bureaucracy.[28] The main duty of the village scribe was to oversee the agricultural taxes of the area. For this, detailed records of each property were kept, including its dimensions and ownership. Crown land would be rented out, but non-crown land was subject to taxes of various sorts. Taxes varied, depending on the crops being grown – even whether the tax would be paid in kind or in silver. Thus, a careful record had to be kept even of the types of crops being planted.

The village scribe was part of a hierarchical network of scribes, answerable to the toparchy scribe (*topogrammateus*) and the chief royal scribe (*basilikos grammateus*) who was above the toparchy scribes. This could lead to a dressing down for not "respecting" the office of his superior, as in a letter in which a relative of the toparchy scribe was alleged to have been given no special treatment.[29] Menches also found himself on the receiving end of various complaints and excuses by those over whom he had responsibility for taxes and the like.[30] Another complaint was of an even more blatant offence, that of breaking into a house and committing armed robbery.[31] Menches himself was not immune from serious legal charges, as is indicated by a petition that he made to the king and queen themselves. He had been arrested because of an accusation of poisoning against him; however, the charges were dismissed because the accusers failed to appear when the court sat. But Menches appealed to royalty so that the same or

---

is found in Giovanni B. Bazzana, *Kingdom of Bureaucracy: The Political Theology of Village Scribes in the Sayings Gospel Q*, BETL 274 (Leuven: Peeters, 2015); his main interest is in applying the model to the origin of the hypothesized Q document.

27. Bernard P. Grenfell, Arthur S. Hunt, and J. Gilbart Smyly (eds.), *The Tebtunis Papyri, Part I*, University of California Publications, Graeco-Roman Archaeology 1; Branch (London: Henry Frowde, 1902): 72–73 (text no. 10); see also the translation in Verhoogt, *Menches, Komogrammateus of Kerkeosiris*, 60.

28. Cf. Grenfell, et al. (eds.), *The Tebtunis Papyri, Part I*, 70–71.

29. Grenfell, et al. (eds.), *The Tebtunis Papyri, Part I*, 94–95 (text no. 23).

30. Grenfell, et al. (eds.), *The Tebtunis Papyri, Part I*, 157–59 (text no. 50); see also the translation in Roger S. Bagnall and Peter Derow (eds.), *The Hellenistic Period: Historical Sources in Translation*, Blackwell Sourcebooks in Ancient History 1 (Oxford: Blackwell; new edn, 2004), 175.

31. Grenfell, et al. (eds.), *The Tebtunis Papyri, Part I*, 152–53 (text no. 46); see also the translation in Naphtali Lewis, *Greeks in Ptolemaic Egypt: Case Studies in the Social History of the Hellenistic World* (Oxford: Clarendon, 1986), 121.

further charges would not be made against him.³²

Although Kerkeosiris was only a village of about 1500 persons, the duties of the village scribe were not carried out in an obscure corner. On the contrary, there was regular correspondence not only with the toparchy scribe but even with the chief royal scribe. Preserved are a number of letters to the various individuals who held the office of *topogrammateus* during the period that Menches held office. Yet the greatest portion of Menches' outgoing correspondence was to the *basilikos grammateus*. The village scribe apparently had the responsibility of letting the chief royal scribe know immediately whenever something went wrong, and the date on the reports indicates they were done with dispatch. In one case, a matter was apparently reported when Menches and Horus the basilikos grammateus were together, since it concerned Menches' own village. As soon as he had further information, Menches made a "supplementary report" to Horus to keep him informed.³³

In the interests of communication – though the ultimate concern was maximizing state revenue – there was evidently an annual meeting in Alexandria, in which all the toparchy scribes and some of the village scribes made the journey down river to report to the chief royal scribe. However often Menches made this journey is not known, but at least one letter seems to order him to do so.³⁴

To summarize briefly, the village scribe held an important office and was responsible for keeping track of records in the local area, especially relating to the assessing and collection of taxes on crops. This would also have applied specifically to village scribes in Judah but also in general to scribes in other spheres. Even though the village scribe will not provide our main model, many scribes had not only the important function of record keeping but also often a significant role in administration. This scribal model is important.

2.5 EXAMPLE OF HOMERIC POEMS

A recent study on the origins of the Homeric poems is Jonathan Ready's *Orality, Textuality, and the Homeric Epics*;³⁵ one of its values

---

32. Grenfell, et al. (eds.), *The Tebtunis Papyri, Part I*, 146–49 (text no. 43); see also the translation in Lewis, *Greeks in Ptolemaic Egypt*, 116–17.

33. James G. Keenan and John C. Shelton (eds.), *The Tebtunis Papyri, Volume IV*, Graeco-Roman Memoirs 64 (London: Egypt Exploration Society, 1976), 27–29 (text no. 1099); see also the translation in Verhoogt, *Menches, Komogrammateus of Kerkeosiris*, 91.

34. Grenfell, et al. (eds.), *The Tebtunis Papyri, Part I*, 103–5 (text no. 26).

35. Jonathan L. Ready, *Orality, Textuality, and the Homeric Epics*: *An Interdisciplinary Study of Oral Texts, Dictated Texts, and Wild Texts* (Oxford: Oxford University Press, 2019).

is that it summarizes some of the debate on the origins of the *Iliad* and the *Odyssey* and also draws on a good deal of comparative studies, especially modern studies relating to oral literature in various parts of the world. As I shall suggest, some aspects of Homerica study have very interesting implications for the study of the origins of biblical literature; on the other hand, there are also crucial differences, especially when we investigate certain genres of biblical writings.

Two main theories about how the Homeric poems became written down are discussed by Ready.[36] One is the "dictation theory", which suggests that a poet dictated, i. e., performed or recited, the poem to a scribe. One variation on this (that of M. L. West) is that the poet himself acted as the scribe or perhaps engaged a scribe as an amanuensis. The other is the "evolutionary theory", in which various versions of the poems were written down, beginning at an early date, though these eventually produced a standardized version by a process of editing. According to Ready's thesis, the written text is a product of a three-way interaction between the collector or sponsor, the poet, and the scribe. In some cases the "collector" might be the poet himself who enlists the scribe to take down the poem in writing. The poet is of course normally performing his recitation before an audience and interacting with that audience. The environment in the process of dictation would be different, even if there was still an audience. The poet would have to give the scribe time to write down the text, which would slow the process of recitation down considerably. It was also likely to make him more self-aware of his poetry and more reflective on its content, perhaps leading to some self censorship.

2.6 SUMMARY ABOUT SCRIBES

The following points seem to be suggested by the data examined above:

– Although they were not always distinguished, it appears that there were different types of scribes: those whose job was primarily to copy, though they might well take dictation; scribes who drafted correspondence; village scribes who were responsible locally, especially in assessing and collecting taxes; scribes who had important administrative responsibilities high up in government; and, finally, scribes who composed and edited literature. The types of scribe varied, of course, from culture to culture. Scribes often seemed to have more than one task, but only the elite, with more leisure time, were probably involved in composing or editing writings to be passed down.

– Many scribes in Judah seem to have been members of the

---

36. Ready, Orality, Textuality, and the Homeric Epics, 101–4.

priestly cast, whether altar priests or lower clergy (Levites). Scribes in the temple would have been trained by priests. There are also indications that the scribal office was often passed down from father to son, and training was probably a form of apprenticeship.

– Some scribes were important figures in the administration of the kingdoms of Israel and Judah, as indicated by a number of biblical passages. Similarly, once Judah became a province in the Persian and the Hellenistic empires, with the high priest as the highest native figure, some scribes were high up in the local government. Some scribes in the royal administration may not have been priests, but many even of these scribes were probably priests. Similarly, during the Persian and Hellenistic periods, some of the scribes might still have been temple personnel.

– The *komogrammateus* or village scribe is well documented in Egypt, and these data have been plausibly extrapolated to other regions. This is probably not a good model for the origins of most Jewish literature, however, since village scribes were not likely to be involved in the composition of literature. Such religious and literary writings were probably more often the product of priestly scribes.

– In Mesopotamia such writings as the *Epic of Gilgamesh* and the *Enuma Elish* give examples of how literature might develop in the scribal sphere. Gilgamesh moved from a (hypothetical) oral stage to Sumerian tales to a first (hypothetical) Akkadian version of the Huwawa tale to the full Gilgamesh epic. Similarly, we see the Babylonian creation epic deliberately edited by Assyrian scribes (probably under Sennacherib) to produce an "Assyrianized" version that makes the god Aššur the hero of the tale.

– Some of the work being done on the development of the Homeric poems and their transfer from the oral sphere to writing helps us to understand how oral tradition can become written literature. An important aspect of this is the question of dictation, since the person with knowledge of the oral tradition might dictate to a scribe. An example of this is already found in the figures of Jeremiah and Baruch.

3. Scribes and the Production of Literature

It seems clear that much of the literature that we possess from antiquity is a scribal product. It may be that a book like Qohelet was written by perhaps a literate member of the upper classes rather than by a professional scribe, but this would have been exceptional in the ancient Near East, especially before the Hellenistic period. In the Greco-Roman world we have many writings authored by individuals who were playwrights, philosophers, poets, and historians who did not belong to the scribal profession as such. Nevertheless, when we are looking at the vast bulk of Jewish literature from antiquity, we appear to be viewing a scribal product. The survey of scribalism in the previous section has thrust upon us a number of possible models for the production of the Hebrew Bible and other Jewish literature. We can now consider the usefulness of some of these.

The model of the village scribe is interesting because we have a good deal of information on the office. It has also been used recently as a means of postulating the origin of the hypothetical Q source in the gospels of Matthew and Luke. This thesis might work well with the Q gospel source (though this is a matter for NT scholars to debate). Yet it seems unlikely that it will help us with the origin of parts of the Hebrew Bible, which are more likely to be the product of temple scribes.

Work done over the past century and more on the Homeric poems may help us. It shows us that great literature might have had an oral stage, perhaps even narratives of considerable length only in oral form. The problem with this model is that the narratives we are investigating in this conference are not poetry and are not likely to have had an origin as poetry. On the other hand, an oral stage for some or much of the material is a reasonable assumption. Also, some of the recent discussion of the Homeric epics has emphasized the importance of considering a dictation model, in which the oral material is reduced to writing by the oral poet's dictation of it to a professional scribe. This is important because we have evidence that certain writings from the late monarchy and the Persian period were dictated by individuals to scribes. For example, Jeremiah is pictured as dictating some of his prophecies to Baruch (Jer. 36). At Elephantine Arsames dictated letters to a scribe, as we know from the letters preserved that give the name of the scribe. Such would have been easier than for an oral poet to perform the Iliad or the Odyssey with a scribe taking it down in writing. We shall return to this point below.

4. Examples of Scribal Literary Development

Of particular importance are examples of writings that show actual evidence of scribal development. There are few of these, sadly, but there are some. Here are four such examples that show development that can be catalogued and is not just hypothesized.

First, there is the Gilgamesh epic, which was discussed at length above.[37]

Its investigation is important because the evolution of the epic is significantly documented. There are still gaps that have to be filled, but its development over perhaps 1500 years can be observed in ways that Hebrew Bible scholars can only dream of because the many copies have given us variant versions, some of which seem to be intermediate between others. Therefore, even though the process of editing is nowhere described, it can be inferred from the various copies of the epic over the centuries. What we find is that the original 3rd-millennium Sumerian tale (the "Huwawa story") – which probably had an oral stage – was turned into Akkadian at the beginning of the 2nd millennium in the Old Babylonian period, but the Akkadian version was not a translation of the Sumerian tale as such but a new creation by the "translator" who retold the story in his own words. The story was then further adapted by having other narratives relating to Gilgamesh edited before and after it, to give an epic of Gilgamesh.

What this model indicates is that narratives or other traditional elements can – indeed, usually do – evolve over time, normally becoming longer and more detailed in the later stages. This has long been the hypothesis in Hebrew Bible studies but, unfortunately, often difficult to find concrete evidence for it. This is why such models are so important.

This general statement is also illustrated by the book of Jeremiah. Much work has gone into proposing how the book arose at the hypothetical level. For our purposes, though, two stages in this development seem to be preserved in the Septuagint version and the Hebrew Masoretic version. There is wide agreement that the LXX version represents an earlier stage in the writing of the book.[38] This is based not only on comparing the Greek and Hebrew versions but also Qumran manuscript 4QJer^b (4Q71). This is a very fragmentary version, but at Jeremiah 9:21–10:22(?) the Qumran manuscript follows the LXX text in lacking verses 6–8 and 10 and having verse 9 between 5a and 5b.[39] This is a good example illustrating that the LXX translator of Jeremiah was not abbreviating his Hebrew *Vorlage* but translating it faithfully. With a text one-eighth shorter than the MT, the original Hebrew text

---

37. See under the heading, "Scribes in Mesopotamia".

38. E.g., J. Gerald Janzen, *Studies in the Text of Jeremiah*, Harvard Semitic Monographs 6 (Cambridge, MA: Harvard University Press, 1973); William McKane, *A Critical and Exegetical Commentary on Jeremiah*: *Volume I Introduction and Commentary on Jeremiah I–XXV*, ICC (Edinburgh: T & T Clark, 1986); Robert P. Carroll, *Jeremiah: A Commentary*, OTL (London: SCM, 1986).

39. Emanuel Tov, "Three Fragments of Jeremiah from Qumran Cave 4," *Revue de Qumran* 15 (1992): 531–41.

of the LXX has been considerably expanded by later scribes to give us the MT.

Another example focuses on Daniel 4. Already in 1935 Wolfram von Soden argued that the legend of Nabonidus lay behind Daniel's story.[40] The *Nabonidus Chronicle* was available to him,[41] then in the next couple of decades surprising new information confirmed von Soden's inspired proposal. One was the discovery of the Harran inscription in 1956 in which Nabonidus's stay in the area of Teman toward the end of the Neo-Babylonian period in quest of the god Sin was described.[42] Nabonidus's actions were interpreted by many in the establishment of Babylon as madness, especially as exemplified in the *Verse Account of Nabonidus*.[43] Some years later a text found among the Qumran scrolls was published, the 4QPrayer of Nabonidus (4Q242), which was a story of the Babylonian king Nabonidus being ill for seven years but cured by a Jewish exorcist. What we now have are three stages in the story:

(i) Story of Nabonidus's religious quest of ten years in Teman (this may have been only an oral stage circulating in Babylon but is supported by the official accounts): (a) Harran inscriptions: Nabonidus's official statement about what he was doing; (b) The *Nabonidus Chronicle*: the official account of Nabonidus's reign. (ii) 4Q242: Nabonidus's strange behavior has become an illness, and his ten years in Teman have become seven of illness. (iii) Daniel 7: Nabonidus has become Nebuchadnezzar, and the Jewish exorcist from the exiles has transformed into the dream interpreter Daniel.

There may not be a linear development in the surviving documents, that is, Daniel 4 may not be a direct literary development from 4Q242 (or its ancestors), but each represents a stage in the development of the tradition that became Daniel 4 from the original story of Nabonidus.[44]

The final example concerns the Qumran and Cairo Genizah texts

---

40. Wolfram von Soden, "Eine babylonische Volksüberlieferung von Nabonid in den Danielerzählungen," *ZAW* 53 (1935): 81–89.
41. See especially Albert K. Grayson, *Assyrian and Babylonian Chronicles*, Texts from Cuneiform Sources 5 (Locust Valley, NY: J. J. Augustin, 1975), 104–11.
42. *ANET* 560–63.
43. *ANET* 312–15.
44. Further discussion can be found in Matthias Henze, *The Madness of King Nebuchadnezzar: The Ancient Near Eastern Origins and Early History of Interpretation of Daniel 4*, JSJSup 61 (Leiden: Brill, 1999); Carol A. Newsom, "Why Nabonidus? Excavating Traditions from Qumran, the Hebrew Bible, and Neo-Babylonian Sources", in *The Dead Sea Scrolls: Transmission of Traditions and Production of Texts*, STDS 92, ed. Metso, Sarianna, Hindy Najman, and Eileen Schuller (Leiden: Brill, 2010), 57–79.

of the *Damascus Document*.⁴⁵ Already the two copies found in the Cairo Genizah (CD) raised questions about the relationship of their texts, but the discovery of approximately ten copies at Qumran has made it clear to many that there were developments in the text over time. The "Admonition" section (CD 1–8, 19–20) would presumably have needed periodic updating because it contained the regulations about a closed community and its organization. The "Laws" section (CD 9–16) seems to have been more stable, but both sections have now been studied from a traditio-historical perspective.

Already it was determined that CD 19–20 and 15–16 should probably be placed between CD 8 and CD 9. Then 4QDᵃ (= 4Q266) demonstrated a much fuller version of the Damascus Document. It apparently has both the beginning and end of the text, based on the physical presentation of the manuscripts. It demonstrates the order CD 1–8, 19–20, 15–16, 9–14, but it also shows that a section of text beginning the document is not found in CD (at least, as preserved); it also has an ending not found in CD. 4QDᵃ preserves a section of text that preceded CD 1.1. 4QDᵃ, along with 4QDᵇ (4Q267), 4QDᶜ (4Q268), 4QDᵈ (4Q269), 4QDᵉ (4Q270), 4QDᶠ (4Q271), 4QDᵍ (4Q272), and 4QpapDʰ (4Q273), also give various statements in the "Laws" section which add further regulations not addressed in CD, including disqualifications for various categories of priests, on diseases, on agriculture, on the jubilee years, clothing for male and female, appropriate marriages, to name some of them. Of particular interest is that 4QDᵉ, frag. 7, i.1–21, is parallel to the *Community Rule* (1QS 7.12–21), as is 4QDᵈ parallel to 1QS 7.14–18. It has often been felt that the *Damascus Document* and the *Community Rule* were somehow related, though few studies seem to have demonstrated this in any detail.

A number of different traditio-historical analyses of the *Damascus Document* have appeared over the years, which will not be discussed further here.⁴⁶ Most of those dealing with the "Admonition" section were done before the Qumran texts became available. The main point, though, is that in the variety of versions now available we seem to see the text developing over time. In this case, the shorter version – CD – is much later than the earlier (Qumran) versions. It may be that CD has been accidentally abbreviated rather than deliberately shortened, though we cannot be absolutely sure.⁴⁷ In any case, the later version of an edited work is not invariably longer; this is only a tendency.

---

45. See especially Charlotte Hempel, *The Laws of the Damascus Document: Sources, Tradition, and Redaction*, STDJ 29 (Brill: Leiden, 1998); Charlotte Hempel, *The Damascus Texts* (Sheffield Academic Press, 2000).

46. See the survey in Hempel, *The Damascus Texts*, 44–53.

47. Hempel, *The Damascus Texts*, 24.

Further study may show a complicated development of this text of the *Damascus Document*.

5. My Proposal for Connecting Chronicles and P

With regard to P, it was probably compiled in the early Persian period, though those members of the "Kaufmann school" who see pre-exilic signs in P are probably right about some or even much of the material in P. But the final product is probably post-exilic, or more likely from the Persian period.[48] If the standard theory (based on Graf-Wellhausen) is accepted, P included a variety of material: directions and descriptions relating to the temple and the cult but also genealogies and narrative material about Israel's past. Priests were interested in giving their own take on Israel's early history, including creation, the primordial period, the post-flood renewal, the patriarchs, and Israel's removal from Egypt to the Promised Land. The classic P hypothesis does not just propose cultic and ritual regulations; it also includes narrative – a *Heilsgeschichte* beginning with creation and leading up to entry into the promised land. The creation story in Genesis 1 seems to be cognizant of the Babylonian creation epic the *Enuma Eliš*. I have argued that a version of the Pentateuch that we now know was compiled in the Persian period, probably in the 4th century BCE, perhaps including the participation of Ezra the priest and scribe.[49] The Deuterono-

---

48. See especially the commentary of Erhard S. Gerstenberger, *Leviticus: A Commentary*, OTL (Louisville, KY: Westminister John Knox, 1996); ET of *Das dritte Buch Mose: Leviticus*, Das Alte Testament Deutsch 6 (Göttingen: Vandenhoeck & Ruprecht, 1993), which argues the case well. The massive commentary by Jacob Milgrom, Leviticus 1–16: A New Translation with Introduction and Commentary, AB 3 (Garden City, NY: Doubleday,1991); Jacob Milgrom, *Leviticus 17–22: A New Translation with Introduction and Commentary*, AB 3A (New York: Doubleday, 2000); Jacob Milgrom, *Leviticus 23–27: A New Translation with Introduction and Commentary*, AB 3B (New York: Doubleday, 2001) argues that P fitted the pre-monarchic phase of Israel, which reflects the small size of the territory. Granted that P seems designed for a small political entity in Palestine, the Persian province is a better fit with the known data (especially the language used) than the alleged pre-monarchic entity.

49. See especially Lester L. Grabbe, "The Last Days of Judah and the Roots of the Pentateuch: What Does History Tell Us?" in *The Fall of Jerusalem and the Rise of the Torah*, FAT 107, ed. Peter Dubovský, Dominik Markl, and Jean-Pierre Sonnet (Tübingen: Mohr Siebeck, 2016), 19–45; also Lester L. Grabbe, "Elephantine and the Torah", in *In the Shadow of Bezalel: Aramaic, Biblical, and Ancient Near Eastern Studies in Honor of Bezalel Porten*, Culture and History of the Ancient Near East 60, ed. Alejandro F. Botta (Leiden/Boston: Brill, 2013), 125–35. On the question of Ezra, see Lester L. Grabbe, "Penetrating the Legend: in Quest of the Historical Ezra", in *Open-Mindedness in the Bible and Beyond: A Volume of Studies in Honour of Bob Becking*, LHBOTS 616, ed. Marjo C. A. Korpel and Lester L. Grabbe (London and

mistic History (DH) seems to have been compiled before the end of the Neo-Babylonian period, though some would want to put it in the early Persian period.[50]

The composer(s) of Chronicles (Chr) probably worked in the early Hellenistic period and thus perhaps a century or even two after P. But he/they already had available to him/them a "history" as laid out in the Pentateuch and DH that extended from creation to the fall of Jerusalem in 587/586 (at least, in outline form, if not as detailed as in the present texts). But to Chr there were some deficiencies in this history, because it did not say enough about the temple and priesthood. Thus, Chr set out to write a version more congenial to their concerns. Whether Chr had P available as a separate document, rather than just as a part of the completed Pentateuch is unlikely, but it is not impossible.

Chr did not repeat the first part of this history as such, but covered it by means of the extended genealogies in 1 Chron. 1–9. Whether it was revised independently from a version of Samuel-Kings,[51] as is conventionally assumed, or had a base text that had been revised by the author of Samuel-Kings (so A. G. Auld argues, based on De Wette[52]), it was important to link the organization of the temple and priesthood to David, the first "proper" king of the people. The author was probably a member of the priesthood or at least someone close to the temple and priests (cf. the later author Ben Sira). In any case, Chr also may have remembered that under the monarchy, the king was the highest cultic official, and all the priests (including the high priest) ultimately answered to him.[53] Some members of the priesthood wanted to present the king as subject to the priests (e. g., Deut. 17:14–20), but this was evidently not the view of Chr – at least, as far as David was concerned.[54]

New York: Bloomsbury T & T Clark, 2015), 97–110.

50. Cf. especially Thomas C. Römer and Albert de Pury, "Deuteronomistic Historiography (DH): History of Research and Debated Issues", in *Israel Constructs its History: Deuteronomistic Historiography in Recent Research*, JSOTSup 306, ed. Albert de Pury, Thomas Römer, and Jean-Daniel Macchi (Sheffield: Sheffield Academic Press, 2000), 24–141, for a discussion of Noth's original thesis and the subsequent developments of the theory.

51. It has been rightly argued that the version of Samuel-Kings used in such a hypothesized revision would have been different from the recension in the Masoretic text (e. g., Werner E. Lemke, "The Synoptic Problem in the Chronicler's History", *HTR* 58 [1965]: 349–63). But it would probably not have been significantly different. Much of the text of Chronicles not found in Samuel-Kings was probably contributed by Chr himself rather than being in the base text he was revising.

52. A. Graeme Auld, *Kings without Privilege: David and Moses in the Story of the Bible's Kings* (Edinburgh: T & T Clark, 1994).

53. Grabbe, *Priests, Prophets, Diviners, Sages*, 20–40.

54. It must be admitted that Uzziah is presented as being cursed by God with a

It is David himself who not only gathered all the material for building the temple but also organized the priesthood and the cultic service, according to 1 Chron. 22–28. Not much was left for Solomon to do, if 1 Chronicles is anything to go by! The history of the monarchy emphasizes the place of the priests and the existence of all sorts of prophets and holy men not found in 1 and 2 Samuel and 1 and 2 Kings. What this suggests is that Chr, although probably (a) priest(s) or Levite(s), belonged to a different school from the compilers of P. Or perhaps it was just that Chr was a generation or more removed from the P school and saw things differently because of the change in circumstance with regard to the priests in the early Hellenistic period.

It seems clear that priestly knowledge was passed down orally, i. e., by apprenticeship. There would have been no need to write it down: it was preserved in the collective minds of the priests and handed on by teaching and example to the new generations of priests learning their trade. Writings such as Leviticus are clearly not for temple personnel but for the wider Israelite community, though based (in part, at least) on priestly knowledge and practice. This means that at some point this oral tradition and practice was reduced to writing, specifically to educate the non-priestly lay Israelites. It might have been a senior priest who wrote it down, but it could well have been that a senior priest dictated the material to a younger priestly scribe.

Thus, the picture of the temple given by the priestly writer(s) of Chronicles is inspired in part by the P section of the Pentateuch, but also by the knowledge of the priestly tradition available to scribes, current cultic practice in the temple and, finally, Chr's utopian imagination of the temple state that he would like to have seen in his own day.

6. CONCLUSIONS

The present study could only go so far because of the sporadic nature of the evidence. I have drawn attention to the hypothetical nature of the standard traditio-historical analysis. Yet the present paper has been disappointing in that it has not been able to obviate the hypothetical aspect of our textual analysis: conjecture and hypothesis have also been a necessary part of this study. Only in four examples has it been possible to provide actual demonstration of some textual development. Also, this study's results might seem to many readers as less exciting than some of the traditio-historical reconstructions in some of

---

disease because of trying to offer sacrifices in the temple (2 Chron 26:16–21), even though Solomon and David had done the same thing (1 Chron 21:28; 2 Chron 1:6). He may, therefore, have distinguished between David and subsequent kings of Judah.

the other papers. This does not, however, licence us to ignore the need for finding evidence, as far as possible, in scribal practice. From that point of view the present study has merit. It has made the following points about scribes relevant to the issue of the conference:

– A variety of scribes with a variety of different duties are documented from various ancient Near Eastern cultures. Not all of them (e. g., the village scribe) are useful models for suggesting how biblical writings originated, but the work of elite and priestly scribes might be more helpful.

– In Judah the bulk of scribes seem to have been priests or other temple personnel. There were also scribes in the royal or local imperial administration, but even these might have been priestly scribes.

– From the examples of Egypt and Mesopotamia we can see that literature was created because of various needs within the scribal profession. Writings were required for teaching purposes, and we have some examples in which the state (i. e., the king) wanted certain writings edited for state purposes (e. g., the Enuma Eliš under Sennacherib). Yet some of the literature appears to have originated and been developed for aesthetic, creative, and even theological reasons (e. g., the *Epic of Gilgamesh*).

– Studies relating to the Homeric poems have led to various theories about how oral material gets put into writing. The question of dictation by the oral poet to a scribe is a model that has been discussed. Although the biblical material was often not in poetic form, the dictation model could still be helpful.

– Yet it has been possible to give a few examples where the development of the text can be witnessed in part because various versions have come down to us, illustrating to some extent the work of scribes in progress. Generally, the progress is from shorter to longer, from simpler to more complex, but this is not invariable: there are examples in which later versions are shorter, though in some cases this is because of deliberate editing for particular reasons.

With regard to the relationship between the P document and the books of Chronicles, the following points can be made:

– Both P and Chronicles appear to be priestly products. P is certainly from the priests, though the author(s) of Chronicles might be individual(s) close to the priesthood without being priest(s) himself(themselves), similar to the situation of Ben Sira.

– P seems to be a product of the Persian period in its final form, even though some or even much of the material might well have been from the period of the monarchy. It looks to reflect the province of Judah under Persian rule.

– The author(s) of Chronicles, probably writing in the early Greek period (perhaps a century or two later than P), had a number of sources and influences:
- A version of Samuel and Kings
- The P document (whether as a separate document or as a part of a completed Pentateuch
- Other priestly and temple traditions, perhaps in oral form
- The author's(authors') vision of a utopian theocratic (i. e., priestly) paradise

From these data, which seem generally accepted, we can then embark on the task of analyzing the present text of the Pentateuch. The results of that analysis remain hypothetical in that we have no intermediate documents that fill the gaps. Instead, we have to bridge these gaps by intelligent conjecture (as we have for the past two or three centuries), but as long as these conjectures keep the scribal evidence in mind and built on it, their plausibility is enhanced and can be better compared and evaluated.

Atonement, Sacred Space and Ritual Time: The Chronicler as Reader of Priestly Pentateuchal Narrative
Benjamin D. Giffone

1. Introduction

The essays in this volume explore the relationship between the so-called Priestly literature and the book of Chronicles. This contribution examines the concept of atonement, which is significant in Priestly Pentateuchal texts, and the application of this concept in Chronicles with respect to ritual time.

It is notable that the כפר word group is rare in Chronicles, occurring only three times as a verb, along with a single reference to the כפרת on the ark. By contrast, the verb כפר occurs dozens of times in Leviticus and Numbers, particularly in relation to consecration rituals, violations of altar purity, and calendric observances. Most notably, the "Day of Atonement" occupies quite a significant place in the structure of the Book of Leviticus (Lev 16) and within the various ritual calendars of P/H (which are more elaborate than the other lists of observances in the Pentateuch). Several commentators have noted that the Chronicler integrates certain uniquely Priestly elements of ritual practice into his narrative, but have struggled to see how "atonement," particularly the Day of Atonement, fits into the Chronicler's presentation.

In investigating the possible conceptual and textual relationships between Chronicles and P, I pose the question in reverse: if the Chronicler *were indeed* a devotee of the Priestly worldview and a reader of the Priestly literature [even as we recognize the subtle difference between those two contentions], and if he indeed wished to present

Israel's monarchic story through the lens of the Priestly concepts of "atonement," ritual space and ritual time – *how* would he have done so, and at which points in his narrative would such concepts have been significant?

I argue that the Chronicler interprets the Pentateuch (including so-called Priestly literature) in something close to its final form, with a sensitivity to its narrative structure. The Pentateuch as a narrative allows the Chronicler a range of ways in which to apply Priestly concepts and rituals within his history of Israel, particularly in moments that are relevant to calendric observances, altar purity and contamination, and "atonement."

The first section of this article situates the Priestly material on atonement, ritual space and ritual time within the narrative context of the Pentateuch, with a particular focus on moments in the narrative that are most relevant to the Chronicler's usage. The second section explores three instances of the Chronicler's appropriation of this Priestly material: Hezekiah's reforms (2 Chr 29–31), Uzziah's transgression (2 Chr 26:16–23), and Solomon's consecration and establishment of the temple (2 Chr 5–8). We will also compare similar appropriation of Priestly "atonement" rituals in Ezekiel 43 and 45. In each of these instances, I argue that certain conspicuous absences of Priestly ideas are not due to ignorance of P or opposition to P, but rather narrative sophistication in the Chronicler's reading of P as (part of) Torah. The concluding third section will draw out some implications for diachronic studies of the Pentateuch, Chronicles, and other narrative literature of the Persian period.

If it can be demonstrated that there is close affinity between Chronicles and the so-called Priestly texts of the Pentateuch, then this could lend support to the idea that the Chronicler is an early reader of a Pentateuch that is close to its final form.

1.1 Methodology and Premises

For Chronicles, more so than for other books of the Hebrew Bible, it can be appropriate to use the singular term "Chronicler" to describe the person or circle who compiled and finalized the book that is very close to the received text. It is plausible to speak of a single author who deliberately brought together disparate materials and perspectives into a work that exhibits some measure of theological coherence.

Chronicles may also be viewed as a document designed to build consensus by drawing together the strands of Israel's and Judah's story that represent different constituencies in his day. The Chronicler focuses on the story of Judah, yet holds out hope that the Northern

Israelite tribes will be joined to the Southern tribes and worship at the Jerusalem temple.[1] I and others have argued that the Chronicler represents a Judah- and Levi-centered view of his people's past, yet also reaches out to Benjaminites, smoothing over the tensions represented by the warring houses of David and Saul, and holding out hope that the historically Benjaminite towns would remain loyal to the Jerusalem cult rather than to other Yahwistic sanctuaries that were available.[2] Gary N. Knoppers, John W. Wright, and others have argued that Chronicles represents an attempt to mediate between the Levites and the priests.[3] Into each of these conflicts between groups that could form the Jerusalem temple's constituency in the Persian period, the Chronicler injects his own perspective that may or may not have been fully representative of those groups' perspectives and stories.[4] We might never know with any certainty how successful was the Chronicler's attempt at building consensus through his revisionist, re-forming history.[5]

Most relevant to this paper is the Chronicler's apparent attempt at blending the legal traditions that prevailed as *torah* in his day and applying them to his historical sources. While the notion of a "Deuteronomistic History" has undergone many permutations and modifications since Martin Noth's original idea,[6] the texts of Samuel–Kings do exhibit a strong affinity to Deuteronomic legal tradition. For the <u>Chronicler, the Priestly tradition is now recognized as authoritative</u>

    1. See, for example, Gary N. Knoppers, *Jews and Samaritans: The Origins and History of Their Early Relations* (Oxford/New York: Oxford University Press, 2013), 71–101.
    2. Benjamin D. Giffone, '*Sit At My Right Hand*': *The Chronicler's Portrait of the Tribe of Benjamin in the Social Context of Yehud*, LHBOTS 628. (London/New York: Bloomsbury T&T Clark, 2016), especially 207–228.
    3. Gary N. Knoppers, "Hierodules, Priests, or Janitors? The Levites in Chronicles and the History of the Israelite Priesthood," *JBL* 118 (1999): 49–72; John W. Wright, "'Those Doing the Work for the Service in the House of the Lord': 1 Chronicles 23:6–24:31 and the Socio-Historical Context for the Temple of Yahweh in Jerusalem in the Late Persian/Early Hellenistic Period," in *Judah and the Judeans in the Fourth Century B.C.E.*, eds. Oded Lipschits, Gary N. Knoppers, and Rainer Albertz (Winona Lake, IN: Eisenbrauns, 2007), 361–84. See also the discussion in Louis C. Jonker, *Defining All-Israel in Chronicles: Multi-levelled Identity Negotiation in Late Persian-Period Yehud*, FAT 106 (Tübingen: Mohr Siebeck, 2016), 106–113.
    4. Giffone, '*Sit At My Right Hand*', 224–226.
    5. I rather like this double-meaning intended by Louis C. Jonker, "Reforming History: The Hermeneutical Significance of the Books of Chronicles," *VT* 57 (2007): 21–44.
    6. For a broad history of perspectives: Thomas Römer, *The So-Called Deuteronomistic History: A Sociological, Historical and Literary Introduction* (London: T&T Clark, 2005). My own perspective is outlined in a forthcoming essay (2022), "Regathering Too Many Stones? Scribal Constraints, Community Memory, and the 'Problem' of Elijah's Sacrifice for Deuteronomism in Kings."

Torah, and so he brings the stories of the monarchy into conformity with both Deuteronomic and Priestly legal requirements. In a previous publication I have shown, for example, that the different conceptions of sacrificial centralization between Deuteronomic and Levitical texts account for key divergences between Samuel–Kings and Chronicles, for this very reason.[7] Yet this distinction must not be overplayed, as Ehud Ben Zvi, Knoppers and Louis C. Jonker[8] have shown that the Chronicler also held Deuteronomistic Torah in high regard and sought in certain places to bring his sources even *more* into line with Deuteronomism – the Chronicler was both Priestly *and* Deuteronomistic.[9]

If Chronicles is a *consensus-building* document that attempts in places to impose a unified – or, unifying – perspective on the source traditions,[10] the Pentateuch by comparison might be viewed as a *compromise* document that blends various traditions using the device of a grand narrative of progressive legal revelation and revision.[11] While the narrative of Exodus through Deuteronomy allows a certain measure of unevenness in the received Torah, we encounter legal divergences that are well-known and impossible to "harmonize," despite some apparent attempts by ancient interpreters (such as the Chroni-

---

7. Benjamin D. Giffone, "According to Which 'Law of Moses'? Cult Centralization in Samuel, Kings, and Chronicles," *VT* 67 (2017): 432–447.

8. Ehud Ben Zvi, "Are There Any Bridges Out There? How Wide Was the Conceptual Gap Between the Deuteronomistic History and Chronicles?" in *Community Identity in Judean Historiography: Biblical and Comparative Perspectives*, eds. Gary N. Knoppers and Kenneth A Ristau (Winona Lake, IN: Eisenbrauns, 2009), 59–86; Gary N. Knoppers, "The Relationship of the Deuteronomistic History to Chronicles: Was the Chronicler a Deuteronomist?" in *Congress Volume Helsinki 2010*, VTSup 148, ed. Martti Nissinen (Leiden: Brill, 2012), 307–341; Louis C. Jonker, "Was the Chronicler More Deuteronomic Than the Deuteronomist? Explorations into the Chronicler's Relationship with Deuteronomic Legal Traditions," *SJOT* 27 (2013): 191–203.

9. Knoppers is cautious in this regard: "It will not do, therefore, to situate Chronicles squarely within an ongoing Deuteronomistic tradition. Fixating on similar verbiage and the affinities between synoptic texts can mislead scholars into thinking that there is more continuity between the Chronistic and the Deuteronomistic works than is actually the case. Rather than thinking of the Chronicler as a Deuteronomist, it may be better to think of the Chronicler as an individual author, who self-consciously imitates and revises Deuteronomistic texts as one important means to construct his own literary work." Knoppers, "Was the Chronicler a Deuteronomist," 332.

10. Giffone, '*Sit At My Right Hand*', 7; David A. Glatt-Gilad, "Chronicles as Consensus Literature," in *What Was Authoritative for Chronicles*? Eds. Ehud Ben Zvi and Diana Edelman (Winona Lake, IN: Eisenbrauns, 2011), 67–75.

11. "… The Pentateuchal law in its final form represents a compromise between different interest groups with their own legal traditions worked out in several stages during the two centuries of Persian rule" (Joseph Blenkinsopp, *The Pentateuch*: *An Introduction to the First Five Books of the Bible* [New York: Doubleday, 1992], 241). See also Glatt-Gilad, "Chronicles as Consensus Literature," 74.

cler).¹² Pentateuchal source criticism is a wide and diverse arena, with entirely different approaches represented in different academic circles and cultures, and identification of sources vigorously contested.¹³ For these reasons one must always approach cautiously – yet this study will rarely attempt to excavate more than a single editorial layer, as the aim is to discover the coherence that the Chronicler apparently saw in the Torah.¹⁴

Scholars have long noted the apparent gap between what is presumed as "Law" in the so-called Deuteronomistic History and in Chronicles, and that this gap can in significant measure be explained by the adoption of material that modern scholars designate as "Priestly." Yet we must remember that these designations are theoretical; without tangible manuscript evidence of development, they remain so. Even as we may find diachronic models historically plausible and compelling, the earliest readers of the Pentateuch as "Torah" did not make such distinctions between Deuteronomistic, Priestly, Holiness, and post-Priestly texts. Rather, they read the text synchronically, with awareness of its narrative progression. On the other hand, Chronicles is a tangible example of development of tradition. The more "Torah" that we can detect within Chronicles, the more finely-tuned our diachronic models for Pentateuchal development can be.

As we consider the Persian context of Chronicles and its Torah, we should note the significance of ritual calendars for a cult that is working to expand its authority through subsuming all these identities and factions within its domain. First, authorities would wish to have the power to summon people to the central location bringing offerings and other resources – pilgrimage feasts. Second, authorities want to tell people what they should do and when in their own towns, on a schedule – sabbaths, new moons, and sabbath years. However, regular observances that never change and do not require pilgrimage could render a centralized authority obsolete, so long as the local authorities follow the initial rulings. Thus, a third exercise of power is the

---

12. See the well-known example of 2 Chr 35:13, "they boiled the paschal-offering in fire according to custom"; Michael Fishbane, *Biblical Interpretation in Ancient Israel* (Oxford: Clarendon Press, 1985), 135–136.

13. See the recent, massive edited volume showcasing these differences: Jan Christian Gertz et al., eds., *The Formation of the Pentateuch: Bridging the Academic Cultures of Europe, Israel and North America*, FAT 111 (Tübingen: Mohr Siebeck, 2016).

14. In this respect I find myself sympathetic with the cautious approaches of David M. Carr, *The Formation of the Hebrew Bible: A New Reconstruction* (New York/Oxford: Oxford University Press, 2011); and Joshua A. Berman, *Inconsistency in the Torah: Ancient Literary Convention and the Limits of Source Criticism* (New York/Oxford: Oxford University Press, 2017).

ability to make changes to the calendar, and to make rulings in exceptional situations. This ability to interpret and apply established rules in changing circumstances is precisely what we will see in the Chronicler's use of authoritative texts.

1.2 Disconnect between P and Chronicles? Preliminary Survey

There are at least three portions of Chronicles that should be kept in view as we consider the narrative background of the concepts of atonement, violations of ritual space, and ritual time in the Pentateuch.

1) Many commentators have seen that the Chronicler adds Priestly elements to the Deuteronomistic account of Solomon's temple dedication and establishment of regular cultic activities (2 Chr 5–8). The Chronicler's "correction" of MT 1 Kings 8:65–66 with respect to the timeline of the dedication, however, leads to potential overlap with the Day of Atonement on the tenth day of the seventh month (m07d10). However, the Day of Atonement is not mentioned where it "should" be in Chronicles – due to oversight, ignorance, polemic, or conscious omission.

2) Uzziah's attempt to burn incense (2 Chr 26:16–23) is recognized as having many echoes of Priestly passages in the Pentateuch, particularly in relation to altar purity violations: the offering of unauthorized fire by a non-priest, and leprosy as a source of impurity.

3) The narrative of Hezekiah's reforms (2 Chr 29–31) includes references to "atonement," and demonstrates some affinities to Priestly חטאת rituals for altar, leadership, and the assembly. Some scholars have noted similarities to the Day of Atonement ritual in Leviticus 16, but dismissed direct connection with this ritual due to Hezekiah's reforms occurring in the first month of the ritual year. Thus, the Priestly ritual calendars and the exception for delayed celebration of Passover (Num 9) in narrative context are particularly relevant for this study.

The puzzle in each of these instances is: if the Chronicler *were* in fact aware of the Priestly material and regarded it as Torah, why are these scenarios not *more* "Priestly" than they appear to be at first glance? What are we to make of the apparent incongruities with the Priestly dimensions of the Pentateuch? At each step, therefore, we should consider the likelihood of the alternatives: that the Chronicler was not aware of Priestly texts in their received form, or that the Chronicler was in fact aware of such Priestly observances but excluded them due to anti-Priestly tendencies.

2. NARRATIVE CONTEXT OF PRIESTLY DAY OF ATONEMENT AND PASSOVER

A narrative approach to the Pentateuch reveals closer alignment between Chronicles and P – which, at the very least, shows us one way that the Chronicler is reading the texts available to him. Rolf Rendtorff aptly proposes:

> We should not think too strictly in terms of literary dependence. I imagine that persons like the authors of the books of Chronicles knew a great deal about their people's national and religious tradition without having constantly to consult written documents. In some cases, of course, they used written material; in others, they might have drawn from their own knowledge gained through experience and education, for authors of texts like Chronicles must have had an excellent education. Hence, in every case, we should seek to identify the authors' sources from among the texts that are extant; if we cannot, we might then ask how we could interpret the tradition behind these utterances.[15]

The Chronicler interprets and applies the Priestly material regarding atonement and calendric observance with narrative sensitivity. Andreas Ruwe has observed:

> Leviticus obviously is not an independent narrative, but is part of the priestly narrative context of the Sinai pericope, Exod 19:1–Num 10:10, which is itself part of the Tetraor Pentateuch. The priestly [*sic*] narrative context of Exod 19:1–Num 10:10 is the primary literary context of Leviticus. Independently of the disputed question whether the priestly formation of the Pentateuch is an independent narrative work or serves as a supplement to the nonpriestly formation of the Pentateuch, it is necessary in any case to examine the inner coherence, the narrative structure and the thematic profile of this formation. Many elements of Leviticus become comprehensible only by contextualizing them with the other priestly texts of the Sinai narrative or with the priestly texts as such.[16]

Regardless of how we might assess the structure of Leviticus and Numbers from the standpoint of modern source criticism, the Chronicler would have read the ritual texts concerning the Day of Atonement as situated within the *narrative* of Leviticus, and perhaps the elements of a Priestly narrative that are embedded within a "Tetrateuch" or Pentateuch. The layers of redaction that we presume to identify within

---

15. Rolf Rendtorff, "Chronicles and the Priestly Torah," in *Text, Temples, and Traditions: A Tribute to Menahem Haran*, eds. Michael V. Fox et al. (Winona Lake, IN: Eisenbrauns, 1996), 259–266, here 259.

16. Andreas Ruwe, "The Structure of the Book of Leviticus in the Narrative Outline of the Priestly Sinai Story (Exod 19:1–Num 10:10*)," in *The Book of Leviticus: Composition and Reception*, VTSup 93, eds. Rolf Rendtorff and Robert A. Kugler (Leiden: Brill, 2003), 55–78, here 58.

Pentateuchal narrative actually provide the Chronicler with the flexibility he needed to apply Torah within his own re-written narrative. The Chronicler saw the causal connection between Leviticus 8–10 and 16, and thus interpreted the "Day of Atonement" ritual as originally performed to purge[17] the altar after the death of Aaron's sons. The Chronicler therefore adopts a "partial *ad hoc*" understanding of the Day of Atonement ritual.

2.1 THE DAY OF ATONEMENT IN NARRATIVE CONTEXT OF THE PENTATEUCH

Leviticus is situated chronologically between the dedication of the tabernacle, which occurs in y2m1d1 (the first day of the first month of the second year) from the exodus (Exod 40:17), and the beginning of Numbers, which occurs in y2m2d1 (Num 1:1). Stackert notes: "The Priestly source's plot continues in the book of Numbers from the exact moment that Leviticus ends. The date in Num 1.1…confirms that the series of divine speeches delivered in Leviticus and the other events recorded in the book ostensibly occurred over a period of one month."[18] Two "flashbacks" occur in Numbers that are relevant for our study: 9:1–10:10, which begins at y2m1 and mentions both the Passover and the assembly of the tabernacle (10:11 continues in y2m2d20); and the anterior reference to Nadab and Abihu's death in 3:4.

Though we find Leviticus's ritual calendar elaborated in the Holiness Code (Lev 23), the actual description of the Day of Atonement is found in Leviticus 16, which is itself a continuation of the narrative begun in chapters 8–10 and interrupted by purity concerns (Lev 11–15). The connection is made apparent by the resumption in 16:1: "Then YHWH spoke to Moses after the death of Aaron's two sons when they had approached YHWH and died…"

The ritual entails the performance of several sacrifices of the תאטח (sin/purification offering), which is also performed several times in the priestly ordination and altar sanctification ceremony of chapters 8–10. The specific instructions for the חטאת (Lev 4:1–5:13) prescribe this ritual for "covering" (כפר) the purity violations of various classes of people: priest (4:3–12), the whole assembly (4:13–21), the "prince" (4:22–26), or any common person (4:27–35). The ritual applies to unintentional sins/errors (ישגו/בשגגה 4:2, 13, 22, 27), and for contamination by an unclean animal carcass or "human uncleanness" (5:2–3).

---

17. Throughout this article I use "atone/atonement" and "purge/purgation" interchangeably.

18. Jeffrey Stackert, "Leviticus," in *The New Oxford Annotated Bible with Apocrypha, Fully Revised Fourth Edition*, ed. Michael D. Coogan (New York: Oxford University Press, 2010), 141.

In each of these scenarios the offerer lays hands on the head of the animal, and the blood is applied to the horns of the altar of incense; in addition, in the cases of חטאת for the priest or for the whole assembly, blood is sprinkled seven times before the פרכט הקדש. The Day of Atonement ritual is a much more grave performance of the חטאת designed to address severe and accumulated purity violations. It includes a חטאת for the priest (16:11–14), a חטאת for the people (16:15– 19), and the live goat לעזאזל (16:7–10, 20–22). Additionally, while blood of the people's חטאת is applied to the altar (16:18), the blood of both priest's and people's offerings is sprinkled seven times inside the veil (16:14–15).

In comparison to the regular prescribed חטאת (Lev 4:1–5:13) and the severe purgation ritual (Lev 16), the eight-day ceremony for the ordination of Aaron and his sons and the consecration of the new altar (Lev 8–9) falls somewhere in between. It includes daily חטאת for the priests, with laying on of hands and blood applied to the altar, but includes the added purificatory step of smearing the blood on the priests' right ears, thumbs, and big toes. The altar is necessary for the consecration of the priests, but the priests would defile the altar if they had not been consecrated – so the eight-day initiation process applies to both. Subsequent minor or severe altar pollution would be addressed with either the regular ritual or the Day of Atonement ritual. Both the *severity* of the purgation in Leviticus 16 and the *initial/foundational* nature of the eight-day purgation in Leviticus 8–9 form the basis for the Chronicler's application of P in his narrative. In fact, these two purification rituals are linked consequentially within the narrative.

Some argue that Leviticus 16 is *not* linked consequentially with Leviticus 10, and thus was not actually performed initially in y2m1 – Stackert explains:

> Some interpreters have argued that ch 16 originally followed ch 10 and that its purification ritual was intended to purge the tabernacle of corpse contamination after the deaths of Nadab and Abihu, and after other emergencies, rather than once a year on Yom Kippur. Alternatively, this reference simply situates ch 16 in the chronology of the overall narrative, perhaps indicating that chs 11–15 were not actually narrated immediately after the events of ch 10 (cf. 16.34b n.).[19]

However, Jacob Milgrom argues that the original description of the Lev 16 ritual envisioned that Aaron would perform it immediately to deal with the impurity brought to the sanctuary due to the death of his sons, and that 16:29–34a is a Holiness insertion designed to fix the date: "The MT strongly indicates that the original form of the pur-

---

19. Stackert, "Leviticus," 166.

gation rite described in vv 2–28 was an emergency measure invoked by the high priest whenever he felt that the entire sanctuary had to be purged."[20] Milgrom asserts that the formulation of 16:2 "implies, with Midr. *Lev. Rab.* 2:7, that Aaron, indeed, can enter whenever he chooses, provided he acts b^{e}zō'ṯ 'in this manner' (v 3)."[21] Moreover, "All of the scapegoat rituals extant in the ancient Near East are emergency rites…They are not fixed calendric occasions but are prescribed whenever a catastrophe threatens or has struck. By the same token, the ceremonial with the Azazel goat originally must have been employed for similar emergencies."[22] Milgrom observes that 16:2–28 contains "unique terms that differentiate them from P…Hence, vv 2–28 must stem from an earlier source, which was only subsequently incorporated into P."[23] Milgrom associates the phrase "once a year" in 16:34a and Exod 30:10 with H, which sought to restrict too frequent high-priestly invocations of "emergency" rites.[24]

---

20. Milgrom, *Leviticus 1–16: A New Translation with Introduction and Commentary*, AB (New York: Doubleday, 1991), 1061. With Milgrom, Bailey argues that Lev 11–15 is an insertion that clarifies the sorts of pollutions that would necessitate an ad hoc ritual cleansing: "It is possible that chapters 11–15 have been inserted into the narrative in order to clarify what is meant by the term 'uncleanness' in chapter 16. In the earlier pre-insertion narrative, it would have been the sins and deaths of Aaron's sons in the sanctuary itself that would have necessitated the purgation that takes place in chapter 16. One result of the insertion is that an ad-hoc emergency ritual (as in 4:1–21) could now be seen as a regular annual requirement (then made explicit by an addition in vv. 29–34)." Lloyd R. Bailey, *Leviticus–Numbers*, SHBC (Macon, GA: Smyth & Helwys, 2005), 191.

21. Milgrom, *Leviticus 1–16*, 1061.

22. Milgrom, *Leviticus 1–16*, 1061; he outlines the scapegoat rituals at length in a later comment (1071–9).

23. Milgrom, *Leviticus 1–16*, 1063. He lists the following: "(1) פשעים 'transgressions' (vv 16, 21), in other words, wanton, brazen sins (contrast Num 15:30–31); (2) אהל מועד 'shrine' (vv 16, 17, 20, 23), whereas in P, this term stands for the entire Tent; (3) P's term for the shrine, קדש (e. g., Exod 28:29, 35) here designates 'the adytum (vv 2, 3, 16, 17, 20, 23, 27), which P labels exclusively by the term קדש הקדשים 'the holy of holies' (e. g., Exod 26:33, 34)."

24. Milgrom, *Leviticus 1–16*, 1062–3. Nihan also allows the possibility that an earlier layer permitted that the ritual could be performed as necessary: "The traditional observation since Benzinger that the ritual described in v. 2–28 does not necessarily presuppose a fixed ceremony remains cogent. Even in the case of the phrase בכל־עת in v. 2, which means literally 'at all times', the context clearly appears to imply that this expression should be interpreted not in a strictly temporal sense (i. e., as a reference to a specific time in the year) but rather in a modal one, i. e., Aaron may not enter the inner-sanctum at free will. This conception agrees with the use of this expression elsewhere in the Hebrew Bible; significantly, it is still retained in part of the rabbinic tradition. It is also consistent with the fact that in Lev 16 itself this phrase does not serve to introduce a specific date but an instruction for the procedure to be followed (v. 3 ff.)" (Christophe Nihan, *From Priestly Torah to Pentateuch: A Study in the Composition of the Book of Leviticus*, FAT II/25 [Tübingen: Mohr Siebeck, 2007], 347).

If Milgrom is correct, then regardless of whether the final hand in the text intended that the Day of Atonement be performed only annually, it is plausible to read Leviticus 16 as the first actual performance of this rite in response to the events of Leviticus 10. Ruwe explains this narrative connection:

> Against this background finally the last detail of time in the book of Leviticus has to be considered, the narrative detail in Lev 16:1. Other than the "eighth day" in 9:1, this chronological notice is not part of the date structure that covers the priestly Sinai story (Exod 19:1; 40:17; Num 1:1; Num 10:11–12). It is a subordinate mark that is *related to a particular event*. The divine speech concerning the יום הכפורים (announced in 16:2–34a) is through this detail closely connected with the death of Nadab and Abihu (narrated in 10:1–20), since it is classified as having been issued after this event. It is not possible to decide whether the detail of time, אחרי מות שני בני אהרון, has to be considered within the horizon of the "eighth day" or whether a distance of a day or a week has to be thought of. Independently of this question, however, it is obvious in any case that the events narrated in 16:1–34 are connected to the events of 9:1–10:20 or to the "eighth day" through this detail of time.[25]

Milgrom,[26] Ruwe (as noted), Nobuyoshi Kiuchi,[27] and Christophe Nihan[28] affirm that the text's conclusion, ויעש כאשר צוה יהוה את־משה "And he did just as YHWH had commanded Moses" (16:34b), indicates

---

25. Ruwe, "Structure of the Book of Leviticus," 66–7, emphasis original.

26. "The subject is not Aaron's successors, the nearest antecedent (v 32), but Aaron himself, who followed Moses' instructions immediately following the death of his sons, Nadab and Abihu (v 1). Thus v 34b originally followed v 28. A fulfillment passage is frequently found at the end of a prescriptive text (e. g., 8:4, 36; 10:7; Num 1:54; 2:34; 5:4; 8:20; 9:5)" (Milgrom, *Leviticus 1–16*, 1059).

27. Nobuyoshi Kiuchi, *Leviticus*, ApOTC (Downers Grove, IL: Intervarsity Press, 2007), 292. Hartley likewise takes this conclusion as being "a report of the first Day of Atonement," but does not connect it to the immediate context of the death of Aaron's sons (John E. Hartley, *Leviticus*, WBC [Dallas: Word Books, 1992], 243). Without textual justification, Stackert asserts regarding 16:34b: "Moses delivers the divine commands to Aaron, but Aaron does not perform them immediately because the Day of Atonement is six months away" ("Leviticus," 167).

28. "… It should be noted that the dating of the ceremony in Lev 16:29–31 stands in tension with the concluding notice in v. 34b stating that the community did 'according to what had been instructed to Moses by Yahweh', and thus apparently performed the ritual of ch. 16. Since, according to P, the instruction of ch. 16 was revealed to the Israelites at some time during the *first* month, between the eighth day (see Lev 9:1) and the end of the month (see Num 1:1), the celebration reported by 16:34b cannot be harmonized with a dating on the tenth of the seventh month, as required by 16:29 ff. in accordance with 23:26–32. On the contrary, the formulation of the notice in v. 34b seems to confirm that the ceremony of Lev 16 was originally *not* connected with a specific date in the year but could be performed on various occasions, provided that the required conditions (as specified in v. 2 ff.) were fulfilled by the high priest" (Nihan, *From Priestly Torah*, 348).

Aaron's performance of the ritual in the first month in response to his sons' catastrophe.[29] Certainly the presence of two corpses and the presentation of "strange fire" (in contrast to the required cloud of incense smoke in 16:11–13) would have constituted such an extreme violation[30] that required immediate action.

2.2 Exceptional Passover in Numbers 9:1–14

Numbers 9 even more explicitly provides for ritual observance outside of the appointed time in exceptional circumstances. Set in y2m1 from the exodus, some men have become ritually impure on the fourteenth of the month due to contact with a corpse (9:6); Moses inquires of YHWH, and answer comes back: in m2d14 they should celebrate the Passover as they would have in the first month, and this is to be a precedent for those who are impure or on a journey during Passover (9:9–13).

Several relevant observations may be made. In terms of Priestly narrative time, Nadab and Abihu's catastrophe would have occurred on y2m1d8; if the standard period of ritual uncleanness for contact with a corpse was seven days (cf. Num 19:14), then Aaron's cousins who removed the bodies of their kinsmen from the sanctuary would have been included in these אנשים who were unable to eat the שלמים of Passover (cf 7:20–21) on m1d14. Even though these cousins are not explicitly noted, the temporal markers between Exodus 40:17 and Numbers 10:11 along with the anterior reference to Nadab and Abihu in Numbers 3:4 are suggestive of this connection.

Second, the use of terms such as הקרב את־פרבן "bring near the

---

29. Wenham seems to endorse this narrative approach to Leviticus: "This flashback to ch. 10 places the laws about the day of atonement firmly in a specific historical context: they were revealed to Moses to prevent any other priests meeting an untimely death when they served in the tabernacle. This shows once again that Leviticus is basically concerned to relate the history of Israel, in the course of which the Law was given" (Gordon J. Wenham, *The Book of Leviticus*, NICOT [Grand Rapids: Eerdmans, 1979], 228). Yet Wenham has no comment on the concluding phrase "and he did just as YHWH had commanded Moses" (16:34b) implying that Aaron performed this ritual in y2m1 to deal with the impurity brought by Nadab and Abihu.

30. "The temple [sic] is to be purged, not merely because of inadvertent ritual 'uncleanness' (as in many of the cases outlined in chapters 11–15), but because of something far more serious. The RSV designates it as 'transgression' (vv. 16, 21), thereby apparently meaning deliberate knowing acts of rebellion against the Deity. Both types of actions were thought to besmirch the sanctuary, and consequently it needed to be cleansed by sprinkling it with a ritual detergent. Inadvertent individual offenses affect the outer altar while communal or priestly ones affect the inner one. Deliberate acts, on the other hand, are more serious: they affect even the innermost room of the temple (the so-called 'Holy of Holies,' curiously here designated only as 'the holy place within the veil') where the Deity symbolically was said to dwell (v. 2; see the diagram with the discussion of Lev 4)" (Bailey, *Leviticus–Numbers*, 192).

offering" and מועד "appointed time," along with the emphasis on the inability to eat the Passover שלם, highlight the Priestly distinction (in both Lev 23:4–8 and Num 28:16–25, but not found in Deuteronomy 16) between פסח and מצות.[31] Strictly speaking, it is only פסח which may be eaten in m2d14 in exceptional circumstances, because מצות involves a מקרא־קדש on d15 and d21. That the exception only applies to פסח is even clearer in light of the next temporal marker in the Priestly narrative: the glory-cloud lifted and the people set out on y2m2d20 from the exodus (Num 10:11).

Third, a time exception and an inclusive exception are coupled together: the one-month delay applies to those who are on a journey (9:10); and, those who are גרים, sojourners in Israel, may celebrate (9:14). These two qualifications would seem to be unrelated – yet their juxtaposition provides warrant for much more inclusive, extensive, exceptional celebration of פסח and מצות in 2 Chronicles 30.

Text	Date (Year 2 from exodus)	Event
Exod 40:17	m01 d01	Tabernacle erected
Lev 8–9	(Seven days)	Consecration of Aaron & sons, and altar
Lev 10 (cf Num 3:4)	m01 d08?	Catastrophe for Nadab and Abihu
Lev 16:1	m01 d08?	Purgation ritual commanded (and performed: 16:1, 34b)
Num 9:6–8	m01 d14	Corpse-contaminated men request a ruling concerning פסח
(Num 1:1)	(m02 d01)	
per Num 9:9–12	m02 d14	Delayed פסח (not 7-day מצות) for corpsecontaminated men
Num 10:11	m02 d20	Departure from Sinai

---

31. Jacob Milgrom, *Leviticus 23–27: A New Translation with Introduction and Commentary*, AB 3B (New York: Doubleday, 2001), 1971–2.

3. LEVITICUS 8–10 AND 16 AS BACKGROUND FOR ALTAR VIOLATIONS AND ATONEMENT IN CHRONICLES

With this narrative understanding of the *foundational* and *emergency* atonement rituals for violations of sacred space, and their relation to ritual time, we may now examine the Chronicler's application of these concepts within his narrative (along with illustrative comparison to the similar use of the same concepts in Ezekiel 43 and 45). I suggest that we cannot conclude that the Chronicler was unaware of the Day of Atonement, nor was he consciously excluding this Priestly observance because of anti-Priestly sentiment. Rather, careful examination of the role of the Day of Atonement in Leviticus suggests its application during the time of Hezekiah, while conversely rendering its observance at Solomon's dedication unnecessary according to Priestly logic.

3.1 HEZEKIAH'S TEMPLE REPURIFICATION AND PASSOVER (2 CHRONICLES 29–31)

A simple reliance on the Holiness calendar in Leviticus 23 (and 16:29–34a) would lead us to wonder about the lack of purgation ritual in 2 Chronicles 5–7 during the seventh month. Conversely, when we search the book of Chronicles for references to כפר or any activities that sound like the Leviticus 16 ritual, we find them in 2 Chronicles 29–30, during Hezekiah's reforms, occurring not in the seventh month but in the first month. Scholars have long noted affinities between the Day of Atonement ritual and the Chronicler's [*Sondergut*] description of the priests' and Levites' re-purification of themselves and the altar (2 Chr 29:15–36), but are reluctant to designate it as an *ad hoc* Day of Atonement (not least because it occurs in the first month and lasts longer than a single day!). I suggest that if we look at the Leviticus 8–10 *and* 16 together as part of the Chronicler's backdrop for this episode, then the similarities become more apparent – especially when we compare to the Priestly or Priestly-influenced texts of Ezekiel 43 and 45. Second, regarding the exceptional celebration of the Passover in the second month, the Chronicler follows the Priestly narrative connection of the Numbers 9:6–14 exceptions to the death of Aaron's sons.

Throughout the narrative, the Chronicler negotiates a balance between the priests – who have the unique responsibility for slaughter and application of blood to the altar – and the Levites, who are named by families, said to be "more upright in heart to consecrate themselves" than the priests (2 Chr 29:34), and who play a significant role in carrying ritual impurities out of the temple (vv 15–16), playing music (vv 25–26, 30), and assisting the priests (v 34).[32]

Just like the consecration of Aaron, his sons, and the altar in Leviticus 8–9, the process of purifying the temple starts in the first month, and involves a weeklong period (2 Chr 29:17b). Given the severity of the situation, it would have been unimaginable for the Chronicler to have written that the king, the priests and the Levites had delayed the altar cleansing and the ensuing חטאת ritual until the "scheduled" seventh month. The חטאת ritual in 29:20–24 is offered "for the kingdom, for the sanctuary, and for Judah" (v 21). This does not precisely parallel the various situations described in Leviticus 4–5, but the comprehensive scope of the ritual and the laying of hands on the sacrificial animal (29:23) aligns it partly with Leviticus 16.[33] The only uses of the verb כפר in narrative within Chronicles are found here in verse 24, and in the following chapter, 30:18.

The failure to recognize a *plausible* ad hoc, first-month reading of Leviticus 16 in connection with Lev 8–10 has thrown some interpreters off of the scent of the "Priestly-ness" of this text. Rendtorff remarks, "Because the text speaks about an ad hoc celebration rather than a regular feast, we cannot compare this list of animals with any particular Priestly text."[34] Yigal Levin[35] and Steven L. McKenzie[36]

32. Jonker, *Defining All-Israel in Chronicles*, 263–6.

33. Ralph W. Klein, *2 Chronicles: A Commentary*, Hermeneia (Minneapolis: Fortress, 2012), 421–2.

34. Rendtorff, "Chronicles and the Priestly Torah," 263. He continues: "But nowhere else in the Hebrew Bible do we find a list of four times seven animals. Seven lambs are mentioned several times in Numbers 28–29; seven bulls are mentioned only once in the descending number of bulls at the seventh day of Sukkot in Num 29:32. The Balaam story (Numbers 23) and Job 42:8 both include seven bulls and seven rams. Seven rams are mentioned as an illegal presentation to the priests in 2 Chr 13:9. So this combination of four groups of seven animals seems to be a product of the Chronicler's imagination."

35. "The closest parallel to this section is the ceremony for the Day of Atonement descripted in Leviticus 16. There, Aaron the high priest is instructed to take two he-goats for *hatta't* and a ram for '*olah* from the people, but to offer up his own bull for *hatta't*, atoning (*kipper*) for himself and his household. One of the goats is then offered as a *hatta't* for the people, and the other sent off to the desert (the so-called scapegoat) after the priest 'lay both hands on its head.' Then, after burning incense, he is to sprinkle blood on the altar seven times, purging (*kipper*) the sanctuary of the sins of 'himself, his household and the whole congregation of Israel' (Lev. 16:17)" (Yigal Levin, *The Chronicles of the Kings of Judah: 2 Chronicles 10–36. A New Translation and Commentary* [London: Bloomsbury T&T Clark, 2017], 304).

36. "Verses 20–24 describe the sanctification and rededication of the temple altar. The list of kinds of animals offered seems drawn from the description of the dedication of the tabernacle altar in Num 7:84–88. But the dedication ceremony also en-

note the similarities, but hesitate to designate this as a Day of Atonement. Here the widely acknowledged affinities between 2 Chronicles 29 and Ezekiel 43–45 show us the connection to Leviticus 8–10 and 16. Dillard, for example, notes: "The inclusion of the sin offerings finds its closest analog in the sin offerings mentioned in Ezekiel as part of the cleansing of the altar and sanctuary, the purification of priests, and preparation for celebration of Passover (Ezek 43:18–27; 45:1–3, 18–20; 44:27); this offering was made for the kingdom, the sanctuary, and the nation as a whole, i. e., for those involved in the apostasy under Ahaz."[37]

My goal is not to make the Procrustean move of forcing the 2 Chricles 29:20–24 ritual to conform with Leviticus 16, but to see how the Chronicler is himself working with the same Torah basis as Ezekiel 43–45 and applying similar narrative logic. The 2 Chronicles 29:20–24 *kipper* ritual is not a straightforward implementation of Leviticus 16, but more like Ezekiel 43 and 45 (see below) – somewhere between Leviticus 16 and 4–5 in terms of severity. Meyer (within this volume) rightly points out that Leviticus does not anticipate a scenario in which the tabernacle/temple would be closed, so there is no ritual precedent: "…There is no ritual in Leviticus prescribed for a scenario after the temple has been closed. There could not be, because Leviticus works within the fiction of Sinai and the tabernacle." Regarding the specifics of 2 Chronicles 29:20–24, he observes:

> …The number of animals referred to in this text is astounding and there is nothing in Leviticus that is similar, or in the Hebrew Bible for that matter…One could say that despite many differences, the Chronicler at least understood that a ritual solution would be necessary before the temple could be used again. This kind of thinking is not that far removed from priestly thinking…[38]

The Chronicler's application of Priestly narrative logic continues in chapter 30, with the celebration of the Passover. As is widely noted, the Chronicler appeals to the good judgment of the community rather

---

tails sin offerings (of the male goats) reminiscent of the Day of Atonement for 'all Israel' (v. 24), thus the northern tribes as well as Judah. The sin offerings for the consecration of the sanctuary and the purification of the priests are also similar to the regulations in Ezek 43:18–27; 45:18–23. The 'they' who do the slaughtering (v. 22) is best understood as impersonal, since it is typically the offerer and not the priests who slaughter the sacrifices; the priests then handle the blood (Lev 1:4–5). The rest of the chapter describes the resumption of cultic activities at the temple and the celebration of this restoration" (Steven L. McKenzie, *I & II Chronicles*, AOTC [Nashville: Abingdon, 2004], 342).

37. Raymond B. Dillard, *2 Chronicles*, WBC (Waco, TX: Word Books, 1987), 235–6.

38. Esias E. Meyer, within this volume.

than explicitly to the "Torah of Moses" when delaying the Passover to m2d14 (30:2–4).[39] Yet this cannot mean that the Chronicler was unaware of the Priestly passage in Numbers 9, given that the two other "inclusive exceptions" are both practiced in Chronicles: those gathering from as far as the extent of Northern Israel would have come on a long journey to Jerusalem (30:18);[40] and the גרים from Israel celebrate as well (30:25). Unlike the narrative implication of Numbers 9:9–13 and 10:11, the exception applies to the whole community, and to both פסח and מצות, which are here conflated as in Ezekiel 45:21.[41] Based on these two exceptions, Hezekiah's prayer that YHWH would כפר the people who are otherwise ritually impure, is answered (30:18–20). The celebration is also extended to two weeks, not in accordance with any Law known to us (30:23). Once again, the Chronicler is applying the Priestly narrative logic, but not necessarily the texts precisely (as we possess them, at least), to these exceptional circumstances.[42]

Finally, we must observe that Hezekiah is described as making provision from his own wealth for the daily offerings, the sabbaths, the new moons, and the festivals "as is written in the Torah of YHWH" (31:3). Despite the very Priestly formulation, the royal role is in keeping not with any Pentateuchal text, but with Ezekiel 45:17–25.[43]

---

39. "In verses 2–4, the Chronicler uses the insufficient number of ritually clean priests and the attendance in Jerusalem to explain the decision to postpone the Passover celebration, rather than the explanation readily available from 29:17 that the cleansing of the temple occasioned the delay. The reason may be that ritual uncleanness allowed him to draw on Num 9:9–11 for legitimation" (McKenzie, *I & II Chronicles*, 344).

40. Regarding Numbers 9:10, the reference to "defiled by a corpse," Milgrom comments: "According to the rabbis, this specific impurity includes all other causes of impurity ... Such certainly was the understanding of the Chronicler, who attributes Hezekiah's postponement of the Passover to the second month most likely to the two reasons cited by this law: the absence of the people, presumably because of the distance, and the negligence of the officiating priests in purifying themselves (2 Chron. 30:3). The nature of the impurity is not stated, nor is it specified even for the people who are impure on the second Passover (2 Chron. 17–20 [*sic*]). Thus one can infer, following the rabbis, that *any kind* of impurity disqualifies the individual from partaking of the Passover sacrifice, which is in keeping with the general law barring those impure for whatever cause from contact with a sacrifice (Lev 7:20–21)" (Jacob Milgrom, *Numbers: The Traditional Hebrew Text with the New JPS Translation*, JPS Torah Commentary (Philadelphia: JPS, 1990), 68–9 [emphasis original]).

41. Milgrom, *Leviticus 23–27*, 1972.

42. Mitchell suggests that in the Chronicler's assessment, one of Josiah's errors is to "formalize" the exceptional practices in Hezekiah's Passover, particularly the overabundance that required Levites to assist with the priests' responsibilities; Christine Mitchell, "The Ironic Death of Josiah in 2 Chronicles," *CBQ* 68 (2006): 421–35, here 430–1.

43. Klein, *2 Chronicles*, 445.

3.2 Initial and Ongoing Atonement in Ezekiel 43 and 45

With the recognition that the "Day of Atonement" rituals could at some point have been understood as allowing the priest discretion in cases of extreme pollution of the altar, as well as the connection to the initial altar purification event (Lev 8–9), affinities between this ritual and those described in Ezekiel 43 and 45 become apparent. Though the phrase יום כפרים and "the tenth day of the seventh month" do not occur in these chapters, we do have what appears to be an initial altar re-purification ritual (43:18–27) and then an ongoing purification ritual to be performed twice annually (45:18–20). The ongoing ritual is performed in m1d1, and then a second time either on m7d1 or m1d7.[44] The initiatory ritual does כפר for the altar, and the ongoing ritual does כפר for the house. In the vision, YHWH's glory-cloud returns to the temple (43:1–5), and the voice speaking articulates the hope/promise that the people will permanently put away their moral and ritual defilements and YHWH will inhabit this sanctuary forever (43:6–12). Thus, the rebuilt altar (43:13–17) will be purified once initially (by the faithful Zadoqites) in a seven-day process involving daily חטאות (43:18–27), which is similar to the Leviticus 8–9 ceremony. In this idealized future, the subsequent regular purgation of the altar on m1d1 and m7d1 (or m1d7) is only for unintentional violations and lands somewhere between the very serious Day of Atonement ritual of Leviticus 16 and the חטאת of Leviticus 4–5;[45] there is no sprinkling of blood within the innermost sanctum as in Leviticus 16:13–15.

One should not overstate the affinities between the Ezekiel 43 and 45 rituals and those described in Leviticus. However, the space between the two Priestly texts is suggestive of the ways in which the Chronicler is reading and applying Torah. Ezekiel anticipates a future in which, after an initial "reset" of the altar, the priests and the people will be sufficiently Torah-keeping so as to render the most extreme atonement ritual obsolete. The presence of the glory-cloud at this initial seven-day "reset" plays a role in the Chronicler's version of the dedication of Solomon's temple (2 Chr 5–7), as we will see below.

3.3 Uzziah Is Not Quite Nadab or Qoraḥ (2 Chronicles 26:16–23)

The echoes of Priestly texts in 2 Chronicles 26:16–23 are numerous,

---

44. The MT is ambiguous (וְכֵן תַּעֲשֶׂה בְּשִׁבְעָה בַחֹדֶשׁ), and the LXX reads ἐν τῷ ἑβδόμῳ μηνὶ μιᾷ τοῦ μηνός. In either case, this is not precisely the m7d10 observance prescribed in Lev 16:29–34 or the H calendar (Lev 23).

45. Compare מֵאִישׁ שֹׁגֶה (45:20) to תִּשְׁגּוּ/וְשָׁגוּ in Lev 4:13 and Num 15:22.

and quite wellknown.[46] Only the priests descended from Aaron may burn incense on the altar of incense (Ezek 44:15–16; Exod 29:38–42; 30:1–10; Num 16–17,[47] esp. 16:40 [MT 17:5]; 18:1–7).[48] The priests' reaction to seeing Uzziah's leprous skin echoes Aaron's reaction to Miriam's affliction (Num 12:10). Uzziah lives the remainder of his days excluded from society, in accordance with Leviticus 13:43–46 and Numbers 5:2.[49]

But though the scene seems similar to Leviticus 10:1–3 and Numbers 16:6–7 inasmuch as Uzziah intends to burn incense, the terms for "firepan"/"censer" are different (מחתה vs. מקטרת), and the key term "strange fire" אש זרה is missing from Chronicles. The priests hurry Uzziah out for fear that he will bring impurity upon the altar/sanctuary (26:20). Uzziah is neither struck down as in Leviticus 10:2 and Numbers 16:35, nor swallowed up in Numbers 16:31–33; but neither is his affliction only temporary, as in Numbers 12. Perhaps because it does not appear from the 2 Chronicles 26 text that Uzziah actually proceeded so far as to burn incense, the Chronicler felt that death was too harsh but temporary ritual impurity was not enough of a deterrent. For the purposes of our comparison to the Day of Atonement ritual and the concept of atonement: despite the near similarities to Leviticus 10, the extreme purgation ritual was not necessary because "strange fire" was not in fact offered, nor did the altar come into contact with ritual impurity (though it was a close call!).

3.4 SOLOMON'S TEMPLE ESTABLISHED (2 CHRONICLES 5–8)

Many commentators have seen that the Chronicler adds Priestly elements to the Deuteronomistic account of Solomon's temple dedication and establishment of regular cultic activities:

1) Japhet notes that 2 Chronicles 5:4 adjusts 1 Kings 8:3 in a Priestly direction: "The 'priests' who bore the ark in 1 Kings 8.6 [sic] are replaced by 'Levites', a change which harmonizes with the Pentateuch Priestly traditions, with their more marked differentiation between the roles of priests and Levites, the latter being responsible for the ark (Num 3.31). This distinction also figures in Chronicles (cf. also on 1 Chron. 23:13–14)."[50] Japhet also notes the parallels

---

46. See especially the contribution of Lars Maskow to this volume.
47. I recognize the discussion of whether these texts should be regarded as post-Priestly; see Louis Jonker's contribution within this volume.
48. This is in contrast to pre-Priestly texts that seem to allow royals to serve as priests or burn incense at YHWH altars (2 Sam 6:17; 8:18).
49. Klein, *2 Chronicles*, 381.
50. Sara Japhet, *I & II Chronicles: A Commentary*, OTL (Louisville: Westmin-

between the Chronicler's plus in 2 Chronicles 5:11–13 (the Levitical song leaders and priestly trumpeters) and the plusses in his version of the ark coming to Jerusalem (1 Chr 15:24; 16:6, 39–42): at the temple dedication the "five [who] were attached to the regular cult of the tabernacle at Gibeon" are named among those who bring the ark and the Gibeon tent and its paraphernalia to its new resting place.[51] Inasmuch as the Chronicler's concern for the Gibeon tent reflects a Priestly layering on top of the source narratives, as I have argued previously,[52] the plus in the 2 Chronicles 5:11–13 is also Priestly (while still being pro-Levite; compare to 7:6).

2) Japhet also notes the Chronicler's plus incorporating Psalm 132:8–10 which gives the passage more of a priestly (little 'p') emphasis;[53] a subtle echo of Numbers 10:35 might be detected (קומה יהוה).

3) The reference within the episode to חנכת המזבח (2 Chr 7:9) is itself a Priestly term drawn from Numbers (7:10–11, 84, 88) which is not present in 1 Kings.

4) The Chronicler adds that fire comes down from heaven and consumes the sacrifice, which explicitly parallels Leviticus 9:23–24.[54] Solomon's exhortation to the people (1 Kgs 8:54–61) is replaced by the people bowing to the ground and responding, כי טוב כי לעולם חסדו "for he is good, and his *ḥesed* is forever" (2 Chr 7:3).

5) The Chronicler omits the words ביום ההוא "in that day" when noting that Solomon also consecrated the middle of the court due to the volume of offerings (cf. 1 Kgs 8:64 to 2 Chr 7:7), perhaps a nod to the Priestly notion that seven days were required for consecration of the altar (Exod 29:37; Lev 8:33–35).

6) Solomon establishes the regular cultic practice in accordance with the Priestly regulations. 1 Kings 9:25 briefly establishes that Solomon offered ושלמים עלות in Jerusalem "three times per year" (perhaps a contrast with his earlier activities at Gibeon; 1 Kgs 3:3–4). Rendtorff observes that the Chronicler clarifies and expands upon this establishment of regular cultic activities (2 Chr 8:12–16). Whereas 1 Kings 9:25 uses the three-feast formula of Deuteronomy 16:16 – clearly implying Unleavened Bread, Weeks, and Booths – the P/H calendars in Leviticus 23 and Numbers 28–29 "recognize more than three feasts"; thus, the Chronicler must clarify which three feasts by name, and also records the daily and weekly provisions "according to the commandment of Moses" (2 Chr 8:13) – from our standpoint, the

---

ster John Knox, 1993), 575.
51. Japhet, *I & II Chronicles*, 579–80.
52. Giffone, "According to Which 'Law of Moses,'" 442.
53. Japhet, *I & II Chronicles*, 602–3.
54. Japhet, *I & II Chronicles*, 609.

Priestly Torah of Moses.[55]

7) The Chronicler appears to have been troubled by the two-week celebration in Kings;[56] thus, he separates the consecration of the court (ויקדש 7:7) and the feast into separate weeks: "Then Solomon performed (ויעש) the feast (חג) in that time (עת) for seven days, and all Israel with him…And on the eighth day they held a solemn assembly (עצרת); for the dedication of the altar they performed (עשו) seven days, and the feast (חג) seven days" (2 Chr 7:8–9). This distinction allows for a "solemn assembly" on m7d15, a full seven-day observance of "the feast," and for the people to leave on m7d23. The observance of a two-week חג may have seemed excessive and not in accordance with either Deuteronomistic or Priestly law – so, the Chronicler clarifies that one week was for חנכת המזבח, culminating in an עצרת, and then the feast constituted the second week.

By aligning the *second* week of Solomon's gathering with the Feast of Booths, the Chronicler has placed the first week (Days 8 to 14 of the month, inclusive) into overlap with the Day of Atonement. Japhet notes the orderly distinction between a seven-day dedication and seven-day celebration of Booths,[57] and the significance of the explicit connection between this dedication and the Feast of Booths, but never comments on the overlap of a Day of Atonement.[58] Raymond B. Dillard notes the overlap with the Day of Atonement, merely that "the author is silent about it."[59] McKenzie similarly makes the observation, but without further explanation.[60] Jonker calls it a "tension in the text."[61]

Here, though, the problem is not with the Chronicler's application of Priestly Torah, but rather with our understanding of it apart from its

---

55. Rendtorff, "Chronicles and the Priestly Torah," 260–1.

56. The LXX reads only, "seven days" (ἑπτὰ ἡμέρας). The MT (ימים ארבעה עשר יום שבעת ימים ושבעת) seems to be reflecting the textual tradition available to the Chronicler, which he is correcting/ clarifying. If he were envisioning only a one-week celebration per 3 Kgdms 8:65, accounting for the second week would be unnecessary.

57. "In order to rule out any possibility of doubt, the Chronicler states that the celebrations ended 'on the twenty-third day of the seventh month' (v. 10a). This remark clearly establishes the exact sequence of dates according to the Chronicler's view: the gathering of the people was on the 8th of the month, the Feast of Booths on the 15th, the solemn assembly on the 22nd, and finally the dismissal" (Japhet, *I & II Chronicles*, 612–3).

58. Japhet, *I & II Chronicles*, 611–613.

59. Dillard, *2 Chronicles*, 58.

60. "Perhaps more problematic, the Chronicler apparently failed to recognize that his dates for the dedication encompass Yom Kippur, the day of atonement, to be observed on the tenth day of the seventh month according to Lev 23:26–32" (McKenzie, *I & II Chronicles*, 249).

61. Louis C. Jonker, *1 & 2 Chronicles*, UBCS (Grand Rapids: Baker Books, 2013), 194.

narrative progression. If we consider how the Chronicler might have viewed the calendar overlap with the scheduled Day of Atonement ritual (m7d10) in light of its restorative purpose, then there would be no obvious necessity for the ritual in this instance. As in Exodus 40 and Ezekiel 43, the glory-cloud of YHWH validates and purifies the sanctuary. Unlike Ezekiel 43, there is no obvious ritual or moral impurity lingering among the people or at the altar (due in no small part to David and Solomon's scrupulous oversight of the priests and Levites thus far). Unlike Leviticus 10, the priests and Levites all conduct themselves properly, so no one defiles the altar by "strange fire" or by unceremoniously dying. Put simply, a purgation ritual is unnecessary at this narrative moment. The activities of the Day of Atonement – self-affliction and the עזאזל-goat ritual (Lev 16) – would be utterly inappropriate.

Moreover, the fact that a new altar is dedicated but new priests are not ordained (like Ezek 44:15–16, but in contrast to Lev 8–9 when both altar and priests are consecrated together) is an implicit validation of the work of both the priests and the Levites who served at Gibeon (with the tent of meeting) and Jerusalem (with the ark) during the "dual centralization" situation between 1 Chronicles 16 and this moment.[62]

4. IMPLICATIONS FOR THE CHRONICLER'S RELATION TO PRIESTLY LITERATURE

The Chronicler, in his adaptation of material from Kings and in his unique material, is reading Priestly texts and applying their language and concepts to his narrative. His method is sensitive to the narrative contexts of these legal texts, which, I have largely presumed, are reflective of the Pentateuch in something close to its received form. Like many believing readers of Torah since his own era, the Chronicler negotiates the uniqueness of the circumstances described in the Torah texts, and their ongoing implications for the community – in regular and irregular situations.

Japhet assesses the apparent incongruities between 2 Chronicles 30 and the Pentateuch:

> One may assume that the Chronicler had in his possession a version of the Pentateuch which was different from the MT, but there is no other

---

[62]. "The Chronicler balances regard for Jerusalem with Priestly regard for the tabernacle and its successor, Solomon's temple. The Chronicler remedies David's apparent lack of regard for the tabernacle in Samuel by 'clarifying' that David most certainly did hold both the ark and the tabernacle at Gibeon in high esteem" (Giffone, "According to Which 'Law of Moses,'" 444).

> support for this assumption than the difficulty which prompted it, and this would then be a circular argument. It seems more likely that the Chronicler did not refer to the written word as it stands, but rather to the way it was understood and interpreted, either by him or at his time.[63]

This is an appropriate word of caution against using Chronicles to excavate too meticulously the developmental layers of the Pentateuch, particularly apart from tangible evidence.

If the argument offered for the Chronicler's application of Priestly law in these texts is correct, then it suggests closer alignment with P than is sometimes assumed. Depending on how finely we choose to parse different Priestly strands that are characterized as proor anti-Levite, or H and anti-H – we would perhaps situate the Chronicler at arm's length from the narrowest understanding of "P." Yet this does not seem necessary, or reflective of the Chronicler's irenic approach to these matters. As an early interpreter of Torah, he seems to be charting a path that is inclusive of both Deuteronomistic and Priestly traditions (understood broadly), and of both Levites and Zadoqite priests in their specific, necessary roles. The Chronicler's circle and the Jerusalem cult's sphere of influence were too small to be unnecessarily exclusive. Regardless of how such debates proceed: sensitivity to the narrative quality of the received Pentateuch is crucial to correct assessment of the debates reflected in our "Bible born out of conflicts."

---

63. Japhet, *I & II Chronicles*, 950.

GRUNDGESCHICHTE UND CHRONIK – KONTINUITÄT UND DISKONTINUITÄT IN ALTISRAELS GESCHICHTSSCHREIBUNG
Thomas Willi

1. DAS NEUE IM ALTEN – DIE FRAGESTELLUNG DER BIBLISCHEN CHRONIKBÜCHER

Die Geschichtsdarstellung von Chr wird durch die Menschheit- sund Bürgerlisten (1 Chron 1:1–9:9 bzw. 10:14) zu Beginn und durch die abschliessende Feststellung „bis zur Königsherrschaft des Königtums von Persien" (2 Chron 36:20) eindeutig begrenzt. Von diesem weitgespannten Rahmen her würde man eine Darstellung erwarten, die entlang der grossen Linien die Themen und Ereignisse erzählt, die diesen zeitlichen Rahmen ausfüllen.

Seltsam berührt nun allerdings, dass ganze Partien und Abschnitte dieser Geschichte eigenartig behandelt oder, noch auffälliger, schlicht übergangen scheinen. Und zwar sind das durchaus bedeutende Epochen, die eine Kennerin der Sache zu dem Urteil bringen: „The intermediate history of Israel, told in Exodus through 1Samuel, is not found in Chronicles. ...As a result, some of the most important events in the history of Israel, such as the descent into Egypt, the exodus, the revelation at Mount Sinai, the conquest of the land of Canaan, the settlement, and the period of Joshua, the judges, and Saul are not described." Folgt daraus: „There is no break, not even any 'history', between Jacob and salvation."[1]

---

1. Sara Japhet, *"Conquest and Settlement in Chronicles,"* JBL 98 (1979): 205–18, wieder abgedr. in: Japhet, *From the Rivers of Babylon to the Highlands of Judah* (Winona Lake: Eisenbrauns, 2006), 38–52. Die Zitate hier pp. 39 und 50 f.; sehr pointiert p. 50: „The story of the exodus is not told in Chronicles and ... even the ref-

In seiner Neuerzählung aus dem Quell der alten Überlieferung behandelt der Chronist also nur die sogenannt staatliche Zeit Israels, geprägt und überragt durch die Gestalt Davids. Dabei sind es ganz andere Gesichtspunkte, die ihn leiten als jene, die die alte „Davidshausgeschichte" ausmachen.

Seit fast zweihundert Jahren stand unter den Voraussetzungen der von Wilhelm M. L. De Wette und Julius Wellhausen inaugurierten historisch-kritischen Sicht der Geschichte und vor allem der Literaturgeschichte des alten Israel[2] die Frage im Vordergrund, wie die Chronik die Vergangenheit umgebaut habe – *sous entendu* – dass sie das im Dienst und im Interesse ihrer Gegenwart, ihrer Partei und der sie leitenden Vor-urteile getan habe.

2. MOSEZEIT UND DAVIDSZEIT

Für den Chronisten als Historiker ist die Fragestellung aber eine ganz andere: Was unterscheidet die von ihm dargestellte Davidsund Königszeit von der Mosezeit, vor allem – aber nicht ausschliesslich – hinsichtlich des Kultes? Wenn David nach der chronistischen Erzählung den „altneuen" Dienst in Jerusalem einrichtet, bestätigt und bekräftigt – was ist daran alt, was ist neu?

1) Der Kult der Exodusund Wüstenzeit galt demselben *Gott*, dem David nach chronistischer Darstellung in hervorragender Weise dient. Getragen wurde der alte Gottesdienst, den priesterschriftlichen Überlieferungen zufolge, von dem Israel der zwölf Stämme. Ihre Einheit zeigt sich in der Sicht von Chronik in der Folge gefährdet. Sie löst sich schliesslich unter Saul (1 Chron 10) nahezu völlig auf, bis sie – und hier beginnt der Chronist seine Erzählung – von David neu hergestellt wird. Das bahnt sich an in 1. Chronik 11:1 – ויקבצו כל־ישראל אל־דויד.

2) Während zweitens in den pentateuchischen Zeiten Israels Gottesdienst keinen festen Platz hat und die Lade im Heiligtum des

erences to the exodus ... are often omitted in the parallel texts in Chronicles."

2. Einer kritischen Rekonstruktion trat Chr hauptsächlich als irritierendes und störendes Hindernis in den Weg, so dass es etwa Wilhelm Martin Leberecht De Wette in seinen *Beiträge zur Einleitung in das Alte Testament I: Kritischer Versuch über die Glaubwürdigkeit der Bücher der Chronik mit Hinsicht auf die Geschichte der Mosaischen Bücher und Gesetzgebung* (Halle: Schimmelpfennig, 1806) vorrangig um „Wegräumung der Nachrichten der Chronik" gehen musste. Besonders argwöhnisch wurden dabei die Inhalte beäugt, die dem Chronisten am Herzen lagen und die Israel aus seinem Gottesverhältnis heraus neu bestimmen sollten. Für eine empathische Würdigung der Darstellung des Kults in Chr war ein Jahrhundert kaum disponiert, das auf den Kulturkampf und die Frontstellung gegen den "Ultramontanismus" zulief, der schon in Formulierungen von De Wette anzuklingen scheint. So ist hier gleich eingangs von „einer unpriesterlichen Freiheit des Cultus" in den „BB. Samuelis und der Könige" die Rede, während „die Chronik den Zustand des Gottesdienstes von David an ganz Mosaisch-levitisch" darstelle (4 f.).

Zelts der Begegnung mobil ist, zeichnet sich die neue Ära dadurch aus, dass Israels Gott und sein Kult dank David den verheissenen und gebotenen, aber nicht identifizierten[3] festen „Ort"[4] gefunden haben: das Haus zu Jerusalem.

3) Sowohl in der Wüste wie nun in Jerusalem sind drittens Gottesdienst und Leben Israels durch die Anweisungen Jhwhs geregelt. Der Jerusalemer Tempel ist freilich gewiss kein „Sanctuary of silence",[5] sondern ist vom Wort begleitet und erfüllt. Nachdem dieses am Sinai Mose mündlich gegeben wurde, wird sich das Geschehen von jetzt an ככתוב, „wie geschrieben, schriftkonform" vollziehen.

Während also [ad 1.] eine eindeutige Kontinuität zwischen Wüstenund Davidszeit in dem ein-einzigen *Gott* besteht, dem der Dienst gilt, so leitet David nun anderseits [ad 2.] einen Übergang vom beweglichen Zelt zum festen Haus ein. Den Wendepunkt von der früheren Epoche zum neuen Zeitalter – der nicht etwa mit der Landnahme zusammenfällt – beschreibt das Kapitel 1. Chronik 17.[6] Davids Plan, Jhwh ein Haus zu bauen, erfährt in 1. Chronik nicht minder eine Absage als in 2. Samuel 7. Die Zusage, dass Jhwh selbst es bauen werde, bekommt aber eine völlig andere Ausrichtung und Zielsetzung. Das „Haus" ist nicht im übertragenen Sinne das (davididische) Königshaus wie im DtrG, sondern es handelt sich um ein reales Haus.[7] Als „Gottes-Haus" weist der künftige Tempel zu Jeru-

---

3. Vgl. Stellen wie Ex 15:17; Dtn 12:5, 14.

4. Zur Bedeutung des מקום in Chr vgl. 1 Chron 13:11; 14:11, sodann in 1 Chron 15:1, 3, und zwar als Einleitung zu 1 Chron 16, hier vor allem V. 27, sodann über das diesbezüglich entscheidende Kapitel 1 Chron 21 hinaus bis hin zum Zielvers 2 Chron 3:1. Dazu Thomas Willi, "Die Suche nach dem Ort in der Chronik: Eine U-topie?," in *Worlds that could not be. Utopia in Chronicles, Ezra and Nehemiah*, ed. Stephen J. Schweitzer and Frauke Uhlenbruch, LHBOTS 620 (London: Bloomsbury, 2016), 183–92.

5. Yehezkel Kaufmann, *History of the religion of Israel*, Bd. 2 (Jerusalem: Hebrew University, 1977), 477 f.; vgl. dazu Israel Knohl, *The Sanctuary of Silence*: *The Priestly Torah and the Holiness School* (Minneapolis: Fortress Press, 2005), 148–52.

6. Zur Doppelheit des – mosaischen – Zelts in Gibeon und dem Zelt, in dem David die Lade in Jerusalem unterbrachte, s. Gary N. Knoppers, "Hierodules, Priests, or Janitors? The Levites in Chronicles and the History of the Israelite Priesthood," *JBL* 118 (1999): 61; Jaeyoung Jeon, "The Priestly Tent of Meeting in Chronicles: Pro-Priestly or Anti-Priestly," *JHS* 18, Art. 7 (2018): 1–15. Nach dem oben Ausgeführten handelt es sich aus chr Perspektive weniger um ein Entweder – Oder denn um eine Übergangssituation, in der Salomo das von Mose überkommene „Zelt" nach 2 Chron 1:3 f. zu Gibeon aufsucht, während die Lade gleichzeitig in dem ihr von David behelfsmässig errichteten „Zelt" zu Jerusalem aufbewahrt ist. Die Situation ergibt sich dem Chr durch die ihm vorliegenden Angaben in der Tradition.

7. Dazu ausführlich Thomas Willi, Gibt es in der Chronik eine "Dynastie Davids"? Ein Beitrag zu Semantik von *bajit*: *FS E. Jenni*, AOAT 336, ed. Jürg Luchsinger, Hans-Peter Mathys und Markus Saur (Münster: Ugarit-Verlag, 2007), 393–403 = ders., Israel und die Völker. Studien zur Literatur und Geschichte Israels in der Perser-

salem allerdings übermenschliche, ja überirdische Dimensionen auf, denn der Bau-Herr ist kein anderer als der König und Herr der Schöpfung selber, der von hier aus sein Weltkönigtum über Israel und über die Völkerwelt ausübt.[8]

3. MOSE IN DAVIDS ISRAEL

Bei allen damit eintretenden Veränderungen ist der Kult am künftigen Tempel zu Jerusalem keine komplette und radikale Neuerung, sondern er geschieht bei allen Unterschieden nach den Standards der alten – als solcher in Chronik nicht thematisierten – Früh- oder Ursprungszeit, chronistisch gesprochen „gemäss der Tora Moses". Mose wird in Chronik 21mal erwähnt, und zwar in unterschiedlicher, aber insgesamt doch zusammenlaufender Perspektive. An erster Stelle ist dabei der genealogische Gesichtspunkt zu nennen: 1. Chronik 5:29 und 23:13 wird er dezidiert als Sohn Amrams angeführt, diesbezüglich auf einer Ebene mit seinem älteren Bruder Aaron und seiner jüngeren Schwester Mirjam. Bereits darin verrät sich der genealogisch interessierte historische Zugang des Chronisten zur Mosegestalt. Aussagekräftig ist sodann die Näherbestimmung durch den עבד-Titel in 1. Chronik 6:34; 2. Chronik 1:3; 24:6, 9. Die drei Vorkommnisse sind anders gelagert als das Gros der 36 Belege in den mehrheitlich (nach-)deuteronomistischen Stellen des MT, wo er meist den "Gesetzesmittler" bezeichnet.[9] Auf Mose als „Gottesknecht" gehen in Chronik die alten Opfer- und weitergehenden Anordnungen zurück (2 Chron 1:3; 24:6, 9), ja er steht „mit Hilfe der Nennung des דבע-Titels" explizit für „die Wüstentradition".[10] Die Bezeichnung איש אלהים in 1. Chronik 23:14

---

zeit, SBS 55, ed. Michael Pietsch (Stuttgart, Katholisches Bibelwerk, 2012)183–95, und vor allem ders., Chronik, Biblischer Kommentar (BK) XXIV/2.3 (Göttingen: Neukirchener Verlag in de Gruyter, 2019) 164–67, 181, 187–89.

    8. Dazu Matthew J. Lynch, *Monotheism and Institutions in the Book of Chronicles. Temple, Priesthood, and Kingship in Post-exilic Perspective*, FAT II/64 (Tübingen: Mohr Siebeck, 2013), besonders 72–136. 2 Chron 2:4 als chr Schlüsselstelle „Und das Haus, das ich nun baue, ist gross, denn gross ist unser Gott, mehr als alle Götter" versteht er im Sinne einer „vertical, or categorical, distinctiveness" zwischen Gott und Tempel (p. 131), wonach dem Chronisten zufolge „Humans could not add anything to all that Yhwh owned" (p. 112), so dass der Tempel im eigentlichen Sinne allein auf Gott "as creator" zurückgeht: „The temple was not…the 'Solomonic' temple", vielmehr "Yhwh initiated its construction, and provides Solomon with wisdom…" (p. 114, vgl. p. 117).

    9. Ernst M. Dörrfuss, *Mose in den Chronikbüchern. Garant theokratischer Zukunftserwartung*, BZAW 219 (Berlin: Walter de Gruyter, 1994), 217. Die Beobachtungen, die Ernst Michael Dörrfuss in seiner so betitelten Untersuchung beibringt, sind sorgfältig zu erwägen, gerade wenn man seine Ansicht, dass Mose „ausschliesslich in sekundären Texteinheiten" vorkomme und insofern "Mose…für den Chronisten bedeutungslos",,sei (p. 277), nicht–mehr–teilt.

    10. Dörrfuss, *Mose in den Chronikbüchern.*

f. teilt er sich dagegen mit David (2 Chron 8:14). Der „Gottesknecht Mose" beschreibt in den meisten chronistischen Belegen Mose als den, der dem Israel der Wüstengeschichte in JHWHs Auftrag die nötigen Anordnungen für sein Leben vor Gott und in der Welt übermittelt hat. In *seiner Person* ist also die sonst in Chronik nicht behandelte, aber nichtsdestoweniger normative, Exodus- und Sinaizeit gegenwärtig. Mose ist und bleibt die Instanz, die Israel wie seine kultischen Vollzüge geprägt hat und – wie auch immer – prägen wird.

Genealogisch und im Blick auf die „historische Anciennität" steht Mose auf *einer* Ebene mit seinem älteren Bruder Aaron. Durch das ihm anvertraute Wort erscheint er aber als weisungsbefugt, und zwar auch für die opferdienstlichen, das heisst, spezifisch priesterlichen, Belange. Der Gottesdienst, wie David ihn für das neue, auf Dauer erwählte Heiligtum in Jerusalem einrichtet, geschieht „wie geschrieben steht," das heisst nach der von Mose vermittelten und schriftlich aufgezeichneten Tradition: Die Priestertora ist in der Mosetora aufgegangen.[11]

Die Institution des Kults ist dadurch charismatisch begründet und eingebettet. Diesbezüglich – und das ist wichtig – zieht die Chronik im Grunde mit ihrer Darstellung der staatlichen Geschichte Israels nur die Linien aus, die bereits in einschlägigen Teilen der – insofern zu Unrecht – als (exklusiv) „priesterlich" apostrophierten Partien des Pentateuch angelegt sind. Ich beziehe mich hier nachdrücklich auf Levitikus 9–10 nach der eingehenden Analyse von Andreas Ruwe.[12] Levitikus 9–10, formuliert als „Kopfstück" jedenfalls die Gesichtspunkte und Leitlinien des anschliessenden Grossabschnitts in Levitikus 11 ff.[13] Dabei ist Aaron der Inbegriff des Priestertums. Mose dagegen personifiziert die prophetische – oder charismatische – Tradition[14] mit ihrer Betonung von Auszug, Gerechtigkeit, usw. Die ihm entgegengebrachte Observanz bürgt nach Levitikus 9–10 für die positive Auswirkung des von Israel dargebrachten Kults; Missachtung seiner Anweisungen hingegen führt zu todbringenden Effekten. Was nicht "mosaischer" beziehungsweise – in der Mosenachfolge – „levi-

11. Vgl. zu diesem, "priesterliche" Tora und "prophetisches" JHWH-Wort einenden, Konzept Mi 4:2b, aufgenommen in Jes 2:3b.

12. Andreas Ruwe, "Das Reden und Verstummen Aarons vor Mose. Lev 9–10 im Buch Leviticus," in *Behutsames Lesen, FS C. Hardmeier*, ABG 28, ed. Sylke Lubs, Louis Jonker, Andreas Ruwe und Uwe Weise (Leipzig: Evangelische Verlagsanstalt, 2007), 169–96. Es spielt dabei eine untergeordnete Rolle, ob man mit Knohl, *The Sanctuary of Silence*, bzw. mit Jacob Milgrom in seinem Leviticus-Kommentar (AB 3, 1991) zwischen Teilen einer älteren "Priestly Torah" und einer jüngern "Holiness School" differenziert, obwohl die Ausgangsposition der Chr eher der letzteren entspricht.

13. Ruwe, "Das Reden und Verstummen Aarons vor Mose," 176.

14. Dazu vgl. Thomas Willi, *Die Chronik als Auslegung*, FRLANT 106 (Göttingen: Vandenhoeck & Ruprecht 1972), 228–30.

tischer" Lehre und Verhaltensnorm entspricht, ist demgemäss זר. Mit diesem Begriff werden "Elemente im Jerusalemer Kult" bezeichnet, die als „fremdreligiös" gelten.[15] Den Textpartien liegt demnach an einem „konstitutionell verfassten Priesteramt," das „kultisch auf Mose bezogen" ist.[16]

Wie eine solche bereits im Pentateuch angelegte „Konstitutionalisierung des Priesteramts" dereinst aussehen würde, davon vermittelt die in Chronik entworfene Geschichte des davidischen Israel ein lebendiges Bild, vorrangig dank der Rolle, die die Leviten in ihr spielen. Wenn es zutrifft, dass „die P-Texte keineswegs die ungezügelte Macht priesterlicher Interessen" vertreten und vermitteln, sondern in ihrer Weise den „Impuls des Deuteronomiums" fortsetzen,[17] so ist das der Hintergrund und die Motivation für das auffällige und immer beobachtete Interesse der Chr nicht eigentlich an einem besonderen Priestertum, sondern an „den Leviten" im umfassenden Verständnis.

4. Levi in Davids neuem Israel

Denn es ist nicht allein die historisch lange zurückliegende Gestalt des Mose, der mittels seiner Tora für die Kontinuität zwischen dem Gottesdienst am einstigen „Zelt der Übereinkunft" und dem Gottesdienst am neuen „Haus" zu Jerusalem bürgt. Sondern dafür steht auch sein Stamm, der Stamm Levi, der durch seinen Umgang mit der Tradition, mit dem Wort und mit der Lehre dem davidischen Jerusalem den Stempel aufdrückt. Was die „Leviten" in die Waagschale zu werfen hatten, war der geistige Aspekt des an sich rein materiellen Bauunternehmens, wie es der entstehende Tempel darstellt. Gerade dieses einzigartige „Haus" beruhte auf der Tora als der umfassenden Bildungs-, Rechts-, Religionsund Lebensgrundlage „Israels". Die Leviten „wachten" darüber und garantierten durch ihre Existenz, dass schon der Bau wie dann der Kult am Jerusalemer Tempel nicht irgendwie, sondern „gemäss der Tora Moses" – des Erzleviten! – geschah.[18]

Der Übergang vom mobilen zum stabilen Heiligtum betrifft – immer laut Chr – ganz speziell den Stamm Levi. In ihrer Rolle verkörpern die Leviten sozusagen die Kontinuität in der Diskon-

---

15. Ruwe, "Das Reden und Verstummen Aarons vor Mose," 181 f. mit Anm. 42.
16. Ruwe, "Das Reden und Verstummen Aarons vor Mose," 186.
17. Ruwe, "Das Reden und Verstummen Aarons vor Mose," 193. Schon Knoppers, "Hierodules, Priests, or Janitors?," 49–72 spricht, speziell im Blick auf Chr, von "a false and misleading dichotomy" (p. 69) zwischen Priestern und Leviten.
18. Zur technischen Bedeutung der Wurzel šmr vgl. die Bemerkung bei David Talshir, "A Reinvestigation of the Linguistic Relationship between Chronicles and Ezra-Nehemiah," VT 38 (1988): 177: Im Unterschied zu $mah^a l\bar{o}qet$ ist "$mišmeret$ a word connoting the fulfilment of a certain cultic role or the appointement to such a role".

tinuität. Das spiegelt sich in verschiedenen kleineren wie grösseren Eigentümlichkeiten im Aufriss von 1. Chronik. So eröffnen beispielsweise die Leviten – nicht etwa die (natürlich in den Stamm Levi integrierten) Kohanim, die Priester – das Bevölkerungstableau des gegenwärtigen und damit auch künftigen Israel, das David zu Ende seiner Lebzeiten Revue passieren lässt (1 Chron 23). Ihre prominente Rolle ist aber mit 1. Chronik 5:27–6:66 bereits in einer Bestandesaufnahme aus früheren Zeiten, in den „Bürgerrechtslisten" Israels (1 Chron 1–8, 9), präludiert. Schon hier nimmt Levi – nicht Aaron, nicht die Priesterschaft – eine zentrale Stellung ein: Levi ist die Mitte, das Herz des chronistischen Ganz-Israel. Mit seiner Einordnung und Anordnung Levis geht der Chronist dort schon seinen eigenen und neuen Weg. Seine Konzeption unterscheidet sich dabei von den älteren Darstellungen Levis, obwohl diese zum Teil auch die Quellen für 1. Chronik 6 sind.[19] Wo nach Numeri 1:49–53; 26:57–62 und Josua 13–19 Levi gerade nicht „inmitten" (בתוך) Israels, sondern als Grösse *sui generis* berücksichtigt werden soll,[20] da gehört Levi nach dem chronistischen Konzept im Gegenteil mitten ins zwölfstämmige Israel hinein. Levi wird nicht im Zusammenhang mit Jerusalem, nicht wie in der Priesterschrift zusammen mit dem Heiligtum und dem Kult behandelt, sondern als vollgültiger und gleichberechtigter Teil des Volkes! Levi ist in der Königszeit von David an, der Chronik zufolge, etwas anderes geworden als in der Priesterschrift. Aus dem ausgesonderten Stand von Kultsachverständigen der Frühzeit ist ein ins zwölfteilige Israel eingegliederter Stamm geworden.[21] Für den Chronisten ist Levi eine, ja die Funktion Israels, Levi verkörpert Israel *at its best*, und umgekehrt ist Israel das Volk Levis.[22]

Die hier berührten Vergleichsbeziehungsweise Quelltexte

---

19. Am ehesten liesse sich 1 Chron 6 noch mit Ex 6:14–27 vergleichen, wo die levitischen Sippen an die Familienhäupter Rubens und Simeons angeschlossen werden, allerdings nicht als deren Mittelpunkt, sondern mit Achtergewicht auf Mose und Aaron.

20. Num 1:49–53 trennt Levi ausdrücklich vom übrigen Israel; nicht anders Num 3 als Nachtrag zur Ordnung der Israelstämme von Num 2. Num 26:57–62 ist ein Sonderanhang zu den bereits komplett aufgezählten Sippen der Israelstämme, und in Jos 13–19 fehlt Levi überhaupt und wird deshalb in Jos 21 separat abgehandelt. Ganz anders 1 Chron 6 und schliesslich erst recht 1 Chron 23:6–24:31 im Rahmen des in 1 Chron 23–27 geschilderten davidischen Israel – kein Mensch käme hier auf den Gedanken, mit Num 1:49 oder 2:33 zu behaupten, dass Levi *nicht* gleich allen anderen Angehörigen Israels "mitten unter den (übrigen) Israeliten zu berücksichtigen" sei.

21. Dazu ausführlicher Willi, BK XXIV/1, 197–99.

22. Dass dadurch eine auf die geschichtliche Ebene herabgebrochene Verbindung zu dem Konzept des "priesterlichen" Textes Num 3:11–13, nach dem die Leviten die Stelle der "ausgelösten" erstgeborenen Israeliten einnehmen, ist nicht zu verkennen.

entstammen dem Pentateuch. Leviten begegnen zwar auch in Esra-Nehemia. Aber nur der Pentateuch und Chronik bemühen sich, je auf eigene Weise, die zweifellos lange zurückreichende Geschichte des Levitums und des Levitismus systematisch einzuordnen, und einzig Chronik gewährt den alten Überlieferungen schon in den Bürgerrechtslisten Raum und sucht sie nun für die Darstellung der staatlichen Geschichte Israels fruchtbar zu machen. Gerade darin erweist sich der Chronist als umsichtiger Historiograph, der aus den alten Nachrichten als Quellen schöpft und die einschlägigen Texte neu zu lesen und zu exegesieren weiss, um sein Tableau über David und die Davidszeit zu entwerfen.

Die chronistische Auffassung von Levi hängt dabei mit dem alten, vorexilischen Stand Levi nur sehr indirekt zusammen.[23] Und auch mit der realen Situation und Funktion von Leviten im Betrieb des zweiten Tempels ist sie kaum deckungsgleich. Was einst zu den hervorragendsten charismatischen Phänomenen nordisraelitischen religiösen Lebens gehört hatte, war durch die Entwicklung der Umstände dreifach bis ins Mark ihrer Existenz getroffen. Israel, das Nordreich, hatte als selbständiges Gemeinwesen aufgehört zu existieren. Im Süden liefen die Reformmassnahmen Josias auf eine Stärkung der Priesterschaft Jerusalems hinaus. Zu ihr gehörte dann auch der von Haggaj und Sacharja erwähnte Seniorpriester Josua ben Jozadak, mit dem sich der Wiederaufbau des Heiligtums verbindet. Leviten erscheinen hier und auf lange hinaus überhaupt nicht auf der Bildfläche.[24] Das Levitentum war keine *condicio sine qua* non für die Ausübung der priesterlichen Funktionen. Der Jerusalemer Klerus war eine lokale Priesterschaft

---

23. Zum Folgenden vgl. einführend und begleitend Thomas Willi, "Leviten, Priester und Kult in vorhellenistischer Zeit. Die chronistische Optik in ihrem geschichtlichen Kontext," in *Gemeinde ohne Tempel/Community without Temple. Zur Substituierung und Transformation des Jerusalemer Tempels und seines Kults im Alten Testament, antiken Judentum und frühen Christentum*, WUNT 118, ed. Beate Ego, Armin Lange und Peter Pilhofer, (Tübingen: Mohr Siebeck, 1999), 75–98, vor allem 89–95. Für die Leviten der Vor- und Frühzeit existieren nur ganz wenige aussagekräftige Nachrichten, und man wird Jaeyoung Jeon, "Levites: I. Hebrew Bible/Old Testament," in *EBR* 16 (2018) Sp. 336–46 nur zustimmen können, wenn er resümiert, dass "no consensus has yet been made among critics concerning the date and origin of the Levites or Levitical priesthood" (Sp. 339).

24. Signifikant für die Zurücksetzung der Angehörigen levitischer Gruppen und Familien ist die Evidenz aus dem 6. Jahrhundert in Ez 44 und aus der Mitte des 5. Jahrhunderts in Esr 8. Esra ist sich nach diesem Kapitel der Bedeutung des levitischen Elements für das neue Jerusalem insofern bewusst, als er die Karawane nicht aufbrechen lässt, bis er ein wenn auch höchst bescheidenes Kontingent von rückkehrwilligen Leviten beisammen hat. Die Zeiten waren längst vergangen, wo jemand wie in Ri 18:3 f. qua Levit und dank seiner Vertrautheit mit Überlieferung und Gesang zum Priesterdienst qualifiziert war. Gewiss mochte es einzelne Priester geben, die sich der levitischen Tradition verpflichtet wussten.

unter Hunderten, ja Tausenden anderer im weiten achämenidischen Reich. Sollte er „israelitisch" im Sinne der Konformität mit Tradition und Schrift sein, dann konnte und durfte er aber auf das levitische Element nicht verzichten.

Das Zeugnis des Maleachibuches verrät manches von dieser Spannung zwischen Realität und Norm, zwischen gegenwärtiger Wirklichkeit und altehrwürdigem Ideal, zwischen Praxis und – vielleicht auch hier schon weitgehend schriftlicher – Tradition. Eine sorgfältige syntaktische Untersuchung kommt zu dem Schluss: „While the Book of Malachi equates the function of *kohen* and *lewî/benê-lewî* the book offers no contextual ground by which to explain this equation."[25] Ein Stamm wie die anderen Stämme zu sein, setzte familiäre, ortsbürgerliche, landschaftliche, territoriale Bindungen voraus. Und genau diese fehlten dem charismatischen und oft auch nomadisierenden Levitentum der Frühzeit – sein „Anteil" war JHWH, wie es die alte Levitenregel Exodus 32:29 im Positiven wie im Negativen festhält: „Da sprach Mose: Füllt heute eure Hände zum Dienst für den HERRN – denn ein jeder ist wider seinen Sohn und Bruder gewesen – damit euch heute Segen gegeben werde." (Vgl. auch den Levi-Segen in Dtn 33:8).

Wenn also, wohl im ausgehenden 5. Jahrhundert v. Chr., die chronistische Darstellung der Geschichte Israels ab David die Leviten als eine Art „Stamm der Stämme" Israels behandelt, so hängt das mit der Eigenart der chronistischen Historiographie zusammen. Nicht das DtrG ist für die Chronik bei ihrem Geschichtsentwurf massgebend, sondern – und das ist etwas durchaus Anderes – die in ihm aufbewahrten und von ihm tradierten Überlieferungen und Materialien. Aus chronistischer Optik handelt es sich bei dem, was heute als DtrG bezeichnet wird, um ein Florilegium diverser Quellen und Nachrichten aus der Feder von Propheten unterschiedlicher Epochen und Regionen.

Diese auch literarisch fassbare Hochschätzung[26] der Boten Gottes macht es von vorneherein unwahrscheinlich, dass entsprechende Überlieferungen und Äusserungen aus einer der behandelten Zeit vorangehenden Epoche einfach übergangen, ja eskamotiert und gezielt verdrängt sein sollten. Auch wenn sie nicht als prophetisch anzusprechen sind, so haben sie eigentlich nicht weniger, sondern im Grunde noch mehr Anspruch auf Autorität und Gültigkeit. Was Mose in seiner ihm aufgetragenen Tätigkeit und Tora, was Aaron in seiner Einrichtung des Kults einst gebracht haben und für Israel auf Dauer bedeuten,

---

25. Julia M. O'Brien, *Priest and Levite in Malachi*, SBLDS 121 (Williston, VT: SBL Press 1990), 47, wo auch verschiedene Versuche zur Lösung des Problems genannt sind.

26. Vgl. Thomas Willi, *Die Chronik als Auslegung*, FRLANT 106 (Göttingen: Vandenhoeck & Ruprecht, 1972), 216–41.

ist und bleibt nicht nur unvergleichlich, sondern schlicht elementar.

Genau diese bleibende Gültigkeit bringt es mit sich, dass die – nach moderner Nomenklatur – pentateuchische Überlieferung mit ihren so vielfältigen Facetten (den sogenannten vorwie nachexilischen „Quellenschriften") eine besondere Qualität aufweist, last not least für die Chronik, die sich zwar explizit überhaupt nicht mit diesen Zeiten und Dingen befasst, implizit dagegen um so mehr auf sie bezogen bleibt.[27] Gerade weil der Pentateuch die Grundlagen der Entstehung und Entwicklung des Israels der zwölf Stämme dokumentiert, sieht sich der Chronist als Historiker vor die Frage gestellt, wie diese Grundlagen bewahrt und im Laufe der Geschichte von Fall zu Fall neu realisiert werden, wenn sich die Voraussetzungen ändern.[28] Der Chronist musste mit dem Kern des Pentateuchs in seiner Letztfassung davon ausgehen, dass die „Stiftshütte" das „Zelt der Übereinkunft/Begegnung," die Mitte nicht bloss des kultischen Geschehens, sondern des Lebens der Israelstämme insgesamt bildete. Dann erhob sich folgerichtig die Frage: Inwiefern ist der Jerusalemer Tempel noch das alte Heiligtum, und inwiefern ist er es nicht? Was ist aus dem reich ausgebauten Gottesdienst in der Wüste und mit denen, die ihn verantworteten und ausführten, eigentlich geworden?[29]

Genau diese in Israels Geschichte eingetretene Transformation hat der Chronist im Blick. In einprägsamer Bildhaftigkeit macht er sie an einer ganz bestimmten Stelle, anhand des Wandels in der Funktion der Leviten dingfest. Früher hatten sie nach Deuteronomium 10:8 rein physisch die Aufgabe, die Lade zu tragen, wie die Erzählung von der Überführung der Lade in 1. Chronik 15:2, 15, 26 f. einschärft. Nun aber, da diese ihren festen Platz gefunden hat, sind die Leviten mit

---

27. Auch die pentateuchischen Überlieferungen sind für den Chronisten nicht als – gar im Skopus unterschiedene – Konzepte im Sinne von "Quellenschriften" von Belang, sondern als Erzählungen und Anweisungen aus Israels Frühzeit von Belang. Was etwa seine Haltung gegenüber "dtr" *versus* "priesterlicher" Traditionen angeht, so wird man mit Knoppers, "Hierodules, Priests, or Janitors?," 68 sagen müssen: "The Chronicler is heir to and interpreter of both traditions."

28. Daher ist der der Chronik gemachte Vorwurf, sie beschreibe ihr Israel nach dem Bild des Pentateuchs, vorab seiner insgesamt "priesterschriftlich" gestalteten Endfassung, weitgehend unbegründet, und man wird Julius Wellhausen nicht einschränkungslos folgen, wenn er behauptet, dass im DtrG die Vergangenheit verurteilt werde, während dagegen "in der Chronik…die Geschichte des alten Israel nach Massgabe des Priesterkodex umgedichtet" werde. Sie disqualifiziere sich in ihrer Geschichtsdarstellung als williges Vollzugsorgan kultisch motivierter Programmatik. Dem Chronisten als Historiker geht es wesentlich darum, alle ihm vorliegenden Überlieferungen, Nachrichten, Quellen zu berücksichtigen. Er kennt und anerkennt sodann – und auch das gehört zum Rüstzeug der Geschichtsschreibung – die Differenz der Zeiten und Epochen.

29. Explizit stellt sich der Chronist dieser Frage in 2 Chron 1:3 f.

der Überlieferung und dem Wort betraut, sollen die Tora anwenden und die Schrift auslegen. In bemerkenswert gegensätzlich-paralleler Formulierung zu 1. Chronik 15:2 hält aber nun David am Ende seines Lebens als Vermächtnis fest:

> ²⁵Denn David sagte: JHWH, der Gott Israels, hat seinem Volk Ruhe verschafft und in Jerusalem Wohnung genommen auf Weltzeit. ²⁶So haben auch die Leviten *nicht mehr* das Wohngemach und all seine Geräte zu seinem Dienst *zu tragen*. ²⁷Aber tatsächlich sind sie in den letzten anordnenden Worten Davids (da, und zwar) als Zahl der Leviten im Alter von zwanzig Jahren und darüber, ²⁸denn ihre Stellung ist an der Seite der Söhne Aarons, zum Dienst am Hause JHWHS...

Diese „Wahrung" der Tradition, von der 1. Chronik 23 abschliessend mit Verwendung der hebräischen Wurzel שמר spricht (V. 32), stellt die Fortführung der alten Levitenobliegenheiten unter den neuen Bedingungen des festen Heiligtums dar und weitet die physischen Verrichtungen aus, indem sie vergeistigt als Handhabung des Wortes, der Tora, ja der Schrift, erscheinen.[30] Aus dem *Stand* der charismatisch inspirierten Outsiders ist in Chronik vermittels kreativer Auslegung[31] der *Stamm* Levi geworden, dem der grundsätzlich gleiche Auftrag obliegt, jetzt freilich als Herz des Zwölfstämmevolks.

Die Leviten, an ihrer Spitze Mose, „wachten" darüber, dass der Kult nicht einfach als *opus operatum* vollzogen wird, sondern dass er nach der Israel anvertrauten Art, der Mose von Gott zuhanden *Israels* übergebenen und als Schrift vorliegenden Grundlage geschieht! Darauf bezieht sich die Schriftkonformität des jeweiligen Sachverhalts. Diese Schriftkonformitätsklauseln (nicht Zitationsformeln!) betonen die Selbigkeit der Autorisierung, die Identitätsstiftung zwischen der grundlegenden Offenbarung von einst und ihrer Realisierung von jetzt, wie sie in Chronik auf David zurückgeführt wird. Im Rückgang auf Mose betont Chronik (wie auch Esr-Neh), diese oder jene Massnahme sei nicht zufällig oder arbiträr nach menschlichem Gutdünken vollzogen worden, sondern sei geschehen *kakkatuv*, „wie geschrieben – nämlich niedergeschrieben und vor„geschrieben" – steht".[32]

---

30. Vgl. den Versuch von M. Gertner, "Masorah and Levites. An Essay in the History of a Concept," *VT* 10 (1960): 242–72, das frühjüdische Levitenamt über einen Rückschluss von den mittelalterlichen Masoreten auf die persisch-hellenistischen Verhältnisse zu bestimmen und in den „medieval masoretic masters" geradezu ein „revival ... of the earlier, pre-talmudic, ideals" zu erkennen (p. 242).

31. Nicht anders werden auch die Texte von Qumran ihr Bild von den Leviten mittels einer „simply text-centered creative exegesis" entwerfen, vgl. Harald Samuel, „Levites: II. Judaism," in *EBR* 16 (2018): Sp. 348.

32. 1 Chron 16:40; 28:19; 2 Chron 23:18; 30:5, 18; 31:3; 35:4, 12, 26; in etwas anderer Weise 1 Chron 24:6. Die Ausdrucksweise wird variiert a) in der Formulierung „nach (dem Buch, der Verschriftung) der Weisung JHWHS durch Mose":

Die Verschriftung der dem Mose mündlich erteilten Tora ist sozusagen die technische Seite der Sache. Davids Vorbereitungen für Heiligtum und Kult hängen aber mit der Grundgeschichte der Wüstenzeit nicht nur dadurch zusammen, dass sie über die schriftliche Fassung mit dem göttlichen Wort zusammenstimmen, sondern auch dadurch, dass nun in der Linie des Mose auch sein Stamm für dessen Geltung bürgt. Die *Personalisierung* durch Levi begleitet und schützt sozusagen die *Skripturalisierung* der Tradition.

5. "Grundgeschichte" und Chronik nach chronistischem Selbstverständnis

Von diesen Voraussetzungen her gestaltet der Chronist seine Geschichtserzählung. Weil er die Zeit des Tempels als eine von der Väter- und Exoduszeit grundsätzlich unterschiedene kennt und beschreibt, sieht er sich vor die Aufgabe gestellt, dem fundamentalen Übergang, der sich mit David vollzieht, und dem Altüberlieferten, das da neu wird, nachzuspüren. Das historische Bewusstsein für den Bruch der Zeiten – der im DtrG so nicht existiert – macht es möglich und nötig, eine neue Darstellung der Geschichte zu schreiben.

Die alten Überlieferungen zur Schöpfung und den Vätern, zum Exodus und zur Wüstenzeit in ihrer ganzen Vielschichtigkeit haben nicht erst die moderne Forschung angezogen und irritiert.[33]

Auch der Chronik sind diese Überlieferungen, paradoxerweise gerade weil sie nicht ihr Thema sind, alles andere als eine bedeutungslose Nebensache. Im Gegenteil: Dank der chronistischen Historiog-

---

2 Chron 23:18; 2 Chron 25:4 (zit. Dtn 24:16); 30:16; ähnlich 33:8; dann 34:14 und 35:12; b) mit der Betonung „ganz wie Mose [...] geboten hat": 1 Chron 6:34; 15:15; etwas modifiziert 22:13 und 2 Chron 25:4; c) schliesslich auf der Ebene der Ausführung (nicht der Übermittlung und daher ohne Bezug auf Mose) „nach dem Gebot/der Regelung/der Vorschrift Davids (und Salomos)", aber auch "des Königs (sc. Hiskia oder Josia)": „Nach dem Gebot (*mizwa*)": Neh 11:23; 12:24, 45; 2 Chron 8:13, 14 (mit *mischpat*), 15; 29:15 (mit *dibre* Jhwh), 25bis; 30:12 (mit *debar* Jhwh); 35:10, 15, 16. Bzw. Verbalwurzel *zwh*: Esr 4:3; Neh 8:1, 14; 1 Chron 6:34; 15:15; 16:40; 22:6; 24:19 (neben *mischpat*; 2 Chron 25:4 // 2Kön 14:6. „Nach der Regelung (*mischpat*)": Esr 3:4; Neh 8:18; 1 Chron 6:17; 15:13 (mit *darasch*); 23:31; 24:19 (neben *ziwwah*); 2 Chron 4:7, 20; 8:14 (neben *mizwa*); 30:16 (neben *tora*); 35:13. „Nach der (Vor-)Schrift (*ketab*)": 1 Chron 28:19; 2 Chron 2:10; 35:4. Das aramaisierende Substantiv *ketab* begegnet weitaus am häufigsten im Buch Esth.

33. Das zeigt sich schon am Spektrum ihrer Bezeichnungen: Rein technisch ist von *Bereschit*, *Schemot* usw., elementar ist von *hakkatuv*, dem „schriftlich Festgehaltenen" oder ebenso allgemein von *sefär*, „Verschriftung" die Rede, die nach dem Übermittler als ספר משה, nach der Gattung als ספר תורה, präzisiert wird, die sich später zum *Pentateuch* als dem *Fünf-Buch* zusammenfassen lassen.

raphie und ihrer Anlage gewinnen sie eine ganz neue Qualität. Sie bilden die unabdingbare Voraussetzung, die Basis und den Hintergrund für die mit David anhebende Geschichte Israels im Zeitalter des Ersten Tempels, gerade dort, wo es um ihre Transformation geht. Für die Geschichte, die nach Chronik mit David neu beginnt, sind jene nicht thematisierten, wohl aber selbstverständlich vorausgesetzten Traditionskomplexe sozusagen die Grundgeschichte im Sinne einer *basic story*.[34]

Eine solche *Grundgeschichte* ist etwas anderes als eine Gründungs- oder eine blosse Vorgeschichte, die die Voraussetzungen für das, was danach kommt, klärt, selber aber abgetan und vergangen und insofern bedeutungslos ist. Die Grundgeschichte, das, was in ihr „aufgeschrieben" ist, bildet vielmehr die Referenz, den Massstab für die neue, anders gelagerte Zeit: jene des – in diesem Falle – Ersten Tempels, des davidisch-salomonischen Jerusalemer Heiligtums, in dem das einstige mobile Ladeheiligtum sein Ziel und Ende gefunden hat und den Anspruch erhebt, als Residenz des Weltreichskönigs zu dienen.

---

34. Der Ausdruck *Grundgeschichte* ist als solcher nicht neu. Wenn er auch in der neueren alttestamentlichen Wissenschaft, vorab in ihrer Formund Literaturgeschichte, u.W. bislang nicht angewendet wurde, so hat er doch seinen Platz im werdenden historischen Denken der Barockzeit und vor allem dann in der beginnenden universalgeschichtlichen Betrachtungsweise des 19. Jahrhunderts, anders ausgedrückt im Umfeld der Untersuchungen Wilhelm Martin Leberecht de Wettes oder Karl Heinrich Grafs und im Vorfeld der darauf aufbauenden Entwürfe Julius Wellhausens. So spricht etwa der christliche Kabbalist Christian Knorr von Rosenroth (1631 – 1689) im Blick auf Ri 11: „Die Grundgeschichte von des Jephtha Tochter lautet…" (*Des vortrefflichen Engelländers Thomae Brown…Psevdodoxia Epidemica. Das ist Untersuchung derer Irrthümer, so bey dem gemeinen Mann…im Schwange gehen: In Sieben Büchern…und dann ferner in denen übrigen sechs Büchern von den Irrthümern, die Mineralien, Gewächse, Thiere…betreffend. Aus dem Englischen und Lateinischen übersetzt durch Christian Peganium, in Teutsch Rautner genannt* [Frankfurt a.M. 1680]: p. 820). Bei Ernst Moritz Arndt bezeichnet der Begriff „das Unmittelbare und Ursprüngliche, was als *Grundgeschichte des Lebens der Völker* in der Fabel und dem Mythos liegt" (*Schriften für und an seine lieben Deutschen*, Band 4 [Berlin: Weidmann, 1855]: p. 305). Nach Friedrich Schlegel in seiner *Philosophie der Geschichte* haben „die tieferen Forschungen…wiederholt hingewiesen" auf "diese *Grundgeschichte*…der Griechen." (*Philosophie der Geschichte 1: Sämtliche Werke* Bd. 13 [Wien: Mayer 1846]: p. 223).

CONVERSATIONAL IMPLICATURES IN THE BOOK OF CHRONICLES: THE PENTATEUCH AS HORIZON OF THE CHRONICLER

Lars Maskow

„Der Wirklichkeitsbegriff einer Epoche bleibt in ihren Zeugnissen in eigentümlicher Weise stumm, und das nicht zufällig, sondern aufgrund der eigentümlichen Selbstverständlichkeit, mit der eine Epoche sich an das hält, was ihr für wirklich gilt. Von ihrem Wirklichkeitsbegriff macht eine Epoche Gebrauch, aber sie redet nicht von ihm, sie kann von ihm gar nicht reden, und in diesem Sinne ‚hat' sie ihren Wirklichkeitsbegriff nicht."[1]

1. INTRODUCTION

The literary correlations between the Books of Chronicles and the Pentateuch have always been observed in historical-critical research. Two prominent camps were formed with regard to the directions of reception. Julius Wellhausen, on the one hand, focused strongly on the reception of priestly writings. In doing so, he used striking parallels between P and Chronicles to elaborate his dating of the priestly source. Whereas in the Vorlage (Samuel/Kings) less priestly but rather deuteronomistic use of language could be recognized, priestly influence could prominently be observed in Chronicles:

> In the Chronicles the pattern according to which the history of ancient Israel is represented is the Pentateuch, i. e. the Priestly Code. In the

---

[1] "The concept of reality of an epoch remains mute in its testimonies in a peculiar way. This is not by chance, but because of the peculiar self-evidence by which an epoch keeps to that which has a real significance for it. An epoch makes use of its concept of reality, but it does not speak of it, it cannot speak of it at all, and in this sense it does not 'have' its concept of reality." (Translation, L. M.) Hans Blumenberg, *Realität und Realismus* (Berlin: Suhrkamp, 2020), 11.

source of Chronicles, in the older historical books, the revision does not proceed upon the basis of the Priestly Code, which indeed is completely unknown to them, but on the basis of Deuteronomy.[2]

In this sense Gerhard Von Rad has come to a completely different conclusion on the basis of his own observations. For him the reception of Deuteronomy is particularly important. Among other facts, he built his thesis on the term 'Ark of the Covenant.' In his eyes this term was a typical deuteronomistic expression. All in all, Von Rad achieved a balanced result, however, the tendency is clear:

> Das eine ist allerdings gewiß geworden, daß sowohl was eigentliche Zitation und Verweisung wie allgemeine theologische Einstellung anlangt, von einer Abhängigkeit der Chronik von P vor anderen Quellen nicht die Rede sein kann. Wir haben im Gegenteil gesehen, daß an ganz ausschlaggebenden Punkten deuteronomische Gedanken in der Chronik Eingang gefunden haben; ja es will fast scheinen als seien sie in ihrer Bedeutung für den Gesamtaufriß des Werkes höher anzuschlagen, als die Abhängigkeit von P in mancherlei kultischen Angelegenheiten.[3]

With regard to these contradictions, recent research on the Pentateuch has brought decisive progress. In particular, a differentiation of the priestly layers of the Pentateuch, but also the question of the extent to which there have been reciprocal adaptations between the priestly and the deuteronomistic texts, has sharpened our heuristics for the fact that, roughly speaking, there have been approximations in the priestly texts as well as priestly influences on the deuteronomistic texts and *vice versa*.[4] So it turns out, to give just one example, that the term 'Ark of the Covenant' in Deuteronomy 10:8; 31:9, 25 is not a genuine deuteronomistic term, but rather presupposes the connection of P and D.[5]

---

2. Julius Wellhausen, *Prolegomena to the History of Israel. With a Preface by William Robertson Smith* (Cambridge: Cambridge University Press, 2013), 294.

3. "However, one fact has definitely turned out to be true. There can be no question of a dependence of Chronicles on P prior to other sources. Both with regard to the actual citation, reference and to the general theological attitude. On the contrary, we have seen that at quite decisive points deuteronomic ideas have been incorporated into Chronicles. It almost seems as if their importance for the general structure of the work is more important than the dependence on P in many cultic matters" (Translation: L. M.). Gerhard von Rad, *Das Geschichtsbild des chronistischen Werkes* (Stuttgart: Kohlhammer, 1930), 63.

4. Decisive are those approaches that have searched for alternative models in the context of the so-called crisis of Pentateuch Research.

5. Achenbach attributes the authorship of the expression ארון ברית יהוה to a Hexateuch-Redactor (HexRed) who combines D and P: "HexRed bildet mit der Bezeichnung der Gotteslade als *'ărôn bərît jhwh* einen aus dtr. und priesterschriftlicher Tradition integrierten Begriff." Cf. Reinhard Achenbach, *Die Vollendung der Tora. Studien zur Redaktionsgeschichte des Numeribuches im Kontext von Hexateuch und Pentateuch* (Wiesbaden: Harrassowitz, 2003), 75 In Achenbach's opinion the process

A closer look at the reception of Torah in Chronicles reveals a paradox. To be more precise, one can speak of a two-fold reception. In a peculiar way, the texts of the Pentateuch do not appear where תורה is spoken of. Nevertheless, the texts of the Pentateuch are received in different ways in Chronicles, but nearly always without referring to the term תורה. In other words, talking about Torah is fundamentally different in Chronicles than talking *out of* Torah. Wherever certain reception formulas appear in Chronicles, they most of the time do not indicate a specific Torah quotation.[6] I have shown elsewhere that this bivalent reception is like a rhetorical call to order (Back to the Torah!).[7]

In Chronicles there are now numerous references to the Penta-

---

of integration consists of a synthesis of Exod 34:28 and Exod 25:10–22, which combines the tradition of the priestly source with the דברי הברית to *arôn berît adonai*. Cf. Achenbach, 191. It is all the more significant that this term is not taken up in 2Sam 7:1 but in 1Chron 17:1.

6. This insight has been particularly emphasized by Willi who, with regard to the term ככתוב including all subsidiary phrase formations, does not speak of a "Schriftzitationsformel" but of a "Schriftkonformitätsklausel". Thomas Willi, "'Wie geschrieben steht' – Schriftbezug und Schrift. Überlegungen zur frühjüdischen Literaturwerdung im perserzeitlichen Kontext," in *Religion und Religionskontakte im Zeitalter der Achämeniden*, ed. Reinhard G. Kratz, 257–277 (Gütersloh: Gütersloher Verlagshaus, 2002).

7. This call to order is obeyed by the Chronicler himself through significant changes of his Vorlage and implementation of texts of the Pentateuch. This means that we have to differentiate between the rhetorical reception of תורה as an ideal concept and the use of the concrete texts of the Pentateuch. I have tried to give a comprehensive description of these reception processes in a contribution submitted shortly before the beginning of the Lausanne conference, of which the conference volume is now available in print. (Cf. Lars Maskow, *Tora in der Chronik: Studien zur Rezeption des Pentateuchs in den Chronikbüchern*. Göttingen: Vandenhoeck & Ruprecht, 2001). It was a stroke of luck for me to be able to discuss the results of my research during the Lausanne conference immediately after publication and I am pleased to be able to present a part of my book here in English. It seems to me that the texts of the Pentateuch are reflected in Chronicles as a kind of Fortschreibung, be it affirmative or contradictory. This becomes particularly clear when we compare the influences of the Pentateuch on Chronicles synoptically with Sam/Kgs. All in all, my impression is that the direction of reception can be understood most clearly as a continuation of what Achenbach called *Theocratic Revisions*. (Cf. also his contribution in this volume, page 53.) I was rather cautious about post-chronistic *Fortschreibungen* in the Pentateuch due to the advanced developments and my dating of Chronicles to the Hellenistic era. Nevertheless, some proposals – not least the name Moriah – were brought into discussion. (Cf. Susanne Rudnig-Zelt, *Glaube im Alten Testament: Eine begriffsgeschichtliche Untersuchung unter besonderer Berücksichtigung von Jes 7,1–17; Dtn 1–3; Num 13–14 und Gen 22,1–19*. (Berlin: De Gruyter, 2017), 326–331). Jonker has made a striking advance in a recently published article. (Cf. Louis C. Jonker, "Melting pots and rejoinders? The interplay among literature formation processes during the late Persian and early Hellenistic periods," *VT* 70/1 (2020), 42–54.) It seems to me that particularly at this interface intensive research is required in the future.

teuch, not only on a conceptually explicit but also, and above all, on an implicit level. It is therefore advisable not only to identify intertextual connections on a conceptual level, but above all also to examine where discourses overlap without being made explicit. It seems to me that the texts of the Pentateuch are in a way "selbstverständlich" as Hans Blumenberg speaks of the "Wirklichkeitsbegriff einer Epoche."[8] If this holds true, we have to take into account that the texts of the Pentateuch appear somehow latent or as a background; or, to put it in the language of the title of this contribution, as a horizon of the Chronicler. This means that we need other methods than the indication of textual similarities or other incidences of intertextual correlation. At this point the phenomenon of Conversational Implicature which was observed by Grice comes into play.

2. SAYING AND MEANING: THE GRICEAN THEORY OF CONVERSATIONAL IMPLICATURES

In the main argument of this essay, the Pentateuch will be made visible as the horizon of the Chronicler. I will show that the Chronicler uses *Conversational Implicatures* that can only be made explicit against the background of an implicit world knowledge. This means that there are cases of reception in Chronicles in which references are made to an implicit knowledge of the torah without making this explicit. I would like to discuss this aspect in the following with regard to 2 Chronicles 26:16–21 unfold. For this purpose, I will first give a short insight into the theory of conversational implicatures, which represent a subfield of linguistic pragmatics.

Pragmatics is – generally speaking – "die Wissenschaft vom Ungesagten," or, "what is meant without being said."[9] Eckard Rolf follows Grice when he calls these approaches "Inferentielle Pragmatik."[10]

---

8. Of course, the quotation does not match in every sense of the word because the concept of תורה is not completly "stumm" (engl. mute). But despite this the observation of Blumenberg is helpful to understand the chronistic approach – not with regard to the term תורה but to the texts of the Pentateuch. In almost any case where the Chronicler refers to the Pentateuch this is not made explicit. This means that the Pentateuch at all is somehow a silent or latent presupposition in the book of Chronicles. I will show in this paper what this really means.

9. Eckard Rolf, *Inferentielle Pragmatik*: Zur Theorie der Sprecher-Bedeutung (Berlin: Erich Schmidt Verlag, 2013), 22. For an introduction to Pragmatics, especially the phenomenon of Conversational Implicature, see also the most influential introduction in English by Stephen Levinson, Pragmatics (Cambridge: Cambridge University Press, [19]2008), 97–166.

10. Rolf, *Pragmatik*.

Pragmatics is the science of the "Ungesagten-aber-Gemeinten. Als solche versteht sich die inferentielle Pragmatik als Theorie der Sprecher-Bedeutung, als eine Theorie dessen, was vom Sprecher gemeint wurde in Fällen, in denen er etwas zu verstehen geben wollte, was von dem, was er gesagt hat, abweicht."[11] The main purpose of inferential pragmatics is to determine the *meaning* of the speaker's utterance.

Paul Grice, one of the patriarchs of the so-called *pragmatic turn*, is the one who for the first time systematically applied the distinction between *what is said* and *what is meant*. He laid the foundation for this in his "William James Lectures" held in 1967 which was posthumously published as "Studies in the Way of Words." In this lectures Grice uttered the idea that language as such represents a maxim-oriented behaviour and designed a way to distinguish between what is said and what is implied with the help of conversation maxims. The core of the theory, which Eckard Rolf[12] calls a kind of "Konversationsethik", is formulated in the essay "Logic and Conversation."[13] It consists of the Cooperative Principle and eleven Conversational Maxims.[14] With the help of this inventory, Grice succeeds in tracking the implied and making it visible. This essay also introduces the term "Conversational Implicature," which plays a key role in this process. Grice puts the so-called "Cooperative Principle" in front of his eleven maxims: "Make your conversational contribution such as is required, at the stage at which it occurs, by the accepted purpose or direction of the talk exchange in which you are engaged."[15] Grice then introduces the eleven maxims he discovered and divides them "echoing Kant"[16] into four categories:

> I Quantity – 1. Make your contribution as informative as is required (for the current purposes of the exchange). 2. Do not make your contribution more informative than is required. II Quality – Supermaxim: 'Try to make your contribution one that is true' 1. Do not say what you believe

---

11. "Unsaid-but-meant. As such, inferential pragmatics is understood as a theory of speakermeaning, as a theory of what was meant by the speaker in cases where he wanted to give something to understand that differs from what he said" (Translation: L. M; Rolf, *Pragmatik*, 60).

12. Eckard Rolf, *Sagen und Meinen: Paul Grices Theorie der Konversationsimplikaturen* (Opladen: Westdeutscher Verlag GmbH, 1994), 9.

13. Paul Grice, *Studies in the Way of Words* (Cambridge, Mass.: Harvard University Press, 1989.), 22–40.

14. Rolf, (*Pragmatik*, 7.26) speaks of "elf, wenn nicht sogar zwölf." Thus, on the one hand he reacts to the completely inadmissible, albeit widespread, custom of reducing the number of maxims to four. At the same time, he integrates an addition to the maxims of the modality, which was considered by Grice later on. For discussion, see Rolf, *Pragmatik*, 47.

15. Grice, *Studies*, 26.

16. Grice, *Studies*, 26.

to be false. 2. Do not say that for which you lack adequate evidence. III Relation – 'Be relevant.' IV Manner – Supermaxim: 'Be perspicuous' 1. Avoid obscurity of expression. 2. Avoid ambiguity. 3. Be brief (avoid unnecessary prolixity). 4. Be orderly.[17]

Rolf, who wrote a fundamental study of Grice's theory, asserts that the maxims developed by Grice are irreducible and complete. The most important of the eleven or twelve maxims, "die mit dem größten Implikaturerzeugungspotential, lautet (verkürzt wiedergegeben): 'Mach deinen Beitrag so informativ wie nötig!'"[18] Following the introduction of these maxims, Grice lists four ways in which a speaker can violate one or more maxims.

> 1. He may quietly and unostentatiously violate a maxim; if so, in some cases he will be liable to mislead. 2. He may opt out from the operation both of the maxim and of the Cooperative Principle; he may say, indicate, or allow it to become plain that he is unwilling to cooperate in the way the maxim requires. He may say, for example, I cannot say more; my lips are sealed. 3. He may be faced by a clash: He may be unable, for example, to fulfill the first maxim of Quantity (Be as informative as is required) without violating the second maxim of Quality (Have adequate evidence for what you say). 4. He may flout a maxim; that is, he may blatantly fail to fulfil it.[19]

Grice also speaks of "[E]xploitation,"[20] of a maxim. Especially the fourth kind of non-fulfilment of a maxim "gives rise to a conversational implicature."[21] Grice characterizes the notion of a Conversational Implicature as follows:

> A man who, by (in, when) saying (or making as if to say) that p has implicated that q, may be said to have conversationally implicated that q, provided that (1) he is to be presumed to be observing the conversational maxims, or at least the Cooperative Principle; (2) the supposition that he is aware that, or thinks that, q is required in order to make his saying or making as if to say p (or doing so in those terms) consistent with this presumption; and (3) the speaker thinks (and would expect the hearer to think that the speaker thinks) that it is within the competence of the hearer to work out, or grasp intuitively, that the supposition mentioned in (2) is required.[22]

---

17. Grice, *Studies*, 26–27.
18. "The maxim with the greatest potential for generating an Implicature is the following (in brief): 'Make your contribution as informative as necessary!'" (Translation: L. M.; Rolf *Pragmatik*, 26).
19. Grice, *Studies*, 30.
20. Grice, *Studies*, 33.
21. Grice, *Studies*, 30.
22. Grice *Studies*, 30–31.

In a nutshell, it can be said: By flagrantly violating one of the conversational maxims, the speaker thus makes clear that he intends to say more than he literally says. In other words: By failing to comply with one of the conversation maxims, the speaker makes clear that he does not mean just what he says, but also something beyond it. According to Grice, Conversational Implicatures now have the property of being "cancellable." Grice speaks of "cancelability."[23] The Conversational Implicature can therefore be cancelled by adding a remark. Thus, a speaker/ writer can, after producing a Conversational Implicature, take the position of not wanting to have said something. He can even take the position of not having said it. After this now almost negligent abbreviation of Grice's theory, however, the range and functionality of this interpretament can be shown clearly.[24]

The recourse to the Conversational Implicature will shed to light, on the analysis of the following text, which has to be understood as a symptom of a discourse of leadership. In 2 Chronicles 26:16–21 for example this discourse is not conducted directly, but indirectly. The implicit discourse will be made visible in the following analysis and interpreted in terms of the chosen means of expression.

Of course, since it is a maxime-guided inferential procedure, the approach is to a certain extent speculative. But on the other hand, especially because we naturally have to expect Conversational Implicatures in all human utterances and communications, it is at the same time the best method available to us. Consequently, there is the necessity to incorporate as much evidence as possible into the analysis.[25]

---

23. Grice *Studies*, 44–46.

24. In the brevity provided for the given purpose, numerous details of Grice's theory must be left out. In particular, the criticism and metacriticism of Grice's theory cannot be addressed here. I am only concerned here with the introduction of an *interpretament* for determining the speaker's meaning, which lies beyond what is literally said. For further details, I refer to Kent Bach "Saying, Meaning, and Implicating". In *The Cambridge Handbook of Pragmatics*, edited by Keith Allan and Kasia M. Jaszczolt (Cambridge: Cambridge University Press, 2012), 47–67; Laurence R. Horn: "Implicature". In *The Handbook of Pragmatics*, edited by Laurence R. Horn and Gregory Ward (Malden: Blackwell Publishing, 2004), 3–28; Yan Huang: "Implicature". In *The Oxford handbook of Pragmatics*, edited by Yan Huang, 155–179 (Oxford: Oxford University Press, 2017); Levinson, Pragmatics; Rolf, Sagen; Rolf, *Pragmatik*.

25. Typically, at this point the question arises whether it would be anachronistic to transfer such an approach to the Ancient Orient. At this point I would like to counter the possible concern with two comments. Firstly, we need to be very aware that the research of linguistic pragmatics prominently speaks of the fact that Grice *uncovered* the Implicatures, and did not *invent* them (Cf. Rolf, *Pragmatik*, 62). Secondly, the design of the theory is related to human language activity in general: "The cooperative principle and its attendent maxims are essentially principles of language use based on the rational nature of human communication, and indeed any shared-goal human ac-

The recourse to the Conversational Implication will now bring to light in the analysis of 2 Chronicles 26:16–21 that it has to be understood as a symptom of a leadership-discourse, which is not directly but indirectly (or implicit) carried out. The implicit discourse will be made visible in the following analysis and interpreted with regard to the chosen means of expression. The influence of the Torah will play the decisive role in this context.

3. CONVERSATIONAL IMPLICATURES IN 2 CHRONICLES 26:16–21

In 2 Chronicles 26 the hierarchy between two conflict parties is negotiated in form of an "incense scene".[26] After the definition of hierarchy between the different families of Priests (Lev 10) and between priests and Levites (Num 16), the relationship between Priesthood and Kingship is determined in 2 Chronicles 26. Second Chronicles 26:16–21 is part of the Uzziah narrative, which has been greatly expanded compared to its *Vorlage*. It tells the story of king Uzziah, who is called Azariah in 2 Kings 15:2. The Chronicler reports, in accordance with its *Vorlage*, that the king did what was right in the eyes of YHWH (יהוה הישר בעיני).

At a certain point during his reign, however, it is stated that his heart became haughty (לב גבה) to his own destruction (להשחית) and he acts disloyally against YHWH (וימעל ביהוה). After the successful and God-fearing years an unprecedented decline begins. The bottom of the decadence is then reached in 2 Chronicles 26:16–22.6 The synopsis of 2 Chronicles 26 and 2 Kings 14–15 shows that the text has been considerably enriched by verses 5–20. The point of the decline seems to me to be in verses 16–21 and to have been formulated in the form of a Conversational Implicature, as I will now demonstrate in a close *reading* of this text.

Zwickel has proposed to stratify the text.[27] However, since the

---

tivity" (Huang, *Implicature*, 157). I therefore suggest that we may also expect to find Implicatures in texts of the Hebrew Bible and to assume the validity of Grice's maxims until this assumption is falsified.

26. In at least two striking texts of the Old Testament, Lev 10 and Num 16, a new formulation of the hegemonial structures is established with the help of the motif of incense: In Lev 10 the two first-born sons of Aaron, Nadab and Abihu, are killed by YHWH because of the offering of foreign fire (שא הרז); in Num 16 Datan, Abiram, 250 men as well as Korah and his family are also killed by YHWH after the execution of incense.

27. Wolfgang Zwickel: *Räucherkult und Räuchergeräte: Exegetische und archäologische Studien zum Räucheropfer im Alten Testament* (Freiburg, CH: Universitätsverlag, 1990), 321–22.

reasons given seem unconvincing to me, I maintain the uniformity of the text.[28] Japhet considered, with good reason, that the mentioning of 80 priests in v. 17 is a later gloss.[29] The actual one-to-one confrontation between Uzziah and Azariah is thus largely defused and has already been decided on the basis of the indicated physical superiority of the priests.[30] It is significant that, while otherwise the king commands brave men (cf. e. g. 1 Chron 12; 2 Chron.13:3; 2 Chron 14:7), he is now facing, so to speak, an army of priests. All in all, it should be noticed that this pericope is not just about a confrontation of two characters but of two institutions. Uzziah's sacrilege against the sanctuary, consisting of the intention to burn incense, is stylized exemplarily as a case of precedent. The etymon קטר dominates the narrative and is used seven times. This expands exactly the motif that the Chronicler omitted from his *Vorlage*. While the people offer (ומקטרים מזבחים) in the *Vorlage* (2Kgs 15:4), the Chronicler omits its violation of the prohibition of incense offerings and attributes the sacrilege to the king instead: Uzziah enters the temple (לכיל) with the intention of offering incense. In this context, the Chronicler seems to parallel his narrative with 1 Kings 12:33, 57.

According to the genre, the motif of the illegitimate incense offering is connected with texts like Leviticus 10:1; 16:1, 12–13; Numbers 16:7, 17–18, 35; 17:5, 11–12, 58 and also Ezekiel 8:11. Already in 1 Chronicles 6:34 the privilege of the incense offering is explicitly assigned to the Aaronidic priests. In the present pericope the king claims this privilege for himself and thus indirectly also to the hegemony of the priesthood. However, the narration is highly artificial because implicitly it formulates a diametrically opposed proposition: The priestly claim to kingship.

The artificiality of the narrative already exists in the fact that Uzziah – although with the intention of burning incense – goes into the temple, but he does not burn incense at all. Similarly, as in 1 Chronicles 13:9, it seems that already the intention of trespassing in the holy

---

28. Cf. for discussion: Georg Steins: *Die Chronik als kanonisches Abschlußphänomen. Studien zur Entstehung und Theologie von 1/2 Chronik* (Weinheim: Beltz Athenäum, 1995), 408–414. Steins wants to adhere to the addition of the incense altar in vv. 16b and 19b with Zwickel. However, neither in 16b nor in 19b are syntactic or content-related reasons to be found that make this assumption necessary. On the contrary, these motifs fit harmoniously into the overall narrative.

29. Cf. Sara Japhet: *1&2 Chronicles. A Commentary* (Louisville, Kentucky: Westminster/John Knox Press, 1993), 885.

30. The incongruence of numerus in v. 17 (בוא) and v. 20 (פנה) would also support this assumption, although an adjustment was apparently possible in v. 18–19. On the other hand, Japhet's assumption that the report is pre-chronistic is by no means convincing because of the entire artificial constellation. Cf. Japhet, *Chronicles*, 876–77.

precinct is severely punished. Apart from the similarity of the names Uzzah and Uzziah,[31] these figures' conduct is thus also paralleled. The intended violation of the *lex sacra* by the king is therefore only the superficial development of a hierocratic discourse on hegemony. In v. 17 the antagonistic priest עזריהו is introduced. His name is frequently mentioned in the post-exile period and the name is often mentioned in priestly genealogies.[32]

In v. 18 Azariah the priest confronts Uzziah the king. The appositions, (הכהן v. 17) and (המלך v. 18), show that Uzziah and Azariah represent not only two conflicting persons, but two conflicting institutions. In particular the official title המלך is over-informative and need not be repeated in vv. 1, 3, 11, 13. This over-informativity violates the second maxim of quantity[33] and produces a Conversational Implicature, indicating that there is more at stake than Uzziah's qualification as king: It is about the conflict of leadership between the institutions of kingship and priesthood and about the outcome of the conflict in favour of the second party. The institutional conflict becomes completely apparent when Azariah is described in v. 20 as כהן הראש. Verse 18 introduces the condition known from Exodus 30:7–8 that only an Aaronide priest may sacrifice, since they are sacred for burning incense (קדש, pual): להפטיר לא לך להקטיר ליהוה כי לכהנים בני־אהרן המקדשים.

In the context of that instruction it is also commanded that no unauthorized incense offering may be offered on the altar of incense: זרה לא־תעלו עליו קטרת (cf. Exod 30:9aα) Even the kings of the Davidic dynasty are thus denied any participation in cultic ceremonies; only

---

31. Cf. Louis Jonker: *1&2 Chronicles* (Grand Rapids, Mi: Baker Books, 2013), 256.

32. He is always identified as a high priest. In the priestly genealogy in 1 Chron 5:29–41 Azariah is listed (depending on the evaluation of the doublet) in at least three different positions. What is important here is that it is said of him, and only of him, in 1 Chron 5:36 that he served as priest under Solomon (בבית אשר־בנה שלמה בירושלם הוא אשר כהן). Thus, already the name patron of the descendant has the highest dignity, since Solomon's reign is stylized by the Chronicler as the ideal epoch. At the same time, Azariah is highlighted among the Zadokites in this way, since according to the representation in 1Kgs 1; 2 and 4 Zadok should actually have been named here. However, the rise of Azariah can also be seen in a short note in 1Kgs 4:2. There, a certain עזריהו בן־צדוק is introduced, of which it is said that this person was a שר of Solomon. He is listed as a priest הכהן, too. This is strange in so far as Zadok and Abiathar, the two conflicting parties, are also introduced as priests in v. 4. In addition to this, the apposition הכהן has no counterpart in the LXX and therefore seems to be a post-chronistic addition – depending on 1 Chron 5:36; 9:11 and 2 Chron 26:17, 20 as well as 31:10. Azariah is described in 1 Chron 9:11 and 31:10 as the leader of the house of God (נגיד בית האלהים). The title appears only twice in Chronicles and is apparently on the same level as 1 Chron 27:17, where Aaron is listed next to Levi as a separate tribe and Zadok is designated as its נגיד.

33. See above page 261 → Second Maxim of Quantity.

the priests are allowed to burn incense.³⁴

Precisely in this context it is stated "You have acted arrogantly" (כי מעלת). On this, Pancratius Beentjes comments that "[a]lléén in 2 Kron. 26:18, en nergens anders in het geschrift, vinden we dit verbum in de directe rede."³⁵ This comment in the text possibly reflects the *Sitz im Leben* of the Chronicler: it is apparently up to the priest to determine מעל-offenses.

The order to leave the sanctuary (מקדש) (יצא, Imp.) directed to the king by the priesthood, provokes anger in Uzziah (זעף). In this incendiary situation the king is described with an incense pan (מקטרת) in his hand.³⁶ The wrath is announced twice by the Chronicler (v. 19). This overemphasis expresses the idea that Uzziah obviously presumes himself as a legitimate priest to act in this manner. Through this perspective, the narrative suggests to the reader that a trial of power between kingship and priesthood is at stake here.³⁷

The wrath of Uzziah (זעף Inf.+ ב+ePP) is followed by his immediate punishment with leprosy that appears on his forehead (זרח). This symbolically pronounces the conflict in favour of the priesthood. In this way he is treated very similarly to King Asa, whose anger (זעף) also brought about a punitive illness (cf. 2 Chron 16:10, 12–13). It becomes apparent that the Chronicler shapes his narratological intention, on the one hand, with free variation, but on the other hand, the narrative also unmistakably takes up the basic constellations of Leviticus 10, 16 and Numbers 16.³⁸

---

34. At this point, a tendency becomes apparent in a radicalized way, that Rudnig shows in the sacral layer he worked out in Ez 40–48, especially with regard to Ez 46:1–3, 8–11 he described: the complete laicization of the Davidic dynasty, which henceforth no longer plays a role in cultic practices. Cf. Thilo Rudnig: *Heilig und Profan. Redaktionskritische Studien zu Ez 40–48* (Berlin: Walter de Gruyter, 2000), 319–322.

35. "Only in 2 Chron. 26:18, and nowhere else in the bible, do we find this verb in direct speech" (Translation: L. M.) Cf. Pancratius Beentjes: *2 Kronieken* (Kampen: Uitgeverij Kok 2006), 338.

36. Uzziah holds a מקטרת in his hand (cf. Zwickel *Räucherkult*, 239–244 as well as Rainer Albertz and Rüdiger Schmitt, (eds. *Family and household religion in ancient Israel and the Levant* (Winona Lake, Ind.: Eisenbrauns, 2012), 70), while in Lev 10 and Num 16 the term used is מחתה. The מקטרת is only mentioned in 2 Chron 30:14 and Ezek 8:11.

37. Beentjes *Kronieken*, 338 rightly points out that the anger in connection with the smoking pan "benadrukt [...] dat hij zich gedraagt alsof hij een priester is."

38. Greenstein, for example, has argued that 2 Chron 26 is a midrash to the Nadab and Abihu episode. (Cf. Edward L. Greenstein: "An Inner-Biblical Midrash of the Nadab and Abihu Episode" (Hebr.). *Assaf* (1994): 71–78.) However, this is questioned by Beentjes due to the sparse linguistic consistency. (Cf. Pancratius C. Beentjes: *Tradition and Transformation in the Book of Chronicles*. (Leiden: Brill, 2008), 88). However, it is incomprehensible that Beentjes, who is one of the few exegetes to have in-

Due to the outbreak of leprosy on the forehead of Uzziah the setting is once again brought into focus. Whereas in v. 16 it was merely indicated that Uzziah went into the temple of YHWH, the scenery is now described in detail. Apparently, the confrontation between Uzziah and the priests happens directly in front of the פרכת at the incense altar.³⁹ Thereby, the priests prevent Uzziah from sacrificing on the altar of incense. One has to imagine that they stood between Uzziah and the altar of incense and obviously turned their backs on the altar while they stood opposite it (לפני). The altar represents the legitimate place of burning incense. This means the מקטרת carried out by Uzziah is currently identified as illegitimate. Because, with the introduction of the incense altar in addition to the requirement for special incense personnel, the offering of incense on the altar excludes the use of an incense pan.⁴⁰

As a consequence, Uzziah is now punished with leprosy. This punishment is documented only three times in the Old Testament, in Numbers 12; 2 Kings 5 and in 2 Chronicles 26. The offences are of varying severity and the penalties therefore of varying duration. While

---

dicated clear links with the Pentateuch, completely denies a connection to Lev 10 and also Num 16–17. Nevertheless, it is precisely this connection that seems to me to be constituted by the motif of strangeness (זרה). Also, the reference of the priests להקטיר לא־לך עזיהו להקטיר ליהוה כי לכהנים בני־אהרן המקדשים (2 Chron 26:18) seems to presuppose both episodes. For this reason alone, 2 Chron 26 can certainly be read as a *topos* in the horizon of these texts, even if the discourse has developed further and no inner-clerical conflict was carried out here, but rather the relationship between kingship and priesthood is negotiated and decided in favour of the priesthood.

39. Cf. on the location of the altar of incense in the temple Exod 30:6. It is particularly striking that after the introduction of the incense altar in Exod 30, which is only mentioned again in Chronicles (מזבח הקטרת Exod 30:27; 31:8; 35:15; 37:25; 1 Chron 6:34; 28:18; 2 Chron 26:16, 19.). The popularity of incensing in post-exile times gets also visible on a literary level. Thus, the incense altar in Exod 30:1–10, as Kuenen and Wellhausen have already shown, is a late addition. This can be reconstructed by various observations. First of all, it is conspicuous that the altar of incense is mentioned later than Exod 25–29 (Cf. Wellhausen, *Prolegomena*, 65–6), since it actually belongs to the inner life of the Mishkan. The Samaritan Pentateuch has therefore introduced the altar according to the factual logic of Exod 26:35. Wellhausen, *Prolegomena*, 66 has also pointed out that with the introduction of the smoking altar, the distinction between מזבח העלה and הקטרת מזבח becomes important: "[T]he altar of incense occurs only in certain portions of the Priestly Code, and is absent from others." Nihan (Christophe Nihan: *From Priestly Torah to Pentateuch. A Study in the Composition of the Book of Leviticus* (Tübingen: Mohr Siebeck, 2007), 32) and Achenbach, *Vollendung*, 95 have confirmed this hypothesis. Analogical observations can also be made for the introduction of the פרכת. Cf. Exod 26:31, 33, 35; 27:21; 30:6; 35:12; 36:35; 38:27; 39:34; 40:3, 21–22*, 26; Lev 4:6, 17; 16:2, 12, 15; 21:23; 24:3; Num 4:5; 18:7; 2 Chron 3:14.

40. Vgl. Erhard S. Gerstenberger: *Das dritte Buch Mose – Leviticus*. (Göttingen: Vandenhoeck & Ruprecht, 1993), 109.

2 Kings 5 describes a different situation, Numbers 12 is actually the only salient parallel.[41]

In Numbers 12, Miriam and Aaron rebel against the Mosaic claim of leadership because of Moses' marriage to a Cushite woman. However, YHWH himself justifies Moses by stating that he speaks face to face (פה אל פה, v. 8) only with him. His anger is inflamed by this conflict and he punishes Miriam with leprosy.[42] In 2 Chronicles 26, as we have seen, Uzziah's pride in connection with his intention to bring incense to YHWH on his own, but especially his wrath leads to him being punished with leprosy.[43] Both scenes are similar in their representation of the diagnosis of leprosy. The high priest turns to the patient for examination (הנפ לא)[44] and confirms the leprosy.

2 Chron 26:20aα	Num 12:10b
ויפן אליו עזריהו כהן הראש וכל־הכהנים	ויפן אהרן אל־מרים
והנה־הוא מצרע במצחו	והנה מצרעת

The intertextual comparison of the initial diagnosis makes it clear that Miriam's skin disease is diagnosed quite unspecifically, whereas the diagnosis of Uzziah is more specific. In his case the leprosy has broken out on the forehead (במצחו), which is stated twice (v. 19–20). Thus, the leprosy is immediately obvious to the priest. But more than that: the Chronicler apparently points specifically to the forehead of the leper. This deictic motif represents the hermeneutic key of the entire episode, which shifts the antagonism between haughty king Uzziah and high priest Azariah to the level of the institutional conflict between kingship and high priesthood.

The interpretation now is derived from the fact that the redundant description of the leprosy is strikingly over-informative: It does not

---

41. Apart from an exact semantic congruence, the topic is also attested in Deut 28:27 and Job 2.

42. Strangely enough, Aaron is spared from leprosy. Perhaps the punishment of Aaron is blocked at this point by a taboo. Presumably, the high priest remained free of leprosy, since he had to diagnose the disease according to Lev 14:57) himself. With regard to leprosy, neither the ritual of self-diagnosis nor that of self-purification was intended for the priest. See also the analysis of Achenbach, *Vollendung*, 281–301.

43. Dillard has pointed out that for the Chronicler illness as punishment is by no means atypical. In 2 Chron 16:12–13 King Asa gets seriously ill at his feet. However, he does not trust in YHWH, but in healers (רפאים). (Cf. Raymond B. Dillard: *2 Chronicles*. (Waco, Texas: Word Books, 1987), 211). This emphasis is significant, because Asa could have known better according to the theology of Exod 15:26 (אני יהוה רפאך). In 2 Chron 21:12–19, Jehoram too, gets so seriously ill that his intestines are spilling out, after Elijah's announcement in a letter. Ironically, Elijah's letter criticizes the fact that he had left the ways of Asa (דרכי אסא).

44. The confrontation is illustrated quite well by the preposition לפני (v. 19) and the direct inspection (פנה).

contribute anything to the progression or dramaturgy of the scene. Nor is it mentioned either in Numbers 12 or in the catalogue of the torah of leprosy of Leviticus 13–14.[45] The Chronicler thus creates another Conversational Implicature, which indicates that he wants to give more to understand than what he literally says.[46]

What is expressed by the implication, that is, what is meant by the Chronicler, can be explained against the background of the Torah, more precisely of Exodus 28:36–38. This connection is rarely identified; only Johnstone[47] and Beentjes[48] indicate this. An analysis from the perspective of inferential pragmatics can assist us here. As part of the instruction for the designing of the high priest's vestment, the order is given to make a flower[49] of pure gold[50] (ציץ זהב טהור). Like a seal (פתוחי חתם)[51] this should bear the engraving קדש ליהוה. Furthermore, it shall be bound with a cord of blue purple at the front (אל מול) of Aaron's headband (על המצנפת). Verse 38 specifies this instruction chiastically:

A	והיה על־מצח אהרן	So it shall be on Aaron's forehead.
	ונשא אהרן את־עון	Since Aaron bears whatever
	הקדשים	

---

45. Kurt Galling: *Die Bücher der Chronik Esra Nehemia, übersetzt und erklärt.* (Göttingen: Vandenhoeck&Ruprecht, 1953), 147) already noticed this over-informativity, but did not provide any further interpretation of it.

46. To speak with Grice, that would mean: The Chronicler exploits the second maxim of quantity (see above page 261).

47. William Johnstone: *1 and 2 Chronicles. Vol. 2, 2 Chronicles 10–36.* (Sheffield: Sheffield Academic Press, 1997), 169.

48. Cf. Beentjes, *2 Kronieken*, 339 as well as Beentjes, *Tradition*, 85.

49. The flower motif of the high priest is also attested in Exod 28:36; 39:30; Lev 8:9; Num 17:23.

50. The use of "pure gold" as a working material also creates an exclusive connection between the Sinai pericope and Chronicles (Exod 25:11, 17, 24, 29, 31, 36, 38–39; 28:14, 22, 36; 30:3; 37:2, 6, 11, 16–17, 22–24, 26; 39:15, 25, 30; 1 Chron 28:17; 2 Chron 3:4; 9:17). No other book of the Hebrew Bible mentions this material.

51. The instruction to make and engrave the golden flower, is contrasted with that related to the two gold-encrusted carnelian stones in Exod 28:9–12. The names of the 12 tribes of Israel according to their order of birth are engraved on these stones. While the name Levi is attested there in third position, Aaron – who at this level of literary development – has already been institutionally separated from the Levites, is thus designated by his own engraving as holy to YHWH. In the same way, then, as in Num 17:23 with the staff of Aaron symbolically flourishing from the tribe of Levi, the engraving of the high priest on the precious stones of the high priestly vestments is to be understood as a gesture emphasizing their superiority.

אֲשֶׁר יַקְדִּישׁוּ בְּנֵי יִשְׂרָאֵל לְכָל־מַתְּנֹת קָדְשֵׁיהֶם	B	guilt the Israelites may incur in consecrating any of their sacred gifts,
וְהָיָה עַל־מִצְחוֹ תָּמִיד לְרָצוֹן לָהֶם לִפְנֵי יְהוָה:	A'	this plate must always be over his forehead, so that they may find favor with the LORD.

The motif of the flower frames the guilt (עון) here, which Aaron apparently has to bear (נשא) on behalf of all those cases in which the Israelites take it upon themselves to offer holy gifts.

The motif of the golden crown with the inscription "holy to YHWH" is further developed in Exodus 29:5–7, where the term "holy crown" (נזר הקדש) is used:

וְשַׂמְתָּ הַמִּצְנֶפֶת עַל־רֹאשׁ וְנָתַתָּ אֶת־נֵזֶר הַקֹּדֶשׁ עַל־ הַמִּצְנָפֶת	v.6	You shall put the turban on his head, and put the holy crown on the turban.

The giving of the crown is supported by a royal act of anointing.[52] This development is then synthesized in Exodus 39:30:

וַיַּעֲשׂוּ אֶת־צִיץ נֵזֶר־הַקֹּדֶשׁ זָהָב טָהוֹר וַיִּכְתְּבוּ עָלָיו מִכְתַּב פִּתּוּחֵי חוֹתָם קֹדֶשׁ לַיהוָה	Then they made the plate of the holy crown of pure gold, and wrote on it an inscription like the engraving of a signet: holiness to the lord.

The motif is then executed in the investiture of Aaron by Moses in Leviticus 8:9.[53]

---

52. The act of anointing is later extended to all priests and has been assigned by Albertz to the last of the priestly revisions for which he especially introduced the signum PB[Salb] ("Ex 28:41* [nur 'du sollst sie salben']; 29:21.36b; 30:26–30; 40:1–16; [vgl. Lev 8:10aβ–11.30]). Cf. Rainer Albertz: *Exodus. Bd. 2: Ex 19–40*. (Zürich: TVZ, 2005), 14.

53. Nihan, *Torah*, 138, is of the opinion that Lev 8:9 does not necessarily presuppose Ex 39:30 MT. However, he also considers Lev 8:9 to be a "conflation of Exod 28:36 (ציץ זהב טהור) with 29:6 (נזר הקדש)." Nihan is, however, sceptical about using the connection as a reason for literary stratification. However, this is not further relevant for the considerations made here.

וישם את־המצנפת על־ראשו וישם על־המצנפת אל־מול פניו את ציץ הזהב נזר הקדש כאשר צוה יהוה את־משה	And he put the turban on his head. Also, on the turban, on its front, he put the golden plate, the holy crown, as the LORD had commanded Moses.

Achenbach has shown that the development of the high priestly crown has to be read against the background of a theocratic revision of the Enneateuch. It must of course also be taken into account that this development does not take place as P[S], but, as H[S] and took place somtime in the second half of the fourth century BCE: "Mit der Verbindung des Stirnblattes und des altisraelitischen Symbols der Königsweihe des Gewählten durch den *nezer*, das Weihdiadem, wird dem Hohenpriester die königliche Würde Israels i. S. eines 'Königreichs der Priester' (Ex 19,6) zugewiesen."[54] In any case, the flower (ציץ) on the crown (נזר) of the priest is in some way derived from the Davidic tradition of a royal diadem. This is apparent, for instance, in Psalm 132:18, where, in the conflict situation between an anonymous Davidic king – called the anointed one – and an equally anonymous enemy, the crown of the anointed one literally flourishes (ציץ), whereas, in contrast, the enemy is dressed in shame.[55] Against this background, the tension of the direct confrontation in 2 Chronicles 26 between king and high priest becomes obvious. In particular, the overwriting of the earlier narrative with the discourse of high priest leadership is expressed in this constellation.[56] In other words: In the presence of the golden diadem

---

54. "By combining the front leaf and the ancient Israelite symbol of consecration of the chosen one with the *nezer*, the diadem, the high priest is given the royal dignity of Israel in the sense of a 'kingdom of priests' (Exod 19:6)." Cf. Reinhard Achenbach, "König, Priester und Prophet. Zur Transformation der Konzepte der Herrschaftslegitimation in Jesaja 61," in *Tora in der Hebräischen Bibel. Studien zur Redaktionsgeschichte und synchronen Logik diachroner Transformationen*, eds. Reinhard Achenbach and Martin Arneth (Wiesbaden: Harrassowitz, 2007), 196–244, 239. A particularly important starting point of the theocratic revisions can be seen in Isa 61, where – according to Achenbach – the royal insignia of the king are transferred to the post-exilic high priest.

55. Cf. here the observations of Reinhard Müller "David und die Lade, Zion und der Gesalbte," in *Psalmen und Chronik*, eds. Friedhelm Hartenstein and Thomas Willi (Tübingen: Mohr Siebeck, 2019), 199–222., 216–219.

56. A similar nuance is attested in the revision of 2Kgs 11:4–16 in 2 Chron 23:1–16, where 2 Chron 23 describes how the priest Jehoiada makes Joash king over Judah. However, before the actual enthronement, a number of cultic regulations are introduced which do not come from the *Vorlage* (cf. vv. 4–8). E.g., the gatekeepers are organized (v. 4 f) and access to the sanctuary is reserved exclusively for priests and Levites on service. The specific regulation for entering the sanctuary is not only unknown to the *Vorlage*, but also not in full congruence with Num 4:20. Whereas in 2 Chron 23:6 it is stated יבוא בית־יהוה כי אם־הכהנים והמשרתים ללוים המה יבאו כי־קדש המה

of the high priest – which I consider to be presupposed – the leprosy mark of Uzziah's forehead unfolds its full effect. It shines (זרח) as a diadem of shame. And even more: the breaking of taboo gets apparent not only symbolically; the engraving on the diadem of the high priest also refers back to v. 18: כי לכהנים בני אהרון המקדשים להקטיר. All of this remains latent in literary terms. However, it is implied on the one hand by the tight-meshed texture of the intertextual references, and on the other hand by the presumable fact that the high priest's figure in this scene simply could not have been imagined otherwise than with the golden flower diadem on his head.[57]

Certainly Zechariah 6:9–14[58] is another horizon of this text, where a similar situation is created by the production of two crowns.[59] While the high priest Yeshua ben Jehozadak, according to 1 Chronicles 5:27–43 a Zadokide, is insigned with a crown (עטרות) there, and it is said of him that he will wear majesty (הור), it is stated in the present text that a second crown is deposed in the temple for a coming Davidide with the "Ehrenbezeichnung צמח."[60]

James C. Vanderkam also pointed out that the golden leaf of the high priest's forehead was part of the implicit world knowledge of the intended addressees of certain texts. Thus he suspects with regard ואל, the Levites in Num 4:20 were forbidden to access the sanctuary; if not abeying, they would even risk punishment of death: ולא־יבאו לראות כבלע את־הקדש ומתו. In addition, specific Leviltical services to the king are established (v. 8). The anointing of the king is carried out in v. 11 where a synoptic comparison brings the chronistic ideology to light:

2 Chron 23:11	2Kgs 11:12
ויוציאו את־בן־המלך ויתנו עליו את־הנזר ואת־העדות וימליכו אתו וימשחהו יהוידע ובניו ויאמרו יחי המלך	ויוצא את־בן־המלך ויתן עליו את־הנזר ואת־העדות וימלכו אתו וימשחהו ויכו־כף ויאמרו יחי המלך

The Chronicler omits the hand clapping of the *Vorlage*, but instead explicates that Jehoiada and his sons were the executors of the anointing. The insignia of authority, including the initial anointing, thus quite explicitly belong to the sovereignty of the priest. 2 Chron 26 is to be read against this background.

57. It is precisely at this point that the text apparently relates to another text for the historical background, showing that the transitions between the perception of reality and the reception of intertexts become fluid at a certain point.

58. On the redactional classification of the text in the Book of Twelve, cf. Jakob Wöhrle. *Die frühen: Sammlungen des Zwölfprophetenbuches Entstehung und Komposition*. (Berlin: de Gruyter, 2006), 340–342.

59. On the question of whether two crowns were made or only one, cf. Wöhrle, *Sammlungen*, 343–345. Wöhrle, in contrast to more recent trends in research, emphazises that there were originally two crowns. After the failure of Zerubbabel, the passages mentioning him were omitted from the text, which resulted into the conflict in number between עטרות (v. 11) and עטרט (v. 14). Wöhrle assigns this ommission to a "Jeschua-Redaktion" (Wöhrle, *Sammlungen*, 345).

60. Wöhrle, *Sammlungen*, 344.

to Zech 6:12 that with the ruler (צמח).⁶¹) mentioned there a significant paranomastic (with metathesis of Mem and Zade) allusion to the forehead of the priest is given. Vanderkam refers specifically to the connection with Exod 28:36–38.

However, as the literary development appears from the perspective of Chronicles, the direction of dependence seems to be rather the other way around. Zecheriah 6:9–14 stands at the beginning of a literary development which – as can be assumed together with Wöhrle – associates Zerubbabel with the honorary title צמח. In contrast to this, the omission of Zerubbabel and the corresponding revaluation of Yeshua by the coronation seems to be the result of a "Jeschua-Redaktion", which already prepares the idea of a kingdom of priests (Exod 19:6). Reinhard Achenbach describes this development in Zecheriah 6 also as theocratic revisions. Other נזר texts also belong to this process of revision (Exod 28:36–38; 29:5–7; 39:30; Lev 8:9). The ideology of these revisions is later reflected in Chronicles in the form of the post-Salomonic decline of the Davidic kingdom. Jeremiah 23:5 and 33:15, of course, also belong to this field of association.

A later reference is attested in Josephus who describes the historically fictitious journey of Alexander to Jerusalem. In his *Antiquities* (X 331) it is told that Alexander inspects Jerusalem from the suburb Sapha. Out of the distance he sees the priests in white robes. The priests' garments are described in detail by Josephus, including the gold-trimmed headband (ἐπὶ τῆς ἔχοντα ἔχοντα τὴν κίδαριν καὶ τὸ χρυσοῦν ἐπ᾽ αὐτῆς κεφαλῆς ᾧ τὸ τοῦ θεοῦ πρῶτος ἐγέγραπτο ἔλασμα), and even the engraving of the name of God is mentioned, too.⁶² It is then stated of Alexander that he alone approaches the high priest (προσελθὼν μόνος) and first prostrates himself before the name (προσεκύνησεν τὸ ὄνομα). Only after this does he salute the high priest (καὶ τὸν ἀρχιερέα πρῶτος ἠσπάσατο). Josephus uses the inscription τό ὄνομα in his narrative as a metonymy. In portraying Alexander's bowing before the name of God, he therefore leaves the material aspect of the flower unmentioned. From this alone it can be deduced that in later times the golden attribution became not only a sign of recognition of the high priest, but also a symbol for the presence of the deity itself. This leads to the subthesis that the במצחו of the Chronicler fulfills a similar (better said: antonymical) function in the same way as Josephus metonyimically uses the phrase προσεκύνησεν τὸ ὄνομα.

---

61. James C. VanderKam: *From Joshua to Caiphas. High Priests after the Exile*. (Minneapolis: Fortress Press, 2004), 34.

62. The production of the headband is narrated in ant. VIII 93. There, it is told that Solomon made only one headband and that this headband still exists till the present day.

At this point it is now sufficiently obvious that 2 Chronicles 26 is about an implicit discourse on leadership. However, it must not be overlooked that in the present text this is not mentioned explicitly. The discourse on leadership is rather cultivated implicitly by four elements: a) priest vs. king; b) anger; c) punitive leprosy; and d) the overemphasis of the forehead. How inevitable this conclusion is, becomes particularly apparent in the second mentioning of the forehead. During the diagnosis by all the priests, the king gets into a pitiful position: he is the only one who cannot see what literally illuminates the army of 81 priests facing him: YHWH has beaten him (נגע). Accordingly, not only the priests are hurrying (בהל) to expel the king from the sanctuary; instead, at the moment of recognition, the king literally flees (דחף).

As a consequence, the sin of the incense offering is severely punished by two penalties (v. 21):

Firstly, Uzziah is infected by leprosy for the rest of his life (מותו עד יום). But secondly, the concomitant impurity also means that he will be cut off (גזר) from the house of YHWH, that is, from the cult. Accordingly, he had to live in a separate house (בית החפשית).[63] Thus, as the progress of the episode shows, he loses his right of residence in the palace and consequently his function as king. There are now two readings:

(1) Against the background of Leviticus 10 it becomes quite clear that Uzziah basically intended a crime worthy of death penalty. The Chronicler, however, could not let Uzziah die, since he was obliged to his *Vorlage* in 2 Kings 15, and at the same time was anxious not to change the sequence of kings and their reigns.[64] But basically his death began with leprosy, since because of this diagnosis, he was not just cut off from his family while alive, but also buried in the open field and not in the graves of kings. Accordingly, his dignity was still denied even after his death. A closer look at Numbers 12:12 also confirms this impression. After Miriam has been punished with leprosy, Aaron begged Moses: "Do not let her be like the stillborn baby that comes forth from its mother's womb with its flesh half consumed!" (בשרו אל-נא תהי כמת אשר בצאתו מרחם ויאכל חצי). The death-like condition of leprosy can hardly be described more clearly than by "stillbirth".

(2) However, a closer look at 2 Kings 15 reveals a completely different reading. The synoptic comparison shows that an incense

---

63. Wilhelms Rudolph: *Chronikbücher*. (Tübingen: Mohr Siebeck, 1955), 284 emphasizes the clear mocking euphemism with his translation "Haus der Freiheit".

64. Cf. Ehud Ben Zvi: "About Time: Observations about the Construction of Time in the Book of Chronicles". In *History, Literature and Theology in the Book of Chronicles* ed. Ehud Ben Zvi (London/Oakville: Equinox, 2006), 144–157.

offering of Uzziah was not even mentioned there. On the contrary, the *people* slaughter (זבח) and burn incense (קטר) on the heights. In contrast to this, the punishment of lifelong leprosy on the king, as mentioned in v. 5, seems extremely draconian. Although Azariah could be buried with his fathers in the city of David without further complications in 2 Kings 15:7, the Chronicler was obviously concerned – supporting Evans[65] – to invent a crime fitting of the punishment. He apparently used the narrative background of Leviticus 10 and Numbers 16 for this offence and adapted it to the intended narrative purpose. Due to the lifelong leprosy, the Chronicler could not recur to the regulation of the seven-day separation (סגר, hif.) from Leviticus 13, but had to use the stronger motif of "cutting off" irrevocably beyond death.[66] By crossing this border beyond life, the sanction of exclusion and the death penalty were transformed to commensurable forms of retribution. Even worse, whereas Korah and his rotting gang, for example, sink into the ground in Numbers 16, Uzziah faces a much more severe punishment: the visualization of guilt in the form of the leprosy mark.

Against this background the strange fact of the double naming of Uzziah (vv. 17–20) comes into view. Its sense is generated against the background of v. 15b, where Uzziah is portrayed as hero. Verses 17–20 on the one hand emphasizes the extent of Uzziah's dramatic fall from heroism, but on the other hand also uses the name עזריהו to mock the king: ויצא שמו עד-למרחוק כי-הפליא להעזר כי חזק. It is stated that Uzziah's name (שמו) spread far and wide (יצא), because he was given help in a miraculous way. Through the possessive suffix (3rd sg. masc.) in ומש the name announcement refers cataphorically to Uzziah in v. 14 and demonstrates once again to every reader that it is the *name* of Uzziah that is in the foreground here. The anadiplosis from v. 15 to v. 16 in form of the verb חזק marks the turning point of the episode and the anathema that begins with the king's pride.[67] The Chronicler thus offers post-factually an aetiology which transfigures the name עזריהו with the infinitive להעזר and the revocation. The mockery is made clear by the fact that Azariah, who is now called Uzziah, is no longer receiving divine help after the attempt of the ille-

---

65. Paul S. Evans, "Let the Crime Fit the Punishment: The Chronicler's Explication of David's 'Sin' in 1 Chronicles 21," in *Chronicling the Chronicler. The Book of Chronicles and early Second Temple Historiography*, ed. Paul S. Evans and Tyler F. Williams, (Winona Lake, Indiana: Eisenbrauns, 2013), 65–80.

66. Beentjes, *Tradition*, 86 even assumes a connection with Lev 16:22 here. However, I cannot see anything but the striking conceptual similarity of sin which is taken away once and for all in both passages.

67. Beentjes, 2 Kronieken, 336 as well as Ibid., *Tradition*, 81 has pointed out that the phrase וכחזקתו is inevitably connected with Rehoboam's abandonment of the Torah (2 Chron 12:1).

gitimate incense offering. It is not without irony that Uzziah finds his antagonist in vv. 16–20 in Azariah of all people, the כהן הראש. The transfer of the sovereignty of the temple, that is, the claim to power over the post-exilic community, is indicated by the permutation of the names of king and priest and is symbolically sealed by the contrast between the mark of leprosy and the implicated diadem of the priest. The consequences for Uzziah are devastating. Already in his lifetime, Jotham his son, took charge. Significantly, however, he is not referred to as king in this interim solution, but as judge in the king's house: ויותם בנו על-בית המלך שופט את-עם הארץ. The motif represents nothing less than a regression into the time of the judges (הם אין מלך בישראל בימים). Thus, in addition to the development of the chronistic theology of retribution, a narrative trait analogous to the time of the judges is taken up. It appears for a brief moment as if there was no longer a king in Judah. Or, to put it otherwise, as if the royal dignity had – at least for the moment – passed to the priest. From now on every generation, even every generation of kings, has to prove itself anew in its relationship to God. However, in contrast to the fiction of the age of judges, the institutional framework cannot be neglected in this narrative. The story continues in the genealogical paradigm according to the *Vorlage*. Unlike the book of Judges, the evaluation of the epoch is therefore no longer carried out by taking into account the behaviour of the people (see, for example, Jdg 2:12-14: יהוה...בישראל ויחר אף יהוה ... ויעזבו את יהוה אלהי אבותם ... בני ישראל את הרע בעיני). Quite the opposite, in Chronicles, the Torah observance of the king alone in the broadest sense, that is, both literal and non-literal, is made the distinctive criterion. From this point of view the overcoming of the disastrous time is understandable: After the death of his father, Jotham becomes king (v. 23) – thus ending the interim of the episode as judge – and immediately does again what is right in the eyes of the Lord (הישר בעיני יהוה [2Chr 27:2]).[68]

Finally, the question arises why the Chronicler has emancipated the priesthood from the Davidic kingship in this indirect way. To be clear: We have seen, that the Chronicler – by overemphasizing the forehead of the king – means what he writes, and he means even more than that. This means that – in terms of Rolf – this is a case of indirectness. The question is: Why did the Chronicler not describe the issue more clearly or directly? Moreover, the question arises why such an important topic is moved to a minor location in Chronicles by its integration into the Uzziah narrative?

From my point of view this is correlated with the importance of

---

[68] Of course, one has to take into account that in the narrative time ("Erzählzeit") no king existed anymore and the priestly option was therefore even closer.

King David and his dynasty for the Chronicler. In hardly any other book of the Old Testament does the Davidic dynasty attain greater significance. Only the Psalter ascribes a similarly extensive significance to David, of course in textual interaction with Chronicles.

The unbroken appreciation for this king is shown by the fact that the Chronicler describes David's comprehensive preparations for the temple extensively (1 Chron 22–29), although David himself did not build it himself. Nevertheless, the Chronicler is not only embarrassed to explain David's failure of building the temple, but in the end, he also has to deal in narrative means with the complete decline of the whole Davidic dynasty. Although a pro-Davidic narrative thread – as it is attested in 1Chr 3; 1Chr 17, 2Chr 13:5 and 2Chr 35:4 – is counteracted by an anti-Davidic narrative thread,[69] the side view on the priesthood remains positively focused throughout. The rule of Judah is always pleasing to God, provided that the royal rule is limited and restricted by the priestly rule.

A hermeneutic key to the understanding of the Chronicler's indirect manner of expression is the moment of cancelability, which, as has been shown at the beginning,[70] is a necessary condition of the Conversational Implicature. Rolf states: "Die Annullierbarkeit ist eines der wichtigsten Merkmale der konversationalen Implikaturen. Das, was lediglich impliziert, nicht aber gesagt worden ist, kann, aufgrund seiner materiellen Ungreifbarkeit, leichter wieder aus dem Verkehr gezogen werden, wenn es denn aus dem Verkehr gezogen werden soll."[71]

In the present case, the writer of the text, who inscribed the anti-royal sentiment, could at any time cancel his implicature. He could do this by taking the position that he did under no circumstances want to elevate the dispute between king and priest to an institutional level – and thus dispute the king's claims to power – by explicitly mentioning the leprous forehead. The writer could, for example, state that he only wanted to name a visible part of the body and that he had constructed an offence appropriate to the punishment of the *Vorlage*. In view of the explosiveness that is caused in discourses on leadership – all the more by the proposal of a non-Davidic option of leadership – the Conversational Implicature thus represents a caution to any messianic aspirations. To what extent this caution was necessary, is evident, of course,

---

69. The first anti-Davidic peak begins already with Rehoboam (cf. 2 Chron 12:14) and then completely culminates in the Jehoram narrative.

70. Cf. page 263 → Cancelability.

71. "Cancellability is one of the most important features of Conversational Implicatures. Something which has only been implied, but has not been said, can be withdrawn from circulation more easily, because of its material non-concreteness, if it should be withdrawn from circulation at all" (Rolf, *Pragmatik*, 27).

from the fact that Chronicles is a reformulation of the history of the Davidic kingship. After all, the Chronicler also portrays David as a second Moses and somehow as a second Aaron, too.[72] For example, in 2 Chronicles 13:5 there is an explicit reference to a salt covenant ברית מלח between YHWH and David and his sons.[73]

The Chronicler cannot hide the conception generated by him in the first place, but must handle it as a narrative burden. At this point the "Putative Kinship"[74] created between the Judean kingship and the Zadokide high priesthood plays a constitutive role in the justification of the priestly claims to power. At the same time, it should also be noted that 2 Chronicles 13:5 is restricted by v. 8, where the reading of the preceding formulation ישראל נתן ממלכה לדויד על-ישראל לעולם כי יהוה אלהי (v. 5) is restricted by the phrase ממלכת יהוה בני דויד (v. 8). The Torah restriction of the Davidic kings by the law of the king (Deut. 17:14–20),[75] which is only enforced in Chronicles, plays the most important role here. In so far, the king is not only subordinated to divine Scripture, but also to the cultic scribes who wrote it. On the whole, the Chronicler creates a dramaturgical caesura after the idyll of Solomon's reign, which responds to the dilemma of the division of the kingdom. Even for the Chronicler, the progressive decline of kingship and the final exile cannot be stopped. Therefore he follows the principle: *Le Dieu règne, mais il ne gouverne pas* from the very beginning.[76] Whereas the act of government could still be taken over by the kings themselves in the time of David and Solomon – well recognizable in the appointment of the priests by David (1 Chron 24) and the anointing of Zadok parallel to the anointing of Solomon (1 Chron 29:22) – this concept of leadership seems to remain in force in later phases, but the government seems to be successively replaced by the priests. However, with regard to the exile, it is also stated of the priests that they impurify the house of God (טמא), participate in the abominations (תעבות) of the nations, and become unfaithful to YHWH (מעל). Nevertheless, the Chronicler is able to implement a positive exile interpretation by integrating Jeremiah. In doing so he obviously

---

72. Note the attribution of David as איש האלהים and the fact that he makes his own מצוה (2 Chron 8:14).

73. This motif is prefigured in Num 18:19, where the covenant of salt serves to supply Aaron and his sons.

74. On the concept of putative kinship between the tribes of Judah and Levi, see the contribution by Achenbach in this volume and Lars Maskow, *Tora in der Chronik*, 257–259, 293–295.

75. The reception of the so-called law of the king is of course a neuralgic point of research. See Maskow, *Tora*, 96–100.

76. The potential of this concept is nowhere else so obvious than in the addition of the edict of Cyrus to Chronicles.

leaves the Davidic option and positions himself ideologically on the side of the observance of the Torah.

The indirect portrayal in 2 Chronicles 26:17–21 indicates that this discourse of leadership could only be conducted in an indirect modality. For it would undoubtedly have provoked harsh opposition from those who longed for hierocratic leadership. In this modality, no matter how clearly the implication appears in 2 Chronicles 26, there was always the opportunity in circumstances of conflict to withdraw to the hierocratic position by claiming that *that* was actually not said.

4. Conclusion

At this point, the result is relatively short compared to the argumentative effort. It can even be summarized in one sentence:

The leprosy erupting on the forehead of King Uzziah in 2 Chron 26 represents, from a pragmatic point of view, a Conversational Implicature that contrastingly evokes the golden headband of the Aaronide high priest and thus disavows or rather transmits royal leadership to the high priest. It should be noted at this point that the priestly claim to power is *not expressed directly, but indirectly*. The whole argumentative effort presented here is necessary to determine what the indirect statement – the Conversational Implicature – of the text consists of. At the same time, this provides a methodological approach to the determination of texttext relations, which can determine connections between two texts and the world knowledge constituted by them, beyond literal or terminological similarities. For the Torah reception of the Chronicler it follows at this point that it seems to be a "Wirklichkeit" in the sense of Hans Blumenberg[77] and that it unfolds highest potential especially at those places where it is not *literally* mentioned. We should bear in mind that this is only one example and that in interpreting the texts we should always be prepared for the appearance of other implicatures, for which a methodology has been offered here for finding and evaluating them.

---

77. Cf. the quotation at the beginning, page 279.

LEVITES OF MEMORY IN CHRONICLES AND SOME CONSIDERATIONS ABOUT HISTORICAL LEVITES IN LATE-PERSIAN YEHUD

Ehud Ben Zvi

1. INTRODUCTION

I was invited to examine the roles that remembering Levites in the context of the world/s of the past conjured by Chronicles had among the literati of Yehud. Certainly, the Levites played an important role in the past world/s conjured by Chronicles. But to what effect? What impact did the references to Levites in Chronicles have in the memory-scape of the literati who read this book as part of a larger core, authoritative repertoire of texts, and why did the Levites of the past, as such and with their diversity, become an important, but complex site of memory?[1]

That said, it is unfeasible to properly address these questions without first dealing with the historical society in which these literati lived. For this reason and given the general context of the workshop and the issues it explores, in what follows I intend to raise a strong note of caution about historical reconstructions that assume (a) an ongoing social struggle about the roles and status of actual Levites *vis à vis* priests in the late Persian period and its close aftermath, (b) the existence of a substantial group of Levites who as such served as agents for the production of texts and memories advancing their case, and (c) the usage of acts of writing, rewriting, editing, and I would

---

1. The approach taken here on matters of social memory is elaborated in e. g., Ehud Ben Zvi, *Social Memory among the Literati of Yehud*, BZAW 509 (Berlin: de Gruyter 2019).

add, reading the relevant texts about the past as key tools used by all in their putative, actual struggle to impose their particular vision on the matter of the roles and status of the Levites in the present of the late Persian Yehudite community and its close aftermath.[2]

Thus, this paper both explores the social roles of imagining and remembering Levites of old among these literati by reading and rereading their Book of Chronicles and also questions widely-agreed assumptions to provide additional lenses to approach the general issue of the Levites in late-Persian (or early Hellenistic) Yehud. This questioning may, in turn, provide an impetus for future reconsiderations of the social roles of remembering past and future Levites in late-Persian Yehud through readings and rereadings of texts other than Chronicles within the authoritative repertoire of these literati.[3]

2. LEVITES OF MEMORY: MATTERS OF BACKGROUND, TEXTS, MEMORIES AND MENTAL LIBRARIES

It is certainly understandable that if one focuses only on texts such as Chronicles or Ezekiel 40–48 (e. g., Ezek 40:44–46; 44:10–15; 48:8–14) or several sections of Numbers,[4] one would think that Levites

---

2. These positions have encountered increased acceptance in the field and were advanced or implicitly assumed by many of my good friends and thoughtful colleagues at the workshop. I assume that these positions will be well represented in this volume. For earlier works that represent or build on this approach, see, e. g., Louis C. Jonker, "Holiness and the Levites: Some Reflections on the Relationship between Chronicles and Pentateuchal Traditions," in *Eigensinn und Entstehung der Hebräischen Bibel. Erhard Blum zum siebzigsten Geburtstag*, ed. Joachim J. Krause, Wolfgang Oswald and Kristin Weingart, FAT 136 (Tübingen: Mohr Siebeck, 2020), 457–74; Louis C. Jonker, "Numbers and Chronicles: False Friends or Close Relatives?," *HeBAI* 8 (2019), 332–77 and the substantial bibliography cited in these works. See also, though from a perspective narrowly focused on the Korahites, Itamar Kislev, "What Happened to the Sons of Korah? The Ongoing Debate Regarding the Status of the Korahites," *JBL* 138 (2019): 497–511. For another, historical approach that construes the Levites as a central group throughout ancient Israel, including the Persian period, see Mark Leuchter, *The Levites and the Boundaries of Israelite Identity* (New York: Oxford Univ. Press, 2017).

3. It goes without saying that these reconsiderations of the social roles of remembering past and future Levites in late-Persian Yehud through readings and rereadings of e. g., Ezek 40:44–46; 44:10–15; 48:8–14 or the relevant sections of Numbers within the context of Numbers or the Pentateuch cannot be carried out within the limits of this paper. It is hoped, however, that the present paper will provide both an impetus for and research questions for subsequent studies on these matters.

4. As it is well known, and unlike the case in Genesis-Leviticus, Levites play important roles in Numbers. On Numbers and its Levites, see, e. g., Christian Frevel, "Ending with the High Priest: The Hierarchy of Priests and Levites in the Book of

were a very hot issue in late-Persian Yehud, and likely that Levites were a strong separate group with agency in the matter of shaping social memory.[5] But these texts never existed alone. They were part of a repertoire of core texts shaping the community that imagined itself shaped around texts, each mutually informing the other.[6] This repertoire constituted a mental library that, as a whole, informed and was constantly informed by their readings of each of these texts. In other words, books or texts for that matter did not exist in a vacuum but carried meaning within and in relation to an eco-system, the mentioned library.[7]

To be sure, this library, as a whole, embodied, reflected, shaped and communicated a comprehensive memory-scape, as most if not all the relevant books conjured images of the past and at times also of the future. Since their imagined, socially-shared, comprehensive image of the past, i. e., their social memory, was not and could never have been informed only by their readings of Chronicles or some sections of other books (e. g. Ezek 40–48) then, for the present purposes, a key question is how they imagined and remembered their Levites, on the grounds of the mentioned mental library.

When one looks at the entire repertoire of the Late Persian/early Hellenistic period in this way, the crucial observation is quite simple: they were rarely mentioned.[8] Moreover, when there are references to them, they tended to concentrate in some books or even sections

Numbers," in *Torah and the Book of Numbers*, ed. Christian Frevel, Thomas Pola and Aaron Schart, FATII 62 (Tübingen: Mohr Siebeck, 2013), 138–63 and bibliography.

5. These texts, of course, are the very reason that the positions about which I want to raise a note of caution are so popular and seemingly so well-supported.

6. It is widely agreed that the Yehudite literati construed Israel (and themselves) as a group centered around tōrâ and that this tōrâ was largely considered to be instantiated in the Pentateuch as they understood it, that is, in a way strongly informed by the rest of their core textual repertoire including, inter alia, the prophetic books, the deuteronomistic historical collection, Chronicles, Proverbs, and thus as a Jerusalem-centered *tōrâ*. On this concept and its eventual spread outside Yehud see Sylvie Honigman and Ehud Ben Zvi, "The Spread of the Ideological Concept of a (Jerusalem-Centred) tōrâ-centred Israel beyond Yehud: Observations and Implications," *HeBAI* 9/4 (2020): 370–97.

7. I explored these issues at some length in my *Social Memory among the Literati of Yehud*, BZAW 509 (Berlin: De Gruyter 2019), and needless to say, the conceptualization of these issues in terms of 'library' owes much to the work of Umberto Ecco.

8. The following observations are in line with, and further develop those advanced in Yigal Levin, "Were there Levites in the Second Temple?", paper read at the EABS Annual Conference, University of Warsaw, 11–14 August 2019; cf. Yigal Levin, "The Role of the Levites in Chronicles: Past, Present, Utopia?," in *Ben Porat Yosef: Studies in the Bible and Its World. Essays in Honor of Joseph Fleishman*, ed. Michael Avioz, Omer Minka and Yael Shemesh, AOAT 458 (Münster: Ugarit Verlag, 2019), 133–46 and note especially the earlier work of Cana Werman; see C. Werman, "Levi and Levites in the Second Temple Period," *DSD* 4 (1997): 211–25.

thereof, thus leaving minimal references to them elsewhere.

If one focuses, for instance, on the Levites that populated the monarchic world as it existed within the memory of these literati, one cannot but notice that, with the exception of Chronicles, the Levites play only marginal roles in the worlds of memory about the monarchic period shaped by the other "historical" books.[9]

In fact, Levites are almost nowhere to be seen in the large imaginary world of memory of the monarchic period conjured by Samuel or Kings. Levites played no memorable role in the larger historical scheme in these books, except for carrying the Ark, and even that not consistently and not necessarily alone.[10] Significantly, when readers vicariously experienced the great event of David bringing the Ark to Jerusalem through their reading of 2 Samuel 6:12–19, their attention was not drawn to Levites as a distinct group that carried a particular role, or to Levites at all, for that matter. One may even argue that as they read the text and imagined themselves partaking in the events

---

9. Levites appear as prominent characters in-the-land, but still pre-monarchic world, evoked by Judges 17–21. This section of Judges was meant to evoke and communicate a need for a king. As Amanda Davis (Bledsoe) put it, the Levites were imagined as cultic specialists and deviants and as the "ultimate example of moral decay" in this section, but just as importantly, also as powerless figures in their own putative society. Thus, unlike the doomed dynasty of Elide priests whose memory confirms the necessity (alongside the problematic character) of kingship in Samuel, the Levites of Judges may only contribute to the construction of a general sense of societal chaos. In any event these Levites are nothing like those of Chronicles (or Numbers, for that matter). See Amanda M. Davis, "Structure, Repetition, and the Characterization of Levites in Judges 17–21," *Glossolalia* 3/2 (2011), 1–16.

10. Levites are explicitly mentioned in 1 Sam 6:15; 2 Sam 15:24 and 1 Kgs 8:4 and all three associate them with carrying the Ark. 1 Kgs 12:31 does not refer to Levites as a group distinct from the priests, but advances the point that all proper priests are from the tribe of Levi. In 2 Sam 15:24–26 the Levites are under the charge of Zadok, the priest. In 1 Kgs 8:4 the text indicates that the priests and the Levites carried the Ark, and thus it balances the impression caused by v. 3 that seems to indicate that only the priests carried it. Josephus in *Ant* 6.15 appears to reflect a tradition in which the Levites are not mentioned in 1 Sam 6:15. The text of 1 Sam 6:19 appears in two different versions (MT and LXX; the latter reading "and the sons of Iechonias were not pleased") and may raise questions relevant to the matters discussed here. One may mention that neither Eleazar the son of Abinadab of Kiriath-jearim who was in charge of the Ark (1 Sam 7:1) nor Uzza and Ahio are anywhere referred to as a Levites (or 'proper' priests for that matter) in Samuel. Moreover, it is likely that none of them was understood by the Chronicler as Levites (or priests). See Gary N. Knoppers, *1 Chronicles 10–29*, AB 12A (New York: Doubleday, 2004), 587, and see 1 Chr 15:13 in the context of the world of Chronicles. It is also worth noting in this context that Obed-Edom the Gititte who takes care of the Ark is not a Levite in 2 Sam 6:10–12, but Chronicles that explicitly refers to him as a Gittite (1 Chr 13:9–14) may have, by implication, conjured an image of him as a Levite (cf. the cumulative weight of 1 Chr 16:5, 38; 26:4, 8, 15). No similar, explicit and cumulative evidence exists regarding Uzza, Ahio, or Eleazar son of Abinadab in Chronicles.

they saw no Levites, as none is mentioned in this text, and can only compare and contrast 2 Samuel 6:12–19 and the world it conjures with that of 1 Chronicles 15:25–16:4 and its world.[11]

As important as historiographical narratives were for shaping constructions of the monarchic past, other texts also contributed much to "sculpting" memories of the monarchic past of long ago in the minds and imagination of the Yehudite literati. Among all these texts, none were more important than the prophetic books. Most significantly, the Levites were mostly unseen in the worlds of memory shaped by most of the prophetic books. In fact, Levites rarely populated these books at all and when they did, they tended to appear in the context of shaping memories about the utopian future, not the past.

To be sure, Levites were important in Ezekiel 40–48, but significantly only in this section of Ezekiel. Ezekiel here (and I along with others would argue in many other respects) was indeed substantially different from all the other prophetic books. Moreover, the absence of Levites from the late monarchic period conjured by Ezekiel 1–39 is at least as remarkable as the condemnatory reference to them in e. g., Ezekiel 44:9–15. Further, a section of Ezekiel (Ezek 40–48) is certainly not weightier than the cumulative weight of the books of Isaiah and Jeremiah in terms of its contribution to the construction of the late monarchic past as a whole or memories about it.[12]

Where are the Levites in the world of imagination communicated by Isaiah? They occurred only once and in the usual second slot to the pair 'priests and levites', that in itself appeared in the context of conjuring memories of a utopian future (see Isa 66:21).

What about the book of Jeremiah, the other central prophetic book

11. On these texts and esp. Chronicles' reconfiguration of the narrative, both at large and in many details, see Knoppers, *1 Chronicles 10–29*, 578–661. It is worth stressing that in Chronicles, the clothing of David *partially* overlaps that of the Levites (and the singers); see 1 Chr 15:27. The *partial* Levitization of David and its corresponding *partial* 'Davidization' of the Levites in Chronicles requires a separate discussion that cannot be carried out here. That said, it is worth stressing that neither process could have led to an image of Levites as "priests" or "priest-like." The opposite holds true, for these processes would have stressed the differences between these relevant groups.

12. The Prophetic Books Collection (i. e., Isaiah-Malachi; hereafter PBC) focuses on the late monarchic period. The collection does not contain a prophetic book putatively associated with, e. g., the days of David, or Solomon or, for that matter, Jehoshaphat, despite the presence of prominent prophetic characters in all these periods as remembered by the very same literati reading the PBC. The generative grammars responsible for this distribution cannot be discussed here. See E. Ben Zvi, "Remembering the Prophets through the Reading and Rereading of a Collection of Prophetic Books in Yehud: Methodological Considerations and Explorations," in *Remembering and Forgetting in Early Second Temple Judah*, ed. Ehud Ben Zvi and Christoph Levin, FAT 85 (Tübingen: Mohr Siebeck, 2012), 17–44.

for shaping and reflecting memories of the late monarchic and early postmonarchic periods and partially covering a period similar to that of Ezekiel? It refers to Levites only in Jeremiah 33:14–22 (18–22), again in the context of conjuring a memory of the utopian future, associated with David. Moreover, the text refers to the Levitical priests, using a language clearly reminiscent of Deuteronomy (cf. Deut 17:9, 18; 18:1; 24:8; 27:9; Josh 3:3) that likely refers to priests who are from the tribe of Levi, rather than Levites as a group separate from the priests (see esp. Jer 33:18).

Within the Twelve Prophetic Books Collection (Hosea-Malachi), none of those directly shaping and conjuring memories about the monarchic period (e. g., Hosea, Amos, Micha, Zephaniah) draw any attention to the presence of Levites as a separate group. In fact, they never refer to Levites at all.

To be sure, Levites are mentioned in two books among those that do not claim to directly portray (and thus ask the readers to imagine themselves as direct observers of) the monarchic past, namely Zechariah and Malachi. The text in Zechariah 12:12–14 conjured among the literati a memory of a future, great mourning that would serve as a prelude to a utopian future (Zech 13:1). The text draws their attention to three main groups of mourners represented in the text by the formula "the family of the house of X," with X standing for, in order of appearance, David, Nathan and Levi (vv. 12–13). The first stands for the clan associated with political leadership (but significantly, the text does not necessarily refer to a king; cf. Zech 14:9, 16, 19, in which YHWH is king), the second, for the clan of prophetic leadership, and the third (v. 13) for the clan of priestly leadership.[13] In other words,

---

13. There is a reference to a fourth group, the family of the Shimeites, although it is not referred to as the family of the house of Shimei. It is very unclear what it might have stood for. One possibility is that the reference was to be construed as enigmatic by the readership and as such contributed to the general atmosphere of the future world of mourning portrayed in the text. To be sure, some have suggested that it refers to a second Levitical family, but only on the grounds that some of the other individual called Shimei in the HB were Levites (see, e. g., Paul Redditt, *Zechariah 9–14*, IECOT [Stuttgart: Kohlhammer; 2012], 112 and bibliography). But one must take into account that all of the Levites called Shimei were only secondary and indeed extremely minor characters. In fact, of all the Shimei mentioned in the HB, the two most memorable were the Saulide Shimei and Shimei son of Gera, both opponents of David. Gonzalez attempts to solve this difficulty by claiming that "the mention of the unimportant Levitical clan of Shimei beside the clans of the houses of David, Nathan, and Levi is probably an indication that it is precisely this Levitical group that developed Zech 9–14" (see Hervé Gonzalez, "Zechariah 9–14 and the Continuation of Zechariah during the Ptolemaic Period," *JHS* 13 [2013], article 9, p. 31 n. 113, https://doi.org/10.5508/jhs.2013.v13.a9. But this is just an ad hoc solution to a problem that arises only because one claims beforehand that the House of Shimei was a reference to a second Levitical clan, which then must be separated from Levi. The list concludes in

again, the text conjured memories of the future, providing hope – even the act of mourning was portrayed as expression of YHWH's favor (see Zech 12:10) – and as it did so, it included a reference to Levites who (most likely) did not stand for a group separate from the priests.

The literati encountered references to Levites (i. e., descendants of Levi) in another book within the Twelve Prophetic Books Collection. Levites are mentioned in Malachi 2:1–9 (vv. 4, 8) and 3:1–4 (v. 3). The first concerns the covenant of Levi and appears in the context of a condemnation of post-monarchic priests. The latter occurs in the context of shaping memories of a utopian future. Although using 'Levi' as a signifier of choice is relevant, the key question for our present endeavor is what was signified by 'Levi.' In both cases, 'Levi' stands for the priests, not the Levites as a group separate from the priests.

In sum, imagining and remembering a monarchic period in which Levites were a powerful group related but separate from priests, stood as an exception to a widely attested tendency whose presence is not only overwhelming but also independent of usual considerations of literary genre.

Since references to Levites in general, and particularly to them as a group separate from the priests, are so rare in the relevant repertoire and memory of the literati, and since they were concentrated in a few particular texts or sections thereof, references to them should *not* be taken as a default, expected feature, but as a rare, 'odd' feature of certain texts. Of course, what is 'odd' always calls for explanation. Moreover, each one of the texts in which the Levites appear prominently in the manner mentioned above requires a distinct explanation since, *inter alia*, meaning depends on the literary context in which the text appears.[14]

This contribution focuses on a prominent case, Chronicles – an entire book in which Levites appear often and frequently as a group separate from the priests. Why would literati whose world of memory of the monarchic period was certainly not suffused with Levites, never mind powerful Levites who are not priests, advance images and evoke memories of a world in which all the above are regularly present?

---

v. 14 with a reference to כל הנשארות המשפחות, i. e., the remaining clans. The text also explicitly refers to the women of each of these groups and to their separate mourning. Any substantial discussion of this text is well beyond the scope of this paper.

14. As per its title the present contribution focuses on Chronicles. That said, the implications of the observation above may have relevance for the study of Levites of memory in other books or sections thereof. Of course, each one of these texts should be studied on their own, with an eye to the world of memory evoked by them and its own specific preferences. As suggested in n. 3, it is hoped that this contributing may end up encouraging the development of such future studies.

3. Constructing Historical Reconstructions of Late-Persian Yehud Levites and Barriers to the Acceptance of the Mentioned Common Positions

Within the world of studies on Chronicles, a somewhat 'traditional' approach to address the questions that conclude the previous section would be to assume that the book constructed a world in which Levites were very present in the monarchic period, because it projected into the past either the current historical circumstances of the society in which it emerged or what a significant group considered to be a different and better society. In other words, from this perspective, it projected a society in which the Levites are a central group. In the first case, the book would be directly mimetic of the present and in the second, it would be a testimony to a desire for change that was accepted and integrated into the larger authoritative repertoire of the literati and their mental 'library.' Both these options require, in one way or another, that the Levites be a powerful group in Late-Persian Yehud. If the Levites were indeed the powerful, historical group described by many scholars (see Introduction) then it would be relatively easy to write the rest of this essay. But in what follows I will argue that it is difficult to make the case that the Levites were indeed such a historically powerful group and thus that a substantially different approach is required. But first things first, why is it so hard to make that case?

For one it is difficult to make the case that the Levites were such a powerful group among these Yehudite literati (or society at large), when the authoritative texts of the literati of the time drew so little attention to them in images of the monarchic past, or the utopian future, and for the most part are completely silent about them in the present *from an overall perspective*.[15]

15. To be sure, theoretically one might argue that there existed at the time multiple, separate groups of literati in Yehud and that each had its own authoritative repertoire and that these repertoires, in turn, contributed to the creation and maintenance of social and ideological boundaries among them. Besides the methodological concerns raised by any approach that keeps constructing separate historical communities for a 'different' book (or section thereof, or even proposed redactional level), there exists the very basic problem of the small number of literati in Yehud, their likely shared socialization/education as literati, and the very integrative, multivocal character of the various works in their authoritative repertoire. This integrative, multivocal character is not incidentally most prominent in Chronicles, and most relevant to the present purposes since it is abundantly attested on matters of Levites and priests. Chronicles cannot be pinned down as pro-priestly or pro-levitical but as a multivocal, multi-per-

Second, there is an understandable tendency among scholars today to associate the development of texts shaping social memory with relatively powerful groups struggling with each other, writing and reading these texts as important tools in their struggles, either as an attempt to socialize the other into the 'proper' way or, and more often, as tools to 'preach to the choir' which is a way to socialize the in-group into particular ways of thinking, countering the possibility of deviance, and as important tools in cultural hegemony battles.

The reasons for this tendency are not difficult to grasp: we are all children of our times and we are all aware of multiple such cases in the last two centuries, especially in Europe. In all these cases, memory-shaping agents on opposing sides worked hard to construe each other as a dangerous enemy Other. Most significantly, these memory agents had powerful social, cultural and political structures supporting them, such as the nationalizing states of this period, or massive political movements battling for control of, or at least increased social, political and cultural power within a particular state, or liberation movements.

But the literati reading, producing, and re-producing these texts were a really small group in the late Persian Yehud, in and around Jerusalem. This group of highly sophisticated writers (and readers) were most likely socialized together and in a similar way, despite all the personal differences one might imagine. Moreover, this group did not have any important political power, nor could they have been supported by any internal group with significant political power. Small groups with no political power and no expectation to achieve it under normal circumstances, may and usually do find ways to resist imperial attempts at hegemonic power, but they tend to use their socially shared memory to emphasize social cohesion, to facilitate the group's social reproduction. They tend to avoid actual, long-standing divisive struggles that relate to their present, unlike large, powerful groups engaged in struggles with others.

Further and directly related to the Yehudite literati and their sub-altern society, why should we assume that among people for whom authoritative texts per se did not play a normative role in the establishment and policing of prescribed or actual behaviour, would anyone consider as their most effective way to accomplish, practical, internal change to write, re-write, read and re-read texts, and in our case, just a few of them, most of which are not even self-standing.

Third, there is the cumulative evidence from later periods in Judah.

---

spectival, and integrative book on these matters. See below for the social-anthropological background underlying these features. On Chronicles as neither pro-priestly nor pro-levitical see notes 34 and 35 below.

The authoritative texts of the literati of late-Persian Yehud are not the only ones to draw very little attention to Levites and be silent about them in the present of the community *from an overall perspective*. Later textual corpora from the Late Second Temple as different as Sirach, 1 and 2 Maccabees, Philo, Josephus and the Dead Sea Scrolls also fail to provide evidence for the Levites as the kind of powerful, independent group in tension with the priests that scholars have proposed existed in late-Persian Yehud. Leaving aside Ezra-Nehemiah,[16] the Levites *as a separate group* in the Jerusalemite cult play no role in Sirach,[17] nor do they later in 1–2 Maccabees. Moreover, actual Levites populating the historical present of the Late Second Temple are difficult to find in Philo, Josephus and the Dead Sea Scrolls (hereafter DSS), despite the fact that the Levites are mentioned in these corpora in various ways in reference to constructions of pre-monarchic and monarchic pasts and, in some texts from DSS, also in reference to future situations.

In fact, more than two decades ago, Cana Werman proposed that the Aramaic Levi Document (hereafter ALD), and several other texts of the Late Second Temple period attempted in their own ways to address and respond to the problem that the scarcity of Levites in their own times created for their own imaginaries.[18]

In other words, scholars who maintain that there was a very substantial, and powerful group of Levites engaged in an ongoing struggle with the priests of late-Persian period Yehud (or early Helle-

---

16. There exist considerable questions about whether Ezra-Nehemiah provides a historically reliable image for Yehud in the Persian period, and if so, in relation to which selected issues and portrayals that may be the case. For one, the lack of any reference to the prominent presence, and from an administrative and political perspective key role of Ramat Raḥel in Yehud raises poignant questions about writing history in the form of a paraphrasis of the book. Whether the image projected by this book is a reliable historical guide for the actual roles and positions and even the relative number of Levites in the Persian period is highly debatable. The cumulative weight of the other sources – see below – raises significant doubts on the matter. To be sure, none of this means that the voice embodied in Ezra-Nehemiah is not important in terms of memories about the Persian period in Hellenistic times (i. e., the likely time in which Ezra-Nehemiah emerged). Moreover, Ezra-Nehemiah clearly represents another 'odd' book, on account of its construction of the Levites, and as widely known, on account of a large number of other matters. Again, 'odd' books require explanations. Needless to say, any exploration of possible answers requires a separate discussion that cannot be carried out in this paper. For my own approach to some of the oddities of this book, though not those associated its portrayal of the Levites, see E. Ben Zvi and S. Honigman, "Remembering Three Nehemiahs in Late Second Temple Times: Patterns and Trajectories in Memory Shaping," *JHS* 18 (2018), article 10, https://doi.org/10.5508/jhs.2018.v18.a10.

17. Sir. 45:6 refers to Aaron, and Moses his brother as a "son of Levi." Levi, Levites and the like are not mentioned anywhere else in the book.

18. See Werman, "Levi and Levites."

nistic) have to deal not only with the lack of clear evidence for their existence in this period, but also need to propose an explanation for the dramatic discontinuity between this period, as they construe it, and the later Second Temple era, from Sirach on.

In contrast, not only is the position advanced here of a basic continuity between these two periods on this matter easier to maintain, but also, as I will argue below, in both cases uneasiness about the scarcity of Levites in the present led to a discursive, ideological and memory need to address through socially shared memories about the past and the future, so as to attenuate some tensions within the imaginary of the group.

For the purposes of the later argument, it is worth dwelling – even if briefly – on the Levites populating the works of Philo and Josephus. The former, seldom writes about them in his large oeuvre, but when he does, he often mentions Levites in the context of his reconfigurations and recontextualizations of some Pentateuchal themes.[19] These themes are, for the most part, the violent actions taken by Levites in the golden calf episode which, not incidentally Philo relates to that of Phineas (e. g., *Spec.* 3.126–27; cf. *Spec.* 1.79),[20] the Korah rebellion and the confirmation of the primacy of the priestly line in its aftermath (e. g., *Moses* 2.174–79, 276–87), and the Levitical cities and at times, along with it the general characterization of Levites as substitutes for the first-born and landless (e. g. *Sacr.* 118, 127–30; *Spec.* 1.157–58, and which Philo also links to the golden calf episode). There is, however, one brief note in Philo's oeuvre that bears a different tone, namely the 'operational' portrayal of the tasks of the Levites in *Spec.* 1.156. To be sure, the question of whether Philo's portrayal of the Levites in *Spec.* 1.156 may be accepted as reliable evidence for the roles of the Levites at the Jerusalem temple during Philo's days remains an open question, but whatever that case may be, the depiction of the Levites's roles there is worth noticing. The relevant text reads:

> After bestowing these great sources of revenue on the priests, he did not ignore those of the second rank either, namely the temple attendants. Some of these are stationed at the doors as gatekeepers at the very entrances, some within in front of the sanctuary to prevent any unlawful person from setting foot thereon, either intentionally or unintentionally. Some patrol around it turn by turn in relays by appointment night and

---

19. For a summary listing of the references to Levi and Levites in Philo and a brief discussion of the way in which they are both informed by the relevant Pentateuchal texts and advance a meaning of their own, see the famous index by J. W. Earp in F. H. Colson, *Philo vol. X*, LCL 379 (Cambridge: Harvard University Press, 1962 – reprint. 1991), 365–70.

20. Cf. David Lincicum, "Philo on Phinehas and the Levites: Observing an Exegetical Connection," *BBR* 21 (2011): 43–50.

day, keeping watch and guard at both seasons. Others sweep the porticoes and the open court, convey away the refuse and ensure cleanliness (*Spec*. 1.156; translation by F. H. Colson; *Philo VII*; LCL 320).

This text does indeed refer to a common feature in many characterizations of the Levites as gatekeepers, but it is particularly interesting that it does not refer to Levites as singers, which is the other common feature attributed to them (see below).

As for Josephus' *Antiquities*, despite the many references to Levites in and of earlier times,[21] when it comes to the Levites close to his own time,[22] he has almost nothing to say, except that they were singers of hymns (see *Ant*. 20.216–18) and that on an occasion reported here, they persuaded the king (Agrippa II) to allow them to wear linen garments, like the priests, and to learn certain hymns. Josephus opposed these 'novelties.' This event, if it happened as it is depicted, is most likely to be understood as part and parcel of the tense relations between Agrippa II, who served as a kind of (Roman-appointed) temple supervisor with the power to appoint and remove high priests, and the Jerusalemite priests and local leadership.

A final observation concerning these matters, within the incredible variegated corpora of literature from the late Second Temple, the relation between the priests and Levites is consistently framed as complementary, with the priests in the higher hierarchical position, whether projected into the past, the future or into a normative textual performance of the present that should exist, (see, e. g., 1QS 2.19–23;[23] 1QWar 7:9–18, the imaginary of the Temple Scroll; CD 14:3–6; Philo's cited text, the normative value attached to memories of the confirmation of the role of the priests after Korah's rebellion). Levites may be present or absent in hierarchical constructions of society, but priests are always present (cf. 1QS 2.19–23 and 1QS6.3–9). Finally, Levi, the ancestor, is, at times, lionized, but mainly as the ancestor

21. Josephus' Levites of old fulfill multiple roles and are certainly significant. On these Levites of old, see esp. Christopher T. Begg, "The Levites in Josephus," *HUCA* 75 (2004): 1–22.

22. One should also note Josephus' account of the establishment of Onias IV's temple at Leontopolis, which is earlier than his period, but still in the late Second Temple period. As one would anticipate, in a report shaping memories about the establishment of a Temple, both priests and levites are mentioned (see *Ant* 13.63–73; and cf. other images of temple establishment in e. g., the Temple Scroll, in which both priests and levites play complementary roles).

23. Which reads "The priests shall enter in order foremost, one behind the other, according to their spirits. And the levites shall enter after them. In third place all the people shall enter in order, one after another, in thousands, hundreds, fifties and tens, so that each Israelite may know his standing in God's Community in conformity with an eternal plan. And no-one shall move down from his rank nor move up from the place of his lot."

of the priestly line, not as a group separate and engaged in severe struggle against the priests.[24]

In sum, the evidence from the late Second Temple does not allow us to construe the Levites as a powerful, substantial group like that proposed by many scholars for late-Persian Yehud, nor does it provide any comparative evidence for the kind of struggle in which these Levites engaged according to these proposals. The latter is particularly noteworthy, because the social and historical circumstances of the late Second Temple, unlike those in late-Persian (and early Hellenistic) Yehud supplied a fertile ground for social and ideological struggles, sectarian battles and the like.

To be sure, none of the above means that there were no Levites at all in these periods. To begin with, levites as singers in the Late Second Temple period appear, even if only once in Josephus (*Ant.* 20.216–18). Psalms seems to support their role as singers and performers (see multiple references to the Qorahites and the Asaphites),[25] and Levites were remembered as singers of an earlier period multiple times in the Mishna.[26] All this suggests that the association between temple singers and Levites in Chronicles was likely to reflect social reality (1 Chr 9:33; 15:19; 16:4–5; 2 Chr 20:19). Perhaps, the same may hold true for the gatekeepers (cf. 1 Chr 9:17–28; and see Philo Spec. 1.156). It is conceivable that actual singers, and likely gatekeepers and perhaps some comparable figures (see 1 Chr 9:25–29) already in Yehud ended up being identified as Levites and given genealogies that construed them as close as possible to the lineage of the person who embodied the temple and its service, Aaron, without being included in it (notice the clear disjunction at the beginning of 1 Chr 9:30).

To be sure, singers were directly responsible for the public performance of (authoritative) texts, had to 'know' them,[27] and contributed to

---

24. E.g., Philo writes "while Reuben is the firstborn of Jacob, Levi is the firstborn of Israel...the fountain of that devout contemplation of the only wise being, on which Israel's rank is based, is the habit of service to God, and this service is symbolized by Levi" (*Sacr.* 119–120). Needless to say, Aaron is explicitly referred to as Aaron the Levite (*Worse*, 135). Comparable processes of memory-shaping and characterization of the great priestly ancestors are evident in texts as different from Philo, such as *ALD* (Aramaic Levi Document), *The Visions of Amram*, and the *Testament of Qahat*.

25. See Pss 42; 44–49; 84–85; 87–88 (cf. 2 Chr 20:19) for the former; and Pss 73–83 (cf. 1 Chr 15:17–19; 16; 25:1–6; 2 Chr 19:30; 35:15) for the latter. The Qorahites are also explicitly singled out as gatekeepers in 1 Chr 9:19; 26:1. See below.

26. See, e. g., m. Tamid 7.4; Pesaḥ 5.7; Bik. 3.4; Sukkah 5.4; Mid. 2.5.

27. There is no reason to assume that all the literati had to be priests, or Levites, or for that matter, that they had to be one of these two, even if the literati were directly or indirectly supported by the temple. This being so, it is possible, even likely that some of the singers might well have been among the literati, but levites as such were

the 'proper' performance of the cult. Gatekeepers might have constituted the only 'force' that was 'in the hands' of the priests and the temple as an institution. That said, these singers and gatekeepers were neither as influential and certainly not as *memorable* as the priests on the whole, but also and more importantly not as the Levites who were closely associated with the priests in the worlds of memory about monarchic times shaped by Chronicles.[28] In fact, one might argue that Chronicles is somewhat comparable to Josephus, since it expands significantly on a group that was so memorable in the past, but relatively marginal and certainly marginal as a group in relation to the priests in their respective present situations. That said, two major and very substantial differences must be kept in mind. First, Chronicles still talks proportionally much more about Levites of the monarchic period than Josephus, and second, Josephus and his world of knowledge and that of his readers was influenced by the very existence of Chronicles and its construction of monarchic Israel. Chronicles, of course, did not have Chronicles to rely upon, but texts about monarchic Israel such as Samuel-Kings and the prophetic books and none of them constructed the monarchic period in that manner. This being so, why did Chronicles construe the Levites as it did?

4. Exploring a Different Approach

The previous section raises the necessity of a new approach for addressing the last and related questions. In what follows I would like to explore one such approach, one whose starting points or assumptions include:

(a) a guiding concept of a shared, ongoing mental library, alongside a shared, ongoing world of knowledge/encyclopedic knowledge, and of a shared ongoing memory-scape and social mindscape among the literati in which Chronicles emerged;[29]

not literati any more than priests as such were.

28. Contrast this with Ezra-Nehemiah which, as required by its basic story, conveys images of a restoration. Of course, as all restoration stories, it evokes and reshapes the past. Thus, Ezra-Nehemiah carries a voice that is evocative of that of the Chronicler, while at the same time overturning some important positions communicated by Chronicles. To some extent, one may argue that Ezra-Nehemiah appropriates (or at least attempts to appropriate) and reconfigures (or at least attempts to reconfigure) Chronicles. These matters require a separate discussion.

29. The underlying assumption implied here is that the Pentateuchal collection, the Deuteronomistic Historical Collection, the Prophetic Books Collection, most of the Psalms and Proverbs and a few other books that were eventually included in the Hebrew Bible (e. g., Lamentations, Ruth, but not e. g., Esther, Daniel) serve collectively as an *approximately representative* of the general authoritative repertoire of the literati in the late Persian-early Hellenistic Yehud and as such, that they may be used, from a *bird's-eye* view perspective, to construct a representative approximation to the

(b) a historical reconstruction in which the literati tended to focus not on their manifested present world when reading, producing and re-producing their authority but mainly on worlds of imagination about their past and future. And that this was done as a way to not only support hope, and social cohesion and reproduction in the present, but also for exploring their various ideas about social order, the past, theological/ideological core matters, and in which fluidity and diversity of constructions, often in logical tension among each other, easily co-ex-

mental, authoritative library of those few literati who read and reread, copied and edited, who likely read to others (cf. 2 Chr 17:7–9) these texts, and who ideologically construed their "Israel" and themselves as a text/*tōrâ*-centered community.

It is worth stressing that within the ideological world of these literati *tōrâ* stood for *their* own, Jerusalem/Jerusalem temple-centered, understanding/social construction of divine *tōrâ*. Given that the literati imagined themselves as a group constituted around authoritative written texts, a cultural, systemic need emerged among them for the presence of a strongly Jerusalem/Jerusalem temple-centered (and thus, David-centered, to an extent) authoritative textual repertoire to inform and shape the understanding of core texts such as those included in the Pentateuch which were not textually inscribed as Jerusalem/Jerusalem-centred texts, because they emerged in collaboration with Samarians and were shared with them. Most of the non-Pentateuchal book in the Yehudite authoritative repertoire mentioned above, including obviously Chronicles, served very well these purposes. To put it differently, within a self-construed text-centered, Jerusalem temple-centered community, the presence of a shared text required a non-shareable reading of it, and thus required the existence of a substantial authoritative repertoire to reflect, generate, support, and make "natural" such un-shareable reading. In other words, historians dealing with the world of thought and literature of these literati stand before an outstanding example of a "mental library" and of the systemic roles that such a "library" may play, at least in a particular group. It goes without saying that the authoritative, textual repertoire of these late Persian/early Hellenistic Yehudite literati may have included some books to which contemporary historians have no access. But given that (a) the books and collections mentioned at the beginning of this note existed among the literati of the late Persian/early Hellenistic period, in some textual form or forms more-or-less similar to those historians have access, (b) the small number of literati in Yehud, their shared socialization, the scarcity of resources necessary for developing and maintaining the high literacy necessary to produce and re-produce both the mentioned corpus and the literati themselves, and (c) the already existing, very substantial number of authoritative books along with both their wide variety and impressive multivocality, which are even more remarkable given the small number of literati and the scarce resources in Yehud, it is very *unlikely* that (d) there existed among these literati an even larger, additional, completely unattested, but highly complex, corpus of authoritative texts that was so *drastically different* from the one mentioned above to the point of making the latter completely unrepresentative even as an approximation to the mental library of the said literati. For a more substantial discussion of these matters and additional arguments in favor of the above conclusion see, e. g., E. Ben Zvi, *Social Memory Among the Literati of Yehud*, passim and previous literature.

Needless to say, the social, political, cultural, economic, demographic (and so on) situation in late Second Temple period Judah was extremely different from that of the poor and marginal Yehud of the Persian/early Hellenistic, and simplistic comparisons between the two periods should be avoided.

isted, because they had no 'operative' applications in the present, except to favor and perform social, horizontal cohesion;

(c) a historical reconstruction in which (i) there were few Levites, (ii) Levites were neither among the central or powerful groups, nor were engaged in an ongoing confrontation with the priests, and (iii) the most severe, practical/ this worldly challenges to 'proper' order were far more likely to come via interventions of political authorities outside the group, authorities that were unlikely to be swayed by texts they could not read (cf. *Ant.* 11.297–301).[30]

The default position within this approach is that when substantial references to Levites occur in a book (or section thereof) within that repertoire and mental library, one has to explain why they appear in this one, unlike all the others. Or phrased slightly differently, why did Levites populate the world of imagination and memory evoked through reading this book (or section thereof) unlike the others? Within these parameters, the first research question related to our topic would be: why do Levites not only populate the monarchic world shaped by Chronicles, but are widely-found inhabitants who play important roles in the book, unlike in the other books that shaped images of that period among the literati?

By looking into the difference that the inclusion of Chronicles in the mentioned library made to the literati's memory-scape on this matter, we may begin to consider which issues this difference was meant to address. Moreover, since Chronicles rarely does only one 'thing,' it is important to investigate what references to Levites in

---

30. The replacement of the top-leader of a sub-altern group by the dominant one constitutes one of the most impactful challenges to 'proper' order from a sub-altern perspective. Moreover, the challenge becomes much more problematic when the sub-altern sees itself as organized around a cultic/religious central institution, in which case the replacement not only affects 'ordinary' aspects of the life of the group, but also interferes with its ability to carry out properly the kind of cultic activities deemed necessary for the proper maintenance of the cosmos, in addition to the very existence of the group. Inner struggle leading to foreign intervention in the leadership in the temple was construed and remembered as an ominous danger for Judah and its Jerusalemite temple during the Second Temple period. The appointment of the Jerusalem High Priest by a foreign king, of course, remained a problem for the legitimacy of the Maccabean priests, which was dealt with in various ways that cannot be discussed here. It is worth noting that Ezra was not imagined or remembered as a High Priest in Ezra-Nehemiah for this reason, despite being depicted as the most pious, and prominent priest, and despite its extended, legitimizing genealogy (Ezra 7:2–5). The reason for this approach to remembering Ezra is, likely, that construing him as High Priest would have raised an indirect potential implication of a royal Persian appointment. In contrast in 1 Esd 9:39, 40, 49, Ezra is referred to as the High Priest. This shift serves as a testimony for the underlying changes in historical and discursive circumstances. These matters, however, require a separate discussion.

Chronicles did help the literati to explore, and how these matters and references may relate to other generative grammars of memory at work in the book. For obvious reasons, it is impossible to address all these issues in full in a single chapter, but a few, significant observations can be advanced.

Before doing so, I want to make clear that in what follows, I will not be proposing sufficient and necessary causes. Such proposals raise too many conceptual questions and evoke the dangerous phantom of historical determinism. Instead, I will focus on factors that facilitated the construction of the Levites in the world shaped by Chronicles and seem to be at work in various forms in Chronicles as a whole, both in relation and not in relation to matters of Levites. This is because potential facilitating factors that are proposed only as an *ad hoc* response to a single issue (in this case, the presence of so many references to Levites) are by definition problematic.

The most important facilitating factor, in my opinion, is the widespread tendency in Chronicles to contribute to a 'normalization' of social memory as it concerns the monarchic period. By this I am referring to the tendency of Chronicles to edge memories of the monarchic period towards better alignment with expectations raised by, and within the world of knowledge and social mindscape of the literati among whom the book emerged. Thus, for instance, when the literati imagined the monarchic past of Judah through their reading of Kings, they failed to see individual prophets prophesying in the kingdom between the establishment of the temple and the period of Hezekiah. Moreover, when they were transported to their monarchic period of memory through readings of the prophetic books, the same thing happened. Chronicles, as is well-known, 'normalized' matters by populating this lengthy period within the monarchic era with memorable prophets. In other words, it edged the comprehensive social memory of the literati towards a closer alignment with expectations.[31]

Similarly, the world conjured by reading Kings was not that deuteronomistic,[32] or, as was important by that time, Pentateuchal. Chronicles edged these memories towards normalization. Likewise, by drawing attention away from the misdeeds and sins of David, Chronicles contributed to a construction of the 'builder' of the temple that

---

31. I elaborated on these matters in my "Chronicles and its Reshaping of Memories of Monarchic Period Prophets: Some Observations," in *Prophets, Prophecy, and Ancient Israelite Historiography*, ed. Mark J. Boda and Lissa M. Wray Beal (Winona Lake, Ind.: Eisenbrauns, 2013), 167–88.

32. Cf., e. g., Gary N. Knoppers, "The Relationship of the Deuteronomistic History to Chronicles: Was the Chronicler a Deuteronomist?," in *Congress Volume. Helsinki 2010*, VTSup 148, ed. Martti Nissinen (Leiden: Brill, 2012), 307–41.

is more aligned with common expectations of such builders.[33] Examples of this tendency in Chronicles, large and small, may be multiplied (e. g., 1 Chr 18:17 and cf. 2 Sam 8:18). Although Chronicles does not construe a world as it 'should have been,' it edges social memory to imagine and remember things in terms more consistent with expectations generated by the world of knowledge and the social mindscape of the literati.

Directly pertinent to our case, the worlds of imagination about the monarchic past evoked by Samuel and Kings and the prophetic books could not but raise a nagging question about the Levites among the literati. Levites played important roles in what they thought to be the foundational period (see esp. Numbers) and Levites as separate from, but alongside priests, are to play roles in the future (see esp. Isa 66:21; and cf. Ezek 40–48). They may have been able to 'live with' the scarcity of Levites in their own historical situation; after all, they had no alternative. But what about Levites in their ideal monarchic period, especially during the foundational time of the temple, i. e., the Davidic-Solomonic period? What about their remembered times of restoration, such as those associated with Jehoshaphat, Joash, Hezekiah and Josiah? Or what about the regulations by David that complemented Moses' *tōrâ*, and which together set the 'proper temple rules' for all times (2 Chr 23:18)? Or the majestic and most memorable (Davidic) performance of bringing the Ark up to Jerusalem?

When late-Persian, Yehudite literati engaged in vicarious time-travel and experienced all these crucial events, all they knew would have led them to expect to see Levites, in fact many of them, alongside priests. Chronicles 'normalizes' social memory by fulfilling their expectations. In all these cases, Levites appear and play significant roles in Chronicles.[34]

Of course, as in all other instances of 'normalization,' Chronicles asked the readers to construe a world with its own flavours. In the case of the Levites, Chronicles, as demonstrated more than twenty years ago by Gary N. Knoppers,[35] has its own construction of the roles of the Levites, which is distinct from those of all other books and texts within the authoritative repertoire of the literati, including, e. g., Deuteronomy, the relevant portions of Numbers, the relevant portions

---

33. Cf. with the construction of Solomon, the builder of the temple in Kings, and notice that his 'unfaithful' actions as portrayed 1 Kgs 11 were set well after he built the temple, when he was old and his abilities were severely diminished.

34. See, e. g., 2 Chr 4; 7:6; 8:14–15; 17:8; 19:8, 11; 23–24; 29–31; 34.

35. Gary N. Knoppers, "Hierodules, Priests, or Janitors? The Levites in Chronicles and the History of the Israelite Priesthood," *JBL* 118 (1999): 49–72.

of Ezekiel.[36] As such, Chronicles contributed, here and elsewhere, to a communal imagination and a shared memory of the monarchic period among the literati that was strongly characterized by multivocality, fuzziness and acceptance of various, seemingly contradictory images. The mentioned multivocality contributed to the richness of their discourse and served them well to explore ideas through multiple perspectives, scenarios and partial memories. Significantly, the general socio-cultural tendency towards multivocality, works well with (intellectual) groups devoid of existential anxiety and that, due to their (sub-altern) social location, tend to involve themselves in shaping worlds of imagination concerning the past (and future), rather than practically exercising much political agency.[37] The very scarcity of Levites in the present, beyond likely singers and perhaps gatekeepers, facilitated acts of imagining them in the past (or future).

The very fact that Chronicles mentions Levites far more than any other book in the late-Yehudite (or early Hellenistic) repertoire was facilitated by another indisputable factor: namely the centrality of the Temple, and of human performances at the temple in Chronicles.

That said, although time travelling to the world of Chronicles indeed meant meeting Levites far more often than mentally travelling to the world portrayed in any other book of the literati's repertoire, it also meant meeting many more priests. Actually, priests and Levites served in Chronicles as a most common type for the "Complementary Other." Priests and Levites appear as separate, but complementary groups numerous times in the main historical narrative (e. g., 2 Chr 7:6; 13:10; 17:7–9; 19:8; 23:4–8; 29; 31:4, 9, 17–19; 35:2–3). Neither priests alone nor Levites alone could carry out the service of

---

36. Of course, there is a lengthy history of scholarship that attempts to separate the relevant texts in Chronicles into distinct layers and redactions, each shaped to be more logically consistent with assumed pro-priestly or pro-levitical groups and more consistent with other texts. For a discussion, in addition to Knoppers, "Hierodules," see, e. g., Matthew Lynch, *Monotheism and Institutions in the Book of Chronicles*, FATII 64 (Tübingen: Mohr Siebeck, 2014), 140–48. I have argued often and extensively against the tendency to first create multiple layers and sources so as to have univocal texts, and then construct an historical group with a consistent voice (and a coherent inner-logic, in our terms) to whom one may assign authorial agency, or vice versa. The fact is that all the "biblical" texts, and prominently among them, Chronicles, are multivocal and sustain inner (logical) tensions, and often stand in tension with other books within the same repertoire. From a historical perspective focused on how the community read these books, these are key features of these books, whatever forerunners they might or might not have had. In addition, the omnipresence of these features in this repertoire strongly suggests that there existed a strong generative grammar that preferred books with such features.

37. Cf. the Seleucid period, 'Babylonian' repertoire; the sages responsible for the Mishna.

the Temple. But complementarity does not mean a lack of hierarchy. Chronicles clearly conveys a sense of hierarchy between the two (e. g., 1 Chr 16:39–40; 26:18 and esp. 1 Chr 23:28).[38]

Significantly, although Chronicles resorts here and there to the notional concept of a "Proximate Other,"[39] only the "Complementary Other" is ubiquitous in this work,[40] which is only a reflection of the value attached to social cohesion (see above).

As hinted to above, the very concept of complementarity went hand in hand in Chronicles – and in the general social mindscape of the literati – with a strong acceptance of social hierarchies and the construction of their maintenance as a key structuring, ordering factor in the world. In fact, piety in this world included accepting the structuring order and maintaining it.[41] Particularly in light of the literati's knowledge of the revolt of Korah, the Levite, and Dathan and Abiram and On, son of Peleth, against Moses and Aaron (Num 16), it is worth keeping in mind that the Levites populating so much of the world of

---

38. There has been some debate on the meaning of 1 Chr 23:28 (אהרן לעבדת בית יהוה על החצרות ועל הלשכות ועל טהרת לכל קדש ומעשה עבדת בית העלהים כי מעמדם ליד בני) which is a key-text on this issue, and particularly on the meaning of ליד within the context of Chronicles. The most similar instance of its use here in this book is in 1 Chr 18:17 (הראשנים ליד המלך ובניהו בן יהוידע על הכרתי והפלתי ובני דויד) and here, as in 1 Chr 23:28, whether one translates X ליד "at the side of X" or not, the clear connotation is X is hierarchically higher than to the other individual or groups mentioned in this context.

39. See my forthcoming contributions to *About Edom and Idumea in the Persian Period*: *Recent Research and Approaches from Archaeology, Hebrew Bible Studies and Ancient Near East Studies*, eds. Benedikt Hensel, Ehud Ben Zvi, and Diana V. Edelman. WANEM (London: Equinox, forth. 2022).

40. For instance, in Chronicles, kings and officers and even the people are often portrayed as working together in harmony and existing in complementarity, at times with negative outcomes, but still complementarity. According to Sara Japhet, this ubiquitous feature of the historical narratives in Chronicles might be understood in terms of a 'democratizing' trend. See S. Japhet, *The Ideology of the Book of Chronicles and its Place in Biblical Thought*, 2nd rev. ed., BEATAJ 9 (Frankfurt am Main/New York: P. Lang, 1997), 417–28. It seems to me that complementary within hierarchy (see also below) expresses more precisely the tendency (and generative grammar for the shaping of narratives and social memories) at work in Chronicles.

41. Thus, for instance, a pious priest such as Zechariah, the son of Jehoiada, may warn the king and utter godly words, and die for that (2 Chr 24:17–22), but can only imagine himself as asking YHWH to observe the matter and draw conclusions (דרש). He cannot even think of taking upon himself the status of a Davidic king or usurping his roles and duties, for such an action would be utterly impious. His father, Jehoiada who is portrayed as close as possible to a royal (and pious) figure in the world of Chronicles (see esp. 2 Chr 24:15) – and thus prefiguring, the later communal leadership of the High Priest – could never have been imagined as unsettling the Davidic king and reigning in his stead. Within this world, pre-ordained, hierchical structures had to be maintained, and what works for the line of Davidides works as well for the priests.

Chronicles were never construed as threatening the main roles of the priests, or the 'proper' order of society, and needless to say, Moses and *tōrâ*. Within the world of Chronicles, the threat to the status of the priests (and from the literati's perspective, the proper, and even cosmic, order) was imagined in the sphere of political power (see the case of Uzziah in 2 Chr 26:16–21, cf. Babylonian texts from Seleucid period). Of course, imagining that the true threat was to be found in political power in the context of the Yehudite literati, meant construing it as external and requiring inner social cohesion among those responsible for the Temple to decrease the risk of external intervention (cf. *Ant.* 11.297–301).

That said, as significant as vertical social cohesion was in the world of Chronicles, it was placed in proportion by a complementary concept that vertical barriers are porous and flexible on some central axes and matters. Levites could, for instance, at times be remembered as behaving much better than priests (e. g., 2 Chr 29:34), without changing their prescribed roles. Whereas, due to the status of the priests and the realities of a late Persian/early Hellenistic Yehud, no Levite could be remembered as a *quasi*-king (unlike the priest Jehoida, see above) in monarchic Judah, the crucial role of serving as prophetic voices and thus guarding Israel was open to them (see 2 Chr 20:14, and in their roles as singers/performers), just as it was open to priests, kings, and anyone else, with some restrictions.[42]

A final observation to matters of complementarity is that, as the imagined and remembered monarchic period fades away in Chronicles, and Zedekiah completely disappears from the text (2 Chr 36:13), incipient features of post-monarchic Yehud begin to emerge in Chronicles. The focus on the leadership shifts from the complementarity of king (and 'his leading officers,' שרים) and people, to the complementarity of שרי הכהנים ('the leaders of the priests') and the people. As the priests begin to be characterized as the internal leaders of the community, Levites disappear; precisely, because both at that moment in the world of Chronicles, as in historical late-Yehud (or Ben-Sira's Judah, for that matter), Levites as such are not to be found as complementary

---

42. On matters of guardianship, prophetic voices and political thought, see Ehud Ben Zvi, "Memory and Political Thought in the Late Persian/Early Hellenistic Yehud/Judah: Some Observations," in *Leadership, Social Memory and Judean Discourse in the 5th–2nd Centuries BCE*, WANEM, ed. Diana V. Edelman and Ehud Ben Zvi (London: Equinox, 2016), 9–26. As for the restrictions, slaves, for instance, were not included among the prophetic voices, no women served in these roles in Chronicles, except for Hulda in 2 Chr 34:22–28, probably a non-malleable 'fact' agreed upon among the literati (cf. 2 Kgs 22:14–20). The question of which 'facts' appearing in Kings (or other relevant texts within the authoritative repertoire of the literati) the Chronicler could not change, and why these ones, requires a separate study.

partners to the priests' in-group, temple-centered communal leadership.

An additional facilitating factor was that Chronicles emphasizes performances and particularly public performances, which it saw as constitutive of the community. Thus, in the world of Chronicles, the temple singers were particularly important.[43] Moreover, when the literati empathetically visited this world of memory, they could not but engage in some conceptual slippage between singer, performer, author/writer and even prophet (cf. 1 Chr 25:1; 2 Chr 34:13).[44]

This slippage, of course, is not restricted to Chronicles, but is well-attested in Chronicles and carried important implications for its construction of the Levites. For one, it created a general realm of meaning that could be activated and associated with Levites; thus a Levite could exist within the world of imagination and memory evoked by Chronicles as singers, a prophetic voice, and as scribes (1 Chr 24:6;[45] 2 Chr 34:13), and therefore also as people responsible for some areas of the administration, including the roles of שטרים (see 1 Chr 23:4; 26:29; 2 Chr 19:11). To be sure, Levites were not the only ones performing these duties. Scribes did not have to be Levites (see 2 Chr 2:55), even a foreign monarch could serve as a prophetic voice, and so on. Even musicians playing instruments in the cult were not exclusively Levites (see the priests with the trumpets in 2 Chr 29:26). But Levites could indeed be imagined as singers, 'gatekeepers' and as fulfilling all these positions.

The more a site of memory serves as a playground for safely exploring some key issues within the ideological discourse of the remembering groups, the more it would tend to populate the memory-scape of a group. Levites served as an excellent playground to point at and even embody some key temporal trajectories and explore their significance. For instance, the Levites were supposed to live all over the country and in some Levitical cities. But, according to Chronicles, the Levites left the territory of the northern Kingdom and settled

---

43. On the Levitical singers in Chronicles, see Ming Him Ko, *The Levite Singers in Chronicles and their Stabilizing Role*, LHBOTS 657 (London: T&T Clark, 2017).

44. Cf. my previous work, Ehud Ben Zvi, "Who Knew What? The Construction of the Monarchic Past in Chronicles and Implications for the Intellectual Setting of Chronicles," in *Judah and the Judeans in the Fourth Century B.C.E.*, ed. Oded Lipschits, Gary N. Knoppers and R. Albertz (Winona Lake: Eisenbrauns, 2007), 349–60; "Observations on Lines of Thought Concerning the Concepts of Prophecy and Prophets in Yehud, with an Emphasis on Deuteronomy-2Kings and Chronicles," in *Words, Ideas, Worlds. Biblical Essays in Honour of Yairah Amit*, Hebrew Bible Monographs, 40, ed. Athalya Brenner and Frank H. Polak, (Sheffield: Sheffield Phoenix Press, 2012), 1–19; "Chronicles and its Reshaping of Memories."

45. Note what the Levite scribe records according to this text, and the complementarity rather than competition between priests and Levites that this text suggests.

in Judah at the time of Rehoboam (2 Chr 11:13–14). This complete spatial transfer served as a manifestation of a larger issue, the turning of 'Israel' into Yehud/Judah and 'the land' into the land of monarchic Judah.[46]

Needless to say, this is not the only case in which the Levites of memory shaped and filled a space for exploring important issues in the discourse of the literati. Perhaps the most obvious one concerns the minimum age at which Levites could be counted in a census. According to Numbers 4:3, at the time of Moses and Aaron, that age was thirty years old (and see also 1 Chr 23:3 in reference to the time of David), but according to 1 Chronicles 23:24–27, David changed the minimum age to twenty, which in Chronicles seems to have been the standard age for assuming full adult responsibilities. This change, which is clearly approved by Chronicles, serves as an excellent ground to explore cases of some 'Mosaic' laws that were deemed to be temporarily contingent.[47] Of course, the same holds true, inter alia, for the rules of the Passover at the time of the Exodus, within the imaginary of the literati. More observations may be advanced, but the preceding ones suffice to illustrate the kind of potential outcomes that the approach outlined above may offer in terms of addressing the social roles and effects of remembering Levites in the context of the world/s of the past conjured by Chronicles, and why Levites populated the world of Chronicles so much, unlike the case in most other books in the authoritative repertoire of the community, and particularly those conjuring the monarchic past. In addition, the preceding observations illustrate ways in which the emergence of Chronicles altered to an extent the comprehensive memory-scape of the literati, and even more importantly, the dynamic character of the social memory system at work among the literati.

Obviously, had their world of memory reflected *only* the monarchic past evoked by the books of Samuel and Kings and the relevant prophetic books, their image of monarchic period Levites would have been drastically different. But, as shown here and by multiple other cases, the main generative grammar at work among these literati showed a strong dis-preference for across the board homogenization,

---

46. This conceptual theme appears in various ways in Chronicles. I have recently explored its significance for Chronicles' dealings with the notion of Israel as the 'twelve tribes of Jacob' in my "Chronicles and the Concept of 'The Twelve Tribes of Israel'," to be published in a forthcoming memorial book.

47. I discussed this example with bibliography in Ehud Ben Zvi, "One Size Does Not Fit All. Observations on the Different Ways That Chronicles Dealt with the Authoritative Literature of Its Time," in *What Was Authoritative for Chronicles?*, ed. Ehud Ben Zvi and Diana V. Edelman (Winona Lake, IN: Eisenbrauns, 2011), 13–35.

both at the inner and inter-book/collection level.[48] The authoritative repertoire and the memory-scape of the literati were both consistently characterized by a multiplicity of voices and of imagined and remembered pasts and futures, interacting and informing each other. In our case, Chronicles, the mentioned prophetic books and Samuel-Kings each kept recalling their own particular monarchic past/s, and, as a result, the literati kept "seeing" or "not-seeing" Levites as they time-traveled to these respective pasts.

At the same time, the literati's mental library and general world of knowledge could not but keep informing their readings of any book in that library, and in our case, also the images of the past that they conjured. Acts of "not seeing" were thus performed time and again against background knowledge and vicarious experiences of "seeing" and vice-versa, and thus causing, by necessity from a systemic viewpoint, ongoing interpretative loops and raising significant questions.[49] Moreover, since the literati read and were fully aware of both texts conjuring different pasts and vicariously, due to empathy, "experienced" these diverse "past realities", their comprehensive memory-scape was unequivocally, strongly multiperspectival, dynamic, continuously self-balancing, and self-complementing.

This paper has focused on the contribution that Chronicles made to the shaping of memories of the Levites of the monarchic period among the literati of the Late Persian/early Hellenistic period, and on factors that facilitated the particular character of the memories of Levites that this book encoded and conjured. It also represents an invitation to reconsider common positions about the Levites in late-Persian Yehud and explore additional research paths, which may apply to Chronicles, as shown above, but perhaps may also be helpful to study other texts, books or sections within books in which the Levites play

---

48. There was indeed a consistent preference for keeping inconsistency at the inner-book level and at the level of core sites of memory (e. g., Moses). I discussed these matters in E. Ben Zvi, *Social Memory Among the Literati of Yehud*, passim, and literature. The same holds true at the inter-book or inter-collection of books levels. No one would doubt that, for instance, that Josiah is the main hero of the (separate, kingdom of Judah) in the world portrayed and communicated by Kings, but no one "updated" the book of Zephaniah to include a positive image of Josiah in it. Similarly, no one "updated" the books of Jeremiah and Ezekiel so as to have the two characters interacting with other, despite the fact that both were remembered as living in more or less the period. Examples can be easily multiplied.

49. On these matters see my "Chronicles and Samuel-Kings: Two Interacting Aspects of one Memory System in the Late Persian/Early Hellenistic Period," in *Rereading the Relecture? The Question of (Post)chronistic Influence in the Latest Redactions of the Books of Samuel*, ed. Uwe Becker and Hannes Bezzel (FAT II, 66; Tübingen: Mohr Siebeck, 2014), 41–56, and *Social Memory Among the Literati of Yehud*, 317–331 and passim.

an important role either in the foundational past or the utopian future, and which existed alongside all the other books within the authoritative repertoire of the historical literati of the period and were all integral to their mental library.[50]

---

[50] I wish to express my appreciation to the organizers of the original workshop and the editors of this volume for inviting me, for their hospitality and friendship, but above all, for their leadership in shaping a friendly atmosphere in which multiple positions are collaboratively aired and discussed and in which we can all learn from each other. I want to express my appreciation to all the other participants for their contributions and comments on my own work. Scholarship and knowledge production are, by necessity, collaborative projects. My thanks to all those involved in this one.

IV. Ideological Conflicts and Scribal Debates

Genealogies as Tools: The Case of P and Chronicles

Joachim Schaper

1. Introduction

The present paper explores the ways in which genealogies have been used by biblical authors who supported the Levites (in the sense of second-rank liturgical functionaries) over against the Aaronide and other priesthoods, constructed a unified Levi-Aaron-genealogy and at the same time emphasised the importance of the Zadokite Jerusalem priesthood.[1] The paper does so against the background of research into the uses of genealogies conducted by social anthropologists. Research into biblical genealogies – or, for that matter, genealogies in any literature of the ancient world – can immensely benefit from insights won in social anthropology because the latter makes us aware of the social and political uses of genealogies, especially of their function in adopting narratives to changes in societal structures and political constellations. In non-literate societies, such processes of change are accompanied by adjustments to the existing genealogies,[2] and in literate societies they are mirrored in the rewriting of genealogies in the extant authoritative texts: while writing leads to "the freezing of the genealogies",[3] this does not preclude the rearrangement of a written genealogy through rewriting it. This is, of

---

1. For my earlier work on the pre-history and history of the priests and Levites of Achaemenid Judah, cf. Joachim Schaper, *Priester und Leviten im achämenidischen Juda: Studien zur Kult- und Sozialgeschichte Israels in persischer Zeit*, FAT 31 (Tübingen: Mohr Siebeck, 2000).

2. See Jack Goody & Ian Watt, "The Consequences of Literacy," in *Literacy in Traditional Societies*, ed. Jack Goody (Cambridge: Cambridge University Press, 1968), 27–68 (= *Comparative Studies in Society and History* 5 [1963], 304–45), especially pp. 31–34, and Jack Goody, *Myth, Ritual and the Oral* (Cambridge: Cambridge University Press, 2010).

3. Jack Goody, *The Logic of Writing and the Organisation of Society*, Studies in Literacy, Family, Culture and the State (Cambridge: Cambridge University Press, 1986), 40.

course, particularly pertinent with regard to the uses of genealogies in Chronicles, in which written genealogies play a crucial role (1 Chr 4:33; 5:1, 7, 17; 7:5, 7, 9, 40; 9:1, 22; 2 Chr 12:15; 31:16–19; cf. Ezra 2:62; 8:1, 3; Neh 7:5, 64).

This essay is divided into three parts, devoted to (1) genealogies as explored by social anthropologists, (2) genealogies in P and Chronicles, and (3) the struggle for interpretative supremacy in Judah during the Achaemenid period.

2. GENEALOGIES AND THEIR FUNCTIONS FROM A SOCIAL-ANTHROPOLOGICAL PERSPECTIVE

Kinship is one of the great and central themes of social anthropology, and genealogies are the key devices used by social groups for the purposes of social organisation and identity-formation. One might say that genealogies are tools because they are the instruments forged by a social group's key functionaries in order to establish, promote and perpetuate their view of the group's (supposed) kinship structure and because those genealogies, once they have been devised and established, can be used in the service of fighting those who resist that order and attempt to change it. This is one of the uses genealogies can be put to, and have been put to, in social and cultural confrontations throughout history.

But, of course, this is just one element of a complex picture. Social anthropologists have much more to say about the social and cultural functions of genealogies:

> Eine Genealogie stellt ein Ordnungssystem dar, das auf die Frage nach der eigenen Herkunft ebenso antwortet wie auf die nach den verwandtschaftlichen Relationen innerhalb einer Gesellschaft. So manifestiert sich in der Genealogie eine Form der historischen Darstellung. Die genealogische Zuordnung, zum Beispiel in der einfachsten Form der Nennung des Vaters (und Großvaters), stellt eine Person in einen geschichtlichen Zusammenhang. Die Genealogie dient dabei jedoch nicht nur der Identifikation, sondern zugleich der Feststellung der Identität, insofern als sie Anteil hat an der Vorstellung, dass die *Herkunft* einer Person oder Sache etwas über ihr *Wesen* verrate. Die Herstellung der Identität durch den Aufweis der Abstammung korrespondiert der Wissensvermittlung vom Vater auf den Sohn usf. ebenso wie der Kongruenz von Gesellschaftsstruktur und Familienstruktur.[4]

---

4. This is the apt summary of social-anthropological approaches to genealogies, produced by a biblical scholar (Jürgen Ebach, "Genealogie," in *Handbuch religionswissenschaftlicher Grundbegriffe*, vol. II, ed. Hubert Cancik, Burkhard Gladigow

Let us give some thought to what this might mean for our investigation of genealogies in the Hebrew Bible, and especially in the Priestly Writing and in Chronicles. In those genealogies, the relations between different groups of the priesthood are expressed as relations of kinship. Thus, relations in society at a particular point in history are expressed as natural relations, as actual kinship relations. Social relations are thus *invested with all the weight and significance of kinship relations*. This is why the statement on the father-son succession in our quotation is so important: "Die Herstellung der Identität durch den Aufweis der Abstammung korrespondiert der Wissensvermittlung vom Vater auf den Sohn usf. ebenso wie der Kongruenz von Gesellschaftsstruktur und Familienstruktur." In ancient Israel and Judah, as in most or all ancient societies, the priestly office and priestly education was handed on from father to son; there was a congruity between being the *descendant* of a man, being his *pupil*, and being his *successor in office*. Once again it is obvious how completely intertwined societal relations and kinship relations really were.

Also, and very importantly, genealogies are instruments that reflect, integrate, and make sense of *change*, while at the same time pretending that change has not taken place. Consider the following example adduced by Goody and Watt, an example taken from a non-literate society that was in transition towards being an at least partly literate one:

> Early British administrators among the Tiv of Nigeria were aware of the great importance attached to these genealogies [which "stretch some twelve generations in depth back to an eponymous founding ancestor", according to Goody; J.S.], which were continually discussed in court cases where the rights and duties of one man towards another were in dispute. Consequently, they took the trouble to write down the long lists of names and preserve them for posterity, so that future administrators might refer to them in giving judgement. Forty years later, when the Bohannans [Laura and Paul Bohannan, two social anthropologists; J.S.] carried out anthropological field work in the area, their successors were still using the same genealogies. However, these written pedigrees now gave rise to many disagreements; the Tiv maintained that they were incorrect, while the officials regarded them as statements of fact, as records of what had actually happened, and could not agree that the unlettered indigenes could be better informed about the past than their own literate predecessors. What neither party realized was that in any society of this kind changes take place which require a constant readjustment in the genealogies if they are to continue to carry out their function as mnemonics of social relationships.[5]

& Matthias Laubscher [Stuttgart, Berlin, Cologne: W. Kohlhammer, 1990], 486–49, here 486–87).

5. Goody & Watt, "Literacy", 32

Genealogies as "mnemonics of social relationships" – this captures the essence of the problem. The Nigerian example was situated in the context of a non-literate society in which the changes in social relationships "require a constant readjustment in the genealogies", but such readjustments remain imperceptible and can, in the context of a non-literate society, hardly be traced and reconstructed. And if genealogies that only existed orally are, so to speak, brought to a standstill *by being written down*, they can no longer function as "mnemonics of social relationships" because they cannot be flexibly adjusted when the social relationships change. Conversely, in a literate society with its written genealogies, such written genealogies can also be continuously adjusted whenever social relationships change, but any such adjustment requires writing activities that result in modified records. Any literate person can then identify the difference between the original version and the modified one. In oral societies, such changes can be identified only by the functionaries who memorise the genealogies and modify them when they see fit.

In the case of the Tiv genealogies, the colonial administrators, who argued on the basis of the decades-old written records of the genealogies as they then presented themselves, did not understand the ways in which genealogies in non-literate societies evolve and therefore thought that they had fixed a precise account of kinship relations when they wrote down what they were being told by the "indigenes". The administrators did not understand that genealogies are malleable, ever-changing records – records indeed, but not "reliable" records in a modern Western sense, for the simple reason that they provide a *snapshot* of the current social relationships and are not intended to provide a record of actual kinship relations in a distant past. Instead, they construct supposed kinship relations that mirror the actually existing social structure in order to achieve social and political objectives.

While genealogies are particularly malleable in non-literate societies, they can be handled very flexibly even in societies where the practice of writing is well established among the elites and where therefore written genealogies are, at least in principle, open to public scrutiny. The development of priestly genealogies in the Hebrew Bible is a case in point. The modifications introduced in Chronicles to genealogies already found in P were introduced not least because of the political need to confer authority upon a temple hierarchy that had evolved over time and needed to reaffirm its claim to authority. We shall explore this in some detail in the next section.

It must be kept in mind that it is one of the many features of genealogies to regulate access to privilege by defining the group deserving of privilege by means of constructing kinship relations. The Hebrew Bible is full of examples of that function of genealogies; a particularly salient one is found in Ezra 2:62–63//Nehemiah 7:64–65 where those who want to have their supposed priestly status confirmed try to find כְּתָבָם הַמִּתְיַחְשִׂים, i. e., "their written record, [that is,] the enrolled" = "their written genealogy". Such a written genealogy determined whether or not certain persons could be considered legitimate priests and therefore be admitted to "the priesthood" (הַכְּהֻנָּה). It is interesting that a written (!) genealogy had to be submitted in order to be given access – references to oral traditions were obviously not considered sufficient.

3. GENEALOGIES IN P AND CHRONICLES

In the Hebrew Bible, and especially in P and Chronicles, genealogies play a significant role, and in Chronicles (as well as in Ezra-Nehemiah) *written* genealogies have a very special place.[6] The genealogies in Chronicles, to which I shall give special attention, are a particularly complex and salient attempt to use what is passed off as a record of the past as a mirror of the present and a foundation for the future. They have to be seen in the wider context of what David N. Freedman has called "the Chronicler's purpose", stating that

> […] the Chronicler establishes through his narrative of the reigns of David and Solomon the proper, legitimate pattern of institutions and their personnel for the people of God; and they are the monarchy represented by David and his house, the priesthood, by Zadok and his descendants, the city and the temple in the promised land. City and ruler, temple and priest – these appear to be the fixed points around which the Chronicler constructs his history and his theology.[7]

Freedman makes a persuasive case for his understanding of the Chron-

---

6. On biblical genealogies generally, cf. especially Robert R. Wilson, "The Old Testament Genealogies in Recent Research," JBL 94 (1975): 169–89 and Robert R. Wilson, *Genealogy and History in the Biblical World* (New Haven, Conn: Yale University Press, 1977). On the priestly and Levitical genealogies in Chronicles (1 Chronicles 5:27–6:38) and their societal and ideological purposes, cf., among others, Antti Laato, "The Levitical Genealogies in 1 Chronicles 5–6 and the Formation of Levitical Ideology in Post-Exilic Judah," JSOT 62 (1994): 77–99. Laato insightfully differentiates between "*historical* genealogy" and "*ideological* genealogy" (p. 77) and demonstrates some of the purposes which the genealogies of Chronicles were intended to serve.

7. David N. Freedman, "The Chronicler's Purpose," *CBQ* 23 (1961): 436–42, here 437–38. On Chronicles and possible attempts at a restoration of the Davidic monarchy in the fourth century, see David Janzen, *Chronicles and the Politics of Davidic Restoration. A Quiet Revolution*, LHBOTS 655 (London: Bloomsbury T&T Clark, 2017).

icler's purpose and for seeing the significance of the Davidic monarchy as the key to the interpretation of his work. We shall return to this observation later, in the conclusion to this essay.

The genealogies that are of interest to us here were originally devised in writing (possible "forerunners" in the shape and form of orally-transmitted genealogies are impossible to reconstruct), and they are different from genealogies devised in non-literate societies because they do not suffer the problem of "genealogical shrinkage".[8] What both written and oral genealogies have in common, though, is that they are "governed by the concerns of the present".[9]

With regard to the use of priestly genealogies in Chronicles and the relation between them and priestly genealogies in P, the exemplary text, where all the key characteristics of the use of such genealogies converge, is found in 1 Chronicles 5:27–6:38 [English 6:1–53]:

Gary N. Knoppers comments:

> By situating the descendants of Zadoq within a broader genealogical context, the author avoids developing antitheses between priests and Levites, Aaronides and Zadoqites, Eleazarides and Ithamarides. The writer negotiates among established positions and synthesizes disparate traditions. In Chronicles the Aaronides are, broadly speaking, Levites (1 Chr 5:27). To some extent, the Levitical genealogies relativize the distinction between priests and Levites by speaking of Qohathites, Merarites, and Gershonites. Within these large phratries there can be specializations. Some Qohathites are priests (5:27–41), while other Qohathites are singers (6:7–13, 18–23). The Qohatite priests clearly have a privileged position. But the Merarites, Qohathites, and Gershonites who function as singers (6:5–33) can lay claim to the same impeccable roots (6:1–4) as the Qohathite priests (5:27–29). All are Levites, who share a common genealogy. Some biblical and postbiblical authors draw clear

---

8. Goody & Watt, "Literacy", 32: "[…] consequently the added depth of lineages caused by new births needs to be accompanied by a process of genealogical shrinkage; the occurrence of this telescoping process, a common example of the general social phenomenon which J. A. Barnes has felicitously termed 'structural amnesia', has been attested in many societies".

9. 9. Contra Goody & Watt, "Literacy", 34, where they write of the genealogies of the Tiv and others: "But all their conceptualizations of the past cannot help being governed by the concerns of the present, merely because there is no body of chronologically ordered statements to which reference can be made. The Tiv do not recognise any contradiction between what they say now and what they said fifty years ago, since no enduring records exist for them to set beside their present views. Myth and history merge into one: the elements in the cultural heritage which cease to have a contemporary relevance tend to be soon forgotten or transformed; and as the individuals of each generation acquire their vocabulary, their genealogies, and their myths, they are unaware that various words, proper names and stories have dropped out, or that others have changed their meanings or been replaced." Rather, it seems that both oral and written genealogies, while they are differently situated, need to respond to "the concerns of the present". The Levi-Aaron-genealogy is a perfect example of that.

contrasts among sacerdotal groups, but in Chronicles they all are ultimately part of the same organization.[10]

In a previous publication, I drew attention to these same facts and pointed out that this genealogical arrangement is the expression of the desire to consolidate and stabilise the temple hierarchy by promoting the new "inclusive" view by means of the ingenious construct that is the Levitical genealogy placed in what Rothstein called the "genealogische Vorhalle".[11] In the text quoted above, Knoppers makes a similar point, and it is indeed true that Chronicles devises a genealogy that accommodates diverse priestly families under one imaginary umbrella, that of the postulated lineage of Aaron who is seen as a descendant of Levi; even and especially Zadok is integrated into this lineage.[12] The Chronicler's construct thus accommodates just about everyone on the priestly side who can be accommodated. In that sense it "synthesizes disparate traditions", and in doing so it regulates access to the privilege of being considered a legitimate priest: where there is no written genealogy (Ezra 2:62–64//Nehemiah 7:61–65), someone's priestly status cannot be ascertained and the person is precluded from priestly privilege (Ezra 2:62!); conversely, where such a written genealogy confirming someone's priestly status exists, that person is accepted as being a legitimate priest.

But there is another way of looking at the passages Knoppers adduces. While the author of the genealogy "avoids developing antitheses between priests and Levites, Aaronides and Zadoqites, Eleazarides and Ithamarides", he subsumes the priests, *together with* the Levites

---

10. Gary N. Knoppers, *I Chronicles 1–9: A New Translation with Introduction and Commentary*, AB 12A (New York: Doubleday 2003), 415.

11. Schaper, *Priester und Leviten*, 304–5.

12. Alice Hunt, *Missing Priests: The Zadokites in Tradition and History*, LHBOTS 452 (New York/London: T & T Clark, 2006) and Nathan MacDonald, *Priestly Rule: Polemic and Biblical Interpretation in Ezekiel 44*, BZAW 476 (Boston, MA: De Gruyter, 2015) both question, in different ways, the existence of a historical priesthood of Zadokites. There are many observations that contradict such views of the Zadokite priesthood. I shall just mention one. The elusiveness of the figure of Zadok in the biblical texts is often adduced to give a basis to 'minimalist' views of the history of the pre-exilic Zadokite priesthood. But while the eponymous ancestor of that priesthood may well not have been a historical character, the fact that the concept of a Zadokite priesthood plays such a distinct role in the Hebrew Bible indicates that a priesthood claiming descendance from what may well be an ahistorical figure of that name *actually existed historically*, just like – to name just one example – the famous Roman noble family, the gens Iulia, which claimed to be descended from the mythical figure Iulus, the son of Aeneas. On the question of the historicity of a Zadokite priesthood, cf. also Lars Maskow, *Tora in der Chronik: Studien zur Rezeption des Pentateuchs in den Chronikbüchern*, FRLANT 274 (Göttingen: Vandenhoeck & Ruprecht, 2019), 322–33.

(in the sense of second-rank cultic officials), under the same eponymous ancestor Levi. This leads to the result that, indeed, "the Levitical genealogies relativize the distinction between priests and Levites by speaking of Qohathites, Merarites, and Gershonites". At the same time – and that is the point – *they subtly subvert the distinction altogether*. More than that: the genealogies integrate the priests so fully under the general heading of the descendants of Levi that it becomes easier and easier *completely to ignore* the distinction between priests and second-rank functionaries, i. e., Levites.[13]

But that is still not the full picture. There are tensions within Chronicles with regard to the question of the priests' status and their historical, dynastic and theological significance vis-à-vis the status and significance of the Levites. The whole problem comes together in 1 Chronicles 5:27–6:38. At the tail end of this, in 1 Chronicles 6:35–38 [English 6:49–53], we have a reiteration of what one might call the *backbone* of the priestly genealogy in chapter 5:27–41 (i. e., 5:29–34): the segment of the high-priestly genealogy that runs from Aaron to Zadok and his son, i. e. that part of the genealogy which integrates the Zadokite priesthood into the "Levi"-construct and thus constructs a line that artificially unifies historically separate Judahite priesthoods. In so doing, it uses the Levi-Aaron-genealogy of P in Exodus 6:14–25 to great effect as a basis for the genealogical adjustment in 1 Chronicles 5:27–41.[14]

Why is the key segment of the high-priestly genealogy of 5:27–41 found again here in 1 Chronicles 6:35–38? Why would the Chronicler, in a strategically crucial place of his work, wish to stress the importance of certain segments of the *priesthood* (as opposed to the Levites), and especially of Zadok (and thus of the Zadokite priestly tradition)? Interestingly, it has been postulated that 1 Chronicles 6:35–38 is a later addition.[15] Be that as it may, the crucial point is that the passage is part of the final form of Chronicles and is supposed to make sense

---

13. Schaper, *Priester und Leviten*, 269–302.
14. Schaper, *Priester und Leviten*, 35–36, 269–79.
15. On the relationship between 1 Chronicles 5:27–41 and 6:35–38, cf., amongst others, Sara Japhet, *1 Chronik*, HTKAT (Freiburg: Herder, 2002), 167. (This is the updated German translation of the English version of Japhet's commentary.) It should be noted that the majority of Chronicles scholars see the shorter genealogy as the earlier and the genealogy in 5:27–41 as the younger one; cf., amongst many others, Martin Noth, *The Chronicler's History*, trans. Hugh G. M. Williamson, JSOTS 50 (Sheffield: Sheffield Academic Press, 1987), 39–40. Knoppers and others take the opposite view; see Gary N. Knoppers, "The Relationship of the Priestly Genealogies to the History of the High Priesthood in Jerusalem," in *Judah and the Judeans in the Neo-Babylonian Period*, ed. Oded Lipschits and Joseph Blenkinsopp (Winona Lake: Eisenbrauns, 2003), 109–34, here 116–122, and Ralph W. Klein, *1 Chronicles* (Minneapolis: Fortress Press, 2006), 176.

in that context.

On the one hand, placing 1 Chron. 6:35–38 in the overall context of 1 Chronicles 5:27–6:38 may simply indicate that Chronicles pays lip-service to the priesthood while at the same time submerging it in a sea of general "Levitical" respectability. In any case, it is part of the process of redefining what is considered to be the legitimate priesthood, a process that was intended to change the regulation of access to the central instrument of power in the Achaemenid period (in the absence of kingship in Judah): the temple hierarchy.[16]

But what is the crucial point about integrating Zadok into the Levi-Aaron-genealogy in 1 Chronicles 5:27–41 and then repeating that section of the genealogy in 1 Chronicles 6:35–38? Was that done simply with the aim of legitimising the Zadokite line,[17] or was there another, more complex reason for this construct? The Zadokite line did not really need to be "legitimised" (it commanded respect because of its significance in the history of the Jerusalem cult), but – from the perspective of the Chronicler – it needed to be fully integrated into the comprehensive construct of his Levi-Aaron-genealogy, in order for that genealogy to stabilise and perpetuate the new equilibrium of the cultic hierarchy and the liturgical practice of the Jerusalem cult that was emerging in the late Persian period. 1 Chronicles 5:27–41 and 1 Chronicles 6:35–38 thus served the purpose of *integrating* the Zadokite line.[18]

But there is another, more subtle element to the integration of Zadok into the Levi-Aaron-genealogy. A key intention behind this strong emphasis on Zadok is to stress the importance of the sacerdotal service rendered by the Zadokite priests in the Davidic and Solomonic ages, to claim normative status for their way of conducting the divine service, and to construe the Davidic and Solomonic periods as

---

16. I have described the way in which this was accomplished in Schaper, *Priester und Leviten*, 269–302.

17. This is assumed by Maskow, *Tora*, 257, who seems to see this as the *only* reason for integrating Zadok into the genealogy: "Hinter der Liste steckt also die Absicht, der zadokidischen Linie priesterliche Legitimation zu verschaffen, indem sie in den Aaron-Stammbaum eingeschrieben wird. Es liegt demnach keine reale Abbildung von Abstammungsverhältnissen, sondern das Durchsetzungsmittel eines Herrschaftsdiskurses vor." That "keine reale Abbildung von Abstammungsverhältnissen" is attested, is not surprising at all; see the discussion above on the typical functions of genealogies that are found in social-anthropological studies in a range of societies.

18. Given the space constraints, we cannot revisit here in detail the complex scholarly discussion of the function of the genealogies in the history of the exilic and post-exilic recalibration effecting the relations between the priestly families of Judah – families that had entertained complex relations in the pre-exilic period. For a recent in-depth review of that scholarly discussion, focusing on the genealogies in Chronicles, cf. Maskow, *Tora*, 240–333.

a "golden age" of the cult. This was part of the larger objective identified by Freedman in his foundational essay.[19] While it is true that extolling the Davidic age was by no means the sole objective of the Chronicler (as Sara Japhet has pointed out),[20] it is equally true that the Chronicler saw that age as the defining golden age of all "Israel". Most importantly, the temple service is at the heart of hearts of "Israel" in the Chronicler's sense, as we shall see in more detail later.

4. THE STRUGGLE FOR INTERPRETATIVE SUPREMACY IN THE ACHAEMENID PERIOD

What I have drawn attention to in Chronicles (amongst other things, like the concept of the importance of the liturgical activity of the Zadokite priests in Davidic and Solomonic times), is the fact that the Levi-Aaron-genealogy subsumes the priests under the general heading of the descendants of Levi so that it becomes possible *completely to ignore* the distinction between priests and second-rank functionaries, i. e., Levites. This is an interpretative strategy intended by the authors of Chronicles to subvert the position of another group of temple functionaries in Judah in the Achaemenid period, i. e., that of priests opposed to the endeavour of the Levitical circles represented by the Chronicler. That priestly position is exemplified by the Korach episode in the book of Numbers which bears the traces of priestly resistance to the cause of the Levites. Jaeyoung Jeon writes in a recent article:

> Korach is not a well-known figure in the Pentateuch, appearing only in late redactional passages (e. g., Exod. 6.21,24; Num. 26.9; 27.3). In Chronicles, however, Korach is described as an ancestor of several influential Levitical clans responsible for the three main tasks of the Levites: singing, gatekeeping and ancillary temple service (1Chron. 9.19, 31; 26,1, 19; 2 Chron. 20.19). Probably in consideration of such Levitical genealogy, the priestly (most likely Zadokite) scribe chose Korach as the main antagonist representing the Levites.[21]

And as I pointed out elsewhere,[22] the Korach episode in Numbers 16 is indeed an instance of the struggle of (segments of) the priesthood

---

19. See above, note 6.
20. See Japhet, *1 Chronik*, 75–77 in the context of the discussion of the theological tenets of Chronicles, 72–78.
21. Jaeyoung Jeon, "The Zadokite and Levite Scribal Conflicts and Hegemonic Struggles," in *Scripture as Social Discourse*: *Social-Scientific Perspectives on Early Jewish and Christian Writings*, ed. Jessica M. Keady, Todd E. Klutz & C. A. Strine (London: Bloomsbury Academic, 2017), 97–110, here 103.
22. Schaper, *Priester und Leviten*, 298–300.

against the emancipatory efforts of the Levites. The Levites' efforts to level the distinctions within the priesthood were seen, by some priests, as being potentially detrimental to their position and function within the temple system and the society of Yehud in general. The use of the figure of Korach serves to denounce the Levitical efforts at subversion. It is intended to delegitimise the Levites, and the fact that references to Korach show up only in late passages unsurprisingly locates that struggle between priests and Levites in the late Achaemenid period, i. e., the period in which, for a number of reasons, we have come to expect the confrontation between priests and Levites to have taken place.

Let us now make an attempt to understand more precisely the nature of the confrontation between the Levites and the supposedly "Levitical" priests. What did the Levites, represented by the Chronicler, really attempt to achieve? How can we conceptualise the nature of their endeavour? Recently, Jeon has applied Gramsci's notion of cultural hegemony to the interpretation of the situation between the priests and Levites in the late Achaemenid period. Can the Levites' endeavour really be described as a struggle for cultural hegemony? While the confrontation between the priests and the Levites in that period was indeed a power struggle conducted with the intellectual weaponry available to priests and scribes, and in that sense a cultural struggle, I would describe it as a struggle for interpretative supremacy, not as a struggle for cultural hegemony in Gramsci's sense. Gramsci's notion of cultural hegemony was developed under the conditions of the 1920s and '30s and is informed by the political struggles in Italy and elsewhere in Western and Central Europe in that period. It made perfect sense in that context and still makes sense today, especially with regard to the losing battle the Left seems to be fighting, in many European countries and in the USA, against the encroachment of the Right on the political, legal and cultural institutions of those countries. However, a struggle for cultural hegemony in Gramsci's sense can only take place under the conditions of modern capitalist class-societies, focussing on the cultural apparatuses commanded by the ruling classes. It is with the help of these apparatuses that the struggle for hegemony is conducted.

Gramsci's notion cannot be applied to pre-capitalist societies, let alone to ancient ones. Yet one may concede that Gramsci's concept can be used heuristically, in the following sense: the struggle between the priests and the Levites was conducted – not exclusively, but to a significant degree – by means of the tools of the intellectual: the alphabet, the stylus, and the intellectual construct. While it cannot be understood as a struggle for cultural hegemony in Gramsci's sense, it is an attempt by one group of the temple personnel subtly to subvert the power of another. It is an *important* attempt at subversion because it concerns the power balance in the most *important institution of Yehud's society*, its one remaining temple – a temple that was, like other temples in the Near East and elsewhere, not just a religious but also a financial and administrative centre.

The attempted result of the subversion was a levelling of the internal hierarchy of the Jerusalem temple: not a *complete* levelling, as the internal differentiation of the hierarchy and the special interest in the Aaronic line and in Zadok demonstrate. This levelling was the expression of – or laid the basis for; that is hard to tell – a more egalitarian approach to the rights and duties of religious functionaries which started to emerge in the late Achaemenid period. It is the beginning of what I have elsewhere dubbed the "Levitical-Pharisaic tradition," i. e., the tradition of scriptural exegesis ultimately rooted in the work of Levites in the late Persian period, taken up and developed by the earliest Pharisees, and fully established by Pharisaism in the Hellenistic and Roman periods.[23] The members of that movement – and of its later permutation, the early rabbinic tradition – did not have an entirely hostile attitude towards the priesthood, but they were wary of the priests, and they did not like the priesthood to become too powerful. What they therefore tried to do was to channel the available religious energy not exclusively through the ritual sacrifices offered by the priests but also through liturgical and textual practices. Their intellectual tool of choice in that process was the genealogy. While the elite of Yehud was literate, and while, therefore, the manipulation of genealogies was in principle open to scrutiny, the people behind Chronicles nevertheless chose written genealogies to make their point. As we have seen, the ways in which they manipulated the material were quite subtle; they made seemingly minor changes, re-emphasising some of the aspects of the existing material and integrating lineages into contexts from which they had been missing, as in the case of 1 Chronicles 5:27–41 and 1 Chronicles 6:35–38, which build on Exodus 6:14–25. While there are obvious problems with the manipulation of genealogies in a society that is largely literate, the people behind Chronicles nevertheless went in for such manipulation. They executed their self-chosen task subtly and efficiently; the fact that they instrumentalised genealogies, in spite of the obvious problems, is due to the fact that

---

23. Cf. Schaper, Priester und Leviten, 307 and Joachim Schaper, "The Pharisees," in *The Cambridge History of Judaism*, vol. 3: *The Early Roman Period*, ed. William Horbury, William D. Davies and John Sturdy (Cambridge: Cambridge University Press, 1999), 402–27.

genealogies continued to be key instruments of legitimisation.

The Levites started out on a transformation of the cultic practices of the Yahweh religion which ultimately ensured that it could survive without a sacrificial cult. To make do completely without a sacrificial cult had of course never been the intention, but when that point was reached much later, religious survival had become possible because the sacrificial cult had been supplemented with textual and liturgical practices which ultimately proved to be able to supplant it. The importance of the divine service was stressed by affording genealogical "room" to Zadok and his descendants, the practitioners of the temple service of the Davidic and Salomonic ages as seen by the Chronicler, that is, the form of service considered normative by the Chronicler. Without the subtle Levitical reform and the textual strategies employed to bring it about, aimed as they were at countering the preponderance of the priesthood *and* at making use of priestly traditions (like that of the Zadokites) where it suited the Levites,[24] that religious and cultural survival would not have been possible.

Let us now return to the observation that the Chronicler's work is focused on the Davidic monarchy and its importance in the context of the 'restoration' – or rather: reinvention – of Judah after the exile. If we look at the whole of 1 Chronicles 5:27–6:38, it is clear that the genealogical manipulations that were used to construct it betray the desire to unify hitherto divergent priestly traditions. What also emerges is the wish to let the 'actually existing' Yahweh temple hierarchy of Yehud bask in the light of the imagined priesthood of the past (an imagined priesthood in which the difference in authority between priests, Levites and other cult functionaries was blurred or even dissolved), and to do that in the service of the nostalgia for a Davidic empire that was never going to return. In that nostalgic projection, the "Levitical" singers (who are classified as being descended from Gershon, Qohath and Merari) were given the central task of performing the temple liturgy (1 Chr 6:16–18). The importance of the cult in the system created by the Chronicler is also demonstrated by the fact that the "tribe" of Levi receives the greatest amount of attention of all the tribes in the "genealogische Vorhalle" of 1 Chronicles.

By devising the genealogical construct of a system of cult func-

---

24. Cf., from another perspective, Benjamin Giffone, "Atonement, Sacred Space and Ritual Time: The Chronicler as Reader of Priestly Pentateuchal Narrative" (in the present volume): "As an early interpreter of Torah, he [the Chronicler; J.S.] seems to be charting a path that is inclusive of both Deuteronomistic and Priestly traditions (understood broadly), and of both Levites and Zadoqite priests in their specific, necessary roles. The Chronicler's circle and the Jerusalem cult's sphere of influence was too small to be exclusive."

tionaries descended from Levi that integrated both the Aaronides and the Zadokites *and* undermined the traditional strict hierarchy between "castes" of temple functionaries, and by also emphatically stressing the historic role of the Zadokites as the functionaries of the normative cult, three things were achieved: (1) a maximum of integration was accomplished, in the sense that historically separate and competing priestly traditions (i. e., traditions that had historically laid claims to priestly authority in pre-exilic Judah) were accommodated under one (imaginary) roof; this integration constituted (2) the basis for a peaceful coexistence of the descendants of the various priestly families; and (3) the integration of the Zadokites enabled the Chronicler further to underline the achievements of the Davidic monarchy by stressing the historic importance and the continuing normativity of the divine service at the Jerusalem temple as conducted by the Zadokites in the Davidic and Solomonic ages.[25]

It has recently rightly been stressed that it is important to "consider[] not just the parallel, but also the new passages in Chronicles that assign greater space, attention, and weight to the altar as compared to the books of Samuel and Kings – mainly in relation to the establishment of the temple [...]", with "the altar" referring to "the outer, burnt-offerings sacrificial altar, not the incense altar".[26] Itamar Kislev's research is not based on the priestly/Levitical genealogies of Chronicles but effectively confirms my conclusion (3), which I have derived entirely from an analysis of the relevant genealogies, by presenting a compelling argument which is derived from the analysis of Chronicles passages that are without parallel in Samuel and King: "Significantly, all these references to the altar are chronistic additions in relation to the accounts in Samuel and Kings; as new additions, they reflect the Chronicler's view of the enhanced importance of the altar."[27] The "enhanced importance of the altar" propagated by the Chronicler represents a new, strong emphasis on the importance of the Jerusalem sacrificial cult as conducted by the Zadokites – an

---

25. This sprang from the growing refinement of the cult and the heightened interest in liturgical music that becomes obvious from numerous passages in 1 and 2 Chronicles, cf. Schaper, *Priester und Leviten*, 280–90, especially 282–84. On the importance of the cult, now see Itamar Kislev, "The Role of the Altar in the Book of Chronicles", *JHS* (2020), article 3. On ritual and atonement in Chronicles, cf. Giffone, "Atonement, Sacred Space and Ritual Time," in the present volume.

26. Kislev, "Role," 5.

27. Kislev, "Role," 8: "By twice describing the sanctification of the location of the temple through the descent of fire on the altar and the divine election of this site, the Chronicler underscores the centrality of the altar in the temple's array. He reinforces this theme through the mention of the altar in David's declaration as well (1 Chr 22:1)."

idealised view of the cultic history of the temple intended to serve as a norm for the present, for the cultic life of the Jerusalem temple in the fourth century. But the Chronicler's endeavour was not just to stress the importance of the altar, and of the *sacrifice as such*, but he also intended to stress the importance of the liturgy (and, importantly, of the liturgical music) that accompanied it: Kislev stresses, with regard to 2 Chronicles 5:11–13, that "[t]he reader may rightly understand that the appearance of the cloud and the glory of YHWH were not a consequence of the bringing of the ark into the temple, but of the priestly and Levitical ceremonial performance of music."[28] Here again, an analysis based on new materials in Chronicles leads to the same conclusion as an analysis focused on the Chronicler's genealogies: in Chronicles, there is a new, emphatic stress on the temple liturgy.

It must remain open whether this stress on the sacrificial cult and the liturgy was part of a concrete programme of Davidic restoration in the late Persian period,[29] but that certainly is an aspect worth exploring. The sacrificial cult and the liturgy that accompanied it (according to the Chronicler's view of the history of the cult) were thus set up as the perennial ideal of worship, as the perfect divine service which ensured the favour of Yahweh and in so doing guaranteed the efficacy of Israel's interactions with the deity.

5. Conclusion

In the present essay, I have attempted to demonstrate how an approach to the Chronicler's genealogies that is inspired by social-anthropological research can help us to understand more deeply how genealogies were devised as tools to be operated in a discourse about priestly and Levitical legitimacy and the function and organisation of the temple cult in the late Achaemenid period. I have also shown that the results thus won, by focusing on the genealogies in Chronicles, are interestingly confirmed by research conducted from a very different perspective, i. e., research that concentrates on those 'cultic' passages in Chronicles that are not derived from Samuel and Kings but come from the Chronicler's own hand. Independently of each other, both approaches arrive at the conclusion that the sacrificial cult and the liturgy

---

28. Kislev, "Role," 5: "Whereas in Kings the filling of the house with the glory of YHWH is clearly a direct result of the bringing of the ark into the temple, in the chronistic account the sequence of events is less clear. The reader may rightly understand that the appearance of the cloud and the glory of YHWH were not a consequence of the bringing of the ark into the temple, but of the priestly and Levitical ceremonial performance of music."

29. Cf. the historical reconstruction attempted by Janzen, *Chronicles* (see above, n. 7).

celebrated at the temple are of crucial importance to the Chronicler's concept of what defines 'Israel', to his view of the history of the Israelite priesthoods, and to his view of the present relations between the priests and Levites and their task in the enterprise of the reinvention of 'Israel' under foreign domination.

DAVID IN THE ROLE OF A SECOND MOSES – THE REVELATION OF THE TEMPLE-MODEL (*TABNÎT*) IN 1 CHRONICLES 28

Jürg Hutzli

1. INTRODUCTION

Commentaries on the book of Chronicles emphasize the important role given to David in this book. In 1 Chronicles 10–29 David in fact plays a major role as king of Israel fulfilling various functions such as political governor, military leader and also founder of the temple in Jerusalem and its cult. The last-mentioned role is prominently described in 1 Chronicles 28. Here David visibly enters into competition with Moses: Like the latter in the Priestly tabernacle account, David receives from YHWH a blueprint (*tabnît*) of the sanctuary to be built. Furthermore, 1 Chronicles 29 reports how David took the lead in donating to the Temple (vv. 2–5). According to 1 Chronicles 23–26, David also appointed the Levites and organized them into divisions. David's acts are visibly reminiscent of the Priestly tabernacle account and other (late) Priestly texts in the Pentateuch.

The importance given to David as initiator of the cult in Jerusalem deserves all the more attention since the Book of Chronicles refers to the Torah as a binding law several times, identifying it as the Torah of Moses.[1] About half of all mentions specify Torah as written law.[2] Among the texts concerned and laws referred to are late Penta-

---

1. 1 Chron 16:40; 22:12; 2 Chron 6:16; 12:1; 14:3; 15:3; 17:9; 19:10; 23:18; 25:4; 30:16; 31:3, 4; 31:21; 33:8; 34:14, 15, 19; 35:26. The specification "Torah of Moses" is found in 2 Chron 23:18; 30:16; 34:14. For an analysis of these texts, see Lars Maskow, *Tora in der Chronik. Studien zur Rezeption des Pentateuchs in den Chronikbüchern*, FRLANT 274 (Göttingen: Vandenhoeck & Ruprecht, 2019).

2. 1 Chron 16:40; 2 Chron 17:9; 23:18; 25:4; 31:3; 34:14, 15, 19; 35:26. As

teuchal texts, such as Numbers 28:3–8; Exodus 29:38–42 and Deuteronomy 17:14–20.[3] Therefore, it seems probable that the Chronicler presupposes the Pentateuch, or at least an early stage of it, and that he considers the latter authoritative.[4] Consequently, regarding the *tabnît*-motif in 1 Chronicles 28, one has to address the question of its relationship to the *tabnît* of Moses. More generally, one should ask whether there is a conflict of competence between the two pivotal figures since both of them appear as founders of the Israelite cult. In the context of this question, it is striking that Moses, the lawgiver and "man of God", is only rarely mentioned in Chronicles. He fades compared to David who plays a major role as king of Israel in a large part of the composition (1 Chron 11–29),[5] and who is also called "man of God."[6]

The present essay aims first to elucidate the diverse activities of King David related to the foundation of the first temple of Jerusalem and its cult. The second part of the paper will consider the question of how David's striking equation with Moses, Israel's cult founder *par excellence*, should be understood. Is he a second Moses? What is the status of the instructions compiled by him in comparison with that of the Torah? This question seems to have attracted only little attention in scholarship.[7] The importance of David in general is often

---

Thomas Willi ("Tora in den biblischen Chronikbüchern," *Judaica* 36 [1980]: 102–5, 148–51, here 104) has shown, the use of the term Torah is nevertheless broader and includes oral instruction and application of the *torâ*. Quite illustrative is the statement of 2 Chron 15:3 ("And for many days Israel was without the true God and without a teaching priest and without *torâ*"). Since the assertion refers to the post-Mosaic era, "*torâ*" here does not mean the written law but rather the application of the Torah by an authorized priest.

3. The mentioned laws are related to the *tamîd*-sacrifice and law of the king, which are considered late by an increasing number of scholars. See the respective treatments in Maskow, *Tora in der Chronik*, 80–81, with n. 78 lit. (*tamîd*-sacrifice); 96, with n. 128 lit. (law of the king).

4. See Martin Noth, *The Chronicler's History*, transl. Hugh G. M. Williamson (Sheffield: JSOT Press, 1987), 100; Hans-Peter Mathys, "Die Ketubim," in *Die Entstehung des Alten Testaments*, ed. Walter Dietrich et al., Theologische Wissenschaft 1 (Stuttgart: Kohlhammer, 2014), 593; Konrad Schmid, *Literaturgeschichte des Alten Testaments: Eine Einführung* (Darmstadt: Wissenschaftliche Buchgesellschaft, 2008), 147.

5. According to Knoppers's word-count, the David-section covers no less than 27,5 % of the entire book. See Gary N. Knoppers, *1 Chronicles 10–29: A New Translation with Introduction and Commentary*, Anchor Bible (New York: Doubleday, 2004), 903.

6. Concerning the attribute "man of God", see below §3.

7. For short treatments of this question, see Gerhard von Rad, *Das Geschichtsbild des chronistischen Werkes* (Stuttgart: Kohlhammer, 1930), 130–31, 136; Sara Japhet, *The Ideology of the Book of Chronicles and Its Place in Biblical Thought*, transl. A. Barber (Frankfurt a/M-Bern-New York: Lang, 1989), 237–38. More elaborate are Simon J. de Vries, "Moses and David as Cult Founders in Chronicles," *JBL*

explained with reference to the Chronicler's hope for a restoration of the Davidic monarchy in the late Persian or early Hellenistic era,[8] or rather as an eschatological messianic expectation.[9] However, if one or the other were the case, why, one should ask, would the author put such emphasis on David's competence for the conceptualization and the establishment of the Jerusalemite cult. In view of this strong focus, one might imagine another main reason for the great importance assigned to David by the author: it might have less to do with his significance as dynasty founder and bearer of messianic hopes than with the high value given to the Jerusalemite temple and its foundation which necessitated an appropriate founder personality.[10] David's importance in the Book of Chronicles consists primarily in his role of founder of Israel's unique sanctuary and the organization of its cult.

2. DAVID AS CULT FOUNDER IN THE BOOKS OF CHRONICLES

The following part explores the different functions David fulfills in Chronicles as founder of the temple and its cult. We begin with the motif that David received the divine plan of the temple, the *tabnît* (cf. 1 Chron 28).

2.1 DAVID RECEIVES FROM YHWH A PLAN OR BLUEPRINT (TABNÎT) OF THE FUTURE SANCTUARY (1 CHRON 28)

The Chronicler takes over this motif from the Priestly tabernacle account (Exod 25–40). Therefore, it is useful to bring to mind the concept of the *tabnît* as it appears in this section. Several statements un-

---

107 (1988): 619–39; Georg Steins, "Chronistisches Geschichtsbild und 'levitische Predigt'. Überlegungen zur Eigenart der Chronik im Anschluss an Gerhard von Rad," in *Das Alte Testament – ein Geschichtsbuch*? ed. E. Blum et al., Altes Testament und Moderne 10 (Münster: Litverlag, 2005), 147–73, here 169–70.

  8. See Noth, The Chronicler's History, 105–6; Wilhelm Rudolph, "Problems of the Books of Chronicles," VT 4 (1954): 404–9; André Caquot, "Peut-on-parler de messianisme dans l'oeuvre du Chroniste?," RTP 3/16 (1966): 110–120; Rudolf Mosis, *Untersuchungen zur Theologie des chronistischen Geschichtswerkes*, Freiburger Theologische Studien 92 (Freiburg-Basel-Wien: Herder, 1973), 162–63.

  9. See J. Wilhelm Rothstein and Johannes Hänel, *Kommentar zum ersten Buch der Chronik*, KAT (Leipzig: A. Deicherstsche Verbuchhandlung, 1927), xliii–xliv; Von Rad, *Das Geschichtsbild des chronistischen Werkes*, 119–32; Walter Brueggemann, *David's Truth in Israel's Imagination and Memory*, 2nd Edition (Minneapolis: Fortress Press, 2002), 101–2.

  10. Similarly Georg Steins, *Chronistisches Geschichtsbild und 'levitische Predigt'*, 159; Pancratius C. Beentjes, *Tradition and Transformation in the Book of Chronicles*, SSN 52 (Leiden: Brill, 2008), 56.

derline that the *tabnît* is "shown" to Moses (הָאר hi.).[11] With regard to this verb, most scholars conjecture that Moses is presented with a *model*; either the three-dimensional celestial proto-type of the tabernacle (the "tent of YHWH")[12] or a real miniature model.[13] The second possibility is supported by the fact that miniature homes and clay model houses have been found throughout the ancient Near East.[14]

What does *tabnît* in Chronicles mean and how does David gain insight in it? The term *tabnît* appears in total four times; all occurrences are found in 1 Chronicles 28. Since the texts in question contain certain difficulties, they are shortly discussed:

2.1.1 1 CHRONICLES 28:11

וַיִּתֵּן דָּוִיד לִשְׁלֹמֹה בְנוֹ אֶת־תַּבְנִית הָאוּלָם וְאֶת־בָּתָּיו וְגַנְזַכָּיו וַעֲלִיֹּתָיו וַחֲדָרָיו הַפְּנִימִים וּבֵית הַכַּפֹּרֶת׃

> Then David gave to his son Solomon **the plan** (*tabnît*) of the porch (of the temple), its buildings, its storehouses, its upper rooms, its inner rooms, and the room for the mercy seat.

Most scholars understand *tabnît* in the sense of a written document. This understanding is supported by verse 19 (see below) in which a written document is mentioned. If correct, the conception of the *tabnît* deviates from the "model"-concept of the tabernacle account. In the latter, the *tabnît* never is associated with a written document. Another difference: David as recipient of the *tabnît* hands it over to another leading figure, Solomon.

2.1.2 1 CHRONICLES 28:12

The subsequent verse mentions another plan (*tabnît*), which David gives to Solomon. Translators and commentators do not agree on the meaning of the expression ברוח in the statement in question. It is rendered either by "in mind" or "by the Spirit (of God)."

> and the plan (*tabnît*) of all that he had (in mind) **by the Spirit**: of the courts of the House of the LORD and all its surrounding chambers, and

---

11. See Exod 25:9, 40; 26:30; 27:8.

12. Umberto Cassuto, A Commentary on the Book of Exodus (Jerusalem: Magnes, 1967), 322; Richard J. Clifford, "The Tent of El and the Israelite Tent of Meeting," CBQ 33: 221–27, here 226.

13. Victor A. Hurowitz, *I Have Built You an Exalted House*: Temple Building in the Bible in Light of Mesopotamian and Northwest Semitic Writings, JSOTSup 115 (Sheffield: Sheffield Academic Press, 1992); William H. C. Propp, Exodus 19–40, Anchor Bible (New York: Doubleday, 2006), 376–77.

14. Cf. Propp, *Exodus 19–40*, 376–77 with reference to Maria G. Masetti-Rouault, "Les maquettes dans les textes mésopotamiens," in '*Maquettes architecturales' de l'Antiquité*, ed. B. Muller, Université Strasbourg Travaux du centre de recherche sur le Proche-Orient et la Gréce antiques 17 (Paris: de Boccard, 2001), 445–61.

of the treasuries of the House of God and of the treasuries of the holy things; (TANAKH, 1985, The Jewish Publication Society).[15]

and the plan (*tabnît*) of all that he **had in mind**, for the courts of the house of the LORD, and for all the surrounding rooms, for the storehouses of the house of God, and for the storehouses of the dedicated things; (The New American Standard Bible, 1977)[16]

Which understanding is preferable? Gary N. Knoppers's argument in favor of the understanding "by the Spirit" in his commentary seems pertinent: "Some (…) prefer to translate 'he had in his mind' (…). This is possible, but one wonders why the writer did not write *hāyâ ʿim lĕbābô*, as one might expect."[17] The expression *hāyâ ʿim lĕbābô* ("he had in his heart [=his mind]") appears in 1 Chronicles 22:7; 28:2; 2 Chronicles 6:7. Regarding the particular choice of vocabulary in 1 Chronicles 28:12 (ברוח), Knoppers opts for the understanding "Spirit." Through divine inspiration, David has insight in the organization of the temple compound, its various parts (courts, surrounding chambers, treasuries). Knoppers's interpretation seems correct also for the following reason: In Chronicles, the motif of the "spirit of God (YHWH)" appears several times. Interestingly, in two other texts רוח is used in the absolute sense, as in the present text, and means "spirit of God".[18] There might be an influence by the book of Ezekiel, in which the expression in absolute use plays an important role (see Ezek 1; 37).[19]

2.1.3 1 Chronicles 28:18

וּלְמִזְבַּח הַקְּטֹרֶת זָהָב מְזֻקָּק בַּמִּשְׁקָל וּלְתַבְנִית הַמֶּרְכָּבָה הַכְּרֻבִים זָהָב לְפֹרְשִׂים וְסֹכְכִים עַל־אֲרוֹן בְּרִית־יְהוָה׃

(and David gave him the weight of the gold) for the altar of incense of

---

15. See also Knoppers, *1 Chronicles 10–29*, 931; Sara Japhet, *1 Chronik*, HThKAT (Freiburg: Herder, 2002), 435 ("was ihm durch den Geist in den Sinn gekommen war").

16. See also Edward L. Curtis and Albert A. Madsen, *Chronicles*, ICC (Edinburgh: T&T Clark, 1910), 298; Sara Japhet, *I and II Chronicles*, OTL (Louisville: Westminster John Knox, 1993), 481; Ralph W. Klein, *1 Chronicles: A Commentary*, Hermeneia (Minneapolis: Fortress, 2006), 525.

17. Cf. Knoppers, *1 Chronicles 10–29*, 931.

18. According to 1 Chron 12:19, "the Spirit" came upon Amasai, the chief of the thirty, and Amasai found the right words to convince David about the honorable intentions of the men who joined David in Ziklag. According to 2 Chron 18:20, in the assembly of YHWH it is the spirit (הרוח) who knows the means how to deceive King Abiah.

19. The movement of the wheels and the creatures besides them is coordinated by the "spirit" (רוח). See Walter Zimmerli, *Ezekiel 1: A Commentary on the Book of the Prophet Ezekiel, Chapters 1–24*, Hermeneia (Philadelphia: Fortress, 1979), 130. Concerning Ezek 37, see Zimmerli, *Ezekiel 1, Chapters 1–24*, 262.

refined gold and **for the model** (*tabnît*) **of the chariot**, *that is* the cherubim, that spread out *their wings*, and covered the ark of the covenant of YHWH.

As for its third occurrence, *tabnît* appears as part of the compound noun "model of the chariot." David indicates the weight of the gold for the *tabnît* of the chariot. In this context, one should not translate *tabnît* with "plan", but rather with "model" or "construction."[20] David indicates the weight of the gold used for (ל) the altar of incense and for (ל) the "model of the chariot." Certain commentators ignore the preposition "for" (ל) and erroneously translate "(and David gave him) the plan of the chariot."[21] The chariot is equated with the cherubim-throne ("the chariot, that is the cherubim"). Probably, the author was influenced by Ezekiel 1, where a similar idea is expressed. The cherubim constitute a vehicle having wheels. However, only in 1 Chronicles 28:18 the designation *merkābâ* for YHWH's "cherubim-chariot" appears; it is, besides Ben Sira 49:8,[22] the only occurrence of this term in the Hebrew Bible, which later on in Jewish mystic movements became so important. Yet, concerning the wording, the question arises of why the author formulates in this indirect way: "for the model of chariot" instead of "for the chariot." Would he like to say that the "chariot" in the Holy of Holies is not the real throne of YHWH but only a model? Such a differentiation between "prototype" and "model" might have been suggestive to the author in light of the chariot-concept of Ezekiel 1. Here, the chariot forms a moving and enormous cloud touching the firmament above (see in particular Ezek 1:15–21). Therefore, according to the author of 1 Chronicles 28:18, the chariot in the Holy of Holies can be nothing more than a *replication* of the real, unseizable and uncapturable chariot of YHWH.

2.1.4 1 Chronicles 28:19

Verse 28:19, where the *tabnît* appears for the fourth time, has a textual difficulty and is, in general, challenging to understand. The Massoretic Text (MT) reads as follows:

הַכֹּל בִּכְתָב מִיַּד יְהוָה עָלַי הִשְׂכִּיל כֹּל מַלְאֲכוֹת הַתַּבְנִית׃

In all this by a writing from the hand of YHWH upon me he (YHWH) gave (me) insight (לְהַשְׂכִּיל), in all the works of the **plan**.

While MT reads עָלַי "on me" or "to me", the Septuagint, which devi-

---

20. Expressing this understanding, Japhet, *1 Chronik*, 435.
21. See Klein, *1 Chronicles: A Commentary*, 515; Japhet, *I and II Chronicles*, 481. See, however, Japhet, *1 Chronik*, 435 ("und für das Modell des Wagens der Cherubim aus Gold")!
22. See the expression ἅρματος χερουβιν in LXX for Hebrew מרכבה זני.

ates in many points from MT, reflects עָלָיו "on him".

> LXX: πάντα ἐν γραφῇ χειρὸς κυρίου ἔδωκεν Δαυιδ Σαλωμων κατὰ τὴν περιγενηθεῖσαν αὐτῷ σύνεσιν τῆς κατεργασίας τοῦ παραδείγματος
>
> David gave all to Solomon in the Lord's handwriting, according to the knowledge given him of the work of the pattern.

If we adopt the reading of MT, verse 19 would include a direct speech by David referring back to verses 11–18. A difficulty of this understanding lies in the fact that the direct speech is not introduced. For this reason, some modern translations insert "and David said", although such facilitating plus is not attested in any textual witness. However, this striking feature, the change to the direct speech, may be explained as a stylistic particularity of the Chronicler. The same sudden shift from the 3rd person to the 1st person occurs also in 1 Chronicles 23:5.[23]

Many commentators read עָלָיו "on him" instead of עָלַי "on me," on the basis of LXX.[24] הִשְׂכִּיל could be understood in the intransitive sense. One may suppose a scribal mistake in MT, namely a haplography of the two similar letters *yod* and *waw*. This reconstructed alternative text would read as follows:

> In all this by a writing from the hand of YHWH upon him he (David) had insight (הִשְׂכִּיל), in all the works of the plan.

Despite the uncertainty in the phraseology, the intention of this verse seems clear: David is inspired by a document written by God. It is through this document, that David has gained insight in all details of the temple architecture.

2.1.5 ORIGINALITY OF THE LITERARY COMPOSITION IN 1 CHRONICLES 28

The specifications of the plan of the temple described in chapter 28 reveal that the author was strongly influenced by the Priestly tabernacle account and Ezekiel:

– The conception of the *tabnît* as written document, which originated in a plan written by God (1 Chron 28:11, 12, 19), is absent from the temple construction report in 1 Kings 6–7. Here, the Chronicler combines motifs found in the tabernacle account of P and in Ezekiel

---

23. According to William Johnstone, *1 Chronicles 1 – 2 Chronicles 9. Israel's Place among the Nations*, JSOTSup 253 (Sheffield: Sheffield Academic, 1997), 282, the author chose the "curious interjection in the first person…in order to emphasize the surpassing authority of the divine revelation of the Temple and its cult to David." Knoppers, *1 Chronicles 10–29*, 923 also follows MT.

24. See for instance, Wilhelm Rudolph, *Chronikbücher*, HAT 21 (Tübingen: Mohr Siebeck, 1955), 188; *Japhet, I and II Chronicles*, 482.

(in Ezek 43:11, Ezekiel is ordered to write down the vision of the temple).

– The Holy of Holies is called "the room of the mercy seat" (28:11, בֵּית הַכַּפֹּרֶת). This peculiar designation is certainly influenced by the tabernacle account, which gives great importance to the "mercy seat" (כַּפֹּרֶת). Yet the designation "room of the mercy seat" is absent in P.

– The depiction of the Cherubim as a chariot (28:18): As shown above, this motif is certainly influenced by the wheeled object described in Ezekiel 1 and 10. At the same time, the protecting function of the Cherubim as it appears in the tabernacle account is mentioned.[25]

However, the reader is also confronted with certain peculiar motifs which do not appear in the mentioned traditions but constitute novelties:

– The temple contains among others "store rooms" (גְּנָזִים) and "upper rooms" (עֲלִיֹּת) (cf. v. 11). Whereas the former expression is a *hapax* but is related to גֶּנֶז "treasury" (cf. Est 3:9; 4:7), the latter term appears only one more time in the Hebrew Bible (in 2 Chron 3:9). Mentioned are furthermore "inner rooms" (חֲדָרִים פְּנִימִים).

– As for the construction material, besides gold, which is the dominant metal, silver is mentioned too. The plan includes silver lampstands, silver tables, and silver bowls (cf. vv. 15–17). Strikingly, none of these items appears in the temple construction report in 1 Kings 6–8, in the tabernacle account and in Ezekiel 40–48.

Summarizing this section, we state that in his development of the intriguing *tabnît* theme, the author of 1 Chronicles 28 borrows elements from different cult traditions, in particular from P and Ezekiel. He furthermore introduces certain items unknown in other biblical traditions apparently in order to provide a legitimation for novelties stemming from the Second Temple era.

2.2 DAVID TAKES THE INITIATIVE FOR THE GENEROUS DONATION IN FAVOR OF THE PROJECTED TEMPLE (1 CHRON 29)

A further remarkable activity of King David related to the building of the temple is as follows: 1 Chronicles 29 reports how David takes the initiative for a generous donation in favor of the projected Temple (vv. 2–5). After having offered enormous donations himself, David summons the leadership of Israel (i. e. a large assembly including the leaders and the representatives of Israel's tribes and army) to contribute to

---

25. Note, however, that the motif of the protecting function of the Cherubim is also found in 1 Kgs 8:7.

the building project in equally substantial manner. As in the previous chapter, David's action recalls that of Moses in the Priestly tabernacle account, who gave the order to donate for the building of the tabernacle in the wilderness. In contrast to Moses, however, David, by offering generous donations himself, serves as a model for the assembled authorities. Another difference of Chronicles in comparison with the tabernacle account is the indication of precise quantities: these quantities are enormous.

Moreover, David addresses a prayer to YHWH in which he puts the donation in a theological perspective. In his point of view, all the vast riches he and the people donate to YHWH belong, in reality, to the deity (vv. 14, 16). At the end of the prayer, he furthermore petitions for the realization of the promised construction of the Temple (v. 19).

Looking on the chapters 1 Chronicles 28–29 as a whole, one becomes aware of how strongly it deviates from its primary *Vorlage* in Samuel-Kings.[26] Together with the following chapter 29 it forms one unit culminating in Solomon's enthronement (1 Chron 29:23–25). While David's speech parallels David's speeches in 1 Kings 1–2 (in particular the farewell address to Solomon in 1 Kings 2:1–9), the two pericopes differ entirely with respect to their content. Whereas the latter, in its present form, may be characterized as "a fairly sordid story of power politics thinly disguised as a morality tale,"[27] the former deals uniquely with important matters of the projected sanctuary: David entrusts the plan of the temple to Solomon, and he encourages the people to donate for it. The two versions of David's testament could not be more dissimilar!

2.3 APPOINTMENT AND DIVERSIFICATION OF THE LEVITES BY DAVID (1 CHRON 23–27)

A third activity of David related to the cult foundation is the appointment of Levites and priests in 1 Chronicles 23–27. These five chapters give an overview of the inner organization of Levites in divisions. The Levites act as priests, as singers and as gatekeepers. Later on, these prescriptions by David are referred to as follows: The Levites are told to act and perform their duties "as prescribed in the writings of King David (בכתב דויד) of Israel and in the document of his son Solomon (שלמה ובמכתב)" (2 Chron 35:4). The author is aware that these detailed descriptions in chapters 23–27 are not found in the Torah given by Moses. Therefore, he refers to them as separate, complementing "writings". This reference to a distinct written document should probably

---

26. See Japhet, *I and II Chronicles*, 483.

27. Cf. Iain W. Provan, *1 and 2 Kings*, NIBCOT (Peabody, Mass.: Hendrickson, 1995), 40.

be seen in close connection with the written plan, the *tabnît*, David received from YHWH and handed over to Solomon.[28]

The chapters 1 Chronicles 23–27 express the Chronicler's particular interest for the development of the cultic institutions, and the organization of the Temple personnel – a theme which is closely related to that of the planning of the sanctuary.[29] The description in 1 Chronicles 23–27 results in a highly complicated differentiation of groups and functions in the cultic community of Jerusalem.[30] Knoppers concludes from his analysis that the responsibilities of the Levites and the priests are complementary and balanced: "Both the priests and the Levites are essential to the success of the Temple cultus. (…) (T)he summary of Levitical duties is evidence for the Chronicler's own distinctive stance, a via media between the positions of Deuteronomy, the Priestly source, and Ezekiel."[31]

3. David as a second Moses: The Chronicler's handling of the Pentateuchal cultic tradition

In his report on the foundation and building of the First Temple, the Chronicler transforms his *Vorlage*, the books of Samuel and Kings, radically. He is highly influenced by the Priestly tradition, in particular

---

28. See Steins, "Chronistisches Geschichtsbild und 'levitische Predigt'," 169 and see further below §3.

29. This interpretation was refuted by M. Noth on literary-critical grounds and with regard to the Chronicler's global plan. According to him, an author having the aim to validate the Levitical claims would not have referred to instructions edited by David. See Noth, *The Chronicler's History*, 100 (for the literary-critical argument, cf. 33). See also Adam C. Welch, *The Work of the Chronicler: Its Purpose and Its Date* (London: Oxford University Press, 1939); Thomas Willi, *Die Chronik als Auslegung. Untersuchungen zur literarischen Gestaltung der historischen Überlieferung Israels*, FRLANT 106 (Göttingen: Vandenhoeck & Ruprecht, 1972), 194–204. The literary classification of 1 Chron 23–27 is disputed, but recent scholarship considers these chapters to be an integral part of the Chronicler's work. See John W. Wright, "The Legacy of David in Chronicles: The Narrative Function of 1 Chronicles 23–27," JBL 110 (1991): 229–42; *Japhet, I and II Chronicles*, 406–11; Knoppers, *1 Chronicles 10–29*, 788–98.

30. For a helpful overview on these chapters, see Louis C. Jonker, "David's Officials According to the Chronicler (1 Chronicles 23–27): A Reflection of Second Temple Self-Categorization?," in *Historiography and Identity (Re)formulation in Second Temple Historiographical Literature*, ed. Louis C. Jonker, LHBOTS 534 (London: T&T Clark, 2010), 65–91; Louis C. Jonker, *Defining All-Israel in Chronicles. Multi-levelled Identity. Negotiation in Late Persian-Period Yehud*, FAT 106 (Tübingen: Mohr Siebeck, 2016), 246–52.

31. Gary N. Knoppers, "Hierodules, Priests, or Janitors? The Levites in Chronicles and the History of the Israelite Priesthood," *JBL* 118/1 (1999): 49–72, here 71.

by the tabernacle account, and also by Ezekiel (see above). This influence of P and late(or post-) Priestly texts is also visible in the chapters of the building and inauguration of the temple in 2 Chronicles 3–7. However, as shown above, in some of these texts it becomes evident that Chronicles deviate from the tabernacle account and compete with the latter. In certain respects, the foundation of the Jerusalem temple *surpasses that of the tabernacle*: the *tabnît* David received is a written document and not only orally transmitted; in contrast to Moses, it is through his personal generous donation that David encourages the assembled Israelites to consecrate their riches to YHWH; also, the tabernacle ("tent of meeting"), constructed by Moses in the wilderness, and at time established at Gibeon (2 Chron 1:3; 1 Chron 21:29), is deposited in the much bigger temple of David and Solomon (2 Chron 5:5). We have also seen that the author integrates certain novelties of the second temple in his report. David's innovations are significant; he plays a role similar to Moses. Yet, David's instructions are called "writing" (כתב), "ordinance" (מצוה), and "law" (משפט) rather than "Torah".[32] Therefore, at first sight, one might think that the author attributed to the ancient prescriptions preserved in the Torah a higher status than to David's writings. As Noth puts it: "(…) in the cultic sphere the age of an ordinance is always a valid legitimation: the older carries greater weight than the more recent."[33] Noth concluded that "the more recent arrangements of David could not make any headway against the older pronouncements of Moses."[34] He was critical of the view that the Chronicler intended to justify certain novelties in the cult. Pursuing such a goal, the reformer of the cult "would have had to expand the tradition of Moses to conform it to his purpose."[35] However, such reasoning does not consider the possibility that at the Chronicler's time the Torah was already a closed corpus. As mentioned above, the redaction of 1–2 Chronicles probably presupposes the achievement of the Pentateuch and the wide recognition of its authoritative status. Therefore, basically, the only way to bring in innovations into the Israelite cultic system was to invent another "collection" of prescriptions and to assign the latter to an authority equal to Moses.[36] The author of Chronicles has found this authority in David whom he conceived as recipient and transmitter of the *tabnît* of the temple and further cultic

---

32. "Writings" and "ordonances" attributed to David are mentioned in 1 Chron 28:19 (כתב);).2 Chron 8:14 (משפט, מצוה); 29:25 (מצוה); 35:35 (מצוה); 35:4 (כתב).

33. Noth, *The Chronicler's History*, 100.

34. Noth, *The Chronicler's History*, 100.

35. Noth, *The Chronicler's History*, 100.

36. Another way was to declare certain novelties as Mosaic Torah. For an example see Willi, "Thora in den biblischen Chronikbüchern," 149–50. In 2 Chron 30:16 (text displayd below) the Torah seems expanded in favour of the Levites.

ordinances. There is indeed an indication that the author is keen to see David and Moses on equal footing. As mentioned above in the introduction, David is given the same extraordinary attribute "man of God" (איש האלהים) as Moses.[37] David receives this title in his function as cult founder, in striking analogy to Moses, the founder of the cult (cf. 2 Chron 8:14 with 2 Chron 30:16).[38]

> "Following the prescription of his father David, he set up the divisions of the priests for their duties, and the Levites for their watches, to praise and to serve alongside the priests, according to each day's requirement, and the gatekeepers in their watches, gate by gate, for such was the commandment of David, the man of God (כמצות דויד איש האלהים)" (2 Chron 8:14; JPS Tanakh).

> "They took their stations, as was their rule according to the Teaching of Moses, man of God (כתורת משה איש האלהים). The priests dashed the blood which they received from the Levites." (2 Chron 30:16; JPS Tanakh)

Furthermore, both, Moses and David, are called "servant of God / YHWH" and "my servant" respectively.[39]

The emphasis put on the equality between the two authority figures should not be interpreted in the sense that David is just Moses' succeeder and imitator. Rather, high status and esteem accorded to David reveal that he is conceived as an innovator of Israel's cult, precisely like Mose was at his time.[40]

4. THE CHRONICLER'S IDEOLOGICAL AGENDA

The above investigation has shown that the Chronicler's presentation of king David's preparation of the temple building and establishment of cult challenges both the tradition of 1–2 Kings and the Mosaic tabernacle account. What are his main motivations to do so? The answer I propose in conclusion to this question goes in three different direc-

---

37. Used for Moses: 1 Chron 23:14; 2 Chron 30:16; applied to David: 2 Chron 8:14.

38. See William M. Schniedewind, *The Word of God in Transition: From Prophet to Exegete in the Second Temple Period*. JSOTSup 197 (Sheffield: Sheffield Academic Press, 1995), 50–51.

39. Moses: 1 Chron 6:34; 2 Chron 1:3; 24:6, 9; David: 1 Chron 17:4, 7; 2 Chron 6:16. To be sure, none of the two expressions is used exclusively for Moses and David; איש האלהים is also applied to Shemaiah (2 Chron 11:2); in his prayer Solomon designates himself as "your servant" (2 Chron 6:19).

40. Similarly, von Rad, *Das Geschichtsbild des chronistischen Werkes*, 130; Jaeyoung Jeon, "The Priestly Tent of Meeting in Chronicles: Pro-Priestly or Anti-Priestly?" JHS 18/7 (2018), 1–15, here 11.

tions:

(1) First, the Chronicler's motivation is *theological-exegetical*: In 1 Kings 6–8, the Chronicler's *Vorlage*, a divine authorization of the chosen temple architecture is absent. Compared with the Priestly tabernacle account in Exodus 25–29; 35–40 which relates that Moses was shown the plan of the tabernacle by YHWH, Solomon's building project in the book of Kings appears theologically deficient. Therefore, the author of Chronicles intended to correct his *Vorlage*, the Book of Kings, at this point. Like with the building of the tabernacle, the construction of the Solomonic Temple should be based on a *tabnît* (see 1 Chron 28). Doing so, the Chronicler provides a better legitimation for the Solomonic temple than that given in Samuel–Kings. He establishes "a long continuity in cultic affairs from the time of Moses to the time of the monarchy" with its emblematic figure David.[41]

Furthermore, the comparison of the two sections 1 Chron 28–29 and 1 Kings 1–2 presenting both a testament by David brings nicely into relief the Chronicler's intention to associate king David primarily with the foundation of the temple in Jerusalem and its cult rather than with the concern of his succession and the maintenance of his dynasty. In general, as argued above in the introduction (§ 1), the great importance assigned to David and his dynasty by the author is primarily due to the high value accorded to to the Jerusalemite temple and its foundation. According to the pointed statement of Beentjes, "David's dynasty only matters as long and in as far as it guarantees optimal conditions for the construction of the temple and the preservation of the cultic institutions."[42]

(2) The Chronicler has a *cult-theological* interest. He aims to provide a legitimate basis for certain novelties of the Second Temple architecture which are unknown in both tabernacle account and 1 Kings 6–8. It would be particularly interesting to know more about the function of the "treasure rooms" and "upper rooms" in the temple at the Chronicler's time (according to 2 Chron 3:8–9 the "upper rooms" were located close to the Holy of Holies and overlaid with gold). Furthermore, 1–2 Chronicles strengthen the position of the Levites and assigns them new tasks. The Chronicler's aim is to put the innovations on a par with the elements stemming from the ancient traditions and thus to legitimize them. By this, the Chronicler brings the continuous tradition into his own time: the tradition runs from Moses through David-Solomon to the Second Temple community.

---

41. Knoppers, *1 Chronicles 10–29*, 941.
42. Beentjes (*Tradition and Transformation*, 103), "David's dynasty only matters as long and in as far as it guarantees optimal conditions for the construction of the temple and the preservation of the cultic institutions."

(3) The Chronicler has a *cult-political* interest: The establishment of a continuous tradition was all the more important because, according to the Chronicler, the Priestly tabernacle account, a composition stemming from the Persian era, could not serve this aim – at least not in an appropriate manner. Regarding the P's tabernacle account, a problematic aspect for the author of Chronicles probably was the location in the wilderness, far away from Jerusalem, and the absence of any explicit link to the temple in Jerusalem. Because of these particularities, the tabernacle account may well have contributed to the decentralization of the cult in the Persian era and may have served as a model for different sanctuaries, even though this was probably not the intention of the tabernacle account.[43] Today, it is known that a YHWH temple existed in Elephantine in Egypt in Persian times and another one on Mount Gerizim close to Shechem. The numerous dedication inscriptions found in the excavations on Mount Gerizim, particularly contain several motifs that are reminiscent of the Priestly tabernacle account and other Priestly texts.[44] The author of Chroni-

---

43. There are important indications that the tabernacle account aims towards the Jerusalem temple as it is described in the report of the building of the Solomon's temple (1 Kgs 6–8). Common points and parallels between the two accounts are as follows: (1) The general structure, orientation and measurements of the tabernacle correspond largely to those of the Solomonic temple. Both sanctuaries are rectangular and have an east-west orientation. Both have a holy of holies (inner sanctum), holy place (outer sanctum), and a courtyard. As for the measurements of the tabernacle (footprint: 30×10 cubits), they correspond to those of the Solomonic temple (footprint: 60×20 cubits), covering precisely half of the area of the temple of Jerusalem. (2) The tabernacle account describes important items of furniture appearing in the report of the construction of Solomon's temple (cherubim, wooden lining, ark, table, lamp[s]). (3) The ornamentation with cherubim on the walls and with curtains respectively, is similar. (4) Both accounts describe similar elaborate architectures reflecting a gradation of sanctity through the subdivision of the sanctuary area, and through the attribution of different building materials to the three areas (gold and precious wood for the furniture of the holy of holies and of the outer sanctum; bronze for the articles of the court). See, among others, Menahem Haran, *Temples and Temple Service in Ancient Israel* (Oxford: Oxford University Press, 1978), 189–94; Suzanne Boorer, *The Vision of the Priestly Narrative: Its Genre and Hermeneutics of Time*, Ancient Israel and Its Literature 27 (Atlanta: SBL, 2016), 306–10; Jürg Hutzli, "Priestly(-like) Texts in Samuel and Kings," in *Writing, Rewriting, and Overwriting in the Books of Deuteronomy and the Former Prophets. Essays in Honour of Cynthia Edenburg*, ed. Ido Koch, Thomas Römer, and Omer Sergi, BETL 304 (Leuven: Peeters, 2019), 224–25.

44. For the editio princeps, see Yitzhak Magen, Haggai Misgav, and Levana Tsfania, *Mount Gerizim Excavations, I: The Aramaic, Hebrew and Samaritan Inscriptions*, JSP 2 (Jerusalem: Staff Officer of Archaeology, 2004). Concerning the dating of the inscriptions: Jan Dušek, *Aramaic and Hebrew Inscriptions from Mt. Gerizim and Samaria between Antiochus III and Antiochus IV Epiphanes*, CHANE 54 (Leiden: Brill, 2012), 6–62; Anne Katrine de Hemmer Gudme, *Before the God in This Place for Good Remembrance: A Comparative Analysis of the Aramaic Votive Inscriptions from Mount Gerizim*, BZAW 441 (Berlin: de Gruyter, 2013), 78–84; Reinhard Pum-

cles, facing this for him problematic reception history of the tabernacle account, wanted to reaffirm YHWH's exclusive election of the Jerusalem temple and its cultic community for all times.[45] The means to emphasize Jerusalem's election was the insertion of the motif of the divine inspiration of the building plan for the Solomonic temple and the depiction of king David as transmitter of this plan and promulgator of cultic laws. By this, the continuity between Moses' tabernacle and the Jerusalem temple was assured and specified: The tabernacle account, as a foundation myth of Israel's cult, should be understood in a strict exclusive way: it aimed only towards the temple of Jerusalem but not to any other Yahwistic sanctuaries as well.

---

mer, "Samaritan Studies – Recent Research Results," in *The Bible, Qumran, and the Samaritans*, ed. Magnar Kartveit and Gary N. Knoppers, Studia Samaritana 10/STJ 104 (Berlin: de Gruyter, 2016), 66–7.

45. Similarly, Noth, *The Chronicler's History*, 100–101.

The Righteousness of the Levites in Chronicles and Ezekiel
Christine Mitchell

1. Introduction

In an article in *Catholic Biblical Quarterly* in 2006, I made a passing remark about 2 Chronicles 29:34, that it seemed to be "a direct response to Ezek 44:12–13…(the play on words is quite obvious)."[1] In that article my focus was on the legitimacy of the expanded role of the Levites in Josiah's Passover in 2 Chronicles 34. In this contribution, I take up the issue of the dialogue between the texts of Chronicles and Ezekiel on the question of the Levites. Because of the linguistic similarities and the tone of both texts, I argue that the dialogue is not a mere discussion, but is a polemic, where the audience of one text sees the implied polemic against the other text. In the case of each text, there is a view of the role, function, and evaluation of the Levites: in the case of Chronicles, it is a positive evaluation; while in the case of Ezekiel 40–48, it is a negative evaluation. In both texts the role and function of the Levites is described in similar terms; it is the aetiology of the role and function that is different, leading to the opposite evaluations. However, unlike the majority of previous scholarship, I do not consider these aetiologies and evaluations to be useful in reconstructing a history of the Judahite priesthood or Levites (cf. some of the work cited below). Instead, I consider both texts to be part of a project of utopian world construction in the Second Temple period: they are texts at play, imagining possibilities rather than reporting actualities.[2] The written form of these imaginings

---

1. Christine Mitchell, "The Ironic Death of Josiah in Chronicles," CBQ 63 (2006): 430.

2. Steven Schweitzer, *Reading Utopia in Chronicles*, LHBOTS 442 (New York: T&T Clark, 2007); Steven J. Schweitzer and Frauke Uhlenbruch, eds., *Worlds That*

should not be discounted: as Donald Polaski has noted, the stability of writing – even though it may be subject to scribal processes such as supplementation – lends authority to these imagined possibilities.[3] More to the point, while it cannot be discounted that these textual visions had either a descriptive or prescriptive relationship with levitical and priestly practices, it is the rhetorical and textual relationships that I am investigating.

While I tend to the view that Ezekiel was composed before Chronicles, and therefore as a matter of literary history Chronicles is a response to Ezekiel, in a web of textuality, or canonically (if you like), or as components of an educational curriculum in the Second Temple period, either can be read as a response to the other.[4] Readers of texts at any point after the composition of Chronicles would not necessarily encounter Ezekiel before Chronicles, so it is important to discuss the mutual effects of the texts if we are interested in the rhetorical and textual relationships. In this, I remain an unregenerate post-structuralist: "il n'y a pas hors texte," as both Barthes and Derrida famously proclaimed. I also continue to be influenced by the work of Mikhail M. Bakhtin and his followers in terms of how inserted texts interact with their surrounding text. These theorists help us to understand the effect that inserted texts have in relationship to the text that surrounds them: the inserted text, which may have had its own independent func-

---

Could Not Be: *Utopia in Chronicles*, *Ezra*, *and Nehemiah*, LHBOTS 620 (New York: Bloomsbury T&T Clark, 2016). The literature on Ezek 40–48 (or Ezekiel as a whole) is more complex: although "utopian" is occasionally used as a way to describe the book, somewhat more often Ezekiel's vision of the temple in Ezek 40–48 is described as "eschatological." For a good summary of a variety of positions, see Steven S. Tuell, "Ezekiel 40–42 as Verbal Icon," *CBQ* 58 (1996): 649–64. He concludes that the envisioned temple is a heavenly temple, not to be built on earth. Although he does not spell out the implications for the Levites in ch. 44, such a vision would suggest an imagined role for Levites and priests. For a critique of Tuell's position, see John T. Strong, "Grounding Ezekiel's Heavenly Ascent: A Defense of Ezek 40–48 as a Program for Restoration," *SJOT* 26.2 (2012): 192–211. His point that Ezek 40–48 was written as an archive of a temple plan that could be studied is well-taken and aligned with an understanding of the text as an imagining of a temple.

3. Donald C. Polaski, "Writing and the Chronicler: Authorship, Ambivalence, and Utopia," in *Worlds That Could Not Be*: *Utopia in Chronicles*, *Ezra*, *and Nehemiah*, ed. Steven J. Schweitzer and Frauke Uhlenbruch, LHBOTS 620 (New York: Bloomsbury T&T Clark, 2016), 129–43.

4. The relationships between the various posited Pentateuchal redactional layers and the formation of Chronicles is spelled out in detail in Louis C. Jonker, "Melting Pots and Rejoinders? The Interplay among Literature Formation Processes during the Late Persian and Early Hellenistic Periods," *VT* 70 (2020): 42–54. As I am not expert in Pentateuchal redaction hypotheses, I leave these arguments aside. On the whole, though, I think Jonker's point is important: the final stages of the formation of the Pentateuch and the writing of Chronicles demonstrate similar tendencies: to merge traditions, and to debate new understandings of holiness (p. 43).

tion and meaning, now both influences the reading of the surrounding text and in turn is influenced by it.[5] The phenomenon of the inserted text is a significant issue for both Chronicles and Ezekiel: Chronicles in terms of how textual fragments are integrated into overarching sections of text, and Ezekiel 40–48 in particular as a component of the larger book of Ezekiel.

Linking two texts, 2 Chronicles 29:34 and Ezekiel 44:12–13, is hardly the formation of a web. In order to form a web of textuality, I bring in texts from Psalms and Deuteronomy. It is through this web that we can see the basis for the connection that forms the polemic between Chronicles and Ezekiel on the topic of Levites: in Chronicles not only are Levites more upright of heart than priests, but they have more righteousness than priests (*tsedeq*). To claim that someone was more righteous than priests might be a serious-enough claim, but when the priests themselves that Ezekiel promotes are Zadokite (whose name Zadok means "righteousness"), it is a more biting polemic.[6]

2. SECOND CHRONICLES 29

The relevant passage in 2 Chronicles 29 deals with Hezekiah's Passover. This Passover is so magnificent, so full of people (especially from the northern tribes), that there are insufficient priests to undertake the sacrifices. In this context, in 29:34, the Levites participate in sustaining or encouraging them, perhaps restoring their numbers (יחזקום); חזק in the Piel can mean "to encourage" or it can have a meaning similar to the Hifil "to strengthen." The LXX translates the verb here with ἀντελάβοντο, which suggests more than simple encouragement: active participation. At this point, the Chronicler makes the comment that seems to justify the Levites' participation and that casts a slur upon the priests: להתקדש מהכהנים כי הלוים ישרי לבב "For the Levites were more upright of heart [conscientious] in sanctifying themselves than

---

5. Mikhail M. Bakhtin, *Speech Genres and Other Late Essays*, trans. Michael Holquist and Caryl Emerson, 1st ed. (Austin: University of Texas Press, 1986); Yury M. Lotman, "The Text within the Text," trans. Jerry Leo and Amy Mandelker, *PMLA* 109 (1994): 377–84. The best evidence for a manuscript used in a Judahite community with an inserted text is the Aramaic copy of the Bisitun text found at Elephantine, although very little work has been done on the text in terms of these dynamics. See Christine Mitchell, "Berlin Papyrus P. 13447 and the Library of the Yehudite Colony at Elephantine," *JNES* 76 (2017): 139–47.

6. Contra Iain M. Duguid, *Ezekiel and the Leaders of Israel*, VTSup 56 (Leiden: Brill, 1994), 81–82. He argues that the link of Zadokite and "righteousness" is a matter of degree, not a binary with "unrighteous." In this reading the Levites are not condemned for their unrighteousness (or un-Zadokite nature) but rather are put into the proper place along the continuum of righteousness and its concomitant responsibilities in the spatial continuum of the temple.

the priests." From a narrative standpoint, this slur is not necessary: it has already been established that the Passover is extraordinarily large, and that because of the number of offerings there were too few priests to do all the work. The Levites' participation as reinforcements makes narrative sense. Therefore, I conclude that there must be a rhetorical purpose to this slur, especially given that throughout Chronicles otherwise there are no negative comments about priests as a whole.[7] The Chronicler's usual stance on priests is that they are necessary, and there are certain functions that only they can perform (blow on trumpets, for example: cf. 1 Chr 15; 2 Chr 7). Normally this includes making sacrifices (e. g. 1 Chr 16:37–43). There is one exception: in 2 Chronicles 36:14, the "chiefs of the priests and the people" continued to commit sacrilege (הרבו למעל־מעל כל־שרי הכהנים והעם). This ultimately led to the destruction of the temple by the Babylonians. However, the point of including the leaders of the priests (not all the priests) at this juncture is to give a picture of the totality of the sin and to provide justification for the destruction of the temple. The sin of Zedekiah alone is not enough, as previous kings had sinned but the temple and Jerusalem had not been destroyed. It took a wider adoption of sinful practice and acts of sacrilege to justify the destruction of the temple; thus, the invocation of the priestly leaders as well as the people (or perhaps just their leaders, if שרי governs העם as well as הכהנים). To recognize the purpose of the slur in 2 Chronicles 29 we must turn to other texts.

3. Ezekiel 44

While the key text is Ezekiel 44:12–13, verses in the middle of Ezekiel's diatribe against the Levites, I shall first examine the relevant passage of Ezekiel 44. This chapter contains the only references to the Levites in the book of Ezekiel. There have been suggestions that these verses (44:10–14) are a later redactional addition to the book, based in part on these unique references to the Levites, and in part on a seeming interruption of the polemic against foreigners found in this chapter.[8] I leave the merits of these arguments to the experts on Ezekiel, only to note that should this passage be a later interpolation, then the question of influence from Chronicles may be pertinent. As I am interested in

---

7. Lars Maskow (in this volume) identifies textual "over-information" as pointing to something else relevant for interpretation that is not directly identified. He points to the "minor incident" of Uzziah's leprous forehead as a way to reinforce Zadokite supremacy over the king.

8. E.g., Walther Zimmerli, *Ezekiel*: *A Commentary on the Book of the Prophet Ezekiel*, Vol. 2, trans. James D. Martin, Hermeneia (Philadelphia: Fortress Press, 1983).

the rhetoric of the final form of the book, the redactional history is not as important.

In 44:4–9, Ezekiel sees the *kabod* of Yhwh filling the temple, and denounces Israel for permitting abominations in the temple in the past. In the future, foreigners are not to be permitted to enter the temple (to serve?). *But*, (note the contrastive כי אם in v. 10), Levites *are* to be servants of the temple, not as an honour, but as a punishment. Rodney Duke attempted to read verse 10, with the Levites "bearing their guilt," as having the same sense as it does in Numbers 18, a Priestly text: the antecedent is Israel rather than the Levites, and the Levites are responsible for Israel's guilt should the Israelites encroach upon the temple in the future as they had in the past.[9] The problem with this argument is that it requires all the verbs in the succeeding verses to have the antecedent Israel as well. Duke's assertion that, "The general theme of Ezekiel's vision in chs. 40–48 is restoration… and not further judgment"[10] is not tenable in the face of the contrastive rhetoric in these verses.[11] Stephen Cook's similar proposal suggests that the Levites are being punished, but their punishment is a form of collective atonement.[12] However, the root שרת is used in chapter 44 in ways that suggest a contrast between the shame of the Levites and the honour of the Zadokite priests. The root is repeated four times in 44:11–12 as applied to the Levites: "And they shall be servants (משרתים) in my sanctuary…and servants (משרתים) in the house/temple (הבית)…and they shall attend them to serve them [viz. the people] (לשרתם) because they served (ישרתו) them before their fetishes…" The root is then found four more times in verses 15–19, where it is used in reference to the service of the Zadokite priests. The Levites' service-punishment is placed in contrast to the Zadokites' service-reward. The polemic against the Levites within Ezekiel is made acute by the repetition of שרת.

4. RETURNING TO 2 CHRONICLES 29

Turning to 2 Chronicles 29 again, in verse 11, Hezekiah does name the Levites as chosen by Yhwh to stand before him to serve him (לשרתו) and to be his servants (משרתים) and sacrificers (מקטרים). However, the whole of the passage is depicting this Passover as unique, a singular

---

9. Rodney K. Duke, "Punishment or Restoration? Another Look at the Levites of Ezekiel 44:6–16," *JSOT* 40 (1988): 66–67.

10. Duke, "Punishment or Restoration," 67.

11. Cf. Nathan MacDonald, *Priestly Rule: Polemic and Biblical Interpretation in Ezekiel 44*, BZAW 476 (Berlin: De Gruyter, 2015), 49–51.

12. Stephen L. Cook, "Innerbiblical Interpretation in Ezekiel 44 and the History of Israel's Priesthood," *JBL* 114 (1995): 204.

set of circumstances leading to the Levites' participation beyond their normal role. There is only this one verse in the Passover episode of 2 Chronicles 29–30 that sets up a contrast between the Levites and the priests, 29:34b, as I noted above. In this slur, the phrase ישרי לבב interests me. It is an unusual although not unique phrase in Chronicles, appearing in a similar form (nominal) also in 1 Chronicles 29:17. Both occurrences are in non-parallel passages with Samuel-Kings.

The root ישר and its derived nouns and adjective appear many times in Chronicles. It is significant that of the eleven occurrences of ישר (adjective), all but two are paralleled in Kings, and the two non-paralleled occurrences are 2 Chronicles 29:34 and 31:20; in the story of Hezekiah. The three occurrences of the verb ישר, 1 Chronicles 13:4; 2 Chronicles 30:4; 32:30 are also non-paralleled, and occur in the stories of David and Hezekiah. The nouns ישר and מישר occur in 1 Chronicles 29:17, describing David. This root is thus not typical of the Chronicler's own general usage; and being used only in texts with either David or Hezekiah is surely significant. In Ezekiel, words from the root ישר are almost non-existent. The adjective occurs twice in its meaning of "straight" in chapter 1, but there are no uses of the verb or of any nominal forms.

The phrase ישרי לבב occurs most frequently in Psalms (nine times: 7:11; 11:2; 32:11; 36:11; 64:11; 94:15; 97:11; 110:7; 125:4) and in five of those occurrences it is paralleled by words from the root צדק, as it is also in Deuteronomy 9:5. "Upright" or "uprightness" more generally is found paralleled by words from צדק nine more times in poetic texts (Ps 9:9; 58:2; 98:9; 99:4; 140:14; Isa 33:15; 45:19; Prov 1:3; 2:9) and is also identified as a word-pair in Ugaritic texts.[13] If this is a stock word-pair, then to say that the Levites were "upright of heart" in 2 Chronicles 29:34 is also to say that they were righteous. Not, on the face of it, particularly controversial, except that in this verse it is a comparative: the Levites were "more upright of heart than the priests in sanctifying themselves."

5. Priests and Levites

Who are the priests that the Levites outstripped in uprightness of heart? At the time of David's establishment of Solomon's succession in 1 Chronicles 28–29, Zadok was anointed as (high) priest, after having been active in the previous chapters. The Zadokite nature of the priesthood, however, is not mentioned again in Chronicles, *except* in 2 Chronicles 31:10 – another episode from the reign of Hezekiah.

---

13. Loren R. Fisher, ed., *Ras Shamra Parallels*: *The Texts from Ugarit and the Hebrew Bible*, *Vol. 1* (Rome: Pontifical Biblical Institute, 1972), 320.

While it is often assumed that the priests in Chronicles are Zadokites, this one explicit mention of Zadok both emphasizes the link between Hezekiah and David and reintroduces Zadokites into the discourse of the book. The priests of 2 Chronicles 29, therefore, are quite plausibly Zadokite, even though it is only the chief priest Azariah who is named as Zadokite in 2 Chronicles 31:10.

The implications of the Levites being more upright of heart should be clear: they are more upright of heart, thus more righteous than the priests, who are Zadokite, or, "Righteous." Within the context of Chronicles, which generally elevates Levites without polemicizing against priests, this slur is difficult to comprehend. Only when placing Chronicles next to Ezekiel do we see the two sides of the polemic. Although Ezekiel does not use ישר except in chapter 1, the way שרת is used in chapter 44 can be read as making the link: it is a pun. This kind of pun: the use of two root letters in common between two root words, is a common form of word-play in Hebrew texts, sometimes called "parasonance."[14]

It can be argued that the priests are not being named as Zadokite in this passage, nor are priests generally assumed to be Zadokite in Chronicles. While there are several references to Zadok as David's priest and to Zadok in the priestly genealogies, there are very few references to Zadok as a priestly family. Jotham's mother in 2 Chronicles 27:1 is named as "daughter of Zadok," but this is taken over from the notice in 2 Kings 15:33 – whether this notice then influenced the construction of Jotham as a "good king" in Chronicles or might be read simply as another piece of evidence for Jotham as a "good king" is still up for debate. The other reference is in 2 Chronicles 31:10. On the other hand, there are a number of references to priests being Aaronide: David assembles the Aaronides and Levites in 1 Chronicles 15:4 as part of the preparations for bringing the ark into Jerusalem; the Levites are complementary to the Aaronides in 1 Chronicles 23:38, 32; 24:31; 27:17; the priests are explicitly named as Aaronides in 2 Chronicles 13:9–10; 26:18; 29:21; 31:19; 35:14. The usual patronymic for priests, when it is given, is Aaron, not Zadok. It may well be that the polemic in Chronicles is not against priests in general – seen as Aaronide – but against a particular priestly family, the Zadokites. By naming Zadok so prominently in the time of David, the Chronicler might be limiting the authority of Zadok to the time of David himself. Yet if that is so, why is the Zadokite nature of the high priest named in the story of Hezekiah? Hezekiah is the king most like David of the post-Solomonic kings, and there are a number of elements of his story

---

14. Scott B. Noegel, "Paronomasia," in *Encyclopedia of Hebrew Language and Linguistics*, *Vol. 3*, ed. Geoffrey Khan (Leiden: Brill, 2013), 26.

that tie back to the reign of David.[15] Ralph W. Klein also notes that the chief priest in 2 Chronicles 31:10 is Azariah, and a previous Azariah is named as the son of Zadok in 1 Kings 4:2.[16] This is another instance of what I followed Lars Maskow in referring to as "over-information" that points to something of importance. It may be pointing to some kind of temporal development in the understanding of the priests and Levites over the course of the book of Chronicles,[17] but I think it more likely, if there are different understandings of the roles of priests and Levites, that the dividing line is at the death of Solomon.

The Levites were part of (even led?) Israel's עוׄן (iniquity); this word is used four times in Ezekiel 44:10–12 (in the passage about Levites), and not at all in the following passage about Zadokite priests, who bear not עוׄן but חלב (fat) and דם (blood). In this comparison, עוׄן is likened to two very concrete things: it becomes a physical thing to be carried by the Levites, just as fat and blood are physical things to be carried by the Zadokite priests. The fat and blood, while concrete, are also symbolic of the abstraction of sacrifice just as עוׄן is an abstraction. While the biblical occurrences do not present a clear antonym to עוׄן, Ezekiel 18:20 and Psalm 69:28 suggest that it might be צדקה: righteousness.[18]

Uncovering the logic of this polemic from the perspective of a reader of Chronicles who already knew Ezekiel, we might say that in Ezekiel, not-Zadok equals not righteous; not righteous equals bearer of עוׄן. Thus, Levites who are not Zadokite are bearers of עָוׄן. Rodney Duke argues that this is not a bad thing – it is more in line with atonement, and therefore the Levites' service is not a punishment.[19] Jacob Milgrom agreed with this position.[20] While this is a plausible reading of Ezekiel 44 (cf. esp. Isa 53), 2 Chronicles 29 suggests that the Chronicler, at least, saw a polemic against the Levites. Therefore, the Chronicler's logic was: more upright of heart equals more righteous (using the well-known stock parallel), therefore Levites are more righteous than priests. Priests are Zadokite, therefore Levites have more צדק

---

15. For a convenient list, see Ralph W. Klein, *2 Chronicles: A Commentary*, Hermeneia (Minneapolis: Fortress Press, 2012), 413.

16. Klein, *2 Chronicles*, 450.

17. Jonker, "Melting Pots and Rejoinders," 51.

18. Klaus Koch, "'āwōn," in *Theological Dictionary of the Old Testament, Vol. 10*, ed. Gerhard Johannes Botterweck and Helmer Ringgren (Grand Rapids, MI: Eerdmans, 2001).

19. Duke, "Punishment or Restoration."

20. Jacob Milgrom, "Ezekiel and the Levites," in *Sacred History, Sacred Literature: Essays on Ancient Israel, the Bible, and Religion in Honor of R.E. Friedman on His Sixtieth Birthday*, ed. Shawna Dolansky (Winona Lake, IN: Eisenbrauns, 2008), 9–11.

than צדוק. Additionally, the uprightness of the Levites is a pun on their "ministering" or "service" in Ezekiel: their service is not a punishment, but a reward.

Were the reader of Ezekiel previously familiar with Chronicles, the polemic is less subtle. The emphasis on Levites in Chronicles, present throughout the book, culminates with the statement in 2 Chronicles 29:34 about the Levites being more upright of heart and therefore more righteous than the priests. The loving descriptions of the Levites' different forms of service found throughout the book have as their conclusion the Levites taking on the responsibilities of the priests. It is important to note that the verb שרת is about as common in Chronicles as Ezekiel, but while twelve of the seventeen occurrences in Ezekiel are in chapters 44–45, eleven of the eighteen occurrences in Chronicles refer to Levites, and are spread throughout the book; only two occurrences refer to priests. It is language typical of Chronicles in that only two of the occurrences are in parallel texts in Kings. One of these, 2 Chronicles 5:14, is important in that it is one of the two uses of שרת for priests, and while Chronicles takes over the Kings text here, the text refers to an event where the priests "were not able to stand to minister before the Cloud of Presence, because the *kabod* of Yhwh filled the House of God." For the reader of Ezekiel who knew Chronicles, the whole passage of Ezekiel 44–45 is a response and polemic against this version of the priesthood, a version of the priesthood in which the priests are not able to fulfill their duties either due to God's presence or to their own incompetence.

Many commentators have suggested that Ezekiel 44–45 is a later addition to the book, or parts of it are later redactional layers. The links between Ezekiel 44 and Numbers have led some to propose that Ezekiel 44 is modeled on the Korahite rebellion in Numbers.[21] If so, those parts may be contemporary with Chronicles. It is typical of scholars writing on Ezekiel to show little awareness of the depiction of Levites in Chronicles, thus reinforcing the "history of the priesthood" model even while explicitly critiquing such an approach. While any of these redactional arguments may be made, from the reader's perspective of the book as we have it now, it does not matter which was written first. The polemic between Ezekiel and Chronicles on the relative worth of Zadokites and Levites can be entered from either direction. While the Ezekielian polemic is blunt and unsubtle, relying on the contrastive use of the same word שרת with respect to Levites and priests, the Chronicler's polemic hinges on the scribal curriculum of stock word-pairs. By making use of a phrase, "upright of heart,"

---

21. Cook, "Innerbiblical Interpretation in Ezekiel 44."

that had a stock complement in *tsedeqah/tsadiq* (or some other word from the root צדק), the root of the Zadokites' name is evoked. The same phrase "upright of heart" also puns on the root שרת, the "service" or "ministry" claimed by the Levites, especially so when the priests were not able to complete their own. The Levites' ministry is righteous, no matter what Ezekiel might say.

6. HISTORICAL DEVELOPMENT OF THE PRIESTHOOD?

In none of the above have I attempted to make any arguments about the development of the Judaean priesthood. Most discussions of priests and Levites in Ezekiel, Deuteronomy, and Chronicles have taken a historical approach to the question, based on their dating of the texts.[22] There is no doubt that the Levites as described in many biblical texts such as Deuteronomy, Judges, Kings, etc. look quite different from the Levites as described in Chronicles. Interestingly, and importantly, the Levites in Ezekiel 44 look a lot like the Levites of Chronicles. It seems that Ezekielian scholarship does not typically pick up on this depiction. Iain Duguid notes the careful construction of the lines between sacred and profane in Ezekiel, both in the temple personnel as much as in the temple itself.[23] Notably there are just as careful lines drawn in Chronicles about the sanctity of the temple and the structure of its personnel: where Chronicles and Ezekiel differ is in what place the line should be drawn. Louis Jonker notes that both Levites and priests are described as sanctified from 2 Chronicles 23:6 onward.[24] Chronicles does not advocate in any way for either kings or the people to take up temple functions, and in fact the episode of Uzziah in 2 Chronicles 26 shows clearly that kings are not qualified to take part in temple rituals.[25] Most Ezekielian scholarship looks for parallels with Numbers and points to Isaiah 56–66 as representing the object of Eze-

---

22. For Ezekiel, e. g. MacDonald, *Priestly Rule*; Milgrom, "Ezekiel and the Levites"; but cf. Cook, "Innerbiblical Interpretation in Ezekiel 44" as already questioning this perspective; even so, he concludes his article with a tentative reconstruction of a social situation that would have led to tensions between priestly groups; for Chronicles, e. g. Gary N. Knoppers, "Hierodules, Priests, or Janitors? The Levites in Chronicles and the History of the Israelite Priesthood," *JBL* 118 (1999): 49–72.

23. Iain M. Duguid, "Putting Priests in Their Place: Ezekiel's Contribution to the History of the Old Testament Priesthood," in *Ezekiel's Hierarchical World*: *Wresting with a Tiered Reality*, ed. Stephen L. Cook and Corrine Patton (Atlanta: SBL, 2004), 58.

24. Jonker, "Melting Pots and Rejoinders," 47–48.

25. Contra Jonker, "Melting Pots and Rejoinders," 48. He sees holiness being "democratized" in this part of Chronicles under the influence of the Holiness Code and associated Pentateuchal redaction.

kiel 44's polemic, rather than Chronicles.[26] Nathan MacDonald even goes so far as to suggest that a later priestly redactor of Chronicles did not even know the text of Ezekiel.[27] Gary N. Knoppers, on the other hand, did show the extensive links between the depictions of Levites, priests, and cultic concerns in Chronicles with the Priestly and Ezekielian material,[28] which suggests that if the Chronicler did not know Ezekiel, the Chronicler knew material that resembles Ezekiel. Knoppers' caution that "Shared terminology does not constitute sufficient grounds to conclude that the levitical (sic) work profile is pro-Priestly in orientation"[29] should be heeded, and indeed provides support for reading a polemic: "Similar verbiage has misled scholars into thinking that there is more continuity between P and the Chronicler than is warranted by the evidence. The Chronicler draws on Priestly terminology, but he does so to expand levitical (sic) responsibilities and to blur some of the clear distinctions advanced by the Priestly writers and defended by Ezekiel."[30] Rather than seeing both texts (or redactional layers) as deriving from a specific historical period and stage in the development of the priesthood, I have examined these texts from a purely literary perspective, looking at them as examples of the genre of polemic, and placing the Chronicles reference as the primary referent for understanding the Ezekielian text.

7. Conclusion

Although many have suggested that Chronicles is a dull book, a simple cut and paste job with some other bits sandwiched in; and although many have commented on the relentlessness of Chronicles in promoting certain themes: David, Levites, temple, etc., a great deal of subtle artistry went into producing such a dull book. The book of Chronicles is filled with sly allusions, complicated word-plays, irony, and other forms of literary artistry. That the "Levites were more upright of heart than the priests in sanctifying themselves" is one more example of this artistry and erudition. In this case, a polemic between the books of Chronicles and Ezekiel can be discerned; although it is not possible to discern with certainty which is a polemic against the other, Chronicles as a polemic against Ezekiel seems most likely.

---

26. But see Benjamin Kilchör, "The Meaning of Ezekiel 44,6–14 in Light of Ezekiel 1–39," *Bib* 98 (2017): 191–207 as a welcome corrective to the search for an external referent, instead placing Ezek 44 in the context of Ezek 1–39.
27. MacDonald, *Priestly Rule*, 121.
28. Knoppers, "Hierodules, Priests."
29. Knoppers, "Hierodules, Priests," 58.
30. Knoppers, "Hierodules, Priests," 64.

THE LEVITES AND IDOLATRY: A SCRIBAL DEBATE IN EZEKIEL 44 AND CHRONICLES

Jaeyoung Jeon

1. INTRODUCTION

The stratification within the Levitical priesthood, namely the distinction between the priests and the non-priestly, second-tier Levites in the Jerusalem temple, has been at the core of the reconstructed history of the religion of ancient Israel. According to the classical scheme constructed by Julius Wellhausen, which has thus far been the most influential theory, this stratification originated from the Josianic reform between especially the Jerusalemite priests and the priests from local sanctuaries (2 Kgs 23:9). Alternative explanations have been suggested by scholars such as Kurt Möhlrenbrink, Antonius H. J. Gunneweg, and Frank M. Cross especially in favor of a pre- and early-monarchic dating of the division.[1] Nevertheless, both Wellhausenian and alternative views share the basic notion that the Josianic reform was a critical juncture for the internal division within the Levitical group. However, a more recent tendency, especially in Europe, has dated the relevant biblical texts to the Persian period,

1. Kurt Möhlenbrink, "Die levitischen Überlieferungen des Alten Testaments," ZAW 52 (1934): 184–231; Antonius H. J. Gunneweg, *Leviten und Priester: Hauptlinien der Traditionsbildung und Geschichte des Israelitisch-Jüdischen Kultpersonals*, FRLANT 89 (Göttingen: Vandenhoeck & Ruprecht, 1965); Frank Moore Cross, *Canaanite Myth and Hebrew Epic* (Cambridge, MA: Harvard University Press, 1973). For a more comprehensive review of scholarship, see, Jaeyoung Jeon, "Levites, I. Hebrew Bible/Old Testament," in *EBR* 16 (2018), 337–346. Especially, for a sharp contrast on this issue between North-American and European scholarship, see, Peter Altmann, "What Do the 'Levites in Your Gates' Have To Do with the 'Levitical Priests'?: An Attempt at European-North American Dialogue on the Levites in the Deuteronomic Law Corpus," in *Levites and Priests in Biblical History and Tradition*, ed. Mark A. Leuchter and Jeremy M. Hutton, AIL 9 (Atlanta, Ga.: SBL Press, 2012), 135–54.

therefore dating both the formation of the Levitical priesthood and its internal stratification to that period as well.[2]

Whatever its historical origin may have been, it is during the Persian period that the more intensified struggles for, and probably against, the stratification were documented. The priestly scribal efforts to codify and perpetuate the distinction between the Aaronite and/or Zadokite priests and the rest of the Levites are visible in the late-Priestly or post-Priestly texts in Numbers, such as chapters 3–4, 8, and 16–18 as well as Ezekiel 44. The latter in particular provides an alternative origin of the stratification, being the Levites' service in idol worship vis-à-vis the Zadokites' loyalty to Yhwh. This is a humiliation and the harshest criticism of the non-Zadokite Levites.

In Chronicles, however, the Levites' possible connection to a previous idol worship is totally eliminated, suggesting a conscious and deliberate muting effort by the Chronicler. Could this have been a Levites's scribal response to the priestly polemics against the Levites? Based on the scholarly consensus that Chronicles represents Levitical interests or was written by a Levitical scribe, I seek to investigate here the contradictory attitude toward the Levites' connection to idol worship in Ezekiel 44 and Chronicles. I then prove that the Chronicler acknowledged the Zadokite accusation against the Levites and responded to it through a reshaping of a history of the Levites as always piously faithful to Yhwh worship in Jerusalem. Since this scribal response was subtle and implicit, it would be helpful to employ relevant theoretical frameworks in order to present it clearly. The argument in the last part of the essay will suggest that the social theories of Pierre Bourdieu and social memory can enhance our understanding of the implicit intertextuality.

2. THE ACCUSATION OF IDOL WORSHIP AGAINST THE LEVITES

2.1 THE LATENESS OF THE ZADOKITE REDACTION

The accusation against the Levites appears in Ezekiel within a section that regulates the clerical order of the future temple (Ezek 44:6–31). In this section, Yhwh denounces the people for defiling the temple by

---

2. See, e. g., Nadav Na'aman, "Sojourners and Levites in the Kingdom of Judah," ZAR 14 (2008): 237–79, at 261–72; Daniel E. Fleming, *The Legacy of Israel in Judah's Bible*: *History, Politics and the Reinscribing of Tradition* (Cambridge: Cambridge University Press, 2012), 72–90; Jean-Daniel Macchi, *Israël et ses tribus selon Genèse 49*, OBO 171 (Göttingen: Vandenhoek & Ruprecht, 1999); Harald Samuel, *Von Priestern zum Patriarchen*: *Levi und die Leviten im Alten Testament*, BZAW 448 (Berlin: De Gruyter, 2014). See further, Jeon, "Levites" with references.

allowing foreigners to enter the sanctuary and especially assigning to them duties of the temple (vv. 7–8). Yhwh's solution for this prior situation is to separate the temple space by different degrees of holiness and assign control of the spaces to a hierarchy of two clerical groups. The preeminent group, the sons of Zadok as the Levitical priests, shall be exclusively responsible for the altar service in the sanctuary (מקדש משמרת, vv. 15–16); the secondary group, the remainder of the Levites, shall not be permitted to access to the sanctuary (v. 13) but instead assigned duties outside the sanctuary such as gatekeeping, temple service (משרת הבית), and slaughtering sacrificial animals for the people (vv. 11, 14).

The accusation against the Levites appears as the rationale for this distinction. Here, the Levites have been deprived of their priesthood because of their participation in the people's previous idol worship (v. 10); they even served the people in the presence of the idols, and thus Yhwh swore to prohibit them from accessing the sanctuary and serving as priests (v. 12–13). Yet, the Zadokites kept charge of the sanctuary when Israel went astray from Yhwh (v. 15). The priesthood of the new temple thus exclusively remains among them (vv. 15–16).

The classical Wellhausenian view of the history of ancient Israelite religion dates the present passage to the exilic period, attributing it either to Ezekiel himself or to his disciples and regarding it as an important link between the priestly hierarchy from the Josianic reform (2 Kgs 23:5–9; Deut 18:7) and the perpetuated class-division between the Aaronite priests and the Levites in P.[3] However, since Hartmut Gese's redaction-critical study of Ezekiel 40–48,[4] the present passage has been regarded as one of the youngest layers or additions in Ezekiel 40–48, which is itself a series of late expansions of Ezekiel's prophecy. Gese identified three independent sources/layers, defining the passages mentioning the privilege of the Zadokites (Ezek 40:46c; 44:6–16, 28–30a; 45:13–15) as the youngest "Zadokite layer" (*Ṣadoqidenschicht*). Walther Zimmerli developed this independent source model into a model of multiple stages of reworking (*Fortschreibung*) and attributed the passages to an early post-exilic expansion

---

3. See further, Jeon, "Levites." See, also, e. g., George A. Cooke, *A Critical and Exegetical Commentary on the Book of Ezekiel*, ICC (Edinburgh: T. & T. Clark, 1936), 480–83; Walther Eichrodt, *Ezekiel: A Commentary*, OTL (London: SCM Press, 1970), 560–66; Walther J. Zimmerli, *Ezekiel: A Commentary on the Book of the Prophet Ezekiel 2: Chapters 25–48*, trans. by James D. Martin, Hermeneia (Philadelphia: Fortress Press, 1983), 447–59.

4. Hartmut Gese, *Der Verfassungsentwurf des Ezechiel (Kap. 40–48): Traditionsgeschichtlich Untersucht*, Beiträge Zur Historischen Theologie 25 (Tübingen: J.C.B. Mohr, 1957).

with further verses (e. g., Ezek 45*; 46:19–24; 48:30–35).[5] Gunneweg narrowed the scope of the Zadokite passages by assigning mainly Ezekiel 44:6–31 to the "Zadokite section," rather than a literary layer, with other small additions.[6] Some later studies have suggested models with two or three layers in Ezekiel 40–48, still attributing the Zadokite passages to a younger (sometimes the youngest) layer dating to the Persian period.[7] Although the models are complex, our passages are thought to be very late additions dated to the fifth and fourth centuries BCE.[8]

The unity of the present section of Ezekiel 44:6–16 is doubted by some of these scholars, mainly because the issue of idol worship in vv. 9–16 shows no direct relationship to the presence of the foreigners in the temple (vv. 6–8). Thilo A. Rudnig, for instance, separates Ezekiel 44:6–8 and vv. 9–16 and claims that the former belongs to an earlier layer containing an original accusation against the exiles, while the latter develops the former as the distinction in the priestly class.[9] Nathan MacDonald further argues that the reproach of the foreigners in vv. 6–7*, 9 was originally followed by the commissioning of the Levitical priests (vv. 15*). For him, the distinction between the Zadokite priests and Levites is altogether a late addition.[10] The entire passage of vv. 6–16, however, forms a structured and coherent literary unit. As shown above, Yhwh reproaches the presence of the foreigners in the sanctuary and their temple duties in vv. 6–8 and sets a two-fold protection for the sanctity of the future temple by the priests and Levites (vv. 9–16). The issue of idol worship by the Levites is mentioned as the rationale for the division between the Zadokites and Levites, which is a logical premise of the two-fold protection. This issue needs not to be

---

5. See Gese, *Verfassungsentwurf*, 31–33, 108–23; Zimmerli, *Ezekiel 2*, 447–59.

6. Gunneweg, *Leviten und Priester*, 188–203.

7. Vogt, for example, assumes three stages of literary expansion in Ezekiel 40–48 and assigns Ezek 44–46 to the second phase. Tuell suggests only a single phase of expansion – including the Zadokite passages – conducted during the reign of Darius (522–486). Konkel reconstructs two stages of expansion, assigning our passages to the second stage, after 515 BCE. See Ernst Vogt, *Untersuchungen zum Buch Ezechiel*, Analecta Biblica 95 (Rome: Biblical Institute Press, 1981), 127–75; Steven S. Tuell, *The Law of the Temple in Ezekiel 40–48*, HSM 49 (Atlanta: Scholars Press, 1992), 75–77; Michael Konkel, *Architektonik des Heiligen: Studien zur Zweiten Tempelvision Ezechiel (Ez 40–48)*, BBB 129 (Berlin / Wien: Philo, 2001), 240–43.

8. For example, Rudnig reconstructs thirteen redactional insertions. He separates Ezekiel 44:6–7* and Ezekiel 44:6–16* and dates them to the fifth and fourth centuries, respectively. See Thilo A. Rudnig, *Heilig und Profan: Redaktionskritische Studien zu Ez 40–48*, BZAW 287 (Berlin: De Gruyter, 2000), 224–330.

9. Rudnig, *Heilig und Profan*, 205–7. This position is followed by Samuel, Von Priestern, 367–68.

10. Nathan MacDonald, *Priestly Rule, Polemic and Biblical Interpretation in Ezekiel 44* (Berlin, Boston: Walter de Gruyter, 2015), 51–55.

directly connected to the problem of the foreigners.

It is neither necessary nor my purpose to evaluate the different compositional models for Ezekiel 40–48 in this essay; the relative lateness of those Zadokite passages (Ezek 40:46c; 44:6–16, 28–30a; 45:13–15) in their literary context seems obvious. For instance, the distinction between those responsible for the temple duties (שמרי משמרת הבית) and those serving at the altar (שמרי משמרת המזבח) is presented already in Ezekiel 40:45–46. They are all priests, however, and there is no hierarchy between them. Only a relative clause attached at the end (v. 46b) defines the altar priests as sons of Zadok who are privileged over other Levites. However, the mention of the sons of Zadok is rather alien to its literary context, and this half-verse is usually regarded as a late addition.[11] If we remove v. 46b, the present passage (vv. 45–46a) knows neither the distinction between the Zadokite priests and the Levites nor the guilt of the Levites. The Zadokite redaction developed the earlier division of the priests according to their functions into the hierarchal system of Zadokites and Levites. In addition to Ezekiel 44:46b, two other passages mentioning the Zadokites (Ezek 43:19a*; 48:11) were also inserted later to the existing texts. In Ezekiel 43:19, the lengthy description of the "seed of Zadok" has been inserted between ונתתה אל הכהנים and פר בן בקר, producing an awkward gap between the two closely related clauses. The following verses simply designate the priests as הכהנים (vv. 24, 27). Ezekiel 48:11 recapitulates the division between the Zadokites and Levites with the language of Ezekiel 44:9–16 and has been attached redundantly to v. 10. The latter already has לכהנים as the beneficiary of the sacred portion of the land and is a complete sentence by itself, while the attached v. 11 only complicates the syntax. These three Zadokite additions presuppose texts in different sections of Ezekiel 40–48, which strongly indicates the lateness of the Zadokite redaction.

The lateness of the Zadokite redaction, especially in Ezekiel 44, is also confirmed by its intertextual connections with other biblical passages usually dated to the Persian period. For example, our passage is often viewed in a polemical relationship with Isaiah 56 (Trito-Isaiah) that allows gentiles to enter the sanctuary.[12] Also, the division

---

11. See, e. g., Gese, *Verfassungsentwurf*, 21–22; Gunneweg, *Leviten und Priester*, 188 Zimmerli, *Ezekiel 2*, 368.

12. See, e. g., Michael Fishbane, *Biblical Interpretation in Ancient Israel* (Oxford: Clarendon Press, 1985), 138–143; Joachim Schaper, "Rereading the Law: Inner-Biblical Exegesis of Divine Oracles in Ezekiel 44 and Isaiah 56," in *Recht und Ethik im Alten Testament*: Beiträge des Symposiums "Das Alte Testament und die Kultur der Moderne" anlässlich des 100. Geburtstag Gerhard von Rad (1901–1971), Heidelberg, 18–21 Oktober 2001, eds. Bernard M. Levinson and Eckart Otto (Altes Testament und Moderne 13. Münster: Lit, 2004), 125–44. And see the referenc-

of duties between the Zadokite priests and the Levites shows a close literary affinity to Numbers (16–)18, regarded as one of the youngest parts of the Priestly text.[13] The Zadokite passages are often thought to be influenced by Numbers 18 or attributed to the same hand.[14] All of these redactional and intertextual studies indicate the lateness of the Zadokite redaction.

2.2 THE GUILT OF THE LEVITES

2.2.1 A HISTORICAL OR LITERARY REFERENCE?

According to the Wellhausenian view, the guilt of the Levites mentioned in Ezekiel 44:10, 12 stems from their service at the local sanctuaries before the Josianic reform. This view is still attractive for those who agree with the classical scheme of ancient Israelite religion, especially about the priest/Levite division.[15] Nevertheless, the Levites' guilt is described in very general terms – the worship of idols (גילולים) – without specifying any historical context. Further, the recent late dating of the passage to the mid- or even late Persian period creates a chronological gap between the Josianic reform and the present passage. Scholars have thus suggested alternative explanations, mainly by finding reference to the passages in the canonical history.[16] Some

---

es there. See also, Steven S. Tuell, "The Priesthood of the 'Foreigner': Evidence of Competing Politics in Ezekiel 44:1–14 and Isaiah 56:1–8," in *Constituting the Community: Studies on the Polity of Ancient Israel*, eds. John T. Strong and Steven Shawn Tuell (Winona Lake, IN; Eisenbrauns, 2005), 183–204; MacDonald, *Priestly Rule*, 26–33.

13. See, e. g., Gese, *Verfassungsentwurf*, 64–65; Gunneweg, *Leviten und Priester*, 198–203; Raymond Abba, "Priests and Levites in Ezekiel," VT 28 (1978): 1–9; Fishbane, *Biblical Interpretation*, 138–143; Rodney K. Duke, "Punishment or Restoration? Another Look at the Levites of Ezekiel 44,6–16," JSOT 40 (1988): 61–81, here 64–75; Stephen L. Cook, "Innerbiblical Interpretation in Ezekiel 44 and the History of Israel's Priesthood", JBL 114 (1995): 193–208; Daniel I. Block, *The Book of Ezekiel*. 2 vols., NICOT (Grand Rapids: Eerdmans, 1997), 628–29; Rudnig, *Heilig*, 295–304; Konkel, *Architektonik*, 311–13; MacDonald, *Priestly Rule*, 41–47.

14. While most of the scholars mentioned in n 13 regard that Ezekiel 44 is dependent on Numbers 18, Cook assigns them to the same hand. See, Cook, "Innerbiblical Interpretation."

15. See, e. g., Keith W. Carley, *The Book of the Prophet Ezekiel*, Cambridge Bible Commentary (Cambridge: Cambridge University Press, 1974), 294; Nigel Allan, "The Identity of the Jerusalem Priesthood during the Exile", HeyJ 23 (1982): 259–269, esp. 265–269; Aelred Cody, *Ezekiel: With an Excursus on Old Testament Priesthood*, Old Testament Message 11 (Wilmington, DE: Michael Glazier, 1984), 159–160; Joachim Schaper, *Priester und Leviten im achamenidischen Juda: Studien zur Kult- und Sozialgeschichte Israels in Persischer Zeit*, FAT 31 (Tübingen: Mohr Siebeck, 2000), 79–95.

16. See, e. g., Jon D. Levenson, *Theology of the Program of Restoration of Ezekiel 40–48*, HSM 10 (Missoula: Scholars Press, 1976), 134–140; Raymond Abba,

have identified it in the Hexateuchal stories: for example, the rebellion of Korah (Num 16–18),[17] idol worship of Baal Peor (Num 25),[18] and the story of the Gibeonites (Josh 9).[19] Others suggest that our passage refers to idol worship during the monarchic period, such as Jeroboam's golden calves[20] and the idolatry under Manasseh's reign,[21] or to foreigner involvement, such as the Carites (2 Kgs 11:4–8)[22] and the temple servants (נתינים) from Solomon's reign (Ezra 2:43–54).[23]

Whereas these different views, whether classical or alternative, endeavor to identify a certain (or multiple) historical or literary event(s) behind the guilt of the Levites, skepticism about such attempts has also been expressed, in line with the growing recognition of the passage's late nature.[24] This skepticism has led some scholars to focus on the literary context of the book of Ezekiel and to find literary connections between Ezekiel 1–39 and the present passage. Steven Tuell, for example, argues that the idols (גלולים) in Ezekiel 44 refer to those in Ezekiel 6:3–6; 8:10; 14:3–4;[25] Alice Hunt regards

---

"Priests and Levites in Ezekiel," *VT* 28 (1978): 1–9; Menahem Haran, *Temples and Temple-Service in Ancient Israel: An Inquiry into the Character of Cult Phenomena and the Historical Setting of the Priestly School* (Oxford: Clarendon Press, 1978), 104–111; Gordon J. McConville, "Priests and Levites in Ezekiel: A Crux in the Interpretation of Israel's History," *TynB* 34 (1983): 3–32; Duke, "Punishment or Restoration?" 66–72; Tuell, *Law of the Temple*, 150–151; Iain M. Duguid, *Ezekiel and the Leaders of Israel* (VTSup 56. Leiden; New York: E.J. Brill, 1994), 79–80; Cook, "Innerbiblical Interpretation," 193–208; Joseph Blenkinsopp, "The Judaean Priesthood during the Neo-Babylonian and Achaemenid Periods: A Hypothetical Reconstruction," *CBQ* 60 (1998): 25–43, here 41–42; Rudnig, *Heilig und Profan*, 291–295; Konkel, *Architektonik des Heiligen*, 304–317. See further Benjamin Kilchör, "The Meaning of Ezekiel 44,6–14 in Light of Ezekiel 1–39," *Biblica* 98 (2017): 191–207, here 192–93.

17. See Cook, "Innerbiblical Interpretation."

18. Levenson argues that the present Zadokite stratum combines an old Aaronite polemic against the Mushites (e. g., Num 25 and 1 Kgs 31–32) with the newer polemic against all of the priests of the shrines; see Levenson, *Program of Restoration*, 136–39.

19. Zimmerli, *Ezekiel 2*, 455.

20. Abba, "Priests," 5; Levenson, *Program of Restoration*, 136. See also criticism of this view by Levenson, *Program of Restoration*, 134–35.

21. Harran, *Temples*, 106.

22. Leslie C. Allen, *Ezekiel 20–48*, WBC 29 (Dallas: Word Books, 1990), 261; Jacob Milgrom, "Ezekiel and the Levites," in *Sacred History, Sacred Literature: Essays on Ancient Israel, the Bible, and Religion in Honor of R.E. Friedman on his Sixtieth Birthday*, ed. Swana Dolansky (Eisenbrauns: Winona Lake, IN, 2008), 3–12.

23. Zimmerli, *Ezechiel 2*, 1125. For further summary of the different views, see Kilchör, "Meaning," 192–93.

24. See, e. g., Eichrodt, *Ezekiel*, 565; McConville, "Priests and Levites," 25–26; Rudnig, *Heilig*, 295; Konkel, *Architektonik*, 317.

25. See Tuell, *Law of the Temple*, 149.

Ezekiel 44 as midrash upon Ezekiel 23;[26] MacDonald suggests that Ezekiel 44:10–14 is an inner-biblical interpretation of Numbers 18 and Ezekiel 14;[27] Benjamin Kilchör claims similarly that the present passage refers via Ezekiel 14:1–11 to Ezekiel 8, in addition to Numbers 18.[28] For our purpose, those views emphasizing the intertextuality within the Book of Ezekiel has primary relevance.

2.2.2 Understandings of the Levites's Guilt by the Audiences/Readers of Yehud

The scholarly views introduced thus far have generally been author-oriented approaches concerned mainly with what the author/redactor meant by the "guilt" of the Levites. The focus of this essay is, nevertheless, how the passage was understood by the audiences/readers of Persian Yehud, particularly by the Levitical scribal circle including the Chronicler and also by their expected audiences/ readers. Although we have a very limited knowledge of how much and among whom the Ezekiel scrolls were preserved, circulated, read, and recited during the period, reasonable inferences should still be possible. When the present Zadokite redaction was completed, it was included as an integral part of a scroll of Ezekiel's prophecy. Once the additions were included in the scroll and the latter was accepted by the religious community, all of the prophetic discourses in the scroll, including the additions, would have been regarded as the prophet's own words. The redactor's scribal work gained the authority of the prophet Ezekiel in this way. This was presumably the purpose of the ancient redactors for choosing to add their own words to existing authoritative texts rather than write their own texts.

When the Zadokite passages were added to a scroll of Ezekiel[29] and this version was accepted by the community as authoritative, those passages including that of Ezekiel 44 would have naturally been understood as a continuation of the preceding prophecy of Ezekiel himself. In this context, the worship of idols and the guilt of the Levites in our passage should have been understood by the audiences/readers based on what they had heard/read previously from the scroll; namely, our passage was primarily understood in the context of the Book of Ezekiel.

---

26. See Alice Hunt, *Missing Priests. The Zadokites in Tradition and History*, LHBOTS 452 (New York: T&T Clark, 2006), 141–42.

27. See MacDonald, *Priestly Rule*, 41–51.

28. See Kilchör, "Meaning," 204–5.

29. Here I would prefer to use the term "a scroll of Ezekiel" in order to include the earlier stages of the text during its expansion before the present form of the book of Ezekiel.

As mentioned above, scholars have discussed our passage's intra-textual connections to other Ezekiel passages mentioning idol worship, especially Ezekiel 6; 8; 14; 23.[30] Although their arguments concern the redactors' literary activity, the literary connections (including verbal correspondences) should also have influenced the audiences/readers to understand the Levites' guilt in line with the blame of the Israelites' idolatry in the previous parts of Ezekiel.[31] These judgement speeches of Ezekiel are delivered mainly to the inhabitants of Jerusalem and Judah from the waning decades of the Judean monarchy. Their worship of idols (גלולים) thus stems mostly from this period, except for several verses in Ezekiel 20.[32] The idolatry in which the Levites participated was most likely understood by contemporary audiences/readers as that of the late monarchic period.

Understandings of the present passage was possibly broader among the literate elites, especially the scribal circles, depending on the range of their knowledge of other authoritative texts. The Chronicler, the focus of the second part of this essay, constructed his view of the history of Israel primarily based on the Deuteronomistic history, especially Samuel and Kings, though he exhibits a familiarity with some Pentateuchal and prophetic texts.[33] It is thus most likely that the Chronicler understood the Levites' guilt in Ezekiel 44 through background knowledge of his primary source. The Books of Kings also employ the term גלולים for describing idols throughout the monarchic period: the idols made before the reign of Asa (1 Kgs 15:12), Ahab's idols (1 Kgs 21:26), Manasseh's idolatry (2 Kgs 21:11), the idols eliminated by Josiah's reform (2 Kgs 23:24), etc. In the literary context of Kings, a general description of idolatry such as Ezekiel 44:10–12 can be understood not only for the later period of the Southern kingdom but also as for the Northern and Southern Kingdoms throughout the entirety of their existences. This was presumably the way in which the Chronicler, whose major source is Kings, understood the idolatry in

---

30. It has been broadly recognized that the description of the sins of the past in Ezekiel 44:6–15 was written with formulaic language and phraseology deeply rooted in the judgement speeches of Ezekiel 1–24; see, e. g., Zimmerli, *Ezekiel 2*, 456; Levenson, *Program of Restoration*, 134.

31. For instance, the term גלולים is a expression for idols that is typical to Ezekiel, occurring approximately 35 times in Ezekiel among 45 occurrences in the Hebrew Bible.

32. Ezekiel 20:7–8 blames the exodus generation for worshiping the idols of Egypt, whereas vv. 16, 24 speak of the idolatry during the wilderness period.

33. For further discussions, see Ehud Ben Zvi, "Who Knew What? The Construction of the Monarchic Past in Chronicles and Implications for the Intellectual Setting of Chronicles," in *Judah and the Judeans in the Neo-Babylonian Period*, ed. Oded Lipschitz (Winona Lake, IN: Eisenbrauns, 2003), 349–60. See also the references below in n 34.

Ezekiel 44. Should this be the case, it would be interesting to examine how the Chronicler, who strongly advocates for Levitical interests, responded to the Zadokite accusation of the Levites's participation of idolatry. Yet before this examination, I would like to clarify two questions as its logical premises: (1) Did the Chronicler know the Book of Ezekiel? (2) Was it necessary to respond to the accusation in Ezekiel 44? The following sections address these two questions.

3. EZEKIEL AND CHRONICLES

The questions of the Chronicler's knowledge of the prophetic literature and its acceptance as an authoritative source has long been discussed.[34] Scholars commonly recognize the Chronicler's knowledge through explicit mentions of prophets or prophetic books, such as Jeremiah, Isaiah, and Zechariah, or quotations therefrom.[35] The mention of prophetic texts as well as some other biblical texts mentioned only in Chronicles attest to their recognition and use by the Chronicler as authoritative sources.[36] Hugh G. M. Williamson further maintains that "the use he makes of them in his work shows that within his community they had already been accepted as authoritative religious texts."[37] Ezekiel must have been among the prophets who attained preeminent authority in the community of Yehud, considering its profound (mutual) influence on the formation of the different layers of the Priestly texts in the Pentateuch. Interestingly, however, the Chronicler never mentions the prophet Ezekiel, nor has Chronicles scholarship regarded Ezekiel as one of the Chronicler's authoritative sources,[38] so that

---

34. Gerhard von Rad, "The Levitical Sermon in I and II Chronicles," in *The Problem of the Hexateuch and Other Essays* (London: SCM, 1984), 267–80 (first published in German as "Die levitische Predigt in den Büchern der Chronik," in *Festschrift für Otto Procksch* [Leipzig: Deichert and Hinrichs, 1934], 113–24); Sara Japhet, *The Ideology of the Book of Chronicles and Its Place in Biblical Thought*, 2nd ed., BEATAJ 9 (Frankfurt am Main: Peter Lang, 1997), 183; Louis Jonker, "The Chronicler and the Prophets. Who Were His Authoritative Sources?" *SJOT* 22 (2008): 275–95; Ben Zvi, "Who Knew What?"; Ben Zvi, "One Size Does Not Fit All: Observations on the Different Ways That Chronicles Dealt with the Authoritative Literature of Its Time," in *What Was Authoritative for Chronicles?*, ed. Ehud Ben Zvi and Diana V. Edelman (Winona Lake, IN: Eisenbrauns, 2011), 13–35; Steven J. Schweitzer, "Judging a Book by Its Citations: Sources and Authority in Chronicles," in *What Was Authoritative for Chronicles?* ed. Ehud Ben Zvi and Diana V. Edelman (Winona Lake, IN: Eisenbrauns, 2011), 37–65.

35. See further the elaborate list of quotations or allusions of biblical texts in Steven Schweitzer, "Judging a Book by Its Citations".

36. See, e. g., Jonker, "The Chronicler and the Prophets"; Ben Zvi, "Who Knew What?"

37. See Hugh G. M. Williamson, *Studies in Persian Period History and Historiography*, FAT 38 (Tübingen: Mohr Siebeck, 2004), 243.

38. For example, even Schweitzer's elaborate list of intertextual connections

the possible relationship between the two texts has generally been neglected.

For an ancient author knowing a certain text versus making explicit literary reference to it belong to two different realms of cognitive activity. Ancient scribes could react to other texts in various ways, not only by accepting concepts and language but also by negating, manipulating, polemicizing, or intentionally ignoring them. The Chronicler was not an exception. Given the various avenues available for scribal reaction, there are a few clues that imply the Chronicler's knowledge of Ezekiel. Firstly, the Chronicler's mention of Nebuchadnezzar making Zedekiah swear an oath by God (2 Chr 36:13) may refer to the same notion in Ezekiel 17:11–17, 19.[39] Japhet sees in this parallel the Chronicler drawing on the depiction in Ezekiel but using different terminology.[40] While this case as a reference to Ezekiel is up for debate, what is directly relevant to the current discussion are the possible references in Chronicles to the Zadokite passages in Ezekiel, in particular those about the Levites.

Gary N. Knoppers made a thorough comparison between the Levitical duties described in 1 Chronicles 23:28–32 and the relevant passages in P and Ezekiel.[41] Although the literary affinity between 1 Chronicles 23:28–32 and P has already been acknowledged by scholars,[42] the former's relationship with Ezekiel has been either ignored[43]

("Judging a Book by Its Citations") does not include Ezekiel.

39. See, e. g., Ralph W. Klein, *2 Chronicles*: *A Commentary*, Hermeneia (Minneapolis, MN: Fortress Press, 2012), 539; Raymond B. Dillard, 2 Chronicles, WBC 15 (Waco: Word Books, 1987), 300; Christopher Begg, "The Non-Mention of Ezekiel in the Deuteronomistic History, the Book of Jeremiah and the Chronistic History," in *Ezekiel and His Book*: *Textual and Literary Criticism and Their Interrelation*, ed. Johan Lust, Bibliotheca Ephemeridum Theologicarum Lovaniensium 74 (Leuven: University Press, 1986), 340–343: 342. Begg claims that the report of defiling temple in 2 Chr 36:14 also presupposes Ezekiel 8.

40. Japhet, *Chronicles*, 1070.

41. See Gary N. Knoppers, "Hierodules, Priests, or Janitors? The Levites in Chronicles and the History of the Israelite Priesthood." *JBL* 118 (1999): 49–72. Some scholars regard the Chronicles passage as a secondary addition; see, e. g., Wilhelm Rudolph, *Chronikbücher*, HAT 21 (Tübingen: J.C.B. Mohr, 1955), 155–156; Hugh G. M. Williamson, "The Origins of the Twenty-Four Priestly Courses," in *Studies in the Historical Books of the Old Testament*, ed. John A. Emerton, Studies in the Historical Books of the Old Testament, VTS 30 (Leiden: Brill, 1979), 251–68: 258. However, Sarah Japhet and others have effectively proven that the passage is interconnected in its concepts and language with other parts of Chronicles and thus an integral part of the book; see Japhet, *Chronicles*, 421; Knoppers, "Hierodules, Priests, or Janitors," 71; Peter B. Dirksen, *1 Chronicles*, Historical Commentary on the Old Testament (Leuven: Peeters, 2005), 281; Jonker, *1 & 2 Chronicles*, 151.

42. See, e. g., Japhet, *Chronicles*, 418–421; Dirksen, *1 Chronicles*, 281; Louis C. Jonker, *1 & 2 Chronicles*, 151.

43. See above n 34.

or deliberately denied.[44] Rodney Duke, for example, claims that "what the Chronicler recorded is not inconsistent with P and does not extend as far as the regulations of Ezekiel."[45] Nevertheless, Knoppers presents concrete examples of the Chronicler's knowledge not only of P but also of Ezekiel, including the Zadokite passages. For example, the terms describing the Levitical duties in 1 Chronicles 23:28–32 are unique to P and Ezekiel: choice flour for the cereal offering (למנחה) סלת (1 Chr 23:29; Num 15:4, 6; 28:5, 9, etc.; Ezek 46:14) and the griddle מחבת (v. 29, Lev 2:5; 6:14; 7:9; Ezek 4:3).[46] There are also close parallels among the three texts, according to Knoppers, in terms of Levitical assignments, such as the work for the Temple of God in general (v. 28; Ezek 44:14), and the watch over the tent of meeting/ house sanctuary of Yhwh (v. 32, Num 18:3; 31:30, etc.; Ezek 44:14).[47] These examples are certainly not decisive evidence of the Chronicler's knowledge of Ezekiel, since it is not impossible that P was a common source for both Ezekiel and Chronicles. However, some parts of the Chronicles passage are closer to Ezekiel than P. For example, the expression שמר משמרת combined with עבדת בית ה' (v. 32) is quite similar to that of the Zadokite passage שמר משמרת with הבית לכל עבדתו (Ezek 44:14).[48] In P, it is naturally עבדת אהל מואד (Num 8:24; 18:6, etc.) or עבדת המשכן (Num 3:7, 8); the Chronicler's phrase (v. 32) rather awkwardly mentions both משמרת אהל מועד and עבדת ביה ה', probably the former from P and the latter from Ezekiel.

A more intriguing observation by Knoppers concerns the way the Chronicler responds to the Priestly and Ezekiel texts. He observes that the Levites are responsible for the choice flour for the cereal offering, which are unleavened wafers (1 Chr 23:29), while P (Num 6:1–21; 15:1; 28:1–31) and Ezekiel (46:11–14) do not mention the Levites; maintaining a balance in measuring capacity and length is a Levitical duty (1 Chr 23:29), while it is the duty of the whole people in P (Lev 19:35–36) or the prince (נשיא) in Ezekiel (45:9–12); the watch over the sanctuary (משמרת הקדש) is assigned exclusively to the priests (Num 18:4–5, cf. Num 3:28), which is defended in Ezekiel 44, while all Levites are responsible for this task in Chronicles (1 Chr 23:25–26).[49] Knoppers then concludes:

---

44. For denials of the relationship, see, e. g., Roddy Braun, *1 Chronicles*, WBC 14 (Waco: Word Books, 1986), 235; Duke, "The Levites of Ezekiel," 78–79 n 30.
45. Duke, "The Levites of Ezekiel," 79.
46. See Knoppers, "Hierodules, Priests, or Janitors," 55–57.
47. Ibid., 59–62. See also, Klein, *1 Chronicles*, 455.
48. The עבדה in v. 32 may apparently be read as the work of only the sons of Aaron. Yet, when it is read together with other relevant passages (1 Chr 6:33; 23:24, 28 etc.), עבדה here includes Levitical work as well.
49. See Knoppers, "Hierodules, Priests, or Janitors," 62–64, and further exam-

The Chronicler draws on Priestly terminology, but he does so to expand Levitical responsibilities and to blur some of the clear distinctions advanced by the Priestly writers and defended by Ezekiel.[50]

The Chronicler did not simply repeat P and Ezekiel regulations about the Levites and priests, but instead creatively modified and revised their presentations to promote Levitical status. This is a good example of the strict hierarchical division between priests and the Levites in P and Ezekiel being blurred and reputed in favor of the Levites in Chronicles. If the Chronicler not only knew the Zadokite passages in Ezekiel 44 but also modified them to counter the negative perception of the Levites, one may have a safer ground to inquire how the Chronicler responded to the Zadokite accusation of Levitical participation in idol worship (Ezek 44:10–12).

4. THE LEVITES AND IDOLATRY IN CHRONICLES

We saw above that the accusation of idol worship against the Levites (Ezek 44:10–12) was made in very general terms, so that it is hardly connected to a specific historical event. Nevertheless, for the contemporary audiences/readers receiving the book of Ezekiel as a whole, the idolatry in question would have pointed primarily to the time of the late Judean monarchy. Furthermore, literate elites like the Chronicler who were familiar with the written history of the monarchy, such as from the Books of Kings, could have understood the sinful past broadly, as the entire monarchic period. It is thus necessary to examine the Chronicler's accounts of the major historical events connected to idolatry in order to find responses to this accusation. Among many, the accounts of Jeroboam's golden calves and Josiah's reform may constitute two exemplary cases. Before the analysis of the two accounts, however, a closer look into a notable aspect of the Chronicler's terminology of idols would be helpful for further discussion.

4.1 NO IDOLS (גלולים) IN CHRONICLES

In the Zadokite redaction, the Levites are blamed for their involvement in the people's worship of idols (גלולים, Ezek 44:10–12). The term for idols, גלולים, is used most frequently in Ezekiel, yet the Chronicler was admittedly familiar with it through legal texts (Lev 26:30; Deut 29:16) and his major source, Kings (1 Kgs 15:12; 21:26; 2 Kgs 17:12; 21:11; 21:21; 23:24). Among the six verses in Kings, three have parallels in

---

ples therein.
50. Ibid., 64.

Chronicles (1 Kgs 15:12; 2 Kgs 21:21; 23:24). Interestingly, however, the Chronicler modifies the verses by replacing גלולים with other terms. Further, he never uses the term גלולים in his entire writing. The three other passages in Kings are omitted in Chronicles due to the latter's lack of interest or a theological revision;[51] the omission of גלולים in Chronicles seems to be neither accidental nor coincidental, but rather deliberate, if we assess the parallels in detail:

(1) Asa's Reform (1 Kgs 15:12): According to the brief report of Asa's reform (vv. 11–13), he removed all the idols (כל הגלולים) his ancestors had made (v. 12). This verse references the time of Solomon, Rehoboam, and Abijam, implying that these Judean kings made גלולים. This is an important verse that summarizes the idolatry in Judah in the early period of the divided monarchy and its parallel is found in 2 Chronicles 14:3 that also describes Asa's religious reform. The report of the reform seems unexpected in its literary context, since in Chronicles, Rehoboam is humbled before Yhwh and Abijam is also described positively. This verse is thus almost certainly from 1 Kgs 15:12.[52] The Chronicler, however, alters the account of reform by adding more details, such as foreign altars, high places, pillars, and sacred poles, but omits גלולים. As Japhet has observed, this alteration is "neither incidental nor merely stylistic,"[53] considering the Chronicler's repetition of the verses preceding and following 1 Kings 15:12 without much modification (1 Kgs 15:11a, 13 // 2 Chr 14:2; 15:16).[54]

(2) Amon's Idolatry (2 Kgs 21:21): The verse describing Amon's idolatry is paralleled in 2 Chronicles 33:22. The Kings passage says that Amon served (ויעבד) and worshiped (וישתחו) "the idols (הגלולים)" that his father had served. The Chronicler rephrases this so that Amon served (ויעבדם) and sacrificed (זבח) to "the idols (הפסילים)" that his father had made. The basic meanings of the two verses are identical; the term for "idols" is modified from גלולים to פסילים.

---

51. 1 Kgs 21:26 mentions גלולים in describing Ahab's idolatry; the Chronicler is not interested in Ahab and mentions him only in relation to Judah (e. g., 2 Chr 18; 21:6; 22:3, etc.). In the Chronicler's description of Ahab, however, his idolatry is mentioned very generally as adultery (ז.נ.ה, 2 Chr 21:13) or evil (הרע, 22:4), without the term גלולים. Similarly, the historical summary of the sins of Northern Israel in 2 Kgs 17:12 that contains גלולים is entirely omitted in Chronicles. The term appears in the account of Manasseh's transgressions (2 Kgs 21:11), yet the entire section of the judgement speech (vv. 11–15) is replaced by the account of his rehabilitation through punishment, repentance, and religious restoration (2 Chr 33:11–17).

52. See Klein, *2 Chronicles*, 213.

53. Japhet, *Chronicles*, 706.

54. The Chronicler also removes "like his father David" (כדיד אביו, 1 Kgs 15:11b), because David is an incomparable cultic founder for the Chronicler. The mention of male cult prostitutes (הקדשים, v. 12a) is removed in Chronicles in an intentional silence about them. See Japhet, *Chronicles*, 706.

(3) Josiah's Reform (2 Kgs 23:24): The Chronicler's account of the purge of the idolatrous objects (2 Chr 34:3–7), though brief, parallels the account in 2 Kings 23:4–20. Several verses later, 2 Kings 23:24 briefly reports Josiah's removal of the abominations from Judah and Jerusalem, including mediums, wizards, teraphim, and idols (גלולים), motivated by the book found in the temple. The parallel of the verse can be found in 2 Chronicles 34:33, which briefly recapitulates Josiah's removal of the abominations motivated by the book found in the temple (vv. 30–32). The Chronicles passage (esp. v. 33), however, omits the details in its *Vorlage*, including גלולים, and only designates them generally as all the abominations. (כל התועבות)

In these three passages, the avoidance of גלולים is hardly accidental but appears to be purposeful. Japhet also notices the lack of גלולים in Chronicles and argues that the Chronicler is probably following the spirit of the Deuteronomic precept in Deuteronomy 7:5, which lacks the term.[55] Yet, as discussed above, גלולים also appears in Deuteronomy 29:16 and other passages in Kings. The intentional absence of the term is also perceivable by considering that Chronicles readily employs other terms for idolatry. For example, another typically Ezekielian term for idolatry (or idol), תועבה, is used without reluctance (2 Chr 28:3; 33:2; 34:33; 36:8, 14). Equally, other biblical terms for idolatrous objects, such as פסילים (2 Chr 33:19, 22, etc.), מפלצת (2 Chr 15:16), מצבה (1 Chr 14:2; 31:1), מסכה (2 Chr 28:2; 34:3), and אשרה (2 Chr 14:3; 15:16, etc), are employed without avoidance. It is only גלולים that Chronicles avoids, even though it appears in the *Vorlage*.

It seems that the absence of גלולים was a deliberate and careful choice by the Chronicler related to the Levites' idolatry in Ezekiel 44. Whether the accusation was true or false, any account of idolatry, especially of גלולים, in the monarchic period may have been reminiscent of the Levites's idolatry to those who were acquainted with the Ezekiel text. The Chronicler probably endeavored to prevent this possibility through a strategic ignorance of the term in order to neutralize the possible influence of Zadokite accusations for the audiences/readers of Chronicles.

4.2 Jeroboam's Golden Calves

The case to be examined in detail is the account of Jeroboam's golden calves (1 Kgs 12), which is denounced by the Deuteronomist as the primary cause of the generations of idol worship in Israel and its subsequent destruction (e. g., 2 Kgs 17:22–23). Including Jeroboam's two calves, as discussed above, the idols that Israel worshiped are ex-

---

55. Japhet, *Chronicles*.

pressed with the term גלולים (2 Kgs 17:12, 16). 1 Kings 12:26–33 reports three grave sins of Jeroboam: (1) establishing the cult of the golden calves in Dan and Bethel and building houses for the high places (vv. 26–31a); (2) appointing non-Levite priests for the high places and the Bethel sanctuary (vv. 31b, 32b);

(3) setting a new date for the Autumnal festival (v. 32a). Scholars argue for an editorial nature of the main part of the passage, pointing out that v. 30 is already the conclusion of the account:

ויהי הדבר הזה לחטאת וילכו העם לפני האחד עד דן
And this thing became a sin, for the people went to worship before the one as far as Dan.

The following vv. 31–33, the accounts of the non-Levite priests and the new festival date, are consequently assigned to a late addition.[56] Juha Pakkala further distinguishes between layers in this passage.[57] He argues that the original layer ends with vv. 31a and 33b, and that the intervening passage, vv. 31b–33a, is a series of later expansions. The major part of the expansion is, according to Pakkala, the passage about appointing non-Levite priests: "and appointed priests from among all the people, who were not Levites" (v. 31b). Defining this redactional phase as "Levitical redaction", Pakkala claims that it intended to undermine the status of the Northern cultic sites by emphasizing the non-Levite priesthood there.[58] This is, however, only one side of the coin. As Mordechai Cogan has rightly observed, none of the Mosaic laws would legitimize idolatrous cultic sites by the presence of Levitical priests.[59] If we assume, with Pakkala, that a Levitical scribe was responsible for this addition, the purpose should be to deny the Levites's involvement in Jeroboam's idol worship.

Nevertheless, as a result of this redaction, the present form of Jeroboam's account in Kings gives the impression that there were Levites in the Northern Kingdom and that Jeroboam should have appointed priests from among the Levites for his sanctuaries (vv. 31–32). Further, the passage in the present form implies that the

---

56. For example, see Alfred Jepsen, *Die Quellen des Königsbuches*, 2nd ed. (Halle: Niemeyer, 1956), 6; Volkmar Fritz, *Das Erste Buch der Könige*, ZBKAT 10.1 (Zürich: Theologischer Verlag, 1996), 127–128; Christoph Levin, "Die Frömmigkeit der Könige von Israel und Juda," in *Verheißung und Rechtfertigung: Gesammelte Studien zum Alten Testament II*, BZAW 431 (Berlin: Walter de Gruyter, 2013) 144–77, here 138–39.

57. Juha Pakkala, "Jeroboam Without Bulls," *ZAW* 120 (2008): 501–25, here 509–11.

58. Pakkala, "Jeroboam", 522.

59. Mordechai Cogan, *1 Kings: A New Translation with Introduction and Commentary*, AB 10 (New York: Doubleday, 2001), 360.

Levites in the North might have served at the royal sanctuaries and local high places if the circumstance allowed. This, however, would not be what the "Levite redaction" intended.

The Chronicler's parallel account (2 Chr 11:13–17) mentions Jeroboam's transgressions only briefly, in a single verse (v. 15, cf. 2 Chr 13:9); in the same passage, the Chronicler focuses on the immigration of the Northern priests, Levites, and pious laity. The major difference from Kings is that all of the priests and Levites had left Jeroboam and the Northern Kingdom and came to Jerusalem to worship Yhwh. The Levites were thus completely disconnected from the idolatrous Northern cult. This "complete disconnection" between the Levites and the Northern cult precludes all possible "misunderstandings" about the Levites by the audiences/readers of Kings. The complete disconnection is precisely achieved through details of the Chroniclers' account.

Firstly, vv. 13–14a justify the presence of the Levites in the Northern Kingdom by referring to the Levitical cities distributed to the Levites (Josh 21; 1 Chr 6:39–66 [ET 6:54–81]; 13:2).[60] It is the Chronicler's view that the Levites (and priests) already settled in towns distributed to them in both the North and the South before the monarchic period (1 Chr 13:2) and in turn served the Temple in Jerusalem (1 Chr 24:19, 31). They were thus present in the North not because of service in local sanctuaries, but because Joshua had allocated towns and pastureland to them. They had not inhabited the Northern towns since the very beginning of the Northern Kingdom, for the Chronicler, so that they were always pious to Yhwh and the temple of Jerusalem and never had contacts with Northern idolatry. Notably, only the Levites, and not the priests, are mentioned in describing their royalty and pious deeds, such as abandoning their lands and holdings (v. 14a),[61] in contrast to most of the other verses mentioning both the priests and the Levites together in the same context (2 Chr 11:13; 13:9–11).[62] As a consequence, the Levites' roles appear more dominant in the pious deeds of leading the Northern laity to Jerusalem and strengthening Rehoboam's reign.[63]

---

60. The terms אחזה and מגרש (v. 14a) also occur together in Josh 21 (vv. 12, 41). See further James T. Sparks, *The Chronicler's Genealogies: Towards an Understanding of 1 Chronicles 1–9*, Academia Biblica 28 (Atlanta: Society of Biblical Literature, 2008), 150–52.

61. Williamson has argued that v. 41a is late addition. See Hugh G. M. Williamson, *1 and 2 Chronicles*, NCB (Grand Rapids, MI: Eerdmans, 1982), 243. Cf. Klein's criticism on this view (*2 Chronicles*, 174).

62. Cf. Japhet, *Chronicles*, 669. Japhet argues that the Levites here include the priests, but this is not a wording typical of the Chronicler, who also designates the priests as הלוים.

63. For example, ואחריהם (v. 16) literally indicates only the Levites. In addition,

The following half-verse (v. 14b) further eliminates any possible connection between the Levites and the Northern cult. Dillard rightly observes that the Chronicler "has also made explicit Jeroboam's rejection of the Levitical priests: rather than simply reporting his indiscriminate hiring practices as done in 1 Kings 12:32; 13:33."[64] The Chronicler explicitly indicates that Jeroboam rejected the Levites serving as "priests of Yhwh," rather than serving as priests of his high places (cf. 1 Kgs 12:31; 13:33–34). This slight revision clarifies that the Levites served and expected to serve Yhwh alone and effectively denies the possible implication of those Kings passages concerning Levites and the Northern high places. The severance between the Levites and the Northern cult is perpetuated in Chronicles by the addition of "ובניו" (and his sons, v. 14b), which is missing in the Kings account: Not only Jeroboam but also his successors rejected the Levites,[65] thus permanently separating the Levites from the Northern cult. This may have been an effective additional explication to prevent overinterpretation of their service to Rehoboam for only three years (v. 17), which could have been interpreted as the Levites' return to the Northern Kingdom.

Further, in the brief description of Jeroboam's idolatry (v. 15), the Chronicler adds goat-demons (שעירים) in addition to calves and high places. As commentators agree, the goat-demons refer to Leviticus 17:7, which forbids the sacrifices offered in the open fields and outside the legitimate sanctuary (the Tent of Meeting).[66] With this addition, the Chronicler projects the dichotomy between the legitimate sanctuary and the others expressed in Leviticus 17:7 to the Jerusalem temple and the Northern cultic sites. This implied dichotomy further enhances the ideological and theological distance between the Levites and Northern idolatry.

The present form of the Jeroboam account in 1 Kings 12–13 distinguishes between his transgression of building idolatrous cultic sites (1 Kgs 12:31a, 32a;13:1–3) and his appointment of non-Levitical priests there (1 Kgs 12:31b; 13:33). The distinction was, as shown above, caused by the Levitical additions. In Chronicles, however, the legitimate place and personnel are not separate matters but are intrinsically combined into one (also 2 Chr 13:9–11).[67] Again, the Levites

---

the grammatical subject of ויחזקו and ויאמצו is only the Levites and the northern people led by them, and not the priests.

64. Dillard, *2 Chronicles*, 97.

65. Here, "his sons" should be understood as his successors. See also Japhet, Chronicles, 669. Cf. Dillard, *Chronicles*, 97.

66. See Japhet, *Chronicles*, 668; Dillard, *Chronicles*, 97; Klein, *2 Chronicles*, 175. For Lev 17:7, see Jacob Milgrom, *Leviticus 1–16: A New Translation with Introduction and Commentary*, AB 3 (New York: London [etc.]: Doubleday, 1991), 1462.

67. See Japhet, *Chronicles*, 669.

cannot be related to cultic sites other than the temple of Jerusalem in the Chronicler's theological scheme.

4.3 JOSIANIC REFORM

The Chronicler takes pains to deny all possible connections between the Levites and idol worship in Judah as well. Among many examples, the Chronicler's account of the Josianic reform deserves a close examination, particularly because its *Vorlage* (2 Kgs 23) is thought to explain the origin of the priestly hierarchy in Jerusalem.[68] According to the majority view of 2 Kings 23:8–9, Josiah gathered the deposed local priests in Judah in Jerusalem, but they had no priestly right to participate in the sacrificial service in Jerusalem (cf. Deut 18:7).[69] The assembled priests were also Yahwistic priests distinguished from the idolatrous priests, called כמרים (2 Kgs 23:5).[70] The passage thus reports that the Josianic reform caused a stratification between the two Yahwistic priestly groups in the Jerusalem temple, between the Jeru-

---

68. The Kings account of Josiah's purge of idols is, like the whole of Kings, thought to have been subjected to multiple stages of expansion from the time of Josiah to the postexilic period. Therefore, Steven McKenzie, for example, argues that the Chronicler had only the Josianic version of Kings (Dtr¹). Boyd Barrick uses this conception for explaining differences between Josiah's accounts in Kings and Chronicles. See Steven L. McKenzie, *The Chronicler's Use of the Deuteronomistic History*, HSM 33 (Atlanta: Scholars Press, 1985); W. Boyd Barrick, *The King and the Cemeteries: Toward a New Understanding of Josiah's Reform*, VTSup 88 (Leiden: Brill, 2002), 61–63. However, most redaction-critical studies of the Kings account of Josiah puts the gathering of the priests to Jerusalem (2 Kgs 23:8a) in the original account. Even Christoph Levin, who reconstructs a very brief original account, regards the passage as original; see Christoph Levin, "Joschija im deuteronomistischen Geschichtswerk," *ZAW* 96 (1984): 351–71; reprinted in Christoph Levin, *Fortschreibungen: Gesammelte Studien zum Alten Testament*, BZAW 316 (Berlin: Walter de Gruyter, 2003), 198–216.

69. This has been the majority view since Wellhausen. Against the majority view, some alternative interpretations have been suggested. See, e. g., Roland de Vaux, *Ancient Israel: Its Life and Instructions*, trans. John McHugh (Grand Rapids, MI: Eerdmans, 1961), 363; Ernest Nicholson, "Josiah and the Priests of the High Places (II Reg 23,8a.9)," *ZAW* 119 (2007): 499–513; idem, "Once Again Josiah and the Priests of the High Places (II Reg 23,8a.9)," *ZAW* 124 (2012): 356–368; Mark Leuchter, "'The Levite in Your Gates': The Deuteronomic Redefinition of Levitical Authority," *JBL* 126 (2007): 417–36; Barrick, *Cemeteries*, 189–93.

70. See, e. g., John Gray, *I & II Kings: A Commentary*, 3rd ed., OTL (London, SCM Press, 1977), 732–733; Gwilym H. Jones, *1 and 2 Kings*, NCBC (Grand Rapids, MI: Eerdmans, 1984), 618; Jimmy J. M. Roberts, *Nahum, Habakkuk, and Zephaniah: A Commentary*, OTL (Louisville, KY: Westminster/John Knox Press, 1991), 172; Gary N. Knoppers, *Two Nations Under God: The Deuteronomistic History of Solomon and the Dual Monarchies*, 2 vols., HSM 52 (Atlanta: Scholars Press, 1993), 188; Phyllis A. Bird, "The End of the Male Cult Prostitute: A Literary-Historical and Sociological Analysis of Hebrew qādēš-qédēšîm," in *Congress Volume, Cambridge 1995*, ed. John A. Emerton, VTSup 66 (Leiden/ New York/Köln; Brill, 1997), 65 n 91.

salemite priests serving at the altar of Yhwh (v. 9a) and those from the local sanctuaries without access to it (v. 9b). Although the account never mentions a Levitical identity for either group, the described situation looks quite similar to the Zadokite passages in Ezekiel. As shown above, a distinction appears between the priests serving at the altar and the priests serving in the house (Ezek 40:45–46a); the Zadokite passages develop the distinction and identify the two groups of priests as the Levitical Zadokite priests and the Levites, respectively (e. g., Ezek 44:10–15). The similarity becomes closer if one regards the sons of Zadok (בני צדוק) as the Jerusalemite priests, following the majority view. The situation reflected in Deuteronomy 18:6–7 is also similar in its recognition of two groups of Levites or Levitical priests; those officiating at the chosen place and those coming from other parts of the land. The similarities among the three passages led earlier generations of scholars to believe that all of them were describing one historical event, the Josianic reform.

I am not arguing here that the Josianic reform was the definite historical origin of this distinction, nor would I say that Ezekiel's account of the Levites' idol service indicates the time of Josiah. I am simply suggesting the possibility that, regardless of the historical reality, the similarity of the situations described in these passages caused them to overlap among the literate elites of Yehud. In other words, the Chronicler or his primary audiences/readers may have naturally made a connection between the clerical stratification in Ezekiel 44 and the similar distinction between Jerusalemite and local priests in 2 Kings 23 (Deut 18:6–7). Were this the case, it would not be without benefit to examine whether the Chronicler is responding to the accusation of the Levites in Ezekiel 44 in his account of Josianic reform.

The Chronicler significantly shortens the *Vorlage* of 2 Kings 23:4–21 in describing Josiah's purging of idolatry (2 Chr 34:3–7), while he extends other accounts such as the observance of Passover and Josiah's death at the hands of Pharaoh Neco (2 Chr 35).[71] Regarding the idol purge, Josiah is a major hero in the Deuteronomistic history of Israel; he is one of the many Judean kings who enacted religious reforms in Chronicles (Asa, Jehoshaphat, Hezekiah, Manasseh, etc.).[72] Josiah continued and completed the reform that his grandfather Manasseh started (cf. 2 Chr 33:15–17), rather than initi-

---

71. See Japhet, *Chronicles*, 1018; Louis C. Jonker, *Reflections of King Josiah in Chronicles: Late Stages of the Josiah Reception in II Chr. 34 f.*, Textpragmatische Studien Zur Literatur- und Kulturgeschichte Der Hebräischen Bibel 2 (Gütersloh: Gütersloher Verlagshaus, 2003), 31–33.

72. See further Jonker, King Josiah, 32 n 17; Japhet, *Chronicles*, 1020. Cf. Dillard, *2 Chronicles*, 278.

ating it by himself. Nevertheless, the Chronicler's account of Josiah's reform makes an interesting modification in terms of the fate of the local priests that has not received much scholarly attention thus far.[73]

Two points of the modification are especially noteworthy: First, the Chronicler combines the different motifs of defiling in 2 Kings 23 into one action. According to Kings, the purge of the high places was implemented with three different measures: Josiah defiles (טמא) the high places in Judah and Solomon's high place in Jerusalem and gathers the priests to Jerusalem (2 Kgs 23:8, 13); at Bethel, he destroys and crushes high places to dust and defiles the altar by burning human bones on it (vv. 15–16); he does the same to the high places in the towns of Samaria but also sacrifices (ויזבח) the priests on their altars (vv. 19–20). Josiah's purges become more severe as he moves northward. The priests at the high places in Judah survive and are called up to Jerusalem, while the priests at the Samarian towns are slaughtered.

Chronicles, however, eliminates the contrasting treatments of the Southern and Northern local priests. The Chronicler combined the burning of human bones on the altars at the Samarian towns with the killing of the local priests, saying that Josiah "burned bones of the priests on their altars" (2 Chr 34:5). This purge is made at the high places in Judah and Jerusalem (v. 3). The fate of these local priests

---

73. There have been some recent studies on the Chronicler's account of the Josianic reform; see, e. g., Ehud Ben Zvi, "Observations on Josiah's Account in Chronicles and Implications for Reconstructing the Worldview of the Chronicler," in *Essays on Ancient Israel in Its Near Eastern Context: A Tribute to Nadav Na'aman*, ed. Yairah Amit et al. (Winona Lake, IN: Eisenbrauns, 2006), 89–106; idem, "Revisiting 'Boiling in Fire' in 2 Chron. 35.13 and Related Passover Questions: Text, Exegetical Needs, Concerns, and General Implications," in *Biblical Interpretation in Judaism and Christianity*, eds. Isaac Kalimi and Peter J. Haas, Library of Hebrew Bible/Old Testament Studies 439 (London: T&T Clark, 2006), 238–250; Jonker, *King Josiah*; Christine Mitchell, "The Ironic Death of Josiah in 2 Chronicles," *CBQ* 68 (2006): 421–435; Mordechai Cogan, "The Chronicler's Use of Chronology as Illuminated by Neo-Assyrian Royal Inscriptions," in *Empirical Models for Biblical Criticism*, ed. Jeffrey H. Tigay (Philadelphia: University of Pennsylvania Press, 1985), 197–210; Christopher T. Begg, "The Death of Josiah in Chronicles: Another View," *VT* 37 (1987): 1–8; Zipora Talshir, "The Three Deaths of Josiah and the Strata of Biblical Historiography (2 Kings xxiii 29–30, 2 Chronicles xxxv 20–25, 1 Esdras i 23–31)," *VT* 46 (1996): 213–36; Hugh G. M. Williamson, "The Death of Josiah and the Continuing Development of the Deuteronomic History," *VT* 32 (1982): 242–48; idem, "Reliving the Death of Josiah: A Reply to C. T. Begg," *VT* 37 (1987): 9–15; Michael A. Fishbane, *Biblical Interpretation in Ancient Israel* (Oxford: Clarendon, 1985), 137–43; Kenneth A. Ristau, "Reading and Rereading Josiah: The Chronicler's Representation of Josiah for the Postexilic Community," in *Community Identity in Judean Historiography: Biblical and Comparative Perspectives*, eds. Gary N. Knoppers and Kenneth A. Ristau (Winona Lake, IN: Eisenbrauns, 2009): 219–248. These works, with an exception of Barrick (*The King and the Cemeteries*), mostly focus on the Chronicler's extended accounts of Passover and/or Josiah's death.

is not explicitly mentioned, yet their bones burning on their altars presupposes that the local priests died already.[74] In other words, the Chronicler is trying to suggest the death of the local priests in Judah and Jerusalem. Further treatment of the priests in Kings, such as gathering or slaughtering them, is thus no more relevant to the Chronicler. Most importantly, no local priests came to the temple of Jerusalem, and, consequently, the separation between altar priests and non-altar priests never occurred.

This modification seems to be deliberate, considering that it betrays even the Chronicler's own historical reconstruction of the Judean high places. Worship in high places is not attacked in Chronicles as harshly as in Kings. Especially after Manasseh's purging of idols, the Chronicler adds that the people of Judah continued to sacrifice at the high places, but only to Yhwh (2 Chr 33:17). Japhet maintains that this is "the clearest biblical expression of the distinction between two kinds of high places: for idolatry and for the worship of the Lord."[75] Josiah's reform started only ten years after Manasseh's death in Chronicles,[76] which is not a long enough time for the natural demise of all priests of the high places. For the Chronicler, therefore, there must have been priests who sacrificed to Yhwh at the Judean high places in Josiah's time.[77] Several tricky questions may then arise here: Who were these priests for the Chronicler? Were they Levitical? David once appointed Zadok as the priest of the high place of Gibeon (1 Chr 16:39); did Manasseh appoint "legitimate" priests of Yhwh at the high places he built? Furthermore, what happened to those priests of Yhwh after the Josianic reform? The Chronicler is totally silent about these issues. The high-place priests are simply regarded as already dead, and only their bones are humiliated. In this way, the Chronicler evaded these tricky questions by mentioning them as if they did not exist at the time of Josianic reform.

The Chronicler's lack of consistency with his own historical

---

74. Dillard interprets the passage as implying that Josiah executed the priests of Baal (*2 Chronicles*, 278), but the "bones" motif presupposes a certain length of time for body decomposition and is used as such in 2 Kings 23:16, 20. Especially in 2 Kings 23:20, Josiah's burning of bones and slaughtering of the priests are described as two separate actions. See also the criticism of Dillard in Barrick, *Cemeteries*, 23 n 20.

75. Japhet, *Chronicles*, 1011.

76. Amon reigned only two years (2 Chr 33:21), and Josiah started purging the idols during the eighth year of his reign in Chronicles (2 Chr 34:3) rather than eighteenth year (2 Kgs 22:3).

77. Barrick similarly argues that "in terms of narrative continuity, the 'bamoth' in question must be those which Manasseh rebuilt (2 Chr 33:3a) and at which 'the people continued to sacrifice, only to Yahweh their god' (2 Chr 33:17); this passing mention is the Chronicler's equivalent of 2 Kings 23:8a (where the priests are presumed to be Yahwistic [cf. v. 9])"; Barrick, *Cemeteries*, 20.

scheme implies that another strong factor influenced this process. This was probably the Chronicler's concern with and response to the notion of a hierarchy within the priestly circle mentioned in 2 Kings 23. The Chronicler's revision eliminates this issue and successfully precludes the possible connection made by Kings between the second-tier Levites in Jerusalem and the former priests of the Judean local sanctuaries. The Chronicler implicitly, but strongly, argued for the Levites' freedom from any accusation of a historical connection with idolatrous worship not only in the Northern Kingdom, but also in Judah.[78]

In summary: The Chronicler neither explicitly mentions nor quotes Ezekiel, yet there are some clues for his knowledge of the prophetic book. Further, the profound (mutual) influence of Ezekiel in the composition of the Pentateuch can serve as circumstantial evidence for the acceptance of the former in the community of literate elites around the temple of Jerusalem to which the Chronicler belonged. Given the Chronicler's knowledge of the Zadokite accusation of idolatry against the Levites, the revision of the accounts of Jeroboam's golden calves and Josiah's purge against Judean idolatry can be understood in terms of the Chronicler's implicit reaction thereto. The two revised accounts preclude any possible connection between the Levites and idolatry both in the Northern Kingdom and in Judah. Further, the term גלולים, possibly reminiscent of the Zadokite accusation, is deliberately avoided throughout Chronicles. This is a subtle and careful way of scribal reaction that is intentional, consistent, and polemical, while simultaneously implicit, indirect, and hidden. In order to sharpen the understanding of the nature of this scribal work, it would be helpful to reinterpret the passages handled above within a theoretical framework of social theories in a heuristic manner.

5. SOME SOCIOLOGICAL OBSERVATIONS

5.1 ZADOKITES' SYMBOLIC CAPITAL

We have observed so far that the Zadokite priestly circle justified the degradation of the Levites through the accusation of idol worship especially in Ezekiel 44. As discussed above, the Levitical scribal works deliberately deny the Levites' possible connection to idol worship. The conflicting Zadokite and Levitical scribal activity may be more

---

78. This interpretation also explains the omission of the slaughter of the Northern priests in 2 Kgs 23:20. The Chronicler does not mention the priests in the Northern towns, presumably because the Northern priests are not within his realm of concern. Cf. Barrick, *Cemeteries*, 61, who argues that the absence of a report about the priests of the Northern towns was because of his *Vorlage*, which was an unaugmented version of Kings.

systematically understood within the theoretical frame of French sociologist Pierre Bourdieu. His studies focus on the division of social classes and how higher or more dominant classes justify and perpetuate class distinction. Already in early twentieth century, Italian sociologist Antonio Gramsci revealed that the dominant class acquires hegemony over a society, not only through economic power but also by manipulating cultural and academic institutions.[79] In an agreement of Gramsci's theory, Bourdieu delves into smaller scale strategy of the bourgeoise to perpetuate class divisions.[80] He argued that "capital" is not only limited to economic assets but also includes invisible assets on cultural and social levels. For Bourdieu, the dominant class is also distinguished from the lower classes by its access to and possession of social capital, such as social relationships as well as cultural capital such as the embodied habitus of the class members, the objectified state like pictures, texts, and academic qualifications. The possession of economic, social, and cultural capital by the dominant class is justified by "symbolic capital" that is represented by values such as honor, authority, and respect. Bourdieu claimed that symbolic capital exercises its power in a specific historical and social context that he defines as a "field."

The Zadokite redaction in Ezekiel can be understood as an attempt to create symbolic capital to justify their dominance in the temple and the community. The Zadokites' exclusive loyalty to Yhwh and their divine selection described in Ezekiel 44 should have been very powerful symbolic capital, especially in the social field of the temple. It shapes in its audiences/readers an honorable memory of the Zadokites, which could sufficiently justify their exclusive priestly prerogatives.

This symbolic power, according to Bourdieu, is exercised violently against the lower classes, especially when it imposes meanings in regard to the dominance of the ruling class and the social structure made by them.[81] Bourdieu coined the term "symbolic violence" for this phenomenon. The accusation against the Levites as the rationale for their degradation in Ezekiel 44 serves as a good example,

---

79. For the application of Gramsci's hegenomy theory to the Zadokite and Levite scribal conflicts, see Jaeyoung Jeon, "The Zadokite and Levite Scribal Conflicts and Hegemonic Struggles," in *Scripture as Social Discourse*: *Social-Scientific Perspectives on Early Jewish and Christian Writings*, eds. Todd Klutz, Casey Strine, and Jessica M. Keady (New York: T & T Clark, 2018), 97–110.

80. Pierre Bourdieu, *In Other Words*: *Essays Towards a Reflexive Sociology* (Stanford: Stanford University Press, 1990); idem, *Language and Symbolic Power* (Cambridge, MA: Harvard University Press, 1991).

81. See also David Swartz, *Culture and Power*: *The Sociology of Pierre Bourdieu* (Chicago: University of Chicago Press, 2012), 82.

with the value of loyalty to Yhwh violently exercising its symbolic power against the lower-class Levites. This value served as symbolic capital for the Zadokites on the one hand; on the other, the lack of such loyalty violently deprives the Levites of priesthood.

According to Bourdieu, "the boundaries between the social classes are crystalized through codification, which indicates formalization of the class boundary."[82] This is an objectified frontier of the classes transformed by the symbolic power standing behind it.[83] The Zadokite redaction in Ezekiel 44 can hereby be understood as a codification of the boundary between the priests and the second-tier Levites.

The Levitical scribal works may be interpreted in a similar manner. As I have discussed elsewhere, the Levites seem to have expanded their power and influence at a certain point in time during the Persian period, probably by assuming different tasks in temple service. The manual workers, gatekeepers, and the singers, who were separated in Ezra-Nehemiah, united themselves as a tribe with an organized genealogy in Chronicles.[84] Joachim Schaper coined a term "united Levites" for the Levites in this stage.[85] The Levites came to possess scribal capabilities as well, as seen in Chronicles and the so-called Levitical Psalms. To be sure, the Levitical roles in Chronicles are ideological and should not be taken as a historical reality of the Second Temple. One may accept, however, that their ideological scribal activity reflects their ambitions projected within the book, in their desired system of temple service in particular.[86] The existence of professional scribes presupposes a certain degree of economic capital, and the resultant texts become cultural capital for the group. Given that the Levites possessed a certain degree of both economic and cultural capital, they must have also sought symbolic capital for justification. The Chronicler's description of David's appointment of the Levites for various tasks as well as their consistent loyalty to Yhwh worship in Jerusalem could function as the Levites' symbolic capital justifying their desirable status. The Chronicler created symbolic capital for the Levites equivalent to that of the Zadokites. At the same time, the deliberate scribal efforts to deny any possible Levitical connection to idol worship can be understood as an effective way of resisting the

---

82. Bourdieu, *In Other Words*, 82.

83. See Bourdieu, *Language and Symbolic Power*, 236.

84. See further, Jaeyoung Jeon, "The Zadokites in the Wilderness: The Rebellion of Korach (Num 16) and the Zadokite Redaction," *ZAW* 127 (2015): 381–411, esp., 401–403.

85. Joachim Schaper, *Priester und Leviten im Achamenidischen Juda: Studien zur Kult und Sozialgeschichte Israels in Persischer Zeit*, FAT I 31 (Tübingen: Mohr Siebeck, 2000), 230–40.

86. See for a further discussion, Jeon, "Hegemonic Struggle."

symbolic violence of the Zadokite scribes.

5.2 Active Remembering, Reshaping, and Forgetting

The scribal debates between the priestly and Levitical circles may also effectively be understood in terms of active ways of shaping and forgetting social memory in a community. The Zadokite redactor's work in Ezekiel 44 formulated a social memory of pious Zadokites and idolatrous Levites in the community that accepted Ezekiel as an authoritative text. Its repeated reinforcement in the memories of the readers/ audiences justified and strengthened the distinction between the two clerical classes on the one hand, while honoring the priests and humiliating the Levites on the other.

For the Levites, the Zadokite accusation should have been forgotten rather than remembered. The Chronicler performed this task by reshaping major "sites of memory" (*lieux de mémoire*) of Israelite idolatry.[87] Firstly, the Chronicler deliberately ignored the term גלולים despite its presence in the *Vorlage*, since this term could be a site of memory that was strongly connected to the Levitical idolatry in Ezekiel 44. Additionally, the Chronicler reshaped the narrative of Jeroboam's golden calves, which is the major site of memory for idolatry of the Northern Kingdom in the Deuteronomistic History. He explicitly described the Levites' piety in leaving the North and abandoning their possessions and, in this way, completely removed them from this "crime scene." Josiah's religious reform is the site of memory for the division between the altar priests and other temple priests/ personnel related to purging of illegitimate sanctuaries. This site likely overlapped with the memory site created by Ezekiel 44 among the reader/audience community. The Chronicler completely eliminated this memory site by reshaping the memory of Josiah's reform, according to which the priests of the high places were already dead and could not have come to Jerusalem.

The Chronicler's efforts to reshape memory were also an active

---

[87]. I use the phrase "site of memory" in a broader sense employed by Ben Zvi, who defines it as "any constructed space, place, event, figure, text of the like – whether it exists 'materially' or only in the mind of members of a social group – whose presence in the relevant cultural milieu evokes or was meant to evoke core images or aspects of images of the past held by the particular social group who lives in that cultural milieu"; see Ehud Ben Zvi, "The Study of Forgetting and the Forgotten in Ancient Israelite Discourse/s: Observations and Test Cases," in *Cultural Memory in Biblical Exegesis*, eds. Trine Hasselbach, Pernille Carstens, and Niels P. Lemche, Perspectives on Hebrew Scriptures and its Contexts 17 (Piscataway, N.J.: Gorgias Press, 2012) 139–157: 141. See also Ehud Ben Zvi, "Chronicles and Social Memory," *Studia Theologica: Nordic Journal of Theology* 71 (2017): 69–90.

way of collective forgetting the Zadokite accusation. According to Umberto Eco, an Italian literary critic and semiotician, one forgets not by a cancelation of memory but by confusion of memories caused by superimposition of different notions and terms; that is, not by producing absence but by multiplying presences. Therefore, an effective strategy for producing "oblivion", according to Eco, is to superimpose different memories on the same issue.[88] The Chronicler's revision of the monarchic history was an effective strategy in this manner. The Chronicler superimposed the alternative history of the pious and loyal Levites upon the Zadokite version in Ezekiel 44, strategically confusing and destroying the relevant memory sites in the social memory of the community. In this way, the negative memory of the Levites is confused and forgotten. This is an effective way of forgetting, against the priestly attempt of active remembrance.

6. Conclusion

This essay has investigated the Zadokite redaction of Ezekiel 44 and the possible scribal reaction of the Chronicler in favor of the Levites. This investigation had yielded the following plausible scenario: The Zadokite scribe endeavored through the redactional work in Ezekiel to enhance their exclusive priestly rights through perpetuating the class distinction between them and the rest of the Levites. Once this text was accepted as an authoritative prophetic book, first by the priestly circle in Jerusalem and subsequently by the wider community, it attained position in the social memory of the community regardless of its historicity. The created memory of exclusive Zadokite loyalty to Yhwh provided them with symbolic capital justifying their monopoly of the priesthood in the socio-religious realm of the temple. The remembrance of the accusation of idolatry against the Levites inflicted symbolic violence against the Levites. Chronicles represents a resistance by the Levitical scribal circle against the symbolic violence of the priestly scribes and, at the same time, Levitical attempts to gain their own symbolic capital. Furthermore, the Chronicler endeavored to collectively forget the memory of the idolatrous Levites in Ezekiel 44 by reshaping and producing the memory of pious Levites during the monarchic period. This result makes it possible to see Chronicles not only as an ideological text promoting the status of the Levites, but also as a Levitical response to the priestly ideology and temple order.

---

[88]. Umberto Eco and Marilyn Migiel, "An Ars Oblivionalis? Forget It!" *PMLA* 103.3 (1988): 254–261: 259. See also Doron Mendels, *Memory in Jewish, Pagan and Christian Societies of the Graeco-Roman World*, Library of Second Temple Studies 48 (London; New York: T&T Clark, 2004).

V. Ezra-Nehemiah: Between P and Chronicles

The Role of Priests and Levites in the Composition of Ezra-Nehemiah: Some Points for Consideration

Deirdre N. Fulton

1. Introduction

The text of Ezra-Nehemiah focuses on events related to the settlement and establishment of Judah, more specifically, Jerusalem, from the period directly after Cyrus' conquest of Babylon to the periods of Ezra and Nehemiah.[1] The priests and Levites (along with other groups connected to the temple administration) are depicted as central to the settlement and establishment of Judah and Jerusalem within the different narrative vignettes. Interspersed throughout the

---

1. Scholars continue to debate the exact dates that Ezra and Nehemiah came to Jerusalem. Scholars who support a return for Ezra and Nehemiah during the kingship of Artaxerxes I (ca. 458 and 445 BCE) include: H. G. M. Williamson, *Word Biblical Commentary. 16*: *Ezra, Nehemiah*, 5 (Waco, Texas: Word Books, 1985); Jacob M. Myers, *Ezra, Nehemiah*, AB 14 (New York: Doubleday, 1987); Joseph Blenkinsopp, *Ezra-Nehemiah*: *A Commentary*, Old Testament Library (London: SCM Press, 1989); Joseph Blenkinsopp, *Judaism, the First Phase*: *The Place of Ezra and Nehemiah in the Origins of Judaism* (Grand Rapids: Eerdmans, 2009); Kyung-Jin Min, *The Levitical Authorship of Ezra-Nehemiah*, JSOTSup 409 (London: T&T Clark, 2004); Frank Charles Fensham, *The Books of Ezra and Nehemiah*, NICOT (Grand Rapids: Eerdmans, 2007). Scholars who support a return for Ezra during the kingship of Artaxerxes the II (398 BCE) include Joachim Schaper, *Priester und Leviten im achämenidischen Juda*: *Studien zur Kult- und Sozialgeschichte Israels in persischer Zeit*, FAT 31 (Tübingen: Mohr Siebeck, 2000); Diana Vikander Edelman, *The Origins of the "Second" Temple*: *Persian Imperial Policy and the Rebuilding of Jerusalem*, BibleWorld (London: Equinox, 2005); Lisbeth S. Fried, *Ezra: A Commentary* (Sheffield: Sheffield Phoenix Press Ltd, 2015); Bob Becking, *Ezra-Nehemiah*, Historical Commentary on the Old Testament (Leuven; Bristol, CT: Peeters, 2018). See Becking, *Ezra-Nehemiah*, 98–100 for a more thorough list of scholars who support Ezra's return during Artaxerxes I or II.

405

narrative vignettes are lists that mention the priests, Levites, and temple personnel, as well as non-cultic personnel who made up the Jerusalem and broader Judahite community.[2] Since the priests and Levites are central figures in both the narratives and lists, certain scholars have examined the role these two groups may have played in the composition of Ezra-Nehemiah.[3] Additionally, while earlier scholarship focused on compositional unity or disunity with Chronicles, more recent scholarship has focused on more specific questions about the unity or disunity of Ezra-Nehemiah itself.[4] This focus on priestly and/or Levitical authorship of Ezra-Nehemiah is hardly surprising, given that one of the most significant moments is found in Nehemiah 8 when Ezra presents the Torah of Moses to the community.

While the priests and Levites are prominent in Ezra-Nehemiah, the close geographical proximity of these groups leads other scholars to argue for a scribal community that is in close contact with both priestly and Levitical guilds.[5] Through these inter-group debates, the text of Ezra-Nehemiah underwent textual changes that preserve decidedly pro-priestly and pro-Levitical (as well as antipriestly and anti-Levitical) editing to the text. In what follows, I explore certain passages

---

2. These lists include Ezra 2//Nehemiah 7, Ezra 7, 8, 10:18–43, Neh 3:1–32, 10:2–28, 11:4–24, and 12.

3. Cf. Williamson, *Word Biblical Commentary. 16*; Min, *Levitical Authorship*; Juha Pakkala, *Ezra the Scribe: The Development of Ezra 7–10 and Nehemiah 8*, BZAW 347 (Berlin: De Gruyter, 2004). Pakkala argues for several different editorial changes to Ezra over two centuries (at least), and one of these editorial changes is Levitical in nature, but preserving both priestly and Levitical interests.

4. For a discussion of Chronicles-Ezra-Nehemiah, see Sara Japhet, "The Supposed Common Authorship of Chronicles and Ezra-Nehemia Investigated Anew," *VT* 18 (1968): 330–71; Thomas Willi, *Die Chronik als Auslegung*, FRLANT 106 (Göttingen: Vandenhoeck & Ruprecht, 1972); H. G. M Williamson, *Israel in the Book of Chronicles* (Cambridge: Cambridge University Press, 1977); Tamara Cohn Eskenazi, *In an Age of Prose: A Literary Approach to Ezra-Nehemiah*, Society of Biblical Literature Monograph Series 36 (Atlanta: Scholars Press, 1988); Blenkinsopp, *Ezra-Nehemiah*. For a discussion of the unity or disunity in Ezra-Nehemiah, see James C. VanderKam, "Ezra-Nehemiah or Ezra and Nehemiah?" in *Priests, Prophets, and Scribes: Essays on the Formation and Heritage of Second Temple Judaism in Honour of Joseph Blenkinsopp*, ed. Eugene Ulrich et al., Journal for the Study of Judaism Supplement Series 149 (Sheffield: Sheffield Academic Press, 1992); Mark J. Boda and Paul L. Redditt, eds., *Unity and Disunity in Ezra-Nehemiah: Redaction, Rhetoric and Reader* (Sheffield: Sheffield Phoenix, 2008); Christopher Jones, "Embedded Written Documents as Colonial Mimicry in Ezra-Nehemiah," *Biblical Interpretation* 26 (2018):158–81; Nissim Amzalag, "The Authorship of Ezra and Nehemiah in Light of Differences in Their Ideological Background," JBL 137/2 (2018):271–97; Becking, *Ezra-Nehemiah*.

5. Cf. Williamson, *Word Biblical Commentary. 16*; Jones, "Embedded Written Documents," 162. Jones does not argue for priestly or Levitical authorship, but rather "an educated scribal literati." See below for discussion.

to investigate priestly and Levitical portrayals within the Ezra-Nehemiah corpus. Some of the key passages referring to priests and Levites include their first and last appearances in Ezra-Nehemiah (Ezra 1 and Nehemiah 13), the settlement of Judah in the time of Jeshua and Zerubbabel (Ezra 3), Ezra's first appearance and return to Judah (Ezra 7–8), the reading of the Torah by Ezra (Neh 8), and the dedication ceremonies in Jerusalem (Nehemiah 9–10 and 12).

I do not seek to revisit the different compositional models for Ezra-Nehemiah in light of priestly or Levitical authorship, an increasingly growing area of scholarship over the past 20 years, but rather to explore how these texts present the temple elite in light of Torah.[6] The differences in the presentation of the priests and Levites in Ezra and Nehemiah highlight certain issues concerning common authorship of these texts, as well as arguments for priestly or Levitical authorship. As I argue, the behaviors of the priests are functional and less prescriptive in nature. That is, the priests and Levites oftentimes are functionaries on behalf of the people within their cultic roles in Ezra-Nehemiah.[7] Yet these narratives are not meant to enforce established, or accepted, behaviors since the cultic functions are not, at times, exclusively the role of the priests and Levites. Rather, they are the role of the entire community, which is also deemed holy.[8]

2. Priests and Levites in Ezra-Nehemiah

Priests and Levites are central actors throughout the book of Ezra-Nehemiah. Upon first glance, the priests and Levites appear to be represented equally within the cultic and sacral life of the Jerusalem com-

---

6. To be clear, these different compositional models are helpful for understanding textual formation and also help draw attention to textual tensions. My observations in this essay are not negating these diachronic models, but are simply examining the final product of Ezra-Nehemiah. I date the latest editorial layers to the late-Hellenistic Period.

7. Cf. Menahem Haran, *Temples and Temple-Service in Ancient Israel: An Inquiry into the Character of Cult Phenomena and the Historical Setting of the Priestly School* (Oxford: Clarendon, 1977). On p. 94 Haran maintains that during the time of Ezekiel, there was no Levitical class but was created by Ezekiel through "down-grading certain" non-Zadokite priests. He also notes that aside from P and "Ezekiel's code," there is no clear categorical division of rank between the priests and Levites except in Ezra, Nehemiah, and Chronicles.

8. Eskenazi, In an Age of Prose; Hannah K. Harrington, "Holiness and Purity in Ezra-Nehemiah," in *Unity and Disunity in Ezra-Nehemiah: Redaction, Rhetoric, and Reader*, eds. Mark J. Boda and Paul L. Redditt, Hebrew Bible Monographs 17 (Sheffield: Sheffield Phoenix Press, 2008), 98–116.

munity since both are generally found together.⁹ The first reference to the priests in Ezra is accompanied by the Levites (Ezra 1:5). Ezra-Nehemiah ends with a reference to both the priests and Levites (Neh 13:30). The common appearance of both groups is evident throughout Ezra-Nehemiah, revealing their centrality within this text and their importance within the Jerusalem cultic community. In places, then, they seem to function simply as a means by which to denote cultic personnel generally.

Upon closer inspection and in different settings, however, priests and Levites have different functions in Ezra and Nehemiah, and on a smaller scale, the texts of Ezra and Nehemiah do not have unified presentations throughout each book. I offer several examples to highlight certain intertextual tensions regarding the role that the priests and Levites play in the Judahite community and how these moments may enlighten us to the goals of the editors in Ezra-Nehemiah. I begin with the framing narratives of Ezra 1 and Nehemiah 13 since they offer examples of how the portrayal of the priests and Levites differ dramatically.

2.1 Ezra 1 and Nehemiah 13: The Introduction and Conclusion of the Priests and Levites

In the first chapter of Ezra (1:5), the priests and Levites are part of the heads of the families (ראשי האבות) who return to rebuild the house of God in Jerusalem. King Cyrus is credited with giving vessels, originally from the House of the LORD that Nebuchadnezzar had taken away from Jerusalem, and entrusting them to Sheshbazzar, the "prince of Judah" (הנשיא ליהודה) who brings them from Babylon to Jerusalem. Within this narrative, the priests and Levites are part of the prominent returnees – mentioned after the Judahites and Benjaminites – but are given no formal position to aid in the return of the freewill offerings of animals or vessels, including the cultic paraphernalia said to be from the first temple that Nebuchadnezzar destroyed.

Similarly, in the first-person narrative of Nehemiah 13, among his final reforms, Nehemiah (v. 30) claims "I purified them of everything foreign, and I established the duties of the priests and Levites, specific duties for each person" (וטהרתים מכל־נכר ואעמידה משמרות לכהנים וללוים איש במלאכתו). Both priests and Levites are mentioned, and the need for purification is because of their impurity in connection to their marriage to foreign women. It is noteworthy, however, that the only people

---

9. Min, citing Anderson and Forbes, notes that the term כהן appears 78 times in Ezra-Nehemiah and לוי appears 65 times. Min, *Levitical Authorship*, 44–47; Francis I. Andersen and A. Dean Forbes, *The Vocabulary of the Old Testament* (Roma: Pontificio Istituto biblico, 1989).

named are the sons of Joiada, son of Eliashib the high priest, because his son-in-law was Sanballat the Horonite. Thus, certain priests are indicted and named, but not the Levites. In the compositional schema of this passage, certain scholars argue for the dependence of Nehemiah 13:23–31 on Ezra 9–10 (or vice versa), and both texts are dependent on Deuteronomy 7 and 23.[10] Juha Pakkala also sees Nehemiah 13:23–31, which he argues is the "youngest expansion to the book" as well as the older vv. 1–14, as decidedly pro-Levitical albeit from a different compositional stratum.[11] Certainly, Nehemiah 13 is more favorable toward the Levites than the priests.

In both Ezra 1 and Nehemiah 13, the activities one would expect the priests and Levites to perform in light of Torah regulations, namely the transport of sacred vessels and freewill offerings from Babylon to Judah and the purification of the community, are performed by non-cultic officiants: Sheshbazzar the "prince" of Judah and Nehemiah the "governor."[12] To add to this list of activities one would expect cultic officiants to perform, the larger narrative of Nehemiah 13 consistently takes the agency of reform away from the priests – and to a lesser degree Levites – and places it in the hands of Nehemiah. These reforms include the already-mentioned separation from foreign wives, but also include the threat of the Moabites and Ammonites in the community (vv. 1–3), the removal of Tobiah from rooms in the Temple (v. 8), the purification of these rooms and return of temple vessels (v. 9), the gathering of the Levites back to the temple from their villages (v. 11), the appointing of priestly, scribal, and Levitical treasurers (v. 13) and finally, the enforcing of Sabbath regulations (vv. 15–20). Crediting Nehemiah with these reforms may be viewed as a critique of the priests since it would have been their prerogative and not that of the lesser Levites. Additionally, if these texts are prescriptive in nature, they provide further evidence that this is a critique of the priests since they are not performing their cultic roles. Lisbeth Fried argues that Nehemiah's actions may be to curb high priestly powers.[13]

10. Pakkala, *Ezra the Scribe*, 223–24; Jacob L. Wright, *Rebuilding Identity: The Nehemiah-Memoir and Its Earliest Readers*, BZAW 348 (Berlin: de Gruyter, 2004). See Pakkala for a discussion of the textual priority of Ezra 9–10 over against Neh 13:23–31, and see Wright for the opposite view.

11. Pakkala, *Ezra the Scribe*, 224. Pakkala's model addresses the fact that Ezra 1 does not mention Ezra the priest and scribe at all, but rather mentions Sheshbazzar.

12. For a discussion of the titles "governor" in Ezra-Nehemiah, see Deirdre Fulton, "What Kind of Governor was Nehemiah? The Titles פֶּחָה and תִּרְשָׁתָא in MT and LXX Ezra-Nehemiah," *Zeitschrift für die alttestamentliche Wissenschaft* 130/2 (2018):252–67.

13. Lisbeth S. Fried, *The Priest and the Great King: Temple-Palace Relations in the Persian Empire*, BJSUCSD 10 (Winona Lake: Eisenbrauns, 2004), 207–8. Fried argues that the Sabbath regulations, specifically the closing of the gates (13:19), were

Sean Burt counters that the religious reforms may have served the purpose of eliminating "sources of competition for Persian power and tribute."[14] Certainly, giving credit to Nehemiah is a case of eliminating sources of competition controlled by other powerful families, such as the Tobiad family in Amman and Eliashib the priest.[15] This removal of power, in turn, would also lessen control of the priests in Jerusalem in favor of Nehemiah.

Nehemiah 13:1–3 also presents proper Torah observance as enforced by the people and not the priests.[16] Namely, Deuteronomy 23:4–7 prohibits the Ammonites and Moabites in the sanctuary – a law one would expect priests to enforce. Yet in Nehemiah 13, this prohibition is carried out by the people.[17] This prohibition also applies to Nehemiah's removal of Tobiah from the storeroom that Eliashib, the priest, had given to him. Thus, in these two instances the priests are depicted as ineffective leaders, thereby suppressing their powers in favor of Nehemiah or the people. The Levites, however, are not suppressed in comparison to the priests, as evidenced in Nehemiah 13. Specifically, Levites are given a role in the treasury collection, which is a departure from Torah regulations. Yet even these Levitical activities are a consequence of Nehemiah's help. Ezra 1 and Nehemiah 13 provide a framework for the texts and are suggestive of the roles that the priests and Levites played in the Jerusalem community, but not meant to curb high priestly power.

14. Sean Burt, *The Courtier and the Governor*: *Transformations of Genre in the Nehemiah Memoir*, JSJSup 17 (Göttingen: Vandenhoeck & Ruprecht, 2014), 192; see also Marty E. Stevens, *Temple, Tithes, and Taxes*: *The Temple and the Economic Life of Ancient Israel* (Peabody, MA: Hendrickson, 2006). While the text of Nehemiah certainly portrays this as the center of economic and religious life in Nehemiah 13, it is not the center of economic or religious life in other parts of the book. Moreover, the possible role of other nearby economic centers, such as Ramat Rahel, draws into question the assumption that the Jerusalem temple functioned as the only economic hub in Judah. For a discussion of the possible role of Ramat Rahel in Persian period Judah, see Gary N. Knoppers, *Judah and Samaria in Postmonarchic Times*: *Essays on Their Histories and Literatures*, Forschungen zum Alten Testament 129 (Tübingen: Mohr Siebeck, 2019), 153–75.

15. Fried, *The Priest and the Great King*, 210. Fried rightly points out that Nehemiah's biggest enemies are the heads of several families, including Tobiah and Eliashib, as well as Sanballat and Geshem.

16. Eskenazi, *In an Age of Prose*, 122; Eskenazi views 13:1–3 as the "finale" that depicts a community purified. This "finale" is in relation to the events in Nehemiah 12. Others, such as Wright, *Rebuilding Identity*, 315–17; Pakkala, *Ezra the Scribe*, 223–24; Becking, *Ezra-Nehemiah*, 313–14 view the third person narrative vv. 13 as a later addition to the first-person material in Nehemiah 13. Either way, vv. 1–3 are not originally part of the other material in Nehemiah 13.

17. Becking, *Ezra-Nehemiah*, 316. Becking is correct in his observation that "the initiative for the action, unlike the four following episodes, lies with the people themselves and not with Nehemiah."

determinative enough so other texts must be explored.

2.2 EZRA 3

In contrast to the minor role that the priests and, to a lesser extent, the Levites play in Ezra 1 and Nehemiah 13, Ezra 3 presents the priests and Levites functioning in specific cultic roles. Set within the return of Jeshua the priest and Zerubbabel the governor to Judah, an altar is built and offerings are made (Ezra 3:2), in keeping with what was "written in the Torah of Moses the man of God" (ככתוב בתורת משה איש־האלהים). The narrative in Ezra 3:3–6 details the reinstitution of sacrificial practice, as well as keeping the festival of Sukkot. Concerning the priests, Nissim Amzallag states, "their initiative in restoring the altar and renewing the sacrifices (Ezra 3:3) presents them as leaders of the community, the initiators of Israel's postexilic rebirth." Certainly, in this instance the priests stand out as such. But these activities are not just the actions of the priests. In Ezra 3:2, Jeshua and fellow priests, as well as Zerubbabel and his kin, are responsible for rebuilding the altar and establishing sacrifice.[18]

Several scholars have questioned which texts in the Torah influenced the description of sacrificial activities in Ezra 3. Ezra 3:3–6 describes the sacrificial activities which took place on the newly-built altar in Jerusalem. The details of the sacrificial practices are clearly in line with Torah regulations, particularly with reference to the description of Sukkoth. Christophe Nihan asserts that the phrase מועדי יהוה "appointed times of Yahweh," found in Ezra 3:5, indicates the "time set apart in the year by Yahweh himself."[19] This phrase, also found in another postexilic text, 2 Chronicles 2:3, is present in Leviticus 23:2 and 38.[20] Nihan concludes that, while missing from the earlier calendars in Exodus 23 and Deuteronomy 16, Leviticus 23 "reflects a typically priestly conception (see Gen 1:14; Ezek 44:24)." Bob Becking maintains that Ezra 3:3–6 is in harmony with Sukkoth descriptions in Numbers 29:12–38 and Deuteronomy 16:13–15.[21] Amzallag argues

---

18. Sara Japhet, "Sheshbazzar and Zerubbabel: Against the Background of the Historical and Religious Tendencies of Ezra-Nehemiah," ZAW 95 (1982):84; Eskenazi, *In an Age of Prose*, 51.

19. Christophe Nihan, *From Priestly Torah to Pentateuch: A Study in the Composition of the Book of Leviticus*, FAT 25 (Tübingen: Mohr Siebeck, 2007), 510.

20. Nihan, *From Priestly Torah to Pentateuch*. For a discussion of the postexilic nature of this phrase, see Klaus Grünwaldt, *Das Heiligkeitsgesetz Leviticus 17–26: Ursprüngliche Gestalt, Tradition und Theologie*, BZAW 271 (Berlin: De Gruyter, 1999). Nihan also points out that Lev 23 is noticeably different from other calendars that treat feasts as "climactic events in the agricultural cycle, as in the previous calendars (Ex 23 and Deut 16)."

21. Becking, *Ezra-Nehemiah*, 56; Amzallag, "The Authorship of Ezra and Nehemiah," 286.

that the description of Sukkoth in Ezra 3 is in keeping with Leviticus 23:33–43, Numbers 29:19–39, and 2 Chronicles 8:13, namely that the festival focuses on sacrifice. Ezra 3:3–6 presents Sukkoth in keeping with priestly conceptions of sacrifice, and highlights the priestly role in such a celebration as well as the other sacrificial activities throughout the year.

The Levites are not explicitly mentioned until the rebuilding efforts are underway in the second year of their return (3:7–10). After their appointment, the Levites function as overseers in the rebuilding of the House of God (בית האלהים). The Levitical roles, however, do not extend to any sacrificial practices, which are significant sacerdotal activities of the priests in this context.[22] Both priests and Levites are together for the festivities connected to laying the foundation of the temple (3:10).

2.3 Ezra 7 and 8

The special role of the priests in Ezra 3 is also evident in Ezra 7 with the gathering of the family heads during the period of Ezra's return.[23] In chapter 7, Ezra is described as a "priest and scribe," descended from Aaron the "head priest" (הראש הכהן).[24] He is also described in verse 10 as one who "set his heart to study the law of the LORD, and to do it, and to teach the statutes and ordinances to the people" (ומשפט עזרא הכין לבבו לדרוש את־תורת יהוה וללמד בישראל חק). While Ezra is gathering people by the Ahava river (Ezra 8), there are priests who are willing to return, but no Levites (8:15b). Ezra then sends for certain Levites, whom he names and describes as "ones with understanding" (מבינים), as well as other temple personnel.[25] Rather than reading the failure of the Levites to appear upon Ezra's first gathering as a critique on this group, Juha Pakkala argues that 8:15b–20 is an insertion into

---

22. Eskenazi, *In an Age of Prose*; Japhet, "Sheshbazzar and Zerubbabel." Both Eskenazi and earlier Japhet maintain that Ezra 3:2 should be understood as the entire community coming together to rebuild the altar and establish sacrifice. While this may be the case, it is still noteworthy that the Levites are not mentioned.

23. In compositional models of Ezra, ch 7–10 is considered part of the so-called "Ezra Memoir." See Fried, *Ezra*; Becking, *Ezra-Nehemiah* for an overview of different compositional models for Ezra.

24. Pakkala, *Ezra the Scribe*, 242. Pakkala argues that Ezra 7:6a is the original introduction of Ezra, and the position of priest (7:1–5) is a later addition. The original role of Ezra is beyond the purview of this paper, but I take Pakkala's compositional model, that Ezra is first and foremost a scribe and then later a priest, as a given and 1–5 as an addition to the earlier vv. 6 and following.

25. Pakkala notes certain text-critical issues between Ezra 7 and 8. Juha Pakkala, "The Disunity of Ezra-Nehemiah," in *Unity and Disunity In Ezra-Nehemiah*, eds. Mark J. Boda and Paul L. Redditt, Hebrew Bible Monographs (Sheffield GB: Sheffield Phoenix Press, 2008), 200–215.

the text, correcting the lack of reference to the Levites.[26] Pakkala also states, "the purpose of the expansion in vv. 15b–20 was to emphasize the role of the Levites in Ezra's mission…the addition is connected to similar additions that emphasize the role of Levites met throughout the Ezra narrative." These Levitical insertions may have functioned for many different purposes, but at the least they function as a way to make sure the Levites are included in the narrative.

Moreover, this may be evidence for Levitical authorship, or it may be evidence of a writer who understands the need for Levites in temple legislation according to Torah laws.

Although this may be an example of Levitical insertion into the text, nonetheless the text portrays a positive image of the priests. In contrast to Ezra 1, the temple vessels entrusted to Ezra to return to Jerusalem, are entrusted first to the priests and then to the Levites. Ezra "sets apart" (אבדיל) twelve priests, and then entrusts them with bringing back silver, gold, and temple paraphernalia for the house of God. Ezra (8:28) then proclaims to the priests, "You are holy to the LORD" (אתם קדש ליהוה). This holiness is extended over the goods that the priests are to bring to Jerusalem (8:29b–29). The Levites are mentioned in the conclusion to these events (v. 30), but not in reference to holiness. This one reference to the priests as holy (קדש) is exceptional within Ezra-Nehemiah. The word "holy" (קדש) appears 13 times in Ezra-Nehemiah in limited contexts, namely to describe food (Ez 2:63/Neh 7:65), the priests (Ez 8:28), vessels (Ez 8:28), God's "holy place" (Ez 9:8), people (specifically זרע הקדש in Ez 9:2), certain days (Neh 8:9–11, 9:14, 10:31, and 13:22), and the city of Jerusalem (Neh 11:1 and 18).[27] This one instance in which the priests are called "holy" is unusual and all the more remarkable since people are not the common recipients of holiness in Ezra–Nehemiah.[28] The only

---

26. Pakkala, *Ezra the Scribe*, 59–60.

27. See Harrington, "Holiness and Purity in Ezra-Nehemiah" for a discussion of the term "holy seed" and relevant references; See also Louis C. Jonker, "Melting Pots and Rejoinders? The Interplay among Literature Formation Processes during the Late Persian and Early Hellenistic Periods," *VT* 70 (2020): 42–54 for the appearance of קדש in Chronicles which, he argues, is significant for understanding the role of the Levites. On p. 48, Jonker points out that, "…from 2 Chronicles 29 onwards numerous connections are made between the Levites and the status of being consecrated or holy." This change, according to Jonker is because the Chronicler "developed this profile of the Levites, and even the 'whole assembly' as being holy under the influence of the redefinition of holiness in H."

28. Eskenazi, *In an Age of Prose*, argues that Ezra is commissioning both priests and Levites, calling both "holy". Specifically, she points to the names Sherabiah and Hashabiah, both names of only Levites in other settings (specifically, 8:18–19). This example of "holiness" may be a case of the entire community as considered holy, but it is still significant that the Levites are not named.

other use of holy is to describe the people in Ezra 9:2, namely the "holy seed" (זֶרַע הַקֹּדֶשׁ) who are to separate from those who are not part of this group. To summarize, while the Levitical references in Ezra 8:15b–20 aid in bolstering the role of the Levites in this particular narrative, the priests are still the leaders performing the proper cultic responsibilities and are called holy.

These events in chapters 7 and 8 reflect the most-priestly of behaviors that Ezra undertakes in the book that bears his name. A close reading of Ezra reveals that his main function is more closely associated with those of a scribe, and later editing creates an image of a priest.[29] He does not perform activities that one expects of a priest, however, as outlined in the Torah, namely activities connected to the temple such as sacrifice and overseeing festival events.[30] The carrying of holy vessels, which the Torah places into the hands of the priests, is not part of Ezra's duties. As Tamara Cohn Eskenazi summarizes, "Ezra is a scribe at the service of a book; his primary affiliation and primary allegiance are to the Torah."[31] While it is still debated what the Torah of Moses means in Ezra-Nehemiah, Eskenazi's characterization, that Ezra the priest is "first and foremost a scribe," is fitting.[32] This scribal designation for Ezra, however, does not negate the fact that in Ezra 7 and 8, the priests and Levites are performing duties expected of them.

2.4 NEHEMIAH 8 AND 9

In Nehemiah, the priests and Levites are part of the wall building efforts in Nehemiah 3, and part of the returnees in Nehemiah 7. In Nehemiah 8, the community is gathered for a reading of the Torah, led by Ezra who is first described as a scribe (8:1) and then as a priest (8:2). The Levites are also present (8:7). On the second day of reading, they read about the festival of Sukkoth. Amzallag observes that the Sukkoth celebration follows the parallel lists of Ezra 2//Nehemiah 7 in both books. He states "One would expect the celebration of Sukkot in Ezra and Nehemiah to be as similar as are the respective census lists (Ezra 2:1–70 and Neh 7:6–72)", but this is not the case.[33] Whereas Ezra 3 focuses on sacrifice, the text of Nehemiah never mentions this activity, and as a result, downplays the role of the priests. Additionally, in Nehemiah the people are to construct booths and collect branches,

---

29. Pakkala, *Ezra the Scribe*.
30. See Hannah K. Harrington, "The Use of Leviticus in Ezra-Nehemiah," *JHS* 13 (2013): 1–19 for a discussion of cultic behaviors in Ezra-Nehemiah.
31. Eskenazi, *In an Age of Prose*, 75.
32. Eskenazi, *In an Age of Prose*, 75.
33. Amzallag, "The Authorship of Ezra and Nehemiah," 286.

which is inconsistent with the prohibition to work in Leviticus 23:35.³⁴ Amzallag hypothesizes that one of the reasons for the change is that priests underwent a "loss of prestige" within this narrative, in contrast to the role of priests in Ezra.³⁵ He cites Nehemiah 9:1–5 and Nehemiah 12 as examples of their loss of prestige. Specifically, in the "supplication ceremony" in Nehemiah 9, the Levites conduct the ceremony without the assistance of the priests. The characterization of the Levites in Nehemiah 9 is clearly pro-Levitical. Pakkala explains these differences in Sukkoth by tracing the text of Nehemiah 8:13–18 to an earlier form of Leviticus 23:39–43.³⁶ While the Sukkoth differences may be the result of an *Urtext* of Leviticus 23, the change in Sukkoth practices in Ezra 3 to Nehemiah 8 also change the centrality of the priests and Levites in this ceremony. The perceived loss of priestly control may, however, be viewed as a "democratization" (or, at least moving more power into the hands of the people) of ancient Judean religion.³⁷ Rather than the priests as the only actors, the people (with the help of the Levites) are now the central actors of this celebration. This quasi-democratization, however, does not extend to sacrifice that was still in the hands of the priests and may be why there is no reference to such a practice.

Although the priests are not elevated in Nehemiah 8 and 9, Nehemiah 10:36–39 does offer a point of departure from these portrayals. Following the pledge of the people (including priests, Levites, and temple personnel) to bring goods to the temple, the priests are to accompany the Levites with the collection of tithes.³⁸ These tithes, collected by the Levites and the priests, were brought to the storerooms of the sanctuary for, as v. 39 indicates, the "priests who minister" (הכהנים המשרתים) as well as the gatekeepers and singers. This portrayal of the

---

34. Amzallag, "The Authorship of Ezra and Nehemiah," 286.

35. Amzallag, "The Authorship of Ezra and Nehemiah," 287.

36. Pakkala, *Ezra the Scribe*, 163. Pakkala also asserts that the Sukkoth law in Deut 16:13–15 is not responsible for the creation of Neh 8:13–18. He states, "This is significant as it positively indicates that the author regarded another version of this law more authoritative than the one in Deut. This shift in attitude should not be disregarded, as it may be the oldest clear indication within the Ezra tradition that Deut is not the main Pentateuchal source."

37. Japhet, earlier, observes the power moving away from the figureheads and into the hands of the people. She states, "We might call this process 'democratization', with reservations concerning the terminology which does not fully fit the framework of Israelite life, but does hint at the rise of the power of popular representatives in the social-political structure." Japhet, "Sheshbazzar and Zerubbabel," 87; See also Eskenazi, *In an Age of Prose*.

38. The pledge taken in Neh 10 is a promise of the community to not marry their sons or daughters to the nations, not to sell anything on the Sabbath, to pay the temple tithe, and that the priests and Levites will collect the tithe and bring it to the temple.

priests and Levites working together is meant as the ideal situation. Nehemiah 12 provides another moment for the community to gather and work together, set within a festival context.

2.5 NEHEMIAH 12

During the dedication ceremony in MT Nehemiah 12:27–43, the priests are only mentioned in four verses (vv. 30, 35, 41, and 43), whereas the instruments and position of the Levites are much more prominent. Amzallag observes, "by means of a literary artifice, it seems that, in contrast to the book of Ezra, the author of Nehemiah intentionally diminishes the ritual importance of both the priests and sacrifice, elevating instead the musical performance conducted by the singers/ Levites."[39] He highlights the text of MT Nehemiah 12:41, when the priests follow the procession with trumpets.[40] As well, Nehemiah 12:43 states, "And they offered great sacrifices that day and rejoiced, for God made them rejoice with great joy" (ויזבחו ביום־ההוא זבחים גדולים וישמחו כי האלהים שמחם שמחה גדולה). In this example of sacrificing, there are no specific details, but rather sacrifice is presented as a communal activity. Moreover, the placement of this activity, within the part of the ceremony focused on rejoicing rather than the sacrifice, is striking.[41] The only specific cultic behavior of the priests is their role in playing musical instruments, a role usually relegated to the Levites. In this context, even the priests seem to take on a role traditionally associated with Levites.

While the Levites do play a more prominent role in the processional activities, Nehemiah 12:31 mentions both priests and Levites as part of the purification ceremony. Both priests and Levites are leaders in the purification of themselves, the people, and the city. This is an essential part of the dedication ceremony, and both cultic leaders are equally responsible in this purification.

2.6 NEHEMIAH 13 (AGAIN)

Nissim Amzallag's observation regarding Nehemiah 9 and 12 appears to be in keeping with the attention paid to the Levites. Nehemiah 13, however, offers another point of comparison. The priests are guilty of mismanaging the temple, Sabbath, and marriage alliances, and the Levites have returned to their villages. The Levites return because the "portion of the Levites" (מניות הלוים) was not given to them, so they re-

---

39. Amzallag, "The Authorship of Ezra and Nehemiah," 288.

40. The B, S, A, and Aram. manuscripts are missing the texts found in Neh 12:37–42. See Deirdre N Fulton, *Reconsidering Nehemiah's Judah: The Case of MT and LXX Nehemiah 11–12*, FAT 80 (Tübingen: Mohr Siebeck, 2015), 150–51.

41. Amzallag, "The Authorship of Ezra and Nehemiah," 287–88.

turned to their fields. Nehemiah gathers them, again, and places them in their stations. Whether one reads this text as sympathetic to the Levites is entirely dependent on one's view of the Levites in Nehemiah. The author of this passage in Nehemiah may be more neutral or even possibly sympathetic toward the Levites, but the power still rests in the hands of Nehemiah (and to a lesser extent the people). With regard to the Torah regulations, Bob Becking observes, "According to Deut 18:2 the Levites were not allowed to possess their own land." Alternatively, the changes between Deuteronomy 18:2 compared to Nehemiah 13 may be a result of a change in cultural and/or social expectations.[42]

3. THE PRIESTS AND LEVITES IN EZRA-NEHEMIAH COMPARED

These textual loci in Ezra-Nehemiah allow for many places to compare the role of priests and Levites in Ezra-Nehemiah in light of their possible roles in the composition of these texts. While it is true that when one compares the text of Ezra to the text of Nehemiah, the text of Nehemiah appears to diminish the role of the priestly power in favor of community power or Nehemiah's power. The priests offer very little leadership within Ezra as well. The role of priests to perform Torah duties, namely perform sacrifices and keep festivals, is more functional and less prescriptive. By this, I mean that they are functionaries performing the actions on behalf of the people, but they are not connected to the establishment or enforcement of these activities. They are also not prescribing ritual in the way that Moses prescribes instructions in Leviticus, or Ezekiel prescribes instructions in his Temple Vision (for example, the priestly instructions to the people for separating clean from unclean). In the few cases in which the priests are most directly involved, namely Ezra 3, the description of what the priests are supposed to do – in line with their activities in the Torah – are to sacrifice specifically during festival events. Yet these moments are uncommon within the text of Ezra-Nehemiah. Priests are depicted as sacrificing during the time of Zerubbabel and Jeshua, but in the time of Ezra this activity is never mentioned. Priests, at times, help transport temple vessels (Ezra 8), but not all the time (Ezra 1). Similarly, in Ezra 3:8, the Levites supervise the rebuilding efforts and help transport temple vessels from Babylon to Judah (in Ezra 8), but not all the time (Ezra 1).

In Nehemiah, the minor priestly roles are more muted, as one sees

---

42. Becking, *Ezra-Nehemiah*, 319.

by the changes in the Sukkoth activities. Specifically, the people are responsible for Sukkoth. By the end of the book, Nehemiah (or the people) performs certain priestly functions, namely reforming the community. The series of reforms in Nehemiah 13 are almost exclusively in the hands of Nehemiah. Even the collection of tithes, which according to Nehemiah 10:36–39 were to be collected by the Levites and priests, is not fulfilled. Nehemiah steps in to reinstate the Levites but not the priests, which is a noteworthy change in comparison to 10:36–39. Thus, while the Levites may be promoted in Nehemiah compared to their role in Ezra, they, like the priests, are under the jurisdiction of Nehemiah.

4. Conclusion

The final editors of Ezra-Nehemiah synthesized a series of narrative vignettes and lists that focus on the promotion of Jerusalem and Judah. Within this community, the priests and Levites are central figures in the rebuilding efforts. Yet their roles as builders are not a rehashing of Priestly or even Holiness legislation in the Torah. Rather, the priests in Ezra-Nehemiah function in limited cultic settings. In the case of the book of Ezra, the priestly functions are constrained in nature, so much so that festivals are not a main focus of the book. In the example of Nehemiah, priestly functions are even more muted.

In light of these limited roles, it is unlikely that these editorial activities should be credited to the priests. It is true that the Levites fare better in Ezra-Nehemiah. Yet when compared to other postexilic literature, namely 2 Chronicles 29–37 which praises the Levites and calls them "holy" on several occasions, Ezra-Nehemiah does not appear to be solely Levitical in nature.[43] Rather, the performative rather than prescriptive nature of the priests and Levites limits the power that both groups possess. One should consider authorship in the hands of, as Ehud Ben Zvi has argued, certain Judean literati.[44] And, in such case, the authorship is in the hands of the Judean literati in conversation with the Jerusalem temple community made up of

---

43. Jonker, "Melting Pots and Rejoinders?"

44. Ehud Ben Zvi, "Introduction: Writings, Speeches, and Prophetic Books – Setting an Agenda," in *Writings and Speech in Israelite and Ancient Near Eastern Prophecy*, ed. Ehud Ben Zvi and Michael H. Floyd, SBL Symposium Series 10 (Atlanta: SBL, 2000), 1–30; See also Jones, "Embedded Written Documents," 162. Jones does not connect the composition of Ezra and Nehemiah simply to the temple elite, but rather to elite Judeans who were part of the "scribal literati." This "scribal literati" was familiar with textual traditions in Judah and also "exposed to the literary forms of their overlords." This more comprehensive view of authorship helps explain the seemingly different voices and/or divergent textual traditions within Ezra and Nehemiah.

Levites as well as priests.⁴⁵

---

45. My sincerest thanks for the helpful feedback from Tamara Cohn Eskenazi, Chadwick Eggleston, Christopher Jones, and two anonymous reviewers on this article.

Levites, Holiness and Late Achaemenid/Early Hellenistic Literature Formation: Where does Ezra-Nehemiah fit into the Discourse?

Louis C. Jonker

1. Introduction

In recent studies on the question how the book Chronicles fits into the literature formation processes of the Achaemenid/early Hellenistic periods, I analysed how the Levites are portrayed with reference to the notion of holiness in different textual corpora.[1] After describing the interrelationship between the Holiness legislation, the theocratic redactions in the book of Numbers, the book of Chronicles, and Ezekiel 40–48 (particularly ch. 44), I hypothesized that the following literary history played itself out in the late Persian and early Hellenistic periods:

> The Holiness legislation sparked off at least two new literature formation processes, namely two theocratic reworkings of the Priestly material in the book of Numbers, and the emergence of the book of Chronicles. Like H, Chronicles also contains a merging of Deuteronomic-deuteronomistic and Priestly notions. It relied on the "democratised" understanding of holiness in H when it developed the Levites' profile in terms of this concept. Chronicles prompted at least two ideologi-

---

1. Louis C. Jonker, "Holiness and the Levites. Some Reflections on the Relationship between Chronicles and Pentateuchal Traditions," in *Eigensinn und Entstehung der Hebräischen Bibel. Erhard Blum zum Siebzigsten Geburtstag*, ed. Joachim J. Krause, Wolfgang Oswald, and Kristin Weingart (Tübingen: Mohr Siebeck, 2020), 457–74; Louis C. Jonker, "Melting Pots and Rejoinders? The Interplay among Literature Formation Processes during the Late Persian and Early Hellenistic Periods," *VT* 70 (2020): 42–54.

cal "push-backs" in which the understanding of holiness was again restricted to the Zadokite/Aaronite priests, and where the Levites were again painted in a very negative light. These two "push-backs" against the Chronicler's positive portrayal of the Levites were Numbers 16–18 (which brought the Pentateuch to a conclusion) and Ezekiel 40–48 (which brought the prophetic book Ezekiel to a conclusion). Both these final literature formation processes probably emerged in the post-chronistic era, that is, towards the end of the Persian and the beginning of the Hellenistic period. And both were rejoinders to the longstanding argument about the status of the Levites within the priesthood, and particularly whether they could also claim holiness for themselves.[2]

A schematic presentation of the above-described processes could look as follows (without any claim that the diagramme is correct in scale):

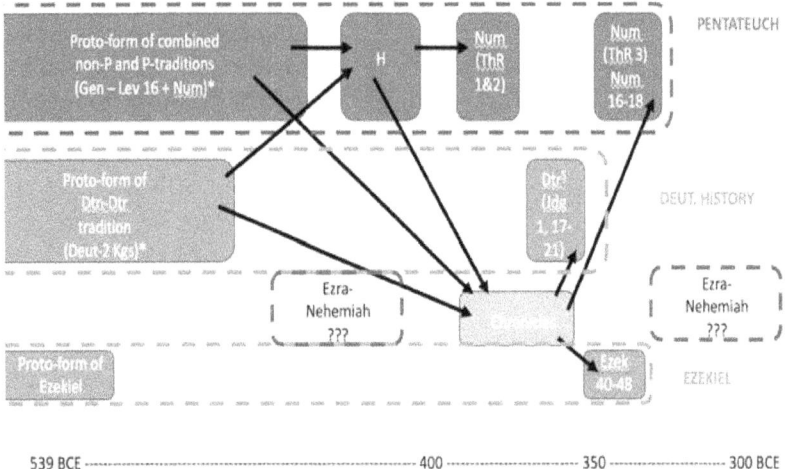

Figure 1: A Hypothesis on (some of) the Literary Formation Processes during the Achaemenid and Early Hellenistic Period (timeline only approximate scale)

If the above hypothesis is accepted (and my expectation is that critical testing will surely follow in scholarly publications), the question remains where Ezra-Nehemiah fits into the picture; and particularly, how does Ezra-Nehemiah contribute to the discourse on the position of the Levites, in contrast or support of Chronicles? Scholarship has come a long way since the days when Chronicles and Ezra-Nehemiah were still seen as part of the same literary work, a so-called Chronistic History.[3] Nowadays, the majority view is that Chronicles and Ez-

---

2. Jonker, "Melting Pots and Rejoinders?" 53–54.

3. Sigmund Mowinckel, *Studien zu dem Buche Ezra-Nehemiah, I* (Oslo: Universitetsforlaget, 1964); Sigmund Mowinckel, *Studien zu dem Buche Ezra-Nehemiah, II* (Oslo: Universitetsforlaget, 1964); Sigmund Mowinckel, *Studien zu dem Buche Ezra-Nehemiah, III* (Oslo: Universitetsforlaget, 1965); Sara Japhet, "Supposed Common Authorship of Chronicles and Ezra-Nehemiah Investigated Anew," VT 18

ra-Nehemiah are separate works by different authors.[4] Chronicles is now seen by the majority of scholars as a unity which was composed towards the middle of the fourth century BCE, most probably by an authorship[5] based in the Jerusalem temple close to the Levites. However, with reference to Ezra-Nehemiah, more issues remain open for debate.[6] Not everybody agrees with the tendency to see the book as one literary work; the majority now view the book as composed of different textual sources, over a fairly long period of time, even into the Hellenistic period.[7] Diachronic theories about Ezra-Nehemiah will, of necessity, have an important bearing on the answering of our question as to where this book fits into the above-mentioned picture. Diachronic theories will help us to a better understanding of the literary engagements with the priestly traditions – "P" and "H" – in the time towards the end of the Persian period and the transitioning to the Hellenistic period (and even beyond).[8]

(1968): 330–71; F. Charles Fensham, *The Books of Ezra and Nehemiah* (Grand Rapids: Eerdmans, 1982); Joseph Blenkinsopp, *Ezra-Nehemiah* (London: SCM Press, 1988); Tamara Cohn Eskenazi, *In an Age of Prose: A Literary Approach to Ezra-Nehemiah* (Atlanta: Scholars Press, 1988); Kyung-Jin Min, *The Levitical Authorship of Ezra-Nehemiah*, JSOT.S 409 (London: T&T Clark, 2004); Lester L. Grabbe, *Ezra-Nehemiah* (London: Routledge, 2005); Lisbeth S. Fried, "Who Wrote Ezra-Nehemiah? – And Why Did They?" in *Unity and Disunity in Ezra-Nehemiah: Redaction, Rhetoric, and Reader*, ed. Mark J. Boda and Paul L. Redditt, Hebrew Bible Monographs 17 (Sheffield: Phoenix Press, 2008), 75–97; Paul L. Redditt, *Ezra-Nehemiah*, Smyth & Helwys Bible Commentary, vol. 9B (Macon: Smyth & Helwys, 2014); Donna Laird, *Negotiating Power in Ezra-Nehemiah*, Ancient Israel and Its Literature 26 (Atlanta: SBL Press, 2016); Bob Becking, *Ezra, Nehemiah* (Leuven: Peeters, 2018).

4. Japhet, "Supposed Common Authorship"; Hugh G.M. Williamson, *Ezra and Nehemiah* (Sheffield: JSOT Press, 1987); Thomas Willi, "Zwei Jahrzehnte Forschung an Chronik und Esra-Nehemia," *TR* 67/1 (2002): 61–104; Thomas Willi, *Esra: der Lehrer Israels*, Biblische Gestalten 26 (Leipzig: Evangelische Verlagsanstalt, 2012).

5. I use the term "authorship" in order to avoid specifying whether it was a single hand (possible, but unlikely), or rather a collective (most likely).

6. Mark J. Boda and Paul L. Redditt, eds., *Unity and Disunity in Ezra-Nehemiah: Redaction, Rhetoric, and Reader*, Hebrew Bible Monographs 17 (Sheffield: Phoenix Press, 2008).

7. For a discussion on the different positions, see Juha Pakkala, *Ezra the Scribe: The Development of Ezra 7–10 and Nehemiah 8*, BZAW 347 (Berlin: De Gruyter, 2004).

8. My approach is thus similar (although with different conclusions regarding the time period) to Raik Heckl's when he indicates in one of his studies on Ezra-Nehemiah: "[Biblical texts] should rather be regarded as intentional literature: literature that served the aim to impart concepts of identity and to reinforce particular forms of religion. That is the reason why it was possible to work on and with these texts over a long period of time. The literary history shows that the biblical authors used their *Vorlagen* in different ways. Transformations, substitutions, and summarizing excerpts of older literary texts are likely as redactions and supplementations. If we accept the intentional nature of the biblical texts on different literary levels, it is possible to ap-

In the present essay, I will concentrate on the distribution of explicit references to Levites and priests in Ezra-Nehemiah, in conjunction with the occurrence of the theme of holiness and purity. As indicated in earlier publications,[9] the portrayal of the Levites in terms of holiness is quite an important element in the argument that I have thus far advanced on the literature formation processes in the late Achaemenid / early Hellenistic periods. The textual observations, mirrored against the background of some diachronic theories (such as those of Williamson and Pakkala) about the composition of the book, will help me to reach a hypothesis about Ezra-Nehemiah's position in the discourses of the same time period.

2. HOLINESS AND THE LEVITES IN EZRA-NEHEMIAH

Our survey focuses on occurrences of terms associated with holiness (קדש),[10] consecration (טהר),[11] separation (בדל),[12] and defilement (גאל II)[13] – collectively called "language of purity" by Hannah Harrington.[14] The textual data are examined with the aim of determining what relationships are reflected in them between the theme of holiness/consecration and the cultic staff, Levites and/or priests. Therefore, only those instances which are clearly related to priests and/or

---

proach them via a discourse analytical concept. During their literary history, the biblical texts belonged to discourses about the national and religious identity of ancient Israel. Changes in the identity emerged together with – and have been enforced by – changes in the texts" (Raik Heckl, "The Composition of Ezra-Nehemiah as a Testimony for the Competition between the Temples in Jerusalem and on Mt. Gerizim in the Early Years of the Seleucid Rule over Judah," in *The Bible, Qumran, and the Samaritans*, ed. Magnar Kartveit and Gary N. Knoppers (Berlin: De Gruyter, 2018), 116.

9. Jonker, "Holiness and the Levites."

10. קרש appears in Ezra-Nehemiah: As verb (6 in total) – Ezra 3:5; Neh 3:1 (twice); 12:47 (twice); and 13:22; As noun (13 in total) – Ezra 2:63∥Neh 7:65 (twice in each); Ezra 8:28 (twice); 9:2, 8; Neh 9:14; 10:32, 34; 11:1, 18.

11. טהר appears in Ezra-Nehemiah: As verb (6 in total) – Ezra 6:20; Neh 12:30 (twice); 13:9, 22, 30; As noun (1 in total) – Neh 12:45; As adjective (1 in total) – Ezra 6:20.

12. בדל appears in Ezra-Nehemiah: As verb (9 in total) – Ezra 6:21; 8:24; 9:1; 10:8, 11, 16; Neh 9:2; 10:29; 13:3. It does not occur as noun or adjective in Ezra-Nehemiah.

13. גאל II appears in Ezra-Nehemiah: As verb (3 in total) – Ezra 2:62 ∥ Neh 7:64 and Neh 13:29. It does not occur as noun or adjective in Ezra-Nehemiah.

14. Hannah K. Harrington, "Holiness and Purity in Ezra-Nehemiah," in *Unity and Disunity in Ezra-Nehemiah: Redaction, Rhetoric, and Reader*, ed. Mark J. Boda and Paul L. Redditt, Hebrew Bible Monographs 17 (Sheffield: Phoenix Press, 2008), 98–116. Additional to the terms discussed here, she also investigates טמא and מעל. See § 3.2 where I will bring more precision in our use of these terms.

Levites, are included in the investigation.[15] The discussion below follows the synchronic, tripartite division in the book – the diachronic aspect will get attention in §3.

2.1 THE TEMPLE-BUILDING ACCOUNT (EZRA 1–6)

There is only one verse in Ezra 1–6 where "language of purity" is used in conjunction with priests and Levites.[16] The term טהר occurs three times in connection with priests and Levites in Ezra-Nehemiah, but here only in Ezra 6:20. In this verse (where it is used twice), it is indicated that both the priests and the Levites consecrated themselves. The context in Ezra 6 is the celebration of the Passover. Very interestingly, it is emphasized here that the priests and Levites consecrated themselves כאחד ("as one"), and that כלם ("all of them") were consecrated. The impression is thereby created that not only did both groups cleanse themselves for the celebration of the Passover (equality of groups), but they also did so in unison (unity of groups). Ezra 6 reminds very strongly of the Passover celebrations under Hezekiah and Josiah, as described in 2 Chronicles 30 and 35 where the Levites also participated in the slaughtering of the offerings after they had consecrated themselves.[17]

---

15. Priests and Levites feature in the following texts: Ezra 1:5; 2:36–63; 3:8–12; 6:16–22; 7:1–5, 7, 11; 8:15–36; 9:1; 10:18; Neh 3:1; 7:39–65; 8:7, 11, 13; 10:1; 12:13. Raik Heckl points out that the Levites occur at very specific junctures in the text: "Besonders thematisiert werden die Leviten in folgenden Zusammenhängen: 1. beim Tempelbau (Esr 3,8–10), 2. bei der Tempeleinweihung und dem anschließenden Passa (Esr 3,16–18.19 f.), 3. bei Esras Rückkehr (Esr 8), 4. bei der Verlesung der Tora und ihrer Vermittlung (Neh 8), 5. bei der Einweihung der Mauer Neh 12,27 ff., und 6. beider Regelung der Anteile der Leviten in Neh 13,10 ff." (*Neuanfang und Kontinuität in Jerusalem: Studien zu den hermeneutischen Strategien im Esra-Nehemia-Buch*, FAT 104 [Tübingen: Mohr Siebeck, 2016], 50). In our discussion, however, those instances where "language of purity" does not occur in relation to the Levites and/or the priesthood, or where the mentioned cultic personnel occur in texts without any reference to "language of purity", are not included in our survey.

16. The genealogy of Ezra 2 will be discussed under the Nehemiah Memoir where the same genealogy also occurs. The diachronic argument for this decision will be explained there.

17. See also the contribution of Esias E. Meyer in this volume. Meyer discusses the language of purity in Chronicles. The verb טהר occurs seven times in Chronicles (2 Chr 29:15, 16, 18; 30:18; 34:3, 5, 8 – all in the Hezekiah and Josiah narratives.) With reference to "holiness", I have hypothesized that those narratives in Chronicles form the climax of the development of the Levite profile in that book. See Louis C. Jonker, "Numbers and Chronicles: False Friends or Close Relatives?" *HeBAI* 8/2 (2019): 332–77; Louis C. Jonker, "Chronicles and Judges: Any Relationship?" in *Jeremia, Deuteronomismus und Priesterschrift. Beiträge zur Literatur- und Theologiegeschichte des Alten Testaments. Festschrift für Hermann-Josef Stipp zum 65. Geburtstag*, ed. Andreas Michel and Nicole K. Rüttgers, ATSAT 105 (St. Ottilien: EOS Verlag, 2019), 179–200; Jonker, "Holiness and the Levites"; Jonker, "Melting Pots

2.2 THE EZRA MATERIAL (EZRA 7–10, NEH 8)

In Ezra 8:24 Ezra indicates (in first person speech) that he has "set apart" (בדל) twelve of the leading priests to guard the offerings for the house of God until they arrive in Jerusalem. Ezra calls these leading priests (שרי הכהנים), together with the temple vessels, "holy" (קדש) in verse 28. This clearly reflects a tradition that considers holiness as a quality that applies to the cultic environment and objects, including the priests officiating in it. However, in verses 29–30 it emerges that the Levites are also counted in – together with the priests – to transport the offerings safely to Jerusalem. Per implication, holiness therefore also applies to the Levites, and not only to the cultic objects and the priests.

As the only occurrence in the Hebrew Bible, the collocation זרע הקדש in Ezra 9:2 has drawn much attention in scholarship.[18] The people of Israel, together with the priests and the Levites (9:1) are accused of not having separated themselves (לא בדל) from the peoples of the lands (מעמי הארצות), and thereby have caused the mixing of the "holy seed", which was considered to be "faithlessness" (מעל).[19] This accusation stands in the direct speech of an official who came to communicate the matter to Ezra. It is noteworthy that the accusation is made about the people of Israel, the priests, and the Levites in equal measure. Although the strong idea of separation from the peoples of the lands is characteristic of priestly ideology, the inclusion of all people of Israel and the Levites in the list of accused, also betrays something of the

---

and Rejoinders?"

18. For some recent studies on this expression, see Willa M. Johnson, *The Holy Seed Has Been Defiled: The Interethnic Marriage Dilemma in Ezra 9–10* (Sheffield: Sheffield Phoenix Press, 2011); Katherine E. Southwood, "The Holy Seed: The Significance of Endogamous Boundaries and Their Transgression in Ezra 9–10," in *Judah and the Judeans in the Achaemenid Period. Negotiating Identity in an International Context*, ed. Oded Lipschits, Gary N. Knoppers, and Manfred Oeming (Winona Lake: Eisenbrauns, 2011), 189–224; Ehud Ben Zvi, "Re-Negotiating a Putative Utopia and the Stories of the Rejection of Foreign Wives in Ezra-Nehemiah," in *Worlds That Could Not Be: Utopia in Chronicles, Ezra and Nehemiah*, ed. Frauke Uhlenbruch and Steven J. Schweitzer (London: Bloomsbury Publishing, 2016), 105–28; Ntozakhe S. Cezula, "The Concept of 'the Holy Seed' as a Coping Strategy in Ezra-Nehemiah and Its Implications for South Africa," *Acta Theologica* 38/1 (2018): 15–36; Pieter M. Venter, "The Dissolving of Marriages in Ezra 9–10 and Nehemiah 13 Revisited," *HTS* 74/4 (2018): 1–13.

19. Olyan remarks: "Lev 18:24–30 and 20:24, 26 were certainly influential on the circles responsible for the Ezra memoir, for their rhetoric of defiling alien abominations and separation from other peoples is reflected directly in Ezra 9:1, 11, 14" ("Purity Ideology in Ezra-Nehemiah as a Tool to Reconstitute the Community," *JSJ* 35/1 [2004]: 7 Fn. 18.). See also Hannah K. Harrington, "The Use of Leviticus in Ezra-Nehemiah," *JHS* 13 (2013): 6–9, https://journals.library.ualberta.ca/jhs/ index.php/ jhs/article/view/20647.

democratized understanding of holines in the Holiness legislation.[20]

The verb בדל is used again in Ezra 10:16, in relation to the priest Ezra. Within the context of the handling of the matter of mixed marriages, it is indicated that Ezra the Priest separated men who were heads of fathers' houses to hear the cases of those who were accused of marrying foreign wives. Although this is not strictly a cultic usage of the term בדל here, it is closely related to Ezra 9:1–2 where the people of Israel, together with the priests and the Levites, were accused of not having separated themselves (לא בדל) from the peoples of the land, and that consequentially, they have mixed the holy seed (זרע הקדש). Ezra, being portrayed as "the Priest" (הכהן) here in 10:16, is the one composing the legal institutions from heads of the fathers' houses to mitigate the situation.[21]

2.3 THE NEHEMIAH MEMOIR (NEH 1–7; 9–13)

The term גאל II "defile"[22] (probably a late form of געל)[23] occurs in connection with the priests in the parallel accounts in Ezra 2:62 and Nehemiah 7:64.[24] It is indicated that some returnees (specified in this case

---

20. For further references on this understanding of the Holiness legislation, see Esias E. Meyer, "From Cult to Community: The Two Halves of Leviticus," *Verbum et Ecclesia* 34/2 (2013): 1–7.

21. The final text of Ezra-Nehemiah indicates an interesting shift in the portrayal of Ezra. Sometimes, like here in Ezra 10, he is prominently portrayed as "Ezra the Priest," while in other cases, for example in the role he plays in Neh 8, he rather features as the scribe teaching the people, which is a function more associated with the Levites. Pakkala (*Ezra the Scribe*) has seen that as one of the features that point towards the redactional history of the book. See also Reinhard G. Kratz, "Ezra – Priest and Scribe," in *Scribes, Sages, and Seers: The Sage in the Eastern Mediterranean World*, ed. Leo G. Perdue (Göttingen: Vandenhoeck & Ruprecht, 2008), 163–88; Willi, *Esra*; Laird, *Negotiating Power in Ezra-Nehemiah*, 289–94.

22. Harrington describes the term as follows: "… a strong term for defilement with the sense of nausea and loathing (e. g. Lev. 26.11, 43)" ("Holiness and Purity in Ezra-Nehemiah," 107).

23. Williamson, *Ezra, Nehemiah*, 27.

24. The repatriation list in Ezra 2 which is repeated in Nehemiah 7, is a diachronic enigma in biblical scholarship. Some, like Williamson, see the Nehemiah 7 version as the primary one, with the implication that Ezra 2 borrowed from the version in Nehemiah 7 (which in itself was composed of earlier lists). Blenkinsopp, however, is not at all convinced by the arguments that underlie such a position. He therefore sees the Ezra 2 version as primary, and indicates how Nehemiah 7 re-used the earlier list, and how further revisions were made there. By placing the discussion on these texts under the Nehemiah Memoir, I indicate that I find Williamson's arguments more convincing in this matter. While Ezra 1–6 is generally accepted as the latest part of the composition of Ezra-Nehemiah which tried to connect the work to Chronicles (see diachronic discussion in §3 below), it is more likely that the Ezra 2 account was taken over from the earlier account in Nehemiah 7. See Hugh G. M. Williamson, "The Composition of Ezra i–vi," *JTS* 34 (1983): 1–30; Hugh G.M. Williamson, *Ezra, Nehemiah, Word Biblical Commentary, Vol. 16* (Dallas: Word Books, 1985), 28–32. See also William-

as descendants of priests – cf. Ezra 2:61//Neh 7:63) could not find their names in the geneaologies of the priests, and that they were therefore excluded from the priesthood because of their defilement. The governor indicated that they could therefore not partake in the holy food מקדש הקדשים before a priest had consulted the Urim and Tummim (Ezra 2:63//Neh 7:65).²⁵ The reference to קדש does, however, not apply to the priest here, but rather to the holy food that was supposed to be eaten by the temple servants (from Ezra 2:58//Neh 7:60). Although it signifies that the priest is instrumental in giving access for the people to the most holy food, it does not qualify the priest as such.²⁶

The text in Nehemiah 10:29, where the term בדל occurs again, indicates an opposite position from the previous occurrence in Ezra 9:1–2. Here in Nehemiah 10, some have indeed separated themselves (with בדל) from "the peoples of the lands" (מעמי האדצות). This anonymous group is mentioned alongside inter alia the priests and Levites as those parties who have entered into a curse and an oath to walk in the Torah of God (v. 30). It thus seems that the priests and Levites are not necessarily singled out as those who have separated themselves from the peoples of the lands, but that they are rather included in a bigger collective.

Two further instances of the root קדש occur in Nehemiah 11:1, 18. The pericope in verses 1–24 provides a list of all the inhabitants of the "holy city" Jerusalem. The ruling is made (by the casting of lots) that 10 % of the people would live in Jerusalem, while the other 90 % would have their residences in outlying towns. It seems from this

---

son's discussion in his review of Pakkala's book: Hugh G. M. Williamson, "Review of *Ezra the Scribe*: *The Development of Ezra 7–10 and Nehemia 8* (BZAW 347) by Juha Pakkala," JTS 58/2 (2007): 587–88; Blenkinsopp, *Ezra-Nehemiah*, 43–44. Blenkinsopp's position is also supported by Pakkala, *Ezra the Scribe*, 137–40. For further discussions on the repetition of the geneology, see Fensham, *The Books of Ezra and Nehemiah*, 47–49; Williamson, *Ezra, Nehemiah*, 24; Blenkinsopp, *Ezra-Nehemiah*, 83; Gordon F. Davies, *Ezra and Nehemiah*, Berit Olam (Gordonville: Liturgical Press, 1999), 103.

25. It is significant that the expression קדש הקדשים also occurs frequently in the Priestly and the Holiness traditions, as well as in the Deuteronomistic history. The genealogies in Neh 7 and Ezra 2 create the impression that the writer(s)/compiler(s) were probably showing allegiance with the Priestly tradition, but simultaneously opened the way towards a wider understanding of who could be involved in the temple-building – a view that reminds of the Holiness tradition's "democratizing" tendency that reflects both priestly and Deuteronomic influence.

26. Interestingly, it is the התרשתא "governor" who orders the temple servants (הנתנים) to refrain from eating the holy food until a priest has consulted the Urim and Tummim. For discussions on the "governor" and "temple servants" mentioned here, see Williamson, *Ezra, Nehemiah*, 27; Blenkinsopp, *Ezra-Nehemiah*, 92; Fensham, *The Books of Ezra and Nehemiah*, 56. See also Baruch A. Levine, "The Netînîm," *JBL* 82 (1963): 207–12, which remains a standard reference on הנתנים.

text (v. 3) that those "heads of the province" were from Judah and Benjamin, and consisted of groups of priests and Levites. Even gatekeepers were allowed to live in Jerusalem, the "holy city" (as indicated in v. 19). It also emerges that some priests and Levites, together with many of the other people, remained living in the towns of their inheritance. Although the "holy city" is thus associated with the Levites and priests, this seems to be a functional arrangement, and not so much on account of cultic status. The fact that Levites and priests also remained living in outlying towns confirms this observation.

We have seen above that the term טהר occurs three times in connection with priests and Levites in Ezra-Nehemiah, in Ezra 6:20 (twice) and Nehemiah 12:30. Whereas the context in Ezra 6 was the Passover celebrations, in Nehemiah 12 it is the dedication of the wall. According to Nehemiah 12:30 both the priests and Levites took part in this occasion, after having consecrated themselves. In addition, it is explicated that they not only have consecrated the people, but also the wall and the gates. Eskenazi has indicated that this information "demonstrates that they (the laity) are brought into the same ritual status as priests and Levites. They become holy people. This amplifies the point made by the Israelite pedigrees: the sanctity of the people, not merely of clergy, matters."[27] Although the consecration of the wall and gates sounds more like a priestly understanding of a holy sphere,[28] the consecration of Levites and the people, together with the priests, rather reflects the theology of the Holiness legislation.

קדש also occurs twice in connection with Levites and priests in Nehemiah 12:47. The pericope in verses 44–47 deals with the portions that were required for the priests and Levites in Jerusalem. These were provided from the rural lands, because "Judah rejoiced over the priests and Levites who ministered" (v. 44). Verse 47 constructs an interesting hierarchy in the provision of the portions: "All-Israel" (and no longer Judah alone) provided the daily portions to the singers and gatekeepers, and they (presumably still All-Israel, on account of the next participle active) declared the daily portions holy to the Levites, who in turn declared holy the portions to the sons of Aaron (the priests). Due to the repetition of "Levites" in the phrase, it is clear that the actors were the Levites in the last instance. All this happened "in the days of Zerubbabel and in the days of Nehemiah", with no indication of "the days of Ezra."

Nehemiah 13 reports Nehemiah's further reform measures. In verse 22 it is mentioned that he called upon the Levites (without

---

27. Eskenazi, *In an Age of Prose*, 117.
28. For a discussion of this aspect, see Williamson, *Ezra, Nehemiah*, 373; Blenkinsopp, *Ezra-Nehemiah*, 344.

mentioning of the priests) to consecrate themselves (with טהר) in order to guard at the gates to keep the Sabbath day holy (with קדשׁ). This command stands in the context of Nehemiah prohibiting merchants and sellers to stay overnight outside the gates on the Sabbath when the gates were closed. Thus, holiness is associated here with the Sabbath, and the Levites' consecration was necessary to perform their service in order to keep the Sabbath holy. The focus is thus specifically on the Levites in this section. It is also quite interesting that Nehemiah, a layman-governor, is the one calling upon the Levites to consecrate themselves. This tendency could clearly be associated with the theology of the Holiness legislation.

In Nehemiah 13:29, where the term גאל II is used again, it is made clear that the defilement is related to the fact that a son of Jehoiada, presumably the high priest during Nehemiah's tenure, married a daughter of Sanballat the Horonite (v. 28). This was in contravention of the law from the Holiness legislation (Lev 21:13–15) which prohibited the marriage of a priest with a woman of foreign descent. Nehemiah 13:29 indicates that this deed has defiled the priesthood, as well as the covenant of the priesthood and the Levites.[29] This indication is therefore an indirect blemish on the priesthood, and the authority relied upon is clearly the Holiness legislation.

At this point, however, we should call attention to the fact that there are scholars who explicitly point out that all "language of purity" terminology in Ezra-Nehemiah cannot be treated on the same level. Jonathan Klawans (supported by Christine Hayes) has made the distinction between "ritual" and "moral" impurity.[30] In their analyses of Ezra-Nehemiah, Klawans and Hayes come to similar conclusions that it is only "moral" impurity that plays a role in this book's alien polemics, and that "ritual" impurity is not at stake here. Saul Olyan,[31] in response

---

29. There is an interesting link in this verse with Mal 2:4–8 where a covenant with Levitical priests is also mentioned (in line with Deut 33:9). This remains a task for another day, but the connection between Ezra-Nehemiah and Malachi, as part of the discourse on Leviticism in the late Achaemenid and/or early Hellenistic periods, could provide an even wider understanding of the issue being investigated in this essay. Some scholars think, however, that the mentioning of the Levites is an addition in Neh 13:29. See e. g. Blenkinsopp, *Ezra-Nehemiah*, 362.

30. Christine Elizabeth Hayes, *Gentile Impurities and Jewish Identities: Intermarriage and Conversion from the Bible to the Talmud* (Oxford: Oxford University Press, 2002); Jonathan Klawans, *Impurity and Sin in Ancient Judaism* (Oxford: Oxford University Press, 2004); Jonathan Klawans, *Purity, Sacrifice, and the Temple: Symbolism and Supersessionism in the Study of Ancient Judaism* (Oxford: Oxford University Press, 2006).

31. Although Saul Olyan also indicates that purity terminology in Ezra-Nehemiah should be correlated to the diachronic development of the book – and should therefore not merely be studied on a synchronic level – he still departs from the tradi-

to the above views, indicate that "[t]hough Klawans and Hayes are correct to suggest an important role for the 'moral' impurity tradition in the shaping of Ezra-Nehemiah's purity ideology, they nonetheless overstate their respective cases."[32] Olyan therefore concludes that "the circles responsible for Ezra-Nehemiah drew upon, combined, and transformed notions from *both* purity traditions in order to shape their novel polemic against aliens and intermarriage."[33]

Hannah Harrington, in her investigation of the relationship between Leviticus and Ezra-Nehemiah (in its final form), not only confirms the priority of Leviticus, but also concludes that "the cultic traditions discussed above derive from both the 'P' and 'H' sections of Leviticus and they are not de novo regulations in Ezra-Nehemiah…"[34]

Benedikt Rausche also engages in this discussion when he indicates that – although cultic vocabulary is at first glance not so prevalent in Ezra-Nehemiah – "a closer look shows that this language is of structural importance for the narrative."[35] After his investigation of the book, in particular the purity language in relation to the temple-building narrative, he comes to the following conclusion:

> Ezra-Nehemiah does not represent a totally unified system of purity. But the idea of an expansion of holiness beyond the sanctuary, to the people as well as to the city of Jerusalem in general, is the base upon which different notions of purity depend. … The question of purity and impurity, exclusion and inclusion, is always related to the holiness of the temple. Purity ideologies remain crucial for the definition of postexilic community according to Ezra-Nehemiah, in so far as they regulate legitimate access to the center of identity.[36]

Particularly Rausche's perspective is valuable for our endeavour,

---

tional position of dating the book according to the tenures of Nehemiah and Ezra. He sees the "Nehemiah Memoir" as the oldest part of the book since Nehemiah preceded Ezra in tenure. Although Olyan's inclination to combine synchronic and diachronic perspectives should be appreciated, his portrayal of the redactional history is no longer the accepted position in light of newer scholarship. See Olyan, "Purity Ideology in Ezra-Nehemiah," 12–16.

32. Olyan, "Purity Ideology in Ezra-Nehemiah," 15.
33. Olyan, "Purity Ideology in Ezra-Nehemiah," 16 (his emphasis).
34. Harrington, "The Use of Leviticus in Ezra-Nehemiah," 19. This shows some development in Harrington's argument. In her earlier publication she did mention that holiness is extended in Ezra and Nehemiah to the profane sphere, but stood more on the side of those seeing a coherent use of "language of purity" in Ezra-Nehemiah. See Harrington, "Holiness and Purity in Ezra-Nehemiah."
35. Benedikt Rausche, "The Relevance of Purity in Second Temple Judaism According to Ezra-Nehemiah," in *Purity and the Forming of Religious Traditions in the Ancient Mediterranean World and Ancient Judaism*, ed. Christian Frevel and Christophe Nihan (Leiden: Brill, 2013), 458.
36. Rausche, "The Relevance of Purity," 472–74.

namely to see whether we can detect influence from the Holiness tradition in Ezra-Nehemiah as well – a tradition which we have argued earlier[37] had played a significant role in the very positive portrayal of the Levites towards the end of the book of Chronicles. Although Chronicles also shows strong influence from the Priestly tradition that worked with a stricter understanding of purity and the role (and priority) of the (Zadokite) priesthood – particularly in the earlier parts of the book – there are clear signs that the Chronicler took his cue from the Holiness tradition to merge the Deuteronomic and Priestly traditions, and to redefine the role of the Levites within a broader understanding of holiness.

The challenge is now to correlate the terminological distribution in Ezra-Nehemiah (synchronic aspect – discussed above) to the processes of growth (diachronic aspect – discussed in the next section) that brought about the unified book Ezra-Nehemiah.

3. DIACHRONIC ORDERING OF TEXTUAL MATERIAL

3.1 THE FORMATION OF EZRA-NEHEMIAH

We have seen in earlier studies (briefly mentioned in the Introduction above) that there is a broad consensus that Ezra-Nehemiah grew over a period of time into its final form, most probably from sometime in the fifth century to the end of the fourth, or even the middle of the third century BCE. Some more extreme positions, such as those of Raik Heckl[38] and Israel Finkelstein[39] who extend the process of growth into the Hasmonean era, have not gained support in Ezra-Nehemiah scholarship yet. It therefore seems that, at this stage of our scholarship, it is more plausible to rather go along with those proposals that see the finalization of the process of growth of this book by the end of the fourth century BCE (Williamson) or middle of the third century BCE (Pakkala). For the purpose of this contribution, the date of finalization is not so important, but rather the position represented in the majority view that the book grew over a period of time that stretched from the middle of the Achaemenid period into the Hellenistic phase. This means that the book's period of growth in its early stages precedes Chronicles, in some part overlaps with the period of origin of Chron-

---

37. Jonker, "Melting Pots and Rejoinders?"
38. Heckl, *Neuanfang und Kontinuität in Jerusalem*.
39. Israel Finkelstein, *Hasmonean Realities behind Ezra, Nehemiah, and Chronicles: Archaeological and Historical Perspectives*, Ancient Israel and Its Literature (Atlanta: SBL Press, 2018).

icles, and in most part postcedes Chronicles. This is in line with Williamson's view who sees Chronicles as a product of more or less the same time period. Pakkala, however, relies for the date of Chronicles on the construction of Steins who places Chronicles much later in history.[40]

This latter position has not been accepted in Chronicles scholarship, though. By accepting some aspects of Pakkala's redactional model of Ezra-Nehemiah in this contribution, I do not concur with his view on the date of Chronicles, however.

Although Hugh G. M. Williamson and Juha Pakkala broadly agree on the period of growth of Ezra-Nehemiah, they do, however, differ about which parts are the earliest, and how this process of growth took place. According to Williamson, three phases can be identified, namely "(1) the writing of the various primary sources, all more or less contemporary with the events they relate;[41] (2) the combination of the EM, NM, and other sources to form Ezra 7:1–Neh 11:20; 12:27–13:31 (11:21–12:26 were added separately);[42] (3) the later addition of the introduction in Ezra 1–6."[43] Apart from the first phase of primary

---

40. Georg Steins, *Die Chronik als Kanonisches Abschlußphänomen: Studien zur Entstehung und Theologie von 1/2 Chronik*, BBB 93 (Weinheim: Beltz, Athenäum, 1995).

41. For Williamson's identification of the sources used in Ezra 1–6, see *Ezra, Nehemiah*, xxiv. This is strictly spoken still not part of the book's development, since these sources developed independently.

42. Pertaining to stage 2, Williamson provides the following detail: "A history of composition must, therefore, start with the combination of the Ezra and Nehemiah memoirs. The same process demands, however, the inclusion of most of the rest of the material in Neh 9–12: chaps. 8–10 are a carefully constructed compilation around the theme of covenant renewal; 11:1–2 and its dependent list are clearly intended as a narrative continuation of 7:4–5; the splicing of other material into Nehemiah's account of the dedication of the wall (12:27–43) is most reasonably to be taken as part of this same editorial activity, and 12:44–13:3 is consciously placed to introduce the remainder of the NM. In fact, only 11:21–12:26 cannot be regarded as part of this major phase in the book's composition" (*Ezra, Nehemiah*, xxxiv.)

43. Williamson, *Ezra, Nehemiah*, xxxv. Stage 3 thus consisted of the bringing of certain primary source texts into a coherent narrative, a construction that departs from the assumption that the repatriation list of Ezra 2 was taken over from Nehemiah 7. Williamson's detailed arguments focusing on the composition of Ezra 1–6 shows that the author of these chapters: "... had at his disposal a number of primary sources of such a nature as could well have been preserved in an official archive, and he also knew several other relevant works which are now found in the Old Testament. There is nothing in Ezra i–vi which cannot be explained on this minimal assumption. Indeed, the consistent editorial handling of primary sources throughout these chapters precludes any intermediate stage in the composition. The author cannot be identified with the Chronicler. Rather, he may be a member of the circle which had earlier sujected the Books of Chronicles to pro-priestly redaction. If so, he probably worked within a few decades of the introduction of Hellenistic rule into Palestine with the purpose of justifying the legitimacy of the Jerusalem temple and its cult after a possible split in its

documents from the sixth and early fifth centuries BCE, the other two phases are dated by Williamson approximately in 400 BCE and 300 BCE.[44] Williamson's dating therefore spans the transition from the late Persian to the early Hellenistic phases, and also of the presumed time of origin of Chronicles.

Pakkala sees the Ezra Material (Ezra 7–10 and Neh 8) as the oldest part of the book, with the temple-building account (Ezra 1–6) and Nehemiah Memoir (Neh 1–7; 9–13) that were added in further stages.[45] Each one of these bigger textual units also went through processes of editing and accumulation (like a "snowball", to use Pakkala's term, or, because of *Fortschreibung* as some German-speaking scholars would call it). According to Pakkala, the earliest literary activities can be dated towards the end of the fifth century BCE, while the final editing was completed in about the middle of the third century BCE.

The main difference between Williamson and Pakkala in terms of the broad description of Ezra-Nehemiah's formation is therefore where the Nehemiah Memoir should be positioned. Williamson sees a merging of the Ezra materials and the Nehemiah Memoir at the start of the process, with the inclusion of Ezra 1–6 at a later stage, towards the end of the the fourth century BCE. Pakkala gives a primary position to the Ezra materials, with a later merging of Ezra 1–6 to form the book Ezra. Only thereafter, the Nehemiah Memoir and the book Ezra was merged by Levitical editors into a proto-form of the book, also towards the end of the fourth century BCE.

How the detail of these processes played out in these centuries, remains unclear, however. Since many different views are represented in scholarship,[46] it is almost impossible to come to final conclusions about these issues at this stage. Pakkala himself admits towards the end of his study that "many uncertainties necessarily have remained, because the preserved text does not allow a precise understanding

---

priesthood, the establishment of the Samaritan community and the first moves to build a temple on Mount Gerizim" ("The Composition of Ezra i–vi," 29–30.).

44. Williamson, *Ezra, Nehemiah*, xxxvi.

45. Pakkala, *Ezra the Scribe*; Juha Pakkala, "The Original Indipendence (sic) of the Ezra Story in Ezra 7–10 and Neh 8," *BN* 129 (2006): 17–24.

46. See e. g. Blenkinsopp, *Ezra-Nehemiah*; Jacob L. Wright, *Rebuilding Identity: The Nehemiah-Memoir and Its Earliest Readers*, BZAW 348 (Berlin: Walter de Gruyter, 2004); Heckl, *Neuanfang und Kontinuität in Jerusalem*; Heckl, "The Composition of Ezra-Nehemiah"; Finkelstein, *Hasmonean Realities*; Benedikt Hensel, "Ethnic Fiction and Identity-Formation: A New Explanation for the Background of the Question of Intermarriage in Ezra-Nehemiah," in *The Bible, Qumran, and the Samaritans*, ed. Magnar Kartveit and Gary N. Knoppers (Berlin: De Gruyter, 2018), 133–48; Benedikt Hensel, "On the Relationship of Judah and Samaria in Post-Exilic Times: A Farewell to the Conflict Paradigm," *JSOT* 44 (2019): 19–42.

of its editorial history."⁴⁷ However, that does not mean that theories cannot be formulated and tested in interaction with other theories. While Williamson's and Pakkala's redactional theories show some convergence, the broad processes sketched above will form the basis of the diachronic view that will be taken as basis in our further investigations below.⁴⁸

---

47. Pakkala, *Ezra the Scribe*, 292.

48. The views of Blenkinsopp and Wright are not considered here as basis for our diachronic understanding. The main difference between Williamson's and Blenkinsopp's views is that the latter sees Ezra 1–6 as the earliest part of Ezra-Nehemiah, which stands in close structural unity with the ending of Chronicles. Blenkinsopp argues against Williamson and Japhet who paved the way in scholarship for seeing Chronicles and Ezra-Nehemiah as separate works by separate authors (as discussed above). Blenkinsopp offers some rejoinders to their arguments in order to see Ezra 1–6 as continuation of Chronicles, at least in terms of the narrative framework. One of the clearest indications, according to Blenkinsopp is the structural repetition that he sees in terms of reformation and infedility, ending in Passover celebration, in the latter part of Chronicles and in Ezra 1–6: "The last part of Chronicles is ordered according to movements of renewal and reform following on periods of religious infidelity: Hezekiah after Ahaz, Josiah after Manasseh, both followed by celebration of Passover (2 Chron. 30; 35:1–19). This pattern continues into Ezra 1–6, where the renewal of the cult concludes with the celebration of the same festival (6:19–22). ... At the celebration of Hezekiah's Passover we are told that 'since the time of Solomon son of David king of Israel there had been nothing like this in Jerusalem' (2 Chron. 30:26). Of Josiah's celebration we hear that 'no Passover like it had been kept in Israel since the days of Samuel the prophet' (2 Chron. 35:18), while the author says of the feast of Tabernacles celebrated at the time of Ezra that 'from the days of Joshua son of Nun to that day the people of Israel had not done so' (Neh. 8:17). There is a progression here which is hardly accidental: the later the point in time, the further back the retrospective allusion goes. It would be difficult to find a clearer indication of unity of conception which binds together the two works into one history with its own distinctive point of view and purpose" (Blenkinsopp, *Ezra-Nehemiah*, 54). Blenkinsopp's views make sense from a narrative perspective, or even canonical (as he indicates in his introduction to the book), but this structure does not exclude that later writers could shape their narrative in such a format that it would link up with an earlier narrative. Furthermore, the textual evidence of 1 Esdras does also not point to the kind of unity that Blenkinsopp suggests. His arguments therefore do not convince in terms of diachrony.

With regards to Jacob Wright's views on the diachrony of Ezra-Nehemiah, his diachronic reconstruction of Ezra-Nehemiah is problematic as well. He relies heavily on his *Doktorvater*, Reinhard Kratz, for the *Literarkritik* and redaction-critical methodology that he is using, and identifies six layers in Nehemiah. His study focuses on the diachrony of the Nehemiah Memoir, but indicates that Ezra was a later attempt to write the history contained in the Nehemiah Memoir in a backward direction. His aim in his study was to let the Nehemiah Memoir speak for itself, before pointing out how this Memoir was re-read in the further development of Ezra-Nehemiah as a whole. His redaction-critical construction, as well as his indications of the relationship to Ezra, are not generally accepted in biblical scholarship (see e. g. the reviews by Fulton, Carr and Klein in Gary N. Knoppers (ed.) *The Journal of Hebrew Scriptures* Vol. 7 Art. 12 (2007), https://journals.library.ualberta.ca/jhs/index.php/jhs/article/view/5646, although the exegetical insights on many of the individual texts are

3.2 THE ORDERING OF THE TEXTS OF EZRA-NEHEMIAH

According to Williamson's broad three-phased development model, the texts discussed in section 2 above can be ordered diachronically in the following way: (i) None of these texts in Ezra-Nehemiah comes from the first stage of primary sources; (ii) All references identified in our study, with the exception of one or two, should be placed in the second phase which could be dated approximately in the period 400–300 BCE; (iii) Only one text possibly belongs in the final phase around 300 BCE, namely Ezra 6:20, while the repatriation list in Ezra 2 was copied from Nehemiah 7 into this late stage of text formation (and thus also belongs to the previous stage).

If Pakkala's theory would be used, it would boil down to more or less the same picture, with some exceptions in the Nehemiah materials. Although Pakkala does not reflect on the formation of the Nehemiah Memoir in detail,[49] it becomes clear from his discussion that the basic form of this Memoir started developing in the second half of the fifth century BCE, and that it must have consisted basically of Nehemiah 2–4, perhaps 5, 6, 11–12. According to this view, the texts we have identified in Nehemiah 11 and 12 would belong to the earliest phase of development, sometime towards the end of the fifth century BCE. Furthermore, Pakkala postulates that the Levitical circles who were responsible for the combination of the book Ezra and the Nehemiah Memoir also edited more materials into the Nehemiah Memoir. This phase, which lasted for quite a long period, probably towards the end of the fourth century BCE (and thus coincided with the time period in which Chronicles was written) probably saw at least three Levitical editors reworking the materials.[50] These editors were not only responsible for duplicating the list of returnees in Ezra 2 and Nehemiah 7,[51] as well as for the relocation of the material that originally stood between Ezra 8 and 9, to become the new Nehemiah 8. Also, Nehemiah 9–10 (including one of our identified texts, namely 10:29) were added in this phase as a reinterpretation of the divine will as articulated in the Pentateuch. It shows that the Pentateuch had been closed by this time for expansions, and that reinterpretation therefore continued outside the Pentateuch. The addition of Nehemiah 1, perhaps considered valuable.

---

[49] Wright, *Rebuilding Identity* discusses that aspect in great detail.

[50] The additions in this Levitical phase identified by Pakkala are: Ezra 6:18; 7:7, 13*, 24; 8:15b–20, 24b, 29*, 30, 33b; Neh 8:7a, 9αa*, 11, 12b, 13; Ezra 10:5, 15b, 18, 20–244; Neh 9–10.

[51] We have pointed out above that Pakkala (together with Blenkinsopp, but contra Williamson who sees it the other way around) holds that the Ezra version is primary. See also Wright's arguments (following Kratz) in favour of Ezra 2's priority (*Rebuilding Identity*, 301–7).

5, and 13 (including Neh 13:22, 29 identified above) also form part of these Levitical editings. These Levitical editors were thus responsible for combining all the material into the book Ezra-Nehemiah.[52] Pakkala remarks that, "[a]s for the political context of the Levitical editors, it is probable that the Israelite society had become more theocratic in comparison with the time of the older editorial phases."[53]

When the above-discussed diachronic theories are taken as point of departure, the following more detailed order can be offered:

---

52. The following information provided by Pakkala is important for our quest: "It is evident that the Levitical circles disfavored Ezra and accordingly tried to diminish his role and importance. This attitude may have been caused by Ezra's prominent role as a Torah scribe, because by the time of the Levitical editors, this sphere had become their responsibility and Ezra was not a Levite. Although the Levitical expansions generally share interest in the activity of Torah scribes with the ES and Ezra's prayer, it is important to distinguish between these two phases. Whereas the authors of the ES and Ezra's prayer should be connected to the (Deutero)nomistic tradition in this respect, the Levitical editors are simultaneously interested in priestly issues. Accordingly, the older editorial stages of the EM witnesses to a scribal tradition that shows no proximity to the temple, whereas the youngest editors may represent a scribal tradition that is close to the temple circles" (*Ezra the Scribe*, 298).

53. Pakkala, *Ezra the Scribe*, 298–99.

Earliest references (from second half of 5*th* century BCE) – pre-Chronistic:

Ch	Context	Terminology	Related to	Comments
Neh 11	List of inhabitants of "holy" city, Jerusalem (1–24)	בעיר הקדש (1, 24)	Priests, Levites, gatekeepers, other people	Reference to holiness as designation of the city, and not explicitly referring to people groups – however, all these groups live in the holy city – "democratized" understanding of holiness
Neh 12	Dedication of wall and gates (27–43)	טהר (30)	Priests, Levites, people, wall, gates purified	Not only priests, but also Levites, people, wall, gates included in purification – "democratized" understanding of purification

Ch	Context	Terminology	Related to	Comments
	Portions required for priests and Levites (44–47)	קדש (47)	Sons of Aaron (priests) and Levites	All-Israel provided portions to singers and gatekeepers, and declared it holy to Levites (as separate category), who in turn declare it holy to the priests – "democratized" understanding of holiness

Later references (during the 4th century BCE) – contemporaneous with Chronicles:[54]

Ch	Context	Terminology	Related to	Comments
Neh 7//Ezra 2	List of returnees (Neh 7:5–73//Ezra 2:1–70)	גאל (Neh 7:64// Ezra 2:62)	Priestly descendants	Priestly descendants were guilty of defilement of the priesthood, and were therefore not found in the family lists

---

54. The texts are listed here in relative chronological order, according to Pakkala's views on the redaction of Ezra-Nehemiah.

Ch	Context	Terminology	Related to	Comments
		מִקְּדֶשׁ הַקֳּדָשִׁים (Neh 7:65// Ezra 2:63)	Holy food distributed through facilitation of priest	Priest associated with holy food, but not qualified as holy himself
Ezra 9	Mixed marriages (9:1–10:44)	לֹא בדל (9:1)	People of Israel, priests, Levites	Levites and people of Israel, alongside the priests, are accused of not separating from foreign women and thereby mixing the holy seed
		זֶרַע הַקֹּדֶשׁ (9:2)		

Ch	Context	Terminology	Related to	Comments
Ezra 8	Guarding the offerings for the temple before arrival in Jerusalem (8:24–36)	בדל (24)	Twelve of leading priests (Levites included according to 29–30)	On account of vv. 29–30 it is clear that Levites were counted among the leading priests who were separated for the task of guarding the holy vessels, and were therefore also considered holy together with the priests – "democratized" understanding of holiness
		קדש (28)	Leading priests and temple vessels (Levites included according to 29–30)	

Ch	Context	Terminology	Related to	Comments
Ezra 10	Ezra the Priest organizes the mitigation of the mixed marriages (10:6–17)	בדל (16)	Ezra the Priest functions as subject, with heads of fathers' houses as object	Associated with accusation in Ezra 9:1–2 – countering of problem caused by Levites, priests and lay people
Ezra 6	Celebration of the Passover (6:19–22)	טהר (20)	Priests and Levites concecrated themselves – "as one" and "all of them"	Equality and unity of priests and Levites emphasized – association of Levites with Passover (like in 2 Chr 30, 35) – "democratized" understanding of holiness

Latest references (from the end of the 4th century to the middle of the 3rd century BCE) – post-Chronistic:

Ch	Context	Terminology	Related to	Comments
Neh 10	Separation from the "peoples of the lands" (10:28–39)	בדל (29)	Laity, Levites and Priests	Not only priests, but also laity and Levites have separated themselves – "democratized" understanding of separation act
Neh 13	Nehemiah's reforms (13:1–22)	טהר (22) קדש (22)	Levites, called by the lay governor, to concecrate themselves to keep the Sabbath holy	Levites portrayed very positively as those who are concecrated to keep the Sabbath holy – "democratized" understanding reflected in action of lay governor

Ch	Context	Terminology	Related to	Comments
Neh 13	Mixed marriages (13:23–31)	גאל (29)	The Priesthood and the Covenant of the Priesthood, and the Levites	Defilement caused by the priest's son marrying a foreign woman which is explicitly prohibited in H (Lev 21:13–15) – priesthood and Levites thereby implicated

With this diachronic ordering of the identified texts in mind, we can now move over to synthesize our results.

3.3 SYNTHESIS

If the hypothesis that was explained in the introduction of this contribution holds truth, and when the diachronic research on Ezra-Nehemiah is considered, there should not be any doubt that the authors and compilers of the Ezra-Nehemiah literature were also exposed to the discourse on the understanding of holiness during the late Persian and early Hellenistic periods. They were exposed to the same literary and ideological milieu of the time, and we may expect some indications in the book that respond to, for example, the status of the priests and Levites in terms of a more limited (that is, cultic and priestly) understanding of holiness, or in terms of a more "democratized" understanding, which redefined the concept of holiness to apply to other priestly factions and officials, and to wider contexts than just the cultic space. The texts we have investigated indeed show engagement with this theme, with the majority reflecting a positive evaluation in terms of consecration and holiness.

The texts in Nehemiah 11 and 12 all reveal a so-called "democratized" understanding of holiness and purification. These are not categories that are restricted to cultic personnel, places, or utensils (like in the priestly understanding), but also include Levites, gatekeepers, lay people, All-Israel, the city wall and gates.

Hannah Harrington remarks that "[w]hile in Ezra and Nehemiah there is a strong boundary between holy Israel and the rest of the world, the level of holiness between priests and laity is less distinct than in the Pentateuch" and "[t]here is an expanded sense of holy space within Ezra-Nehemiah."[55] She furthermore observes that "in both Ezra and Nehemiah Levites gain more prominence than in earlier sources, … The expansion of the holiness of the priest to the laity seems to be a trend in the Second Temple period."[56] On account of these observations, Harrington shows sensitivity for the relationship between Leviticus and Ezra-Nehemiah, as well as for diachronic issues involved when she says: "Taking the position that the tolerant attitude toward the gēr in Leviticus reflects an earlier time of less crisis vis-à-vis foreigners, I beg for reconsideration of the chronology of these traditions. I call attention to elements from Leviticus which are present in Ezra-Nehemiah but are not found elsewhere in the Torah and argue for the chronological priority of these traditions over Ezra-Nehemiah."[57]

We will return to this observation below in the discussion of further texts, but from the texts of this phase, and the observations above, one could agree with Harrington that understandings from Leviticus definitely played a role in the formulation of Nehemiah 11 and 12. The "democratized" understanding referred to in our comments above, but also in Harrington's observations, clearly point towards the Holiness materials (although Harrington does not make that distinction with reference to the book Leviticus). It thus seems that the Holiness legislation must have had an influence in these early discourses of the Nehemiah memoir, even before Chronicles started participating in the discourse.

3.3.1 LATER REFERENCES (DURING THE 4TH CENTURY BCE) – CONTEMPORANEOUS WITH CHRONICLES

In the case of the list of returnees in Nehemiah 7//Ezra 2, various groups are differentiated, inter alia priests (Neh 7:39–42//Ezra 2:36–39), Levites (Neh 7:43–45//Ezra 2:40–42), temple servants (Neh 7:46–56//Ezra 2:43–54), and descendants of Solomon's servants (Neh 7:57–59//Ezra 2:55–57). However, in the section of the name list where the exclusion of some members from the returned community is narrated, a short list of people who came from specific locations (Neh 7:62//Ezra 2:59) are mentioned alongside the priests (Neh 7:63//Ezra 2:61). Levites are not implicated directly in this accusation of defilement, although they are part of the list mentioned earlier.

---

55. Harrington, "Holiness and Purity in Ezra-Nehemiah," 101–2.
56. Harrington, "Holiness and Purity in Ezra-Nehemiah," 101–2.
57. Harrington, "The Use of Leviticus in Ezra-Nehemiah," 5.

Benedikt Rausche, after studying how the term גאל functions in other biblical literature, argues that in Ezra 2:62 "a suitable translation of ויגאלו מן־הכהנה could [...] be 'they were excluded from the priesthood as inadequate'. This does not mean 'inadequate' only in technical terms. ... [T]he text takes a certain polemical tone against the discharged 'wannabe-priests' that goes beyond only technical matters."[58] This observation seems to be in line with Priestly regulations on who may act as priests. This impression is confirmed when one notices that similar terminology (מקדש הקדשים) is used in the next verse and in Numbers 18:9–10 (which I associated with a post-Chronistic theocratic/priestly "push-back" against the Chronicler's very generous treatment of the Levites).[59] Rausche reminds us, however, that the Nehemiah 7//Ezra 2 text does not see this disqualification as something permanent, and it does not apply to all the groups. Thus, what is different here in regards to Chronicles, is that the so-called "wannabe priests" are not associated with the Levites, but with some supposedly priestly descendants. The terminological link with Numbers 18 confirms that this might be part of a priestly "push-back", but the argument is not against Levites overstepping their boundaries.

Ezra 9:1–2, as we have seen above, contains an accusation against "the people of Israel, the priests, and the Levites" that they have not separated (לא בדל) themselves "from the peoples of the lands" (מעמי הארצות), and thereby have contributed to the mixing of the "holy seed" (זרע הקדש). Juha Pakkala sees this text as part of the "prayer" expansion to the older Ezra source, around 400 BCE, in which the author probably appealed to the Torah, Deuteronomy in particular.[60]

Hannah Harrington also weighs in on this section, specifically on the nuances on holiness reflected here. She makes an interesting observation when she indicates that Ezra-Nehemiah's usage of the qualification of holiness is somewhat ambiguous. On the one hand, and particularly through the use of the novel collocation "holy seed" (Ezra 9:2) the book draws a much stricter border between Israel and foreigners than some Pentateuch texts.[61] Harrington indicates in her discussion of the term בדל that "while the concept of separation from non-Israel is a tenet of the Pentateuch and a goal of its ritual purity system, both Ezra and Nehemiah sharpen this distinction and regard

---

58. Rausche, "The Relevance of Purity," 460–61.
59. Jonker, "Melting Pots and Rejoinders?"
60. Pakkala, *Ezra the Scribe*, 296.
61. Harrington, "Holiness and Purity in Ezra-Nehemiah," 100. She also indicates that there are other biblical texts that share Ezra-Nehemiah's rejection of foreigners, such as Ezekiel 44:7–8 that labels foreigners as "uncircumcised in mind and body." Malachi 2:11–15 also falls in this category of texts supporting the position of Ezra-Nehemiah.

people of other races morally and ritually impure in order to reinforce an irrevocable separation between them and holy Israel. This use of separation language 'raises the bar' from earlier texts and is shared by the sources of both books."[62]

As we know from Genesis 1, the term בדל is closely associated with priestly ideology, as also suggested by Harrington above. However, one of the occurrences of this term in priestly material, namely in Numbers 16:21, is quite significant for our purposes. The term is used there in the so-called Korah legend which portrays the Levites as rebellious in terms of their claim towards holiness, to indicate that these rebellious persons had to be separated from Israel. As mentioned above, I have indicated elsewhere that Numbers 16–18 might be a post-chronistic "pushback" against Levitical aspirations as expressed in, for example, Chronicles.[63] Might it be that Ezra 9:1–2 latches onto this same theocratic tendency to "push back" against too liberal understandings of who should be considered to be part of the restoration community?

The texts in Ezra 8 and 10 seem to take part in the same discourse about belonging to the postexilic (cultic) community or not. In Ezra 8:24 and 28, the Levites are clearly in focus, however. They form part of those who are considered holy enough to assist with the guarding of the holy temple vessels. Here, the "democratized" tendency is again visible, where Levites occupy clear priestly functions. Ezra 10:16, on the other hand, indicates that "Ezra the Priest" tried to mitigate the problem of mixed marriages by appointing heads of fathers' houses as judges in these cases. There is no indication of Levites here, except that they were also implicated in Ezra 9:1–2 that they contributed to the mixing of the "holy seed."

Ezra 6 shows very clearly that the Levites are equal to and one with the priests, and that they were also actively involved in the Passover. This is the same "democratized" understanding that is also reflected in texts such as 2 Chronicles 30 and 35 where the Passover celebrations of Hezekiah and Josiah are mentioned, and where the same term (טהר) is also used frequently in connection with the Levites.[64] Ezra 6 surely takes the same position in the discourse on the status of the Levites than those Chronicles texts.

---

62. "Holiness and Purity in Ezra-Nehemiah," 115. See also Harrington, "The Use of Leviticus in Ezra-Nehemiah," 11–12.
63. See particularly Jonker, "Melting Pots and Rejoinders?"
64. See again Meyer's contribution in this volume.

3.3.2 LATEST REFERENCES (FROM THE END OF THE 4TH CENTURY TO THE MIDDLE OF THE 3RD CENTURY BCE) – POST-CHRONISTIC

The texts mentioned above as part of the latest layer of Ezra-Nehemiah are all associated by Pakkala with Levitical editing. In two of these texts, namely Nehemiah 10:29[65] and 13:22, the Levites are portrayed very positively as having separated themselves from the "peoples of the lands" and being consecrated for keeping the Sabbath holy. In the third text, Nehemiah 13:29, the verdict goes against the Levites, however. Although it is the son of a priest who married a foreign woman, the text implicates the priesthood and the Levites for this defilement. Although this is a negative assessment of the situation, the priest and Levites are however obligated in exactly the same way. Ironically, the priesthood and the Levites are on an equal footing, as 'partners in crime.' Olyan observes that – even though this text contains a negative assessment of the Levites, together with the priesthood – the text latches onto understandings coming from the Holiness legislation where the so-called "democratized" tendency is given shape in the earlier literary history of the Persian period.[66]

3.3.3 SUMMARY

To summarize this section: The majority of texts in Ezra-Nehemiah where "language of purity" – particularly understandings of holiness and consecration – is mentioned in connection with Priests and Levites, reveal a "democratized" understanding in line with what we observe in the Holiness legislation. Although it is not crystal clear in all

---

65. Williamson indicates with reference to Neh 10:29: "As seen above, this verse was originally the direct continuation of v 1 and, as such, was a circumstantial clause. While a developed subject would not be impossible in such a construction, it is nevertheless probable that 'the rest of the people' once stood alone. The expansion through the remainder of the verse is to be attributed to the editor, who here shows the same concern for a comprehensive definition as he has in a different way in the list itself. There, he gathered most of the names known to him; here, he amasses every way of describing the people already found in the preceding chapters in order once more to emphasize that the agreement was undertaken by the whole community without exception" (*Ezra, Nehemiah*, 332). This observation reconfirms the "democratized" view expressed here.

66. Olyan, "Purity Ideology in Ezra-Nehemiah," 6–7. See also Harrington's discussion of this aspect: "The Ezra memoir and third-person narrative both consider intermarriage a sin and a profanation…By contrast, intermarriage is allowed in Leviticus, even for ordinary priests, without any ill consequence; only the high priest must marry within his clan (Lev. 21.14). Thus, Leviticus does not ban an ordinary priest's marriage with a foreigner, and,…, Deuteronomy provides a process of conversion; it is only Ezra-Nehemiah that regards such a union categorically impure" ("Holiness and Purity in Ezra-Nehemiah," 107).

cases from where the writers / editors got their cue to portray this understanding, it seems that one can at least argue the following:

(i) The texts in Nehemiah 11 and 12 – being earlier than Chronicles according to the diachronic reconstruction that we used in this contribution – most probably latched onto the Holiness material directly, shortly after the emergence of H as a reinterpretation of the priestly and Deuteronomic traditions. (ii) It is unclear what position vis-à-vis the Levites is represented in the duplicated list of returnees in Nehemiah 7 and Ezra 2. If Rausche is correct that the texts we discussed wanted to push back against "wannabe" priests, it could be an indication that these remarks in the list represented the same position as the (in my view, post-Chronistic) theocratic redaction in Numbers 16–18. However, in these texts – differently than in Chronicles – the theocratic "push back" is against priestly descendants and not Levites. This factor makes it very difficult to decide where Nehemiah 7 and Ezra 2 fit into the discourse, both thematically and chronologically. (iii) The texts in Ezra 8, 9 and 10 also leave us with a vague picture, although an association with the Holiness legislation can be plausibly explained. The portrayal of priests and Levites as being together (and equally guilty) in their defilement of intermarriage, points in the direction of the "democratizing" tendency that we have observed elsewhere.[67] (iv) The one text which clearly shows influence of the "democratized" understanding of the Holiness legislation, and which clearly latches

---

67. Saul Olyan discusses the purity ideology in Ezra-Nehemiah as a strategy to reconstitute the post-exilic community (in response to the work of Jonathan Klawans and Christine Hayes). With reference to the exclusionist stance of this book, he indicates that two distinct strategies were used by the writers to achieve this position: first, "expansive and creative exegesis of earlier texts such as Lev 18:24–30, Deut 23:4–9, and Deut 7:1–6"; second, "the application of the concept of illegitimate profanation of a holy item to intermarriages between Judeans and foreign women" in order "to exclude those constructed as alien." This is particularly witnessed in the casting of Israel as זרע קדש "holy seed" in Ezra 9:2; and third, "a powerful and novel purity and pollution discourse explicitly informs several of the narratives that describe and justify the forced removal of persons classed as alien from temple and assembly." This novel discourse renders, according to Olyan, three results, namely "[f]irst, as in the Holiness Source, Deuteronomistic materials and other texts, alleged acts associated with aliens…as practised by aliens themselves and the Judeans associated with them threaten the purity of the land and even Israel's continued existence…Second, according to Neh 13:28–30, marriage with alien women pollutes the Judean priestly bloodline. And finally, Neh 13:4–9 casts the male alien as a perpetual polluter in ritual terms." Olyan concludes from his discussion: "Thus, in the final form of Ezra-Nehemiah, earlier ideas of both 'ritual' and 'moral' impurity are marshaled to craft a new, complex and unprecedented ideology of alien pollution. This ideology, together with other anti-intermarriage strategies such as expansive exegesis and the application of the notion of illegitimate desacralization to Judean intermarriages, function to buttress Ezra-Nehemiah's exclusionary program" ("Purity Ideology in Ezra-Nehemiah," 2–4).

onto the Chronicler's description of Hezekiah's and Josiah's Passover celebrations, is Ezra 6:20. The text clearly supports the same position in the discourse on the Levites' status than Chronicles.[68] (v) In the texts in Nehemiah 10:29 and in chapter 13 of the Nehemiah Memoir, it became clear that the positive Levitical portrayal has reached a level unprecedented compared to the earlier parts of the book Ezra-Nehemiah (probably with the exception of Ezra 6:20). One could safely argue that these texts were probably *Fortschreibungen* of the narrative development of the Levite profile that we witness in Chronicles. These texts are clearly post-Chronistic, and supported the same position in the discourse on the Levites than the final form of Chronicles.[69]

This summary shows that, as far as the diachronic reconstruction of Ezra-Nehemiah allows us, we can observe clearly that the different parts of the book engage – albeit in a variety of ways – with the more "democratized" understandings of holiness, consecration, and the Levites' position in the cult.[70]

4. CONCLUSION

We have observed the following strategies in the different parts of Ezra-Nehemiah for engaging in the late Persian/early Hellenistic discourse with the issue of the status of the priesthood and the Levites, particularly with reference to holiness and consecration: (a) There is

---

68. See also Heckl, *Neuanfang und Kontinuität in Jerusalem*, 392.

69. Although I agree with Pakkala that clear Levitical editorial activity can be observed in the mentioned texts, I would not go as far as Kyung-Jin Min who concluded the following: "Therefore, from our examination of the authorship issue through the available clues, we now conclude that E-N most likely came from a Levitical group who received Persian backing during the late fifth century BCE and who valued the ideologies of decentralization of power, unity and cooperation among social groups, and dissatisfaction with the religious status quo" (*The Levitical Authorship of Ezra-Nehemiah*, 141). Although Kyung-Jin refers to the debate on the unity of Chronicles with Ezra-Nehemiah, and of Ezra and Nehemiah, his approach is mainly synchronic, and therefore not so helpful for our present endeavour. His detection of strong Levitical interests in Ezra-Nehemiah remains valuable, however. It would therefore be worthwhile to bring Min's study into interaction with studies with a stronger diachronic interest, such as the present contribution. It would be interesting to see how synchronic and diachronic results correlate. However, this remains the task for another day.

70. Harrington observes the same when she says: "[I]t is clear that both books emphasize the notion of purification on a wider scale than found in previous texts. The purification of the laity is emphasized, at least for holy assemblies. Not only priests are in charge of purification, but also other Levites, and even, on occasion, Nehemiah, a non-Levite. …The control of purification rites beyond priestly personnel is unique in the Second Temple period beginning with Ezra-Nehemiah. Clearly ritual purification has taken a giant step toward the centre of Israelite religion" ("Holiness and Purity in Ezra-Nehemiah," 105–6).

emphasis on the holiness and the consecrated status of the Levites, particularly in key events such as the dedication of the rebuilt Temple, the celebration of the Passover, and the dedication of the rebuilt wall. (b) Some texts show a clear push back against "wannabe" priests. (c) In all this, further interpretations of Pentateuchal materials, namely the Deuteronomic, Priestly, and Holiness traditions, can be observed.

Diachronically, it seems as if there are parts of Ezra-Nehemiah that latch directly onto the Holiness legislation, while others seem to engage with the "democratized" tendency in H via Chronicles. The youngest parts of Ezra-Nehemiah (Neh 13) clearly showed a post-Chronistic *Fortschreibung*.

A next step in our research would be to correlate these findings with studies on other related texts, such as Ezekiel 40–48 (particularly ch. 44), Numbers 16–18, Malachi 2, and in more depth also Chronicles. Space does not permit us to take the present attempt into that next phase, and it should remain the task of another day.

www.ingramcontent.com/pod-product-compliance
Lightning Source LLC
Chambersburg PA
CBHW042112100526
44587CB00025B/4025